The Founder of Opus Dei

The Life of St. Josemaría Escrivá

Vol. II

God and Daring

The Founder of Opus Dei

The Life of St. Josemaría Escrivá

Vol. II
God and Daring

Andrés Vázquez de Prada

 Scepter

Library of Congress Cataloging-in-Publication Data

Vázquez de Prada, Andrés.
  [Fundador del Opus Dei. English]
  The founder of Opus Dei : the life of St. Josemaría Escrivá / Andrés Vázquez de
  Prada.
     p. cm
  Includes bibliographical references and index.
  Contents; 2. God and daring
  ISBN 1-889334-85-5 (hb : alk. paper) — ISBN 1-889334-86-3 (pbk. : alk. paper)
     1. Escrivá de Balaguer, Josemaría, 1902–1975. 2. Catholic Church—Spain
  Clergy—Biography. 3. Opus Dei (Society) I. Title.

BX4705.E676 V39 2000
267'.182'092—dc21
[B]

                                                                    00-061238

Cover photo: Father Josemaría Escrivá, taken on Nov. 5, 1946
Courtesy of the Central Archives, Opus Dei Prelature, Rome

Cover design by Carol S. Cates

This edition of *The Founder of Opus Dei: The Life of St. Josemaría Escrivá*,
vol. 2, *God and Daring* is published in the United States
by Scepter Publishers, Inc., P.O. Box 211, New York, NY 10018.
www.scepterpublishers.com

ISBN 1–889334–85–5 hb
ISBN 1–889334–86–3 pb

Printed in the United States of America

Contents

TABLE OF ABBREVIATIONS

AGP	General Archive of the Prelature (*Archivo General de la Prelatura*)
Apuntes	Personal Notes (*Apuntes íntimos*)
AVF	Assorted writings of the Founder (*Autógrafos Varios del Fundador*)
D	Document
EF	Personal letters of the Founder (*Epistolario del Fundador*), cited by number
IZL	Section of AGP corresponding to the Servant of God Isidoro Zorzano Ledesma
Letter	Letters written to all the members of the Work, cited by date and section number
P01, P02 etc.	Collections of printed documents (sections within AGP)
PM	Madrid Process of beatification (*Proceso Matritense*), followed by folio number
PR	Roman Process of beatification (*Proceso Romano*), followed by page number
RHF	Historical Register of the Founder (*Registro Histórico del Fundador* [section within AGP])
Sum.	*Summarium* of the Cause of beatification and canonization. *Positio super vita et virtutibus*, Rome, 1988. The name of the witness, followed by the corresponding section number of the *Summarium*.
T	Testimonial

War and Revolution: Hopes of Evacuation

1. The fruits of hatred

The tragic events that gripped Spain during the civil war years of
1936 to 1939 can hardly be comprehended without at least some
understanding of their political framework. Although the response of
the founder of Opus Dei stands out in this context, to ignore the
historical facts would render unintelligible what he did and why he
did it. This is still more obvious when one considers that religion was
a key factor in the tragedy. There has been no dearth of civil wars in
Spain, but the war that broke out in 1936 was distinctive in that it
unleashed one of the fiercest and bloodiest religious persecutions in
twenty centuries of Christianity.[1] In the brief space of a few months, a
dozen bishops and more than six thousand priests and religious were
killed. This simple fact, stark and objective, sheds a somber light
upon the scene, so that the founder's behavior could hardly be understood apart from it, or without a grasp of the Christian motives
that led him to forgive those guilty with his whole heart, to make
reparation to our Lord for the crimes committed, and to learn, for the
future, the lesson of history.

In July 1936, both in the countryside and in the cities, there was an
enormous tension arising from social demands, the breakdown of the
national economy, the discrediting of government action, and frus-
trated regional sentiments. It was exacerbated by continual strikes,

[1] "The terror in Spain was similar to that of the civil war in Russia in that in both cases
the clergy were among the principal victims of the violence. The persecution of the
Catholic Church was the greatest ever seen in Western Europe, even counting the
harshest periods of the French Revolution. The number of churchmen assassinated,
some seven thousand, was proportionately equal to the number killed by the Communists in Russia, taking into account the difference of population, but it seems that torture
was more common in Russia." Stanley G. Payne, El catolicismo español (Barcelona, 1984),
p. 214. See Fernando de Meer Lecha-Marzo, "Algunos aspectos de la cuestión religiosa
en la Guerra Civil (1936–1939)," in Anales de Historia Contemporánea, no. 7 (1988–1989),
pp. 111–25.

9

hunger, disorder, and revolutionary agitation that incited the alienated workers and unemployed while fostering a counterrevolutionary stance on the part of people who wanted to use force. The regime was reeling on the verge of collapse, while the military was preparing a coup d'état to restore the lost authority of the Republic. How could things have come to such a pass?[2]

It is unnecessary either to go back to past centuries (to the civil wars of the nineteenth century, to the historic delay in establishing democratic principles in political institutions) or to attribute the seriousness of the conflict to the bellicose character of Spaniards.[3] When the monarchy fell and the Republic was established in 1931, half of Spain greeted its coming with rejoicing and hope. Here was a fresh start—an opportunity to rectify mistakes and establish a democratic, just, and representative government. But, from the setting up of a provisional government to the elaborating of the new Constitution, those in power and the delegates in the Constituent Assembly stamped the new government with a frequently radical style that many Spaniards found hard to accept.[4]

From its inception in 1931 to the start of the civil war in 1936, the history of the Second Spanish Republic is extremely troubled. It is easy to distinguish different stages: an initial period of getting orga-

[2] For a summary view of the situation, see Carlos Seco Serrano, "De la democracia republicana a la guerra civil," in *Historia General de España y América*, vol. 17, *La Segunda República y la guerra* (Madrid, 1988), pp. xiii–lx; and Payne, "La quiebra de la Segunda República," in *La Guerra Civil Española (Sesenta años después)*, ed. Miguel Alonso Baquer (Madrid, 1999), pp. 17–32.

[3] The Constitution of 1876 and the Electoral Law of 1890 did indeed establish democratic principles in Spain. The question was whether those principles were really effective in a country that in 1900 had an illiteracy rate of more than 60 percent.

[4] This was an era that is still controversial among historians. "The political history of the Second Spanish Republic is among the most controversial and myth-ridden in Europe in the twentieth century. The Republic began peacefully, with relatively broad acceptance, although naturally there were different attitudes among the diverse elements of Spanish society. In two years it introduced a series of reforms—some of questionable prudence and effectiveness—which produced the greatest political mobilizations Spain had seen up to that time. The result, after three years, was the most notable case of political decline and polarization in Europe in the twentieth century, disintegrating into a massive civil war, both revolutionary and counterrevolutionary.

"Even historians are not in agreement on how this occurred. They no longer accept the propaganda widely accepted abroad during the civil war and the Second World War, which attributed it to a rightist conspiracy against democracy, but there is no clear and simple consensus. The republican experience can be seen as the conflict and collapse of parliamentary forces, as the failure of an attempt at reform, or as a revolutionary process and the breeding ground of a rightist conspiracy. In fact it was all of these things, and more." Payne, *El régimen de Franco, 1936–1975* (Madrid, 1987), pp. 47–48.

nized, followed by a two-year period of radical reforms pertaining to the Church, the army, education, regional concerns, agriculture, and labor.[5] The general discontent generated by the government's actions gave rise to a poorly organized military uprising, by a small group of monarchists, which collapsed in Seville in the summer of 1932. It was neither the first, nor an isolated, attempt to change the course of events by force. Spanish political life, which already had a radical tinge, was becoming more and more violent. General elections were held in November 1933, and the Chamber of Deputies changed color politically. The previous majority, dominated by socialists and leftist republicans, was replaced by another formed by the CEDA (Spanish Confederation of Autonomous Rights) and the Radical, Liberal-Democratic, and Agrarian parties.[6] The representatives of the CEDA, the most numerous party in the new majority, taking a stance of indifference toward the form of government (monarchy or republic), proclaimed themselves conservatives and defenders of Catholic ideals. Policies designed to modify the extremism of the preceding period marked the years 1934 and 1935, along with another attempt—more intense, better prepared, and more widespread than that of 1932—to overthrow the government. This leftist uprising of 1934 collapsed in Madrid and Catalonia but succeeded in Asturias after a bloody revolution.[7] The use of the army was required to put it down and to restore constitutional government.[8]

[5] See Payne, "Antecedentes y crisis de la democracia," in *La Guerra Civil: Una nueva visión del conflicto que dividió España,* ed. Stanley G. Payne and Javier Tusell (Madrid, 1996), pp. 26–27.

[6] Out of a total of 472 delegates, the CEDA had 115, followed by the Radicales of Lerroux, with 102. The group of small right-wing parties (Agrarios, Tradicionalistas, Partido Nacionalista Vasco, Partido Nacionalista Español, and Lliga Catalana, etc.) obtained 124 seats; the small right-republican parties (Conservador, Liberal-Demócrata, and Progresista) gained a total of 30; and the leftist block, composed of various bourgeois parties (Acción Republicana, Esquema Republicana, Federales, and ORGA) and the revolutionary parties (PSOE, Radical-Socialista, Comunista, and Unió Socialista de Catalunya) got 101.

[7] Gonzalo Redondo, on p. 412 of *Historia de la Iglesia en España, 1931–1939,* vol. 1, *La Segunda República, 1931–1936* (Madrid, 1993), gives the following figures for the casualties of this uprising: "Deaths: gendarmery, 100; Army, 98; police force and cavalry, 86; priests and religious, 34; peasants, 1,051. Wounded: Army and police, 900; peasants, 2,051. Buildings burned, blown up, or damaged: public buildings (barracks, city halls, etc.), 63; churches, 58; cultural centers, 5; factories, 26; private homes, 730. In addition, 58 bridges; 31 highways; and 66 rail lines cut."

[8] The most serious development politically was the advance of a decidedly revolutionary orientation among a sector of the socialists which had decided to bolshevize the party, in opposition to its moderate wing. See Burnet Bolloten, *La Guerra Civil española: Revolución y contrarrevolución* (Madrid, 1989), pp. 73–89.

The disintegration of the nation accelerated after the October 1934 uprising. Right and left moved toward political extremism, leaving no possibility for compromise. In the absence of understanding between the moderates on either side, the march toward confrontation advanced implacably, outside the channels of democracy.

In February 1936, the political forces of the right and the left (the latter united under the Popular Front) once more went to the polls in a general election. Many on either side were less interested in seeking democratic legitimacy than in gaining political power to destroy their enemy definitively. By a narrow margin the left won, but this unfortunately did not serve to pacify their spirits. On the contrary, with the forces on the left growing ever more divided, the conflict between the political antagonists continued to escalate until it hurled the country, irremediably, into chaos.[9]

The hatred the adversaries felt toward one another was not purely political. It would be possible to trace its roots through a stormy process running throughout the nineteenth century and pitting conservative traditionalism against progressivist liberalism. To this must be added the resistance of many capitalists and landowners to a solution to the urgent problems of justice for the worker, a resistance that exacerbated old social tensions even as demagogic propaganda fomented the armed uprising of the proletariat. The leaven of hatred entered people's hearts, filling them with enmity and violence.

Other proximate causes of the conflict were the mistakes made by the republican governments. For example, there were the reforms of the president, Manuel Azaña, which mainly affected the army and the Church. The army was unnecessarily humiliated, which alienated many military men from the republican cause and tempted them toward conspiracy and military uprising. As for the Church, the profoundly secularist measures adopted reflected a sectarian ideology that ignored the fact that the majority of the population were practicing Catholics.[10] Other mistakes—such as bribery and corruption

---

[9] See Payne, "Antecedentes," pp. 35–40 and 61–94.

[10] An idea of the complexity of the motives which led to the war can be gotten from reading the "Informe acerca del levantamiento cívico-militar de España en julio de 1936" of August 13, 1936, sent by Cardinal Gomá to Rome. This can be found in María Luisa Rodríguez Aisa, *El Cardenal Gomá y la Guerra de España: Aspectos de la gestión pública del Primado, 1936–1939* (Madrid, 1981), pp. 371–78. See also Lecha-Marzo, "Algunos aspectos," pp. 111–13, and Payne, *La revolución Española* (Madrid, 1972).

among some Radical Party members serving in the government in the second two-year period, lack of sensitivity to social problems on the part of some and loss of a sense of opportunity in others, the general radicalism of European politics in those years and the crisis in the democracies—all helped discredit the government further and confirm the violent in turning to radical solutions.

The spark that set off the explosion and precipitated the decision of those who were still hesitating[11] and the understanding between the Carlists and General Mola, the leader of the rebellion, was the assassination of José Calvo Sotelo, one of the monarchist leaders of the parliamentary opposition, on July 13, 1936. It was carried out by police forces in reprisal for the recent assassination of a lieutenant of the shock troops, José Castillo, and it resulted, within a few days, in the outbreak of the uprisings.[12]

The first, late on July 17, was that of the military garrisons in Africa.[13] The government was not taken by surprise by the military conspiracy, but believed it could subdue the rebellion since the army's key positions were in the hands of generals who favored the government. Within twenty-four hours the situation was rather confused, with some garrisons going over to the rebels while the parties of the left and the labor organizations demanded that the government arm

[11] Included in this group was General Franco.

[12] See Bolloten, pp. 95–97. See also the personal record of a qualified witness of these events: Julián Marías, *Una vida presente, Memorias I: 1914–1951* (Madrid, 1988), pp. 187–92.

These words of the socialist leader Indalecio Prieto, written the day after Calvo Sotelo's assassination (see the July 14, 1936, edition of *El Liberal*), show the level that social tension had reached: "If the reactionaries dream of an unbloody coup d'état like that of 1923, they are completely mistaken. If they think they would face a defenseless government, they are deceiving themselves. To win they would have to leap over the human barricade that the proletarian masses would put up against them. It would be, as I have said many times, a battle to the death because each of the two sides knows that the adversary, if it triumphed, would give no quarter. But even if this were to occur, a decisive combat would be preferable to this continuous bloodletting."

We must point out that on July 12 General Mola set the time for the future military uprising as "Starting at the zero hour of the 17th": see F. B. Maíz, *Mola, aquel hombre* (Barcelona, 1970), p. 264. See also Antonio González-Betes, *Franco y el Dragon Rapide* (Madrid, 1987), p. 107, where an account is given of how the plane which brought General Franco to Morocco at the beginning of the uprising began its trip to Spain on July 11.

What motivated the military to rebel was the crisis that Spain was undergoing. See the "Address of General Franco Broadcast from Tenerife," the "Proclamation of a State of War in Seville" dictated by General Queipo de Llano, and the "Manifesto of General Mola," all three issued on July 18, 1936.

[13] Spain, together with France, at that time held a protectorate over what is now Morocco.

the people's militias.[14] On the critical night of July 18–19, the president of the Republic sought to provide a temporary solution by replacing the government of Casares Quiroga with that of Martínez Barrio and its more moderate ministers, in an attempt to win over the generals in this camp.

The new government, like its predecessors, immediately came under pressure from the workers' parties and unions to arm the socialist and communist militias.[15] The authorities refused to give arms to the affiliates of the unions. At daybreak on July 19, thousands of workers circulated throughout Madrid armed with rifles given to them hours earlier in some barracks. In the Montaña Barracks, however, despite orders to the contrary, the revolutionary militias were refused weapons.

*   *   *

[14] The militias were partially armed paramilitary formations established by different groups. The term "people's militias" arose in connection with the demand to give arms to "the people"—in reality, to the militants of the revolutionary parties and unions who had decided to take control of the situation. This demand was accompanied by a desertion of the army by many soldiers, especially in Madrid, Barcelona, Cartagena, Valencia, and other cities, on the basis of a decree, issued by the president of the Republic shortly after the uprising, which exempted them from their oath of obedience to their officers. At the same moment the army was disintegrating, there was born the militia or people's militia, whose components were grouped according to political leaning. These constituted a serious problem for the government until they were brought under military discipline, something the government often either could not or would not effectuate. In Madrid this objective was not measurably attained until May of 1937. It was the militias, outside any government control, that at least in the first months of the conflict imposed their own law in the streets. See Burnet Bolloten, pp. 411–23; and for the case of Madrid, Javier Cervera Gil, *Madrid en guerra: La ciudad clandestina, 1936–1939* (Madrid, 1998), pp. 109–110.

[15] The cabinet of Martínez Barrio did not last twenty-four hours and was not even announced in the *Gaceta*. It was succeeded on July 20 by another, with José Giral as prime minister. One of the gravest problems at the root of these lightning-like changes was the transfer of weapons, something Casares and Martínez Barrio tried without success to prevent, in the realization that otherwise their governments would be purely nominal, with the real power in the hands of the militias. Precisely this led to the dismissal of Martínez Barrio and the accession of Giral. "But that government," says Bolloten (on p. 109), "was one in name only. Dragged along hopelessly by events, it was helping bring about the rapid dissolution of the republican government of 1931 under the double impact of the military rebellion and the social revolution. According to its prime minister, committees of the Popular Front were immediately established in each of the ministries to assist and supervise the ministers, depriving them of even the appearance of real authority." He therefore speaks of the coming of a "Third Republic" born of the revolution.

"In another order of things," says Cervera Gil (pp. 44–45), "Casares Quiroga, before resigning (which he did at night [on the 18th]), advised Bishop Eijo y Garay, the bishop of Madrid, that for his own safety he should leave the city, which he did, taking the road to Vigo that same evening. . . . The militia then attacked the bishop's residence in Madrid and [on the 19th] riddled the portrait of Bishop Eijo y Garay with bullet holes.

On Sunday, July 19, the Father and some of his sons were working in the new residence at 16 Ferraz Street, and from the balcony they could see police and curious onlookers constantly coming and going in front of the house. On the other side of Ferraz there was at this time no building, just an empty stretch looking toward the esplanade of the Montaña Barracks, which was about two hundred yards from the residence.[16] Toward the end of the afternoon, they began hearing the noise of the people's militias, which had been marching with weapons, flags, and raised fists through the center of the capital. At about ten that night, the Father sent home those who lived with their families, asking them to telephone him when they arrived so he would not worry about them.[17] Isidoro Zorzano and José María González Barredo remained with him that night.[18]

Meanwhile, behind its high walls, the barracks remained closed in menacing silence. Intermittent gunshots were heard throughout the night. Soon after daybreak they began to notice activity in the neighborhood. Preparations were being made for a taking of the barracks. There was a heavy bombardment, to which the besieged replied with rifles and machine guns.[19] Stray bullets ricocheted off the walls of the residence and splintered the balcony, obliging the Father and those with him to take refuge in the basement. At midmorning the attack took place. The patio of the barracks was strewn with bodies. The mass of militia who had burst into the barracks emerged, shouting and excited, armed with rifles.

The Father, who for months had been hearing of murders of priests and nuns and of arson, assaults, and other atrocities,[20] saw that the time had come when wearing the cassock would be tempting Divine Providence—doing something not merely imprudent but foolhardy. He therefore put on the blue overalls he had been using those days when doing repairs, and left his cassock in his

---

[16] "Anyone entering the [Montaña] barracks [on the 19th] had to pass through a blockade composed primarily of the gendarmes and the shock troops, followed by a battalion of socialists and, further back, armed groups of the people of Madrid." Cervera Gil, p. 45.

[17] See Juan Jiménez Vargas, AGP, RHF, T–04152–III, p. 15, and Alvaro del Portillo, *Sum.* 879.

[18] See José Miguel Pero-Sanz, *Isidoro Zorzano Ledesma, Ingeniero Industrial: Buenos Aires, 1902—Madrid, 1943* (Madrid, 1996), pp. 191–92.

[19] A detailed description of this event can be found in Cervera Gil, pp. 45–48. Two cannons and some other military vehicles had been brought to the Plaza de España.

[20] See *Apuntes*, no. 1325 (25 Mar 1936).

room.[21] That afternoon, after praying to our Lady and commending themselves to the guardian angels, the Father, Isidoro, and José María González Barredo left separately through the back door. In his haste, the Father forgot to cover his head, whose ample tonsure plainly announced his clerical status. He walked through groups of militiamen who, excited by their recent combat, did not pay the slightest attention to him.

Upon reaching his mother's house (which was not far from the residence), he spoke by telephone with Juan Jiménez Vargas, and learned that all of his sons were safe and sound. Having left his breviary in the residence, he had extra time on his hands, so he turned on the radio, which continued to give confused and alarming news. The night was going to be long and hot. He prayed rosary after rosary. The apartment was at the top of a building on Dr. Cárceles Street, down from where it crosses Ferraz. Militiamen could be heard running on the roofs and terraces in pursuit of snipers firing from the rooftops.

Father Josemaría decided to begin a diary whose entries would have a telegraphic conciseness—not a detailed historical record. On Monday, July 20, he made the first entry in that journal:

> Monday, the 20th — Worried about everyone, especially Ricardo. — We prayed to the Blessed Virgin and the guardian angels. — About one o'clock, I made the sign of the cross and was the first to leave. — Reached my mother's house. — Spoke by phone with Juan. — Listened to the radio news. — Everyone arrived safely. — A bad night, hot. — All three parts of the rosary. — Don't have my breviary. — Militia on the roof.[22]

The quick brushstrokes depict his soul in the face of what was happening and his concern for his sons, especially Ricardo Fernández

---

[21] As Jiménez Vargas puts it, "The cassock was now a death sentence" (AGP, RHF, T–05152/1, p. 16); see also Santiago Escrivá de Balaguer y Albás, AGP, RHF, T–07921, p. 18. The clerical tonsure carried the same danger: see Alvaro del Portillo, *Sum.* 879. About the blue overalls, see his letter to María Dolores Fisac Serna in AGP, RHF, EF–370813–1. (All the letters of the founder from this period—July of 1936 to October 7, 1937—were written in Madrid.)

[22] The diary consists of two handwritten pages. It has the character of an outline; its many abbreviations are replaced in our transcription by the words they stand for. The original is preserved in AGP, RHF, D–15223. See Appendix 1.

Vallespín, who was caught by events in Valencia. That Monday, July 20, Father Josemaría had said Mass in the residence, without suspecting that he would not celebrate it again for a long time. The notes of that brief diary, which only goes up to Saturday, July 25, show where his thoughts and his heart were. "Tuesday, the 21st — No Mass. Wednesday, the 22nd — No celebrating Mass. Thursday, the 23rd — Spiritual communions. No Mass! Friday, the 24th — No Mass!"

On Thursday he found a missal in the apartment and began, out of devotion, to say "dry Masses," meaning that he performed the ceremonies of Mass, and said attentively and devoutly all the liturgical prayers, up to those of the Consecration (which he could not do since he lacked bread and wine), and when it came time for Communion, he made a spiritual communion.[23]

The week was filled with anxiety. All of Spain was passing through hours of tragic uncertainty. It was not easy to piece together the situation of the country, since nothing in the press or on the radio could be trusted. By telephoning the funeral home across from Santa Isabel, Father Josemaría learned on Tuesday that the church had been burned down. One day four or five years earlier, while leaving Santa Isabel, he had received from God a strong presentiment that the church would be torched.[24] Sadly, the convent too was not spared. Juan Jiménez Vargas brought them the news that other churches in Madrid were already ablaze and the rest had been seized. In the entry for Wednesday, July 22, we read: "They say that priests are being imprisoned."

In view of the recent events at the Montaña Barracks, Father Josemaría had little difficulty realizing the dangers to which the ministers of the Lord were exposed. That very week, as if sounding the alarm, there began an implacable pursuit of priests and religious, with either imprisonment or martyrdom for those caught. Convents and rectories were deserted.[25] The only safety lay in remaining hidden. In

---

[23] See Alvaro del Portillo, PR, p. 1001, and Javier Echevarría, *Sum.* 2420.

[24] See *Apuntes*, no. 1620 (24 Aug 1940).

[25] See Bolloten, pp. 117–18. On July 19 there were still some Masses celebrated in Madrid, and on that same day some ten churches were attacked and sacked. "On the night of July 19 to 20, thirty-four more religious buildings in Madrid were burned. In the period between Saturday the 18th and Tuesday the 21st, the first seventy-two hours of the revolution, there were sacked in the capital of Spain forty-six churches; that is, 34.8 percent of the city's churches." Redondo, *Historia*, vol. 2, *La Guerra Civil, 1936–1939* (Madrid, 1993), p. 20 and note 6. See also Raymond Carr, *La tragedia española: La Guerra Civil en perspectiva* (Madrid, 1977), pp. 111ff.

the apartments below Doña Dolores's, a nun and an Augustinian monk were hidden.[26] Father Josemaría redoubled his prayer and expiation, as a line in his diary indicates: "Prayer: to our Lord, the Blessed Virgin, Saint Joseph, the guardian angels, Saint James."

He searched through the apartment and found a copy of the "Roman Euchology," which enabled him to say the Office of the Dead. With the rest of his family he began a novena to Our Lady of the Pillar. In the extreme heat, he also began an ascetical struggle with thirst. "I will not drink water, and will offer this for everyone, especially our people," he noted on Wednesday. What he could not resign himself to was the lack of news about his sons. He therefore asked Juan to send some postcards to Valencia, in order to reassure Ricardo Fernández Vallespín and Rafael Calvo Serer and get to hear from them.

Father Josemaría wanted to go back to living at the Ferraz Street residence, but Juan, who walked every day from his own apartment to Doña Dolores's, made him see how dangerous it would be if he had to pass through the many checkpoints of the revolutionaries. As it was, he was able to do very little work, because the records and documents of Opus Dei were locked in a trunk in the apartment on Dr. Cárceles Street and he had left the key in the Ferraz residence. On Thursday, Juan and Isidoro took it upon themselves to go to the residence and bring back to the Father the keys, a briefcase, and his ID card, which was his only proof of identity.[27] Now the priest was prepared for the unforeseeable—that is, for a time when he might suddenly have to leave his mother's apartment. He also let his mustache grow, so that he would not be recognized.

At the beginning of Saturday, July 25, the date of the last entry in the diary, neither the republican government nor the rebels knew which

[26] The nun was a daughter of Lieutenant Colonel Paniagua, who lived in the same building as Doña Dolores, and the Augustinian monk was Father Nemesio Morata, a well-known Arabist who had fled from the monastery of El Escorial. See Alvaro del Portillo, *Sum.* 879, and Santiago Escrivá de Balaguer y Albás, AGP, RHF, T–07921, p. 19.

The assassinations of forty-one priests in Madrid are documented as having occurred in the first days of the revolution, up to the end of July. The number of priests of the diocese of Madrid-Alcalá killed during the war was 435 (38.8 percent), according to the most detailed available study: José Luis Alfaya Camacho, *Como un río de fuego: Madrid, 1936* (Barcelona, 1998), pp. 64–88 and 285–309. To these must be added, without leaving this same diocese, the 451 monks and 73 nuns killed or made to disappear during the war: see Redondo, *Historia*, vol. 2, p. 20. The effort to count the lay people who were killed for being Catholics is difficult because there were so many and because it is almost impossible to find sources, although Cervera Gil's book supplies interesting and significant information.

[27] See Pero-Sanz, pp. 192–93.

way the scales would tip. The outcome was most uncertain. Caught up in a kind of formless brawl, its territory capriciously divided and redivided among hostile forces, the nation tottered on the threshold of civil war.

Radio Madrid broadcast an incessant deluge of news served up by the government, announcing the failure of the military uprising, the surrender of the rebels, the bombardment and destruction of those who had fought against the victorious republican forces. To keep his mother's mind off all these catastrophes, Father Josemaría tried to entertain her by playing cards with her or by having her listen to Radio Seville.[28] The talks of General Queipo de Llano, promising an imminent arrival in Madrid of dissident forces that would liberate the capital, were, though untrue, a small source of optimism.[29] As yet no one was thinking of a civil war, but only of a military coup and the repression of revolutionary outbursts.

On the morning of Saturday, July 25, Juan had just entered the foyer of the Ferraz Street residence, in search of some papers, when a band of anarchists broke into the apartment, among them the chauffeur and the cook of the former resident of the house, Count del Real. Probably not knowing who the new residents were, the militiamen inspected the apartment. In the Father's room they found a cassock, a hat, and other objects, such as cilices and a discipline with bloodstains, which clearly announced that a priest had been living there. Juan answered the questions of the searchers as best he could, with vague remarks, trying to get out of the predicament by explaining that some medical students lived there (the militiamen had already seen some skulls and skeletons in the study room), that the owner of the house was a foreigner, and that the chaplain did not come there very often.[30]

Without any further investigation, they declared the building seized in the name of the CNT (the National Labor Confederation, an anarchist union) and went to Juan's house to continue their search. Here the danger was even greater, because in a trunk in his bedroom Juan had a file containing the addresses of the students who went to the residence and some other documents whose possession meant a death

---

[28] See Appendix 1 and Jiménez Vargas, AGP, RHF, T–04152–III, pp. 21ff.
[29] See Ian Gibson, *Queipo de Llano, Sevilla, verano de 1936: Con las charlas radifónicas completas* (Barcelona, 1986).
[30] See Jiménez Vargas, AGP, RHF, T–04152–III, pp. 26–28.

•

sentence.[31] Although the search of his room was meticulous, the militiamen inexplicably did not come across the trunk, which remained hidden behind the closet's opened doors. In any event, when they finished, they invited Juan to "accompany" them, which in their jargon of terror meant they were "taking him for a walk"—in other words, taking him to be executed—something that was the order of the day and was within the authority of the patrols. At that moment, however, his mother dramatically intervened, and the leader of the anarchists, pistol in hand, suddenly changed his mind, explaining, "We don't kill anyone. The ones who do the killing are the socialists. We carry this"—here he pointed to his pistol—"only as a preventive measure. Let him stay!" [32]

That same evening Juan discussed the events of the day with Alvaro del Portillo, and they asked each other how it all would end. "If the communist revolution succeeds," they agreed, "we will not be able to stay here. We will need to make plans for a residence abroad." [33] Both of them had very much in mind their commitment to continue with the Work even if the founder died. Each reaffirmed what they both already knew well: "The Work of God has come into being to fulfill the will of God. Have, therefore, a deep conviction that heaven is determined to see it realized." [34] By such simple logic they maintained a firm, hopeful conviction that nothing would happen to the Father.[35] And in fact, during all the years of religious persecution, all the members of the Work repeatedly escaped from the hands of their

[31] These other documents that were in the same trunk as the address list were blank ID cards for the Association of Traditionalist Students, signed by Juan Jiménez Vargas. He had kept them from the time, some years back, when he was secretary of that organization in Madrid. Since they were in the same trunk as the address list, there was the danger that the militiamen would have connected the students at the residence with the members of this political organization. See ibid., p. 29.

[32] Jiménez Vargas, AGP, RHF, T–04152–III, pp. 29–30. Cervera Gil (pp. 68–78) has carried out a detailed study of the "walks" in Madrid from July to December of 1936. Of the 3,000 cases studied, he concludes that the most "walked" individuals were priests and religious (18 percent), and the least, students and doctors (5 and 4 percent respectively).

[33] Jiménez Vargas, AGP, RHF, T–04152–III, pp. 30–31.

[34] *Instruction* of 19 Mar 1934, no. 47. See also *Apuntes*, no. 1287 (3 Oct 1935), and Alvaro del Portillo, *Sum.* 675.

[35] About that security and optimism Jiménez Vargas writes, "The explanation is very simple. We never had any doubts about the immediate future, convinced, of course, that nothing would happen to the Father. We understood, nevertheless, the need for extreme prudence and care for his personal safety. We knew that he had to carry out the Work, and this gave us a solid hope, a clear certainty that everything would be solved" (AGP, RHF, 04152–III, p. 34).

persecutors in a way that was miraculous, or at least quite unlikely and inexplicable.

Father Josemaría, in addition to his foundational graces, possessed a quality which for some time had helped him in dealing with an adverse historical situation, enabling him to carry out his apostolic mission with daring and naturalness. The Lord undoubtedly had given the young priest an interior peace and even an incredible physical courage, given the circumstances in which he carried out his ministry. As if to acknowledge that gift, he tells in a journal entry of one of the very few occasions when he could not overcome his fear. He experienced, he says, "a physiological, childish fear at being in the church at night, in the dark." This happened in 1930, at the Foundation for the Sick. This fear that he recognized as "foolish," but could not help having, kept him from approaching the tabernacle— until one night when, upon returning from the academy, "I felt an interior divine inspiration: 'Go, without fear. Now you will not be afraid.' Not that I heard those words. I felt them—them or something very similar. Anyway, that was the idea. I went into the dark church. The only light was that of the sanctuary lamp. I went up to the tabernacle and rested my head on the altar. I've never again felt afraid." [36]

Freed from fear, Father Josemaría was able to dedicate himself fully to his activities despite ridicule, insults, and even stoning. The figure of that priest wrapped in his cloak was well known in the poorer districts and slums on the outskirts of Madrid, where he went to visit the sick or to give catechesis.

Father Josemaría needed a good dose of daring and courage to continue carrying out his ministerial functions as if the atmosphere in the streets had not changed. In the months that followed the establishment of the Republic, he had to overcome hatred wherever he turned. "My God," he asked, "why this hatred for those who are yours?" [37] Meeting hatred with love, he resolved to "stone" with Hail Mary's those who insulted him with vulgarities and obscenities, and thus he purified his feelings. Whereas previously he had become indignant, "now, when I hear those vulgarities, my heart trembles." [38]

A few weeks after making that entry in his journal, he confirmed a

[36] *Apuntes*, no. 178 (20 Mar 1931).
[37] *Apuntes*, no. 212 (26 Jul 1931).
[38] *Apuntes*, no. 291 (18 Sep 1931).

priestly resolution that he kept alive to the end of his days: "I must speak only of God."[39] Being involved in a divine enterprise that he had to carry out in the midst of the world, he suffered those daily street confrontations in silence. Immersed in the reality of life, but staying above and outside of any political ideologies, the founder carried out his mission from 1931 to 1936 in an atmosphere of growing agitation and hatred. The whole country appeared to be plunging into an abyss of evil, and his apostolic heart found itself surrounded by people who thought that the first step to the solution to their problems was to destroy the Catholic Church.

"The Work of God," the founder had written, "was not thought up by a man to solve the lamentable situation of the Church in Spain since 1931."[40] He dedicated his energies to fulfilling faithfully the mission, universal and perpetual, that he had been given on October 2, 1928.

2. *Seeking refuge*

Doña Dolores predicted to her family that by the feast of Saint James, the patron saint of Spain, everything would have returned to normal. Father Josemaría's diary includes the invocation of the apostle: "Saturday, the 25th: Saint James, and Spain to the attack!"[41]

When August began, all of Spain was in turmoil and confusion. Fighting continued in villages and whole regions, and the split in military commands during the insurrection was clear. What the leaders of the uprising thought would be a swift seizure of power by the army had turned into a bloody battle resembling a simultaneous revolution and civil war. For the most part, the people in charge were supporters of the republican government, especially in Madrid and Barcelona, where the largest military forces were stationed. However, in the large rural areas of Galicia, León, Castile, Navarre, and Aragón, the population enthusiastically supported the uprising. The result was unforeseeable. In the republican zone, power was theoretically in the hands of the government but in fact fell into the hands of the revolutionary committees of the party militias and the local unions, while in the zone that came to be called "national" the forces of the

---

[39] *Apuntes*, no. 431 (29 Nov 1931).
[40] *Instruction* of 19 Mar 1934, no. 6.
[41] See Appendix 1.

villages and cities placed themselves under the authority of the military commanders of the insurrection.

As the days passed, hopes for a quick end to the conflict vanished. It now looked as if it would continue to the end of that summer. Throughout Madrid homes were searched for suspicious people. Generally, the searches were targeted at addresses lifted from political files or obtained from accusers. The most dangerous of these accusers were neighbors and apartment building porters and janitors who knew the residents' movements and whereabouts.[42] In the apartment below Doña Dolores's there was a communist woman, a cook, who probably knew that a priest was living in hiding in that other apartment. Father Josemaría, realizing this, remained cautious and ready to take flight at any moment of day or night. But, as if these difficulties were not enough, he had no union card or political documentation to show to the militias if stopped. So Doña Dolores gave him Don José's wedding ring, so that they would not think he was single. For him, wearing that ring was like having inherited a holy relic of his father.[43]

Two weeks after he began hiding out in the apartment, search patrols came to the neighborhood. Probably on August 8, what they had feared did happen. Early in the morning, the porter, in alarm, told them that there was about to be a search. Without waiting for a second warning, Father Josemaría took out for the street to begin a long *via dolorosa* that would fulfill his premonition of a special cross starting in 1936. At the end of June he had written in his journal, "Victim! On an unseen cross."[44]

That day of August 8, he walked aimlessly from one part of Madrid to another, constantly in danger of falling into the hands of some militia squad that would carry him off to prison. Finally, late at night, he went to sleep at a rooming house on Menéndez y Palayo Street, where José María Albareda lived. This was a young professor whom he had met at the Ferraz Street residence and who on Thursday, July 23, had visited him in the apartment on Dr. Cárceles Street, accompanied by Juan and by Isidoro Zorzano.

The following day, by prior arrangement, he went to the home of Manolo Sainz de los Terreros, at 31 Sagasta Street.[45] (Manolo was that

[42] See Cervera Gil, p. 189.

[43] See Alvaro del Portillo, *Sum.* 879.

[44] *Apuntes*, no. 1372 (30 Jun 1936).

[45] The apartment was on the third floor, left side, of 31 Sagasta (which later became 33 Segasta), at the corner of Alonso Martínez Street and across from the old bar La Mezquita. See Jiménez Vargas, AGP, RHF, T–04152–III, pp. 40–41.

young man who had begun receiving spiritual direction from the Father at the building on Martínez Campos Street in June 1933, showing him his soul "without leaving out a single thing.") At midday Father Josemaría succeeded in getting up to the apartment without the porter noticing. That same afternoon Juan Jiménez Vargas also arrived. Manolo's family was on vacation and Manolo was living only with Martina, an elderly servant who was deaf and imperturbable. The two guests had to remain completely hidden, without any of the neighbors knowing about them, and especially not the porter, who was supposed to keep the building's political committee informed about the residents' comings and goings. They had to move cautiously and silently so as not to arouse suspicion. Manolo or Martina did the shopping, letting people think they were buying food for two rather than four. Manolo was a resolute and impetuous and not easily intimidated man, but his home had been under suspicion since his brother had been taken to prison at the end of July. The searches were now becoming methodical, and after the Father had been there two days, militiamen searched another apartment in the same building—one in which the Count of Leyva had earlier been arrested.[46]

With Father Josemaría also came order in that home. There was set a fixed schedule for prayer, work, and meals. What worried the Father the most was not having news of his children, and so one can well imagine his great joy when, in mid-August, Manolo brought from the Ferraz Street residence some letters given him by the doorkeeper, including one from Pedro Casciaro. A little later, on the twenty-fifth, there arrived a letter from Ricardo addressed to Isidoro from Valencia, saying he was very well. Through Isidoro and Manolo, the Father kept in touch with those in Madrid—including Doña Dolores, although she preferred not to know exactly where her son was.[47]

Soon after Father Josemaría left his mother's apartment, the feared searches began. There were several. Some members of the family that the communist cook worked for were arrested. Another time the militia went through all the apartments except Doña Dolores's. They

---

[46] See Jiménez Vargas, AGP, RHF, T–04152–III, pp. 36ff. Since 1925 the Count of Leyva had been Don Juan José Conde-Luque y Garay.

[47] See Pero-Sanz, p. 194, and Manuel Sainz de los Terreros Villacampa, AGP, RHF, D–03637. Actually, Father Josemaría's mother went several days before learning where her son was hiding out. This was due to the careful reserve of Manolo, who "would not tell us where he was," says Santiago Escrivá de Balaguer (AGP, RHF, T–07921, p. 19). "Possibly my mother preferred not to know where he was, as long as she received frequent news that he was all right."

even broke into a next-door apartment that was under the protection of the English embassy. Its British owner had left Spain when the revolution broke out.[48] Doña Dolores and her children trembled in fearful silence every time they heard the militiamen noisily mounting the stairs. But, strange as it seems, it never occurred to them to search the Escrivá apartment.

In the apartment was a trunk filled with private papers and documents related to the Academy and to Father Josemaría's apostolic work. He had placed all his trust in the hands of God and of Doña Dolores, who "kept the key with her and would not let it go for anything in the world."[49] But Carmen and Santiago, fearing that the contents of the trunk could compromise the safety of others, talked their mother into giving them the key, and they did in fact find in there a notebook with names, addresses, and phone numbers, which they decided it would be prudent to burn.

In his search, Santiago also came across his brother's spiritual diary. "That was when I read the diary that Josemaría had been keeping for many years," he tells us. "I remember those notebooks covered in black oilskin."[50] Clearly he is referring to the founder's *Apuntes íntimos*. That trunk, which was placed under the protection of Divine Providence and the loving care of Doña Dolores, contained an important part of the spirit and the still brief history of the Work. Here on Dr. Cárceles Street the trunk began a long odyssey that would last throughout the war and leave it unscathed by moves and searches. Three years later, like someone encountering an old acquaintance, the founder noted: "Madrid! April 13, 1939. After almost three years, I restart my Catherines in this notebook that I left off without finishing in July 1936. Our Lord wanted, in a not very ordinary way, to preserve our archive. And he made use of my mother and Carmen as his instruments."[51]

In the Sagasta apartment Juan and Manolo were the Father's only company, until one day, making an exception to his extreme cautiousness, Manolo introduced the other two to a couple of refugees in the apartment below. Manolo did not tell them that Father Josemaría was

---

[48] See Jiménez Vargas, AGP, RHF, T–04152–III, pp 38ff, and Santiago Escrivá de Balaguer y Albás, AGP, RHF, T–07921, pp. 20ff.

[49] Jiménez Vargas, AGP, RHF, T–04152–III, p. 39.

[50] Santiago Escrivá de Balaguer y Albás, AGP, RHF, T–07921, pp. 20–21. See also Jiménez Vargas, AGP, RHF, T–04152–III, pp. 39–40, and *Apuntes*, introductory note, p. 3.

[51] *Apuntes*, no. 1595.

a priest, but because of the familiarity with which he spoke about religious subjects, they soon identified him as one, which was what he wanted to happen, in case they needed his services. One of the refugees, Pedro María Rivas (then a lawyer, and later a religious), says that "in those days of the war" they saw him as a person of "great patience and much peace of spirit." [52]

The refugees enjoyed Father Josemaría's conversation, and so they often went up to Manolo's apartment to chat with him. From experience they knew very well what to do if the doorbell rang while they were there: they at once retreated to the back stairs, while Martina very slowly made her preparations to open the door. Making use of her deafness, she would keep the visitors outside, not letting anyone get through the door. If they looked dangerous, her signal was to speak very loudly and make them identify themselves, giving the others plenty of time to get up the back stairs and into the attic.

On August 28, Manolo brought home a cousin of his, named Juan Manuel. On the morning of Sunday, August 30, they filled him in on what to do in case of a search, and even went through a drill, little imagining how opportune it was. A few hours later, when Manolo was away and Martina was preparing dinner, the others heard loud voices on the stairs, and then the bell rang. The three of them—the Father, Juan, and Juan Manuel—headed for the back stairs while Martina calmly made her way to the door. The militia tried to enter, saying that they had to make a search. Martina detained them by playing to the hilt her role as a deaf person, shouting, "There is no one here! I am deaf! I can't hear anything!"

The three others climbed up the stairs and into the attic, went through the first door they found open, and found themselves in a small space used as a storage room and coal bin. They had to walk stooped over, because the ceiling was so low. The early afternoon heat was stifling. Seated motionless amidst cobwebs and coal dust, they waited. The slightest noise might give them away, and, if found, they most likely would be shot.[53] For several hours they kept waiting, listening to the sounds of the search going on below them. Not know-

[52] Pedro María Rivas García-Calderón, AGP, RHF, T–03175. Rivas later took refuge in the home of some acquaintances, and from October 16, 1936, until the liberation of Madrid in 1939, he found political asylum on Del Prado Street, under the protection of the Chilean embassy. In 1946 he joined the Brothers of the Hospitaller Order of Saint John of God. He died in Madrid in 1993.

[53] See Jiménez Vargas, AGP, RHF, T–04152–III, pp. 50–52.

ing whether Juan Manuel, who had been with them only two days, knew he was a priest, Father told him, and then said to both him and Juan, "This looks bad. If you want, make an act of contrition, and I'll give you absolution." [54]

Juan Manuel received absolution. Later he wrote, "I'll never forget that encounter with Father Josemaría, since it took place at what we all thought was the last hour of our lives. . . . It took a lot of courage for him to tell me that he was a priest, because I could have betrayed him. If the militia had come in, I could have tried to save my life by informing on him." [55]

Juan also received absolution, and immediately afterward he asked the Father, "And if they find us, what will happen?" The Father replied, "Then, my son, we will go straight to heaven." At this point in his memoirs, Juan says that his fear was an unfocused one—that it was not exactly a fear of being shot, but just a sensation of uncertainty that did not rob him of his peace of mind. "With the Father there," he says, "I was sure I had nothing to fear. And to show what a sense of security I had, at three in the afternoon I went to sleep for a while." [56]

While he slept, the militia meticulously searched the house top to bottom and bottom to top—so thoroughly, in fact, that they had no time for the attic. At about nine that night the noise finally stopped. Cautiously, the three men went down the stairs and knocked at the service entrance of the fourth-floor home of the Count of Leyva, and were let in. Sweaty, thirsty, and covered with soot, they asked for a glass of water. There they were told that Manolo had returned home in the middle of the search and that the militia had arrested him, locking the apartment behind them.

The Count's family offered them some shirts belonging to the Count, who was in jail, while theirs were washed, and generously invited them to stay in that apartment, no further searches being expected there for some time. But they were mistaken about that. The next day, at eight in the morning, the militiamen were already back again, continuing the meticulous search that had been suspended the previous night. They entered the apartment next door and the one below. "At times," says the Count's daughter Mercedes, "we were

[54] Juan Manuel Sainz de los Terreros, AGP, RHF, T–05127. See also Alvaro del Portillo, *Sum.* 880.

[55] Sainz de los Terreros, AGP, RHF, T–05127.

[56] Jiménez Vargas, AGP, RHF, T–04152–III, pp. 51–52.

horribly afraid, but the Father kept us in a good mood, making us laugh a lot, although he was thinking much about his family and friends."[57] At one of those moments of danger the Countess suggested saying the Rosary.[58] "I'll lead, since I'm a priest," the Father quickly responded.[59]

Because of the persistence of searches in that area, they saw that they needed to change their hiding place.[60] Two of the Countess's maids went to see José María González Barredo, to ask him to look for a place where the Father could hide. The only one possible was the house of the Herrero Fontana couple, whose two sons knew Father Josemaría and received spiritual direction from him. The family lived in a mezzanine apartment, number 4, in Herradores Plaza.

That move toward safety put them right in the mouth of the wolf. One night the plaza was suddenly surrounded by police patrols and militiamen, who obliged the porters to open the doors of all the apartments so that they could do a roundup. They did their search with great commotion and nighttime confusion. Inexplicably, the porter of number 4 was not notified, and stranger still, the militiamen made no attempt to enter there.

For Juan, that was one more of many incidents showing that "the Father had a special protection," one more of the "episodes in which the guardian angels played a major role."[61] Every time they were saved from death, Juan thought that "not the militiamen, not anyone" could do much in the face of that protection. However, the young priest did have to go from house to house, begging for a haven, not knowing where or how he would be received. The fear of being caught hiding a priest, which would mean prison or martyrdom, made many good Christians close their doors to him. This pilgrimage in search of a hiding place was "a very hard thing." It was "not just a feeling of physical abandonment," but more like a feeling of being completely forsaken.[62]

---

[57] Mercedes Conde-Luque Herrero, AGP, RHF, T–04925, p. 1.

[58] The name of the Countess was Mercedes Herrero y Velázquez.

[59] Mercedes Conde-Luque Herrero, AGP, RHF, T–04925, p. 3.

[60] Their efforts to find a new haven were numerous, risky, and unfruitful. In some cases (that of Miguel Bañón's family, for instance) there was an insuperable fear about hiding a priest in the house. In other cases (like that of the Count of Leyva's household) there were already other refugees in the house, and the danger would have been multiplied. See Alvaro del Portillo, *Sum.* 881.

[61] Jiménez Vargas, AGP, RHF, T–04152–III, p. 55.

[62] Ibid., p. 58.

And yet, in the midst of that ordeal, Father Josemaría felt himself accompanied by God. The whole time that he was beset with insecurity and helplessness, he carried within him, very deeply, a joy and a peace. God let him suffer the abandonment of the homeless, of those without shelter, of those being pursued and having no place to hide. He shared the suffering of the members of the Work who were in danger, some of whom were on the run, some in isolation, several in prison.

His inquiries at the homes of friends and acquaintances proved unfruitful, as did also an attempt made by a daughter of the Count of Leyva to get him into the Cuban embassy. Finally, exhausted and not having found a hiding place, he ended up at the home of Don Alvaro González Valdés (the father of José María González Barredo), at 15 Caracas Street.

The revolutionary terror continued to escalate. The membership files of all kinds of associations (political, cultural, sports, or religious), together with accusations made by neighbors, colleagues, porters, or personal enemies, produced long lists of people to persecute.[63] Those being pursued had to change hiding places so often that their families frequently were in the dark concerning their whereabouts.

This was the case with Alvaro del Portillo, who had managed to find refuge with one of his brothers in a cottage on Serrano Street owned by a friend of the family. He had been hiding out there for a month when it occurred to him, at the beginning of September, to go to the business office of the Department of Bridges and Foundations, where he had worked before the war, to claim the pay he was due. Now, with some bills in his pocket, he decided to have a beer at La Mezquita, a bar in Alonso Martínez Plaza, not thinking about the fact that while sitting at a sidewalk table he could be asked for documentation he did not have. Fortunately it was not the police but Don Alvaro González Valdés who approached him. "Thank God I found you!" he said. "Do you know who is at my house? The Father! He asked me to let him rest for a little while because he couldn't keep standing any longer. But the porter can't be trusted. If he saw him, we're all in danger." [64]

---

[63] See Cervera Gil, pp. 175–79. Cervera discusses in detail the kinds of potential enemies of the revolution in the city, the most common ways of identifying them, and some of the people who were searched for.

[64] Alvaro del Portillo, *Sum.* 882.

Taking the Father with him, Alvaro went at once to Caracas Street. A few days later, Juan Jiménez Vargas joined them, and they went to the hiding place on Serrano Street, where they quietly spent the rest of September. The cottage was close to police headquarters. For what it was worth, the owner had placed on the balcony a sheet of paper with the Argentine flag on it. Errands and all communications with the outside were taken care of by the previous occupants' cook, an elderly woman who was not at all tongue-tied, and by a chauffeur, Selesio, who put in an appearance once in a while.

The Father gave meditations and celebrated "dry Masses" with his sons, and, since they had no books to read, they filled up the rest of the time by discussing many topics. They could hear the police radio station next door transmitting messages around the clock.

The Father spent three weeks in that house with Juan and with Alvaro and Pepe del Portillo. The first of October, the eve of the eighth anniversary of the founding of the Work, found them in relative tranquillity. The Father was expecting a favor from heaven, one of those "drops of honey" that God was habitually giving to sweeten his apostolic endeavors—such as the sending of a new vocation. "Alvaro, my son," he said, "tomorrow is October 2. What caress does our Lord have in reserve for us?" [65]

They soon found out. That same morning, Ramón, another of Alvaro's brothers, arrived with alarming news. They were all in danger: the militia might show up at any moment. They had searched the home of the owners of the cottage where they were staying and had killed six members of the family, among them a priest. Now they were coming to search the family's other houses. It was time to flee; the Argentine flag would not hold the militia back. Before leaving, the Father gave them absolution and felt his soul fill with joy at the thought of martyrdom, even as he had the sensation that his courage was disappearing, his body was weakening, his legs were trembling with fear. [66] The anticipated gift from God was the insight that all his courage was on loan. The grace expected to arrive on October 2 had come on its eve.

He quickly got his feet back on the ground, and they began their

---

[65] Alvaro del Portillo, PR, p. 614. For more on the "drops of honey," see Javier Echevarría, *Sum.* 3267.

[66] See Alvaro del Portillo, *Sum.* 466, 882, and 1499; Javier Echevarría, *Sum.* 2418; and Joaquín Alonso Pacheco, *Sum.* 4632.

search for a new hiding place. The Father called José María González Barredo, and they agreed to meet on Castellana Avenue, a principal north-south artery dividing Madrid, not very far from the cottage. Within a short time, the Father returned to the cottage, in such distress that as soon he got through the door, he broke out in tears. Alvaro asked him, "Father, why are you crying?"

In the short time that he had been out, he had run into someone who told him of the assassination of Father Lino Vea-Murguía, the priest who had gone with him on visits to hospitals and who had tended to the spiritual needs of the women of the Work. He had also been given some details about the martyrdom of his friend Father Pedro Poveda, of whose death he had already heard.[67]

After saying all this, the Father then explained why he had returned so quickly. He had in fact met José María González Barredo at the designated place on Castellana Avenue. Happy to have found a solution to their problem, Barredo had taken a small key from his vest pocket and handed it to Father Josemaría. The apartment in question belonged to some friends who were away; the doorman was trustworthy; so what problem could there be?

The Father listened attentively, to make sure he understood the situation. "But alone in a stranger's house," he said, "what am I going to say if someone comes to the door or calls on the phone?"

"Don't worry," said José María. "There's a maid there. She is totally trustworthy and can take care of whatever you need her to."

"And how old is this maid?"

"Probably twenty-two or twenty-three."

At this, Father Josemaría took the key back out of his pocket and said to José María, "My son, don't you realize that I am a priest, and that what with the war and the persecution, we all have shot nerves? I can't and don't want to put myself in a position of being closed in with a young woman day and night. I have a commitment to God which comes ahead of everything else. I would rather die than offend God by breaking this commitment of love." Then, by way of illustration, to help José María understand, he said, "Do you see this key you

[67] Father Pedro Poveda was arrested on July 27 and killed the next morning. Father Lino Vea-Murguía was seized at his home just after saying Mass and shot hours later, on August 16, in the Del Este Cemetery. For a detailed description of these events, see Camacho, pp. 91–96. See also Antonio Montero Moreno, *Historia de la Persecución Religiosa en España* (Madrid, 1961), p. 594; and Alvaro del Portillo, *Sum.* 1471.

gave me? It's going down into that sewer." And immediately he walked over to the sewer and threw the key in.[68]

On October 2, very early, they fled their refuge—and just in time. Right after they left, the militia showed up to search the cottage. The Father and Alvaro went to Juan's house.

Without papers, and in a haphazard way, they resumed their pilgrimage. It occurred to them to return to Herradores Plaza, where Joaquín Herrero Fontana lived with his sister and also their mother, Doña Mariana, and their grandmother. The older women (both of whom were widows) had welcomed the Father as a guest several weeks earlier.

The Father spent the hours of that October 2 recollected in prayer and begging God to protect his children. All went well until fear escalated into an obsession in the grandmother. She kept repeating, in a frenzy, "A priest in the house! They'll kill us all! A priest in the house! They'll kill us all!" [69] Her daughter and granddaughter tried to calm her, but to no avail. Under such conditions there was nothing anyone could do but think of a quick move for the priest and his companions.

October 3 found the Father, Alvaro, and José María González Barredo sitting exhausted and discouraged on a sidewalk curb at Cuatro Caminos Plaza. Suddenly Barredo had an idea: why not go visit Eugenio Sellés, a young professor of pharmacy who had met the Father at the Ferraz Street residence and who had generously and unwaveringly offered the use of his home? Sellés lived with his wife in the Albéniz development in Chamartín, which was at the end of the trolley line from the garden city, across an empty stretch where patrols brought groups of prisoners at night to be shot. The Father took that route with Alvaro and José María as evening fell the following day, detouring to avoid checkpoints where documentation would be needed. José María, after staying for a little while in the Sellés apartment, returned to Madrid.[70]

The young couple learned a lot in these days from the sagacity, good humor, and warmth of their two guests. Every night the four of them prayed the Rosary on their knees. The Selleses were especially

---

[68] See Alvaro del Portillo, *Sum.* 882 and 883, and Joaquín Alonso Pacheco, *Sum.* 4632.

[69] See Jiménez Vargas, AGP, RHF, T–04152–III, p. 60, and Joaquín Herrero Fontana, AGP, RHF, T–04812.

[70] See Eugenio Sellés Martí, AGP, RHF, T–02012, p. 1; Alvaro del Portillo, *Sum.* 883; and Juan Jiménez Vargas, AGP, RHF, T–04152–III, p. 62.

impressed by the calm confidence of the priest. "He behaved," says Eugenio, "with complete abandonment in God's hands, with no sign of tension, as if nothing out of the ordinary was happening."[71]

The search continued for a permanently safe hiding place for the Father. Finally, on Tuesday, October 6, Joaquín Herrero Fontana came to Juan's apartment to tell him everything had been arranged. Juan and Joaquín had spent several days trying to get Father Josemaría admitted to a psychiatric hospital! Juan had tried this at the Metropolitan Park facility, without success; Joaquín, who worked at the Emergency Hospital, had better luck. Having documentation that allowed him to move freely around Madrid, he spoke with Dr. Angel Suils, a colleague of his—from his own hometown of Logroño—who was in charge of a sanatorium for mental patients.[72] It was arranged that this new "patient" be admitted to the hospital the following day.

The Father and Alvaro left the Sellés apartment Tuesday afternoon. Alvaro went to seek another refuge, and the Father spent the night at Joaquín's place.[73] On October 7, at ten in the morning, they went to Juan's apartment, where a car sent from the Emergency Hospital picked them up. The driver was a militiaman. The "patient" was put in the back seat, alone, while Joaquín sat in front, next to the driver. Joaquín relates, "I told the driver that the person in the back seat was mentally ill, not dangerous but beset with delusions of grandeur, and that I was taking him to the sanatorium for treatment. The Father was talking to himself, and now and then would announce that he was Dr. Marañón. The driver replied, 'If he's that crazy, you might as well just shoot him and not waste our time.' "[74] From this it seems clear what

---

[71] Sellés Martí, AGP, RHF, T–02012, p. 2.

[72] Dr. Angel Suils Pérez was born in Logroño in 1906, and, like Father Josemaría, he went to high school at the Institute of Logroño. His father, Angel Suils Otto, was a doctor who knew the Escrivás and was present at the birth of Santiago. His grandfather had been an associate of Antonio Garrigosa, the man whom Don José Escrivá worked for in Logroño. See Jiménez Vargas, AGP, RHF, T–04152–III, p. 64.

[73] On this point the sources are a little vague and even slightly contradictory, which is understandable after an interval of forty years. We do, nevertheless, have some of the entries in the diary that Juan Jiménez Vargas kept, including those for October 6 to 15. On October 7 he writes, "At 10:00 the Father and Joaquín came to my place. And then Chiqui, to go to confession to the Father. Joaquín's maid said to him this morning, 'Good morning, Father.' I called the hospital to have them send a car here, and I told the porter that they would be asking for Dr. Fontana. We have hidden his I.D. in my apartment. Suils will sign the certificate, surely with a false name." See Appendix 2. See also Sellés Martí, AGP, RHF, T–02012, p. 2, and Jiménez Vargas, AGP, RHF, T–04152–III, pp. 64–65.

[74] Herrero Fontana, AGP, RHF, T–04812. Dr. Marañón was a famous doctor, a well-known writer, and a republican of strong liberal convictions.

the militiaman would have proposed had he known that this "crazy" man was a priest!

3. *In Dr. Suils' sanatorium*

The Father wore a dark blue suit with a gray shirt and sweater, but without a tie. Those who had seen him a few months earlier would have been surprised by his extreme thinness, his mustache, and his close-cropped hair. It was so short that the barber had looked pleased with his work and casting a glance at the wedding ring that had belonged to Don José, said, "Well, now even your wife won't recognize you!" [75] The wardrobe of the new patient was poor and scanty: an old overcoat, charitably donated by the Herrero Fontanas' mother in view of the coming cold weather, an assortment of underwear, and various items from different people.[76]

The clinic was a house on the outskirts of Madrid, in a partially built-up area with extensive building sites and vacant lots. The recently constructed building had a garden outside it and consisted of three floors: a semibasement for the most seriously mentally ill, and the other two floors for patients under observation. The letterhead of the clinic read:

Psychiatric Sanatorium of Ciudad Lineal
A Residence for Rest and Health
Mental illnesses, nerve problems, drug addictions
Modern treatment
Medical Director: Dr. D. Angel Suils
492 Arturo Soria, telephone 51188
Ciudad Lineal (Madrid)
Just off the Aragón highway [77]

Dr. Suils was away from the clinic, so the patient was interviewed by his assistant, Dr. Turrientes. Without beating around the bush, Dr. Turrientes said to Father Josemaría, "Look, I know that you are a priest, but you need to be very careful about speaking of such things around here." [78] The new arrival kept a prudent silence, without prom-

---

[75] See AGP, RHF, EF–370505–4.
[76] See Appendix 2.
[77] See AGP, RHF, D–15348.
[78] See AGP, RHF, D–15348; Jiménez Vargas, AGP, RHF, T–04152–III, p. 64ff; María Luisa Polanco Fernández, AGP, RHF, T–04835; Santiago Escrivá de Balaguer y Albás, AGP, RHF, T–07921, p. 20ff; and Carmen Peñalver Gómez de las Cortinas, AGP, RHF, T–05090.

ising anything. He stopped repeating that he was Dr. Marañón and started pretending that he had lost his voice due to a nervous problem. This gave him the opportunity to study his new environment without any risk to himself.

In his room on the second floor, Father Josemaría must have felt terribly the isolation of the first few days. On Tuesday, October 13, Juan writes in his journal, "Before leaving the house I called the doctor on duty at the sanatorium. The Father is well. We can go see him if we want. . . . The mother of Herrero (he wasn't at home) says that it would be a crazy idea to visit him—that it is understandable if he is worried, not knowing anything about us, but we must restrain ourselves. She's right, although I think of what the Father must be praying for. Completely isolated. We would love to see him too, but we don't want to create new complications by affectionate foolishness. And so I went to Suils' house this afternoon and told him that the Father shouldn't worry about anyone, and should act as if we weren't even in Madrid. No phone calls, or anything. Only if he is in any danger should they call my home. Dr. Suils told me that the Father has been feigning a trauma-induced inability to speak, and that he's now beginning to say something, but very little so as to avoid arousing suspicion." [79]

Juan Jiménez Vargas, being accustomed to danger, had his own ways of going in for "affectionate foolishness." During the last few days he had done nothing else but eagerly serve other members of the Work. He visited Alvaro, who was trying to obtain refuge in the Mexican embassy. He was concerned to find out how Chiqui (José María Hernández Garnica) was doing. He spent time with José María González Barredo, Isidoro, and Vicente Rodríguez Casado, a member of the Work who could not leave his house for fear of being incarcerated. And without the knowledge of the Father he was trying to make it possible for him to say Mass. [80]

In those first months of terror the religious persecution was merciless. Priests who were not incarcerated or killed were in hiding. The churches were either torched or appropriated for secular uses. Sacristies were dismantled. It was a return to the Church of the catacombs. Aware of the tribulation and anguish of Spanish Catholics, the Holy See granted priests permission "to celebrate the Holy

---

[79] See Appendix 2.
[80] See Jiménez Vargas, AGP, RHF, T–04152–III, pp. 65–66.

Sacrifice without an altar, without sacred vestments, and using, in place of a chalice, a decent drinking glass." [81] It took several weeks for these dispositions regarding worship to become widely known to the faithful in the republican zone.

Without knowing either the personnel or the modus operandi of the sanatorium, it would be extremely risky to try to have the Father say Mass there without advance preparations. Eugenio Sellés, who lived not very far away, offered to let him say Mass at his house. But this was not to be.

The last lines of Juan Jiménez Vargas's journal speak optimistically of this matter. "It is a wonderful thing, this 'imprudence' of Sellés," he says. "In his house, no, we can't do it there, but I think maybe at the sanatorium we could. It would, of course, have to be done without anybody knowing about it. A little argument took place at Joaquín's house. His mother told me yesterday that she prays for me constantly because I'm taking my life in my hands by walking around on the streets so much! I answered her that I must have nine lives, like a cat, and still have plenty left, because with all the doctors I've been to and all the blows I've suffered in my years, I haven't managed to use up more than four or five." [82]

This entry, dated October 15, 1936, is the last one because, says Juan, no sooner had he decided to bring the Father to the Sellés house to say Mass than, "just when I was waiting for Isidoro, to go with him to the insane asylum, a patrol showed up and I got arrested." [83]

*   *   *

When María Luisa Polanco, a nurse at Dr. Suils' sanatorium, reconstructs her memories, she is surprised to retain such a clear image of this priest; he is one of the residents that she best recalls. At a distance of almost half a century, she nostalgically remembers the clinic as "a little house, very pretty, surrounded by a garden." There in the garden, she says, on the cold, sunny days at the end of autumn, she saw

---

[81] Because of the extent and cruelty of the religious persecution in the republican zone, and the difficulties in administering the sacraments, some bishops and abbots had written to the Holy See. In a letter dated August 22, 1936, Papal Secretary of State Cardinal Pacelli (the future Pope Pius XII) announced to the superior general of the Missionaries of the Immaculate Heart of Mary that the Pope had granted, officially and to all priests in Spain, the requested permission to celebrate Mass without altar or vestments "while the current sad circumstances last." See Montero Moreno, pp. 99–100.

[82] See Appendix 2.

[83] Jiménez Vargas, AGP, RHF, T–04152–III, p. 66. See also Pero-Sanz, p. 199.

Father Josemaría walking, wrapped up in a blanket, and talking with another fugitive.[84]

The sanatorium admittedly did not have the dreary, depressing appearance of most mental institutions of those days, where inmates endured their miseries behind bars. But it was hardly the place of carefree relaxation that calling it "A Residence for Rest and Health" suggested. Legally it was a kind of limited-partnership collective, approved by the Medical Association of Madrid, which, though directed by "Comrade Angel Suils," was "controlled by its personnel, completely subject to the socialist union."[85]

The permanent staff consisted of two doctors, three nurses, an administrator, a couple of attendants (in charge of guarding the patients), a cook, and a laundrywoman. The nurses were a mixed group as far as political views were concerned. Two were communists who were capable of turning in a priest. But the third, María Luisa Polanco, a confidante of Dr. Suils, was a Falangist. A brother of hers, also a Falangist, had been assassinated in Bilbao, and she herself, because she knew Dr. Suils, had come to the sanatorium as a refugee. At least one of the attendants was a fanatical communist. As for the administrator, we know only that the militia one day came hunting "fascists" at the "Residence for Rest and Health" and told him, "Don't bother changing your clothes, comrade; we just need ten minutes of your time so you can make a statement at the station; you'll return in the same car"—and he was never seen again.[86]

The staff took care of about twenty patients. The situation of the most seriously disturbed, the ones in the semibasement, was very sad, often tragic.

An old lady, Doña Carmen, whose son had killed himself after committing a crime of passion, would suddenly go from profound apathy to rabid rage. Another patient continually stalked the corridors and the garden in a frenzy, spitting at invisible persecutors and threatening them. But the best-known and most picturesque case was that of Don Italo, who was severely schizophrenic. "Don Italo, illustrious pharmacist," they would call him, to which he would invariably reply, with genuine modesty, "Learned pharmacist, which is not

---

[84] See Polanco Fernández, AGP, RHF, T–04835.

[85] See AGP, RHF, D–03414 and D–15348.

[86] See Polanco Fernández, AGP, RHF, T–04835. That administrator was succeeded by Celso Lacalzada, a man from Logroño who was an acquaintance of Dr. Suils.

the same!" "One day," recounts Father Josemaría, "he came up to me and said point-blank, 'Sir, immerse yourself in this environment, stand tall, cast off those thoughts, loosen up those clamps, and you will get well." [87]

Most of the people on the second and third floors, those "under observation," were healthy, sane refugees feigning nervous conditions or mental disorders. There were also a few special cases, such as a six-year-old boy (a nephew of one of the medical assistants) whose parents had been murdered in Extremadura. The woman who had been taking care of him managed to escape with him to Madrid. The murderers were looking for the orphan, determined to eliminate the only heir of those landowners, whose farm they had seized. Finally, there were some individuals who had entered pretending to be mentally ill, but who had ended up truly insane because of the constant tension. [88]

Juan now being in jail, Isidoro Zorzano became the link and messenger. Born in Buenos Aires, he had Argentine documentation and an armband with his country's flag, which enabled him to move around Madrid in relative safety. Fairly often he visited the Father, bringing him news of his scattered family. In October, Vicente Rodríguez Casado was given refuge in the Norwegian embassy. Alvaro del Portillo, after several weeks of looking for one, found a refuge—a local branch of the Finnish embassy—but only for a short time, because on December 3 and 4 militia raided the Finnish branches and he ended up in the notorious prison of San Antón. So did Chiqui. Manolo Sainz de los Terreros and Juan were in the Porlier jail. [89]

The massive detentions of persons not belonging to any of the revolutionary parties were due to the advance of nationalist troops on Madrid. At the end of October they were already at the very gates of the capital. There the republican army, reinforced by the recently arrived International Brigades, stopped them at the beginning of November. [90] To their great joy, the patients at Dr. Suils' clinic could see

---

[87] See AGP, RHF, EF–370505–4 and Alvaro del Portillo, *Sum.* 884. The full name of this pharmacist was Don Italo Della Torre Morasso.

[88] See Jiménez Vargas, AGP, RHF, T–04152-III, pp. 71–74, and María Luisa Polanco Fernández, AGP, RHF, T–04835.

[89] See Pero-Sanz, pp. 197–204; Jiménez Vargas, AGP, RHF, T–04152–III, pp. 67–69; and Alvaro del Portillo, *Sum.* 884. See also Aurelio Núñez Morgado, *Los sucesos de España vistos por un diplomático* (Madrid, 1979); Javier Rubio García-Mina, *Asilos y canjes durante la Guerra Civil española: Aspectos humanitarios de una contienda fratricida* (Barcelona, 1979); Bolloten, p. 119; and Cervera Gil, pp. 79–84 and 229–33.

[90] The International Brigades were formed under the initiative of the Communist International (Comintern) and recruited volunteers all over the world: see Bolloten, pp.

from the garden the flashes from the artillery in the Puerto de Hierro, Ciudad Universitaria, and Casa de Campo districts. Don Italo, mistaking the cannon flashes for festival lights, exclaimed, "Now the crazy people are in Madrid! They're having a party, right in the middle of Madrid. How good it is to be here, how peaceful."[91] That was, however, no beginning of a fiesta, but rather the start of a horrific carnage. Fearing encirclement by enemies, the militias carried out a bloody and subhuman suppression of what was called the "fifth column."[92] Throughout November the overflowing general prisons were systematically emptied on revolutionaries' orders. At night, prisoners were loaded into trucks and taken to the infamous Paracuellos del Jarama or some other place near Madrid, where they were executed en masse.[93]

The district of Ciudad Universitaria, which was near the neighborhood that the apartment on Dr. Cárceles Street was in, had to be

---

205–207. See also George Esenwein, "El Frente Popular: La política Republicana durante la guerra civil," in Payne and Tusell, pp. 367–70.

[91] See Jiménez Vargas, AGP, RHF, T–04152–III, pp. 71–72.

[92] Cervera Gil (pp. 139–40), says, "The term 'fifth column' originated in the Spanish Civil War, in the weeks before the attack on Madrid. It is not certain who coined it, but probably it was General Mola. At the beginning of October 1936, believing that a capture of Madrid was imminent, this nationalist leader said that the capital would fall as a result of the efforts of the four columns of General Varela, which were then approaching it, and of a fifth column already inside it: the supporters of the nationalists. A classically stupid remark, to say the least, considering its effect on violent men who in the first months of the war had already shown no disposition to practice restraint out of moral consideration. The result was a feverish campaign to eliminate fifth columnists and to purge the rear guard clean of traitors. Hugh Thomas, however, attributes the expression 'fifth column' to the British journalist Lord St. Oswald, who used it in a dispatch to the *Daily Telegraph* in September."

[93] After the initial chaos of the military uprising, by August of 1936 the map of Spain was divided in half, with borders separating the zones controlled by the rebels from those controlled by the republican government. The republican forces had an obvious superiority in terms of territorial expanse and of population; they had Madrid, Barcelona, and Valencia, and in their camp were the industrial areas, the financial resources, and the gold reserves of the Bank of Spain. However, the confusion among the republican rulers and a lack of discipline and cohesion in the revolutionary militias made it possible for nationalist offensives to equalize the troop strength, the territory, and the monetary assets of the two sides before winter.

The advance of the nationalist troops on Madrid in October 1936 reached the outskirts of the city, forcing the government to move to Valencia. This was the time of uncontrolled arrests and systematic takings of prisoners to be shot en masse. "Of the seventeen thousand who were executed or murdered in Madrid, almost half died in that fateful November": Ramón and Jesús Salas Larrazábal, *Historia General de la Guerra de España* (Madrid, 1986), p. 161. See also Rafael Casas de la Vega, *El Terror: Madrid 1936: Investigación de víctimas y catálogo de víctimas identificadas* (Madrid, 1994), pp. 191–228; and Matilde Vázquez and Javier Valero, *La Guerra Civil en Madrid* (Madrid, 1978), pp. 118–19.

evacuated. The Escrivás, in the hope that nationalist troops would soon occupy the area, resisted abandoning their home. But because their neighborhood was so close to the battlefront, they were incommunicado for several days, Isidoro being unable to get to them so that he could let the Father know their situation.

Toward the end of November, Doña Dolores had to move her family into a hotel on Mayor Street, near the Puerta del Sol (the center of Madrid). Her luggage, says Santiago, "consisted only of "one suitcase with the indispensable items, and the trunk with the papers of the Work."[94] As soon as he heard of the move, Isidoro went to the hotel and brought the Escrivás to the apartment of Don Alvaro González Valdés, the father of José María González Barredo.[95] The apartment was half empty, his son having taken refuge in Dr. Suils' clinic at the beginning of November, when the searches and arrests had intensified.

The Escrivás came to the apartment at 15 Caracas with all their meager luggage. Then, says Juan, the trunk "became a nightmare."[96] Alarmed at the sight of it (no one knows why), the porter wanted to examine it. Its owners flatly refused to let him do so. The porter would not back down, but neither would Carmen. She told him that "on principle she did not want to open it, and would sooner leave it in the doorway," and there it remained.[97]

Ultimately it was Santiago who paid for that argument. The porter refused to let him live in that building. Perhaps he thought that the boy was of military age and feared that in case of a search, he would be held responsible for having withheld information about new residents. In view of this impasse, and of how complicated things were getting, and of the fact that only a few yards from the building were two "checas" and the barracks of an anarchist column that a few days earlier had killed fifty police officers, Isidoro and Doña Dolores agreed that Santiago should go live with his brother at the asylum.[98] There he

[94] Santiago Escrivá de Balaguer y Albás, AGP, RHF, T–07921, p. 20.
[95] See Pero-Sanz, pp. 199–200.
[96] Jiménez Vargas, AGP, RHF, T–04152–III, p. 77.
[97] Santiago Escrivá de Balaguer y Albás, AGP, RHF, T–07921, p. 21.
[98] The "checas," along with the prisons, were agents of uncontrolled and arbitrary repression in Madrid. "According to Peter Weiden," says Cervera Gil (p. 60), "the word 'checa' was used throughout Spain to refer to the dreaded tribunals (often self-appointed) which sprang up in many neighborhoods for the purpose of eliminating the 'Fascist enemy,' often on the basis of accusations with the flimsiest credibility. 'CHEKA' is a Russian acronym for 'Pan-Russian Special Committee for the Suppression of the

was admitted as "a companion of a patient under observation." Dr. Turrientes picked him up at the apartment and took him to the clinic by streetcar. The trunk with the papers followed soon after.[99]

The tranquility of that "Residence for Rest and Health" did, as one can well imagine, leave something to be desired. On one occasion a militia patrol arrived, strode in very purposefully, and carried off the Duke of Peñaranda, brother of the Duke of Alba.[100] The Father did not learn what had happened until the next day. With deep sorrow he went to the director of the sanatorium to complain about not having been notified. "From now on," he said, "no one is to be taken from here without my hearing his confession and giving him absolution."[101]

Despite the advice given him by Dr. Turrientes upon his arrival at the sanatorium, priestly zeal had led Father Josemaría to begin drawing the refugees to himself, one by one, after a few days. "I have the feeling," says Dr. Suils' assistant, "that he spoke to absolutely everyone."[102] Although the refugees all shared the same danger, they had nothing else in common except the mistrust arising from the fear of betrayal. The Marchioness of Las Torres de Orán, who along with her husband quickly became friends with Father Josemaría, says that the atmosphere among the residents at the clinic "was one of suspicion."[103] Yet they each had their own story, and when they opened their hearts it was because Father Josemaría had let them know that he was a priest.

Aside from the ones who were mentally ill, the people at the sanatorium came from very diverse backgrounds. The staff sought, as the last line of the clinic's statutes reads, "through friendly collaboration in a single ideal to foster material well-being by means of work."[104] Doctors Suils and Turrientes were protecting the refugees in reaction

---

Counterrevolution and of Sabotage,' the first Soviet police force, precursor of the OGPV, the NKVD, and the KGB. The checas proliferated principally in Madrid, Barcelona, and Valencia." Cervera found that in those years there were more than two hundred of them in Madrid. A map showing the location of the most important ones can be found on pp. 64–65 of the work cited. On p. 63, in his account of the "checas most notorious for their repressive activity," he discusses the fate of the Ferraz Street residence. See also Casas de la Vega, *El Terror: Madrid 1936* (Madrid, 1994), pp. 75–120.

[99] See Santiago Escrivá de Balaguer y Albás, AGP, RHF, T–07921, p. 22; and Pero-Sanz, p. 200.

[100] The Duke of Peñaranda de Duero was Hernando Stuart Fitz-James Falco. His brother's name was Jacobo.

[101] Alvaro del Portillo, *Sum.* 896.

[102] See AGP, RHF, D–15348.

[103] Carmen Peñalver Gómez de las Cortinas, AGP, RHF, T–05090, p. 1. The name of her husband, the Marquis, was Don Manuel María Fernández de Prada y Vasco.

[104] See AGP, RHF, D–15348.

to the criminality running rampant in this time of war. For others, the opportunity of running a business, even one dealing with one of the most horrible situations in human life, inclined them to pretend not to be aware of where their clients came from. Juan Jiménez Vargas had already noticed this on October 10. His journal entry for that day reads, "We were a little worried about the sanatorium. They seem a bit too eager about collecting their payments, which doesn't give us much confidence about how safe it's going to be here. But I already knew this, and it seems to me a reason to give it a try, since they apparently are helpful as long as they get their money." [105]

All things considered, the food was neither bad nor in short supply. Santiago says this place was where he was able to "eat best" until the end of the war, although his appetite was conditioned by the hunger he had suffered in the apartment on Dr. Cárceles Street. Meals consisted of a single dish that varied daily—red beans, chickpeas, lentils, rice—and for dessert, oranges. For these provisions they had the clinic's union affiliation to thank. Don Italo, however, was not impressed by the cook's efforts. On calm, sunny days Don Italo could be seen walking in the garden holding a flowerpot with nothing in it (not even soil) and affectionately watering it, drop by drop, waiting for juicy cutlets to bloom.[106]

With the arrivals of José María González Barredo and Santiago, a new stage of sanatorium life began for Father Josemaría. The three of them occupied the room next to that of the Marquis and the Marchioness of Las Torres de Orán. Taking the necessary precautions to do so without sacrilege, Father Josemaría celebrated Mass almost every day. Isidoro provided him the wine and the hosts. The room had a large wardrobe, and he said Mass on one of its shelves, keeping the doors open so that if someone entered suddenly, they would not immediately see what was going on. For greater security, he asked the help of María Luisa. He said to the nurse, "Would you please sit on the sofa and keep watch while I say Mass? If anyone comes, knock on the door or speak in a loud voice." [107] (The sofa was a small one strategically located in the area between the Father's room and the room of one of the communist nurses.) After Mass he would give Communion to some of the refugees and hear confessions.

---

[105] See Appendix 2.
[106] See Jiménez Vargas, AGP, RHF, T–04152–III, p. 71.
[107] See Polanco Fernández, AGP, RHF, T–04835.

When Doña Carmen, the old woman who had gone mad after her son's suicide, was in a state of apathy, she was very courteous and attentive; but in her fits of anger she would spit out atrocious insults at everyone except Father Josemaría, whom she affectionately referred to as "the little old man." "Don Josemaría is so good," she said, "that he must be at least a general." Other times she would say, "Don José is not Don José; he is San José." [108]

Such praise, needless to say, was not music to the ears of the patients or nurses who supported the Popular Front. One of the nurses strongly suspected that he might be a refugee priest, but one day he quickly put those suspicions to rest. Lowering his voice, he told her in a confidential whisper that he was Dr. Marañón, and that she must at all costs keep this a secret.[109]

José María, whom no one seemed to have any suspicions about, began to cause the Father and Santiago some anxiety by trying to appear crazy and not being very good at it. He acted so strangely, going into such exaggerated relapses, that even the demented patients found his behavior bizarre. It included turning on the lights at strange times and jumping repeatedly out the window into the garden and back again—luckily, no big jump, so he suffered no harm.

With the first frosts the Father began to suffer rheumatic pains. Someone brought him a small heater, but he immediately gave it to his neighbors, the Marquis and his wife, saying he did not need it.[110] At the beginning of December, instead of prescribing a simple painkiller, the doctors decided to give him an injection of bee venom, a treatment that was then very fashionable. Dr. Suils may have wanted to kill two birds with one stone: to prevent further rheumatic attacks by provoking a strong reaction that would convince the rest of the staff that Father Josemaría was really sick.

The effects of the poison were "explosive and terrible," his brother relates. Dr. Suils, in fact, "thought they had killed him with those injections."[111] The patient was left paralyzed and in great pain, hardly able to move his head. His only nourishment was orange juice. After

---

[108] See Jiménez Vargas, AGP, RHF, T–04152–III, p. 72.

[109] See Alvaro del Portillo, *Sum.* 885, and Jiménez Vargas, AGP, RHF, T–04152–III, p. 74. José María González Barredo gives a related anecdote: "The Father wrapped his eyeglasses in white paper and wrote on it, 'These are Dr. Marañón's glasses'" (AGP, RHF, T–04202, p. 14).

[110] See Carmen Peñalver Gómez de las Cortinas, AGP, RHF, T–05090, p. 2.

[111] Santiago Escrivá de Balaguer y Albás, AGP, RHF, T–07921, p. 22. See also Jiménez Vargas, AGP, RHF, T–04152–III, pp. 80–81.

fifteen or twenty days in bed, however, he was partially recovered, and in the end, though weak and very frail, he was cured of his rheumatism.

Parties of militiamen continued to show up to inspect the sanatorium. The building was fairly close to the highway to Aragón, which carried trucks to and from the battlefront. If they happened to stop nearby, the troops would get out to stretch their legs, look around, and sometimes fill their canteens at the sanatorium. That was when the demented residents served their purpose as protective shields. The director had given instructions that on those occasions, the patients in the semibasement should be brought out and allowed to walk freely in the garden. The militia, moved either by fear or by a pitying disgust, would quickly leave the garden.

Don Italo was a central figure in one of those encounters. Coming upon a group of militiamen, he went to examine the gas mask one of them was carrying, and in his ever courteous and refined manner he said, "With all respect, and if you would be so kind, could you please explain to me how this wind instrument works?" [112]

Finally Isidoro brought the Father the identity document he had been waiting for. It was a simple sheet of paper imprinted with the seal of the "Madrid Delegation Committee of the Basque Nationalist Party" and bearing the following text: "We ask the authorities and the militias of all the parties of the Popular Front to allow José María Escriba Albás to circulate freely, since he is a person attached to the Government. Madrid, December 23, 1936. For the Committee [here appears a signature]." [113]

---

[112] See González Barredo, AGP, RHF, T–04202, p. 14, and Jiménez Vargas, AGP, RHF, T–04152–III, p. 71.

[113] AGP, RHF, D–15068. Juan's journal entry for October 15 reads, "It would be a good idea to speak with Elordi, to see if we could get the Father a safe-conduct pass as a Basque nationalist" (see Appendix 2). At that time, when nationalist troops were advancing toward Madrid, many people were ordered to produce documentation and many were arrested, since, as this journal entry continues, "The personal ID card is not enough; they demand evidence of being trusted by the Popular Front."
Juan did not get very far with his plan, since that same week he landed in a prison cell. Isidoro then contacted Elordi, who, as a Basque, would know people in the Basque Nationalist Party who were in Madrid. Elordi had received spiritual direction from Father Josemaría and had taken part in the formation classes given at the Ferraz Street residence during the 1934–1935 school year. In the August and September 1935 issues of *Noticias* there is mention of the Father having received a letter from him during the summer vacation (see AGP, RHF, D–03696).
As for "Escriba," that was definitely not a mistake, but rather a deliberate alteration of the spelling, with the irony intended. ("Escriba" is a form of "escribir," meaning "to

Though the Basque nationalists were hardly attached to the ideology of the Popular Front, their hopes of obtaining political autonomy kept them on the side of the republican government.[114] A document without a photo of the person in question, who was not even a member of the Basque Nationalist Party, would be of little value with the inspection patrols, but it might at least get one through a superficial check.

Isidoro, the Father's one contact with the outside world, brought him news from Caracas Street and from his sons in prison, and wrote to the members of the Work in Valencia and carried on other works of mercy.[115] The Father, meanwhile, in his isolation, kept himself spiritually united to the dispersed members of the Work through his suffering and prayer. There are impressive anecdotes from those days when "extractions of prisoners" were made for the nightly shootings,[116] anecdotes illustrating the widely held conviction that the Father's prayers saved some of his sons. Chiqui is a case in point. He was on the truck with other prisoners waiting to be driven to the place of execution when his name was called and he was ordered to get off.

---

write" or "to spell.") This version appears on all the official documents received by Father Josemaría until he left the republican zone. See AGP, RHF, D–15067 (statements given by Dr. Suils on March 14 and August 22 of 1937), D–15070 (the certificate from the Honduran consulate, dated August 1, 1937), and D–15125 (the safe-conduct pass dated October 25, 1937).

[114] See Lecha-Marzo, *El Partido Nacionalista Vasco ante la guerra de España: 1936–1937* (Pamplona, 1992). The republican assembly approved the Statute for the Basques on October 1, 1936, and on October 7 the Basque Provisional Government was set up. Almost all of the Basque province of Guipúzcoa and a great part of the province of Alava had already become part of the nationalist zone, while the rest of the Basque territory was isolated from the Spanish capital. Cervera Gil (p. 354) says, "This permitted the Basques to accentuate their autonomy, through which their delegation in Madrid did in fact acquire a respect and status similar to that of the embassies and legations. . . . The number of persons to whom the Basque delegation provided documents enabling them to live freely in Madrid was somewhere between 2,350 and 2,850. . . . Thus the activity of the Basque delegation in Madrid during the civil war was analogous to that carried out by the diplomatic representatives, and was even broader in some cases." See also Jesús de Galíndez, *Los vascos en el Madrid sitiado* (Buenos Aires, 1945).

[115] See Pero-Sanz, pp. 200–204.

[116] "In November," says Cervera (pp. 84–85), "Madrid's prisons became the scene of some of the most tragic episodes of the civil war: massive removals of prisoners for execution, actions which also made obvious the lack of control of the situation by the republican authorities. These murders, commonly referred to as 'extractions of prisoners,' took place between November 7 and December 4, 1936. . . . The days on which these expeditions took place are known through the documentation of Madrid's General Office of Security and the testimonies contained in its General Office of Prosecution." Cervera offers descriptions of some of those deeds. See also Ian Gibson, *Paracuellos: cómo fue* (Barcelona, 1983); Carlos Fernández, *Paracuellos del Jarama: Carrillo culpable?* (Barcelona, 1983); and Casas de la Vega, pp. 135–90.

The truck then drove away to the killing ground. Chiqui returned to his cell.[117]

Juan Jiménez Vargas says, "Toward the end of 1936 there was a series of episodes in which one can see that all of us were saved, more than once, in ways that were humanly inexplicable. Some of these things happened in the prisons."[118] In November Juan was in the Porlier prison, which was being emptied, corridor by corridor, for the nightly shootings. His turn came on November 26. The prisoners lined up and walked to a truck waiting on the street. It loaded up and drove off, leaving Juan and three others to be taken on a second trip. The truck returned just before daybreak. A half hour passed. Then it was announced that the operation had ended, and those left in his corridor were spared.

*   *   *

The relative calm of the sanatorium was soon disturbed. In January 1937, Isidoro, who had been negotiating for this, finally got Juan Jiménez Vargas released from the Porlier prison. After hiding, un-documented and at risk of rearrest, in his parents' apartment for two weeks, Juan was by the Father's efforts admitted to Dr. Suils' sanatorium.[119]

Two other new refugees arrived at the same time: an air force commander, and a Falangist from Logroño named Alejandro Láscaris Comneno.[120] Fear and mistrust greeted the three newcomers. The "patients under observation" fell suddenly silent; those who had been coming to Father Josemaría for confession or advice did not leave their rooms; no one walked in the garden. Dr. Suils, anticipating an "inspection," strongly urged Láscaris to leave the hospital, and then told José María González Barredo and Juan that they too must leave. For the sake of peace and especially the Father's safety, they went to their homes in Madrid. Meanwhile Father Josemaría consumed the consecrated hosts he had been keeping for giving Communion when he could not say Mass.

Several days passed. As the inspection began to look like a false

---

[117] See Alvaro del Portillo, *Sum.* 888, and Juan Jiménez Vargas, AGP, RHF, T–04152–III, p. 78.

[118] Jiménez Vargas, AGP, RHF, T–04152–III, p. 79.

[119] See Pero-Sanz, p. 201.

[120] See Santiago Escrivá de Balaguer y Albás, AGP, RHF, T–07921, p. 23, and Juan Jiménez Vargas, AGP, RHF, T–04152–III, p. 85.

alarm, the "patients under observation" became optimistic again and started to move around the sanatorium with a restored sense of confidence. But the Father had suffered greatly. When things settled down, he went to see the director and said, "I can't stay in a place my sons have been thrown out of." [121] He strongly reproached Dr. Suils for what he had done and said he had decided to seek another refuge.

In February 1937, Isidoro told him that José María Hernández Garnica (Chiqui) had been transferred on the fifth from the San Antón prison in Madrid to the San Miguel de los Reyes prison in Valencia. After months of communicating through Isidoro with members of the Work in Valencia, he wrote them directly.

> Madrid, February 10, 1937
> Dear friends:
>
> I have been very anxious to write you, and, finally, I am taking advantage of Isidoro's visit to give him this letter.
>
> My head seems to be getting better. I've been in this sanatorium for quite a while now. Although time passes slowly, I console myself by remembering that I am locked up for my own good, by my Father's orders. And besides, I never forget that there is nothing bad that lasts a hundred years.
>
> My great concern, in my loneliness, in the midst of so many poor patients like myself, is my children. How much I think about them and about our family's marvelous future!
>
> At the moment, Chiqui is my top concern (if my heart can make distinctions among my children, all equally dear). See if by means of some friend of yours you can help him in his present predicament.
>
> This poor madman sends you hugs and love.
>
> Josemaría
> (Write to Isidoro.) [122]

*   *   *

From that point on, he poured out his soul in letters to his children. From February until September (when he left the haven in the Honduran consulate that he moved to in March), there are more than one

[121] See Santiago Escrivá de Balaguer y Albás, AGP, RHF, T–07921, p. 23, and Juan Jiménez Vargas, AGP, RHF, T–04152–III, p. 87.

[122] AGP, RHF, EF–370210–1.

hundred seventy letters written from his hiding place to the members of Opus Dei. Those pages are packed with the vigorous ardor of his spirit. The feelings of his heart brim over, sustaining his sons in their faith and encouraging their hopes for the future of the divine enterprise to which they all were committed.

Unable to stay inactive any longer at the "Residence for Rest and Health," he asked God to let him leave as soon as possible. José María González Barredo, through a friend who was a friend of a son-in-law of the Honduran consul, had found refuge in the Honduran consulate, and, once there, he obtained permission for the Father and Santiago to be admitted.[123]

On the eve of his move, the Father again wrote to those in Valencia.

Madrid, March 12, 1937
My dear friends:

I have just spent some time in the insane asylum with my poor brother Josemaría. Knowing how interested you are in him, I will speak to you about practically nothing else.

It was to be expected that he would end up in a mental hospital, since starting in October 1928 he has been completely crazy. Do you know what he says he is? A little donkey. Luckily he doesn't go around braying, although on January 9, when he turned thirty-five, he claimed he was thirty-five brays. As far as his mood is concerned, he is doing very well. He is full of optimism, sure (he says) that the idea he is obsessed with will very soon become a successful reality. He thinks constantly of his children, and, being old-fashioned and crazy, he blesses them, each one specifically, several times a day. It now occurs to him—he knows there's a war going on—that his Chiqui, who is only a year away from being a mining engineer, might do well to go to work for some archi-

---

[123] José María González Barredo tells us that after he had spent a few days in his father's apartment, his friend Manuel Valdés (the friend who knew the son-in-law of the Honduran consul) arranged for a consulate car to be sent to pick him up. As soon as he was in the consulate, he obtained permission for the Father and Juan Jiménez Vargas to join him, without the consul knowing about it; he was presented with it as a fait accompli. See José María González Barredo, AGP, RHF, T–04202, p. 16, and José Luis Rodríguez-Candela Manzaneque, AGP, RHF, T–05120, p. 1. Rodríguez-Candela, the son-in-law of the consul, did not know the Father personally, although he had heard some friends speak about him. They had invited him to go to the DYA Academy.

tect involved in building fortifications. He has asked "the little watchmaker" (a friend of his whom the others haven't met) to find him a highly recommended doctor who can cure him.

He asked me to congratulate Chiqui on his saint's day— that's what he told me, and that's how I'm writing it—and he added, "and for his renewal feast."

Really, poor Josemaría is totally gone; every day he is more daft.

My warmest greetings. Forgive the silliness of this letter.

A big hug from
Mariano[124]

This letter is written in one of the codes he used because of the censors. Correspondence with a priest being extremely risky, information is eliminated that would place the recipient in danger, but the meaning is clear. The convention of speaking of himself in the third person is something he also uses in his journal.[125] Speaking as an old dodderer permits him to say to his "grandchildren" all sorts of "childish" things about divine realities.[126]

Nonetheless, it is surprising that he had no problems with the wartime censors. Apparently no one paid much attention to the letters of a grandfather, even if they were written in a strange jargon. The Father was well aware of the risk he was running—Juan Jiménez Vargas reminded him of it all the time—but his affection for his family, the Work, won out. In this wartime correspondence (sent under the protection of our Lady), and also later on, he used the name Mariano, one of his baptismal names, as a sign of devotion to Mary.

4. *Asylum in the Honduran consulate*

On March 14 he left the sanatorium, with a doctor's certificate reading:

---

[124] AGP, RHF, EF–370312–1.

[125] As, for example, when he writes, "My God—Love—thrash the donkey, who doesn't deserve anything but whacks" (*Apuntes*, no. 388; November 12, 1931). See also *Apuntes*, nos. 1128 (11 Feb 1934) and 1371 (30 Jun 1936).

[126] The Father had for some time been speaking of his divine "wild idea," of his "obsession" with doing the Work, while speaking of new members as "lunatics" entering the "insane asylum." The terms with double meanings included "bread" (the

"Madrid, March 14, 1937. As of today, Don José María Escriba Albás is discharged from this sanatorium. At present he is not completely cured, which means he is restricted from doing any kind of work, bearing any responsibilities, doing any traveling, or engaging in other types of activities. In the sanatorium he was accompanied by his 15-year-old brother Santiago, who should remain near him. The Director, Dr. A. Suils." [127]

The Marchioness of Las Torres de Orán recalls that, after saying Mass and administering Communion, he gave them some small host particles carefully wrapped in cigarette paper, so that after he was gone they could receive Communion without touching the sacred host.[128]

From that of Dr. Suils, he now came under the protection of Don Pedro Jaime de Matheu Salazar, a Salvadoran diplomat who at this time was serving as honorary consul general of the Republic of Honduras. From the outside, the consular residence, at 51 (later 53) Paseo de la Castellana, looked a great deal more comfortable than it was. The first-floor foyer, though spacious, had very little light and some old furniture that looked discarded. Through a door of leaded glass on the left, one came into a large, dilapidated room; it had a large window facing the Paseo de la Castellana, but looking out that window was strictly prohibited. Next to this room was one that was crowded with antique and modern furniture of good quality. Evidently the consul's family had put all their good pieces there in order to make room for the refugees in the other rooms on that floor. Off the passageway leading from the foyer was a large bathroom, the only one the refugees on that floor could use.[129]

On the other side of the foyer, a long corridor, with doors on both sides, led to rooms occupied by groups or families of refugees. At first,

---

Eucharist), "table" (altar), "Doctor" and "Friend" and "Manuel" (the Lord), "Manuel's mother" (our Lady), "roses" (rosaries), "lunch with Don Manuel" (reception of Holy Communion), "the little watchmaker" (his guardian angel), and "renewal feast" (renewal of the commitment made to our Lord by members of the Work).

[127] Original in AGP, RHF, D–15067.

[128] In this way some people were able to keep receiving Communion daily for ten or twelve days. See Carmen Peñalver Gómez de las Cortinas, AGP, RHF, T–05090, p. 4.

[129] See Eduardo Alastrué Castillo, AGP, RHF, T–04695, pp. 10–11. For more on the arrival of the Father with his brother at the consulate, see Santiago Escrivá de Balaguer y Albás, AGP, RHF, T–07921, p. 25.

when the Father and his brother arrived in a car with the Honduran flag, there was no room available for them. But every night that large room, which also served as a dining room, was converted into a "circular bed," new arrivals putting their mattresses under the enormous circular table there.

Three days after arriving, the Father wrote to his sons in Valencia: "I saw poor Josemaría, and he assured me that he is no longer in the insane asylum (this is his current obsession) but has gotten into deep waters [*honduras*]. He is very happy. The Doctor lets me see him every day." [130] (That last sentence means he was able to say Mass every day.)

In the last week of March, Carmen and Doña Dolores came to visit him at the consulate, and afterwards he wrote to Francisco Botella, "My dear Grandmother came to see me, and earlier my sister also came. You can imagine our joy, after not seeing each other for so long. What will it be like when the poor madman is able to embrace his sons?!" [131]

Despite their happiness, the two women found the visit somewhat disconcerting. Doña Dolores could only recognize her son by his voice; it was the only thing about him that had not changed.[132] And the joy of the visit was, of course, followed by the sadness of separation. "You know," he writes to his sons in Valencia, "there being no fool like an old fool, I so much want—so much!—to give Grandmother a hug, and it may not be possible. I have seen her for ten minutes, in nine months. And now it seems as if I love her more, and the same with Aunt Carmen, because they have protected my things so well, and because, when I saw them, they looked so worn out, so much older. Plus, who knows if it won't be necessary to ask them for another sacrifice?" [133]

He was beginning to see how important Doña Dolores' help in the apostolates of the Work would be. The following week he writes to his sons in Valencia, "I ask you to remember Grandmother, because she thinks of you a lot, and also because circumstances have put her in the midst of her grandchildren. And perhaps she might be willing, as I

[130] AGP, RHF, EF–370317–1.
[131] AGP, RHF, EF–370325–1.
[132] He now weighed less than 110 pounds, mainly as a result of his sickness in December, at Dr. Suils' sanatorium (see AGP, RHF, EF–370328–1). And he lost still more weight during his stay at the Honduran consulate.
[133] AGP, RHF, EF–370414–1.

am, to dedicate the rest of her life to them! It's worth some serious thinking about."[134]

During that visit he asked his mother to take over again the care of the famous trunk containing the archives of the Work.[135] A few days before leaving the sanatorium, he had sent it to the Caracas Street apartment and asked Isidoro to bring all the papers and letters to his mother so that from then on she could keep them in the trunk.

When, eventually, it was full, Doña Dolores took to removing the wool stuffing from her mattress and replacing it with papers. Santiago, exaggerating a little, says, "In the mattress my mother slept on, there ended up being more paper than wool."[136] There were no searches, but from time to time the militia came to the apartment looking for blankets and mattresses to take to the battlefront. At those times Doña Dolores would quickly get into bed and pretend to be sick.

In the best-case scenarios the militia's presence was enough to make people tremble. Across from this apartment building was the former Monastery of the Visitation, now turned into the barracks of the anarchist Spartacus Brigade and a checa of the CNT; and not far away was the checa of the General Inspection Office of the People's Militias, which also had a branch office on Caracas Street. During that period, shortly after the Father took refuge in the Honduran consulate, it happened that Doña Dolores had to leave the trunk unprotected for a few hours. She had to flee the neighborhood because in one of the skirmishes between the communists and the anarchists there was a real danger that the Spartacus Brigade's store of explosives would blow sky-high.[137]

*   *   *

[134] AGP, RHF, EF–370421–1.

[135] He says in a letter to his sons in Valencia, "Grandmother will be staying in Madrid, to keep an eye on the odds and ends that haven't been lost yet, and the worthless papers of her elder son" (AGP, RHF, EF–370406–1).

[136] Santiago Escrivá de Balaguer y Albás, AGP, RHF, T–07921, p. 24.

[137] See ibid. and Juan Jiménez Vargas, AGP, RHF, T–04152–III, p. 88. These skirmishes were episodes in the power struggle that took place within the republican ranks when efforts were being made to put the state back together. The communists sought to increase their power by making a deal with the socialists, but they encountered ever more bitter opposition from the anarchists and from Marxist elements that were not pro-Soviet. The result was an internal civil war between these elements of the Popular Front, culminating in the so-called "events of May 1937," which were especially dramatic in Catalonia. The communists succeeded in crushing their opponents (at times simply eliminating them) and gained control of the situation after the middle of 1937. See Bolloten, pp. 587ff.

The Marchioness of Las Torres de Orán, in her testimony about Father Josemaría's stay at the sanatorium, says, "One could see how enthralled he was with the idea of the Work. I don't recall him speaking about anything else. He was in a great hurry to get out of there, this was very urgent to him, he said, because he could not work in that place." [138]

But his impatience at being cooped up continued in the consulate. Soon after arriving, he wrote to his sons in Valencia, "The poor, strange madman is of no use in Madrid. He could continue spreading his madness if he went someplace else." [139]

The founder had only two possible ways to continue building the Work. The first, a practically suicidal one, would be to take to the street. The other was to wait in the consulate until he could be sent from it to join his sons in the other zone of the country, where he would not be persecuted for being a priest. His temperament was not the most suited to putting up with being penned up and inactive. He writes to Isidoro, "More than once—even this very day—the thought comes to me of going out on the street. And right away there also comes the realization that, as you know has already happened to me, I would find myself having no place to sleep, hiding out like a criminal. . . . Given my nature, this life of a refugee is no small torture. But I don't see any way out. Patience. If an evacuation finally comes, I can leave; if not, I'll wait here, shut in, until the storm passes." [140]

With the members of the Work scattered and in danger, coordination was essential, and would be even more needed if the founder were to leave Madrid. One can, then, imagine his surprise when Isidoro mentioned that, being an Argentine citizen born in Buenos Aires, he was thinking of asking the Argentine embassy to send him abroad.[141]

In writing, so that Isidoro could calmly and carefully think them through, Father Josemaría set out the pros and cons of that idea. In the first place, as a foreigner, Isidoro did not have to fear persecution; he enjoyed a freedom that his brothers lacked to look after the needs of the Work. Plus, some of them were far from Madrid. Wouldn't those in Valencia be stranded if he went abroad? On the other hand, if Isidoro

[138] Carmen Peñalver Gómez de las Cortinas, AGP, RHF, T–05090, p. 3.
[139] AGP, RHF, EF–370406–1.
[140] AGP, RHF, EF–370331–1.
[141] See Pero-Sanz, pp. 209–210, and the entry for March 28, 1937, in the journal kept by Isidoro Zorzano during the civil war (original in AGP, IZL, D–1122).

remained in the capital, he could give hospitality and counsel to those who came through Madrid, and be a channel of communication for everyone. And, after all, what danger would he be in? "Surely the same danger," reasoned Father Josemaría, "that women and children in Madrid face, that my mother faces. If I thought the danger so terrible, do you think I could abandon my mother and Carmen? Perhaps also a little bit of hunger."

Having laid out these considerations, he left it to Isidoro to make the decision. "Obviously my view of this problem of yours should not bind you," he writes to him. "Act with the *utmost* freedom. . . . If you see things differently, tell me. My only concern is to do what at the hour of my death I will wish I had done."[142]

Isidoro's decision—not to abandon his post as a communications link in the capital—was noble and altruistic. "I did not expect anything less of you, Isidoro," the founder then wrote him. "The decision you have made is without a doubt what our Lord wants." [143]

Still fresh in Isidoro's memory was the past feast of Saint Joseph, March 19, when he and Manolo Sainz de los Terreros (who was by then out of prison) were invited to dinner at the Caracas Street apartment. Doña Dolores and Carmen wanted to hold, in a family setting, an unforgettable celebration for the people of the Work. It entailed great sacrifice on the part of the two women; probably they fasted for the next few days. But there the founder's two families were symbolically fused.[144]

Meanwhile Juan Jiménez Vargas had received an order from the medical association to join a battalion of the Spartacus Brigade as a medical lieutenant. With the agreement of the Father, he was going to try to cross over into the nationalist zone as soon as he arrived at the Jarama front, but when the time came he made only a few halfhearted attempts. Something seemed to hold him back. "Almost without thinking about it," he explains, "at the moment of making the leap

---

[142] AGP, RHF, EF–370328–2.

[143] AGP, RHF, EF–370330–2. Isidoro made his decision quickly. In fact, before writing it to the Father, he had already communicated it to Doña Dolores. "Your family was happy to know that you can go with Ricardo and that I will stay here," he says in his letter of March 31, 1937 (AGP, IZL, D–1213, 130). Isidoro notified the founder of his decision by means of this letter, instead of in person, because at that time he was not allowed to go to the Honduran consulate: see AGP, IZL, D–1122. On April 16 he communicated it to Pedro Casciaro in Valencia, writing to him, "I am staying to keep the others company and to be able to take care of the house when things get back to normal" (AGP, IZL, D–1213, 132).

[144] See Jiménez Vargas, AGP, RHF, T–04152–III, p. 92.

I found myself unable to cross over with the Father remaining in Madrid."[145]

At that time they were waiting for a visit from Ricardo Fernández Vallespín, who would be coming to Madrid on a three or four days' leave from the military fortifications office in Valencia, where he was being very closely watched. (At the outbreak of the war Ricardo had joined the socialist union, with the endorsement of a communist architect in his group of enlistees. He was assigned to constructing fortifications on the Teruel front.) Their idea was to have Ricardo seek asylum at the consulate, where he would be presented as a relative of the Father. But when he got to Madrid, he told the Father about his plan to cross over to the nationalist zone from the Teruel front. This left it open for someone else to be "Ricardo Escrivá." So Juan, instead of deserting, returned to Madrid and entered the consulate under that name, and Ricardo a short time later crossed over from the Levant battlefront into the other zone.[146]

The Father made no effort to hide his concern. "I am on pins and needles from not having news of my sons out there," he wrote. "How eager I am to see my little ones!" He was especially concerned about the situation of Chiqui, who was in a prison in Valencia. He affectionately urged the others to take care of him, "because Josemaría will be heartbroken if the little one's health is not soon restored"—in other words, if he was not soon released from prison.[147]

The Father was extremely worried about their bodily health, but even more so about the danger to their spiritual health and to their perseverance in their vocations. He protected members of the Work with his prayers and by offering himself in expiation. "Health is so important!" he wrote to them. "Of course, Josemaría has asked, and he asks every day, that his Friend take from him the payment needed for his sons and safeguard them from the dangers of this catastrophe. And he is sure that their perseverance will be unanimous."[148]

He was vividly aware of the suffering of so many innocents, the

---

[145] Ibid., p. 95.

[146] Although Ricardo told the people in Madrid that he would let them know of his safe arrival in the other zone by means of a coded signal to be transmitted by nationalist radio, nothing was heard of him for several weeks. But he did cross over at an opportune moment, providentially, and he "got away by a hair's breadth, because on the following day they were after him" (see ibid., p. 95). But his friends were not sure he had made it until the beginning of June 1937 (see AGP, RHF, EF–370605–1).

[147] AGP, RHF, EF–370328–1.

[148] AGP, RHF, EF–370406–1.

many Christians deprived of the sacraments, those silently languishing in prison. And the war had already lasted "nine months, which is a lot of months, Lord." [149]

At that time, nine months into the war, the international public began to receive and react to authoritative information regarding the bloody atrocities in Spain. These crimes were broadcast to the whole world by Pope Pius XI in his encyclical *Divini Redemptoris* (March 19, 1937), in which he condemned the errors and evils arising from Marxism. The communist scourge has been unleashed in Spain, he said, "with a more than frenzied violence. It is not this or that church, this or that convent which has been destroyed, but wherever possible, they are destroying all of the churches, all of the convents, and every trace of the Christian religion, even where this is linked to the great monuments of art and science. The communist frenzy has not been limited to the murder of bishops and thousands of priests and members of religious orders of men and women . . . but they have found a much greater number of victims among all classes of laymen who, still today, are being murdered en masse for the mere fact of being good Christians, or, at least, opposed to communist atheism." [150]

That summer, forty-eight Spanish prelates signed a collective letter on the religious persecution. Dated July 1, 1937, and directed to the bishops of the world, it said: "The Church did not want or seek this war. . . . Anyone who accuses the Church of having provoked it or schemed to bring it about, or even of not having done all it could to avert it, either does not know the truth or is falsifying it." [151]

The Marxist revolution ruthlessly sought to eradicate every trace of Christianity. "The most eloquent proof that the destruction of churches and the murder of priests was something premeditated," says Antonio Montero Moreno, "was the terrifying numbers. . . . Some six thousand priests were martyred. They were chased by dogs; they were pursued across mountains; they were zealously looked for in every

[149] AGP, RHF, EF–370409–1.

[150] *Acta Apostolicae Sedis*, vol. 29, 1937, p. 75.

[151] See Montero Moreno, p. 728. A few lines further on, one reads: "Even if the war was of a political or social nature, its repercussions on religion were very grave and from the beginning it was clear that one of the warring parties was bent on the elimination of the Catholic religion in Spain." On the international repercussions of the "Collective Letter from the Spanish Bishops to the Whole World on the Subject of the War in Spain," see Redondo, *Historia*, vol. 2, pp. 310ff, and Lecha-Marzo, "Algunos aspectos," pp. 116–19. See also Isidoro Gomá y Tomás, *Por Dios y por España: Pastorales, Instrucciones pastorales y Artículos, Discursos, Mensajes, Apéndice, 1936–1939* (Barcelona, 1940).

possible hideout. Most of the time they were murdered on the spot, with no trial, for no reason other than their social function." [152]

5. *"The good pipe story"*

The safest hiding places were the embassies. From the first days of the uprising, when the militias brought terror to Madrid, these diplomatic headquarters took in hundreds of refugees, a high percentage of whom were priests and religious. Later, in the autumn of 1936, when the persecution intensified and mass executions began, not only the official headquarters but also the branch offices and subsidiary buildings became filled with refugees. Within a few months these places were so crowded that, it being obvious that the war would continue, the ambassadors of several countries tried to secure an evacuation of the refugees, who in Madrid alone now numbered more than thirteen thousand.[153]

On March 27, 1937, the republican government finally issued general regulations for the evacuation of refugees from embassies, setting

[152] Montero Moreno, p. 733. For more on the religious persecution in Madrid, see Camacho, passim.

At the end of the civil war the number of victims of the religious persecution, says Montero Moreno, came to 13 bishops, 4,184 diocesan priests, 2,365 religious-order priests and brothers, and 283 nuns. Not included in this number, of course, were the thousands of persons murdered simply because they were Catholics. (See Montero Moreno, p. 762.) To comprehend the impact of the slaughter, one must bear in mind that it took place in only half of Spain's territory; that is, in the republican zone.

An analysis of the figures shows that Montero's numbers are low. See Vicente Cárcel Ortí, *La persecución religiosa en España durante la Segunda República, 1931–1939* (Madrid, 1990), pp. 234ff. See also the martyrologies of various dioceses or regions, such as A. Garralda's two-volume *La persecución religiosa del clero en Asturias, 1934 y 1936–1937* (Avila, 1977), or Santos Lalueza Gil's *Martirio de la Iglesia de Barbastro, 1936–1938* (Barbastro, 1989). See also, in the first volume of this biography, chapter 2, "Logroño Years (1915–1920)," note 7.

Between October 7 and 25, 1936, three weeks after the entrance of Franco's army into San Sebastián, one religious-order and nine diocesan priests, on charges of being Basque nationalists, were shot by the nationalist troops. When, on October 26, Cardinal Gomá informed General Franco of this, Franco assured him the executions would immediately be stopped, and gave orders to that effect. Nevertheless, between October 27 and November 7 three more priests were shot. To date, no documentation has been found for the hasty trials possibly carried out by the military. See Anastasio Granados, *Cardinal Gomá, primado de España* (Madrid, 1969), p. 145, and Rodríguez Aiso, pp. 49 and 62–65. Father Antonio Bombín, OFM, was killed in Laguardia (Alava); see Joseba M. Goñi Galarraga, *La guerra civil en el País Vasco: una guerra entre católicos* (Vitoria, 1989), p. 229.

[153] In his chapter on the search for hiding places in Madrid, Cervera Gil says that the safest ones were the embassies. His study is thus far the most complete and well-documented one with regard to the number of refugees in diplomatic headquarters. His count (given on pp. 369–74) sets the number at the beginning of 1937 at close to 14,000,

as a condition that "no new refugees are to be admitted there, regardless of the circumstances." It was agreed that the heads of the various diplomatic missions would have to make the evacuation requests via sealed detailed lists with photographs of the refugees.[154]

The Honduran consulate offered a second-rate shelter. It was not the headquarters of a diplomatic mission but only a consular office, wherein lived Don Pedro Jaime de Matheu, whose status, for negotiating purposes, was only that of honorary consul general.[155] In February and March of 1937, hundreds of refugees who had been under the protection of the Argentine and Mexican embassies left Spain. It was reasonable for Father Josemaría to think his move to the Honduran consulate would open the doors for him to leave Madrid, but that thought, as he would later learn, was a mistaken one.

He and Santiago and Juan had left Dr. Suils' sanatorium with the idea of being included on the list being prepared by the Honduran consulate. And after they paid in advance the price of the trip, they were given the numbers 23, 92, and 35, respectively. But soon the Father began to suspect that negotiations were at a standstill. On April 20 he wrote a letter to Isidoro asking him to meet with the ambassador of Chile and give him the enclosed note, in which Father Josemaría notified him that they were registered on the Honduran consulate's evacuation list. "They tell me," he explained to Isidoro, "that a group leaves every week. If the ambassador were to put in a word for us, we could be out of here by next week. If not, who knows!"[156]

---

not counting those mentioned in reports that do not give numbers. According to these figures, the embassy that took in the most refugees was that of France, with 2,240. See also María del Carmen Gómez Reoyo, *Madrid 1936–1939: El asilo diplomático en la Guerra Civil Española* (master's thesis, Universidad Completense [Madrid], 1985). Gómez Reoyo distinguishes officially recognized refugees from de facto refugees, who were more numerous, and gives 11,000 as the number of the former. See also García-Mina, passim, and Camacho, pp. 181–93.

[154] See García-Mina, p. 476: "General Conditions of March 17, 1936, for the Evacuation of Refugees from Embassies." The last line of this decree leaves a wide margin for arbitrariness: "The Minister of State, always within the above-written norms, will proceed in a manner consistent with criteria of political relationships." What is granted, therefore, is not a right to evacuate, but only authorization to negotiate, country by country, national interests, taking into account political pressure and the international importance of the country involved.

[155] See Consuelo de Matheu Montalvo, AGP, RHF, T–05050, p. 1, and José Luis Rodríguez-Candela Manzaneque, AGP, RHF, T–05120, p. 1. It was, then, a matter of an extension of consular asylum.

[156] AGP, RHF, EF–370420–3. Aurelio Núñez Morgado, the Chilean ambassador, was then the dean of the diplomatic corps in Madrid; his reminiscences are also in EF–370420–3.

The effort came too late. Aurelio Núñez Morgado, the Chilean ambassador, had to leave Spain that very week because of his strained relations with Spain's secretary of state, Alvarez del Vayo.[157]

By the end of April the founder was sure the day was near: "Nothing is set, but it seems imminent." Nevertheless, eight days later, he could see no way out except through the negotiations then being carried on by José María Albareda, that young professor he had met at the Ferraz Street residence. "We will never get out of here if José María doesn't make progress with Chile," he wrote to his sons in Valencia. "I don't know when Josemaría will go. Perhaps soon, perhaps later. . . . Perhaps never."[158]

As it turned out, those who did not leave the Honduran consulate voluntarily would remain trapped there till the end of the civil war. But of course no one knew that then.

In the first week of May, Father Josemaría turned over in his head other possible solutions. "Chile or China, what's the difference?" he wrote to his sons in Madrid. "We have to keep trying."[159] Again Isidoro went to the Chilean embassy. They told him their lists for admissions of evacuees were closed and that it would be impossible to add another name because the names had already been sent to the government. But the Father still would not admit defeat. He wrote to his sons in Madrid, "As for Chile, look, what they told you is what they say here to get rid of pests. . . . *If they want to, they can arrange it. It's their job to fix what most needs fixing!*"[160]

Arguments given by the diplomats could not discourage the Father. He next tried to get through to the Turkish embassy, after warning his sons not to buy the excuse that "the lists are already closed." "Keep insisting, keep pestering, opportunely and inopportunely," he told them. "I know you are already doing what you can—and I appreciate that very much—but it's necessary that you do more than what you can."[161]

In the middle of May his correspondence is entirely about evacuation, but is not without a touch of humor. To Isidoro he writes, "Saturday, May 15, 1937—From the bottom of the depths [*honduras*]!"[162] A letter at the end of the month to Valencia is filled with a healthy

[157] See García-Mina, p. 47, and Cervera Gil, p. 367.
[158] AGP, RHF, EF–370421–1.
[159] AGP, RHF, EF–370503–1.
[160] AGP, RHF, EF–370504–1.
[161] AGP, RHF, EF–370506–1.
[162] AGP, RHF, EF–370515–2.

skepticism about evacuation. "It's sad to feel oneself a foreigner and evacuee without ever managing to get evacuated. Once more—it's the good pipe story—we seem to be making progress in the matter of leaving. . . . Frankly, I'll believe it when I see it." [163]

In June hope seems reborn, and references to evacuation again become frequent and insistent in the Father's letters. "We need to put all the pressure we can on Chile or Switzerland to get the passes," he writes to his sons in Madrid. "Don't let up. We can't stay here. Won't they take us in Switzerland, or in Turkey, or somewhere?" [164]

But twenty-four hours later, that hope has vanished. "All has come to naught." [165] The Honduran consul told them he would make no further efforts to get permission for evacuation. This announcement relieved the refugees of any false expectations, but it was probably also a smoke screen, a way for the consul to avoid letting on how serious the situation actually was. They were now in a real bind. It was questionable enough whether an honorary consul could negotiate with a government minister on equal terms, but Don Pedro had also tied his own hands in making up the list of refugees that was sent officially to the Spanish government. He had listed a total of thirty-two persons, including most of the women and children. If it were discovered that the real number of refugees in the Honduran consulate was three times larger, the consul would be in trouble. He naturally saw it as best to make no further applications and thus avoid unpleasant surprises.[166]

On June 29, Don Pedro's name day, the refugees gave him three sheets of paper filled with their signatures.[167] The heading was:

---

[163] AGP, RHF, EF–370530–1. The "good pipe story" is an expression referring to a complicated issue whose resolution takes a long time and keeps getting more and more bogged down by the efforts made to reach it. A similar expression translates as "a never-ending story."

[164] AGP, RHF, EF–370606–2.

[165] AGP, RHF, EF–370607–1.

[166] According to the official communication of the Honduran consul general to Spain's state department, at the beginning of 1937 there was a total of thirty-two refugees there, twenty-seven being men of military age, and the other five being women, children, and elderly men. At the end of 1938 the list was unchanged. (See García-Mina, p. 32.) But we know from eyewitnesses that in some cases the number of actual refugees was triple the number of the officially recognized ones. See also AGP, RHF, EF–370701–2.

[167] The original set, as a gift from the consul's daughter, is in AGP, RHF, D–11074. See also the testimony of Juan Manuel Sainz de los Terreros in AGP, RHF, T–05127, and that of Recaredo Ventosa García in *Beato Josemaría Escrivá de Balaguer: un hombre de Dios. Testimonios sobre el Fundador del Opus Dei* (Madrid, 1994), p. 419. (This last book will hereafter be cited as *Testimonios.*)

To His Excellency Don Pedro Jaime de Matheu
From the grateful refugees
Madrid, June 29, 1937

There are eighty-eight names on these sheets. The first is that of Juan Manuel Sainz de los Terreros.

Father Josemaría still did not admit defeat. Immediately he launched a new effort—to obtain Argentine passports—even though he realized this was part of the never-ending story. To his sons in Valencia he wrote, "Josemaría? He seems to be seeing once again a possibility of getting out. It's the good pipe story." [168]

* * *

For a long time after their arrival at the consulate, Father Josemaría and his companions lived a nomadic life. By day they were herded through corridors. At bedtime they camped out in the dining room. Under the dining room table they put their mattresses next to each other and set out other items around them. He wrote to his sons in Valencia, "If only you could see the nightly operation of turning the dining room into a big circular bed, or practically that!" [169]

The dilapidated room was strewn with cups, blankets, books, napkins, suitcases, pictures, jars, cleaning rags, and toiletries. "And what about the chairs?" he continues. "They've come from several families; some are even kitchen chairs. But at night we put them in the bathroom. The bathroom!" [170] About thirty people shared that bathroom. Its use in the morning was strictly regulated since it was the only one available to the refugees on that floor.

A few days after their arrival, the Father, Santiago, and José María Barredo were joined by Alvaro del Portillo and Eduardo Alastrué. Eduardo had been imprisoned in a checa on Fomento Street in November; his captors had been about to kill him when inexplicably they let him go.[171]

Until the middle of May the Father and his companions did not

---

[168] AGP, RHF, EF–370701–2. "In this activity [of organizing evacuations]," says Cervera Gil (p. 357), "the embassies of Latin American countries, especially Argentina, Chile, and Mexico, were the most successful. In addition, France, the United Kingdom, and Turkey organized and carried out evacuation programs."

[169] AGP, RHF, EF–370417–1.

[170] Ibid.

[171] AGP, RHF, T–04152–III, p. 55.

have a room of their own. Then they were given one at the end of the corridor, next to the service stairs. In earlier times it had probably been a storeroom for coal. It was so small that at night its tile floor disappeared under the thin mattresses and the blankets. Rolled up and rested against the wall, the mattresses served as seats during the day. A narrow window looked out on an enclosed patio. The room was so dark that even in the daytime they had to turn on the bare electric light bulb that hung from the ceiling. In this tiny, dismal room the Father organized life for himself and his companions. And to amuse his sons in Valencia, he wrote this humorous description of the place:

There isn't room to spread out all five of our mattresses. Four are enough to completely carpet the floor. Can I describe our home? When camp is struck, we have two mattresses, one on top of the other, folded up and put in one corner, the blankets and pillows tucked inside. Then a small space. Then the two mattresses of José B. and Alvaro, arranged in the same way, and on top of them, rolled up very tightly, with a funereal black cloth to cover it, Eduardo's thin mattress. Immediately adjacent is the radiator—five wheezing elements—on top of which is a board from a chest of drawers. This serves as a table for our food supplies and for six big cups, only superficially clean. One window, which looks out on a dark patio— very dark. Beneath the window, a small packing crate, with some books and a bottle for the banquets. On top of the crate, two small suitcases. (I'm writing this letter with one of them on my lap—after writing in a hundred thousand positions, awfully painful for the muscles, totally ridiculous, and unstable.) Next to the crate, two other small suitcases, in a corner of the room, on top of which are a valise and a tin box where we keep everyone's toiletries. Right next to all that, the door. Although we have now reached the door, I won't make you leave the room. (You can enter whenever you like—the door doesn't shut; there's something wrong with it.) The only thing left for you to admire is the rope that cuts across a corner of the room and serves to hold five towels. And also the beautiful lampshade, of genuine newspaper, which in a lighthearted moment this grandfather placed on the bare bulb hanging from a dirty wire. Don't even think about touching the light switch, because if you do it will be a lot of trouble to get the light back on; the switch is broken. Anything else?" [172]

The crowding of more than thirty people in rooms along that hallway made the monotony of the long hours even harder to bear.[173] The only bright spot for the refugees was their hope for something that never seemed to be coming: evacuation or the end of the war. The resulting discouragement frayed their nerves and eventually plunged many of the refugees into such a deep apathy that they lacked even the energy to kill time. And so the time crawled by, leaving only tedium and a feeling of emptiness. Momentary sparks of interest, or flashes of hatred or rebellion, quickly died out.

Social relations in that enforced togetherness were not pleasant or tranquil. Continually there were quarrels, complaints, and recriminations. Lacking the discipline of work, living like caged animals, people just brooded on their many worries, to the point where some of them became mentally unhinged. For almost everyone, life was a fog filled with two obsessions: hunger and fear.[174]

At first the protection of being in a foreign diplomat's headquarters meant freedom from the danger of arrest and the threat of death, but after a while, gradually, an acute sense of insecurity gripped and took over the imagination. The refugees in the Honduran building knew all too well that they were under the protection of a mere general consulate. Rumors of a possible attack, with the insufficient guarantee of asylum, increased the fear, especially when news arrived of a police raid on the Peruvian consulate. On the night of May 5, 1937, the authorities had sent armed forces to arrest all the refugees there—three hundred Spaniards and sixty Peruvians.[175]

---

[172] AGP, RHF, EF–370526–1. "This is a paradise of cockroaches," he writes in another letter. "Some are quite big, as solemn and lustrous as a sacred Egyptian beetle; others are the size of a pinhead. And what a harmony of colors! White, red, silver, russet, gold, brown, black—it makes one want to praise one's Maker. So you see why we're having such a good time." And on another occasion, "Today, when little Eduardo opened a book, a magnificent bedbug emerged. Can you imagine? At least the cockroaches will see they are well accompanied." See AGP, RHF, EF–370701–1 and EF–370725–3, and also EF–370727–3 and 370420–1.

[173] The number living upstairs was about sixty. About the life of those refugees, see *Testimonios,* pp. 420ff.

[174] See AGP, RHF, T–04695, p. 13; T–05120, p. 3; and T–04152–III, p. 95.

[175] As Cervera Gil notes (p. 363), "most of those refugees were set free, but eighteen of them—young men known for their rightist connections—were taken to the General Office of Security." There they were tortured so badly that the General Office of Security

This event sparked a collective panic attack in one group of the refugees at the Honduran consulate. They feared that their security would be endangered if Father Josemaría, who said Mass almost every morning in the foyer, was denounced by someone and the police showed up.[176] Not even the consul, his daughter tells us, considered himself safe. "The people were afraid, they felt endangered," she says, "and so, after my father told him it was dangerous for him to celebrate Mass there, he always celebrated it in the room that he and his companions occupied." [177]

Early in the morning, before the other refugees got up, the Father would give a meditation to those who were with him. "His words," recalls Eduardo, "some serene, some energetic and charged with emotion, but all of them illuminating, poured down on us and seemed to settle within our souls." [178] He would comment on the day's Gospel reading, he would speak to them about the person and life of Christ, and they would all thus be prepared for Mass.

Then he would hang a crucifix on the wall and spread out the corporals on a suitcase. When Mass was over, the consecrated hosts that had not been consumed were placed in a small leather case, which they took turns keeping each day, either to give as Communion to other people there or to give to Isidoro for distribution to members of the Work outside the consulate. Mass in that hovel of a room was reminiscent of Mass in the catacombs. Father Josemaría, with an eye on the censor, gave to his sons in Valencia this cheerful and down-to-earth account:

> And then, good Lord, Don Manuel invites me and the family to lunch. And we go. How can we not, being so hungry? But it turns out that, because of the problems with evacuation in Madrid, there is nothing of what in other times would be considered necessary. From today's experience you can get a good idea of what it's like the other days. There was no table,

---

opened a file on their jailers. After several transfers to different jails, they were condemned to death; but the intercession of other countries and of the International Red Cross resulted in the lifting of that sentence. See Cervera Gil, pp. 244–45, and García-Mina, p. 83.

[176] The priests on the upper floor had to stop saying Mass because of the refugees' fear. See *Testimonios*, pp. 420ff.

[177] AGP, RHF, T–05050, p. 3.

[178] AGP, RHF, T–04695, p. 19.

so one was improvised with a wooden orange crate. On top of it, one, two, three suitcases. Then a napkin, not very clean—poor Don Manuel!—and two smaller ones of the ordinary type. It was seen to—by us—that a picture of our host presided over the banquet. We put it on the wall, nicely fastening it with a nail. Afterwards, to top it all off, despite the deficiencies, we have enough bread left over to last for several days. And now these boys of mine are starting to act as if they're in a play about Monipodio [a character similar to Fagin in *Oliver Twist*, who teaches boys to steal]—they robbed me of my leather case. Yes, can you believe it, that little African case Isidoro brought me! And to keep from fighting among themselves, they each keep it for one day, taking turns in strict order. I keep quiet, acting as though I know nothing about it.[179]

The Blessed Sacrament ("the Friend") was for a time reserved in the foyer, in a desk that could be locked with a key ("the Bread box"). At the end of April, Father Josemaría, because of an attack of rheumatism, could not make his usual visits to our Lord, so he asked two little boys to send messages to his Friend. The boys would come back to report. "And what did you say to him?" Father Josemaría asked one of them. "That he should give you those three things, plus the other things you need," the boy answered.

The priest was touched by the way these boys greeted their Friend. He wrote to his sons in Valencia, "I don't know who taught them this little game, but, maybe because I'm getting senile or something, I really enjoy seeing these two youngsters—who know only too well that one can't live without eating!—go up to the Bread box and give it a kiss, a big, loud one, near the keyhole." [180]

Another cautionary measure taken by the consul was a great restriction of Isidoro's visits to the consulate. The building was protected and controlled by guards who demanded proof of identity from

---

[179] AGP, RHF, EF–370519–1. Starting on the very day he arrived at the consulate (in the middle of March), the Father said Mass in the foyer and reserved the Blessed Sacrament in a small silver box in a desk there. They made visits to the Blessed Sacrament there in the foyer until May, when they had to remove it from the desk by order of the consul, because of the refugees' panicky fear of the police showing up. From then on, they kept the consecrated hosts in that small leather case.

[180] AGP, RHF, EF–370501–1.

anyone entering or leaving it. But this was no problem for Isidoro, because of his Argentine citizenship. And as for the consul's prohibition, he easily got around that by using not the main stairway but rather the service stairs. He would knock softly on the door at the end of the corridor, it would be opened, and no one outside that room would know he was there.[181] At other times it was Alvaro's brother Carlos and sister Teresa who would come. Being eleven and nine, they could safely take letters or documents to Isidoro.[182]

In addition to the uneasiness coming from fear of an attack or of being turned in to the police, there was also the affliction of hunger. Food was scarce and hard to come by in a city almost completely surrounded by nationalist troops. When a system of food rationing was imposed on the general population, hunger became a severe problem in most of the embassies giving asylum, because the refugees had no ration cards. They had to find their own sources of supply.[183] The topic of food was often brought into conversations, obsessively and nostalgically. Yet in the abundant correspondence produced by Father Josemaría in those months of confinement (he seldom went a day without writing), hunger and food are mentioned only very rarely, and then always with a touch of humor. To his sons in Valencia he writes, "Little Santiago is skin and bones. As for me, though they may tell you otherwise over there, I still have too much flesh on me, in spite of not eating more than two ladle scoops of rice at midday. (We are up to *here* with rice—to the height of the tonsure, if you'll allow me to use such a reactionary, obscurantist, and clerical term.) And in the evening, two little scoops of garlic soup. But there's nothing bad that lasts a hundred years, Paco. Sure isn't like me, is it, to be talking about food?" [184] And later, "Now they're varying our menu from time to time. The grandfather, talking about things culinary!—as an old novel might say. But hunger, or, I should say, appetite, works wonders. Yesterday, at midday, they gave us rice with beans—beans of a respectable age, still sporting their shells. And in the evening, raw onions with orange slices. (We thought it was great, but revolutionary—boy, do things move fast the next day!) And in those big cups that you already know about, a good amount of a very watery liquid

---

[181] See Pero-Sanz, pp. 205–206.
[182] See AGP, RHF, EF–370420–1.
[183] See García-Mina, p. 176, and Cervera Gil, pp. 355–56.
[184] AGP, RHF, EF–370406–1. See also AGP, RHF, T–04695, p. 16.

with a faint taste of cinnamon that sticks to one's throat. They told us it was chocolate. So many new discoveries these days!"[185]

The jocular tone he used in writing to his sons in Valencia, as a way of entertaining them and keeping them from worrying, was in stark contrast to his letters to those in Madrid, who knew very well what hunger they were suffering in the consulate, where even crumbs of bread were cherished.

Isidoro undoubtedly made requests to those in "the happy Levant," as the Valencian provinces were then being called because of being far from the battlefront and having an abundance of food, thanks to the fertile soil. "Oh! If they send anything from Valencia," the Father wrote to Isidoro, "don't forget that we have four *hungry* fellows here. As for me, I have more than enough with what they give us. But Santiago and the others need more. . . . How it bothers me to even talk, let alone write, about food."[186]

Two days later he writes to those in Madrid, "Bread? We have more than enough. . . . Oh, and make absolutely sure you don't send us anything that you need for yourselves. I want, I demand, that you take care of yourselves first. I think I make myself clear?"[187]

Some idea of the seriousness of the food shortage can also be gotten from the excitement that greeted a replenishment of their supplies on May 5. "Today," the Father writes to those in Valencia, "they brought us cheese and eggs, from my nephew Isidoro. It's been months since we've seen or even smelled any food of that sort."[188]

Above all, he was concerned with distributing among the others whatever food they got. Certainly he did not go by the popular saying, "Whoever does the dividing and distributing gets the best part." In fact, while trying to give the impression that he was eating as well as the others, he surreptitiously gave himself the smallest portion, while tightening his belt. Even so, some of his fasting did not go unobserved. Santiago tells how the refugees looked forward to Sunday night like children waiting for a treat. Sunday's supper was fried bread crumbs with chocolate. But, he says, "on Sundays Josemaría

---

[185] AGP, RHF, EF–370426–1. Among the joking remarks in his correspondence, there appear from time to time some unadorned truths. For instance, "Today they gave us rice with lentils, and nothing else. . . . It's a miracle that we're still alive, don't you think?" (AGP, RHF, EF–370508–2).

[186] AGP, RHF, EF–370430–3.

[187] AGP, RHF, EF–370502–1.

[188] AGP, RHF, EF–370505–1.

never had supper."[189] The Father, meanwhile, continued his old custom of eating bitter aloes, which were readily available. War and
privation did not seem to him sufficient reason to exempt himself
from living, even in the smallest details, with a spirit of penance.[190]

*   *   *

One striking thing about the copious correspondence written by the
founder from the Honduran consulate is the absence of comments on
political matters. There is not a word about governments, zones,
battlefronts, cities liberated or occupied, allies or enemies, victims or
guilty parties. Similarly, although the refugees' conversations often
turned to what was going on in the war, Father Josemaría avoided
talking about the fratricidal conflict tearing the nation apart. His four
companions were also not contentious, and in his presence they said
nothing about military operations or about crimes committed behind
the scenes. The rule was to forgive and forget.

The Father's kindly presence inspired calmness. His conversation
was so consoling and supernatural, so soothing to their spirits, that
they actually came to look on their confinement itself as a gift from
God. Eduardo recalls, "Sometimes we thought, If only this could last
forever! Had we ever known anything better than the light and
warmth of that little room? As absurd as it was in those circumstances,
that was our reaction, and from our way of seeing things it made
perfect sense. It brought us peace and happiness day after day."[191]

When necessary, the founder did touch on the subject of the war,
and always he referred to it as a catastrophe, but his priestly spirit was
open to souls in both zones and all factions. His general intercessions
at Mass took in the whole ocean of suffering produced by the conflict—everything suffered at the battlefronts, in prisons, hospitals,
homes, places of refuge.

Father Josemaría's attitude was not one of lofty indifference. It was
one of consummate charity, stemming from a higher, supernatural
vision of world events. "He was always very concerned with what
was happening," says the consul's son-in-law, "though at the same
time he was very much above it. . . . Never did he speak with hatred

---

[189] AGP, RHF, T–07921, p. 26.
[190] See AGP, RHF, EF–370530–3, Alvaro del Portillo, *Sum.* 365, and Eduardo Alastrué
Castillo, *Sum.* 5552.
[191] AGP, RHF, T–04695, p. 18.

or rancor, or judge anyone. On the contrary, he was always saying: 'This is a barbarity, a tragedy.' He was saddened by what was happening, but not in a merely human way. When the others celebrated victories, Father Josemaría remained silent." [192]

*   *   *

The miserable little room at the consulate became a sort of center of operations. From that office came letters from the Father that were full of picturesque descriptions, news of joys and sorrows, instructions, spiritual reflections, and advice on material concerns. Because he was so eager for information about his children and had so many matters in hand, he adopted the custom of sometimes numbering the paragraphs of his letters, "not as an obsession," he explained, "but in order to make sure that you answer all my questions." [193]

One thing he wanted them to do was to present a claim for the goods that had been lost at the Ferraz Street residence when it was taken over by the anarchist militia of the CNT on July 25, 1936. Upon learning that the father-in-law of one of the consul's children had filed a claim after his house was broken into by the militia, the Father thought, Why not file a similar claim in the name of the residence's titular company, the Civil Society for the Encouragement of Advanced Studies? He took up the cause as earnestly as if the future of all of them depended on its outcome—when they had yet to see if they would survive the war.

And thus began an all-out battle. On April 23 he asked Isidoro to inquire at the Argentine embassy as to what steps needed to be taken and what documents presented. That same evening, he wrote again, giving an account of his recent conversation with that relative of the consul and asking Isidoro to get a notary to make copies of the documents relating to the creation of the Society and to the purchase of the Ferraz Street residence.[194]

[192] AGP, RHF, T–05120, p. 1.

[193] AGP, RHF, EF–370523–1. Some of his letters had as many as seventeen separate sections on different topics; see, for example, EF–370525–1. Just two days before writing that letter, he had sent them one with eight sections; and one day after, he wrote them one with seven.

[194] AGP, RHF, EF–370423–1.

In about 1933 the Father gave spiritual direction to "the illustrious and most virtuous Countess of Humanes," Doña María Francisca Messía y Eraso de Aranda. She was a Spanish blue blood, and yet she lived in great poverty, in a spirit of detachment from her wealth. An anecdote about her is included in *The Way*, no. 638. Among other things,

From the start, Isidoro ran into difficulties.[195] Neither the inventory of goods nor the documents establishing the Society nor the deed were obtainable. They had been left in the building and could not be retrieved, if indeed they still existed. They then decided to present the Society as an "international association," since some of its members were not from Spain. Isidoro, as an Argentinean and as president of the Society, submitted at the Argentine embassy a claim against the Spanish state for losses amounting to 1,078,900 pesetas.[196]

Not even a week after the Father came up with the idea of submitting the claim, he wrote Isidoro a letter that began:

---

she donated her jewelry, intending for it to be sold and the profits used to help spread the Work. It is likely that when the militia searched the Ferraz Street residence in July 1936, they stole those jewels and other objects of value which the founder was saving to pay for the building. The Countess of Humanes died on July 23, 1936, a few days after the civil war broke out.

The reproduction of the Society's constitution was made and notarized at the office of Don Juan José Esteban y Rojo. The constitution bore the date of November 2, 1935. The original members of the Society were Isidoro, Ricardo Fernández Vallespín, José María González Barredo, and Manuel Sainz de los Terreros Villacampa.

The reproduction of the deed of the Society's purchase of the house at 16 Ferraz Street from Don Javier Azlor-Aragón was made and notarized at the office of Don Luis Siera Bermejo, and is dated June 17, 1936. Appearing before the notary "as the sole members and in the name of the Civil Society for the Encouragement of Advanced Studies" were these same original members.

[195] See Pero-Sanz, pp. 220–22.

[196] Among the listings in the claim were the following:

    Academy (furniture, labs, etc.):154,820 pesetas
    Residence (furniture, clothes, equipment, etc.)240,400
    Building (16 Ferraz Street): repair work110,000
    See AGP, IZL, D–1213, 139.

As can be seen, there was no claim for the building itself, but only for repair work. Stipulation 4 in the deed of purchase reads, "The purchasing entity takes possession of the purchased property by the sole fact of the granting of this deed." The agreed-upon price for 16 Ferraz Street was 400,000 pesetas, to be paid over fourteen years at 43,032 pesetas a year. As stipulation 3 indicates, this annual amount was to paid "in four equal installments, every three months, with the first payment due on September 30 of the current year." When the deed was drawn up, on June 17, 1936, the Society handed over 6,000 pesetas as part of the first quarterly payment.

The situation from a legal point of view was somewhat complicated. The deed of purchase was presented on July 20 (probably by Isidoro) at the Real Estate Department, but in view of the political situation, nothing was done. "By indications given us in August," says Isidoro in a note about "the matter of the notary," the sale taxes were not paid, "for which reason the property has not been put in the name of the Society. For all legal purposes, the present owner of it continues to be the former one. And therefore they cannot give us an authorized copy of the document" (AGP, RHF, D–15711).

The presenting of this claim involved many difficulties, not the least of which was that of obtaining proof that the inventoried objects had been destroyed or had disappeared. This was impossible at that time because 16 Ferraz Street was in a war zone.

Saturday, May 1, 1937

Very good, the matter of your putting in the claim through your country's embassy. But *we have to hurry*! A delay of even one or two days could jeopardize our success. *Impress this on the mind* of the secretary. Don't leave any loose ends. Let's get those papers moving *as soon as possible*.[197]

The Father did not have many people to help him in this effort. There were in Madrid only three members of the Work who were out free, the others being the refugees in the Honduran consulate and Vicente Rodríguez Casado, a refugee in the Norwegian embassy. In Valencia there were only two free members, since Chiqui was in prison. Those two were Rafael Calvo Serer, who was then in Alicante and sick, and Pedro Casciaro, in Torrevieja. The others were either in hiding or in the nationalist zone. In one way or another, all those available got mobilized for Operation Residence, Isidoro having told those in the Levant that the Father wanted them to pitch in. Valencia was now the official seat of the government (the cabinet having left Madrid at the beginning of 1936), and was where the administrative matter they now had in hand would end up.

Pedro Casciaro, who already had plenty to worry about, now had his life complicated even further by the assignment of enlisting in the project his grandfather, a British subject who, because he had made a contribution to the Society, was in a position to direct a claim for compensation to the British embassy.[198]

---

[197] AGP, RHF, EF–370501–2.

[198] Here (from AGP, IZL, D–1213, 139) is the letter from Isidoro to Pedro: "Madrid, May 3, 1937 / My dear friend: / Mariano has asked me to bring you up to date on some business that I have transacted today. As you know, my house on Ferraz Street has been half destroyed and the furniture that was in it has disappeared, and on the basis of my situation as a foreigner I have presented a claim to the Argentine embassy against the Spanish state for the value of what was damaged in that house and of the furniture. The house belonged to the Society for the Encouragement of Advanced Studies, of which I am president. As such, I have presented the claim, since as co-owner of what has been destroyed and of what has disappeared, I have a right to consider as mine those goods of the Society and to request the proper compensation, which amounts, according to the inventory which I attached to the claim, to 1,078,900 pesetas. I have just written to Paco and Eugenio asking them to work on this matter in Valencia. Mariano has asked me to find out if your British grandfather could do something in this matter. Entrust it to the G.A.'s [guardian angels] and to Don Nicolás [Saint Nicholas], who have a lot of influence. Do all that you can, spare no effort, butter them up with gifts if necessary; you can't imagine how much interest Mariano has in this matter. Keep me posted on whatever you can do in this regard. I am mailing a letter to Paco and Eugenio at the same time as this one. An embrace from your good friend, Isidoro."

Two joined concerns were now consuming the Father's energy: the claim and the evacuation. "Hurry. There's a need to hurry, for everything: to get us out of the country, and to get our compensation," he wrote to those in Madrid.[199]

But this was in the middle of a war, in a country whose administrative departments had suddenly moved to another region; they had gone to Valencia, leaving their records behind in Madrid. And this was a request for compensation for a house requisitioned and sacked by CNT anarchists and later destroyed by artillery-fire. The chances of succeeding were slim, and the Father could see that. And yet, "Whether we accomplish anything or not, what peace it will give everyone to know that we did everything possible to protect the patrimony of the Society! Right?"[200]

One thing he was doing was to give them a quick lesson in how to handle the affairs of God and of the Work. "Carry on with this matter of the house, despite the potholes and the ruts in the road. It may happen that the car will turn over. Then we just put it back on its wheels, fix what is messed up, and continue going forward as before. Always happy, with joy and peace, which never, for any reason, should you lose."[201] In adversity they would learn to be orderly and diligent and not put things off till "the convenient tomorrow."[202] "'Mañana! Mañana!' And I repeat to you, 'Today! Right now!' 'Tomorrow' and 'later' are words permanently deleted from our lexicon. Agreed?"[203]

When this activity had been going on for a month, he wrote to Isidoro to urge him and the others to be persistent in pressing the claim. He wanted them, he said, to do it like this:

> ... without impatience, but with perseverance; to be like water constantly dripping on the rock of obstacles. They receive me well? Good. They receive me badly? Better. I will go on, like water dripping, with holy shamelessness, putting

[199] AGP, RHF, EF–370502–1.

[200] AGP, RHF, EF–370513–1. And in another letter to these sons in Madrid, "It is necessary to pursue this matter, even if nothing is accomplished. I assure you that in any case we will have accomplished a lot. Being the old man that I am, I do know well what I am talking about" (AGP, RHF, EF–370518–1).

[201] AGP, RHF, EF–370516–1.

[202] AGP, RHF, EF–370519–2.

[203] AGP, RHF, EF–370513–1.

up with frustrations and humiliations and harsh refusals and rudeness (what riches!), very happy and at peace, until they grow weary (I must not grow weary: this should be your resolution) and they end up receiving me kindly, as a friend—or as an unavoidable calamity. . . . If you knew how to speak clearly! Don Manuel has confided this to us.[204]

(In other words, that "holy shamelessness," that business of being armed with stubbornness and ready to take humiliations, was not a merely human tactic, but rather a behavior adopted in obedience to an inspiration from the Lord.)

My sons: Did you have the idea that it's possible to make progress without overcoming resistance? Well, it is a fact that always and in everything we have to encounter sometimes great difficulties and other times smaller ones. Of course, the first kind are usually less of a problem, since great difficulties get us fired up. It is in the second kind, the ones that sting our pride and do nothing more, that the Lord is waiting for us. Yes—in those waiting rooms; in those rude remarks; in hearing oneself referred to as "that individual"; in yesterday's friendliness turned to today's discourtesy.[205]

But, for all that, they inevitably ran into dead ends, given the bureaucracy they were up against.

It's only natural that people each do what's most convenient for them. Thus you will learn to hold out and be stubborn. Let's not have the courage of the snail, who, as soon as his antennae meet an obstacle, withdraws completely into his own little shell of selfishness. Rather, we need the drive, assertiveness, and perseverance of the brave bull who flattens, with the means he has available, whatever obstructions

[204] AGP, RHF, EF–370521–2.

On this point he was so sure of the will of God that on the following day he wrote to Isidoro to have him communicate it to those in Valencia by way of Paco Botella. "When you write to Paco," he says, "copy the first paragraphs of my letter of Friday—the ones about the need to be a pain in the neck. I think they will do a lot of good." (See AGP, RHF, EF–370522–1.)

[205] AGP, RHF, EF–370513–1.

stand in his way. It is true that we do not lack—and never will lack—obstacles and obstructions. But it is also true that we have more than enough means, if we want to use them. Right? Well, let's use them. Our own, that's fine, and at the same time, those of Don Manuel. Oh, and always be very happy.[206]

Certainly they were not lacking obstacles. Even as the Father was congratulating Isidoro for having put in that claim at the Argentine embassy, Isidoro was running into problems. After three weeks of negotiations, little progress had been made.[207]

As the Father had foreseen, they needed the help of Saint Nicholas, the Work's intercessor in financial matters. He asked the saint to help make sure the papers did not get lost in the labyrinth of administrative offices, which would have meant yet another continuation of the never-ending "good pipe story." He wrote to his sons in Valencia, "Don Nicolás now has the ball in his hands. Our job is to go on being persistent."[208]

Father Josemaría's fears were not unfounded. Things kept getting bogged down, and the "good pipe story" continued.

Pedro Casciaro's grandfather, Don Julio, did not get much better results. His citizenship claims were shaky, since his British passport, issued in Valencia on April 21, 1937, and signed by the British consul in that city and by the provisional vice-consul of Alicante, was valid for only six months and was not renewable unless the person concerned could document his citizenship. Even as Isidoro was sending Pedro Casciaro all the documents needed for "a written claim against the Spanish state, via the British embassy, for compensation ... ," a painstaking search for Don Julio's papers in the archives of the consulates in Cartagena and Valencia continued to produce noth-

[207] For him to submit the claim, the offices of the Argentine embassy in Valencia demanded a certificate of nationality. So he had one sent from Madrid. But a copy of his birth certificate, the only proof he had of his citizenship, was not enough; he had to apply for an original from Buenos Aires. And later he was told that even then he could not officially be considered an Argentine citizen, since he had not done the required military service. This was the situation in July. The birth certificate arrived, and the Father wrote him, "Well, better late than never." See AGP, RHF, EF–370701–4. For more information on the claim and the required documentation, see AGP, IZL, D–1018 and D–1213, 147, 148, 151, 173, 190, 191, 230, and 234. In this last letter (234) Isidoro asks those in Valencia to bring some documents to the Argentine embassy to add to the claim's file. See also Pero-Sanz, pp. 221–22.
[208] AGP, RHF, EF–370601–1.

ing.[209] Nor did other possible mediators suggested to Isidoro—a Swiss co-worker, a Bolivian who had spent some time at the Ferraz Street residence, a Paraguayan friend of Manolo Sainz de los Terreros—look promising.[210]

6. *"The worst days of this period"*

Life in the Honduran consulate went by quietly. The Father's companions rose early and took turns using the bathroom. Later the priest would usually give a meditation and celebrate Mass. Breakfast was a cup of tea. The rest of the morning was filled with work.[211]

Father Josemaría, in the role of kindly grandfather that he played for the censors, mingled serious points for meditation with affectionate, playful comments in letters to his "grandchildren" in Madrid and Valencia. Afterwards, in mid-morning, the room was transformed into a classroom where they studied or read French, English, and German.

In one letter to his sons in Valencia, Father Josemaría pretends that he is in the midst of a terrible racket. He is obviously just pretending, or wildly exaggerating, because it is a known fact that the refugees down the hall from them called their group "the whisperers" because no loud sounds ever came from that room.[212]

> Madrid, April 30, 1937
>
> . . . Nothing; this grandfather was not wanting to write you anything more. But today, when I tried to do something worthwhile and, after a few preliminaries, started really getting into the first stage of my work, these noisy children I have to put up with started shrieking, and no human patience

---

[209] See AGP, RHF, D–15702.

[210] "I only have a little news to relate today," says Isidoro in a letter of June 6, 1937. "First, the Swiss friend of Miguel's was not able to do anything, because it was a holiday. And second, we're thinking that the Bolivian from the So-Co-In [Sociedad de Colaboración Intelectual], Pablo García de Paredes, could be used as a "member" for the claim; maybe Barredo knows where he lives. And Manolo tells me he's thought of a Paraguayan friend of his." See AGP, IZL, D–1213, 185. For more on the So-Co-In, see vol. 1, p. 451, of this biography.

[211] The meditations which the Father gave were taken down "with considerable accuracy" by Eduardo and, once transcribed, were picked up by Isidoro, along with the correspondence, so that the other members of the Work could also benefit from them. See AGP, RHF, T–04965, p. 19, and Pero-Sanz, pp. 206–207.

[212] See AGP, RHF, T–05050, p. 1, and T–05127.

could bear it, nor could any mind concentrate on serious work. Oh, to be in my room, *my* room, with my solitude and my silence! Old people need quiet. The racket, the boisterous laughter, the running around of these reckless kids mixes poorly with my years. Patience, right? Right! And to top it all off, they keep bumping into this desk, and even into my poor skeleton of a body. Mariano, get to work. I don't want to; let somebody else do it! . . .

Very monotonous, my life, little ones. But I'm always a hundred miles from the physical place I'm in, so I can hardly speak of monotony. I chat as much as I can with my old Friend. I think of my family, perhaps more than I should. I am at peace. I look somber, but I am happy. And because of my happiness, and because of my years, the memories, thoughts of possible dangers for my children and grandchildren, and other excusable selfish reasons, hardly a day goes by that I don't cry, also more than I should.

Josemaría, who has gotten more rational since we took him out of the insane asylum, assures me that this painful environment of war in which Spaniards find themselves will be good for my young ones and help give them a manly character. And, moreover, that as the foreigners that they are, they can and should remain foreigners to avoid the contamination of certain places. And that since they have been well vaccinated, if they follow the doctor's norms it should be hard for them to lose their health—which is what I am concerned about. . . .

When I see myself at the end of all the years since I set up a household, with my family scattered around and growing more numerous by the day, I think I need to have a heart that is bigger than the world. And I apologize for my spells of melancholy and childish foolishness (children and old folk!), and I want to embrace all of you with all my soul, like the doting grandfather I am, so that whatever blows you might receive would fall on the strong back of the one writing to you. Isn't it strange that, having as many debts of my own as I do, I have been allowed to co-sign for everyone in these times of economic collapse? And I hope the payments will be asked of me. If they are, how joyfully I will give all that is needed, down to the last penny! . . .

Stay strong. And don't get upset because your grandfather embraces you with all his soul.

Mariano[213]

At lunchtime they went to the dining room with the round table, and usually were served a little bread and a bowl of rice soup, occasionally fortified with lentils or carob beans.[214] They then returned to their room for a get-together. After that, they read or worked. The Father would visit with the family of the consul, whose wife was then very ill. He also made his afternoon prayer and visits to the Blessed Sacrament there, until he decided to no longer keep the Blessed Sacrament reserved in the consul's living area.[215] After supper—a thin soup with bread, or cooked vegetables, or a salad—they said the Rosary, had another get-together, spread out their thin mattresses, and went to sleep.

A day spent with the Father was one filled with affection and security. The consul's son-in-law says, "Never did he show any sign of anxiety or depression. He was a person who made living together easy and pleasant, who never created problems of any kind, who never made any comment that was less than positive—not about the red government, not about the white government, not about the bombings, not about any of the difficulties."[216] Even in the midst of such circumstances, he was such enjoyable company that one member of the Work accidentally said out loud what everyone was thinking: "This can't go on, it's too much happiness."[217]

*   *   *

Arguments and loud voices often filled the consulate during the day, but at night it was fairly quiet, even though, as the Father jokingly called it, that room was "a cage of crickets,"[218] not very suitable for his soul, which craved recollection. He spoke to God about his sons,

---

[213] AGP, RHF, EF–370430–1.

[214] See AGP, RHF, EF–370406–1.

[215] See AGP, RHF, EF–370530–1, and AGP, RHF, T–05050, p. 3. This must have occurred at the beginning of May, certainly not before, because one of his journal entries reads, "Thursday, May 6, 1937: They want to have the Blessed Sacrament removed" (*Apuntes*, no. 1377).

[216] See AGP, RHF, T–05120, p. 2.

[217] It was José María González Barredo who said this, and Eduardo Alastrué Castillo who related it, in AGP, RHF, T–04695, p. 16.

[218] See AGP, RHF, EF–370508–2.

mentally reviewing the situations of them all: the prisoners, the refugees, those in hiding, the sick, and those of whom he had no news. He implored his Friend to keep them safe in body and soul, and to give him a big heart, a very big one with room for them all.

In a letter dated May 1, he reminds those in Valencia of the promise he had made the previous day for his entire family: "Little ones—poor little ones!—now that you know that your little grandfather has made a formal commitment to pay all the family's debts, don't become spendthrifts." [219] Did they understand? Yes. They knew of the commitment he had made to our Lord to make expiation for his own faults and those of others, to pay for the innumerable sins tearing the Spanish nation apart. And they knew that he was offering his own back to be beaten so that his "grandchildren" would not have to suffer these blows. The recipients avidly read his letters and memorized them, as Pedro Casciaro told Isidoro: "I can say, with only a little exaggeration, that I memorize everything he writes, because here, so far away from the family, I am very much alone and the only warmth I find is in his very expressive words. He complains sometimes about difficulties in expressing himself. Ah! If he were in my shoes! I am, if the donkey will forgive me, the proverbial jackass who reads but can't articulate." [220]

Having quite often heard him speak of this, his sons knew well enough what he considered the spirit of penance to consist of: taking advantage of the tasks, irritations, and frustrations of everyday life, elevating them to the supernatural plane, "divinizing" pain and suffering. Shortly before the civil war broke out, he had written: "In the prose of the thousand small daily happenings, there is poetry enough to make one feel that one is on the cross." [221]

In August 1936, when he had to leave his mother's house, he took full advantage of the "thousand small daily happenings" in the hiding places that sheltered him—all the instances of loneliness, hunger, persecution, sickness—using them to make divine poetry. His exile was cruel and prolonged. He suffered great hunger. Illness in the sanatorium had reduced him to skin and bones. But he took up his new crosses without abandoning his old mortifications. His penance was aimed at making the lives of those around him more bearable. He sought to console the afflicted, to avoid creating problems with those

[219] AGP, RHF, EF–370501–1.
[220] AGP, RHF, D–15702.
[221] *Apuntes*, no. 1372 (30 Jun 1936).

he lived with, to do small services for the refugees. He tried not to speak about the war or about himself. He suffered the hunger without complaint. He kept his curiosity in check. He smiled and cultivated good humor, transmitting to everyone serenity and joy, being courteous, punctual, and orderly, offering up to God the privations and annoyances.

And, every now and then, he added to all this some bloody disciplines. Sometimes, without explaining why, he would ask the others to leave him alone for a while; other times he would take advantage of the fact that they were in the dining room. One day, however, Alvaro was there, in bed with a fever. "Cover your face with the blanket," the Father told him. The blows were hard and rhythmic. Out of curiosity, Alvaro counted: a thousand, all delivered with equal force. The floor was spattered with blood, but before the others got back, the Father carefully cleaned up.[222]

The crimes and offenses committed in connection with the war also weighed on him as he writes to his sons in Valencia:

> Today, Grandfather is sad, downcast, in spite of the love and affection of his family, and in spite of the heroic patience of his nephew Juanito—who is *not* "being bossy." It's just that when he looks back on his youth and contemplates the present life, he has a great desire to behave well, for those who are behaving badly; to play Don Quixote, making reparation, suffering, putting things right. Then his intellect and will (Love) start to race. Love arrives first—but so weak, with so few deeds! Grandfather is sad because he can't get things right (being so old, having so little strength) unless the grandchildren of his soul help him with their youth.[223]

In a letter written on May 6 to those in Madrid, he makes an even more distressing comment. "The worst days of this whole period," he says, "have been those spent in these pits [*honduras*]. One would surely be better off in prison. One suffers, and one offers up the suffering; but it's not the way."[224]

---

[222] Alvaro del Portillo, PR, p. 486. Alvaro had also been sick once before, during the days just before March 10, 1937. See *Apuntes*, nos. 1381 and 1382.

[223] AGP, RHF, EF–370421–1.

[224] AGP, RHF, EF–370506–1.

The hours of his day were filled with activity, but for long stretches of the night he could not sleep.[225] On May 30, he unburdened himself at the end of a long letter to those in Valencia: "Do you want me to tell you, Paco, what's going on with the grandfather? I'll tell you, in part. First, very personal concerns, very much his own. (But I have nothing that is my own!) Then, he's been hit where it hurts him the most, in his grandchildren. And that's almost everything." [226]

Lacking news and imagining their sufferings, the Father suffered over his sons. But this communication he made to Paco Botella is put in carefully chosen, reticent words. What was really burdening him?

Whatever it was, this was not its first occurrence. In his journal there is an entry where he uses similar expressions. It was written on September 9, 1931, in the midst of a period of great suffering and great graces. The symptoms were "great tribulation and great helplessness," with temptations to rebellion and lack of conformity to God's will, and "low and vile things." And what was the cause? "Really, the same as always. But it's something very personal that, without taking away my trust in my God, makes me suffer. . . . And, as a remedy, I think of the serious illness I know God will lovingly give me when the time is right." [227]

Although he had already been raised to the heights of mystical contemplation, to "looking directly at the sun," [228] these "very personal concerns," these very private things which made him suffer, reflect the passive purification by which God was detaching him from every affection that was not in keeping with the divine will. From this period of passive purification the founder left some notes, written at the consulate. One, dated May 8, 1937, reads, "The worst days of this period are those I am spending in Honduras." (He had said the same in the letter of May 6 to those in Madrid.) "I think that rarely have I suffered as I do now." [229]

---

[225] AGP, RHF, EF-370519-1

[226] AGP, RHF, EF–370530–1.

[227] *Apuntes*, no. 274.

[228] *Apuntes*, no. 244 (31 Aug 1931).

Bishop Alvaro del Portillo, commenting on the richness of the founder's life of prayer, says, "The Holy Spirit undoubtedly led him to the highest summits of mystical union in the midst of ordinary life, while he was also undergoing very painful passive purifications of the spirit and the senses." See "Sacerdotes para una nueva Evangelización," in *La formación de los sacerdotes en las circunstancias actuales. XI Simposio Internacional de Teología* (Pamplona: University of Navarre, 1990), p. 989.

[229] *Apuntes*, no. 1379 (8 May 1937). In the general archives of the prelature there are some notes written by the Father, on small sheets of paper, in the Honduran consulate.

Before the war broke out, he had foreseen being nailed to a cross. It was a cross he lovingly accepted, in reparation for sins.

*   *   *

The floor above theirs was considered an extension of the consulate but was also filled to overflowing with refugees, among them Father Recaredo Ventosa and other priests of the Sacred Heart. Father Josemaría made his confession to Father Ventosa every week.[230] How surprised must that priest have been when, in the wee hours of the morning of Sunday, May 9, he was awakened by this visitor from the floor below who just had to talk with him right then. The Father writes:

> Sunday, May 9, 1937: I've suffered terribly this night. Thank goodness I was able to unburden myself, at 1:30 or 2:00 in the morning, by speaking with the religious-order priest in our refuge. I have asked many times, with many tears, to be allowed to die soon in God's grace. It's cowardice: I think this immense suffering is simply the result of my self-offering as a victim to the Merciful Love. Let me die, I prayed, because from heaven I will be able to help, whereas here below I am an obstacle and I fear for my salvation. On the other hand, I realize that Jesus wants me to live, suffering, and work. It's all the same. His will be done.[231]

So terrible was his anguish that he came down sick and was not able to get up again until Saturday, May 15. The following Friday he wrote, "Like an open wound, that's how you are. Everything makes you suffer, in your faculties and in your senses. And everything is for you a temptation. Poor child!"[232]

The interior suffering of his passive purification went on:

He began this writing of notes in April of 1937, but the first twenty-two are missing. The "Honduran notes" are recorded in *Apuntes*, nos. 1374 to 1394.

[230] "He started out having a great affection for me," says Father Ventosa, "and after our first conversation, he asked me to hear his confession. The Father came to confession to me many times during his stay at the consulate. . . . I also heard the confessions of those who were with the Father." See *Testimonios*, p. 420.

[231] *Apuntes*, no. 1380.

[232] *Apuntes*, no. 1388.

Sunday, May 23, 1937: My prayer last night, because of my fear that I am not fulfilling the will of God and the worries I feel about my salvation: "Lord, take me. From the next world, from purgatory, I will be able to do more for the Work and for my sons and daughters. You will raise up a better instrument than me—and a more faithful one—to carry forward the Work on earth." [233]

On May 26, another cry from the battle taking place in his soul:

Jesus, if I am not going to be the instrument you desire, take me *right now,* in your grace. I am not afraid of death, despite my sinful life, because I keep in mind your Love. Typhoid, tuberculosis, pneumonia, or four bullets, what's the difference?[234]

And, in the same journal entry, yet another cry:

I suffer terrible doubts and distress when I think about my salvation. O my God! O my Mother! Will you allow me to be condemned? Saint Joseph, my father and lord! Little watchmaker! Saint Peter! Saint Paul! Saint John! [235]

In his letters, nevertheless, he tried to keep a cheerful face, regaling them with entertaining—though slightly embellished—news and commentary.

His companions knew nothing about the spiritual purification he was undergoing, but they did notice the physical ravages. In a letter to María Dolores Fisac, dated June 4, 1937, Isidoro gave this description:

Yesterday I went with Manolo to see our grandfather. It having been several months since I last saw him, I found him looking very worn down. He really is a lot thinner; all that remains of his former appearance is the liveliness of his eyes; but he has the same temperament as always. His words pick you up and infuse life into you. It really shakes you up and

---

[233] *Apuntes*, no. 1389.
[234] *Apuntes*, no. 1391.
[235] *Apuntes*, no. 1391.

makes you care nothing for all those little material things that, with their many imperfections, you are still so attached to. After talking to him you feel much lighter, as though you've been relieved of something that was weighing you down. We must do our utmost to show our affection and care for him, because he is constantly thinking of his little ones; he thinks about us all the time. He remembers us especially when he makes his daily visits to our great protector Don Manuel.[236]

7. *"Grandfather's business"*

From his place of confinement, the founder continued to carry on the Work, by intense prayer and by his letter-writing apostolate. The biggest obstacle to that apostolate was the censorship, but he got around that with ingeniousness and good humor. There is, for example, this letter of April 29, 1937, in which he reminds his sons in "the happy Levant" of their responsibility to carry on Opus Dei should he die:

I hope—I *hope*—that it won't be long before I can give you big hugs. In the meantime, don't forget this poor old fellow. And if the old man (it is the law of nature) marches on, it's your job to carry on the family business more vigorously every day. I'll tell you something in confidence, the confidence between a grandfather and his grandchild: on discovering all these bones I have that I didn't know about, I find myself in excellent health. Come what may, I think that my life will be extended for many years, and that I will see all my children and grandchildren well situated and getting ahead. But—*but!*—don't forget, I'm insisting on this, that if I do march on, you must never for anything abandon my business. It will make you all rich and benefit everyone. I almost don't know what I'm writing. Did I speak of "life"? Bah! I meant "Life," with a capital L! . . .

My young ones! I can see that this business will in the near future be such a marvelous venture that it would be foolish

---

[236] AGP, IZL, D–1213, 183.

for anyone to let this opportunity to be rich and happy slip away. How right they are to say that when one reaches seventy (and I'm eighty), one's greed increases! I long to see all of you gilded by the rays of the Sun, my loved ones radiating the pure gold acquired—very well acquired—by their efforts to make our family's patrimony grow.

Mariano, you're talking a lot of foolishness. That's true. But a leopard cannot change its spots. I have always been ambitious. I've always wanted everything. And besides, since this doesn't seem to me to be the wrong way to go, I do hope to guide my family along it.

Ambition! Blessed ambition! How many obstacles you can overcome! With a thirst for the heights it's hard to fall into pools of stagnant water, which are the opposite: the abyss. Blessed ambition! Most noble ambition! If I save myself for great things—and I was born for great things!—I will know how, with the necessary help, not to get sidetracked by the small stuff. Now, notice that I'm not talking about *neglecting* the small stuff. That would be a big mistake, since great things, the very greatest, are won by small efforts.

Then he tells them, in a veiled way, about the serious commitment he made to the Lord to make reparation for himself and others, imploring protection for his "business":

I don't know if you've heard about the financial mess that, for the good of my family, which is always my weakness, I've gotten myself into. I've pledged to pay all the debts myself. No need to say more. Surely you must know that I have plenty of debts of my own. Thus the chaff gets mixed with the grain. Now is when I really feel old, weak, and awfully shaky. But what I've said stands. There's no turning back. Help me out as much as you can, you and my other grandchildren. It would be a pity if my ambitions were to terminate in bankruptcy, or at least in a suspension of payments! I shudder at the thought. I trust I can count on the effort and sacrifices of all my family.[237]

---

[237] AGP, RHF, EF–370429–1.

Two months later, interiorly strengthened by the hard trials to which our Lord had subjected him, he returned to the management of his enterprise, his "business," with redoubled optimism. "This grandfather of yours," he writes on June 24, "has once again taken up the reins. What news! And I assure you, he has more strength than he did before he got sick, although now he weighs twenty pounds less."[238] The adversities of that period did not discourage him, since, as he told them, "the war not only does not slow things down, but can actually give greater impetus to many undertakings, if those in charge don't fall asleep."[239]

The founder was burning with impatience to get on with the task God had given him. He wrote to those in Madrid:

> As soon as I can start working again (hopefully very soon), I'm going to be reborn.
>
> Let it be known that the grandfather is very satisfied with all his grandchildren, without exception. Is that clear? And he thinks they will always know how to be optimistic, joyful, stubborn, convinced that our business ventures must necessarily prosper, and deeply certain that everything works for the good.[240]

But did it? In the middle of June he heard that Pepe Isasa, one of the members of the Work in the other zone of Spain, had died in April at the front. Isidoro immediately informed the others, as the founder wished, so that they could offer suffrages for his soul, praying all three parts of the Rosary and offering their Communion. He wrote, "The grandfather said to me: Tell my grandchildren to bring three bouquets of roses to the Mother of Don Manuel on Pepe's behalf, and if they can, to have lunch with this good friend."[241]

For the grandfather, the loss of this grandchild is "bittersweet news." He writes to those in Valencia:

> There's one thing I would like you to do, which Ignacio[242] will also request: place roses—three bouquets—on Pepe's tomb. And make a visit to Don Manuel. Don Manuel! How grateful

---

[238] AGP, RHF, EF–370624–1.
[239] AGP, RHF, EF–370421–1.
[240] AGP, RHF, EF–370605–1.
[241] AGP, IZL, F–1213, 196. Pepe Isasa died on April 23, 1937.
[242] "Ignacio" was Isidoro's code name.

I am to him! My tears (I'm not ashamed to tell you that I've cried) are not tears of protest at the death of my dear grandson. I accept it. But I do ask you to put in a good word for the rest of my little ones, as will I, that no more of them be taken from me.

Be happy, okay? Haven't I told you many a time that the grandfather has a very large House, where a number of his grandchildren are waiting for him?

That is all too easy. We have to remain here, and even grow old, to keep the business going—the totally magnificent business!—that your family has been involved in for more than eight years.[243]

It was obvious that this great and universal business—Opus Dei—would need many people. The founder's zeal knew no bounds, although he was still in confinement.

I've been infected with the crazy longings of my brother Josemaría. (He is mad, fit to be tied; it's not for nothing that he's been in the madhouse.) I, too, long to crisscross this tiny world, from pole to pole, and thaw out the icy wastes, and level the mountains, and uproot all the hatreds, and bring happiness to all men and women, and make that desire for one flock and one shepherd a blessed reality.

My head feels like it's about to burst, like a firecracker. It seems like a miracle that it doesn't happen. There just won't fit into a person's head (though in the heart, yes) so many great things. Therefore, may I be given many heads and many hearts, youthful and clean, to fill with noble, exalted ideas and desires!

Although a guy like you may find it hard to believe, less than half an hour ago I was mending a pair of socks for one of my wildest grandsons. Madness is no excuse for not keeping one's feet on the ground.[244]

While he kept his feet on the ground, his soaring apostolic imagination carried him to the scattered members of the Work. With the

243 AGP, RHF, EF–370615–1.
244 AGP, RHF, EF–370815–1.

invaluable help of Isidoro, who served as secretary in charge of mailing the correspondence from the consulate, the letters destined for "the happy Levant" ("From Grandfather to Perico, via Paco, for all his grandchildren") went to Valencia, addressed to Paco Botella, and from there were sent to Torrevieja, where Pedro Casciaro was for some time. Later they were read by Rafael Calvo Serer, who was convalescing at Alcalalí, a place in Alicante. After everyone—including Chiqui, who was in a prison in Valencia—knew what the Father had said in them, the letters were stored away.

Father Josemaría poured his heart into those letters. Juan Jiménez Vargas, reflecting on the odd manner of expression that was made necessary by the censorship, once remarked, "How ridiculous this will all seem, in the course of time." "The ridiculous doesn't exist," replied the Father.[245] His communications were treasured by those who received them. "We began to do our prayer with the letters," Paco Botella recalls. And once everyone had read them, he says, "Pedro took them and carried them off to be kept in a good place. It was this way until the end of the war. These letters from the Father were waiting for us in a safety-deposit box in a bank."[246]

Having no fear of sounding ridiculous, he unabashedly showed the affection he had for his grandchildren. Isidoro, when telling the Valencians how happy everyone was at learning that Chiqui had been released from prison, added, "You can't possibly imagine how concerned the grandfather has been; he's been on pins and needles. Really his affection for his grandchildren borders on delirium. It's his main obsession. What a responsibility his little ones have to respond in like manner."[247] He read and reread their letters. Alvaro even once asked him jokingly if he was going to pin them to his lapel so that he could keep them always in view.[248]

[245] AGP, RHF, EF–370515–1.

[246] AGP, RHF, T–00159/1, pp. 15–16.

[247] AGP, IZL, D–1213, 217.
The censorship made it necessary that, where spiritual matters were concerned, some things be communicated in a vague way or through silence. It annoyed the grandfather when this was carried too far, and sometimes he complained to Paco Botella about his not having really answered his questions. "Paco," he said, "don't you realize that your poor grandfather's concern about his little ones is like an unhealed wound?" (AGP, RHF, EF–370725–3).

[248] That was not much of an exaggeration, as the Father himself admits. "Rafael," he says, "I've read your letter three times in the last two hours. It's true that I do the same with the letters of all my grandchildren. Jeannot and Alvarote, who always notice these things, have made a big fuss about it" (AGP, RHF, EF–370624–1).

Chiqui, after his months in prison, had gone to rest for a few days at Alcalalí, where Rafael Calvo Serer was staying. Both received letters from Madrid on the same day.

From the grandfather to Chiqui, July 27, 1937
My dear child:
Knowing the joyful surprise your last letter was to me, you can guess how apprehensive it made me that it was Paco, and not you, who wrote me when you were discharged from the clinic. Isn't that just like an old man!

I have thought of you so often. I have accompanied you more than you think. I have pestered Don Angel constantly, asking him to give my grandson all the care I would have given, and more. I guess he listened to me, and I trust that he will continue to listen to me. He is a very good friend of mine!

Possibly soon (I seriously think so) my brother Josemaría will set out, with his son Jeannot, to visit our country. When this happens, I'll ask Ignacio to let you know.

How did the visit with Rafa go? That boy, by loving his brothers so much when he's still so young himself, has won my heart.[249]

And to Rafael Calvo Serer:

From the grandfather to Rafa. Greetings. July 27, 1937
Little one! Here are some lines for your eyes alone.

I've read your letter I don't know how many times, even though Alvarote laughs at me. Now it might be your turn to hear the war whoops of these big kids who live with their grandfather. How bad they are! But of course you know that's not true. My little ones are very good.

The affection you show your brothers—now our Chiqui!— touches my heart. Don Manuel and I are truly grateful to you for all your *natural* good behavior. What a hug I'm going to give you, Rafaelín, when I have you with me!

Take heart. Even though you have an ulcer, may you recuperate to the point where you are brimming with good health.

---

[249] AGP, RHF, EF–370727–4.

If possible, go see the Son of Doña María every day. He's a great Friend, isn't he?

Keep the family very much in mind. (Grandfather doesn't dare ask that you keep him in mind.) Take on, more every day, our family characteristics.

Everyone sends you a big hug, along with mine.

Mariano[250]

*   *   *

It was obvious that the "business" would require manual labor, and that the few workers already in it needed looking after. Even from his confinement in the consulate, the founder had to watch over his sons or ask Doña Dolores to take care of those who were at large in Madrid. "Mama, keep in mind that you're the grandmother of my children," he wrote her.[251]

He was also aware that the storm of war had swept away many of the first women of the Work. "I think I have lost a grandson, my Pepe, and I don't know how many granddaughters," he reflected sadly.[252] Of the handful of women who had asked admission to Opus Dei, he had been able to locate only one. He asked Isidoro to tell this young lady that if she saw the others, she should ask for their prayers but not give them her address, to avoid risks and worries.[253] Yet even in these untoward circumstances, a new vocation for the women's branch arrived. News of it came through the mail, with allowance for the wartime censorship.

Miguel Fisac, when he was living in the Ferraz Street residence, had asked admission to the Work. Now he was hiding out in his parents' home in Daimiel, a village in La Mancha. Father Josemaría wrote to him there through his sister Lola. It was Miguel who took the initiative of suggesting to his sister that she might have a vocation to the Work, and later the Father asked her to consider that possibility.[254] Meanwhile, he kept asking our Lord ("Don Manuel," "Manolo") to

[250] AGP, RHF, EF–370727–2.
[251] AGP, RHF, EF–370529–2.
[252] AGP, RHF, EF–370707–1.
[253] AGP, RHF, EF–370525–1.
[254] The letter to María Dolores (Lola) Fisac is brief: "For Daimiel. What joy it gave me to read your letter, Lola! Know that I keep you always in mind, as I do all your family. Oh, and it would make me very happy if you were to become my granddaughter. Yours, Mariano. Madrid. May 21, 1937." See AGP, RHF, EF–370521–1.

grant her a vocation. On the vigil of the feast of the Visitation of our Lady, thanking her for food packages she had sent from Daimiel, he wrote:

> From Grandfather to Lola, from Tegucigalpa!
> July 1, vigil of my Mother's saint's day, 1937
> My dear child:
>   If you could only see how thankful I am for your repeated kindnesses! Well, well. There's no way that Manolo won't make you fall in love and fulfill my desire, that grows stronger every day, that you become part of my family.
>   Just know that I am hoping for this. And forgive me for speaking so frankly. It's my advanced years, and the affection I have for all of you! Forgiven, right?[255]

Our Lord soon granted him his wish. Two weeks later the founder wrote her, "Well, little one: I am delighted to call you my granddaughter."[256] And the following month, when Lola had had time to think over her decision, he wrote her again.

> For my granddaughter Lola
> My dear child:
>   The grandfather, with all your gifts, is going to become a glutton, that's all I can say. How tasty, those sweet rolls! We licked our fingers—even Jeannot, with his impressive schnozzle.
>   Don Manuel . . . I'll keep quiet. Only one question: How is your courtship going? And one more: Is it really, really true that you prefer him to all others and truly want to become part of this grandfather's family?
>   Forgive me, my child. We old folks like to ask so many questions! And I imagine they have told you how much Mariano likes to have people confide in him, especially secrets of Love.
>   I suppose that to answer my question will make you blush. Well, since I'm not there to see it, what does it matter? Besides, you do have an easy way to do it. Just say to me, "Grand-

---

[255] AGP, RHF, EF–370701–1.
[256] AGP, RHF, EF–370714–1.   ·

father, to your question, my answer is yes." Frankly, Lola, I can't even imagine your saying no. So—as you already know—I hope that soon you will begin to confide in me.

Whenever I speak with Manolo, I remember your parents and your whole family to him. I do this every day. And when I mention you by name, I always say the same thing: it depends exclusively on you to make what we talked about a reality. But don't forget that there's a lot of work waiting for you in my house, and hard work at that. We're at the beginning; and the foundations have to be set in stone. Nevertheless, you will also find something that you won't find just anywhere: joy and peace; in a word, happiness.

Well, that's all for now. Affectionate hugs for your parents, and don't forget your grandfather.

Mariano [257]

*　　*　　*

When things finally quieted down at night—insofar as that was possible "in this solitude that we enjoy, so excessively accompanied," as the Father put it[258]—he chatted with Alvaro about the "family business." What did he say to him?

Between the lines of a letter that he wrote to those in Valencia, there are remarks written in a very small hand by Alvaro, which read as follows:

> We are overjoyed by the news about Chiqui. How much we would all love to get together and, all together, for a good long while, get ourselves good and revived! It would be great for all of us. And it may perhaps, I don't know, be necessary for us to undertake with a new spirit the business that the grandfather and the rest of us have in hand. At night, when the others are still up, the grandfather and I, sprawled out on our mattresses, chat about all these family matters.
>
> It's true that circumstances have made it difficult to develop the business. Everything is a problem. The financial question, the lack of personnel, everything. Nevertheless, and despite his age, Grandfather never lets himself give in to

[257] AGP, RHF, EF–370805–1.
[258] AGP, RHF, EF–370505–4.

pessimism. He accepts the lack of money, we all do, without worrying. Everything depends on our working with much spirit; this and much faith in a successful outcome will overcome everything. This is what the poor old man says. But what makes him sad—a feeling consistent with the hope that animates him—is the lack of personnel. Counting all the members of the family, there are very few, and what will happen if some die or prove useless for the business! . . . From now on, for when it is possible to start working, let us each be firmly resolved to stay very united to the rest of the family and, above all, to Don Manuel and our poor grandfather. He certainly deserves it! And besides, it makes perfect sense. It is impossible to get good results without a blind adherence to those who, in whatever matter, are in charge. Don't complain. Even though you are so far away, you've now been let in on the bedtime conversations the grandfather and I have.[259]

Work and responsibilities were good for the founder. He forgot about himself in order to live the Gospel saying, "I have come not to be served, but to serve," which he freely paraphrased as, "I have come not to be a nuisance, but to put up with nuisances."[260]

Being responsible "for six mouths and the stomachs coming with them,"[261] he had to acknowledge and do something about the hunger, if not for his sake, then at least for the sakes of the young people with him. Overcoming his aversion to talking about food, he timidly begged for it, as in this brief note to Isidoro: "If this is possible for you, I would be grateful if you could bring me something to eat, because there is hunger these days. If it's not possible, don't worry. Patience. We're starting to get used to it."[262]

Isidoro received this note from the consulate via Alvaro's little brother and little sister. The following day he replied, "We are very low on food we can bring you, because these days we don't even have fruit. We will send the packages from Daimiel they told us about when they arrive. . . . The ham that comes with this note was sent by

---

[259] AGP, RHF, EF–370707–1. Between the lines of this letter from the founder, there is also a note from Juan Jiménez Vargas for those in Valencia.

[260] AGP, RHF, EF–370526–1.

[261] AGP, RHF, EF–370505–1.

[262] AGP, RHF, EF–370629–1.

Pedro. Wine is given out a few droplets at a time." [263] "Don't worry about provisions," Father Josemaría responded. "We'll just tighten our belts another notch. By the way, I'm getting fat. Believe it." [264]

The wine he could get hold of was very little, and there were days when he could not celebrate Mass because it had turned to vinegar. This was worse than any hunger. "The grandfather would be happy if only he had wine," he writes his sons in Valencia. "I'm not a drunk, but since Don Manuel is fond of it, I would like to have it on hand. . . . Poor Grandfather, who has no wine for his bad stomach! Of the thousand privations, this is the one I find hardest." [265]

From time to time provisions were sent to those in Madrid from the Levant or from Daimiel. However, with the rigor of his fasting and penances, he still was reduced to skin and bones. He bore his weakness with cheerful good humor, describing his pitifully thin self as "this half pound of dried tuna that is your grandfather." [266] But Isidoro, who saw him frequently, reported, "He's gotten terribly thin. He laughs about it, but he's only a shadow of what he was." [267]

*   *   *

On July 24, 1937, twelve months after the anarchists took over the Ferraz Street residence (now uninhabitable, having been hit again by artillery shells on the third floor and roof), Isidoro sent the founder his reflections on that year: "Juan says, and with good reason, that we have to rectify, with deeds, the outrages committed in this past year. I would be the first to go along with that." [268] The founder agreed entirely, adding, "We've been too naïve this year." [269] Their combined efforts toward an evacuation convinced them that they were in the hands of God. That same day, the founder wrote to Lola Fisac: "The departure of Josemaría? Who knows! If Don Manuel, who has so much influence, doesn't arrange it with the consul of his country, it could be a long time coming. As I told you before, it's the good pipe story." [270]

---

[263] AGP, IZL, D–1213, 214.

[264] AGP, RHF, EF–370701–3.

[265] AGP, RHF, EF–370707–1.

[266] AGP, RHF, EF–370601–1.

[267] AGP, IZL, D–1213, 247. "Do you want to know how much I weigh? Well, it's 125 pounds" (AGP, RHF, EF–370905–1).

[268] AGP, IZL, D–1213, 230.

[269] AGP, RHF, EF–370725–6.

[270] AGP, RHF, EF–370725–2.

Isidoro felt the same way about this. He writes to Pedro Casciaro, "Sometimes the evacuation seems like something you could almost touch with your hands, and other times you can only see the possibility of it with a high-powered telescope. We are now in a telescope phase."[271] And, in fact, having been disillusioned by their many failed attempts to use diplomatic connections, Father Josemaría was ready just to leave the Honduran consulate, no matter what. Impatient to get on with his apostolate, he even set a date: "At the beginning of August, it will be time to leave, without hesitation."[272]

During those days negotiations were underway to get him an Argentinean passport. For this, an Argentinean birth certificate was required. Since Isidoro had just gotten two copies of his, they thought of using them, properly altered, for passport applications by the Father and Juan. On July 31 they went to have photos taken, and on the next day they asked Carmen to make armbands with the national colors of the Argentinean Republic, like the one that Isidoro wore.[273]

Also around that time, Tomás Alvira, a friend of José María Albareda, got a birth certificate from another Argentinean, with the idea of obtaining a passport and leaving Spain. He and Isidoro decided, however, that it would be better to use that birth certificate for getting the Father's passport. When they erased the personal information on it, it got so wrinkled that they had to go over it with a hot iron. Then, using a typewriter that had the same style of letters as the certificate, they substituted the Father's data and delivered the certificate to the consulate. They were to return in three or four days to pick up the passport.

But the erasing liquid they used had produced an embarrassing blotch on the paper. When Father Josemaría went there in person, the consul (or it may have been an embassy secretary) reproached him. He replied, "I am a lawyer and a priest. Given the circumstances, as a lawyer I defend this act and find it justified, and as a priest I give it my blessing."[274] He received apologies, but no passport.

The priest took this setback calmly, to judge by what he wrote Isidoro: "I am very resigned, even delighted. Believe me."[275] Two

[271] AGP, IZL, D–1213, 229.
[272] AGP, RHF, EF–370725–4.
[273] AGP, RHF, EF–370801–3.
[274] AGP, RHF, T–04373, p. 3. This must be seen in the context of the times, the extraordinary circumstances of a grave breakdown of the social order and its ordinary norms of conduct.
[275] AGP, RHF, EF–370804–2.

days later he wrote to those in Madrid, "Let everyone start pestering Don Manuel," and to those in Valencia, "Give Don Manuel a hard time, so that, if it's a good thing, an evacuation to our country can be arranged." [276]

Although the uncontrolled terrorism of the revolutionary militias had not disappeared, it had considerably declined.[277] Santiago now lived with his mother and sister and could move freely around Madrid, dressed in overalls and carrying two passes, one as an anarchist of the CNT and the other from an academy of the International Relief Organization. Isidoro, meanwhile, had received from the Argentinean embassy the work certificate needed to stay in Madrid.

Another matter of vital importance, that of food, was partly taken care of, thanks to the generosity of those in the Levant and in Daimiel. As Isidoro put it, "We almost have to eat by correspondence." [278] The packages sent by mail or by messenger contained a small amount of food for so many mouths, but they helped.

On August 20, along with a packet of food, Isidoro received a letter from Daimiel marked "For the Grandfather." It was a brief answer to his question of two weeks earlier: "Grandfather, my answer to both of your questions is yes. Truly and without the least doubt I prefer him to all others, and I consider myself very blessed to become part of your family. Your granddaughter does not forget you. —Lola." [279]

Father Josemaría wrote back:

> August 22, 1937
> My dear child:
>   Your last letter gave me great joy. More, of course, than the ham—although the ham (since you ask about it) is the most delicious one we've ever eaten in this part of the world. We're very grateful. Now (I'm telling you this in confidence) it's my

---

[276] AGP, RHF, EF–370806–2. In a letter dated August 12, Isidoro notified those in Daimiel that the plan for getting the grandfather out had failed. "However," he added, "since everyone in the family is very obstinate, we're going to continue pestering until Don Manuel gives in to our request" (AGP, IZL, D–1213, 244).

[277] To some extent the nation had been put back together, and there were greater assurances of safety, although the campaign against the "fifth column" was still going on full force. Political activity was intense and was in the hands of the communist elements. They had taken over most of the channels of political power. See Cervera Gil, pp. 104–105.

[278] AGP, IZL, D–1213, 171.

[279] AGP, RHF, D–15703.

turn to blush. It's not right to live off someone else, as I'm doing. But—Don Manuel pays very well.

Nevertheless, I don't want to impose on you. You've already done too much for your poor grandfather.

My warmest greetings to your family, and much love to you.

Mariano[280]

Still, the problem of how to get him out of Madrid remained unresolved. He planned to leave his refuge and go live with his mother in the Caracas Street apartment, protected by a medical certificate from Dr. Suils,[281] but complications arose. He would need to get a union card and a work certificate before the "house committee" controlling the comings and goings of residents would let him live there.[282] Juan's evacuation plan, on the other hand, was making good progress. But in the end, it too fell through. Said Isidoro: "Anyone would think Don Manuel doesn't want them to leave, but all the same we are continuing to make efforts in other directions." [283]

That same week, at the end of August, Chiqui showed up in Madrid. "And he was in luck, the big rascal," writes Father Josemaría, "because I brought him Don Manuel's marvelous breakfast." [284]

At long last, persistence paid off. Father Josemaría thought of another possible way to get documentation that would allow him to pass police and military inspections: Could the consul give him a work certificate as an employee of the consulate?[285]

[280] AGP, RHF, EF–370822–1.

[281] See AGP, RHF, EF–370822–1. Isidoro went to see Dr. Suils, and he made out the certificate as follows: "Madrid, August 22, 1937. I certify that José María Escribá Albás, 35 years of age, has been treated by me since the age of 29 for an endogenous psychosis, which affects him periodically. He is discharged as of today, having recovered from the latest outbreak (period) of this illness, which required him to be interned in this sanatorium for several months, given the difficulties of treating at home under the present circumstances. From today on, we are allowing him to go live with his sister. — The Director / Dr. A. Suils." The original is in AGP, RHF, D–15067.

[282] There were other problems as well. Don Alvaro González Valdés, in whose home Doña Dolores was living with her children, was full of doubts and fears. But on the other hand, if the Father presented himself before the committee as a sick person, they were likely to send him to some village far from Madrid, since he did not have a job or occupation. See AGP, IZL, D–1213, 253.

[283] AGP, IZL, D–1213, 256.

[284] AGP, RHF, EF–370825–1. By this "breakfast" he means, of course, holy Communion.

[285] AGP, RHF, EF–370828–1.

He had his doubts about whether he could talk Don Pedro into this, but in the end he did succeed. Don Pedro appointed him "Chief Supply Officer" and provided him with a document certifying that "José ESCRIBA ALBAS, 35 years of age, single, is in the service of this Ministry of Foreign Affairs as Chief Supply Officer."[286] On it is a photo of him, in dark suit and tie, and beneath that, the "Signature and fingerprint of the above-mentioned." (Without thinking, he signed himself "Josemaría Escrivá," and when he realized his mistake, corrected the "v" with an oversized "b.")

Now he wrote to those in Daimiel, ready to begin a new phase and not forgetting that, best of all, it would mean he could bring them Communion:

August 31, 1937
My dear granddaughter:

I'm writing to let you know that my brother Josemaría has been named Chief Supply Officer of the General Consulate of Honduras. That means, of course, that he is responsible for obtaining provisions for the consulate. And it occurs to him that if by any chance one can in your area buy, in quantity, kidney beans, chickpeas, lentils, olive oil, flour, etc., he—Josemaría—would be happy to travel to Daimiel (accompanied by Don Manuel) in an official consulate car. See, then, if there is any possibility of buying over there the items I listed, and if so, send me the prices and the quantity of each that is available for purchase. If the quantity is not substantial, the consul will never agree to authorize the trip.

What joy if Josemaría gets to see you!

Looking forward to your reply, I send you a hug.

Mariano[287]

---

[286] The document reads: "General Consulate of Honduras / Telephone 4507 / 51 Paseo de la Castellana / Madrid / The general consulate of the Republic of Honduras, Central America, with its official residence in this city, certifies that José ESCRIBA ALBAS, 35 years of age, single, is in the service of this Ministry of Foreign Affairs as CHIEF SUPPLY OFFICER, and we ask the CIVIL AUTHORITIES to provide him, in return, complete support and protection, and thus freedom of movement to carry out his duties. / Madrid, August 1, 1937 / Consul General / F. Matheu." See AGP, RHF, D–15070.

[287] AGP, RHF, EF–370831–1.

2

1. *Activities of a "Chief Supply Officer"*

Father Josemaría walked briskly down the street, quite at ease in the too-large suit the consul had given him. He wore a clean shirt and a nice tie, emblems of the fortunate few—usually foreign diplomats or civil authorities—who, possessing good documents, could walk the streets of Madrid with self-assurance. With a small flag on his lapel and his accreditation as an official of a Latin-American republic in his pocket, Father Josemaría could, for the first time in almost a year, move around in Madrid in relative safety. Add the pallor resulting from his having been indoors for months, and who would recognize this emaciated bureaucrat as the former rector of Santa Isabel?[1]

From the consulate he went directly to Isidoro's apartment, where he was reunited with Manolo, Rafael, and Chiqui. Rafael had come from Valencia on a two days' leave, just to see the Father; after talking with him, he returned to Valencia to join the International Brigades, to which he had been assigned. Chiqui was staying for a few days in Madrid, before rejoining the army of Andalusia.[2]

[1] See AGP, RHF, T–04152–III, pp. 154ff. Up till then he had been wearing Chiqui's blue overalls, the ones he had put on before leaving the Ferraz Street residence on July 20, 1936; see AGP, RHF, EF–370813–1.

Father Josemaría also carried with him some identity cards saying, "José Escriba Albas—Chief Supply Officer of the Consulate of Honduras — Madrid."

[2] The republican zone now had an army combining volunteers with regulars. The republican government, in which the Communist Party was gaining more and more power, proceeded to militarize the militias and create a People's Army, as it was called, under the supreme command of the Ministry of War. The communists managed to dominate the new military apparatus by controlling the General Commissariat of War, created to exercise sociopolitical control over the armed forces through political commissars—commissar delegates, as they were officially called. See Ramón Salas Larrazábal, *Historia del Ejército Popular de la República*, vols. 1 and 3 (Madrid, 1973). See also Michael Alpert, *El Ejército Republicano en la Guerra Civil* (Madrid, 1986), especially pp. 93ff. and 219ff.; Rafael Casas de la Vega, "Ejército Nacional y Ejército Popular de la República," in *La Guerra Civil Española (Sesenta años después)*, ed. Miguel Alonso Baquer

The new consular official's role demanded naturalness and daring. His first step was to move into a rented room that Eduardo Alastrué's father had found for him, on the fourth floor of a building on Ayala Street.[3] Accustomed to having in his room a picture of our Lady to glance at affectionately from time to time, he went to a store at Angel Plaza, thinking he might find one there even though the shop window displayed only frames and mirrors. His request for an image of our Lady—something prohibited and dangerous to have—caused a small stir at the back of the shop. To convince the shop owner that he was not an undercover police officer, he showed his documentation as foreign consular official. Then, nervously, they produced a lithograph of Our Lady of Sorrows.[4]

The next day, on the recommendation of a friend of José María González Barredo, he went to the Panamanian consulate and obtained an identity card in the name of "Ricardo Escriba." This was for Juan Jiménez Vargas, who two days later came to live with the Father in the Ayala Street apartment. The plan was that they would pass themselves off as brothers.[5] But all that Juan did by way of disguise was to use an old prescription to get glasses with black frames; Isidoro picked them up. And despite the Father's efforts to get him to speak with him as an equal, Juan had too much respect for him to be able to use toward him the word for "you" that brothers would use. So the plan was not a success, even though physically they were not that dissimilar.

During early September, Father Josemaría visited his family and members of the Work every day, and usually ate with Doña Dolores. On September 4, though, all the members of the Work who could circulate freely in Madrid went to Heidelberg, a restaurant where they had eaten on a special occasion in 1934. Little had changed in its

---

(Madrid, 1999), pp. 183–231; and Burnet Bolloten, *La Guerra Civil española: Revolución y contrarrevolución* (Madrid, 1989), pp. 247–59 and 439–43.

[3] The room looked out on the street. It had no bed, only mattresses on the floor. As one can tell from the receipt for September, it was a bedroom: "I have received from Don José Escribá the amount of seventy pesetas, the rent for the month corresponding to this date, for the bedroom of my apartment at 67 Ayala Street, fourth floor, left side. Madrid, September 13, 1937. Juan Zafra. Total: 70 pesetas." See AGP, RHF, D–05201.

[4] It was a small reproduction of "L'Addolorata," by G. B. Salvi, a seventeenth-century painter also known as Sassoferrato. When Father Josemaría left Madrid, he left the picture behind, letting Santiago keep it.

[5] See AGP, RHF, T–04152–III, pp. 118 and 121–23. The document for Juan certified that "Don Ricardo Escribá is the Purchasing Agent in the Supply Department of this Consulate."

appearance, but the waiters were different, the menu was much more limited, and the prices were much higher.[6]

*   *   *

The Spanish bishops' collective letter on the religious persecution, dated July 1, 1937, and published in August, had important repercussions on international public opinion.[7] In the republican zone the charges made in the letter were hushed up as much as possible, but the letter did have the effect of reducing the persecution that had been raging since the outbreak of the civil war.[8] In the Negrín government, formed in May 1937, a Catholic Basque Nationalist, Manuel Irujo, was named Minister of Justice. Irujo tried to convince the republican government of the grave danger it was putting itself in by that fierce opposition to the Church. He even presented a legislative proposal to restore worship and assure religious freedom.[9] His colleagues in the

---

[6] See AGP, RHF, EF–370905–1. In his correspondence from all those months of his stay at the Honduran consulate, and in Isidoro's as well, one can see the detail, orderliness, and punctuality with which they did their accounting for the Work. In one letter, for example, he says to Isidoro: "Today you sent one peseta less, 55." (See AGP, RHF, EF–370725–5.) The purpose of such exactness was to live poverty well. They had to deal with hunger and prepare for the expenses of trying to get out of the country, which would undoubtedly be high. For doing all this, the founder sketched out a practical rule: "Let us adjust our expenses to the precarious situation. In war, as in war." (See AGP, RHF, EF–370704–1.)

But he was not stingy. A few days later he wrote, "Spend what you need to for your personal needs, without scruples" (AGP, RHF, EF–370710–1).

Finally, this orderly accounting made it possible to keep expenses of the Work separate from those of the Escrivá family. He writes to Isidoro, "Please do me up a balance sheet of our financial situation, going into as much detail as possible. It is, of course, understood that all the expenses for Santiago should be taken care of by my mother, not one penny being charged to the Work. Also send me a note listing in detail the monthly expenses we will keep having to meet as long as the present circumstances hold. Show this to Aunt Carmen too." (See AGP, RHF, EF–370630–1.)

[7] As was the case with almost everything that happened during the civil war, this letter provoked a lot of controversy. See Gonzalo Redondo, *Historia de la Iglesia en España, 1931–1939*, vol. 2, *La Guerra Civil, 1936–1939* (Madrid, 1993), pp. 343–53.

[8] See Vicente Cárcel Ortí, *La Gran Persecución: España, 1931–1939* (Madrid, 2000), pp. 126–46.

[9] The revolution of July 1936 had driven the Church back to the catacombs. The only exception in the republican zone was the Basque Provinces, where the practice of religion continued under the shelter of that region's autonomy and the fact that the vast majority of the population was Catholic. In the churches there, public worship was never interrupted. See Fernando de Meer Lecha-Marzo, *El Partido Nacionalista Vasco ante la guerra de España: 1936–1937* (Pamplona, 1992).

On January 9, 1937, Irujo presented to the Council of Ministers of the Republic a memorandum (dated January 7) showing how much harm the religious persecution had already caused the Republic. Its opening sentences sum up the outrages and the responsibility of the republican rulers: "Opinion in the civilized world looks with

government did not support him, but they did take advantage of his efforts by publicizing his proposals internationally for purely political purposes.

Hostility toward Catholics continued, in a more underhanded but still dangerous fashion, and the Church continued to have to operate undercover.[10] Assassinations and imprisonment of priests and religious had practically ceased, the initial campaign to hunt them down having attained its objective. Catholic worship was clandestine; even the possession of religious books or images was taken as a sign of hostility to the regime. Many churchmen had been martyred in the violent phase, and those still alive were in prison or in hiding, some in large cities where they heroically exercised their ministry, at risk of being apprehended and killed. Father Josemaría became one of them.[11]

---

dismayed astonishment, not to say revulsion, at the conduct of the government of the Republic in failing to prevent these acts of violence and in consenting to their continuance. The revolutionary outburst might have been considered blind, overwhelming, and uncontrollable at first. But the systematic destruction of churches, altars, and objects used for worship can no longer be considered a spontaneous eruption." See Vicente Cárcel Ortí, *La persecución religiosa en España durante la Segunda República, 1931–1939* (Madrid, 1990), pp. 286–87.

The government of Largo Caballero rejected Irujo's proposal for religious freedom. On July 31, 1937, Irujo submitted to the Council of Ministers a similar proposal, which also failed.

The one thing he was able to accomplish along these lines came a year later. On April 30, 1938, Negrín made public a policy statement which included an allusion to the government's desire to respect freedom of conscience and assure religious freedom. Unfortunately, however, this declaration of intent had little effect in practice. Irujo, for other reasons, resigned in August of that year. See Bolloten, pp. 784–85, 918, and 951–52; Manuel de Irujo, *Memorias*, vols. 1 and 2: *Un vasco en el Ministerio de Justicia* (Buenos Aires, 1976 and 1978); and A. de Lizarra [Andrés María de Irujo], *Los vascos y la República Española: Contribución a la Historia de la Guerra Civil, 1936–1939* (Buenos Aires, 1944), pp. 155–59 and 172–97.

[10] An attempt was made to restore Catholic worship in a few places, such as Catalonia, where the communists had less power, but the effort never amounted to much. See Josep Maria Solé i Sabaté, "Las represiones," in *La Guerra Civil: Una nueva visión del conflicto que dividió España*, ed. Stanley G. Payne and Javier Tusell (Madrid, 1996), p. 595.

[11] Cervera has found that while priests were the most numerous group among those killed without trial (18 percent), clerics charged before the People's Courts in Madrid during the war made up only 1 percent of the total tried (between twelve and thirteen thousand). "Of the priests tried by the People's Courts," he says, "something over 25 percent were considered enemies of the regime," and the rest were acquitted. He also notes that "religious practices . . . were considered a sign of hostility to the Republic," and that simply having religious books could lead to arrest. See Javier Cervera Gil, *Madrid en guerra: La ciudad clandestina, 1936–1939* (Madrid, 1998), pp. 76, 155, 191, and 179–80. For more on the clandestine exercise of priestly ministry, see José Luis Alfaya Camacho, *Como un río de fuego: Madrid, 1936* (Barcelona, 1998), pp. 119–93. The risks and dangers entailed by religious practices are reflected in the fright of the people who sold that picture of the Blessed Virgin to Father Josemaría; Tomás Alvira recalls that he saw

The first thing he did now was to seek news of his children. Vicente Rodríguez Casado was a refugee in the Norwegian consulate on Abascal Street. When the Father unexpectedly showed up there, Vicente did not recognize him until he heard him laugh. From then on they saw each other almost every day, meeting in the entryway and going to the garage to chat, comfortably seated in one of the cars. During that time the Father would give a meditation to his companion.[12]

He also visited the family of Ricardo Fernández Vallespín, who told him they had received a letter from Ricardo, re-mailed from France, telling them he was well. He then went immediately to see José María Albareda, in the boardinghouse on Menéndez y Pelayo Street. This good friend had done a lot for the Work since the beginning of the civil war, and the Father in a very special way prayed for his vocation during those days. When Tomás Alvira, a friend of Albareda, showed up there, the priest spoke at length with both of them.[13]

He then visited two families who had offered him shelter in more perilous times, the Leyvas and the Herrero Fontanas, in order to let them and their friends know where he was living and to offer them his services as a priest.[14] Father Josemaría tried not to let even one day go by without his saying Mass and afterward going from house to house to bring Communion. The hosts were wrapped in some small corporals made by his sister and were put in a metal cigarette case decorated with a Honduran flag, also sewn by Carmen. Some nights he would fall asleep during prayer and remain that way all night, fully dressed and with the consecrated hosts on his breast.[15]

One person he visited often was Don Ramón del Portillo, Alvaro's father, who was gravely ill. The family was dispersed; some members were in the nationalist zone. Alvaro's mother, Mexican by birth, had moved to an apartment owned by the Mexican embassy in Madrid. A woman with great strength of character, she was awaiting her hus-

---

someone arrested "because a medal of our Lady was found on him" (see AGP, RHF, T–04373, p. 2). This was still the situation in the summer and autumn of 1937.

[12] See AGP, RHF, T–04152–III, p. 126.

[13] See Antonio Vázquez Galiano, *Tomás Alvira—Una pasión por la familia—Un maestro de la Educación* (Madrid, 1997), p. 80.

[14] See AGP, RHF, T–04373, p. 1, and T–04152–III, p. 125.

[15] See *Beato Josemaría Escrivá de Balaguer: un hombre de Dios. Testimonios sobre el Fundador del Opus Dei* (Madrid, 1994), p. 421. (Hereafter this book will be cited as *Testimonios*.) See also AGP, RHF, T–04152–III, p. 128; Santiago Escrivá de Balaguer y Albás, *Sum.* 7344; and Alvaro del Portillo, *Sum.* 889.

band's death with two little children, Teresa and Carlos—the ones who had picked up Father Josemaría's letters for Isidoro from the consulate. Not all of the neighbors could be trusted, so as soon as Father Josemaría arrived, the children would shout, "The doctor is here! The doctor is here!" Neither they nor Alvaro knew how seriously ill their father was; and with no documentation, Alvaro could not risk leaving the consulate.[16]

One day José María Albareda informed the Father that the wife of an acquaintance of his, Domingo Díaz-Ambrona, who was then (with his family) in refuge at the Cuban consulate, had had a baby girl in Riesgo Hospital, which was under the protection of the British embassy. A priest was needed to baptize the child. Albareda told them Father Josemaría was willing, and they settled on a certain day at seven in the evening. One would think it would not have been necessary to warn them to be careful, but Father Josemaría learned that Señor Díaz Ambrona, in his excitement, had invited other people besides the godparents. Therefore he arrived two hours early, and after baptizing the little girl he quickly took his leave, even though the parents wanted him to stay for a family celebration. Since they were scheduled to be evacuated soon, he told them, they would have the opportunity to supplement the ceremony in a parish church.[17]

On September 8, José María Albareda asked to be admitted to Opus Dei.[18] Father Josemaría decided to give for him and his friends, and for Tomás Alvira and other acquaintances he had managed to locate in Madrid, a retreat like the ones he had given at the Ferraz Street residence, although now they had no oratory, no terrace to take a walk on during free time, and no certainty that they would not fall into a police trap and all end up in prison.

In a letter dated September 10, he tells those in Valencia about the events of that first week outside the consulate:

---

[16] See Alvaro del Portillo, *Sum.* 901.

[17] On January 9, 1992, Díaz Ambrona wrote a letter to Bishop Alvaro del Portillo which can be found on page 23 of del Portillo's *Immersed in God* (Princeton: Scepter, 1995).

[18] See AGP, RHF, T–04152–III, p. 121 (testimony of Juan Jiménez Vargas, who used to eat at Albareda's rooming house), and Enrique Gutiérrez Ríos, *José María Albareda— Una época de la cultura española* (Madrid, 1970), p. 109. For some time the founder had been praying intensely every day for Albareda. "Tell José María Albareda that I remember him very especially every day," he wrote to Isidoro Zorzano (AGP, RHF, EF–370701–3).

I take up my pen today with very little enthusiasm. Not because of any lack of desire to, but because of the thousand little things weighing on me. If I'm not careful, they put me in a wretched mood.

Alvaro, poor fellow, is going through some really hard times, because his father, who stayed behind in Madrid with his wife (Alvaro's mother) and their two little ones (nine and eleven years old) when the rest of the family left Spain—his father, I was saying, is very gravely ill, with tuberculosis. You can imagine the conflict. Alvaro's mother is very spirited, but it is not possible for the poor lady to do without the company of her son in these circumstances. We will see how this works out.

Ricardo and Josemaría live in a small room they have rented—very cheaply—in the Salamanca district. Josemaría has lunch with the grandmother, and Ricardo with my son José María Albareda. Breakfast? Good! Dinner? Well, is there really dinner?

I'm sending you an authentic sketch of my brother, as he is now. They say it looks just like him.

These days, that lunatic has gotten it into his head to give some conferences, like the ones he used to give in his house along with little strolls on the rooftop. He claims he will have seven or maybe even nine professors listening to him. Well, that's his business. As for me, I wish him luck.

I get out fairly often and occupy myself with things that I like. Being old-fashioned, I hold on to my time-honored traditions—water, wine, and bread—everywhere I can. Also—prerogatives of an old man—I hear confidences and give advice, prudent advice because of all these years of experience, to all my little ones, and even to some who are no longer children. My legs? For now, no rheumatism. But I don't know how much they can endure.

On the 8th, José María Albareda came to see me, to ask permission to become part of our family. Since he's a well-mannered suitor and a serious person with a bright future ahead of him, I consented. Ask Doña María to take an interest in these love affairs, all right?

Many thanks for your frequent gifts, which take care of our

midday gastronomical problems. But the grandfather doesn't want you to make financial sacrifices. You have certainly done more than you can afford to. And I don't like it. I don't want you to, in any way, deprive yourselves of anything for us. Is that clear?

Rafa! Any news of him? How joyfully I embraced him, and how it hurt me when he departed! Tell me something.

I'm not hearing anything from Lola. I would like to come see everyone, accompanied by Don Manuel. I hope it can be arranged.

I am worried about Alvaro.

Write me often. Your grandfather sends the three of you (and the others yet to be born?) much love.

Mariano

P.S. My brother asks you to keep in mind his conferences.[19]

2. *"They had seen Josemaría dead"*

There had been more than a year of fighting since Doña Dolores made her prediction that the war would end by July 25, the feast of Saint James, Spain's patron saint. During the summer of 1937 nationalist troops gradually took over the coastal regions of northern Spain. Once Santander fell, they dislodged the republican forces from the province of Asturias, and now had control of the entire northern coast of the peninsula. The Negrín government thus lost its superiority in military strength, and with the opposing forces now roughly equal, the war promised to be a long one, even though optimists continued to predict that it would end soon.

The founder reflected on the events of recent months. The hunger in Madrid was getting worse every day. How his sons in prison must be suffering! For a few months Alvaro and Chiqui had been in the San Antón prison, and at times the militiamen had given them human excrement to eat.[20] Now, at the beginning of September 1937, Chiqui

---

[19] AGP, RHF, EF–370910–1.

[20] See AGP, RHF, EF–370406–1. Alvaro had been in refuge in a branch office of the Finnish embassy. He landed in the San Antón prison when that office was invaded by the militia. He tells an interesting anecdote about his time in San Antón. One day a guard named Petrov put a pistol to his temple and said he was going to kill him since he was obviously a priest. (Alvaro was wearing glasses, which for the militiaman must

was back in Madrid, tanned and looking great, enjoying a few days of military leave. Isidoro writes jokingly, "Chiqui is wonderful. He's even putting on weight, because he hogs everything. He eats at the camp and then goes home and does the same all over again. He doesn't want anyone to benefit from his having eaten at the camp." [21]

The Father found all of his sons who were in the republican zone. He even had good news from Ricardo, who had made it into the nationalist zone. No one knew until years later that he had crossed over just a few days before an order for his arrest as a "Fascist" arrived from Madrid.[22]

It was rare to find a family without a loved one on the list of the fallen in battle, missing, or murdered. This was also the case among the members of the Work. Pepe Isasa had fallen in battle. Manolo had lost two brothers, one in battle and the other murdered. José María Albareda's father and a brother of his had been murdered when the war broke out.[23]

Among all the discomforts he had suffered during his confinement in the Honduran consulate, what Father Josemaría had found especially trying was having to live with filth. Although there was never a lack of water and soap and other products with which to free oneself, as he said, quoting Saint Teresa, from the "bad populace"—bedbugs, fleas, and lice—the lice had put up a stiff resistance in that tiny room in the consulate. (Which is certainly understandable, considering that this room had been a storing place for coal, and that the real intruders were the refugees.) And there had been plenty of other crawling creatures besides.

The room that Father Josemaría shared with Juan in the apartment on Ayala Street was incomparably better. Now there were only two mattresses on the floor, and it was a lot easier to get access to the bathroom. And although the late-summer mornings were becoming chilly, the priest never omitted the mortification of a cold bath. Whether this was a good idea in view of his physical condition is another question. Worn out by hunger and low spirits, he was at the point of exhaustion. He also was showing signs of rheumatism and

---

have been a sure sign that he was an ecclesiastical intellectual.) See Alvaro del Portillo, *Sum.* 884. Petrov, or Petrof, was the nickname of Santiago del Amo; see Cervera Gil, p. 80.
[21] AGP, IZL, D–1213, 265.
[22] See AGP, RHF, T–00162, p. 37.
[23] See AGP, IZL, D–1213, 254, and AGP, RHF, EF–370725–5.

possibly the first symptoms of diabetes, such as having to urinate frequently. He also seems to have suffered some bouts of fever. In a letter written in the summer of 1937 we read: "Madrid is excessively hot, and one feels the heat more than ever. And—a paradox—at times I'm so cold that I have to stay wrapped up in a blanket until I recover. Stomach problems, no doubt." [24]

For meals, Father Josemaría went to his mother's place, and often he would take her for a walk in the afternoon. And so Doña Dolores grew accustomed to her son's emaciated face. Suffering and privation had left their mark on everyone in Madrid, including her—her hair was turning gray. But her son saw in her face a serenity in affliction that reminded him of the picture of Our Lady of Sorrows that he had bought in Angel Plaza.

Now the two of them could speak at length about all they had experienced in the year since—on July 20, 1936—Father Josemaría had showed up at his mother's apartment dressed in overalls. Right after that there had begun the attacks on churches and monasteries and the hunting down of priests. And one day, Santiago tells us, a communist woman who worked for one of their neighbors "informed the authorities that there was a priest hiding out in our apartment, and that they should kill him." [25]

When news came a few days later that the house was about to be searched, Father Josemaría fled. The militia arrested several members of a family on the floor below, but, for some reason, did not search the Escrivás' apartment, even though everyone in the neighborhood knew that a priest lived there.[26]

A few days after the flight of Father Josemaría, the Escrivás witnessed a frightening event: "a murder in the street, in the early hours of the night," reports Juan Jiménez Vargas. "They heard a big commotion, and, thinking it was one of the patrols that were searching the houses, they looked down from the balcony, staying hidden, of course, peeking between the closed blinds. . . . Some militiamen were chasing a man, and he couldn't escape; they killed him right there and left the body in the street." [27]

Street murders were not uncommon. A couple of months later, in

[24] AGP, RHF, EF–370725–3. See also AGP, RHF, T–04152–III, p. 119, and Alvaro del Portillo, *Sum.* 889 and 890.

[25] Santiago Escrivá de Balaguer y Albás, *Sum.* 7326. See also AGP, RHF, T–07921, p. 19.

[26] AGP, RHF, T–04152–III, p. 139.

[27] Ibid.

October 1936, Santiago tells us, two sisters of Father Norberto, the priest at the Foundation for the Sick, came to the apartment "to ask us for money which, they claimed, was owed to their brother. Since this was not true, the conversation became pretty heated, to the point where they said to my mother—I don't know where they got this from—that they had seen Josemaría dead, hanging from a tree. Unable to restrain myself, I then told them what I thought of them and threw them out." [28]

But there was a body. Other neighbors had seen it and heard the militia boasting of having killed a priest. At the time that the murder took place, Father Josemaría was in refuge in Manolo's apartment, on Sagasta Street, and it was not uncommon for several days to pass before they heard anything from him. Quite possibly Doña Dolores had heard from a neighbor that her son had suffered a violent death, and mother and daughter had suffered a few days of anguish but had not said anything to Santiago. He, meanwhile, naturally thought that the story told by Father Norberto's sisters was a total fabrication, since in October his brother was in refuge, safe and sound, in the clinic of Dr. Suils.

The last person to hear that he had been murdered was the supposed victim himself. On September 18, 1937, he wrote to his sons in Valencia: "A bit of old news: A number of people have told me—right to my face—that they saw my brother Josemaría hanging from a tree. Some say it was on Moncloa; others, on Ferraz. One person even claimed to have identified the corpse. Another version of his death: they shot him." [29]

The one hundred seventy letters written from the consulate contain no mention of this "old news." Presumably, the reason is that it was not until now that he was able to have a good, long conversation with his mother. It was, no doubt, Doña Dolores who filled him in on the different stories going around about his supposed death. The letter continues: "You can imagine the look on the grandfather's face when he received this news. Actually, for a madman like my brother, such a death would be something to envy, especially with the addition of a common grave. What more could the poor fellow have wished for, when he was lying at death's door in a luxurious room of an expensive sanatorium! But what am I saying? This kind of death (normal, without noise or show)—a death like that of a bourgeois pig—best

[28] AGP, RHF, T–07921, p. 20.
[29] AGP, RHF, EF–370918–1.

suits his life, his work, and his path. To die thus—oh, Don Manuel!—but mad, with the madness of Love."

Later he would put it this way: "You talk of dying 'heroically.' Don't you think that it is more heroic to die unnoticed, in a good bed, like a bourgeois . . . but to die of Love?" [30]

Elsewhere in that same letter, trying to raise the spirits of someone who had not yet recovered from the pain of his father's death, he wrote: "Cheer up, man! I myself have no intention of dying. I'll be marching on, just marching on." [31]

In a letter written in 1943 there is another reference to that incident:

> Neither before nor after 1936 have I taken part either directly or indirectly in politics. If I have had to hide out, pursued like a criminal, it has only been for professing my faith, even if our Lord did not consider me worthy of the palm of martyrdom. On one of those occasions, in front of the house we were living in, they hanged a man they had mistaken for me.[32]

He never found out who that man was, but he never forgot him. "I know for a fact," says Bishop Javier Echevarría, his second successor as head of the Work, "that he prayed for that man throughout the rest of his life, while also begging our Lord's forgiveness for those who committed the murder." [33]

3. *"Don Manuel knows best"*

After a year spent in one refuge after another, Father Josemaría now felt the joy of being able to minister to many souls. But his idea of taking a consulate car to Daimiel, accompanied by "Don Manuel," in order to visit Miguel Fisac and his sister Lola, did not work out. Perhaps it was impossible to get permits. In any case, on September 19 he wrote: "Dearest Lola: Patience. Don Manuel knows best. What a pity that the trip fell through!" [34]

However, his plan to give a retreat for young men who were students or teachers did bear fruit. The first talk was given on September

---

[30] *The Way*, no. 743.
[31] AGP, RHF, EF–370918–1.
[32] *Letter May 31, 1943*, no. 45.
[33] Javier Echevarría, *Sum.* 2418. See also Alvaro del Portillo, *Sum.* 877.
[34] AGP, RHF, EF–370919–1.

20 or 21, in the morning. Attending were Isidoro Zorzano, José María Albareda, Juan Jiménez Vargas, Manolo Sainz de los Terreros, Tomás Alvira, and another friend, Angel Hoyos. A group of young men meeting together would naturally have drawn attention, so the Father gave the meditations at different times and places during the three days of the retreat. Sometimes they met at Isidoro's place, sometimes at Doña Dolores's apartment, and sometimes at Alvira's and Albareda's boardinghouses, whose proprietors were trustworthy. After giving the half-hour morning meditation, points for examination of conscience, and a few suggestions, Father Josemaría would leave. Then the retreatants, separately, would stroll on the street or in Retiro Park, continuing their reflections and saying the Rosary. In the afternoon, at the time and place earlier decided on, they would meet for another meditation.

On the last day of the retreat, the Father celebrated Mass in Tomás Alvira's boardinghouse, in secular clothes and without any vestments.[35] The landlady, Doña Matilde Velasco, had carefully prepared a table for the Mass, but she did not attend, her job being to watch from the hallway those going up or down the stairs, in order to head off interruptions.[36] Even so, the landlady was impressed by the priest's conversation and manners during breakfast. What really stuck in her memory was that he caressed an orange, and then, mortifying his hunger, left it there, eloquently forgotten on the table. After breakfast, Doña Matilde reverently reclaimed it. "That orange," Juan Jiménez Vargas tells us, "is still kept by that family, forty years later." [37]

In his last months of confinement in the consulate, the Father had stayed in contact with his daughters through Isidoro. On several occasions Isidoro had passed on to Hermógenes García the Father's instructions that the women pray for him and the Work, but not try to see him. But now that he had a certain freedom of movement, he thought of repeating for them the spiritual exercises he had just given the men.[38]

He learned that one of the young women in the Work, Antonia

---

[35] See Vázquez Galiano, p. 85.

[36] See AGP, RHF, T–04373, p. 2, and Joaquín Alonso Pacheco, *Sum.* 4636.

[37] AGP, RHF, T–04152–III, p. 128.

[38] He optimistically expected to give the meditation to sixteen or eighteen ladies; see AGP, RHF, EF–370924–1. At his request, Isidoro had contacted Hermógenes to try to find out what had happened to some documents that Father Lino Vea-Murguía had been unable to deposit in a bank. When Father Lino was assassinated, on August 16, 1936, they had lost track of those papers. See AGP, RHF, EF–370828–1, and AGP, IZL, D–1213, 251.

Sierra, was in Castellón, near Valencia. She had been sick with tuberculosis since 1933. As had earlier been the case with María Ignacia García Escobar, Father Josemaría regarded the dying woman as a treasure, an expiatory soul. He wrote to those in Valencia:

> Here is the address of a granddaughter of mine who is sick and poor and extremely good, a treasure that the madman they killed has been exploiting for years: Antonia Sierra / Sanatorio Hospital / Villafranca del Cid / Castellón. For I don't know how long, she's been in one hospital after another. If you could go see her, I would be most grateful. At least try to get into her hands the fifteen pesetas that Isidoro is sending to you, and, if possible, something that a person in the advanced stages of tuberculosis can eat. How happy it would make me if you could give her the consolation of a visit! [39]

It was a rare day that he did not celebrate Mass for a group, and give them a homily. Often, these groups were communities of nuns. In contrast to the six thousand priests killed during the persecution, the number of nuns martyred was less than three hundred.[40] Jailing them would have been a problem, given that every prison in the country was full to overflowing, so it was not uncommon for communities to take refuge in apartments or boardinghouses, with the knowledge of the neighbors and the police. On one occasion, Father Josemaría was about to enter the house of his friend Don Alejandro Guzmán when a woman approached him with the warning that militiamen were searching the building.[41] A community of Reparation nuns had taken up residence there, and two or three of them, including a sister of Don Alejandro's, lived in the apartment next door.[42] Father Josemaría must

---

[39] AGP, RHF, EF–370918–1.

[40] See Ortí, *La persecución religiosa*, pp. 238–39.

[41] See AGP, RHF, T–05399, p. 36. This woman was María Teresa Villanueva Labayen. The daughter of a minister during the monarchy, Miguel Villanueva, she had met the founder at the Foundation for the Sick. In 1931 she joined the order Jerónimas de la Adoración, and moved to Gijón. She returned to Madrid as a result of the revolution that took place in October 1934. During the civil war she remained in the capital, helping Catholics at the risk of her life. She died in 1942. Her identity is known because the Father told this story to her nephew, a diplomat who lived in Rome in the fifties.

[42] See Alvaro del Portillo, *Sum.* 889. On the religious activities in the apartment at 12 Hermosilla Street, known as "the Cathedral of Hermosilla," see Antonio Montero Moreno, *Historia de la Persecución Religiosa en España* (Madrid, 1961), p. 104; Alfaya Camacho, pp. 139–43; and Cervera Gil, pp. 191 and 371.

have attended to their spiritual needs more than once, because a year later—in Avila, in the nationalist zone—he ran into two of them, and one of them cried out in surprise, "It's the diplomat!" Father Josemaría did, in fact, look quite the diplomat with the little flag in his lapel, his well-tied tie, and a large briefcase with the Honduran coat of arms. The briefcase contained a piece of dry bread, in case he did not make it home in time to eat.[43]

Having witnessed the savagery of militia terrorism, some of these congregations of nuns were still living in a state of nervous tension. A community of Third Order Capuchin nuns that in 1936 had run Villa Luz Hospital on General Oraá Street had taken refuge at the beginning of the war in a boardinghouse, thanks to the generosity of a benefactor. A year later they were still there, living a somewhat relaxed convent life. "We were afraid, very afraid," confesses Sister Ascensión Quiroga. "And to hide the fact that we were nuns, we wore regular clothes and used makeup so that no one would report us. I myself went a bit overboard, not just concealing my state in life, but enjoying showing off and fixing myself up."[44]

When they heard about Father Josemaría, they wrote to him, and soon he came to the boardinghouse to give them a spiritual talk. In it he said to them, "We are cowards, we are afraid to stand up for God." "I was impressed," says Sister Ascensión, "by his way of addressing us. It wasn't preaching, but rather the personal prayer of a saint, spoken aloud. It renewed our desire to give ourselves totally to Jesus Christ, as on the day of our religious profession." From that day on they no longer tried to disguise themselves by using makeup.[45]

Not much else is known about Father Josemaría's priestly work at this time. Occasionally, when going to take care of a group of refugee nuns, he was accompanied by Juan to the vicinity of their house.[46] Other people came to see him in the room on Ayala Street. Sometimes, too, in his incessant traveling around the city, our Lord brought him in contact with souls that needed help. This was the case with a "straying nun" whose secret thoughts and intentions he seemed to penetrate by divine grace, thereby moving her to ask him to hear her confession.[47]

---

[43] See AGP, RHF, EF–380813–1.

[44] AGP, RHF, T–04388, p. 1.

[45] Ibid., p. 2. See also Joaquín Alonso Pacheco, *Sum.* 4638.

[46] See AGP, RHF, T–04152–III, p. 125.

[47] A journal entry dated January 11, 1938, reads: "Your light, Jesus, has made me see very clearly that it was not an intuition of mine, but rather an inspiration of yours, that

*   *   *

In the letters he had written while in confinement in the consulate, Father Josemaría was always having to pour oil on troubled waters. One day recommending patience, another day urging action on some matter, in one way or another he was always lifting the spirits of his children. In a letter to Isidoro he says, "Peace of soul, all right? With the help of Don Manuel, never to lose self-control—that is the spirit of our family. Thus we will always have joy and peace. Everything in this world, except for death, can be fixed. And sometimes a thing that has been fixed is better than it was before it needed fixing." [48]

There was only one solution: to pester Don Manuel, insistently begging for his help. The Father wrote to his sons in Valencia:

> Since you're planning to visit my old and dear friend Don Manuel, I ask you to remind him of three matters that I have already brought to his attention: (1) the evacuation of my poor mad brother, Josemaría, to our country; (2) the success of the claim submitted, through the embassy, to the government of the Spanish Republic; and (3) that he use his influence with the grandmother to encourage her, if this is appropriate, to be willing to make a certain sacrifice for the good of the whole family.[49]

Apart from the request about Doña Dolores, who was always ready to make a sacrifice, all of that came to nothing. But even so, on July 25, 1937, the Father wrote to his sons in Valencia:

> Today, the feast of Saint James, it's exactly a year since I had to evacuate my house. Nevertheless, I am happy. Manolo knows very well what he is doing, and I am quite hopeful that our family's affairs will be set right *sooner, more, and better* than we could have dreamed. Of course, with us using the means.[50]

---

spoke during the revolution to that straying nun, that moved her to make her confession to me, and to confess and repent of what I—sinner that I am—appeared to divine in her heart" (*Apuntes*, no. 1482).

[48] AGP, RHF, EF–370805–2.

[49] AGP, RHF, EF–370505–4.

[50] AGP, RHF, EF–370725–3.

They did use the means, and they were at peace, but their efforts kept going nowhere. After the failure of his plan to go to his mother's under the cover of a certificate from Dr. Suils, he wrote from the consulate on August 25:

> All his plans for returning to his former professional life fall apart, despite his certificate of discharge from Dr. Suils? Well, so what? Being from Aragón, he goes right on sticking to his guns and leaving no stone unturned. . . . Have confidence. Thanks to Don Manuel, we can never—never!—doubt the speedy success of our family's business. Certainly there will be difficulties, but people grow when faced with obstacles. Come on! G. and daring! Right? So at every moment, live in the assurance of success.[51]

"Don Manuel knows best, as my brother the madman always says."[52] In all of his consulate correspondence, in fact, "Don Manuel knows best" appears to be the founder's favorite expression. No matter how many plans and projects fell through, the priest calmly stuck to his guns, saying, "Don Manuel knows best. Come what may, it's all for the good."[53] Well he knew that everything comes from the hands of God our Father.

He saw everything with the eyes of faith. But he also had his weak spot: a compassionate heart that made him deeply respectful of others' freedom and rights. He writes to his sons in Madrid:

> I'm not going to tell you anything. It's my custom to keep quiet and almost always just say, "Good," or "Very good." No one can truthfully say at the end of the day that he did this or that thing by order, or even by an implied order, of the grandfather. When I think I have to say something, I limit myself to setting out clearly the facts of the problem at hand. In no way, even if I very clearly see one, do I or will I give a specific solution to it. I have a different way, a gentler and more effective way, of influencing the wills of my children

---

[51] AGP, RHF, EF–370825–1. (Because of the censorship, even "God" could not safely be spelled out.)
[52] AGP, RHF, EF–370822–2.
[53] AGP, RHF, EF–370825–2.

and grandchildren: I give myself a hard time and pester my old Friend Don Manuel. May I never stray from this path, of always letting my children act with complete freedom . . . until the time comes to tighten the rope! That time will come. But, of course—I think you know this about me—despite my human frailty, I could never use anyone's life, not even a minute of it, for my own comfort or consolation. So much is this true that I will keep my mouth shut (though later I will speak with Don Manuel about it) even when what my children have in mind looks to me like a real disaster.[54]

Certain that the Work had to go forward even in those very difficult times, the founder had begun to think about crossing over to the nationalist zone to rejoin the members of the Work there and carry on his apostolic efforts unhindered. Not wanting to impose his will, he consulted his sons, and they insisted that he should do it. The decision, obviously, was his, but only after a lot of prayer and vacillation was he able to make it. Bishop Alvaro del Portillo explains:

The idea of leaving a number of his sons and daughters behind in the Red zone, in a dangerous situation, hurt him. Plus, his mother and and brother and sister would also be staying in Madrid. The founder of Opus Dei was in doubt for quite some time. Sometimes he saw clearly that he should escape; other times, it looked to him that his duty was to stay and, if necessary, face martyrdom. Finally, after a lot of prayer, he made the decision to escape.[55]

But that was not so easy to do. He could move freely within Madrid, but finding a way to leave the Red zone was a different story. On September 18 he wrote his sons in Valencia: "My little ones! Grandfather so much longs to give you all big hugs, but his plans always seem to fall through. I'm sure it's for the best. Nevertheless—who knows!—I'm not giving up hope that what I want will soon become a reality. Don Manuel knows best." [56]

Of course, his situation had already improved considerably. There

[54] AGP, RHF, EF–370505–5.
[55] Alvaro del Portillo, *Sum.* 907. See also AGP, RHF, T–04152–III, p. 134.
[56] AGP, RHF, EF–370918–1.

was quite a difference between being cooped up in that "cricket cage" in the consulate and being out in the Madrid sunshine. But he was still having to exercise his priestly ministry with caution, in danger.

He had accumulated a whole collection of documents of various kinds, though none of them gave him total safety. The oldest was the paper from the "Madrid Delegation Committee of the Basque Nationalist Party" made out on December 23, 1936, granting him the right to "circulate freely" as "a person attached to the Government." [57]

He also had a certificate, dated March 15, 1937, issued by a lawyer of the Madrid courts. The lawyer in question was Juan José Esteban Romero, a former classmate of his at the Piarist high school in Barbastro; the certificate stated that "José María Escrivá Albás, of this district, 35 years of age, provides services in this office, during office hours." [58] Of course, in the Madrid of 1937, where strict official orders had already been given that anyone who did not have a permanent job there had to leave the capital, no one was going to get very far with this kind of certificate. And in this case nobody was even going to bother checking to see if what was said there was true or not, because in the summer of 1937 the authorities had already decreed that certificates made out for legal assistants had no validity.[59]

However, he did have the certificate dated March 14, 1937, that Dr. Suils' clinic provided when he left the Residence for Rest and Health, the one saying, "At present he is not completely cured, which means he is restricted from doing any kind of work, bearing any responsibilities, doing any traveling, or engaging in other types of activities"— saying, in other words, that he should be left in peace. And he had that other certificate from Dr. Suils, dated August 22, 1937, declaring that he had been suffering for six years from "an endogenous psychosis which affects him periodically." [60]

The most important document in his arsenal was that new one certifying him as "Chief Supply Officer" of the Ministry of Foreign Affairs of "the General Consulate of the Republic of Honduras, Central America," and requesting that he be provided "freedom of movement to carry out his duties." [61] Though it was not a bona fide appointment, the paper did command respect.

[57] See AGP, RHF, D–15068.
[58] See AGP, RHF, D–15069.
[59] See AGP, IZL, D–1213, 255, and D–1122.
[60] See AGP, RHF, D–15067 and AGP, RHF, EF–370723–1.
[61] See AGP, RHF, D–15070.

He also had the indispensable revolutionary credentials: a union card from the CNT, in the name of José Escribá Albás, with the membership number 522 and June 9, 1937, as the date of admission, and bearing the seal of the Union of Judicial Officials, Lawyers, and Officials in General; and a copy of the union charter. Dues payments were recorded for June, July, August, and September, at the rate of 2 pesetas and 25 centimos per month. The copy of the union charter was number 908930.[62]

Father Josemaría seems to have obtained the union documents with no great difficulty, probably just by presenting his work papers.[63] But a CNT card, with a dues book that began in June of 1937, that is to say, a year after the revolution broke out, could very well have given rise to suspicions in certain sectors.

Except for Doña Dolores, all the adults in the Escrivá family obtained documents from that anarchist union. Circumstances compelled many good Catholics to enlist in the army alongside avowed enemies of the Church, simply because they lived in the republican zone.[64] The situation can be illustrated by a story Father Josemaría

---

[62] See AGP, RHF, D–15071. This document contained a number of maxims and policy statements for the member to reflect on, such as "Your emancipation has to be your own work," "Don't grovel before anything or anyone," and "Your fatherland is the world; your family is humanity." It is quite possible that Father Josemaría made use of some of these aphorisms in his own preaching, either to affirm parts of them or to change people's minds about them. Of course, the openly Marxist sayings about fomenting class struggle would have been of no use to him.

[63] The first reference to the attempt to obtain union cards for Father Josemaría and Juan Jiménez Vargas is found in a letter written by Isidoro on May 13, 1937, when they were still refugees in the Honduran consulate. He says: "*The union*: Albareda has applied for the union documents. He wants to know if it would be best to describe Ricardo as a lawyer or an employee." And on June 17 the founder wrote to those in Valencia: "If Eugenio sends them a pass to travel to Valencia, José and Ricardo will leave immediately for Valencia to lend their services to the fatherland, since they now have their documentation in order (identity card and union card with photos)." José and Ricardo are the founder and Juan. See AGP, IZL, D–1213, 151, and AGP, RHF, EF–370617–1.

[64] See Alvaro del Portillo, *Sum.* 903, and AGP, RHF, T–04152–III, p. 112. Of course, not all those aligned with the republican government were enemies of the Church. One must bear in mind the grave disturbance that the military uprising produced in Spanish life, especially in places where it did not prevail, by unleashing precisely what it sought to prevent, namely, an anarchist or socialist-Marxist revolution. In consequence, when the republican state disappeared in August of 1936, there were convinced republicans, many of them agnostics, who were eager to defend the Republic but lacked any military or judicial means of securing what they called a freedom-of-conscience regime. Their fate was unfortunate, but many of these people (including agnostics) were not anti-Catholic. More problematic, personally and from the point of view of conscience, was the situation of the Basque nationalists and of Carrasco and Formiguera's small Christian party, the Democratic Union of Catalonia.

told about a country bumpkin who visited the cathedral in Saragossa. When he came in, some practical jokers pointed out to him that its floor was paved, like a chessboard, with large slabs of black and white marble, and told him he must be very careful not to step on the white slabs, because the cathedral guards had orders to take a stick to anyone who did. The bumpkin hopped like a sparrow from one black slab to the next. The guards, thinking he was crazy, told him to leave. And very proudly he answered them, "You just can't stand it that I landed on the black." [65] Overall, half of Spain had landed on the white and half on the black, and in many cases happenstance settled it. Either way, everyone had to make the best of the situation. But still, many homes were broken, and many parents were separated from their children.

In the spring of 1937 an internal conflict broke out behind republican lines, between different revolutionary forces. The CNT came out of it badly shattered and suffering a fierce persecution by the Stalinists. Emulating the socialist and communist unions, the anarchists then opened their ranks to new members without caring about their ideology or background. The Escrivás were among those who took advantage of the opportunity to join the CNT, since this was the only way one could get out and about in Red-controlled Madrid. [66]

One day, as a result of these events, some socialist militiamen came to Caracas Street asking to see work documents. Neither Carmen nor Doña Dolores had any. They were told to pack up their belongings—the militiamen would return in a few days and they would be taken to Valencia. [67] (Orders to remove from Madrid anyone

[65] See Alvaro del Portillo, *Sum.* 903.

[66] In early May 1937, the streets of Barcelona were the scene of a real war between the militias of the different political factions. Four hundred people were killed and a thousand wounded. These power struggles between socialists and communists, Catalonians and Libertarians, Stalinists and Trotskyites were such that the government finally had to send in from Valencia the air force, a motorized column, and two destroyers, with troops, to reestablish order.

The government of Largo Caballero collapsed as a consequence of these battles, and Negrín formed a new government excluding the anarchists, Libertarians, and anti-Stalinists. Then political and religious repression began again with the use of Bolshevik methods, including the "checa" torture centers. Anarchists and heterodox communists were systematically persecuted and eliminated. In accordance with the dictates of Stalin and the instructions of the Bolsheviks, they were represented to public opinion and the government as undesirable elements and infiltrators serving the "fascist" Francoists. See Bolloten, pp. 525–730, and Ramón and Jesús Salas Larrazábal, *Historia General de la Guerra de España* (Madrid, 1986), pp. 225–31 and 246.

[67] See AGP, RHF, T–04152–III, p. 129.

without a work permit had been in force since January 1937.) When Isidoro heard of this, he went to see José María Albareda, who knew people working in the teachers' union of the CNT. The CNT was short on members for this union, since most teachers and other school personnel were in the socialist UGT union. For that reason, quite a few members of religious orders had enrolled in the CNT at the beginning of 1937, and thus gotten their work permits. (However, later there was a purge, and some of these religious ended up in prison.)[68]

José María Albareda, who was a professor at the Velázquez Institute in Madrid, volunteered to obtain from the CNT union the work permit that Carmen needed, since she had a degree in education from the teachers college in Logroño. Everything seemed to be going fine, and then suddenly there was a big commotion and the office was closed. Several days later, Carmen, accompanied by Isidoro, went to the union building to pick up the document. A middle-aged official who seemed very good-natured, possibly a disguised religious, gave her a typed union certificate, along with a serious warning: that she should

---

[68] Tomás Alvira says: "On Castellana Avenue there was, and still is, an insurance building. Because it had a large clock on top, people called it the clock building. This building was taken over by the CNT for 'the Education CNT.' The CNT did not have a teachers' union in Madrid, so a group of teachers organized one, and it was accepted. A large number of teachers with rightist political leanings joined, including a good number of priests and men and women religious who were high school teachers. It was a way to get documentation. One person on the committee running the union was Father Manuel Mindán, who, after the war, became a philosophy professor at the Ramiro de Maeztu Institute. He was from Aragón and had been in the seminary with the Father. I myself had been in that clock building several times; I had some professional acquaintances there." See AGP, RHF, T–04373, and T–04152–III, pp. 129–30 and 135–38. See also Manuel Mindán Manero, *Testigo de noventa años de Historia: Conversaciones con un amigo en el último recodo del camino* (Saragossa, 1995); on pp. 339–50 he tells the history of the foundation and the functioning of the teachers' union of the CNT.

Javier Cervera points out that since the beginning of hostilities the CNT had sought members in Madrid, and that its battle with the UGT continued until an agreement was reached in 1938. See also Alfaya Camacho, pp. 155–58.

"The CNT's objective of gaining a position of power," says Cervera Gil (pp. 225–26), "had as a consequence the relaxation, if not the elimination, of all control over the loyalty of the new members. . . . We have found hardly any cases of disaffected members, or of infiltrators from other organizations of the Popular Front, except among the anarchists. This situation was the cause of more than one confrontation within the Madrid Defense Committee, between the communists . . . and the anarchists' representatives, who repeatedly ignored the warnings they received about how dangerous it was. Nevertheless, in contrast to this attitude, the CNT itself created in its own defense committee a statistics subcommittee directed by Vicente Santamaría Medina, who was also in charge of the counterespionage division of the Ministry of War. It was assigned to check the backgrounds of new members of the union to uncover disaffected or hostile persons in its ranks."

never, for any reason, even think of coming back there. Wrote Isidoro in June:

> Finally the problem of a work permit for Carmen has been resolved. I accompanied her to the union this afternoon and they gave it to us. Everything had come to a standstill because the secretary had taken all the funds and crossed over to the other side. Today there are rumors that the whole Spartacus battalion has crossed over. Ricardo will have fond memories of it.[69]

Juan Jiménez Vargas (alias Ricardo) did have vivid memories of his brief service as a medical lieutenant in the Spartacus Brigade of the CNT on the Jarama front and of the "inner force" that held him back every time he tried to desert to the other zone. Apparently the rumors of the treachery of the Spartacus Brigade were part of the Bolshevik campaign to discredit the CNT politically.

Doña Dolores decided to celebrate the work permit with a family gathering. "The grandmother has invited us to tea on Sunday; all the grandchildren are going," writes Isidoro.[70] Now that, thanks to the permit, his mother and sister could remain in Madrid, Father Josemaría suggested that they also try to obtain documents that would allow Santiago to leave the consulate and move about freely. The labyrinthine process extended from May to the second half of July.

Neither Carmen nor Doña Dolores had any real idea of the conditions of that confinement in the consulate. In the midst of his efforts to get himself out, the founder wrote to Isidoro: "I am extremely interested in arranging for the youngster to go live with the grandmother. My mother doesn't realize what life here is like." [71]

First they tried to get Santiago a student ID and enroll him in a summer-school program at a high school. This required signatures

---

[69] AGP, IZL, D–1213, 182. Actually, José María Albareda contacted Tomás Alvira, and it was Tomás who obtained the work certificate for Carmen, as he himself explains: "When they told me about the situation of the grandmother and Aunt Carmen, I went to obtain a certificate stating that Aunt Carmen worked in the office of the teachers' union. It was a bit of a struggle to talk them into it, but in the end, in consideration of the reason I was requesting it, they gave it to me. It certified that she was a typist in the primary education department of that organization. . . . A few days later, the militiamen came to take them to Valencia, but when shown Aunt Carmen's work certificate, they left them alone" (AGP, RHF, T–04373).

[70] AGP, IZL, D–1213, 182.

[71] AGP, RHF, EF–370624–2.

from two people with pre-revolution ID cards—evidence of their loyalty to the regime. But these ID cards had to be inspected by the students' union, and every attempt they made here led to a dangerous dead end.[72] So they changed tack, and Santiago was enrolled in some classes offered by the International Red Cross. And now that an ID card had boldly been gotten for him from the CNT, and he had a certificate from Dr. Suils that would pass muster with the committee that controlled the apartment building on Caracas Street, he was able to go live with Doña Dolores.[73]

On July 27 the Father wrote joyfully to Pedro Casciaro, "Did I tell you that Uncle Santi, as of several days ago, is living with the grandmother? They tell me he's not just happy, but ecstatic! He belongs to the International Red Cross and the CNT. They tell me he wears overalls and attends classes held by the Red Cross."[74]

Among the different plans for leaving the zone controlled by the Popular Front, the most direct and least risky was that of politically arranged evacuation; but God had not willed this for Father Josemaría. Of what value, then, was his whole arsenal of documents if he was not able to get out?

4. *Departure from Madrid*

Toward the end of September, José María Albareda received a letter from Barcelona. Some members of his family had escaped to France by way of the Pyrenees, and the letter was from a priest friend, Father

[72] José María Albareda first took on the task of getting a student ID for Santiago. His first impression, according to Isidoro, was that "this was not going to work, since it required certifications of the identity of the students, and those certifications would be investigated by the students' union" (AGP, IZL, D–1213, 187). In the end, José María turned over the job to Tomás Alvira, and it was he who got the ID card, as he himself testifies: "I also obtained an ID card for Uncle Santiago in that same union of the CNT, which gave him the documentation he needed to go out in the street" (AGP, RHF, T–04373).

[73] On July 18 the Father wrote to his sons in Valencia: "Yesterday afternoon, with a joy you can easily imagine, Uncle Santi went to live with the grandmother. They have been separated for I don't know how many months. As for me, I'm very delighted too, because this leaves me much freer" (AGP, RHF, EF–370718–1). Santiago says in his testimony: "I was the first to leave the Honduran consulate. Tomás Alvira got me an ID card from the CNT and another from the Libertarian Literary Club. I went to live on Caracas Street with my mother and Carmen. With my ID card I could go often to the consulate to visit them and bring them things. I came in through the servants' entrance and did not have any problem with the militiamen who guarded it" (AGP, RHF, T–07921). See also AGP, IZL, D–1213, 226.

[74] AGP, RHF, EF–370727–3.

Pascual Galindo, who was passing along information about the people who had helped them cross the border.[75]

Albareda told the Father, and, after carefully thinking it through, they decided to go that same route, with all its risks. Then they started trying to get safe-conduct passes and money for the trip. But right then, when everyone had agreed on the escape plan, Father Josemaría began to waver. One day he was willing to accept the idea of going to Barcelona with Juan and José María, and the next day he was backing out. He was thinking of the members of the Work who would be left behind in that dangerous situation, and of his mother and brother and sister, and of Alvaro del Portillo's father, who was gravely ill and could die at any time. But finally he did accept the idea of leaving Madrid, accompanied by all those who could get the necessary documentation.[76]

Thanks to the generosity of friends and even people they hardly knew, they got hold of a good sum of money.[77] To get their safe-conduct passes, they had to present their work permits and testimonials to their political acceptability; and since they wanted to leave Madrid as soon as possible, they needed help from people skilled in cutting through all this red tape.[78] They were aiming for the first week in October.

---

[75] See Gutiérrez Ríos, p. 108.

[76] See Alvaro del Portillo, *Sum.* 908; see also AGP, RHF, T–04152–III, p. 136.

[77] On the eve of their departure for Barcelona, Manolo Sainz de los Terreros was given 3,000 pesetas by neighbors of his on Sagasta Street, the Corchado family. This was a considerable sum, roughly equivalent to the annual wage of an unskilled worker. On the help given on that and earlier occasions to people of the Work, see AGP, RHF, T–04152–III, p. 140, and AGP, IZL, D–01051 and D–01199.

It would take a long time to detail all the efforts made to get the needed money. In broad outline, both José María Albareda and Tomás Alvira, who were employed by the state, contributed the savings from their salaries, and the rest—Juan Jiménez Vargas, Manuel Sainz de los Terreros, Pedro Casciaro, Francisco Botella, and Miguel Fisac—got help from their families and friends, in Madrid, Valencia, and Daimiel. There was also the remainder of the funds earmarked, before the war, for the new residence at 16 Ferraz Street, and there were donations from other friends and acquaintances. Even so, there did not end up being enough to pay the guides in full; they received after the war what was owed them.

[78] José María Albareda got his safe-conduct pass by asking for it directly from the Undersecretary of the Interior, Bibiano Fernández-Osorio, a high-school classmate he had not seen since before the war. He was a rather gruff man, but had the heart to help Albareda get to Barcelona to see his mother, who had lost her husband and a son, both killed by the militia.

Other documents were faked. Manolo Sainz de los Terreros, for instance, used a sheet bearing the letterhead of the director of the San Antón prison, where he had worked, to certify that he needed to make a trip to Barcelona for job-related purposes. See AGP, RHF, T–04152–III, pp. 137–38.

On October 1, the eve of the ninth anniversary of the founding of Opus Dei, the Father wrote to his sons in Valencia: "Tomorrow my little girl will be nine! I will be giving thanks all day long! She's still very little, but one can see that she will grow up strong and healthy." [79] Then he announced that "within a few days" he and Juan would be making a visit to Valencia.

In the offices of the CNT's Regional Union for Public Services, "Comrade José Escribá" got a political testimonial to use for getting a safe-conduct pass in the police headquarters. It read:

Madrid, October 5, 1937
To the Passport Division of the Police Headquarters
  Greetings, comrades. We hope you will authorize and grant safe conduct for travel to Barcelona and return within a period of 30 days, for taking care of family matters, to the comrade of this "Lawyers' Group" José Escriba Albas, ID number 522.

Yours and for the cause,
on behalf of the Committee,
Guillermo Zendón, Secretary[80]

(The explanation "for taking care of family matters" was one of the few true things said in that huge mess of "falser than Judas" documents, as Father Josemaría called them.[81])

October 8 was set as the departure date. Two days earlier, Juan left for Valencia to arrange for a place for them to stay. Father Josemaría made last-minute visits to people he was looking after and gave the last sacraments to Don Ramón del Portillo, realizing sadly that he would not be with him when he died.[82] Everything was "very rushed, because it was a matter of opportunity," Isidoro wrote on October 9.[83]

---

[79] AGP, RHF, EF–371001–1.

[80] The original document is in AGP, RHF, D–15072.

[81] See AGP, P03 1981, p. 367.

[82] See Alvaro del Portillo, *Sum.* 901.

In a letter dated October 15, to those in Valencia, Isidoro writes of the death of Don Ramón. "Yesterday," he says, "I went to visit the family of Alvarito, and was present at the death of his father. Alvarito couldn't leave the household he has been evacuated to, because he's hoping that through its mediation he will be able to follow the grandfather" (AGP, RHF, D–1213, 270). The "household," is, of course, the consulate. See also AGP, IZL, D–1213, 271 and 273.

[83] AGP, IZL, D–1213, 268.

The capital was then a besieged city. Juan left Madrid in a truck carrying barrels of wine, and was dropped off in Tembleque. From there he took the train for Valencia, and on the morning of October 7 he showed up at the home of Paco Botella. Later he visited Eugenio Sellés, who offered to have the Father stay with him.[84]

For Pedro Casciaro and Paco Botella, especially since Juan was now with them, October 7 and 8 were days of great expectation. They talked for hours on end, discussing what they had learned in the letters from Madrid, from the Father and Isidoro, about that whole year of isolation and extraordinary events.[85] Valencia at that time was swarming with outsiders: government officials, foreigners, and people coming in from all over Spain to live there. Unlike Madrid, it was a city that many people just passed through, where the arrival of the Father's group would not attract attention.

Pedro was attached to a cavalry support group at a barracks in Valencia. Paco worked in the army auxiliary services, and was free to get out and about and to live at home with his family. On the evening of October 7, relates Juan, he and Pedro went for a walk, "talking on and on about everything that had happened during our separation. Around eleven, we got to Pedro's boardinghouse. He wanted to go on hearing more news. But after praying the Preces, I fell into bed and slept like a log, while he did his mental prayer and said a Rosary."[86]

---

[84] See AGP, RHF, T–04152–III, p. 140, and T–02012, p. 1.

[85] "The important news was that the Father would be arriving the next day, to continue on to Barcelona," writes Francisco Botella (AGP, RHF, T–00159/1, p. 23). A very brief letter that came from Madrid said: "Greetings—Just want to let you know that tomorrow, Friday, my sisters will arrive in Valencia. Yours always, Mariano" (AGP, RHF, EF–371007–1).

[86] See the pages of introduction to the journal of the crossing of the Pyrenees, in which Juan Jiménez Vargas describes these earlier travels of his. The narration of the crossing begins on November 19, 1937, and ends on December 10, in Andorra. During their stay in the district of Rialp, those who were with the Father took turns writing down each day's events. When they reached Andorra, they incorporated into the journal the brief notes written while they were on the move.

The following year, when the Father was in Burgos, those handwritten records were typed, and the journal was given the title "The Road to Freedom." In this transcription, some clarifications were introduced and a few words were omitted. Some of the changes, as we will see, give us deep insights into Father Josemaría's behavior and interior life. In other cases, as he told Ricardo Fernández Vallespín, there is some touching up. "I've enjoyed typing up the 'Road to Freedom' journal," he says. "Of course, I've had to leave out some phrases that were too explicit" (AGP, RHF, EF–381010–3).

There were seventy-one manuscript sheets, written on both sides; the typescript was sixty-one pages. Both originals are in AGP, RHF, D–15323.

The "Preces," by the way, are special prayers said daily by members of Opus Dei.

Not knowing whether those coming from Madrid would be arriving by train or by automobile, the three spent the morning going back and forth to the railroad station. Then they decided to wait at Paco's apartment. At eight that night the doorbell rang. It was the Father! Between the strain of waiting and the shock of seeing the Father emaciated and wearing a suit, Pedro and Paco felt strangely uneasy until they found themselves getting a big hug. The others then came in, and the group split up according to plan: the Father and José María Albareda going to Eugenio Sellés's apartment, Manolo Sainz de los Terreros and Tomás Alvira going with Pedro to his boardinghouse, and Juan staying in Paco's apartment.[87] They all dined together at a restaurant called Merchants' Inn, and while they were there, some policemen came in and for some reason thought Pedro looked suspicious. They came over to their table and asked to see only the documentation for Pedro—who was the only one who had all his papers perfectly in order.[88]

The following morning everyone met at Eugenio Sellés's apartment for Mass. When the Father learned that the porter of the building was a priest, he told them to let him know that he too was one, in case he was in need of his ministerial help. The two priests made their confessions to each other and served each other's Masses.[89]

This priest who was serving as porter was named Pepe. That he was alive at all was a miracle. As he was being driven off to be shot and thrown in a ditch for being a priest, a communist had talked the revolutionaries into leaving him in his hands. This man, a recent party recruit who disapproved of his bloodthirsty comrades, managed to find him cover as a porter.[90]

To ward off suspicion, the Father asked Pedro and Paco to use the familial word for "you" when speaking to him, but, as had been the case with Juan, they could not do it. He took that opportunity to speak to them at length about the importance of being faithful to their vocations and having unlimited confidence in God our Father. He told them how eager he was to get into an atmosphere of freedom so that he could carry on his apostolate and be reunited with the young men

---

[87] See AGP, RHF, EF–371009–2.

[88] See AGP, RHF, D–15323, and AGP, RHF, T–00159/1, p. 25.

[89] See Alvaro del Portillo, *Sum.* 910. That priest came up and said Mass in Eugenio Sellés's apartment every day. And the Blessed Sacrament was reserved there. See AGP, RHF, T–02012, p. 2.

[90] See AGP, RHF, T–04152–III, p. 141.

who had been at the Ferraz Street residence and were now in the other zone. He also asked them to be generous enough to sacrifice some of their professional goals, since once the war was over there would be urgent apostolic work to do.[91] And since the train for Barcelona was not leaving until eleven that night, the Father still had time to write to Isidoro, even though during the trip there would be times when he could not write, when they were going through inspections. (At one point on their trip to Valencia, militiamen had demanded, while kneeling on the ground and aiming their rifles at the car, to see their documentation.)[92]

His letter to "Ignacio" is filled with his usual good humor.[93]

Saturday, October 9, 1937
Dear Ignacio,

We got here in great shape, at eight o'clock at night. We had set out at one. In the first town after Tarancón we stopped for lunch: ham, brought by José María and Tomás, and our biscuits and nougats. Ah! And wheat bread (yes, there is wheat bread), plus some salad with tomatoes that our Saragossan companion sniffed out. Along the way we bagged two pieces of game: a partridge that hit the car while crossing the road, flying at low altitude, and a dog that, elevated to the status of a ram, will be eaten today, Saturday, by rich Madridians.

My grandchildren are doing fine. . . .

I will remember you and all my little ones, as well as Lola and her children, in my talks with Don Manuel on the trip.

Much love,
Mariano[94]

---

[91] See AGP, RHF, T–00159/1, p. 25.

[92] See AGP, RHF, T–04152–III, p. 143, and Alvaro del Portillo, *Sum.* 909. In the hurry to leave Madrid, they had to leave behind some things in the room on Ayala Street, including the picture of our Lady from the frame and mirror store. When Isidoro and Santiago went to retrieve it and other items, they found that a howitzer shell had penetrated the front of the building, spraying the room with shrapnel. This image of our Lady was then kept in the grandmother's apartment; later the Father gave it to Santiago; and eventually it ended up in Rome, in the office of the secretary general of the Work, where the founder usually worked. See Alvaro del Portillo, *Sum.* 889; AGP, RHF, T–04152–III, p. 143; and AGP, RHF, EF–371027–1.

[93] Only rarely did his good humor fail him in his letters to his sons. In June he had written to those in Valencia: "I would like to try to tell you a joke, but I can't get it out. It keeps sticking in my throat" (AGP, RHF, EF–370601–1).

[94] AGP, RHF, EF–371009–2.

At eleven the train left for Barcelona, with Pedro and Paco seeing the travelers off. If the expedition went well, a second one would be organized for those still in Madrid and Valencia. As the train began moving, the Father blessed them; with his hand half hidden by his suit coat, which held the little metal box with the Blessed Sacrament (the cigarette case with the Honduran-flag cover and the corporals made by Carmen), he made a sign of the cross while saying with a slight movement of his lips, "Beata Maria intercedente, bene ambuletis, et Dominus sit in itinere vestro et angeli eius comitentur vobiscum." [95] Pedro and Paco watched the train pull out, wondering when they would see him again and imagining the dangers the travelers would soon face. "I got little sleep that night," Paco recalls.[96]

The travelers got even less sleep. The coaches had no compartments, and the train was already filled when it left Valencia. The wooden seats were broken and dirty. The middle aisle became packed with people getting ready to sleep on the floor, mostly militiamen on furlough, whose conversations were marked by frequent blasphemies and foul language. The Father spent the night making acts of reparation to our Lord; and given the possibility of a sacrilege resulting from an inspection, he decided very early in the morning that the sacred hosts should be consumed. So, in the bathroom, the cigarette case was passed from one to another so that all could receive. On Sunday, October 10, a little before noon, the train entered Barcelona. The Father immediately wrote Isidoro a few lines announcing their arrival.[97]

José María Albareda went to stay at 60 Argentina Street, where the widow of a man named Montagut had taken in his mother with her two grandchildren. A daughter of the widow had placed on the front door of the house a sign saying that it had been seized by the F.A.I., a group of anarchists. Thus protected, they were living a quiet life. Even Father Pascual Galindo, the priest who had sent the information to Madrid about how to get to France, had stayed there.

The Father and the rest of the group went to "Centric Hotel," on Rambla de Estudios Street. Despite their sleepless night on the train, they spent Sunday afternoon walking around the city; soon their legs would have to make the arduous trip across the mountains.

[95] "Through the intercession of our Lady, may you have a good trip, and may our Lord be with you on your way and his angel accompany you." See AGP, RHF, T–00159/1, p. 27, and T–04152–III, p. 145.
[96] AGP, RHF, T–00159/1, p. 27.
[97] See AGP, RHF, T–04152–III, p. 145, and T–04373, p. 4.

On the next day Father Josemaría celebrated Mass for all of them in the house on Argentina Street. Afterwards Doña Pilar, José María Albareda's mother, explained how to find people who could get them over the border. Wasting no time, they went to a café on Ronda de San Antonio and casually asked for Mateo. This turned out to be the man at the counter—a white marble counter like those in stores specializing in milk and dairy products. Later they learned that the rest of his name was Molleví Roca, but from the start they gave him the nickname of Mateo the Milkman. He was a middle-aged, level-headed man who inspired confidence.[98]

After a lot of beating around the bush, they agreed to meet the next day. When they did, Mateo told them that the contact would be a man named Vilaró, whom they would find the next day on the corner of Gran Vía de las Corts where the Flora Bar was. Juan was there on Wednesday the 13th, at the appointed time, with the signal, a newspaper folded in half. But Vilaró never showed up. Perhaps he had found other clients. According to Mateo, his price per person was 2,000 pesetas.[99]

5. *A stay in Barcelona*

After three days in Barcelona, the Father was getting more optimistic, to judge by the tone in which he wrote of the planned crossing into France. "My impressions are very good," he writes to Isidoro on Sunday, October 10. And on October 12 he writes to him, "Slowly but surely, I am improving," giving him to understand that the plan is moving ahead.[100] On Wednesday the 13th, in a long letter to Isidoro, after saying they are thinking of setting out "within a few days" although "it might be a little later," he outlines his plan of organizing a second expedition for all the members of the Work still in Madrid. They should, he says, get all their documents in order so that they can meet in Valencia as soon as they receive instructions from Pedro Casciaro. Anticipating an imminent departure from Barcelona, he ends the letter thus:

> I may leave before your letter gets here. I will ask a good friend of mine to receive your reply and forward it to me. So

[98] See AGP, RHF, D–15323 and D–15373, and AGP, RHF, T–04152–III, pp. 146–48.
[99] See AGP, RHF, T–04152–III, p. 148.
[100] AGP, RHF, EF–371010–1 and EF–371012–1.

don't write me at the hotel, but use the address I will put below.

Warmest greetings and much love, and best regards to Don Manuel and his Mother.

Mariano

Address your reply to:
Cecilia Sánchez
60 República Argentina
Barcelona
(You can put another envelope inside, with the words "Please forward to Mariano.")[101]

At the same time that he sent this letter to Isidoro, designating Pedro Casciaro as the coordinator of a second expedition, he sent a telegram to Valencia inviting Pedro to come to Barcelona in order to "hear the plan explained in detail and meet Mateo and the other intermediaries." Pedro and Paco were alarmed by this, taking it to mean that the Father wanted Pedro to join the expedition that was about to leave Barcelona. But Pedro immediately went into action. Getting some papers from the cavalry support service, he made out a pass for himself, and that same night he took the eleven o'clock train for Barcelona.[102]

When Juan came back to the Central Hotel with a long face, looking tired and holding under his arm the folded newspaper, they had been waiting for him for three hours. He informed them that the plan had failed; that the contact had not shown up.

Thus they had to postpone their departure from Barcelona. Since they were running short of money, they considered leaving the hotel and going to stay at Doña Rafaela's boardinghouse, on Gran Vía

---

[101] AGP, RHF, EF–371013–1.

[102] Juan Jiménez Vargas, in "Road to Freedom" (AGP, RHF, D–15323, p. 4), speaks of a letter the founder sent to Valencia ("The letter was received by Paco, who brought it to Pedro at the entrance to the barracks"). Francisco Botella also speaks of a letter ("In the afternoon we received a letter from the Father"; see AGP, RHF, T–00159/1, p. 27). This letter, however, does not appear in the founder's correspondence. There are many indications that what was sent was not a letter but a telegram. For one thing, this would explain something said in the manuscript written at that time: "Pedro arrived in Barcelona at 2:00 p.m., with the aforesaid faked permission." Only if it was a telegram could he have received the news from Barcelona that quickly, three days ahead of those in Madrid. (The Father's letter of October 13 was received in Madrid on the 16th. In consequence, Isidoro gave instructions to everyone to make sure they had their documents for "evacuation"; see AGP, IZL, D–1213, 272.)

Diagonal, where they would also be at less risk of being reported to the police.[103] On October 14, all except Albareda moved to Doña Rafaela's. She was aware of their plans and knew that Father Josemaría was a priest. That same day, Pedro arrived in Barcelona, and the Father told him about the contacts and the plan for a second expedition. That night, he returned to Valencia by train, but when he showed up at the barracks, he was sentenced to sixteen days in the guardhouse.[104] Meanwhile, there was a considerable commotion when Isidoro shared with the other members of the Work the Father's letter of the 13th suggesting that they join Pedro in Valencia; but things quieted down in a few days, after they received information sent by Pedro from the guardhouse. (Actually there was no guardhouse; they had to find a room to put him in.)

In a letter dated October 21, Isidoro tries to clear up the misunderstanding. He tells those in Madrid: "The Grandfather called Perico to go to Barcelona. Upon his return to Valencia, Pedro wrote to say that 'within ten or twelve days they will be in José Ramón's house,' and "What one must have is thirty years of age and three books. For now this is not viable; we'll see later on. . . .' These are the grandfather's words, as transmitted by Radio Pedro." [105] In other words, the departure from Barcelona had been delayed; the ones in Madrid would need 3,000 pesetas each; and they should not leave Madrid yet. "José Ramón" was José Ramón Herrero Fontana, the youngest member of the Work. The beginning of the civil war found him in the nationalist zone, while his mother and brother remained in Madrid, on Herradores Plaza. "José Ramón's house," therefore, was the code for freedom, and for the nationalist zone.

Pedro's willingness to run such a big risk for the Work moved the Father. He began again to reflect on the dangers to which his sons were being exposed. The result was a fresh round of doubts centering on the thought that he was acting in a cowardly manner by abandoning the people who most needed him—the people in Madrid.

On October 15, when the two of them were alone in the boardinghouse, the Father told Juan emphatically that he was going to return

---

[103] The change of residence in Barcelona and some details of the conversation of the Father with Pedro on that October 14 are recorded in a note written by Pedro; see AGP, RHF, D–15374.

[104] See AGP, RHF, T–00159/1, p. 28.

[105] AGP, IZL, D–1213, 276. The situation had changed from October 13 (when the Father wrote Isidoro) to October 14 (when he met with Pedro in Barcelona).

to Madrid, but that Juan and the others should follow through with the plan they had made. And he actually walked out the door. "It was, without doubt, the worst moment of my life," Juan writes. "After all these years I remember it as though it were happening right now." [106] What was he going to say to the others when they got back to the house?

A half hour later Father Josemaría had changed his mind. Evidently he was seeing clearly what God's will for him was. "What really struck me," Juan continues, "was the humility with which he asked my forgiveness for having made me go through such a bad time. At that time I didn't tell the others anything about what had happened." [107]

Father Josemaría had managed to find where Father Pou de Foxá was hiding out and to go see him. That visit was just what he needed, as he wrote Isidoro a few days later.

> Barcelona, October 20, 1937
> My good friend:
>
> I have received your letters. I am very sorry to hear of the death of Don Ramón, even though it was to be expected. Let that dear family know that I share deeply in their pain.
>
> We keep all of you very much in mind. I hope the grandmother and her young ones are well. Soon we will see José Ramón.
>
> Tell Lola that I have spoken at length with Pou, and that they're all doing fine.
>
> It will be some time before I write again.
>
> Did you receive Pedro's letter?
>
> > Much love to you all,
> > Mariano[108]

The Father celebrated Mass almost every day, usually in Doña Rafaela's boardinghouse and occasionally in the home of the Albareda family, with others attending. (He kept the Blessed Sacrament with him, in order to give Communion to those who could not attend Mass.) These gatherings involved their share of danger. Perhaps at

---

[106] AGP, RHF, T–04152–IV, p. 1.
[107] Ibid., p. 2. See also AGP, RHF, T–04152–III, p. 159.
[108] AGP, RHF, EF–371020–1. For more on Father Pou de Foxá, see volume 1 of this biography, pp. 124, 132, 166–67, 170, and 246–47.

Father Josemaría's suggestion, Doña Rafaela usually kept watch in the corridor in case anyone came to the door.[109]

While they were waiting for news from Mateo the Milkman, Father Josemaría filled his free time with priestly work. As was the case in Madrid, there was in Barcelona a secret network of priests who risked their lives giving the sacraments to the faithful.[110] But it was not so easy to get in contact with them. One day Tomás Alvira ran into a friend from Saragossa, Francisco Gayé Monzón, whose mother, he told Tomás, was living in Badalona and had since 1936 been unable to find a priest to go to confession to. Having set the date and time, Tomás and Father Josemaría traveled to Badalona with Francisco. Once they were off the bus and walking toward the sea, the priest began praying aloud the Salve Regina (Hail, Holy Queen). That evening, when saying good-bye to Tomás, Doña Pilar Monzón told him that the Father had said things to her about her spiritual life that no one had ever said to her before.[111]

Tomás had good social connections. Soon after arriving in Barcelona, the group read in the papers that Pascual Galbe Loshuertos had been appointed to the Catalonian Court of Appeals for the Generalitat, the highest authority in Catalonia. He had been a high-school classmate of Tomás's in Saragossa. Father Josemaría also remembered him, from the law school—he was that fellow who had had a reputation for being a nonbeliever. They had last seen each other on a streetcar in Madrid. As soon as Pascual had caught sight of him, he had made a beeline for him and given him a big hug. It had required a lot of courage to show a priest such affection so openly in those days.[112]

But how would he react now? Tomás, feeling confident also because of his own long-standing friendship with Pascual, got the Father's permission to appear one day at the court. The judge, when he caught sight of his old friend, could not contain his joy. In the course of their conversation, Tomás told him Father Josemaría was also in Barcelona and wanted to see him. "Not here! Not here!" Pascual exclaimed in alarm. "Better that he come to my house for dinner." [113]

[109] See AGP, RHF, T–04152–III, pp. 159–60; T–00874; and T–04373, p. 4.

[110] See Joan Marqués i Suriñach, *La força de la fe a Catalunya durant la guerra civil, 1936–1939* (Girona, 1987), especially pp. 131–45, 167–95, and 253–80.

[111] See Vázquez Galiano, pp. 94–95.

[112] See AGP, P03 1981, p. 596, and volume 1 of this biography, p. 165.

[113] See AGP, RHF, T–04152–III, pp. 161–65; Alvaro del Portillo, PR, p. 1130; Alvaro del Portillo, *Immersed in God*, p. 17; and Vázquez Galiano, pp. 95–97. Juan Jiménez Vargas gives October 15 as the date of this meeting at the court.

The visit having been arranged by telephone, Father Josemaría, who, as we know, was not rolling in money, bought some toys for Pascual's two children and, accompanied by Juan, went to the judge's house. The two friends gave each other a big hug, and after a wonderful meal, when Pascual's wife and children had left the room, their conversation continued.

"What a joy to see you, Josemaría," said Pascual. "You don't know how much I suffered—thinking you had been killed." He then offered his friend the possibility of remaining in Barcelona, and working as a lawyer, with documentation that would guarantee his safety. Father Josemaría thanked him, but declined. "I've never practiced law before," he said, "because all I cared about was being a priest. So how can I do it now when I could get shot just for being a priest?" [114]

Father Josemaría explained that his reason for being in Barcelona was to cross over into the other zone. Pascual at first tried to dissuade him, reminding him of how tight the controls on the border were, and of the harshness of the punishments—those caught trying to escape were executed. And then, seeing that he was getting nowhere, he made him this unconditional offer: that if he did have the bad fortune to get arrested, he should not fail to let him know.

Pascual then opened his heart to his friend. He told him of his political disillusionment. He was not doing well. The anarchists had given him a bodyguard, but more to keep an eye on him than to protect him, because they did not trust him. Father Josemaría spoke about God, trying to rekindle the other man's faith, but the judge took refuge in his old prejudices and arguments.

"Look, son, you say these things," the priest interrupted, "because you've read four or five books that you needn't have read. But to acquire a minimum of theological culture, you have to read a lot more things. When you've read everything you need to, you'll be in a position to form a sound opinion on these matters." [115]

Tears came to Pascual's eyes, and the two friends agreed to meet again in his office. When they got together this second time, some people who had been arrested while trying to escape to Andorra were being sentenced in the courtroom: they were found guilty and

---

[114] AGP, P03 1981, p 597.
[115] See AGP, RHF, T–04152–III, p. 165.

condemned to death. "You see what awaits you," Pascual told him. "But if they catch you, tell them you are my brother."[116]

*   *   *

Their escape now depended entirely on Mateo the Milkman. Ever calm and easygoing, he advised them to be patient. After they had been in Barcelona for over a week, Mateo gave them the address of Rafael Jiménez Delgado, a soldier who had documents from the General Workers Union (UGT) and a lot of ideas about possible ways to escape. But after meeting with him in his home, they found that most of his plans were impossible to carry out, if not utterly harebrained.[117]

On October 22 Mateo had good news for them: the expedition was arranged, and would begin soon. Any day now, someone named Pallarés, a friend of Mateo's son and a very tough and resourceful man, would be arriving in Barcelona. At the request of Father Josemaría, Juan headed for Valencia to bring back Paco and Pedro to join the expedition.[118]

On Sunday, October 24, there was alarming news in the papers. The guards on the Pyrenees frontier had ambushed one of the expeditions. *La Vanguardia*, Barcelona's principal newspaper, gave the story this headline: "Nine Fugitives Captured. One Killed, Three Others Wounded." It is very probable that this expedition was the one organized by Vilaró, the man who had not shown up for his meeting with Juan Jiménez Vargas.

As if by magic, all traces of the contacts disappeared. Mateo himself came close to falling into the hands of the police. At the end of November he would flee to Argentina, where he would remain until the end of the war. At the end of December, Pallarés, while trying to save the life of a person wounded on his expedition, would be captured and then executed.[119]

Meanwhile, Father Josemaría and his companions worked on getting in shape for the long mountain hikes that lay ahead. Every day, they tramped up and down Barcelona's hills, from the harbor to

---

[116] See AGP, P03 1981, p. 598. The founder, relates Bishop del Portillo, "always prayed for this upright man who tried to save his life. He offered many suffrages for his soul when, later on, he heard that he had died in a car accident in the south of France" (Alvaro del Portillo, PR, p. 1130).

[117] See AGP, RHF, T–04152–III, p. 169.

[118] See AGP, RHF, T–00159/1, p. 28; AGP, RHF, T–04152–III, p. 177; and AGP, IZL, D–1213, 280.

[119] See AGP, RHF, T–04152–III, p. 170, and T–04152–IV, p. 2.

Montjuic or from the old part of the city to Mount Tibidabo. The last days of October were cold and rainy. Thinking of the frost and snow there would be in the mountains, they bought raincoats and winter clothing.

Another physical enemy was hunger. This one had no easy remedy, since they had little to spend on food. Their last dinner deserving of that name was the one they had on October 24, the feast of Saint Raphael; it cost them 15 pesetas each. Also on that day, at Father Josemaría's suggestion, Doña Rafaela was presented by her guests with a bouquet of flowers. Nothing like that had been done for the widow in a long time, and least of all by her boarders.[120]

Money was already getting short before they had to pay the fees of the expedition organizers. If the price was 2,000 pesetas per person, as Mateo had indicated, they would not be able to sign up. Mateo had also specified that these had to be "good" pesetas, which were bills issued by the Bank of Spain and in circulation before July 18, 1936. These bills were recognized as legal tender in the other zone, and for that reason were highly coveted. But they were very hard to come by. Evidently quite a few people in the republican zone were expecting the nationalists to win, or at least were prudently preparing for that eventuality.

The group started looking for "good" money immediately, and, surprisingly, they found it, in a way that could only be called providential. It was Francisco Gayé, the friend of Tomás Alvira, whose mother had made her confession to Father Josemaría, who took care of the problem. At Tomás's urging, Gayé, an employee of the Hispano-Americano Bank, took the risky step of exchanging other bills for "good" ones, and he got away with it, even though the "good" pesetas were kept under extremely vigilant control by the banks.[121] Once more, everyone had occasion to see the guardian angels' hand in events.[122]

On October 25, when he showed up unannounced in Valencia, Juan got a big surprise. He had not heard anything about Pedro's sentence.

---

[120] See AGP, RHF, T–04152–III, p. 171.

[121] See Vázquez Galiano, p. 93.

[122] See AGP, RHF, T–04152–III, p. 176. The matter of the "good" currency was common knowledge. The government of Burgos had announced by the nationalist radio station which series of bills would be exchangeable at the end of the war. See Pedro Casciaro, *Dream and Your Dreams Will Fall Short* (London and Princeton, 1994), p. 138; and AGP, IZL, D–1213, 286.

Pedro still had a week to go before his release, so Juan went with Paco to visit him. Then and there, they resolved to leave for Barcelona the very day Pedro got out. In the meantime Juan would go to Daimiel, where Miguel Fisac (Lola's brother who was also a member of the Work) had been hiding out in his parents' home for over a year. Miguel would need papers, and also some physical conditioning after all those months of inactivity. The first problem was the more easily solved—Pedro had in his apartment some stamped letterheads of his cavalry support division that could be used to counterfeit a pass.[123]

Juan went to Daimiel on October 27 and on the 30th was back in Valencia with Miguel, who was pale as a ghost. The next day, at nine in the morning, Pedro was released, with a strong warning from the commandant, who threatened severe punishment for a repeat offense. Pedro contritely assured him that that offense would not be repeated.[124] (He had already decided to desert.) On November 2, at eight in the morning, just as the Father was finishing Mass, the four from Valencia arrived at Doña Rafaela's boardinghouse. The Ebro River had overflowed its banks at Amposta, forcing them to spend a night there. The next morning they had crossed over to the other shore and caught a train. To avoid suspicion, three of them now went to stay at a house on Argentina Street that the widow Montagut had found for them.[125]

As Mateo the Milkman kept telling them, all they could do was wait for more favorable conditions. In the last week of October, matters were complicated by a widespread flood in Catalonia. On October 30 the Father sent to Isidoro a postcard saying, "My dear friend: A few words of greeting, to tell you that, with the rains, my trip has been postponed for four to six days." [126]

To make matters even worse, on October 31 the republican government moved from Valencia to Barcelona, increasing the police presence and communist influence in the area.[127] It was not unusual to

[123] See AGP, RHF, T–04152–III, p. 178. Following the instructions that the Father had sent from Barcelona in his letter dated October 13, Isidoro had written to Lola Fisac about preparations for getting her brother to Madrid; see AGP, IZL, D–1213, 274. Juan anticipated those plans and brought Miguel, along with Pedro and Paco, to Barcelona.

[124] See AGP, RHF, T–00159/1, p. 29.

[125] See AGP, RHF, T–04152–III, p. 181, and T–00159/1, p. 30.

[126] AGP, RHF, EF–371030–1.

[127] Despite strong opposition by the Generalitat, the government made this move in order to consolidate its authority in Catalonia. "The government's move to Barcelona in November 1937," Bolloten tells us, "exacerbated the discord between the central and

read items like this one from the October 31 issue of *La Vanguardia*: "Law and order: The undocumented. For being undocumented, some eighty individuals have been arrested by the police in bars, restaurants, handball courts, and other places of relaxation." By now they themselves were the next thing to undocumented, since both the military passes that Pedro had provided the Valencians and the safe-conduct passes of the Madridians had expired.

The only solution was to erase the old dates and substitute new ones. An uncle of Tomás's who was a hospital administrator and had his own office was able to make the changes with a good ink eraser and a typewriter that had the same style of letters as the passes.[128] Some of the documents were easy to amend. The safe-conduct passes for the Father and Tomás, for instance, had been valid for thirty days starting October 5, so they only needed a "2" inserted before the "5" to become valid until November 25. The military passes, on the other hand, were usually given for only a few days, with both the starting and the ending dates specified. By mid-November, the ones for their group had suffered more than one erasure in the same spots. Obviously, not all of those documents would pass a rigorous police inspection. The Father always turned to the guardian angels in such difficult situations, and he taught his followers to do the same, with results that, as Juan puts it, were sometimes "quite spectacular."[129]

Meanwhile, Mateo was able to revive their hopes: a new expedition was being organized. On November 6 Father Josemaría wrote to Isidoro, "I trust that everyone in the family will be fine. Here we're doing great, and, at any moment now, the grandfather will be leaving for José Ramón's house with his seven little grandchildren."[130]

But what actually kept happening "at any moment now" was that the departure was put off for another couple of weeks. Hunger was getting to be a real problem. They had no ration cards, and to try to get them would be too risky. Food could, of course, always be bought on

---

regional authorities with regard to public order. . . . The most deeply felt complaint in all sectors of society in Catalonia was the omnipresent terror of the SIM and its special courts and the police apparatus controlled by the communists" (Bolloten, pp. 861 and 913–17). The SIM, the counterespionage service of the People's Army, was controlled by Alexander Orlov, who had been appointed by Stalin as head of the Soviet NKVD (later KGB) in Spain. His much-dreaded police employed brutal methods in all sectors of the republican zone. See Bolloten, pp. 897–912.

[128] See Casciaro, pp. 91ff., and AGP, RHF, T–04152–III, p. 183.

[129] See AGP, RHF, T–04152–III, pp. 161 and 183–87, and T–00159/1, p. 32.

[130] AGP, RHF, EF–371106–1.

the black market, but not without more money than they had. All they had plenty of was hunger. They ate one meal a day, and a very small one at that. Long walks were needed for getting into condition, but that expenditure of energy made the hunger worse.[131]

Of course, many other people were also hungry. The priest felt very sorry for the two little nephews of José María Albareda who lived with their grandmother Pilar. When he had breakfast in a café—on days when he had breakfast at all—he would usually get a malt, as a substitute for coffee, and a couple of salted biscuits, and save all this for the two boys.

"Entertain the little ones," he would say to Pedro. And Pedro, armed with paper and pencil, would ask them what they wanted him to draw. Invariably, it was something to eat. One day he drew a plate with a couple of fried eggs, and generously added some delicious-looking sausages. The youngsters were delighted, but the Father, taking him aside, said to him, "Don't you think, my son, that it might be mental cruelty to give a picture like that to these hungry children?" [132]

To walk out on the street in groups of four or five would have been dangerous; it would have attracted attention. But the Father saw to it that, fairly often, they all got together as a family in one or another of the boardinghouses in which they were staying. These get-togethers were not, of course, risk-free, but they were a way of cheering people up and preventing them from growing cold in their spiritual life or giving in to depression.[133] The Father was the heart and soul of the group, but when it came to the material organization he made it clear that his role was to obey. "On one of the first days of our stay in Barcelona," relates Paco, "the Father told us that as far as the departure from the Red zone was concerned, he was putting himself in Juan's hands like a child and that he would follow his instructions. And we did in fact often see Juan and the Father speaking together by themselves." [134]

In mid-November, Mateo announced that they would be leaving Barcelona on Friday the 19th. He informed them of the means of transportation, the stopping places, and the passwords for the contacts. The documents were altered for the last time. Some of the safe-

[131] See AGP, RHF, T–00159/1, p. 32, and Casciaro, pp. 99–101.
[132] See Casciaro, pp. 100–101.
[133] See AGP, RHF, T–04152–III, p. 184.
[134] AGP, RHF, T–00159/1, p. 31.

conduct passes, including the Father's, were again easy to adjust, requiring only that a new destination be typed in.[135]

The last-minute preparations were made with a close eye on expenses. They bought first-aid items, six more raincoats, several pairs of rope-soled shoes, and some boots for the Father. He was still wearing a coat and tie, in keeping with his position as a consulate official, but very soon he would have to change into much sturdier clothes.[136]

When the time for the departure came, the Father sent a few letters and postcards: to Isidoro, to the Honduran consul, and to Lola Fisac. To her he sent two postcards, the second of which reads:

Barcelona, November 19, 1937
My dear friend: Just a few words to tell you that today the grandfather leaves for José Ramón's house, with his grandchildren. He says he will write you within a month.
Much love,
Josemaría[137]

Then, showing him their deep gratitude, they took leave of Mateo the Milkman. Doña Rafaela was also sorry to see them go. She would never forget the fear she had of what might have happened to that priest if he had been caught saying Mass. But at eighty-five she would still remember him as a "very prudent" person, with very refined sensibilities.[138] Undoubtedly she was thinking of his good manners and great dignity, but perhaps also of something that can be illustrated by the following incident. In Barcelona, after a good deal of hunting about for eating places they could afford, they found two: a squalid, dirty tavern and a modest place on Tallers Street called L'Aliga Roja Bar and Restaurant. At L'Aliga the tables had tablecloths, the dishes were clean, and the prices were almost as low as in the other place. But the portions were larger at the grimy tavern. The Father preferred the cleanliness and simplicity of L'Aliga, but almost always he let his sons drag him to the place with the more plentiful helpings.[139]

---

[135] See AGP, RHF, D–15125. See also AGP, RHF, T–04152–III, p. 183, and T–04152–IV, p. 3.
[136] See AGP, RHF, T–00159/1, p. 32, and T–04152–III, p. 172.
[137] AGP, RHF, EF–371119–1.
[138] See AGP, RHF, T–04152–III, pp. 156 and 158, and T–00874.
[139] See Casciaro, pp. 102–104, and AGP, RHF, T–00159/1, p. 32.

6. *The rose of Rialp*

As the doctor of the group, Juan was worried that their physical resistance might be too low for the difficult passage ahead. He was particularly concerned about the health of the Father, who at the end of October had spent several days in bed with a high fever.[140] Also, Tomás and Manolo had not yet recovered from recent attacks of colitis.

Fortunately, José María did not have any special problems, and neither did Paco and Pedro, who had been living a normal life since the beginning of the war. And as for Miguel, his muscles were quickly regaining strength as a result of the walks around Barcelona.

On Friday, November 19, at 1:00 P.M., six of them took the bus for Seo de Urgel. (Manolo and Tomás would leave Barcelona two days later, so that the group would not be so large as to arouse suspicions.[141]) The Father, José María, and Juan rode in front, and Pedro, Paco, and Miguel, further back.[142] In accord with their instructions, this latter group, being young men of military age whose documents were not in the best condition, got off the bus in Sanahuja, where a guide was waiting for them. From that point on, inspections by the police and by militiamen would become more frequent and rigorous as the bus got closer to the border.

The Father, Juan, and José María got off a little past Oliana, near where the road to Peramola begins.[143] (It was in Peramola that the other three were to rejoin them.) A prearranged signal immediately identified their contact, who followed them at a prudent distance until they reached a secluded spot. He told them that his name was Antonio Bach, but that people called him Tonillo. A mail carrier and an employee of the town government, Tonillo was a brave and decisive man to whom more than one fugitive owed his life. He quickly made friends with Father Josemaría—who was now wearing tobacco-colored corduroy pants that were loose-fitting and fastened at the ankle, a navy-blue turtleneck wool sweater that was too big for

[140] See AGP, RHF, T–04152–IV, p. 2.
[141] For the trip to France from the point of view of Tomás Alvira, see Vázquez Galiano, pp. 89–106.
[142] For an extensive description of José María Albareda's escape to France, see Gutiérrez Ríos, pp. 118–34.
[143] See AGP, RHF, T–00159/1, p. 34, and Casciaro, p. 107.

him, rubber-soled boots of a sheepskin leather that became terribly soft the first time it rained, and a black beret.[144] "Soon after we started walking," recalled Tonillo years later, "that gentleman in the blue sweater had already told me he was a priest and the rector of the Church of Santa Isabel in Madrid. He said it just like that, of his own accord, as if he had no concern about it being known that he was a priest."[145]

Night had fallen by the time they reached Peramola. They made a detour around the village, and then Tonillo put them up in a barn, promising to come at dawn to wake them. As soon as they lay down, the place came alive with the sounds of rats and mice running around. Possibly Juan and José María, in their exhaustion, slept soundly, but not the Father. His thoughts went back to his family, to the members of the Work still in Madrid, and to those at the battlefronts. And he started praying, holding to what he had written to Lola Fisac two days earlier: "The poor old fellow keeps you very much in mind, each and every one of you. He talks with Don Manuel at length every day about his concern for the whole family."[146]

It was still dark when Tonillo showed up at the barn. His son Paco, a boy of about fourteen, was with him. When Tonillo asked if they had slept well, the Father replied, "We've had company." Tonillo was alarmed, until the Father explained that he meant rats.

There was no news of the three who had gotten off at Sanahuja. Perhaps they were resting after a night of walking. To lift their spirits, the Father left a few lines for them at Tonillo's house:

In the mountains of Rialp, November 20, 1937

I imagine you're dead on your feet after a sleepless night. Well, everything worthwhile costs effort. Plus, if you want, not a single step you take will be unfruitful.

All right, enough philosophizing. Take good advantage of the straw—just don't try to eat it, okay?—and sleep soundly, without paying any attention to the troop of rats that will come out to greet you.

As for us, we are doing very well—we're deeply grateful to these good friends here—and are just sorry that our good

[144] See Casciaro, p. 106.
[145] See AGP, RHF, T–04152–IV, p. 4.
[146] AGP, RHF, EF–371118–1.

Madridian friends (José María, Alvaro, and the others) couldn't also come.

Eat well and don't forget about Don Manuel.

The other two send their regards.

> Much love,
> Mariano

Till tomorrow.

P.S. Pedro, see if you can draw a nice picture of the boy who will hand you this note—a picture where he looks dressed up.[147]

Guided by Paco Bach, they set out on a trek to the Vilaró farm. When they were halfway there, dawn began to break through the thick pine trees, but soon they arrived at the farmhouse, which was built on a small elevation affording plenty of visibility—if police or militiamen approached, there would be time to hide. The person running the farm, Pere Sala, was overjoyed when the Father said he was a priest and would like to celebrate Mass. A table was set up in one of the rooms of the house, and they laid out the items they had so carefully put together in Barcelona: hosts, a small crystal glass to serve as a chalice, some small corporals, purificators, a crucifix, a small bottle of altar wine, and a notebook in which the canon of the Mass and several texts for votive Masses had been copied.[148]

They spent the rest of that day hiding out in the barn, and then when night came, they went over to the farmhouse to sleep. But still having received no news of Pedro, Paco, and Miguel, the Father hardly slept a wink. Finally, early the next morning, word came that they had reached Peramola. It was now Sunday, November 21. The Father, wanting to wait for them, put off saying his Mass as long as he decently could, but as it turned out, they showed up in the middle of it. Afterward, they all had breakfast with Pere Sala and his family. The newcomers recounted their adventures, starting with when they had gotten off the bus in Sanahuja. They had had trouble giving the password to the guide, and had gotten lost in the middle of the night, because the guide was a foreigner who was not very familiar with the terrain and who spoke neither Spanish nor Catalan. They had not reached Peramola until the evening of the following day, after walk-

---

[147] See AGP, RHF, D–15323.
[148] See Casciaro, p. 107, and AGP, RHF, T–04152–IV, p. 5.

ing for over twenty hours, and had had to wait at the outskirts of the village until night fell and they could share the barn with the rats. After reading the Father's note, Pedro had made a pencil sketch of Tonillo's son Paco.[149]

Pedro was so exhausted that he could hardly think straight. But despite that fact, and despite the joy they all felt at being together again after all the uncertainties of the previous day, he knew that something was wrong. Here they were, seated at table, enjoying a hearty breakfast: potatoes, peppers, bacon, bread, and wine. "However," Pedro wrote in their journal that day, "we are all like strangers. And the reason is that the Father is worried, and can't hide it. Back in Madrid there is this little group of our people who have not been able to leave . . ." [150]

*   *   *

They were in the barony of Rialp. The area got its name from the Rialb River (the "rivus albus," or "bright river," of Roman times), which picked up the waters of a multitude of small streams before flowing into the Segre River. Peramola and the Vilaró farmhouse lay between these two rivers. The area had many low mountains, whose valleys and spurs were covered with oaks and pines.

In the middle of the afternoon, Pere Sala came to tell them that they would need to get on the move, because they would not be safe staying at the farmhouse. At nightfall, when they had been walking for a quarter of an hour, the parish church at Pallerols came into sight. On a smooth hillside, between the trees, they could make out the silhouette of a tower and a small church, with a large rectory attached.[151] The nearby houses and stables looked abandoned. The rectory door had no lock. Following Pere Sala, the fugitives climbed the stairway to the second floor, where their guide lit a candle. They were in a large, nearly empty room that had several doors and a balcony looking out over the valley. Pere opened one of the doors, and

---

[149] See AGP, RHF, T–00159/1, p. 36, and Casciaro, pp. 108–109.

[150] AGP, RHF, D–15323.

[151] The church at Pallerols was so small that it looked like a chapel, but it was a parish church, dedicated to Saint Stephen. This church is mentioned in the record of the consecration of the Cathedral of Seo de Urgel, which took place in 839. The construction of the building existing in 1937 took place at the end of the eighteenth century, and probably involved an expanding of the two naves of the early Romanesque church. The rectory was connected to the sacristy, by means of a stairway behind the sanctuary. See AGP, RHF, D–15369.

in the dim light they could make out a small room with a low arched roof. The walls were darkened, the plaster was grimy, and the floor was covered with straw. Air came in only through a small window badly covered with boards. In the flickering light of the candle that little room resembled an oven.[152] This was where they were to sleep that night—after barring the door, their guide advised them.

They followed Pere Sala back down the stairs, into the sacristy, and out into the church. The walls were completely bare. The paintings and statues, the reredos and altars, and even the bells had been ripped out and destroyed in 1936 by militiamen. In fact, not content with mere destruction, they had used their plunder to make a bonfire outside.[153] By the light of the candle the Father went looking for a memento to take with him, for the purpose of making reparation for such savagery, but could not find anything.

They went back up the stairs and into the rectory living room, and Pere took his leave, saying that he would come get them in the morning. They dined on bread and sausage that they had been given at the farmhouse, and after a short get-together and the praying of the Preces of the Work, they set up for the next day's Mass on a table in the living room. Then they retired to the room with the vaulted ceiling, put out the candle, and stretched out on the straw. Juan and the Father were at the back of the room; Paco and Pedro were very near them; and José María and Miguel were near the door.[154]

They had been lying there for a while when Paco heard the Father stirring and breathing in an agitated way. Juan got up and opened the little window to let in some fresh air, but this did not calm him. As Paco relates it, "There came from the Father first a low, pain-filled moan, and then a soft sobbing that grew in intensity." [155]

---

[152] Pedro Casciaro's impression was that they actually were in "a kind of oven," and Francisco Botella describes it as similar "to the oven in my grandfather's country house." See Casciaro, p. 110, and AGP, RHF, T–00159/1, p. 35.

[153] On August 24, 1934, Father Joan [Catalonian for "John"] Porta Perucho came to Pallerols as pastor. Ordained in 1931, he had been serving at Peramola. In 1977 he was still tending Pallerols and other places nearby. As Father Porta testifies, as of 1934 he was living in the rectory next to the church. His parish was made up of twenty-five families.

In 1936 the feast of Spain's patron saint, Saint James, was celebrated in the parish with all solemnity. This was July 25. A few days later, groups of militiamen came and burned the parish books and the vestments. A month later they returned and destroyed the altars, statues, and altarpieces, making a large bonfire outside the church. See AGP, RHF, D–05429 and D–15369.

[154] See AGP, RHF, T–00159/1, p. 38.

[155] Ibid.

Juan spoke to the Father very quietly, but the whispering woke Pedro, and he asked Paco what was going on. Paco, in turn, asked Juan, but Juan did not reply.

The Father was now sobbing more deeply and his breathing was becoming more labored. Then Pedro clearly heard Juan say something that stunned him: "We're taking you to the other side, dead or alive." He could not believe that one of the Father's sons would speak to him in that way. Frightened and unable to bear any more, he prayed to our Lady and fell into a deep sleep.[156]

Only Juan knew about that terrible trial of October 15 in Barcelona, when the Father had left the house determined to return to Madrid by train because he couldn't stand the thought of going against the will of God by leaving abandoned the people there. Only he knew that this trial had come back, this time even more forcefully. But for all of them, it was one long night of suffering. "Never," says Paco, "had I seen anyone cry like that. And never since then have I seen anything like it. It was an anguish that made him shudder, a deep pain that made him tremble. It lasted a long time, hour after hour, until dawn. Long enough to burn itself into my memory forever."[157] Toward the end of that anguished night, the Father asked our Lord for a sign that he was doing God's will, not his own.[158]

At dawn the Father grew quiet, but kept praying, asking our Lady's intercession for the calming of his conscience, still suffering from the fear that he was not doing God's will. He got up to open the little window, and he looked exhausted and sorrowful, but calm. He told Juan that he would not be celebrating Mass—he was thinking that to do so might be contrary to the will of God—and asked him to take everything off the table in the living room. Then he rapidly disappeared down the stairs to the sacristy.

After a short time he reappeared in the living room, radiant with joy. Every trace of the exhaustion had disappeared from his face. In his hand he held something made of gilded wood. It was a rose.

"Juan," he said, "take good care of this. And get everything ready. I'm going to celebrate Mass."[159]

---

[156] See Casciaro, p. 110, and Alvaro del Portillo, *Sum.* 913.

[157] AGP, RHF, T–00159/1, p. 38.

[158] See Alvaro del Portillo, *Sum.* 913, and Ernesto Juliá Díaz, *Sum.* 4244.

[159] See AGP, RHF, T–00159/1, p. 39, and Casciaro, p. 111. One of the five altars of the church was dedicated to Our Lady of the Rosary. The altar and the statue of Our Lady of the Rosary were burned in 1936. Father Porta does not remember exactly what the

*   *   *

Whether out of humility, embarrassment, or respectful reticence, Juan left no record of what had happened during that night. Skipping it entirely, he just entered this in the journal:

> The next morning, Monday the 22nd, there occurred an event that, in order to avoid sensationalism and any attempt at interpretation, I think I should recount in very few words. . . . He left the room and apparently went down to the church. A little while later he returned. His worry had disappeared. Although he didn't say anything to this effect, he looked like he was very happy. He was holding a gilded rose. We all got the impression that the rose had a deep supernatural significance. He kept it with very special care, and we packed it carefully in the knapsack, together with the items used to celebrate Mass.[160]

Pedro explains his own reticence in this way: "I should be sorry for having slept so soundly that night, but to be perfectly honest, I am really glad I did. I have to admit that whenever I sensed something extraordinarily supernatural happening in the life of the Father, I felt a special fear. For me it was very traumatic." [161]

Out of humility, and also because he wanted to keep his children from dreaming of "miracles" instead of exerting human effort to solve problems, the founder was never inclined to say much about that rose. "It's a wooden rose, gilded, nothing important," he told a group in 1961. "It was in the Catalonian Pyrenees that I first held it in my hands. It was a gift from our Lady, through whom all good

---

statue looked like, but he does say that it was similar to the one at Puig, which dates back to the beginning of the seventeenth century. A little over three feet in height and of gilded wood, it shows our Lady with a symbolic rose in her right hand. See AGP, RHF, D–05429 and D–15369.

In 1758, on the occasion of the annual visitation by the bishop, this note was entered in the registry book of the diocese of Seo de Urgel: "Pallerols. Altars: Besides the main altar, this parish has a chapel, as big as the parish church, with an altar dedicated to Our Lady of the Rosary, decently furnished with altar stone, cross, candlesticks, and other prerequisites." (See AGP, RHF, D–05429 and D–15369.) In 1980, people in Pallerols still remembered that the altar of Our Lady of the Rosary had a reredos in which Mary's image was surrounded by roses. (See AGP, RHF, T–04152–IV, p. 7.)

[160] AGP, RHF, T–04152–IV, p. 7.
[161] Casciaro, p. 112.

things come to us. How many times we have addressed her as Mystical Rose! But I no longer call to mind that event. I just remember to give thanks to the Lord for his mercy toward the Work and toward myself."[162]

The first time he related explicitly and in writing what had happened in Rialp was on December 22, 1937, in an entry in his personal journal.[163]

The wooden rose is now in the headquarters of Opus Dei in Rome.

7. *"Saint Raphael's Cabin"*

That same morning (Monday, November 22), after Mass, they met up with Manolo and Tomás, who had left Barcelona the day before. (Tonillo had put them up at his house, saving them from a night with the rats in the barn at Peramola.) They breakfasted together at the Vilaró farmhouse, enjoying sausage and fried potatoes, washed down with a good jug of red wine. In the evening their guide, Pere Sala, led the fugitives back into the woods. About a half hour's walk past the Pallerols church, they reached a spot with a lot of pine trees, near the top of a hill. There, built into the hillside, they found a log cabin with a pine-branch roof. The "hut," as Pere Sala called it, was behind a rise and not visible from the valley. From up there, however, one could see far and wide, all the way to Mount Aubens in the north.[164]

---

[162] AGP, P03 1978, pp. 254–55, and P03 1982, pp. 27–28. On another occasion he said, "When I was eaten up with worry, stuck in the dilemma of whether or not I should try to cross over, during the Spanish Civil War, from the one zone to the other—in the midst of that persecution, when fleeing from the communists, I received another external sign: that wooden rose. That's how it is. God treats me like a hapless child who needs to be given tangible signs, but in an ordinary way" (*Meditation* of 14 Feb 1964).

When typing out the journal of those days' events (*Road to Freedom*: AGP, RHF, D–15323), the founder added on a separate sheet, in handwriting, "journal entry missing." And in fact, in the manuscript, Pedro Casciaro (it being his turn to write the notes) ends his narration of the breakfast at the Vilaró farm by noting the time and signing off ("9:15 on November 21, 1937. —P."), and immediately after that we read, "Monday, November 22. The day started off cloudy . . ." There is no mention of what happened on either the day or the night of Sunday, November 21. The founder quietly called attention to this fact with his laconic "journal entry missing."

[163] "Then, in response to an interior inspiration that compelled my will, I said to our Lord, 'If you are happy with me, let me find something,' and I thought of a flower or some other wooden adornment from the destroyed reredos. I went back into the church (I was in the sacristy), and looked in the same places I had looked before, and right away I found a rose of gilded wood. I was very happy and grateful to God, who gave me that consolation when I was so worried about whether Jesus was happy with me or not" (*Apuntes*, no. 1439). See also Alvaro del Portillo, *Sum.* 913.

[164] See AGP, RHF, D–15323, fol. 18v, p. 16, and AGP, RHF, T–04152–IV, p. 8.

The Father christened it "Saint Raphael's Cabin," in honor of the archangel, a patron of the Work and of wayfarers. Obviously there had already passed through it an expedition that included a priest, because there was an altar made of boards and pine branches. The new arrivals added a vertical pole on which to hang a crucifix.

The following day, very early in the morning, the Father said Mass on that rustic altar. Afterward, some of them went down to the Vilaró farmhouse in search of breakfast. Others went to a nearby spring to fetch water. There they ran into Peramola's parish priest, Father Josep Lozano. He had been living in the forest for fifteen months, hiding in a shack with his brother.[165]

To lift their spirits, the Father jovially announced that there would take place on that day a general constituent assembly, opening in mid-morning under his honorable presidency. Its purpose was none other than to distribute duties and set a schedule for work and for the norms of piety. The following schedule was unanimously approved:

Rise 7:00
Prayer 7:15
Holy Mass 7:45
Preces
Breakfast and Joyful Mysteries of the Rosary
Gathering wood, walking, etc.
Angelus and Sorrowful Mysteries 12:00
Lunch, visit to the Blessed Sacrament, walk
Prayer and reading the paper 5:00
Conference 7:00
Supper and Glorious Mysteries
Examination of conscience, resolutions, retire 10:00
D.O.G.[166]

---

[165] See AGP, RHF, D–15323, fol. 21, p. 17. Tomás Alvira writes, "The Mass was a dialogue. I'll never forget those Masses: the forest as our church; the celebrant utterly recollected, praying very slowly, putting his whole heart and soul into what he was doing, and above all at the moment of the Consecration. Hundreds of birds, waking with the sun's first rays, sang incessantly, contributing to the enchantment of our Father's Masses in the Rialp forest. Always he set aside a consecrated host, which was borne devoutly by one of us." See AGP, RHF, T–04373, p. 7.

Father Josep Lozano i Eritjà had been named pastor for Peramola in March 1936. Joaquim, the brother he was hiding out with, was also a priest. On January 24, 1939, Father Josep was killed by retreating republican soldiers. See Jesús Castells Serra, *Martirologi de l'Esglesia d'Urgell, 1936–1939* (Seu de Urgel, 1975), p. 104.

[166] See AGP, RHF, D–15323, fol. 20v, p. 17. "D.O.G." stands for "Deo omnia gloria" ("All the glory to God").

They soon came to appreciate the importance of that schedule as a mainstay of discipline, a defense against idleness and discouragement, and a means of bolstering optimism.

Also specified were each person's chores: cleaning, fetching water, preparing meals, writing in the journal. . . . Pedro used one of his free periods to describe in detail his adventures of November 19 and 20. In their forest shelter, after a decent meal, those long hours of exhausting night-time hiking had taken on a certain lyrical aura. "The moon," he writes, "rose almost full, casting its serene silver light over mountains and valleys." However, he quickly comes down to earth. "Here, with a pen," he says, "it is very easy to climb up and down mountains and traverse valleys, but reality is usually not that poetic." [167]

By now those back in Madrid had learned that they had left Barcelona on the 19th. "How wonderful! The youngsters on the other side will be able to receive the grandfather's care. How much I miss them!" wrote Isidoro to those in the consulate. And then he added, "How much *we* miss *you*! There are only nine of us on this side, and most of us are separated. If only those of us who are here could live as a family!" [168]

Even though Saint Raphael's Cabin was bathed in sunlight and pine-scented breezes, life there was far from comfortable. At night the cold was intense, and of course a fire was out of the question. And despite all their efforts, they could not rid the cabin of lice, a legacy of previous tenants. To wash, they had to go to a pool of clear water halfway between the Vilaró farm and the cabin. While some, the Father first of all, bathed in the frigid waters, "I didn't dare," confesses Pedro. "That whole scene reminded me of the martyrs of Sebaste." [169]

Still, they were happy—very happy. For the first time they could sing without fear. At one of the get-togethers, the Father gave the first performance. He sang, among other things, a Christmas carol he had

---

[167] AGP, RHF, D–15323, fol. 12, p. 13.

[168] AGP, IZL, D–1213, 289. The ones still in Madrid were Isidoro (who was in charge in the absence of the Father), José María González Barredo and Alvaro del Portillo (in the Honduran consulate), Vicente Rodríguez Casado (in the Norwegian consulate), Miguel Bañón Peñalba (who was living with his mother), and Eduardo Alastrué (who stayed in a boardinghouse and never went out).

Enrique Espinós Raduán, a cousin of Paco Botella's, was doing military service outside Valencia, and was going through a hard time because of the recent death of his father. Rafael Calvo Serer was assigned to the International Brigades and was at this time hospitalized on account of an ulcer, and José María Hernández Garnica (Chiqui) was doing military service in Baza, in the province of Granada.

[169] AGP, RHF, T–04197, p. 23. See also AGP, RHF, T–04152–IV, p. 9.

learned from the nuns at Santa Isabel—one with simple words and a catchy tune.[170]

The food left a lot to be desired. Although it was enough to get by on, it was too little for undernourished young people with hard mountain climbing ahead. They bought it at the Vilaró farmhouse or at the nearby Ampurdanés farm, and almost always it was sausage and potatoes. On the third day, the Father gave their "protector" a piece of his mind about how scanty and expensive the food was. Pere Sala became angry. But the Father ended the discussion with a few affectionate words to calm him down, and from then on, the food improved noticeably in both quality and quantity.[171]

Nature protected them on all sides. Secure in the thick forest, with no fear of being surprised by militiamen, with no one but friendly country people around them, the refugees could move about freely. On Tuesday, November 23, as we have mentioned, they ran into Peramola's priest, Father Josep, while fetching water from the spring. From him the sacristan's son learned that the cabin had new tenants, and at three that afternoon the boy came over and invited them to have coffee in a nearby cabin. And except for the Father and Pedro, they all went. With the sacristan were the tailor and other pillars of the Peramola community. Amid songs and good cheer, everyone got coffee, a cigarette, and a small glass of brandy.[172]

Thursday, November 25, was an eventful day. At five in the morning, Pere Sala came to the cabin and told them that on the next day there would be leaving an expedition with very expert guides who were asking 2,000 pesetas a person—in "good" bills, of course. The Father, without even getting into the question of money, told him that they already had a commitment (to Mateo the Milkman) and would not consider changing it. Pere left, and they went back to bed.

Then, just after they got up, there showed up Father Porta, the pastor for Pallerols. The Father had asked Pere to introduce him to other priests in hiding, in case he could be of service to them. After spending some time with Father Porta, he said Mass, at daybreak. At mid-morning, Father Josep, Peramola's priest, came over and invited them all to join him in picking mushrooms. In the forest there were

[170] Casciaro, p. 123.
[171] See AGP, RHF, D–15323, fol. 27v, p. 22.
[172] See AGP, RHF, D–15323, fol. 22v, p. 19.

lots of them, both edible and poisonous—several varieties of each type. Father Josep showed them how to distinguish the edible ones, and they ended up with so many that, after sautéing them with garlic in a frying pan, they could not eat them all.

In the afternoon their "protector" arrived with food borne by his mule. With him was the pastor of the church at Pons, who was living in hiding at the Vilaró farmhouse. He spent a long time with the Father. Among other things, he had come over to let them know that the expedition Pere had told them about that morning was just a ploy to get more money.

Friday, before they were up, they got a pleasant surprise: a visit from Mateo. He brought word that the expedition would be leaving Monday. The Father and Pedro then went down to the Vilaró farmhouse. Pedro finished some sketches of the parish church of Pallerols, while the Father, accompanied by the priest from Pons, examined its interior. They could not find the slightest trace of the carvings and altarpieces destroyed by the revolutionaries.[173]

The next day, Saturday, word came in the morning that the departure had been moved up and they would be leaving that afternoon. After eating, they made their visit to the Blessed Sacrament, which the Father was still keeping in the metal cigarette case, in his shirt pocket, under the turtleneck sweater. As the afternoon progressed, they were joined by other people who had been hiding out in that area and who would be part of the expedition. Finally, Pallarés (the aforementioned friend of Mateo's son) arrived, and he told them that the guides were now demanding 2,000 pesetas each, instead of the agreed-upon 1,200. This caused quite a disturbance, there now being not enough money to go around. Fortunately, Mateo then arrived and offered to intercede personally with the guides. But just when everything seemed to be taken care of, the Father's affection for his children got the better of him. Pedro, who knew what he was going through, tells what happened:

> He came up with an idea for how to get rid of the predicament, an idea it was just like him to come up with: he would go back to Barcelona, without money. There he would ask for

---

[173] See *Apuntes*, no. 1440 (22 Dec 1937), and AGP, RHF, D–15323, fol. 31, p. 25. The pastor of the parish in Pons was Father Nicolau Auger Ortodó (1865–1942). See Castells Serra, p. 311.

a loan and return to Madrid. (He can never get Madrid off his mind—our people there, and especially Alvaro.) This idea, as one might well imagine, sent Juan into a fit. He used very strong language and then, under his breath, said to him some terrible things. Finally the Father gave in and agreed to set out.[174]

8. *Crossing the Pyrenees*

Those who would remain in hiding in Rialp said good-bye to that expedition, which was taking such great risks for a chance at freedom. Much safer, they thought, to stay hidden in the huts. But one never knows what the best solution is. Only a few weeks before the war ended, Father Josep was killed—one more name on the long list of priests killed in the province of Lérida.[175] Had the Father stayed a few days more in Madrid, he might well have been in the room he rented on Ayala Street when a shell exploded there. And a brief delay in leaving the boardinghouse in Barcelona would have landed them all in prison; police acting on a tip came to search it, and Doña Rafaela did spend a month in a *checa*.[176]

It was six o'clock, and already dark, when they left Saint Raphael's Cabin. The sacristan of Peramola led the way. Next came Mateo, and then came the others, trying their best not to fall behind. The leader stepped up the pace. Juan, who was walking next to the Father, heard him arguing with himself, in a low voice, about whether to go on or to turn back. Juan says:

> He couldn't tell what he should do. It was as though he suddenly felt abandoned, left without supernatural help. It seemed to be a trial permitted by God, that made it a tremendous effort for him to go against the grain and get the better of his worries of the moment. I panicked at the thought that he might decide to return. Without hesitation I grabbed his

---

[174] AGP, RHF, D–15323, fol. 33v, p. 27.

[175] The province of Lérida is divided into three dioceses: Lérida, Seo de Urgel, and Solsona. At the beginning of 1936 the diocese of Lérida had 410 priests. Of these, 270 (66 percent) were killed. The diocese of Seo de Urgel (where Pallerols is) had 540 priests; 109 (20 percent) were killed. And in Solsona, which had 380 priests, 60 (some 15.5 percent) were killed. See Montero Moreno, p. 764, and Castells Serra, pp. 304–305.

[176] See AGP, RHF, T–04152–IV, p. 1.

arm. I was not about to let him turn back, and I told him so in very crude, impolite language. I recall it with horror, but it was necessary, because I knew he had decided not to go on and I felt obliged to fight him on that.[177]

"The Father insisted on staying in Peramola to go back to Madrid," explains Pedro. "Juan was walking right behind him, and he responded by saying things like, 'We're taking you to Andorra, dead or alive.' The Father was giving as his reason that he felt so weak he didn't think he could make it on foot all the way to the border."[178]

The episode of the rose had calmed his conscience, but he still felt an overwhelming paternal pull to be with his children. Considering the dangers there, wasn't he more needed in the republican zone? Juan's love-motivated crudeness did a lot to keep him pressing on. As Paco Botella puts it, "Juan's attitude toward the Father was a combination of filial submission and energetic decisiveness."[179]

In pitch-black darkness they made a stop and waited a half hour in the cold. Juan got sick and threw up his supper. The guide returned with rope-soled canvas shoes for those not well shod for this type of walking. (These helped prevent falls and made less noise.) They then continued their trek through dense woods, along treacherous paths. Juan at one point fell and rolled down a hillside, but was not seriously injured. A little before midnight, the guide led them to a cave at the foot of El Corb. The narrow entrance was half hidden by rocks and adobe, and when they got in, they were reminded of the cave of Ali Baba and the forty thieves. It was a deep cave, with many branching caverns. They lit a fire and saw a dirty floor, a smoky roof, rows of racks for a stable, and a stove. Both men and beasts had left traces of nights spent in that shelter.

In the innermost part of the cave, a man was waiting for them— twenty-something, wearing sandals and a corduroy outfit, looking very stern. He said, "Here I'm in charge and everyone does what I say. We walk single-file, no talking, no noise. When I need to let you know something, I'll tell those in front, and it will get passed on back. No one breaks rank, and no one falls behind. If anyone gets sick and can't continue, he stays behind, and if anyone wants to keep him company,

[177] AGP, RHF, T–04152–IV, pp. 10–11.
[178] AGP, RHF, D–15323, fol. 33v, p. 27.
[179] AGP, RHF, T–00159/1, p. 42.

he stays too." [180] Their previous guide called this guide Antonio, but later they learned that this was not his real name.

They lay down and got whatever rest they could, and then, a few hours before dawn, they set out again, climbing a steep footpath. After they had crossed a gorge in the early morning fog, other people joined their line. As day was breaking, they went around a foothill that was thick with pine and oak and descended beside a vigorous waterfall into the ravine of Ribalera.

Father Josemaría prepared to say Mass, although not without the fear that this might provoke some irreverence, since blasphemous comments had been made during the previous night's trek. They were at the foot of a high cliff that sheltered them from the cold wind. At that moment a boy showed up. His name was José Boix Oste, and he had come there from the Juncás farm, which had an arrangement with the organizers of the expedition. He had brought food for the travelers. José also gladly helped set up an altar—a more or less flat stone placed on top of some rocks that had fallen from the cliff.[181]

It was Sunday, November 28. The Father announced to those with them, about twenty people in all, that he was going to say Mass. Some were curious, others excited. Probably none of them had been to Mass since July of the year before. The altar being very low, the Father celebrated the Mass kneeling. Paco and Miguel, kneeling at either side of the altar, held down the corporal so that the hosts would not be blown away. Some of their companions received Communion with great devotion, among them a student from Catalonia who had joined the group the previous night.[182]

José Boix recorded years later that he had found it strange that the priest, right after arriving, would want to say Mass. The boy had gone out on many a morning to meet expeditions of fugitives, and he knew that in many of them there were priests. But, he says, "out of all the others who showed up at that farm in those years, not one was disposed to say Mass." The reverence of the priest moved him deeply. "I think," he adds, "that I saw in action a priest who was a saint." [183]

The student from Catalonia kept a journal of his experiences on the trip. On November 28 he wrote, "Here the most moving event of the

[180] See AGP, RHF, T–04152–IV, p. 11.
[181] See AGP, RHF, T–01440, and T–00159/1, p. 44.
[182] See Casciaro, pp. 116–17.
[183] AGP, RHF, T–01440.

whole trip takes place: Holy Mass. On a rock and kneeling down, almost prostrate on the ground, a priest with us is saying Mass. He doesn't say it like other priests in churches. . . . His clear and heartfelt words penetrate the soul. Never have I attended Mass like today's. I don't know if it's because of the circumstances or because the celebrant is a saint." [184]

After breakfasting on bread and sausage, with a little wine, they tried to sleep as best they could on that rough, uneven ground. At three in the afternoon they were given a little bit of fried rabbit to eat. Then some of them prayed the Rosary. And at four, wrote that day's journal keeper, "we set out again, poorly fed and poorly rested." [185]

The previous treks had been made at night, but the next stage, the climbing of Mount Aubens, was too risky for that—they needed to reach the summit while it was still light. The route began along slopes that were not very steep, though they were thick with undergrowth. But when they had been walking for an hour, they reached a place where it was necessary literally to climb. The guide, Antonio, tried to hurry the stragglers. Tomás Alvira collapsed, exhausted. The guide ordered the others to keep going. If they wanted to reach the summit, he told them, Tomás would have to be left behind. "The best thing," he said, "would be for him to return. Otherwise we'll have to leave him by the wayside." The Father spoke with him and managed to get him to change his mind. Then he encouraged Tomás. "Don't worry," he said. "You'll continue with us, as will all the others, to the very end." ("We were constantly praying to the guardian angels," Tomás recalls.)[186]

The summit turned out to be a plateau covered with spongy vegetation that was delightfully easy to walk on. After crossing it, they began a steep descent through a damp pine forest, by way of logging trails. Falls were frequent, and everyone ended up with bloody hands from grabbing the thornbushes.

When they got to the valley, they stopped for a brief rest. During

[184] See Appendix 3. This student was Antonio Dalmases Esteva, and the original of this "Journal of My Flight from the Red Zone, November–December 1937" is in AGP, RHF, T–08246. Like almost all the others on the expedition (except for the Father's group, which had only a wineskin, filled with sugared wine, and a bottle of brandy), he carried with him a supply of food. Antonio had a lunch box that was filled with chicken legs. "Smart fellow," the Father remarked. "He's found a way to cross a chicken with a centipede." And thus he got nicknamed the Centipede Kid.

[185] AGP, RHF, D–15323, fol. 37v, p. 29.

[186] See AGP, RHF, T–04373, p. 8; AGP, RHF, T–04152–IV, p. 12; and Casciaro, p. 118.

that time, their guide disappeared for a while and then reappeared without saying where he had been. Now, well into the night, in groups of three or four and with great care, they crossed a highway. They regrouped a little past the bridge over the Valldarques River, and then had to wade across the knee-deep Sellent River. After this they still had more than three miles to go, and the guide started getting nervous. The Father could hardly stay on his feet, but he took Antonio by the arm and tried to calm him down. Soon they passed the town of Montanisell and arrived, exhausted, at the last stretch of this stage of the journey. And just then it began to grow light, which was exactly what the guide had feared would happen. The road to the Fenollet house, where they were to spend the day, could be seen from the village of Orgaña, where several guard units were posted.[187]

In the cold light of dawn they entered Fenollet—a country house, with large corrals, hidden among mountains three thousand feet high. As soon as they arrived, the Father gave Communion to his companions, making sure that all the hosts he had brought with him from the Mass in Ribalera got consumed, because they had again heard blasphemies during the previous night.

The guide warned them that they had three days to go, with no chance of getting supplies, and then, after ordering them not to leave the corral they were in, he disappeared. The fugitives made themselves as comfortable as they could amid the stables and sheds, sleeping all morning to the background music of bleating sheep, cackling hens, and tinkling cowbells. Only the Father, who was half awake, was aware of the danger they got into in the middle of the morning, when two militiamen visited the farmhouse and asked the woman who came to the door if she had seen any signs of fugitives. The woman unperturbedly served them some glasses of wine, and they left.[188]

At about two in the afternoon the group woke up, famished. In anticipation of their arrival, the people at Fenollet had slaughtered a lamb the night before, and the food was so abundant and tasty that their guide told Juan Jiménez Vargas years later, "I've forgotten many things, but that meal I will remember forever." [189] The journal keeper of the day also had high praises for the mutton-and-bean dish. (When

[187] See AGP, RHF, T–04152–IV, p. 16.
[188] See AGP, RHF, D–15323, fol. 41, p. 31, and AGP, RHF, T–04373, p. 8.
[189] See AGP, RHF, T–04152–IV, p. 18.

typing up the journal, the Father added, "They certainly charged enough.")[190]

After the meal, while some of the fugitives were taking a siesta, the women of the house (among whom was a nun in hiding) mended their clothes. Seeing how exhausted his companions were, the Father told them to lighten their knapsacks before the next trip over mountains. Some of their belongings were left behind in the corral.[191]

As sustenance for the trek to Andorra, they bought a small cheese, a loaf of bread, and a refill for the wineskin. Shortly after nightfall they set out again, walking single file to Mount Santa Fe, which faces Fenollet. This route to the Pyrenees involves a constant climbing up and down of a mountain range to the right of the Segre River; the valley of this range forms a natural corridor from the barony of Rialp to the foothills of the Pyrenees. Because this strip they would be traversing was only thirty or forty miles from the French border and had the best hiding places, it was closely watched by militiamen.

After a painful climb of more than an hour, they began to descend the northern slope of Mount Santa Fe into the plain where the village of Orgaña is located. The walking was, of course, much easier now, but the barking of the farm dogs was an ever-present danger. Only a few weeks before, as their guide knew only too well, militiamen had been alerted by the dogs that an expedition of fugitives was approaching, and they had opened fire.

After crossing the Cabo River, they began climbing Mount Ares, which is some 4,500 feet high. The ascent, at night, over rough and uneven and steep terrain, in which one didn't know where to set foot, was the ultimate test of physical endurance. The Father, who had gotten hardly any rest at Fenollet because of the exhaustion of the night before, was now panting painfully, his pulse racing. Paco and Miguel helped him climb, at times almost carrying him, while he kept repeating to himself, "Non veni ministrari, sed ministrare." [192] When they got to the top, they rested for a while. A cold wind was blowing, so everyone tried to huddle together around the Father, while Juan gave him a good swig of sugared wine from the wineskin.[193]

---

[190] See AGP, RHF, D–15323, fol. 42, p. 31.

[191] See AGP, RHF, T–04152–IV, p. 18.

[192] "I came not to be served, but to serve" (see Mt 20:28).

[193] "The Father counted his falls: there were many, many!" we read in the journal. To which the Father added, "Always taken with good humor: Twenty-six! Twenty-nine! . . . We were counting them." "Thinking of the apostolic work that awaits us," the

Despite their exhaustion, they set out again. José María Albareda had become dizzy and disoriented, but after a few good swigs from the wineskin, he let himself be led by the hand.[194] Fatigue and the strain of trying to pierce the darkness, of guessing where to set foot by keeping track of the shadows of what lay ahead, caused them to start seeing lights and farmhouses that didn't exist. And if they tried to pray a Rosary, they soon lost count and ended up with mysteries that had in them twenty or thirty Hail Marys. In their heads, the words of their prayers blended with the tune of the Christmas carol the Father had learned from the nuns of Santa Isabel, which goes: "What a beautiful Child Saint Joseph has got. At the sight there comes over me I don't know what." By some strange phenomenon, says Pedro Casciaro, the melody and rhythm of that carol "became an inseparable part of our belabored breathing." [195]

Suddenly, those at the head of the line halted. The guide had disappeared. He soon reappeared with a straggler who had fallen down, half dead, and given up. Antonio, fearing that it might be a trick done to get them caught by the police, or that he might be found by one of the border guards, forced this man at pistol point to rejoin the group.

Finally, as dawn was breaking, the guide brought them all into a livestock barn that was hidden in a high meadow. Numbed by the cold, dead tired, having almost no food or wine left, they rested there for that day—Tuesday, November 30, 1937.[196]

It was getting dark when the guide returned and they resumed their trek. From the meadow they descended, by a path, to the banks of a stream which runs into the Segre River. In the woods they came across quite a few tree stumps, and, as on the night before, there were a lot of falls and bruises.

In 1938, when typing up the journal of their passage through the Pyrenees, Father Josemaría was deeply touched at the thought of those days when he was so physically broken down and there were so many slips and falls at night in the mountains. Where the journal

journal keeper continues, "he takes it with peace and joy. But it is a hard beating." (See AGP, RHF, D–15323, fol. 44v, p. 36.) That climb remained so vivid in the Father's memory that in the 1940s, when staying at La Pililla (Piedralaves), a house near the mountains, he said to Paco Botella, "Since that climb, Paco, I've lost all my desire for mountain climbing" (AGP, RHF, T–00159/1, p. 46).

[194] See AGP, RHF, T–04152–IV, p. 20.
[195] Casciaro, p. 123.
[196] See AGP, RHF, T–04152–IV, p. 20.

keeper says, "We hold onto one another, it's the only way to walk," Father Josemaría adds this comment: "And this is the exquisite charity that those sons of my soul showed me. They—Juanito, Paco, Miguel—lifted me off the ground and kept me from many a fall, as one lifts a small child that is trying to take its first steps." [197]

When they got near the Segre River, they turned away from the stream and skirted the base of Mount Creueta. Then they crossed the Pallerols River and came up to the highway to Seo de Urgel. Antonio had learned from locals that militiamen had been watching the highway closely during the day. Quickly and silently they crossed to the other side of the highway, and then walked another three miles, skirting the village of Pla de Sant Tirs and turning north. [198]

During one of their rest stops, the guide went to a farmhouse to refill the wineskins, and there he encountered another group of fugitives and three or four men with large bundles on their backs. From the fragrance emanating from their cargo, which contrasted sharply with that given off by the hikers' clothes, it was obvious that these were smugglers carrying perfumery products. Along with these inoffensive aromatic articles, they also carried a good supply of weapons.

In the wee hours of the morning, the expeditionaries set out to follow the course of a stream that led directly north. The going was very rough. For several hours they walked alongside the stream—and sometimes *in* it. Father Josemaría's boots became soggy, making walking in the cold and dark even more unpleasant, and certainly not good for someone susceptible to rheumatism. [199] When they reached the village of Arabell, they left the stream and used their remaining energy to climb a rise, from which they could make out Seo de Urgel in the distance. At daybreak, protected by dense thickets, they made camp near a farmhouse. The expedition had been reinforced the previous night; it now numbered about forty people.

December 1 dawned cold and crisp, with a cloudy sky. Damp and stiff with cold, they hardly touched their meager provisions, and spent the day huddled in their blankets—three blankets among the eight of them.

"In these days full of trouble, fatigue, and hunger," writes the journal keeper, "it is very difficult to do our norms. But we do them. If

---

[197] AGP, RHF, D–15323, fol. 45, p. 37.
[198] See ibid., and also AGP, RHF, T–04152–V, pp. 4 ff.
[199] See Casciaro, p. 122, and AGP, RHF, D–15323, fol. 44v, p. 36.

we cannot dedicate the usual time to them, we shorten things; but we do them." [200] They did the norms—the periods of mental prayer, the Rosary, the aspirations—on the move, between falls, as best they could. In their daytime hiding places they gathered strength for the next leg of the journey. Father Josemaría slept fitfully, usually only half asleep. On Tuesday, November 30, the journal keeper writes, "The Father did not sleep at all today"; and on the next day, "The Father did not sleep." [201]

He spent these hours of wakefulness in prayer.[202] During the treks he usually refused the sugared wine Juan offered him to give him strength, on the pretext that others needed it more than he did. During the rest periods he gave his blanket to others, and when food was distributed he made sure the others got more.[203] It is amazing that his constitution didn't completely give out before they reached the border.

By now they were close to Andorra, and this did rekindle their hope of getting through the final stage, although they were too exhausted to show it. In midafternoon the sky grew dark. Some snowflakes were fluttering indecisively when the guides told them they had to get going again. They finished eating the bit of bread that still remained, while Juan distributed the few lumps of sugar he had left.

They headed north, climbed Cerro el Tosal, and came down into the valley of Civís, their descent slowed by the loose rocks underfoot and by dense undergrowth that tore clothes and skin. "I don't know what the roads of hell are like, but it's hard to imagine them being worse than this," writes the journal keeper of the day. "Today's descent makes those of previous days seem like something to laugh about." [204]

According to the guides, detachments stationed in Argolell had been patrolling the area all day. The fugitives spent two hours lying in bone-piercing cold along the banks of the Civís River before the guides gave word that it was safe to resume walking. Toward midnight, they

[200] See AGP, RHF, D–15323, fol. 44v, p. 36.

[201] See AGP, RHF, T–04152–IV, p. 17. When typing out that entry for November 30, the Father omitted the word "today," evidently to indicate that his wakefulness had been chronic. See AGP, RHF, D–15323, fol. 44v, p. 35, and fol. 46, p. 39.

[202] "He slept hardly at all, when we were resting in those corrals and caves," says Pedro. "I got the impression that he was doing this to mortify himself and to pray more. Although I found it moving, I never could understand all that, and because of the affection I had for him, I wanted to prevent it" (Casciaro, p. 122).

[203] Casciaro, p. 122.

[204] AGP, RHF, D–15323, fol. 47v, p. 40.

quickly crossed the river and began climbing the steep mountain looming before them. When they looked back at the river, they seemed to be standing on a precipice. At about three in the morning they reached the summit and began descending into a wooded area near Argolell. There, for a half hour that felt like forever, they stayed hidden behind tree trunks before being told to start walking again. They passed a house that had a light on, and dogs began to bark. Then they crossed another stream and climbed the hillside in front of them.

As soon as the expeditionaries realized they were in Andorra, they began to disband and scatter. The Father's group, after walking along for some time, decided to stop and wait for daylight, so they could get their bearings. Sitting on the ground, wrapped in their blankets, they prayed to the guardian angels that their guide would show up. A few minutes later they heard someone whistling. Going in the direction of the sound, they came upon a campfire, with some members of their expedition seated around it with the guides and the smugglers. In a spirit of camaraderie, they offered the newcomers a place at the fire and some bread and sausages. The guide, Antonio, told them his real name was José Cirera.[205]

9. *In Andorra*

Before taking leave of one another, these fugitives all prayed together a Hail, Holy Queen. Then, in their separate groups, they made their way toward Sant Juliá de Loria. The Father's group was praying the Rosary when, from the still distant town, there came the sound of pealing bells. Suddenly they felt that indescribable sensation of having gotten back their freedom and being free of fear. "Deo gratias! Deo gratias!" the Father kept saying. It was the morning of December 2, 1937.[206]

At the entrance to the town, French gendarmes stopped them to take down the names of these "political refugees." They had breakfast in a café: milk, cheese, and white, spongy, still-warm bread. Then they asked if the church could be opened for them. It was the first church they had seen since 1936 that had not been desecrated. They made a visit to the Blessed Sacrament, but Father Josemaría could not say Mass because of the liturgical norms on fasting that were then in effect.

[205] See AGP, RHF, D–15323, fol. 50, p. 43, and AGP, RHF, T–04152–IV, pp. 11 and 29.
[206] See Casciaro, p. 125.

By midmorning they were already settled in the Hotel Palacín of Les Escaldes, which was only a short distance from Andorra's capital, Andorra la Vella. In the evening they all went there together to send a telegram to José María Albareda's brother, who lived in Saint-Jean-de-Luz, asking him to arrange for the required vaccinations and for the photos needed to obtain safe-conduct passes. Suddenly Father Josemaría's heart leaped. Walking toward them, right out there on the street, was a priest in a cassock. For his part, the priest, Father Luis Pujol Tubau, saw approaching him six or eight very badly dressed young men whose shoes were falling apart. "From that group," he recalls, "came forward someone who with open arms greeted me, saying, 'Thanks be to God—a priest!' "[207] That embrace was the beginning of a lasting friendship. And Father Josemaría took advantage of that first encounter to find out where he could say Mass the next day.

After sending the telegram and taking care of some other business, he wrote a note to the Honduran consul, Pedro de Matheu Salazar, as a way of getting word to the others in Madrid:

Escaldes (Andorra), December 2, 1937
My dear friend:
    Before returning to the Pacific, where I will see José Luis, I have taken advantage of an opportunity to visit this pleasant principality of Andorra, since the situation in Spain doesn't allow me to travel to Madrid. Tomorrow I will leave, with my brother Ricardo and the rest of the family, for Saint-Jean-de-Luz. Give my regards to Mila and Consuelito.
                                              Best wishes,
                                              Josemaría[208]

Then they returned to their hotel. After dinner they intended to say a Rosary before going to sleep, but, says the day's journal keeper, "I don't think any of us even managed to start it. I'm amazed that we didn't fall asleep taking off our shoes." [209]

The next morning, the Father celebrated Mass in the church of Les Escaldes—not "stealthily and in secret," as in Madrid and Barcelona,

---

[207] See AGP, RHF, T–00675, p. 2, and T–04152–IV, p. 30. Since 1930 Father Pujol had been the acting archpriest in Andorra la Vella. He was ordained in 1925 and was now thirty-six.
[208] AGP, RHF, EF–371202–1.
[209] AGP, RHF, D–15323, fol. 51v, p. 45.

but with the decorum that the liturgy calls for. There were many things and many people to remember during that Mass. The celebrant was overwhelmed by the thought of those he had left behind. Before beginning the Mass he asked his companions to pray for them, and during the Mass he paused for a long time at the Commemoration of the Living and at the Commemoration of the Dead. In the Commemoration of the Living he also remembered the bishop of Vitoria, it being the feast day of the bishop's patron saint (Saint Francis Xavier), and after Mass he sent him congratulations by telegraph.[210]

The telegram they were looking for from Saint-Jean-de-Luz arrived that day. Signed by José María Albareda's sister-in-law, Pilar, who was the Marchioness of Embid, it read: "Jacques Not will come to pick you up tomorrow"—and had been sent the night before. All afternoon they waited impatiently for the car, but it did not arrive. Who did show up was José Cirera, the guide. He had been unable to return to Spain. Had there been a delay of only twenty-four hours, he told them, the expedition would have failed, because heavy snowstorms had closed the mountain passes. He also told them that on their final trek he had had to change the route, because police were waiting for them at one of the fords they would have been crossing.

That day the Father wrote to Isidoro:

Escaldes (Andorra), December 3, 1937
My good friend:
I am quite upset at your failure to answer the last two letters I wrote you: the first in October, from Prague, and the second from Paris, in the middle of November.
Today, taking advantage of having come, on a sports trip with some friends of mine, to this principality of Andorra, I send you this brief note to ask that you write me at my cousin's house. In case you don't remember his address, here it is: "Señor Alvarez / Hotel Alexandre / Saint-Jean-de-Luz / France." You can just put my name at the top of the letter—he'll forward it to me if I'm not there. You know how much I like to travel!

[210] The telegram said, "Javier Lauzurica. Bishop, Vitoria. Remembering you on your saint's day. Managed to escape yesterday with eight of my people. Leaving tomorrow for Saint-Jean-de-Luz. José María Escrivá." See AGP, RHF, D–15323, fol. 52, p. 45; AGP, RHF, EF–371203–2; and Casciaro, p. 126.

My family is in excellent health and happy as always.

Affectionate greetings to your brothers and sisters, and of course to the grandmother, uncle, and aunt.

Love,

Mariano

P.S. I'll be leaving for my cousin's house (in Saint-Jean-de-Luz) today or tomorrow—he's sending a car. Best wishes.[211]

The events of those days are recorded in the journal in detail: "December 4, 1937 (Saturday). It is seven in the morning, and it is snowing as we begin today's activities. The landscape around us, being all covered in snow, now exhibits another aspect of its beauty. The high peaks, clothed in white, have a more elegant, less rustic beauty." [212]

It was half a mile from the hotel to the church where the Father celebrated Mass. He and his companions were joined by five other young men who had been part of the expedition. Afterward Father Luis invited him over for breakfast and then took him to visit some Benedictines from Montserrat who were staying at a school named Meritxel.

Meanwhile, it didn't stop snowing. Obviously, the expedition had by a miracle beat the snow. But now everyone was saying that the En Valira pass to France was closed. This was a serious setback. Was the car waiting on the other side of the pass?

They devoted the afternoon to correspondence. In Spanish, in French, in English, they wrote to relatives, friends, and acquaintances to communicate to them—with great discretion, if they happened to be in the republican zone—that they had gotten out of there. Tomás Alvira and the Father sent to their friend Pascual Galbe Loshuertos, the judge in Barcelona, a brief message that could not put him in any danger: "*Un abrazo*. Josemaría — Tomás." [213]

They also used this delay to bring the account of their crossing of the Pyrenees up to date. During the nocturnal treks they had been able to jot down only the briefest of notes. Now everyone helped flesh them out.[214]

---

[211] AGP, RHF, EF–371203–1.
[212] AGP, RHF, D–15323, fol. 54, p. 47.
[213] AGP, RHF, T–04152–III, p. 165.
[214] See AGP, RHF, T–00159/1, p. 53.

As a result of those marathon hikes in torn-up shoes, Manolo's feet were in such bad shape that he could not walk. Even to get from Andorra to Les Escaldes, he had to go in a car. As for Father Josemaría, his hands were sore and alarmingly swollen. Juan treated them with salicylate, thinking that the swelling was a symptom of rheumatism, but after two days, seeing that it had increased, he took a closer look and discovered a lot of small splinters from the thornbushes the Father had grasped for support. Juan carefully extracted about thirty.[215]

For five days they were at the mercy of the weather. Their hopes kept rising and falling. The snow went on, and the car sent by Albareda's brother did not arrive. December 6 dawned cold but clear, and at midday word came that they could leave the next day by bus. But at suppertime they were informed that so much snow had accumulated in the pass that it would be two or three days before they could leave. The next day a villager who had gotten through the pass brought them letters written in Hospitalet, the French village where their car was waiting; it turned out to be not an auto from Saint-Jean-de-Luz but a taxi from Hospitalet. But in any case, it had not been able to get through because of the snow.[216]

If the villager who brought the letters had been able to get through the pass, why couldn't they? Why would the direction make any difference? They also thought about renting a tractor, but the one available wasn't working. They consulted the gendarmes, and were told that the pass could not be gotten through. Perhaps, they thought, this was the time to get some help from higher authorities. Staying with them in the Hotel Palacín were Colonel Boulard and some other officials whom the French Republic had sent to defend the principality against possible incursions by Spanish militiamen. "Monsieur le Colonel" expressed sympathy for these political refugees whom he had been seeing and greeting every day in the dining room, but when they asked him to help them get into France, he suavely advised them, given the circumstances, not to try to do this.[217]

The journal-keeper wrote:

---

[215] See Casciaro, p. 126, and AGP, RHF, D–15323, fol. 63v, p. 54.
[216] See AGP, RHF, D–15323, fol. 64v, p. 55.
[217] See Casciaro, pp. 126–27.

After having kept trying all day long (impolitely, the Father says), we have shut up. We are now ready to wait until the pass is opened. But let it be soon!

We're gathered in the dining room, near the heater, and thinking of our companions still in the red-zone Calvary. Every time he thinks about that, the Father gets very sad. We have to believe this forced wait is a very good thing, since our Lord has arranged things this way.[218]

During those days Father Josemaría said Mass in various places: in the chapel of Meritxel School, in Les Escaldes' parish church, and, on the feast of the Immaculate Conception (December 8), in the chapel of Holy Family Convent. (This, coincidentally, was the day the nuns renewed their vows. It was a simple ceremony in a simple chapel.) From the prolonged stay forced on him by the snow, there also came memories of delightful get-togethers with Father Pujol. Writing a month later in Pamplona, in his personal journal, he says: "Walking along the river this evening, I thought of our little evening walks in Andorra, from the capital to Las Escaldes, after get-togethers with the good archpriest."[219]

Father Luis Pujol was, as we have mentioned, the pastor and acting archpriest of Andorra la Vella (which had a population of a little over one thousand), and right away he and Father Josemaría had hit it off. The very first day that Father Josemaría said Mass in the capital, Father Luis invited him to his home, a comfortable house on the main square. There he had his office—a small room with a desk, vestry cabinets, and a bookcase, plus an armchair and three or four other chairs. Adorning the walls were pictures with scenes from the lives of Saint Ignatius and Saint Francis Xavier, together with a crucifix. The desk always had on it a pile of letters to be relayed from one zone of Spain to the other. Father Luis would open a letter, transfer it from one envelope to another, and affix a fresh stamp. In some special cases, he passed along messages in letters of his own. But the snow had interrupted this work of his, too.[220]

"Today," Pedro writes in the journal on December 5, "the archpriest did not receive us in the usual room; after we passed through what

---

[218] AGP, RHF, D–15323, fol. 65, p. 55.
[219] *Apuntes*, no. 1463 (2 Jan 1938).
[220] See AGP, RHF, D–15323, fol. 59, p. 50.

looked like a fairly good-sized dining room, he led us into the kitchen. The fact of being received in the kitchen, near the warmth of the chimney, has in Andorra, in the house of the archpriest, all the significance of being offered a seat in the presence of the king." [221]

They were very grateful for Father Luis's hospitality. Along with the cups of coffee and the glasses of anisette that he served them, he would also give them updates on current events, especially those in Andorra. There was, for instance, the arrival of "Monsieur le Colonel." There was also the rebellion of some Andorrans who, incited by Spain's former Minister of Public Education, Fernando de los Ríos, refused to give the bishop of Seo de Urgel his traditional "present": a tribute consisting of a few roosters, several hams, a dozen cheeses made of sheep's milk, and 1,500 pesetas. [222]

The invitation was repeated the following day, and they spent an agreeable afternoon chatting. As they returned to the hotel, along the banks of the snow-swollen Valira River, an icy wind took their breath away.

On the feast of the Immaculate Conception, the archpriest invited Father Josemaría to dinner, and during that dinner he asked him about their crossing of the Pyrenees. Many fugitives had arrived in Andorra, each with their own story and tragedy, but what struck the Andorran priest more than any of those stories was the silence of Father Josemaría. "What impressed me the most," he says, "was to hear him say, with regard to everything that happened in those days in the mountains, 'I suffered so much that I've resolved not to mention any suffering.' And so it was, because neither then nor later did I hear him say anything about the torments he underwent." [223]

That evening the Father told his companions about the menu the archpriest had treated him to: hors d'oeuvres, cannelloni, calf's head, cutlets, pastries. The journal keeper does not mention that, after such

[221] AGP, RHF, D–15323, fol. 59, p. 50.

[222] This rebellion began during the time that Fernando de los Ríos was Minister of Public Education, that is to say, between December 1931 and July 1933. Since the beginning of the war, the bishop of Seo de Urgel, Justino Guitart, had had other problems. On July 23, 1936, he had to leave Spain, taking refuge in Andorra. He stayed there until August 13, and then left for France because his life was in danger. See Castells Serra, pp. 265–67.

[223] AGP, RHF, T–00675, p. 5. In Pamplona a month later, on January 2, 1938, in the privacy of his personal journal, the Father writes: "My feet still bother me, although the swelling is almost gone. It's not from the cold; it's an effect of the harsh treks of our escape" (*Apuntes*, no. 1463). See also AGP, RHF, D–15323, fol. 66v, p. 57.

a long period of hunger, Father Josemaría had such a shrunken appetite that he hardly wanted to eat.[224]

News came that the pass would be open December 10. A bus would leave at 7:30 in the morning. They rose at six, went to Las Escaldes' parish church for Father Josemaría's Mass, and had a quick breakfast. An awkward moment came when they went to pay their hotel bill. Eight people, for eight days at 20 francs a day, plus ten percent, came to 1,408 francs. They had to haggle over this, because the little money they had left was going to have to last them till they got back to Spain. They were so poor that they hadn't even been able to buy shoes in Andorra. The bill ended up reduced to 1,300 francs, to the satisfaction of the guests and the hotel owner. While the account was being settled, the travelers donned all their warm clothing and stuffed newspapers in their socks and around their legs for protection against the cold.[225]

At eight o'clock, in brilliant sunshine, a truck left with twenty-five passengers in improvised seats. Many of these people had been part of José Cirera's expedition. As they passed the hamlet of Encamp, the motor began to sputter, and they had to get out. After walking beside the truck for a while, they got back in and reached Soldeu. The vehicle could go no farther, and it was eight miles to the border at Pas de la Casa. At first the snow was pleasant to walk on—a nice thin, crunchy layer. But little by little it got deeper, ending up knee-high. The melting snow soaked their shoes and made liquid paste out of the newspapers that were supposed to protect their feet.

Waiting at Pas de la Casa was a bus with fourteen seats. The Spanish fugitives squeezed into it. A French brigade had cleared the highway from the pass to Hospitalet, where the customs station was located. They presented their documentation and were granted permission to cross into France, but only for a stay of twenty-four hours. Nevertheless, the Father decided to stop in Lourdes before going on to Hendaya.[226]

The taxi driver whom Albareda's brother had contracted with had an old Citroën—big, but not for a passenger load of eight adults. The slowness of the border police and the driver's evident hesitation delayed their departure, and by the time they left Hospitalet it was growing dark and foggy and they were shivering with cold, even

[224] See *Apuntes*, note 1064 (written by Bishop Alvaro del Portillo).
[225] See AGP, RHF, D–15323, fol. 69, p. 58.
[226] See AGP, RHF, D–15323, fol. 71, p. 61, and AGP, RHF, T–00159/1, p. 53.

though they were blanketed with newspapers and crammed together in the car. As they passed through Tarascon, Father Josemaría tried to cheer up his companions by recalling Alphonse Daumet's comic character, Tartarin, that brave hunter of lions. He is the hero of several adventure books, one of which is *Tartarin de Tarascon*.[227]

They slept in the Hotel Central at Saint Gaudens, and the next morning, December 11, they squeezed back into the Citroën. It was still very early when they reached Lourdes. Everything was closed except the basilica's crypt. In the sacristy Father Josemaría spoke in Latin with the priest on duty, and the priest allowed him to say Mass, although he still seemed taken aback by his shabby appearance. The Father asked Pedro to serve the Mass, since he would be celebrating it for the intention of Pedro's father, who was in a difficult political situation and estranged from religious practice. Pedro followed the Mass with great emotion, as he himself relates: "This manifestation of our founder's priestly zeal and affection for my family so moved me that all other recollections of his first Mass in Lourdes have faded from my memory."[228]

The Father celebrated Mass at the second side altar on the right side of the nave, near the entrance to the crypt. Afterward they had breakfast at a café and then prayed a Rosary at the grotto, thanking our Lady for her protection. "We remembered, one by one, all those who remained behind in the Red zone and all those we hoped to find as soon as we got to the other zone," says Juan Jiménez Vargas.[229]

They reached Saint-Jean-de-Luz at six in the evening. José María Albareda's brother was waiting for them. It was already dark when they crossed the international bridge back into Spain.

---

[227] See Casciaro, pp. 128–29, and AGP, RHF, T–04152–IV, p. 32.
[228] AGP, RHF, T–04197, p. 50. See also T–00159/1, p. 54, and T–04373, p. 10; and Alvaro del Portillo, *Sum*. 915.
[229] AGP, RHF, T–04152–IV, p. 33.

3

Interlude in Burgos (1938–1939)

1. Resuming the "Catherines"

Father Josemaría was eager to begin again to record the events in his turbulent life, including the day he entered the Nationalist zone. He tells what happened in the first few entries of a new notebook of his personal journal.[1]

> Pamplona, December 17, 1937: Today, before beginning my retreat, I am—with the help of the notes I've been taking since the 11th of this month—going to start up again the journal, the Catherines.[2]

He starts with the events of his first week in the nationalist zone.

> December 11: A lot of emotion, very justified, on crossing the international bridge. Fervent prayers, when the Spanish flag came into view. . . .
>
> To be able to enter our own country, we need somebody to vouch for us. I tried to call His Excellency the bishop of Vitoria. "I'm sorry, Bishop Lauzurica is in Rome." Some ladies who work at the phone company catch on to my little problem—and they turn out to be friends of my mother's family. They offered to vouch for me, and invited me to their home. I thanked them, but didn't accept.[3]

He tried another avenue:

---

[1] He began this notebook (the no. 8 duplicate) on December 11, 1937, and ended it on January 23, 1939. When the war ended, he found the old notebook no. 8, in Madrid, and he went back to putting his entries in it, starting on April 13, 1939. See *Apuntes*, note 1034. (For the *Apuntes*, "no." refers to a journal entry, by Father Josemaría, whereas "note" refers to an explanatory comment made by Bishop Alvaro del Portillo.)

[2] *Apuntes*, no. 1396.

[3] *Apuntes*, no. 1397.

I then called His Excellency the bishop of Pamplona: a very warm welcome. How good this holy bishop is! He immediately asked to be connected by telephone with the military headquarters in Fuenterrabía and vouched for us. He wants to see me tomorrow, in Zumaya, and tells me, with genuine affection, that I must come with him to his residence.[4]

The Father's group all spent the night at Fuenterrabía's Hotel Peñón. In the morning he said Mass for them, and one by one they took off. José María Albareda went home to his family in Saint-Jean-de-Luz. Manolo stayed in Fuenterrabía, also with family. Tomás Alvira made preparations to leave for Saragossa. The others, all being of military age, presented themselves to the authorities at Camp Loyola in San Sebastián. Father Josemaría, meanwhile, wrapped his few belongings in a newspaper, tied it with a string, and left the package with the hotel concierge. Then he left for Zumaya, a vacation resort near San Sebastián, for his meeting with the bishop. When he got there he was told that the prelate was in Zarauz, a village nearby. So off he went to meet him there. Still wearing the clothes and boots he had worn on the long expedition, he finally met up with Bishop Olaechea in the house of the Marquis of Warros, where a party celebrating Italo-Spanish solidarity was underway. "The bishop," he writes, "gave me a hug and greeted me very cordially, in the midst of all these people, and introduced me to the Italian ambassador. They invited me to the banquet."[5] Just then he spotted someone he had given spiritual direction to in Madrid. The two of them went to a restaurant to have lunch and to chat.

He spent the afternoon with the bishop, and on the way back to San Sebastián, the bishop made Father Josemaría promise to come to his residence in Pamplona for a few days' rest. In San Sebastián, members of the Teresian Association found him a boardinghouse. He said Mass for them the following day, offering it for their founder, Father Pedro Poveda, who had been martyred the year before.

December 13: I offered the Mass for Father Pedro. Besides offering suffrages for his soul (holy, even without the martyrdom), I asked him to intercede for me.

[4] *Apuntes*, no. 1398. The bishop of Pamplona was Marcelino Olaechea.
[5] *Apuntes*, no. 1400 (12 Dec 1937).

The Teresians offer me money. I ask for some toiletries for those with me. They said they would buy us four combs, four pairs of scissors, and soap.[6]

The members of the Teresian Association gave him clothes and some used shoes, which allowed him to get rid of those tattered boots from his passage through the Pyrenees. The shoes came at a very welcome time, because the next week was filled with social engagements and apostolic activity. He made visits to some relatives of Don Alejandro Guzmán, the Aguilar de Inestrillas family,[7] the Count and Countess of Mirasol,[8] the Guevara family,[9] the Bernaldo de Quirós and Vallellano families,[10] and the de Cortazar family. He also visited María Machimbarrena, her sister the Marchioness of Los Alamos,[11] and María Luisa Guzmán, three of the ladies who had accompanied him years earlier to meet with the undersecretary of the Ministry of Justice and Ecclesiastical Affairs in the time of the monarchy, with a view to obtaining a stable ecclesiastical position in Madrid.[12] While he was visiting the family of the Count of Mirasol, a niece of Luz Casanova, the foundress of the Foundation for the Sick, suddenly announced that she had a vocation to the Work. Father Josemaría took this calmly.[13]

---

[6] *Apuntes*, no. 1403. The affection that Father Pedro and Father Josemaría had for one another did not interfere with their respective foundational vocations. "Father Pedro had no influence on the Work of God," we read in *Apuntes*, no. 1510 (25 Jan 1938). "I met him when I had already been doing this work for a long time. Although, he was never my spiritual director, (for years now, that has been Father Sánchez) God did unite us in such a way that he was my friend, my brother, and my son, as I was for him. . . ." See also *Apuntes*, note 1140.

[7] The Count of Aguilar de Inestrillas, was Agustín Carvajal de Quesada. His wife, Doña Mercedes Guzmán O'Farrill, was a stepsister of Don Alejandro Guzmán and also a cousin of Mercedes Reyna O'Farrill, one of the first Apostolic Ladies. who died in January 1929. (For more on the Congregation of Apostolic Ladies of the Sacred Heart of Jesus, see vol. 1, pp. 188–89, 192, and 208–209, of this biography.)

[8] The Count of Mirasol was Don Rafael Gordon. He was married to Doña María Rodríguez-Casanova, sister of the foundress of the Apostolic Ladies.

[9] The Marquesa de Guevara was Doña María del Perpetuo Socorro Travesedo. She was married to Don Florentín Rodríguez-Casanova, brother of the foundress of the Apostolic Ladies.

[10] The Countess of Vallellano was Doña María de la Concepción Guzmán O'Farrill, another stepsister of Don Alejandro Guzmán and cousin of Mercedes Reyna O'Farrill.

[11] The Marquis of Los Alamos del Guadalete was Don José Ramón de Goytia, and their home in Madrid was on Covarrubias Street, next to the Foundation for the Sick. The couple's friendship with the founder dates from that time.

[12] See *Apuntes*, no. 192 (20 Apr 1931), and vol. 1, pp. 253–54, of this biography.

[13] See *Apuntes*, no. 1410 (15 Dec 1937).

But he had not crossed the Pyrenees to live a high-society life in the Basque Provinces. During these visits he inquired into the whereabouts of individuals with whom he had been doing apostolic work. With a telephone call to Bilbao, he found two young men who had lived at the Ferraz Street residence: Carlos Aresti and Emiliano Amann Puente. In San Sebastián he met with Vicente Urcola and the family of Joaquín Vega de Seoane.[14] And as one person led to another, he soon began reassembling his apostolic-work card file.

In the entries for December 16 we read, "I still don't feel well, but I try to hide it. . . . I said Mass for Victor Pradera. Delighted not to receive stipends. Lord, now that I am truly poor, let's see what you do with your little donkey." [15]

His clothing still left much to be desired. Some photos were taken in San Sebastián, and, as he himself could see, he looked really bad with that emaciated face right above the too-big collar of that blue sweater from the days in Rialp. No one had yet offered him a cassock. In these circumstances, he had the sudden impulse to renounce completely the receiving of stipends, his only foreseeable source of income. His thought was that the priests of Opus Dei should be detached from everything, including ministerial income, offering a holocaust by way of poverty. This was something he had been thinking about for a long time. One day when he was feeling worried about the lack of money, he meditated on the words of Psalm 55:22, "Cast your burden on the Lord, and he will sustain you." [16] He came out of that meditation determined to put himself completely in God's hands, to carry out this resolve fully.[17]

On December 17 Father Josemaría left for Pamplona. And once again his guardian angel gets mentioned in his journal. "At 5:30 exactly (the time set the night before), the little watchmaker wakes me up. The alarm clock they gave us at the boardinghouse didn't go off." [18] The borrowed car he went in had to stop twice because

---

[14] See *Apuntes*, no. 1406 (13 Dec 1937).

[15] *Apuntes*, nos. 1411 and 1412. Victor Pradera was a politician whom the People's Court of San Sebastián had condemned to death for being a monarchist and supporting the uprising. Sentence was handed down on September 5, 1936, and he was shot the next day. His widow and son were present at that Mass said for him on December 16 by Father Josemaría. See Gonzalo Redondo, *Historia de la Iglesia en España, 1931–1939*, vol. 2, *La Guerra Civil, 1936–1939* (Madrid, 1993), pp. 44–45.

[16] In 1 Peter 5:7 this is paraphrased as, "Cast all your anxieties on him, for he cares about you."

[17] See *Apuntes*, no. 1428 (20 Dec 1937), and also *Apuntes*, note 1065.

[18] *Apuntes*, no. 1414.

of the snow, but evidently this did not dampen his spirits, because when he entered the province of Navarre, he began singing softly a local song to Our Lady of Puy in Estella, a town near Pamplona.[19]

When he finally arrived, half frozen, at the bishop's residence, it was lunch time. During the meal, he told the bishop that he had come with the intention of making a retreat. That was fine with the bishop, but he did not want him to leave the residence, so he provided him with some books for meditation and made him the gift of a copy of Father Carmelo Ballester's bilingual (Latin/Spanish) version of the New Testament.[20]

Running through his mind before his retreat was a question: What had happened to his sons? Juan and Miguel had been assigned to Burgos, but he had heard nothing from Pedro Casciaro and Paco Botella. Finally, in the middle of that afternoon, they called to tell him they were both at the garrison in Pamplona.

Having obtained the address of the vicar general of the diocese of Madrid (who was then residing in Navalcarnero, a village near Madrid but in the nationalist zone), he wrote him:

Pamplona, December 17, 1937
Monsignor Francisco Morán, Navalcarnero
My dear and esteemed Vicar:

After a thousand adventures gotten through by the palpable protection of my Father-God, I managed to escape from the Red camp. . . . I have taken advantage of the warm hospitality of my good friend the bishop of Pamplona. At present I am staying at his residence; tomorrow I will begin a retreat here on my own.

If my Vicar does not tell me otherwise, I will assume that he is happy with my immediately resuming (*fulfilling the holy will of God,* in accord with my specific vocation) my work with the souls that you know about, and that are scattered through-

---

[19] See *Apuntes*, no. 1425 (19 Dec 1937).

[20] Father Carmelo Ballester Nieto was the provincial of the Vincentian Fathers. Shortly thereafter he was named bishop of León, and later he was transferred to Vitoria. Father Josemaría first met him on December 23, 1937. He was very grateful for the gift of that edition of the New Testament. "This is a beautiful edition the bishop has given me," he says. "I rejoice, and I kiss this book, in gratitude to our Lord God and to that blessed Vincentian Father" (*Apuntes*, no. 1423: 19 Dec 1937).

out the nationalist zone. By the way, all, without exception, have been heroic!

I ask my esteemed Vicar to let our beloved Prelate know that, in the midst of so many tribulations, we did not fail to pray daily for His Excellency.

Father, assuring you of my esteem and love, I ask for your blessing.

Josemaría Escrivá[21]

He also wrote to Josefa Segovia, one of the members of the Teresian Association, a letter of condolence (mixed with joy) about their recently martyred founder, Father Pedro Poveda. "My heart won't let me wait any longer," he says, "so here are a few lines, about a father and a brother. What joy, after the sorrow of losing him and many tears, to know that he goes on loving us from heaven! This was precisely the topic of one of our last conversations." [22]

On December 18 he wrote in his journal, "From now on, since I've brought them up to date, these Catherines will have more life," and then he copied into the notebook his retreat plan. The first point was "Purity of intention and the aim of this retreat." Under this heading he wrote:

> I'm going to be very brief in these retreat notes. I bring to this retreat nothing but a most intense desire to *be a better instrument* in the hands of my God, in order to make his Work a reality and extend it throughout the world, as he wants. The *immediate and specific aim* is twofold: (1) interior, purification: renewing my interior life; and (2) exterior, to consider the real possibilities for the Work's apostolate, the means and the obstacles.[23]

After a thorough self-searching, he had to acknowledge before God that "amid so many and such great miseries" he did indeed find "weakness, smallness," but "never a deliberate desire to offend God." [24]

---

[21] AGP, RHF, EF–371217–1.
[22] AGP, RHF, EF–371217–2.
[23] *Apuntes*, nos. 1419–1421.
[24] *Apuntes*, no. 1426 (19 Dec 1937).

During that retreat he "prayed like a child, unburdening himself as a child." He wept with "tears of sorrow—of Love-sorrow" for his lack of response to grace. Examining his conscience, there rose to his view failures and omissions—and, the mercy of God. "I find myself overcome by tears: so close to Christ, so many years, and such a sinner! The intimacy of Jesus with me, his priest, makes me break out in sobs." [25]

But those sobs got in the way of his meditations. "*The prayer of Christ*: I got off the topic. Crying, imploring, imploring and crying—that has been my meditation. Lord, peace!" And when he thought of the example of the saints, tears again welled up in his eyes. "I cried—I am a crybaby—reading a life of Don Bosco, which I asked for this morning from the bishop's secretary. Yes—I want to be a saint. Even though this affirmation, so vague, so general, usually strikes me as foolish." [26]

Well, neither could he contain himself at the time of confession; once more he was overwhelmed with lively sentiments of the sorrow of Love. "I went to confession to Father Vicente Schiralli and the tears streamed down my face in front of that holy priest. A crybaby, truly a crybaby. But these blessed tears, a gift of God, bring me a deep joy and comfort I don't know how to explain!" [27] It got to the point where "this outpouring of my tenderness toward Christ was worrying me." [28]

On one of the retreat days, December 22, in the chapel of the bishop's residence, the vicar consecrated some chalices that were going to be sent to army chaplains. When the ceremony was over, says Father Josemaría, "I stayed behind in the chapel for a few moments by myself, and I left a kiss on each chalice and paten, so that my Lord will find it waiting the first time he comes down to those sacred vessels. There were twenty-five in all, a gift from the Diocese of Pamplona for the front." [29]

It was snowing. The cold penetrated to the bones. The meditation on the final judgment again brought tears to his eyes and prompted resolutions.

---

[25] *Apuntes*, no. 1423 (19 Dec 1937). See also *Apuntes*, no. 1422 (19 Dec 1937) and no. 1444 (23 Dec 1937). "Love-sorrow" ("dolor de Amor") was a favorite expression of his, meaning sorrow born of love for God, or perfect contrition.

[26] *Apuntes*, no. 1437 (22 Dec 1937) and no. 1431 (20 Dec 1937).

[27] *Apuntes*, no. 1439 (22 Dec 1937).

[28] *Apuntes*, no. 1444 (23 Dec 1937).

[29] *Apuntes*, no. 1441. See also *The Way*, no. 438.

A lot of coldness. At first, the only thing shining was the childish desire that "when my Father-God has to judge me, he will be pleased." Then, a strong jolt—"Jesus, tell me something!"—repeated many times, full of sorrow for my inner coldness. And an invocation to my Mother in heaven: "Mama!" And to the guardian angels, and to my children who are already enjoying God in heaven. And then, lots of tears and cries . . . and prayer. Resolutions: "To be faithful to the schedule, in my ordinary life"; and, if my confessor allows this, "To sleep only five hours, except on the night of Thursday into Friday, when I won't sleep at all." Specific and small, these resolutions are, but I think they will be fruitful.[30]

During this retreat he resumed his old penances having to do with food, sleep, and everything else—all the things he used to do before the revolution. He was thinking that this retreat, compared to earlier ones, did not deserve to be called rigorous. But then again, "I couldn't have made a rigorous retreat. One tempered by the charity of the bishop of Pamplona, yes. God, my Father, always arranges things in a maternal way."[31]

Bishop Olaechea engaged him in friendly conversation at mealtimes, and when on December 20 the apostolic delegate, Archbishop Hildebrando Antoniutti, came to visit, Bishop Olaechea asked Father Josemaría (who was still wearing the blue sweater and the corduroy pants from the trek through the Pyrenees) to sit at the right of his illustrious guest.[32]

Regarding the work he wanted to "immediately take up" after the retreat, he wrote: "I should do everything possible to see our fellows often, and keep up a discreet correspondence with them (since mail is censored). And if the war drags on and the retaking of Madrid is

[30] *Apuntes*, no. 1429 (20 Dec 1937).

[31] *Apuntes*, nos. 1433 and 1434 (21 Dec 1937).

[32] Archbishop Antoniutti had arrived in Spain in July 1937, as the delegate from the Holy See on a fact-finding mission to nationalist Spain. On September 7, 1937, Pope Pius XI put him in charge of negotiations between the Holy See and the nationalist government in Salamanca (as apostolic delegate). In May 1938 his role was raised to that of a papal nuncio. See Redondo, *Historia*, vol. 2, pp. 339–41 and 470–72; and Fernando de Meer Lecha-Marzo, "Algunos aspectos de la cuestión religiosa en la Guerra Civil (1936–1939)," in *Anales de Historia Contemporánea*, no. 7 (1988–1989), pp. 120–21.

delayed, I should set up a house—a provisional center—where they can all go, when on leave." [33]

On Christmas Eve, José María Albareda came to Pamplona with good news: those in Madrid now knew about the crossing into the nationalist zone. They had gotten the first postcards sent from Andorra to the consul and to Isidoro. And on the very day they received them, Isidoro had sent to Albareda, in Saint-Jean-de-Luz, this letter for Father Josemaría:

> December 7, 1937
> My dear friend José María:
>
> So that this time you won't complain about my tardiness in writing you, I am answering by return mail sent to the beautiful villa where you are spending your vacation, resting from your work in Paris.
>
> Everyone in my family is doing fine. I have little Chiqui in the south now, for the time being; he will be back soon. In spite of the harsh winter we're having, the grandmother and the uncle and aunt are doing great. I write often to my sister Lola; it's likely that her cousin will come live with us one of these days.
>
> How are your children?
>
> Hoping that your vacation goes well, and sending greetings from all the family, affectionately, your good friend,
>
> Ignacio[34]

Father Josemaría's idea of setting up a provisional center in Burgos had by now already become a firm intention. On the evening of Christmas Day, he dined with his sons who were then in Pamplona: José María Albareda, Pedro Casciaro, Paco Botella, and José Luis Fernández del Amo, a young fellow assigned to the same garrison as Pedro and Paco. They had to open a center in Burgos, he said after dinner. Then and there, they started making plans for the oratory. José Luis promised to do the design for the chalice, which Albareda would then have made by a silversmith in Saragossa. On December 28 the Father writes in his journal: "I bought an altar stone, at the chancery office. In the afternoon, with Fernández del Amo, I went to the silver-

[33] *Apuntes*, no. 1445 (23 Dec 1937).
[34] AGP, IZL, D–1213, 293.

smith where they will make the candlesticks, the cross, etc., for the oratory in Burgos, if this becomes a reality." [35]

It was almost the end of the year. When Father Josemaría mentioned that he was thinking of leaving, Bishop Olaechea jokingly answered, "You have to stay with me for thirty years. Don't even talk about leaving." A few days later, when he brought up the subject again, the bishop took a different approach. "He got angry. He told me that if I go, I have to return soon. And he said he doesn't want me to leave here before they've made the cassock he wants to give me." [36]

On December 29 the tailor came. "January 4: They brought me the cassock. I had asked the tailor not to make it too tight; now I'm swimming in it. He's left room for the eighty pounds I lost." [37] Father Josemaría also needed a hat. Removing the tassel from it, the bishop gave him his own to use until the one he had ordered came. And still not admitting defeat, the bishop also kept insisting that his guest stay and spend his birthday there, January 9, for which he would give him a party. To all these urgings Father Josemaría invariably replied, "The bishop is tired of working, and I'm tired of resting." [38]

The number of names and addresses in his card file was steadily increasing. By letter, by telegram, by telephone, he contacted people who had asked admission to the Work or had been on the verge of joining just before the outbreak of the civil war, and many young men who had spent time at the Ferraz Street residence. [39] Before the year ended, he had communicated personally with all of his sons in the nationalist zone, as he happily informed Ricardo Fernández Vallespín.

> Dear Ricardo,
>
> At last! What a joy to receive your letter! . . .
>
> How many fruitless attempts to get news about all of you! As soon as we crossed the border, the inquiries began. And

---

[35] *Apuntes*, no. 1454. By the beginning of February the chalice was already in the hands of the founder. See AGP, RHF, EF–380207–1. For more on the Saint Raphael work, see vol. 1, pp. 367 and 431–32, of this biography.

[36] *Apuntes*, no. 1455 (29 Dec 1937) and no. 1449 (24 Dec 1937).

[37] *Apuntes*, no. 1465.

[38] *Apuntes*, no. 1457 (30 Dec 1937) and no. 1466 (5 Jan 1938). At the bishop's insistence, he did upon leaving accept 100 pesetas; he had to, in order not to offend the bishop.

[39] In the correspondence of this period appear mentions of Pepe Isasa Navarro and Jacinto Valentín Gamazo, both of whom were killed in battle. There are also letters to José Arroyo López, Miguel Sotomayor y Muro, Enrique Alonso-Martínez Saumell, Joaquín Vega de Seoane, and others.

from the 11th to the 31st, when your letter arrived, an eternity
of twenty days!

Grandfather says that he is very grateful to God, because he
has managed to locate all his grandchildren.[40]

Getting letters to and from Isidoro by way of France was working
well. Considering the wartime conditions, there were no serious de-
lays or mishaps, which was a great consolation to those in both zones.
On the subject of the relief he felt at having news of everyone, the
Father opened his heart to one of his sons in the nationalist zone.

Today I wrote to my poor sons in Madrid, and to the grandmother and my brother and sister. From them, we've already
received five letters, the last one dated January 26. They are
completely up-to-date on our family's situation. It's a pity
that you yourselves hadn't worked out some such system of
communication! Of all the terrible things we suffered, the
worst was not having any news of you when we were in that
Red hell. Our relatives and friends who have not been able to
escape the Marxist tyranny, we have already relieved of that
pain. I think we've written them more than ten times since we
got free.[41]

On January 7 Father Josemaría left for Vitoria. There he was received with great affection by Bishop Javier Lauzurica, the apostolic
administrator of the diocese. They discussed a matter of conscience
that he had come to consult about. Next morning, he left for Burgos.

2. *Burgos*

Juan Jiménez Vargas and José María Albareda were waiting for him in
Burgos. Albareda was living on the city's outskirts—on a street that

---

[40] AGP, RHF, EF–371231–3. He told Isidoro Zorzano the same thing, in a letter dated
December 29 and written in English, with the help of someone who lacked full command of the language. "All my children are very well. In a short time I shall have a
proper house, I think in the town where my grandmother Florencia was died. In my
new house, Sir Emmanuel will have a magnificent room." (His grandmother Florencia
died in Burgos. And that last sentence, of course, refers to the beautiful oratory he is
hoping to have in the "house" there.) See AGP, RHF, EF–371229–3.
[41] AGP, RHF, EF–380204–1.

took its name from a small Romanesque church (Santa Clara)—in a family-style boardinghouse where all the guests sat at the dining room's one table. Apart from that boardinghouse, there was not much to choose from by way of accommodations. Since the start of the war, the population of Burgos had doubled, now reaching about sixty thousand. Burgos was the seat of the government of the nationalist zone and of some of its administrative departments. The city's few hotels and all of its major buildings had been taken over by civil and military authorities. Also located in Burgos was the Madrid diocese's Central Board for Worship and the Clergy, although Madrid's vicar general was in Navalcarnero and its bishop, Leopoldo Eijo y Garay, was usually in Vigo.[42] Its strategic position made Burgos a good place for the apostolic center the founder envisaged.

Right away he started working on this. First with Juan, who was about to leave Burgos to join a unit at the Teruel front. "Juanito spoke with me at length about matters of the Work," he notes in his journal.[43] Among those in the nationalist zone, Juan was the best equipped to lend a hand in the responsibilities of governing the Work.

On January 9, Father Josemaría celebrated his thirty-sixth birthday. He wrote to all his sons a long letter which began:

> Circular Letter, January 9, 1938
> In the name of the Father and of the Son and of the Holy Spirit, and of Holy Mary
> May Jesus bless my sons and keep them safe.
> The Lord also watched over me, safeguarding me from death, which more than once seemed certain. He rescued me from the land of Egypt, from the Red tyranny, despite my sins and surely because of your prayers, so that I might continue to be head and father of his chosen ones in this Work of God.

---

[42] Bishop Leopoldo Eijo y Garay had managed to escape from Madrid at the outset of the revolution. Finding in Father Casimiro Morcillo a man he could trust, he appointed him "Vicar General for Reorganization" and asked him to set up in Burgos, with local offices in other provinces, a "Central Board for Worship and the Clergy." The purpose of the board was to reestablish contact with the priests and faithful of the diocese of Madrid, and to collect funds and liturgical objects. On the organization of the Madrid diocese during the war, and on the functioning of the "Provisional Board for Worship and the Clergy for the Diocese of Madrid-Alcalá," see José Luis Alfaya Camacho, *Como un río de fuego: Madrid, 1936* (Barcelona, 1998), pp. 197–247.

[43] *Apuntes*, no. 1474 (8 Jan 1938) and no. 1573 (4 Jun 1938).

My plan is to visit all of you, one by one. I will try to make this a reality as soon as possible.

Until that moment (which I am so looking forward to), I am sending you, in this circular letter, advice and encouragement and the means that are needed not only to persevere in our spirit but to sanctify yourselves by carrying out our discreet, effective, and courageous apostolate, so similar to that of the first Christians: what a blessed labor of selection and confidence!

With naturalness, as the savory fruit of your interior life, renew your silent and effective mission for the glory of our God—*Deo omnis gloria!*

Nothing is impossible. *Omnia possum. . . .* Could you ever forget our ten years of consoling experience? Let's go, then! God and daring![44]

Looking forward to getting to speak individually with each of his sons, he now reminds them of the fundamental practices of the interior life and gave guidelines for their apostolic work. He also gave useful advice for overcoming wartime obstacles: write to him, study a language, find some kind of professional work, come to Burgos when one gets a pass. . . . He puts himself entirely at their disposal, this being his job as their Father: "If you need me, call me. You have the right and duty to call me. And I have the duty to come to you by the quickest means of transportation."

He concludes with an announcement:

And now, *an important matter*:

For some time we have felt the need to include a petition "pro Patre" in the official prayer of the Work. Beginning next February 14—a day of thanksgiving, like October 2—we will say in our Preces, after the "Oremus pro benefactoribus nostris," "Oremus pro Patre," and then, "Misericordia Domini ab aeterno et usque in aeternum super eum: custodit enim Dominus omnes diligentes se" (May the mercy of the Lord always be upon him; for the Lord watches over those who love him).

[44] AGP, RHF, EF–380109–1. "Omnia possum" is the beginning of the Latin for "I can do all things in him who strengthens me" (Phil 4:13).

Know that you are, to use Saint Paul's expression, my joy and my crown. I'm depending on you. Be faithful!

Your Father sends you his blessing.

Mariano

From San Miguel de Burgos, January 9, 1938[45]

The next day, January 10, he went to the residence of the archbishop of Burgos to request ministerial faculties. Outside, he ran into an old acquaintance from Madrid, a priest who knew a number of the priests in the Albás family, and their conversation briefly took his mind off what people had told him about the archbishop's difficult temperament. Not that he was too worried about this; he had, after all, been well recommended by Bishop Olaechea, and Bishop Lauzurica had taken the trouble to call the archbishop on his behalf. However, when he entered the building, he did notice something strange about the atmosphere there. The place seemed cold and deserted; no one was walking around or waiting to be received.

Then Archbishop Manuel de Castro y Alonso appeared in the corridor, and Father Josemaría heard someone announce, "Escrivá is here."

Father Josemaría entered the visiting room and handed the archbishop the letter from Bishop Olaechea.

"Wait, I'm going to get my glasses," the archbishop said.

In a moment he returned, looking not very friendly. He became engrossed in reading the letter, and although the bishop had sprinkled it with pleasant remarks, he never blinked. When he had finished, he looked at Father Josemaría over his glasses and said sharply, "I don't know this Work."

Father Josemaría tried to explain briefly what the letter had already said about the aims and activities of the Work.

"There are no university students here; I have more than enough priests; I do not give you faculties," was the blunt reply.

"If my Lord Archbishop will permit me . . ."

"Yes, I permit."

"It is true that there aren't any university students here, because all the young men are at the front. But since Burgos is the center for all activities, there are always university students coming through here."

---

[45] AGP, RHF, EF–380109–1.

"I have them very well taken care of. I don't need you." [46]

Thus the visit ended. Father Josemaría thought it could easily have been a theatrical sketch entitled "Interview of a Sinful Priest with His Reverence the Archbishop of Burgos." Obviously he would need to consult again the bishops of Pamplona and Vitoria and try to obtain the faculties by some different approach. Before the month was out, the bishop of Vitoria, en route through Burgos, got the matter taken care of. When Father Josemaría went to see the archbishop again, the prelate was all smiles. "Burgos is a good place for you," he said. "Stay in Burgos. Go to the office and they will give you full faculties." [47]

Next he needed to find a suitable confessor. On January 11 he was introduced to a paralyzed priest, Father Saturnino Martínez, and on that very day he asked this priest to be his confessor. "He understands me perfectly," he says in his journal. It is not hard to see why he hit it off so well with Father Saturnino:

> Our conversation made me very happy because he praised the angels so highly. And he even shares my view that we priests, by reason of our ministry, have not only a guardian angel but also an archangel. I left his house with a deep joy, entrusting myself to the Little Watchmaker and to the archangel. And I felt sure that even if I don't really have an archangel at my side, Jesus will end up sending me one, so that my prayer to the archangel will not be futile. Out on the street, I became a child again and tried to decide what name I should give him. It sounds a bit ridiculous, but when one is in love with Christ, nothing is ridiculous: I named my archangel "Amador." [48]

Since he no longer accepted stipends, Father Josemaría was free to offer his Masses for the needs of the Work and for his family. As an exception, on January 17 he offered his Mass for himself and his own intentions:

> I celebrated the holy Sacrifice for myself, a sinful priest. How many acts of love and faith! And in the thanksgiving after

---

[46] See *Apuntes*, nos. 1476 and 1477 (10 Jan 1938), and also AGP, RHF, EF–380110–2 and EF–380110–3.

[47] See AGP, RHF, EF–380206–1 and EF–380206–2.

[48] *Apuntes*, no. 1480 (11 Jan 1938). (Amador = "one who knows how to love.")

Mass, brief and filled with distractions as it was, I saw how much my children's perseverance (and, now, even their earthly life) depends on my faith and my love, on my penance, my prayer, and my activity. Blessed cross of the Work, that is carried by my Lord Jesus—him!—and me! [49]

For his penitential practices Father Josemaría needed a modicum of independence and freedom of movement. "I would like to have a room for myself alone," he reflects in his journal. "Otherwise it's not possible to live the life that God is asking of me." That life consisted of sleeping on the floor and for only five hours a night (except for Thursday nights, when he did not sleep at all), going without some meals, and using the disciplines (something hardly possible in the close quarters of a boardinghouse). "By the way," he notes, "I could tell a very funny story about an adventure I had in Pamplona and Burgos, which could be called, 'The Hunt for Some Disciplines.'" [50]

On the previous day (January 16) he wrote in his journal: "I made a firm resolution never to visit out of curiosity any religious building—never! Poor Burgos cathedral!" [51] (Given his strength of will, his use of a word like "never" has more than a little impact. Recall that resolution made in 1932 "not to look—ever!" [52])

He needed a place in Burgos where he could receive visitors, put up those who were passing through, and, he hoped, set up an oratory. But, no matter how hard they looked, they could not find such a place. So that impressive-sounding "San Miguel de Burgos" (see the circular letter above) never came to be anything more than a small room in a boardinghouse or hotel. [53]

[49] *Apuntes*, no. 1493. A few days later he wrote to Madrid's vicar general, Monsignor Francisco Morán, "I have made a serious resolution never to accept Mass stipends, which at present are my only possible source of income. Crazy? All right, crazy. But this way I can often offer the Mass for my bishop, and for my Father Francisco, and for my beloved sons—and for myself, a sinful priest" (AGP, RHF, EF–380127–1).

[50] *Apuntes*, no. 1493 (17 Jan 1938). On December 31 he visited the Capuchins in Pamplona to order "some rosaries and other things," and on January 12 he went to see the Carmelites in Burgos "to look for some things that I need." See *Apuntes*, no. 1458 (31 Dec 1937) and no. 1484 (13 Jan 1938).

[51] *Apuntes*, no. 1492.

[52] *Apuntes*, no. 1702 (3 Oct 1932). See vol. 1, p. 366, of this biography.

[53] See *Apuntes*, no. 1491 (15 Jan 1938). On February 4 he wrote to Enrique Alonso-Martínez Saumell, "How hard it is to find a house! We look, but to no avail. If you have any friends or relatives in Burgos who could help, we would be very grateful" (AGP, RHF, EF–380204–1).

He considered it urgent to speak, as soon as possible, with each and every member of the Work. This journal entry written on January 13 makes clear what he was suffering: "My God, my God! All of them equally loved, through you and in you and with you—and all of them dispersed. You have hit me where it hurts me the most: in my children." [54]

It was a pain involving many things: the impossibility of sharing closely in their difficulties and sufferings; the lack of a family home; the isolation and loneliness ("How this loneliness weighs on me! My children, Lord!"); and the disturbing thought that in such conditions it was harder for his children to persevere in their commitment. [55]

Now that he was cut off from the Red zone, his love for those he left behind caused him to magnify in his mind the troubles they were going through. When he read in one of Isidoro's letters, "The grandmother and the uncle and aunt are in perfect health; they're getting through the winter very well," [56] he thought, "How well can they be doing when for the last eight months they've had a lack of everything?" [57] While deprivations and other hardships leapt to his imagination, he had no way of getting at the unvarnished truth, which, naturally, they tended to keep from him. The winter of 1938 was extremely harsh in Madrid. The terrible cold was made worse by the shortages of food and fuel. "I have such an abundance of chilblains," wrote Isidoro to another person in the Red zone, "that I can hardly hold the pencil." [58]

The Father kept careful track of the correspondence. On February 24 he said to Juan Jiménez Vargas, "We have received seven letters from Madrid, and we have sent them eighteen." Being able to receive news was a great consolation, but it could also be a source of anxiety. It was very nerve-racking to be awaiting a reply, not knowing if one had not yet been written or if it had perhaps gone astray or aroused the suspicions of the censor. Father Josemaría could hardly be expected not to be upset. In a letter written to Juan on March 27, he wrote: "I hope that *some* day we'll be hearing something from my poor sons in Madrid! I

---

[54] *Apuntes*, no. 1484.

[55] See *Apuntes*, no. 1510 (25 Jan 1938). In an entry for January 9 we read, "I pray a thousand times each day for all these dispersed sons—perseverance!" (*Apuntes*, no. 1475).

[56] AGP, IZL, D–1213, 312.

[57] AGP, RHF, EF–380602–3.

[58] AGP, IZL, D–1213, 307.

sent them one letter, by way of Saint-Jean-de-Luz, on the 18th, and another, via the Marquis of Embid, on the 26th. They are causing me a lot of suffering. You know me better than anyone, and you well know that on this I'm . . . overboard. The Lord won't hold it against me." [59]

*   *   *

During his year and a half in the republican zone, when he was in constant danger of prison or death, the Father had firsthand experience of the courage and fidelity of Juan Jiménez Vargas. His seniority in the Work and his qualities of decisiveness and command led the Father to put him in charge of their group's crossing of the Pyrenees. Once they were in the nationalist zone, he did everything possible to keep Juan with him to restart the apostolic work. Juan could, the founder was thinking, very well serve the nation in some hospital, combining that patriotic service with his services to the Work. And so, soon after his arrival in San Sebastián, the Father urged Juan José Pradera to speak to General Cabanellas about this possibility. He also phoned the bishop of Pamplona to ask him to use his influence with Dr. Antonio Vallejo Nagera, an army doctor, to get Juan assigned to Burgos. But these and other efforts had no success.[60]

A journal entry dated January 27 clearly shows that he was still not about to give up: "Determined to do everything possible, and even the impossible, to get Juan by my side. It's necessary!" And a letter dated February 24 explains why. With great reserve, the Father tells Juan that, if he remains faithful and lets himself be properly formed, he will be his "immediate successor in the family business." [61] (As we shall soon see, the founder was at this time experiencing some very difficult problems.)

José María Albareda was living in the Santa Clara boardinghouse with Father Josemaría, but was frequently away from Burgos for professional reasons. Pedro and Paco were still in Pamplona, but assigned to Auxiliary Services—a fact that might facilitate their

[59] AGP, RHF, EF–380327–3. What with the censorship and the war, it was not surprising that some letters did not reach their destination. So they soon came to an understanding concerning correspondence: four or five letters a month would go from Madrid to Burgos. "I wrote Grandfather on the 5th," Isidoro tells those in his zone, "because I have a habit of writing him whenever the date ends with a '5.' That's three letters a month, which with yours makes a total of four or five. So he'll get at least one" (AGP, IZL, D–1213, 352). See also AGP, RHF, EF–380224–1.

[60] See *Apuntes*, nos. 1406, 1408, 1410, and 1527.

[61] AGP, RHF, EF–380224–1.

transfer to a military department or office in Burgos. And so, when the Father learned that Luis Orgaz was the Director General of Military Mobilization, he decided to try to get them transferred. General Orgaz knew this priest from back in May of 1931, when convents were being burned in Madrid. Father Josemaría had brought the Blessed Sacrament from the Foundation for the Sick to the home of some neighbors of the general. Later, when the general was imprisoned in Madrid's "Model Prison," he had again met up with Father Josemaría. And now here he was in his office, inquiring about the possibility of transfers for Pedro Casciaro and Francisco Botella.[62]

The one for Paco came relatively fast. On January 23 he reported for duty at his new assignment in Burgos. But Pedro stayed with the Mine Sappers regiment in Pamplona until March, though he did enjoy the "protection" of Corporal Garmendia, with whom the Father had made friends during his visits to the regiment—by, in part, occasionally bringing him a fine, expensive cigar from the stock that Bishop Olaechea kept for important guests.

The landlady of the boardinghouse in Pamplona where Pedro and Paco lived was Doña Micaela Pinillos. A good cook who had been housekeeper for an elderly priest, she had seen in Father Josemaría "something very special." "One can see from miles away that he is a saint," she would often say.[63] Her veneration for the priest led her to give Pedro and Paco, the guests associated with him, special treatment, often including free suppers.

In January Pedro came down with an intestinal infection. He notified his uncle Jorge Claramunt, who came to Pamplona and brought him to Bilbao to rest. After some weeks, he returned to Pamplona. A few days later Paco Botella learned that there was an opening in General Orgaz's office. Father Josemaría immediately requested that Pedro get the position. On March 9 Pedro was in Burgos.[64]

3. *"A traveling salesman for my Lord Jesus Christ"*

Being one of the many optimists who now saw the end of the war as imminent, Father Josemaría began an apostolic campaign to find the

[62] See *Apuntes*, no. 1483 (12 Jan 1938).

[63] See Pedro Casciaro, *Dream and Your Dreams Will Fall Short* (London and Princeton, 1994), p. 136.

[64] See AGP, RHF, EF–380304–1, and Casciaro, p. 138.

people and material means needed to get started again in Madrid.[65] "Lord, give us fifty men who love you above all things!" he prayed before the tabernacle. And to the bishop of Vitoria he wrote: "I need a million pesetas, along with fifty men who love Jesus Christ above all things."[66] But realizing that neither the vocations nor the pesetas were going to just fall into his hands, he got ready to launch himself on a search.

The first plan was to speak with each of his sons. Foreseeing that this could involve long and complicated travels, he wrote to Ricardo Fernández Vallespín, on December 31, 1937: "They have promised me a very broad safe-conduct so that I can visit all the members of my family without hassles. I'll be doing more traveling than a truck driver."[67] He drew up a mental itinerary that also incorporated other errands, such as visiting bishops to tell them about the Work.

"In these days," he announced to the bishops of Pamplona and Vitoria, "I'll be leaving for Palencia, Salamanca, and Avila. Then I go to Bilbao. I've become a traveling salesman for my Lord Jesus Christ!"[68]

He had just received, on January 15, a warm letter from Monsignor Morán, Madrid's vicar general, which gave him the impetus he

---

[65] In a letter to Isidoro, he mentions having met Alvaro del Portillo's mother, Doña Clementina Diez de Sollano, and says that efforts are being made to get Alvaro out of Madrid on the basis of his Mexican citizenship, "although I see that they will be useless, since I will get to Latin America before then and be able to arrange for this personally" (AGP, RHF, EF–380203–1).

And in a letter to Monsignor Morán (written freely, with no need to worry about censors), he says: "I want to reiterate to my dear father the Vicar my offer to go and work in our Madrid, with the first group that goes. For this, it will of course be necessary to have all the documents ready. . . . I beg you, my dear Vicar, to accept my poor services, offered with so much willingness, and to provide me the necessary documents, so that I don't run into any difficulties when the long-awaited conquest of Madrid comes" (AGP, RHF, EF–380303–3). See also AGP, RHF, EF–380327–1 and EF–380425–2.

[66] *Apuntes*, no. 1483 (12 Jan 1938), and AGP, RHF, EF–380206–1. He also wrote to Enrique Alonso-Martínez Saumell, "Son, tell our Lord that we need a million pesetas and fifty men who love him above all things! Then again, how good it is not to have even one peseta! But we have to be persistent in our petition. Oh, and also a car! Yes— a small Chrysler, for example. Know that I am asking our Lord for this, as I am writing to you, with that trustful hope that filled my whole soul when as a little boy I would write to the Three Kings. Let's see what happens!" (AGP, RHF, EF–380204–1). (In Spain, children receive gifts on the feast of the Epiphany.)

[67] AGP, RHF, EF–371231–3.

[68] AGP, RHF, EF–380116–2. In a January 17 journal entry he writes, "I'm planning to take my first business trip—feeling my way—day after tomorrow. My last stop, God willing, will be Bilbao, where I'll go to ask for donations. Sancti Angeli Custodes nostri!" (*Apuntes*, no. 1494).

needed to set out on those rickety trains and buses of wartime Spain. "You can't imagine," the vicar wrote, "the wonderful surprise you gave me. Thank God we have you with us, to labor in his chosen Work! It will always be necessary, but all the more so in the postwar period." [69]

A few days earlier, as if to clear the way, a donation of 1,000 pesetas had arrived. He was excited and very hopeful about the trip, convinced that as a result of it their apostolic work would take a big leap forward. In a letter to Manolo Sainz de los Terreros, he enthusiastically sketches it out:

> Day after tomorrow—traveling salesman for my Lord Jesus Christ!—I start out on this trip: Burgos—Palencia; Palencia—Salamanca; Salamanca—Avila; Avila—Salamanca; Salamanca —Palencia; Palencia—León; León—Astorga; Astorga—León; León—Bilbao; and then, who knows, I may even have to go to Seville.
>
> For seeing the world, nothing beats being dirt-poor. [70]

He also writes in a joyful tone to Isidoro:

> The grandfather is running around, which is a pleasure. Tomorrow he leaves for six or eight cities. Despite everything, the poor old fellow is putting on weight. . . .
>
> By the way, he's doing that running around by himself. And he says he's going to come back with a lot of money that Don Manuel will give him for fixing up his house in Paris. May it be so! [71]

In his private journal, however, the tone is more subdued:

> I decided to undertake a trip that will be somewhat tiring, but is necessary.
>
> If I had my way, I would shut myself up in a monastery and stay there—alone!—till the war ends. I have a great hunger for solitude. However, not my will, but God's. He wants me

[69] See AGP, RHF, EF–380116–2, and *Apuntes*, no. 1490 (15 Jan 1938).
[70] AGP, RHF, EF–380117–3.
[71] AGP, RHF, EF–380118–1.

to work in an environment far removed from isolation. Also, I have a great desire to get out of Burgos.[72]

On January 19, after (as usual) celebrating Mass at 6:15 in the house of the Teresian Association, he took the bus for Palencia. When he arrived at the bishop's residence, the bishop, who had not seen him since before the war, was astonished at his appearance. "He's a different man!" he said to his secretary. They had a friendly chat about recent events. Then the Father took the train for Valladolid, and on the following day celebrated a memorial Mass for Father Pedro Poveda in a house of the Teresian Association. Then he tried to locate the family of Jacinto Valentín Gamazo, a member of the Work who had died at the battlefront of Alto de los Leones.[73]

On January 21, in Salamanca, he said a Mass at the Teresian house of formation. There he had a long meeting with Josefa Segovia in which, with her concurrence, he drew up a program of spiritual assistance for these women.

On January 22 he left Salamanca for Avila, and arrived there in time to say Mass. "I celebrated it for Father Pedro, at the Teresians' house. (How he must be laughing from heaven! 'What a nitwit, offering suffrages for me!' he'll say.) A very warm welcome!"[74]

In a long, cordial talk he explained the Work to the bishop of Avila, Santos Moro. ("He understood everything," he noted in his journal.[75]) In the afternoon, he returned to Salamanca. The next day, to his great surprise, while he was working up the schedule for a day of recollection he was going to give the Teresians, Ricardo showed up. He had

---

[72] *Apuntes*, no. 1494 (17 Jan 1938).

[73] See *Apuntes*, nos. 1499–1501 (19–20 Jan 1938), and AGP, RHF, EF–380204–7. Later, in March 1939, he was with this family in El Boecillo, and celebrated Mass for Jacinto. See AGP, RHF, D–04691.

[74] *Apuntes*, no. 1505. See also *Apuntes*, no. 1503 (21 Jan 1938), no. 1506 (22 Jan 1938), and no. 1508 (23 Jan 1938).

There are two letters of Father Josemaría addressed to Sister Josefa, after the meeting in Salamanca. In one of them, written in Burgos on March 3, 1938, he tells her, "I'm running around all over the place, and wherever I find daughters of Father Pedro, I make them sit through a talk. I did this three times in Bilbao, in Valladolid, in Avila, in León and Astorga, in San Sebastián, in Saragossa . . . Is this all right with you? If you don't give me your explicit approval, I'll keep my mouth shut" (AGP, RHF, EF–380303–4).

Father Josemaría wanted to do all he could to comfort Father Pedro's daughters, who were deeply grieved over the death of their founder. "How can I refuse to help Pepa Segovia?" he writes in his journal on January 25. "I told her I would always call her my sister, my good sister" (*Apuntes*, no. 1510).

[75] *Apuntes*, no. 1506 (22 Jan 1938).

come from the battlefront with a pass that was good for only two days, so Father Josemaría immediately postponed the day of recollection. "All day with Ricardo, thinking about everyone."[76]

As he records the stages of this tiring trip, disquieting symptoms begin to appear.

> January 25: I gave a day of recollection for the Teresian women, with little zest but a lot of good will.[77]

> Burgos, January 28: Back to ordinary life. Caught a cold.[78]

> Vitoria, Sunday the 30th: A great longing to be alone. I see myself as a little ball bounced from wall to wall by my Father-God, getting a good whack with the foot and then, immediately afterward, a caress from his hands.[79]

> Bilbao, February 1: Today I've done a lot of lying around. . . . I've completely lost my voice; can't talk at all. Tomorrow I'm returning to Burgos, to recover. I feel weak. I've put on some weight, and yet I'm doing worse than when I arrived. I get nauseous as soon as the car starts moving. I'm a complete wreck—but I'm not going to tell anyone.[80]

> Burgos, February 2: Back at 51 Santa Clara, and I won't go out of the house. Gargling, compresses, handkerchief around the neck, etc. Pleased with my stay in Bilbao! Hoping it will bear fruit.[81]

> February 3: Got up late. . . . Can't say Mass.[82]

> February 4: Bad night. Coughing: tried some lozenges. Can't even say Mass.[83]

He was hoping that a few days' rest would cure him. But he got worse. He was still confined to bed when he received a letter from Madrid's vicar general setting an appointment for February 10 in

---

[76] *Apuntes*, no. 1509 (24 Jan 1938).
[77] *Apuntes*, no. 1510.
[78] *Apuntes*, no. 1514.
[79] *Apuntes*, no. 1517.
[80] *Apuntes*, no. 1520.
[81] *Apuntes*, no. 1521.
[82] *Apuntes*, no. 1522.
[83] *Apuntes*, no. 1523.

Salamanca. On the 8th he wrote, "Still hoarse. Tomorrow I have to go to Salamanca. . . . I don't know if I should go back to bed." [84] In the end he decided to make the trip, but he had to interrupt the journey. He spent the night in Medina del Campo, running a high fever and getting almost no sleep. But he did rally and make it to Salamanca the next day. He met Monsignor Morán for lunch and spoke with him at length. He sketched his life in Madrid, his escape, the apostolate at the fronts and behind the lines, his visits to bishops. . . . He read his circular letter aloud. He spoke of the retreat he had made and of his interior life. They recalled the times of the Republic when Father Josemaría was not yet incardinated in Madrid and was trying to obtain priestly faculties. Then they talked about the ten years of work with Opus Dei. The vicar laughed heartily when Father Josemaría asked, "What would you have said to me if I had come to you in 1928 and said, 'I need to stay here in Madrid, because Jesus wants me to carry out a really great Work'?" [85]

On February 11, back in Burgos, he found waiting for him "a very affectionate letter from the bishop of Madrid." Bishop Eijo y Garay wrote:

> My dear Father José María:
>
> I was very happy to receive your letter of January 10, and I thank you with all my heart. Monsignor Morán had already given me the great joy of knowing that you had escaped from the Red zone and that God our Lord has preserved you to continue doing so much good. Forgive me for not answering your letter sooner. I have been sick. I am slowly recovering, but have of course fallen way behind in my correspondence.[86]

---

[84] *Apuntes*, no. 1530; see also nos. 1531 and 1534 (9 and 10 Feb 1938). "On the 9th," he writes to Juan Jiménez Vargas, "I set out once more for Salamanca. How little I feel like doing all this stuff! What I would really like to do is to shut myself up in a monastery, to pray and do penance, until the war is over. But it would be the first time I did my own will, and naturally—or rather, supernaturally—I'm not going to start doing that now" (AGP, RHF, EF–380207–3).

[85] There is a handwritten note about this conversation of February 10, 1938, with the vicar general of Madrid. It begins: "I don't think I can put into words the affection he showed for the Work and for me. Monsignor Morán spoke with real enthusiasm about all our endeavors, as if they were his own." There then follows a list of the topics discussed. (See AGP, RHF, AVF–0020.)

[86] AGP, RHF, D–15226/1. The letter is headed, "Vigo, February 9, 1938."

Now feeling much better, Father Josemaría spent February 15–17 in León. There he met with a number of people, including the bishop of Astorga, but his main objective was to see Father Eliodoro Gil, whom he had known since 1931. This priest had frequented the DYA Academy on Luchana Street and later the Ferraz Street residence; now he was a parish priest in León. Father Eliodoro promised to mimeograph the circular letters Father Josemaría would send him, so that they could then be sent to his sons on the various battlefronts. In addition, this good priest paid Father Josemaría's hotel bill, gave him some candy for his sons, and added "a nice donation." [87] "Pleased with the trip. Successful visits with Espinosa and Eliodoro: I won't go into details," he wrote in his journal. (On the same trip Father Josemaría had spoken with Espinosa de los Monteros about his possible vocation to the Work.) "I'm going to bed right now," that entry continues, "because I'm done in." [88]

On Sunday the 20th he left for Saragossa by way of Calatayud.[89] The journal continues: "Monday. February 21. To Pilar. First visit to Saragossa. Afterward stopped by the Teresians. Then to the doctor. I still have a fever and sore throat, and am coughing up blood." [90]

Learning that Enrique Alonso-Martinez was hospitalized in Alhama de Aragon, he went to see him. He returned to Saragossa, then to Pamplona, and from there to Jaca, to see José Ramon Herrero Fontana. (The Father had called him the "Benjamin" of the family just before the war broke out.) He returned to Pamplona. Then to San Sebastian. More visits. More business: On March 2, Ash Wednesday, he returned to Burgos, very tired and with fever. On Thursday the fever continued. On Friday he was still in bed. The next journal entry is dated:

> Thursday, March 10: I haven't written any Catherines for several days now. There's a lot I could write. . . . I see myself as a poor servant whose master has taken away his livery. Nothing but sins! I understand the nakedness felt by our first parents. And I've cried a lot—I've suffered a lot. Nevertheless, I am very happy. I wouldn't trade places with anyone. I haven't lost my *gaudium cum pace* [joy with peace] for years

---

[87] See *Apuntes*, nos. 1540 and 1543 (15 and 17 Feb 1938).
[88] *Apuntes*, no. 1544.
[89] *Apuntes*, no. 1545.
[90] Ibid., no. 1547.

now. Thank you, my God! . . . I can't do vocal prayer. It causes me pain, almost physical, to hear praying done out loud. My mental prayer and my entire interior life are in complete disorder. I spoke about this with the bishop of Vitoria, and he set my mind at rest. I will write him today. *Omnes cum Petro ad Iesum per Mariam* [All with Peter to Jesus through Mary].[91]

Monday, March 21: Lots of days without writing Catherines. . . . In these days, three doctors have been here to see me. The boys insisted. . . . Father Antonio Rodilla came over today. What a good friend he is! I showed him the state of my soul: bare of virtues, a heap of wretchedness. I can hardly say vocal prayers; to hear praying out loud gives me a headache. I don't think I do any mental prayer, either: disorder. But I know that I love God. Yes, and that he loves me. I'm a poor wretch, because I'm a sinner and disordered and have no interior life. I want to cry, and can't. I, who have cried so much! And, at the same time, I am very happy; I wouldn't trade places with anyone. I told Father Antonio all this. That eternal fifteen minutes of thanksgiving, constantly looking at my watch, wanting it to be over! How shameful! And yet I do love Jesus above all things. Then I told Father Antonio that it seemed to me that I was trying to fool him, moved by pride. He consoled me and said I'm doing fine.[92]

April 15, Good Friday: Time has flown past without my being able to write in the diary. . . . I won't say anything about the current state of my soul.[93]

June 4, 1938, Vigil of Pentecost: Almost two months without writing. I will try from now on, as far as possible, to write every day.[94]

* * *

To what extent was the founder aware that something serious was going on? The illness that was filling his mouth with blood was

---

[91] *Apuntes*, nos. 1566 and 1567.

[92] *Apuntes*, nos. 1568 and 1569. Born in 1897 and ordained in 1921, Father Antonio Rodilla Zanón served as principal of San Juan de Ribera High School in Valencia from 1923 to 1939, as vicar general of that diocese from 1938 to 1944, and as rector of its major seminary from 1939 to 1969. He died in 1984.

[93] *Apuntes*, no. 1572.

[94] *Apuntes*, no. 1573.

painful and strange. It was never established with certainty whether it was a problem of the throat or of the lungs. Father Josemaría accepted it with patience, despite his initial fear of not being able to remain with his children if it turned out to be tuberculosis. At the doctor's suggestion, he began receiving injections for his lungs. If it really were tuberculosis, he thought, our Lord would cure him so that he could keep working.[95] And at the end of March he was able to write to Ricardo, "Please do me the favor of not speaking about my illness, since it doesn't exist anymore."[96] The lung specialist had not found anything out of the ordinary.

Father Josemaría seems to have sensed all along that this unusual illness was the prelude to a renewal of his passive purifications. How else account for the fact that after two weeks of silence, he suddenly comes out with the disquieting confession that "I see myself as a poor servant whose master has taken away his livery"?

Father Josemaría had passed through many trials since that day in 1931 when he wrote of feeling like a little bird who, unable to fly high, is taken in the powerful claws of the divine eagle and suddenly lifted to the heights, to be initiated into the sublime flight of the spirit.[97] He endured his tribulations, convinced he was "an inept and deaf instrument,"[98] a sorry excuse for a founder, a sinner. Fierce and prolonged sufferings sometimes tempted him to rebel. He had to overcome strong temptations toward "low and vile things"[99] while anxiously seeking to conform to the will of God. Then came the "cruel trial" culminating in that anguished prayer of detachment from what was the very essence of his life: Opus Dei.[100] Plus what he suffered on account of the poverty of his family, various humiliations, spiritual dryness, persecutions against the Church, and the sacrileges being committed all over Spain. Yet through all of this he had remained abandoned to the hands of God. He had kept in his heart a vivid consciousness of his divine filiation and a deep-rooted love for the cross, living a life of spiritual childhood and burning with apostolic zeal. Intermingled with all his sufferings and joys was grace—which inundated his soul with infused contem-

[95] See AGP, RHF, EF–380323–1.

[96] AGP, RHF, EF–380327–2.

[97] See *Apuntes*, no. 244 (31 Aug 1931), and vol. 1, pp. 279–80, of this biography.

[98] *Instruction* of 19 Mar 1934, no. 7.

[99] See *Apuntes*, no. 274 (9 Sep 1931).

[100] See *Apuntes*, no. 1729, and vol. 1, pp. 386–87, of this biography.

plation and constant prayer day and night, even when he was asleep.[101]

According to Saint John of the Cross, when God wants to proceed with the shaping of a mature soul familiar with affliction and dryness, he ordinarily does not place it in the dark night of the soul at once, but "lets a good amount of time pass."[102] In the mystical life of the founder, however, infused contemplation was present at a relatively early period. And an attentive tracing of the course of his life yields evidence that severe passive purifications at the hands of divine Love did not cease until he died. In the years of the Spanish Civil War, however, his spiritual life was marked in a special way by a craving to make reparation, as he had requested of our Lord a month before the war broke out. Truly he spent those war years "on a cross hidden from the eyes of men."[103]

The trials came in distinct periods. There were those long nights around May 9, 1937, when, as a refugee in the Honduran consulate, he went upstairs to unburden himself to Father Recaredo Ventosa. Then came the piercing doubts before the finding of that rose in Rialp. A third period was that of his illness in the boardinghouse on Santa Clara Street in Burgos, which lasted from February to April of 1938. For this period, the allusions to his purifications are quite veiled. For example, in a letter to Juan Jiménez Vargas he says, "If I were to tell you, Juanito! But I won't tell you."[104] He did not want to burden his children. But he did seek spiritual counsel, such as that of Father Antonio Rodilla, to whom he opened his soul.[105]

In the mystical tradition, such tribulation is understood as God's way of removing imperfections from a soul that he wishes to draw closer to himself. The journal entries from the consulate and from Santa Clara Street are at times quite moving. "I suffered horribly last night. . . . I think that rarely have I suffered as I do now."[106] One can imagine how trying it must be for a holy soul to feel itself rejected, despoiled of virtues and of friendship with God, and cast into

---

[101] See *Apuntes*, no. 877 (24 Nov 1932).

[102] Saint John of the Cross, *The Dark Night of the Soul*, 2, 1.

[103] *Apuntes*, no. 1372 (30 Jun 1936). See also vol. 1, pp. 455–57, of this biography.

[104] AGP, RHF, EF–380227–3. In a letter to Francisco Botella he says something similar: "Do you want me to tell you, Paco, what's going on with the grandfather? I'll tell you, in part. First, very personal concerns, very much his own" (AGP, RHF, EF–370530–1).

[105] See *Apuntes*, nos. 1567 (10 Mar 1938) and 1569 (21 Mar 1938).

[106] *Apuntes*, nos. 1379 (8 May 1937) and 1380 (9 May 1937).

darkness like the man without a wedding garment—"Bind him hand and foot, and cast him into the outer darkness; there men will weep and gnash their teeth" (Mt 22:13).

Father Josemaría felt himself just a step removed from damnation. "I fear for my salvation," he wrote at the consulate.[107] "I suffer terrible doubts and distress when I think about my salvation. O my God! O my Mother! Will you allow me to be condemned?"[108] His soul was overwhelmed by the fear that he was failing to carry out God's will. This suffering, this "sorrow of Love," crushed his soul and caused his tears to flow uncontainably.

During this mystical process, the soul typically experiences a kind of paralysis of its faculties. The masters of the spiritual life speak of a *hebetudo mentis,* a dullness of the mind.[109] "I can't think of anything. I'm in a fog," writes Father Josemaría.[110]

The will also becomes impaired, and one loses all feeling and drive; acts of devotion become nearly impossible.[111] "I can't do vocal prayer. It causes me pain, almost physical, to hear praying done out loud," he writes at the Santa Clara boardinghouse."[112]

The memory, too, loses strength, making one unable to focus on the past. And thus the soul becomes absorbed in the contemplation of its own imperfection and weakness. "My prayer, said with all the energies of my soul, was, 'Jesus, if I am not going to be the instrument you desire, take me to you in a state of grace *as soon as possible.*' "[113]

In the midst of this process of purgation, his heart at times was filled with aspirations, such as "O Lord, you know that I love you!" and "Holy Mary, our hope, our Mother!"[114] Other times brought poignant declarations of trusting love: "I am not afraid of death, despite my sinful life, because I keep in mind your Love. Typhoid, tuberculosis, pneumonia, or four bullets, what's the difference?"[115] But in any case, despite the anguish of fearing that he had lost God, he also sensed his

[107] *Apuntes,* no. 1380 (9 May 1937).
[108] *Apuntes,* no. 1391 (26 May 1937).
[109] See Adolphe Tanquerey, *The Spiritual Life* (Baltimore: St. Mary's Seminary, 1930), no. 1464.
[110] *Apuntes,* no. 1379 (8 May 1937).
[111] On May 10 he again writes, "I can't think of anything; still completely in a fog" (*Apuntes,* no. 1381).
[112] *Apuntes,* no. 1567 (10 Mar 1938).
[113] *Apuntes,* no. 1391 (26 May 1937).
[114] *Apuntes,* no. 1379 (8 May 1937).
[115] *Apuntes,* no. 1391 (26 May 1937).

nearness. Somehow he simultaneously experienced both the presence and the absence of God. Thus he could say, "I haven't lost my *gaudium cum pace* [joy with peace] for years now." [116]

This purification produced a clearer knowledge of God and of his own nothingness, together with a purer love and a stronger joy. "I know that I love God. Yes, and that he loves me." [117] "I am very happy. I wouldn't trade places with anyone." [118] That divine action, of course, leaves unique marks on each of God's saints. One mark it left on the founder was the insight reflected in this journal entry: "Now I understand . . . that Jesus wants me to live, suffering, and work. It's all the same. His will be done." [119] The vision, that is to say, of a fusion of his contemplative life of love for the cross with his life of working: all in one. That enterprise, in those early days, was not an easy one. From those hard nighttime struggles Father Josemaría emerged happy, but also exhausted in both soul and body. From a journal entry written on Friday, May 21, 1937, we can get some idea of how he was feeling:

> Like an open wound, that's how you are. Everything makes you suffer, in your faculties and in your senses. And everything is a temptation to you. Poor child! Be humble. You will see how quickly all this passes, and the pain will turn into joy, and the temptation, into firm steadfastness. But in the meantime, stir up your faith, fill yourself with hope, and make constant acts of love, even if you think they're coming only from your lips.[120]

Who would have imagined that on that same day, he would write to Lola Fisac inviting her to be his grandchild, and then write to his sons in Madrid urging them to keep trying to obtain compensation for the damages to the Ferraz Street residence?

If he did not say much to his children about his interior suffering,

---

[116] *Apuntes*, no. 1567 (10 Mar 1938).
[117] *Apuntes*, no. 1569 (21 Mar 1938).
[118] *Apuntes*, no. 1567 (10 Mar 1938).
[119] *Apuntes*, no. 1380 (9 May 1937). "The founder of Opus Dei not only *accepted* the cross with joy, in sickness, in persecution, in every kind of external difficulty, and in the interior purifications that God made him go through, but also *looked* for it, deeply convinced that to find the cross is to find Christ": Alvaro del Portillo, "Sacerdotes para una nueva Evangelización," in *La formación de los sacerdotes en las circunstancias actuales: XI Simposio Internacional de Teología* (Pamplona: University of Navarre, 1990), p. 992.
[120] *Apuntes*, no. 1388.

this was not because of any concern about the wartime censorship, but because of his fixed resolve to "hide myself and disappear," especially with regard to his personal relationship with God.[121] However, he did allow them glimpses of his interior struggle so that they could accompany him in his love and reparation. In a letter to his sons in Valencia, for example, he wrote this:

> Today, Grandfather is sad, downcast, in spite of the love and affection of his family, and in spite of the heroic patience of his nephew Juanito—who is *not* "being bossy." It's just that when he looks back on his youth and contemplates the present life, he has a great desire to behave well, for those who are behaving badly; to play Don Quixote, making reparation, suffering, putting right. Then his intellect and will (Love) start to race. Love arrives first—but so weak, with so few deeds! Grandfather is sad because he can't get things right (being so old, having so little strength) unless the grandchildren of his soul help him with their youth. But I'm getting philosophical, and rambling so much that you probably don't understand what I'm trying to say.[122]

*   *   *

Around the middle of February 1938, Paco Botella returned one evening from the barracks, and finding the Father in bed, he asked what was wrong. The answer, after a long silence, was: "Paco, for the last few days my throat has been bleeding, and I am wondering if it might be tuberculosis. Don't come near me." [123]

The fever continued. His throat was burning. His mouth kept filling with blood. A doctor whom he consulted on his way through Saragossa on February 21 diagnosed it as "chronic pharyngitis." The symptoms resembled those of tuberculosis in an advanced, incurable stage. Did he have a right to risk infecting his children? It was this painful thought that led him to write to Juan Jiménez Vargas on February 24 and tell him that, if he let himself be properly formed, he would be his "immediate successor in the family business." That letter contained a lot of news and some details about his illness:

---

[121] See AGP, RHF, EF–370521–2, and vol. 1, p. 239, of this biography.
[122] AGP, RHF, EF–370421–1.
[123] AGP, RHF, T–00159/1, p. 63.

Did you hear that I've become an old wreck? I caught a cold over a month ago, and it's turned into chronic pharyngitis. If I have to talk, Jesus will have to cure me, since I often lose my voice completely. *Fiat* [His will be done]. An old man: 80 years old on the inside, and 36 on the outside; total, 116 years; and a cracked pharynx that makes me cough every two minutes. *Fiat.*[124]

He got worse. Some mornings he woke up with his mouth full of blood clots.

On March 9 Pedro Casciaro arrived, assigned to Burgos at the orders of General Orgaz. Upon moving in with the Father and Paco at the Santa Clara boardinghouse, he found the patient in a sorry state, "with a dry and persistent cough, unable to speak, and spitting up blood." On March 19, the feast of Saint Joseph, the three had the joy of being reunited with Ricardo Fernández Vallespín, Manolo Sainz de los Terreros, and José María Albareda. Paco and Ricardo decided to take the Father to a doctor that week, even though they had no money to pay him. On March 23, the Father wrote to Juan:

During their stay, by force of everyone's insistence, I had to go see the optometrist. He gave me a new prescription (half a diopter more), and told me I needed reading glasses— I'm wearing them now—and to make sure both pairs had good lenses. Everything got done on that very day. It cost a fortune!

Then, off to a throat specialist. He examined me carefully and concluded that it could have something to do with my lungs. That mouth filled with blood! He recommended a chest specialist, and wrote us a note for him. We went; long wait; finally, the examination. Stethoscope; again, stethoscope; and then a third time, with other instruments. Then, X rays. Finally, "Doctor, do I have TB?" "No, completely clear of that; not the least chance of it. Just at the bottom of the right lung, some residues of a cold." The truth is that I wasn't concerned, because I thought that even if I did have TB, the Lord would cure me so that I could keep working.

[124] AGP, RHF, EF–380224–1. See also AGP, RHF, EF–380227–3, and *Apuntes*, no. 1547 (21 Feb 1938).

I'm still seeing the ear, nose, and throat specialist. Like the one in Saragossa, he cleans and disinfects my nose and throat. In sum, I hope I'm making you happy, but it's costing us another fistful of pesetas.[125]

Everyone was in on the project of looking after the Father. By serving, cajoling, and pressuring him, they were trying to get him to put on weight and become, as he saw it, "a tub of lard, like a bon vivant." He resisted it as much as he could, in the conviction that the "good life" is not compatible with a spirit of penance. In that same letter to Juan, he wrote:

Everyone in the world thinks they have a right to tell the Grandfather to take care of himself, forget about fasting, eat well, get more sleep, the list is endless. And he feels, deep inside, the exact opposite. The conflict is fierce. Don't you try to become the battlefield for another like it. People suffer if they can't have the chubby cheeks, pomp and vanity of former times. And they're getting their way. Poor soul, wrapped in layers of rancid lard! [126]

His sons had agreed among themselves to make him eat so that he could put on a few pounds. But, in their zeal and good will, they were hounding him day and night. He wrote to Ricardo: "Please do me the favor of not speaking about my illness, since it doesn't exist anymore. I am still going to the throat specialist, but just to keep from getting into a big fight every Monday and Tuesday with these meddling sons of my soul." [127]

Sensing God's hand in the Father's illness, Pedro decided that the only solution was to pray that it be transferred to him. And at least once, that did seem to happen. "When the Father got better," Paco Botella recalls, "Pedro fell sick with a headache, digestive problems, and a fever. And when Pedro got better, the Father got worse again." [128]

[125] AGP, RHF, EF–380323–1.
[126] AGP, RHF, EF–380323–1. See also AGP, RHF, T–00159/1, pp. 64–65, and Casciaro, pp. 149–50.
[127] AGP, RHF, EF–380327–2.
[128] AGP, RHF, T–00159/1, p. 74.

According to Pedro, it was his anxiety about the Father's high fever that "made me think of asking God to take the fever from him and give it to me." He continues, "Perhaps I made this petition without really believing that our Lord would listen to me. So I was very surprised when, that same evening, my temperature skyrocketed and the Father's fever disappeared. They called the doctor, and he said I had typhoid or paratyphoid and ordered tests. The results were negative, but I kept running a high fever." [129]

This was on March 23, the day Father Josemaría wrote to Juan about his visits to the doctors and about how much it was costing them, needlessly, in his opinion. The lung specialist had not found any lesions or even traces of tubercular calcifications. The throat specialist had also found nothing special, and had called the case a no-man's-land.[130] Here was, indeed, a mix of strange pathological symptoms attached to no known illness.

In this same letter to Juan, the Father wrote: "Ricardo has started giving me some balsam injections for my lungs. Wasted efforts—I tell you this with all my soul." And immediately after that he says, "Poor little Pedro has come down sick on us today—for the third time since he's been in Burgos—with a high fever that came on suddenly. I would like you to take a look at the case." [131]

Pedro, with a temperature of 104, and with fear and misgivings at not having done this before, finally told the Father what he had done. "With a lot of embarrassment," he says, "I ended up telling the Father about my request to our Lord. 'Don't do anything like that again,' he told me, 'but don't worry about it.' " [132] The fever disappeared as if by magic, and for some time the Father was also free of it.

But because of his intense work life and the fasting he was doing, his sons, especially Pedro and Paco, kept up their mission of looking out for him. On Sunday, March 27, while he was writing another letter to Juan Jiménez Vargas, they tried to talk him into putting on a sweater. The summer cassock he was wearing was not much protection against the harsh cold of the Burgos winter. They kept pestering and would not leave him in peace.

"These fellows," he writes to Juan, "are giving me a rough time

---

[129] Casciaro, p. 152.
[130] See AGP, P03 1983, p. 445, and Casciaro, pp. 139–40.
[131] AGP, RHF, EF–380323–1.
[132] Casciaro, p. 152.

about my health and the illness. Aside from the fact that I'm getting fat (which, by the way, I find very unpleasant), this subject does not concern me. What I'm concerned about is souls, including mine." [133] Then, after describing how the two young men urged the sweater on him, he wrote:

> What silly things I'm telling you! It's true. But everything we poor humans try to achieve—even sanctity—is a weave of little things which, when drawn together in a certain way, can form an astonishing tapestry of heroism or villainy, of virtues or sins. The epics—those of our El Cid, for example—always relate gigantic adventures, but mixed in with commonplace details about the hero. May you always pay a lot of attention to the little things. May you zero in on them! And I too; and I too. [134]

Good as their intentions were, his sons were suffocating him with their attentions. They kept track of his mortifications and vigils and of whether or not he slept on the floor. They watched over his fasts, asking what he had eaten and when. Pedro and Paco even monitored his thirst (detectable when his voice cracked, or when his dry tongue stumbled over words). And when he refused to take their advice, they kept giving it, undeterred. [135] "They are unbearable," he wrote to José María Albareda. "They make me eat at all hours, after some epic battles. Tell them to leave me in peace." [136]

On April 30 the situation came to a head. Without comment, he left on the table a sheet of paper that read:

> (1) I have decided not to let you order me around in things that are so much matters of my conscience.
> (2) I won't give you any kind of explanation.

---

[133] AGP, RHF, EF–380327–3.

[134] Ibid. "This 'Siegfried sweater,'" writes Pedro, "resulted in my going too far in my desire to take care of the Father. He didn't want to use it, mainly out of mortification and so that we could use it. But one extremely cold day, when the Father was still unable to talk and was coughing a lot, Paco and I, out of love for him but without any tact, almost physically forced him to put it on. A few minutes later he took it off, and then we realized how improperly we had behaved. We asked his pardon and decided to look for other ways to look after his health" (Casciaro, p. 141).

[135] See Casciaro, pp. 150–51, and AGP, RHF, T–00159/1, p. 74.

[136] AGP, RHF, EF–380429–1.

(3) I will eat where and when it seems best to me, guided solely by what I see to be my duty.

(4) If you continue to meddle in this matter, I will, regretfully, find it necessary to leave Burgos.

(5) Same goes for the hours and ways I sleep.

I will not permit any discussion on these matters.[137]

A strong letter to Juan followed:

Although I don't have a director here in Burgos—I'm not going to do anything that would clearly pose a threat to my health. However, I cannot lose sight of the fact that we are trying not just to do something good, but to carry out the will of God, and that for this to happen, I have to be a saint, no matter what it costs! Even if it should cost me my health, which it won't.

This decision is so deeply rooted—I see it so clearly—that no human consideration can get in the way of carrying it out.

I am speaking to you in all simplicity. You, having lived alongside me longer than anyone, surely realize that I need to be hit with an axe.[138]

4. *The Sabadell Hotel*

After his initial concern that he might have contracted tuberculosis and might infect his sons, Father Josemaría acquired a different view of his illness. Very soon he came to see it as a means of purification, and to accept as special favors from God the physical suffering and the spiritual dryness that accompanied it.[139]

The lessons of his recent trip boiled down to two things: "Lord, we need people and money." [140] As to the first, he wanted "fifty men who

---

[137] AGP, RHF, AVF–0095, and AGP, RHF, T–00159/1, p. 75.

[138] AGP, RHF, EF–380430–1. His confessors in Burgos were Father Saturnino Martínez and Father Francisco de Borja López Pérez. The latter belonged to the Missionary Sons of the Immaculate Heart of Mary and was then that order's official delegate to the national government of Spain.

[139] "I'm still seeing the throat specialist a couple of times a week," he writes to Juan, "and I have to tell you that either he doesn't know what he's doing or else this pharyngitis is a really virulent one, since even today I have been spitting up blood" (AGP, RHF, EF–380401–1).

[140] *Apuntes*, no. 1524 (4 Feb 1938).

love Jesus Christ above all things." [141] Not so many, it would seem, among so many resolute young people, with a handful of vocations already. But his sons were scattered about on different fronts, north and south; visits to give them spiritual direction would be slow and irregular. One possible solution was for them to get furloughs and spend some days at "our house of Saint Michael in Burgos," as he said in his circular letter of January 9. But if he expected the religious and patriotic zeal of young soldiers to be easily turned to higher ideals, he was destined to be disappointed. "So many young people ready to die for an ideal! And—?—impossible!" [142]

One institution that Father Josemaría sometimes had to confront, even though it arose from patriotism, was the "madrinas de guerra"— girls who volunteered to write to lonely soldiers to boost their morale. On more than one occasion, he counseled breaking off a relationship. "*The* Love is well worth *a* love," he wrote to one young man.[143]

But how had he, the founder, responded to that Love in these nine and a half years of Opus Dei's existence? That question led him (during his trip to Saragossa in February) to write this to Bishop Santos Moro, the bishop of Avila:

> May Jesus watch over my Bishop.
> Father: This sinner sends his greetings to tell you that he has not forgotten you one single day—and certainly not today, before Our Lady of the Pillar. And I ask you, my Bishop, to help us with your prayers and to bless us. We are finishing the first half of our tenth year of silent and hidden labor. What an account our Lord will demand from me!
> Help me to render it *cum gaudio et pace*.[144]

"I was amused," the bishop answered a few days later, "when you spoke of the 'account' that our Lord will demand of you. No, for you he will not be a judge, in the harsh sense of the word, but simply Jesus.

[141] See AGP, RHF, EF–380206–1.

[142] AGP, RHF, EF–380327–3.

[143] See AGP, RHF, EF–380502–7. (The young man was Miguel Sotomayor Muro.) "Many have as their 'madrina' their fiancée," we read in the July 1938 issue of *Noticias*, "but from this to other extremes that could lead us to stray from the path of spiritual rectitude that we have decided to follow—you understand very well, don't you?" See also *Apuntes*, no. 1502 (20 Jan 1938).

[144] AGP, RHF, EF–380223–5.

If only I could give myself the same promise, working as you all do, if not as a captain, at least *sicut bonus miles Xi Iesu* [as a good soldier of Christ Jesus]." [145]

At the time of these letters, Father Josemaría was going through the darkest phase of his illness, overwhelmed by the thought that he might have tuberculosis.

They continued to look for an apartment. "It's a pity," wrote the Father, "that we haven't been able to find a place of our own. It would have been better and cheaper for us. Of course, in spite of everything, we're doing fine where we are." [146] However, their days in the Santa Clara boardinghouse were quickly nearing their end. That same week, at the end of March, the landlady decided to evict Pedro and Paco, in order to take in two other persons. For the Father's group to stay together, they would all have to move. To make matters worse, the boarding house charge floored them. Father Josemaría spoke of bills "worthy of the den of Monipodio." [147] And he wrote to Ricardo, "If you could only see the pirate's bill we've been presented with." [148]

Monsignor Francisco Morán, Madrid's vicar general, had asked for "a note with the purposes, origin, development, and present state" of his enterprise.[149] Without much enthusiasm, Father Josemaría sent him a sheet covering all of that. He would have preferred to explain things in person, because he realized that some of what he was writing could be misinterpreted. Thus he concludes: "How little one can say in a written note! And yet, even the little I have written seems to me indiscreet. And, of course, very incomplete." [150]

Now, spurred by this note, the Father began to think seriously about returning to Madrid when the war ended, and about the problems that this would entail. To Juan Jiménez Vargas he wrote:

> Being in Burgos is not the same as being in our center. Not by a long shot. As long as the war continues, given the makeup

---

[145] AGP, RHF, D–10989.

[146] AGP, RHF, EF–380323–1.

[147] AGP, RHF, EF–380406–2. Monipodio is a character in Cervantes' novella *Rinconete and Cortadillo*. "The den of Monipodio" signifies a meeting of persons conspiring for illicit purposes.

[148] AGP, RHF, EF–380406–1.

[149] See AGP, RHF, EF–380323–1.

[150] AGP, RHF, EF–380404–1.

of our family (people who are awfully young), I don't think I
will have the tranquillity (the peace, yes) necessary to do deep
apostolic work. I don't mean to say that I'm not doing anything, because, what with one thing and another, something is
always going on. But it's certainly the case that wonderful
work could be done now with people more mature in years.
Well, God knows best.[151]

To get things going again, after a war so tragic and destructive,
would not be easy. He had no illusions that peace would solve
everything.

I can hardly wait for this war to be over! Then we can start (or,
rather, restart) another one that is harder, perhaps, but more
to our liking. I think we may again have to go through what
we did during those terrible years of shortages. No matter: if
we work as hard as we can, our Lord will solve everything
sooner, more, and better than we can imagine.[152]

Meanwhile, whether he liked it or not, he had to stay in Burgos.

* * *

When the Father returned to Burgos from Vitoria on April 3, they
had already moved from Santa Clara Street to the Sabadell Hotel, at
32 Merced Street. The hotel brochure, printed before the war, read:
"Magnificently situated, facing the Arlanzón River. Close to the cathedral and the station. Special prices for families and long-term guests.
Central heating. Hot and cold running water in all rooms. Bathrooms."

Father Josemaría did not sing its praises. Instead he wrote, "I am
not happy with our new home, because it's expensive." [153] (The price
was four pesetas per bed, that is sixteen pesetas a day for their "suite,"
not including meals.)

It was, at best, a third-class hotel, consisting of a ground floor and
three upper floors. Over the entrance was a marquee of iron and glass.
Each upper floor had three rooms overlooking the street. The middle
room had a balcony and the two on either side had glassed-in porches.

[151] AGP, RHF, EF–380406–2.
[152] AGP, RHF, EF–380406–1.
[153] Ibid.

They occupied one of the side rooms on the second floor. At the far end of the room was a small alcove, dark and unventilated, with a basin, separated by a cloth curtain from the rest of the room; here the Father slept. Three beds, one next to the other, were in the room proper, leaving space for a table, two chairs, and a small wardrobe that held their few possessions. The room was decorated with two awful lithographs. Eventually they replaced them with a small wooden crucifix, a picture of our Lady that was modeled on a Byzantine icon, some felt pennants bearing the word "Rialp" and the initials "DYA," and a map of Aragón and Catalonia bearing little flags and markings indicating battlefronts and places where members of the Work were stationed.[154]

The hotel brochure's mention of "Bathrooms" turned out to mean one per floor. The Father, who was the first to use theirs in the morning, saved time by filling the tub with water the night before. The water was bound to be icy on those winter mornings, because the window had a broken pane. When he got done, he would refill the tub. "As, I'm sure, you've already guessed," says Paco Botella, "there was no shower or hot water." [155]

Getting their clothing and luggage to the hotel was not much trouble. Their belongings consisted of some souvenirs of the escape over the Pyrenees—the glass they had used as a chalice, the rose of Rialp, the wineskin, their documents, letters, the journal, and the card file—and a few other things. The most cumbersome item was the typewriter, bought secondhand in a store on Plaza Mayor. It was a Corona with a very peculiar keyboard, made in such a way that one could type well, but only very slowly. They had purchased it to prepare the circular letter sent out in March of 1938, in continuation of an initiative begun in the summers of 1934 and 1935. This "family letter," containing news of friends and Ferraz Street residents, along with spiritual advice, was sent in a sealed envelope.[156] The Father's plan was for it to come out monthly, in the second half of the month. A typewritten original would be sent to Father Eliodoro Gil, in León,

---

[154] See Casciaro, p. 118.

[155] AGP, RHF, T–00159/1, p. 68.

[156] Since at that time all kinds of newspapers, magazines, pamphlets, and other papers were being circulated, the Father wrote in the July 1938 letter: "We don't want these notes to be mistaken for any kind of publication, because they are not public; they're private. So we're not calling them "newsletters" or anything else. Just as the letters you receive from home don't have a name."

who would run it off and send back the mimeographed copies for distribution from Burgos.

Those who received the issue for March 1938 read this:

> Right now, from your barracks, from the trenches, from the ramparts, from your forced stays in hospitals, how much you can help our Work with your prayers and clean living, your setbacks and successes! Let's live a special communion of saints, and each of you, at the hour of interior struggle as well as at the hour of combat, will feel the joy and strength of not being alone.[157]

The spiritual impact of those family newsletters was discernible in the many letters received at the Sabadell Hotel, especially starting in April. "How clearly your letters reflect the joy these lines bring you," we read in the July 1938 issue. "It's like receiving, at one and the same time, letters from many friends, reminders of hours spent working and laughing together, desires and hopes for a new and even more work-filled future." [158]

Pedro and Paco considered the move from the boardinghouse to the hotel "a big improvement," since it meant no longer having to eat with all the other guests at a fixed hour. But life in the hotel also had its drawbacks. The little curtain separating the main room from the alcove where the Father slept was more symbolic than practical. He had to try to find time during the day, when the others were out, to use his disciplines. (He could not do this in the bathroom, because of insufficient sound insulation.) But whether or not he could find a good time for it, he did close the curtain and proceed in the energetic way already familiar to Doña Dolores, Ricardo Fernández Vallespín, and Alvaro del Portillo. Pedro grew nervous. When he intervened with him to try to get him to lessen the blows, the Father replied that they had witnessed his weaknesses and failings, so what did it matter if they now heard him doing penance?[159]

One big advantage of the new lodging was the glassed-in porch.

---

[157] See AGP, RHF, D–03691; AGP, RHF, T–00159/1, p. 71; and Casciaro, p. 155. Father Eliodoro Gil Rivera was at that time pastor of San Juan de Renueva, in León. He had met Father Josemaría at the Teresian Institute in Madrid in 1931, and had continued his friendship and contact with him at the DYA Academy and the Ferraz Street residence.

[158] AGP, RHF, D–03691.

[159] See Casciaro, p. 151.

About seven feet long and only three feet wide, it had room only for a little wicker table and two wicker chairs, but with the windows closed and the green wooden blinds lowered, it became a space for private conversations, a niche that gave the place an air of gentility and decorum and made one forget its poverty. The small space served as confessional and receiving room. Many notable people passed through it: bishops, university professors, doctors, diplomats, priest friends, business leaders, government officials. . . . This is what Father Josemaría had in mind when he spoke of the wonderful work that could be done with "people more mature in years." [160]

For this apostolic work with highly educated people, the only one who could now help him was José María Albareda. He asked Albareda to start assembling a collection of books, the basis for the library of the center that would be opened in Madrid once the war was over. (What he envisioned was a circulating library.) Three months later they sent out a circular letter, in several languages and signed by fifteen professors, asking for books from all over the world. The address they gave was that of Albareda's brother in Saint-Jean-de-Luz. Very few books arrived, and the few journals and reprints that reached them were in bad shape from rough handling in the mail.[161]

*   *   *

Those in the military fortunate enough to get a few days' leave and spend some of it with the Father were very well received. He would walk with them along the banks of the Arlanzón River or to the abbey of Las Huelgas or the monastery of the Carthusians, or else take them to the top of the cathedral tower to enjoy a beautiful view of the buttresses, the pinnacles, and the stone carvings. Back at the hotel, they would have a private conversation in the enclosed porch. And

---

[160] In his journal entries for the first months of 1938, and in his letters, he mentions some of those professors: Inocencio Jiménez Vicente, professor of penal law at the University of Saragossa; Francisco Navarro Borrás, professor of rational mechanics at the School of Science of Madrid's Universidad Central; Mariano Puigdollers y Oliver, professor of philosophy of law at the University of Valencia; Tomás Alvira, professor of science at the Cervera del Río Alhama high school (La Rioja); Enrique Súñer Ordóñez, professor of pediatrics at the University of Valladolid; and Federico García Borruel. Also mentioned are a few doctors (Vallejo Nágera, San Román, Vallejo Simón, and Enríquez de Salamanca) and such old acquaintances as Enrique Giménez-Arnau Gran, chief of the special secretariat of the Ministry of the Interior; José Lorente Sanz, undersecretary of the same ministry; and Pedro Rocamora Valls, a lawyer and journalist.

[161] See AGP, RHF, EF–380104–1 and EF–380323–1.

if they spent the night in Burgos, they were invited to attend his Mass the next morning, usually celebrated at the Church of Saints Cosmos and Damian.[162]

And if one of those soldier sons could not come to Burgos, Father Josemaría would go to him. If someone needed his help and advice, he was there; distance did not matter.

Once he went all the way to Andalusia to see a son of his who was having a hard time.[163] The trip began on April 17 and took quite a while, because of the war. Soon after his arrival in Córdoba, he sent to his sons in Burgos a letter with entertaining descriptions of the places and people he had encountered along the way:

> I went to the hotel. What saluters the people of Córdoba are! Everyone gives the military salute, or tips their big sombrero to this priest they don't even know!
>
> In the hotel they give me room number 9—the number I'm so enamored of. (That theology of mathematics!) In León they did even better; they gave me room 309. And I thought: 3, my Father-God; and 0, myself, a sinner (*mea culpa!*); and 9, my sons. How good Jesus is, to bring us to himself with something so little!
>
> I start writing letters, to these sons of my soul, and in walks Miguel. A hug. "Pax!" "In aeternum!" Night falls, and in filial confidence, nobly and with great simplicity, he unburdens himself of these almost two years of separation. And the Father—who always wants to be, for everyone, very much a father—gives counsels and practical guidelines. And he also gives—he wants to give—Love of God and that affection of ours which is a spark of that Love.
>
> Miguel doesn't return to Alcolea. He stays here with me, in the hotel. Dinner, a walk, the Preces, a blessing.[164]

From Córdoba the Father went to Seville, to make more visits, and there he ran into a problem. When he went to the station to return to Burgos, the trains were full and he did not have a reservation for the night train. He was advised to go to Utrera, because the chances of

---

[162] See Casciaro, pp. 142–45, and AGP, RHF, T–00159/1, p. 75.
[163] See AGP, RHF, EF–380408–7.
[164] AGP, RHF, EF–380419–2.

getting a ticket were better there. At six in the evening, in Utrera, he approached the ticket agent, explained his problem, and ran into another one: the only seats available were first- or second-class. He had only enough money for a third-class seat. The letter to Burgos continues: "I explained my situation. With great patience and kindness, he tells me the third-class fare, which I do have the money for, and the second-class fare, which I don't. Then he takes another look at the fares, and shortens the trip. Going second-class, I have just enough money to reach Salamanca."

He would have to wait until the train left Cádiz and Utrera received the telegraph saying how many and what kind of seats were left. With only the remotest hope of getting a third-class ticket to Burgos, Father Josemaría handed the problem over to his guardian angel. He returned to the station a little after eight, and found a surprised ticket agent. "The agent had a third-class ticket reserved for me. And he said with disbelief in his voice (I had turned this over to my guardian angel), 'This evening they telegraphed us that they have seventeen tickets available—and all third-class!' I didn't find it hard to believe."

Two nights and a day on the train. At four in the morning on April 23, he reached the Sabadell Hotel. The next month was also filled with trips and visits. He wrote to the bishop of Avila, "I spent almost the entire month of May traveling all over the place, including the front lines at Teruel." [165] He went to the active and dangerous front at Teruel to visit Juan, whom he had not seen for a long time.

*   *   *

The Work continued to be blessed with unity, strength, and cohesion. The founder wrote of the future: "We are going to meet with obstacles, but—so many are the obvious favors from God in these months!—we will overcome them." [166] Two weeks earlier he had written: "We only have reasons for thanking God. However, I am overwhelmed when I think of what we will soon have to confront." [167]

In his writings of this period there are occasional glimpses of his life of contemplative union with God. On Monday, June 6, for example, he noted in his journal: "My prayer this morning on the way to Las Huelgas: guided by Saint Joseph, I placed myself, with the light of the

---

[165] AGP, RHF, EF–380607–2.
[166] AGP, RHF, EF–380408–5.
[167] AGP, RHF, EF–380323–1.

Holy Spirit, in the Wound of the right hand of my Lord." [168] And on his return home that evening, he wrote to Juan Jiménez Vargas:

> Burgos, June 6, 1938
> + May Jesus safeguard you, for himself.
> Dear Juanito,
>   This morning, on my way to Las Huelgas, where I went to do my prayer, I discovered a new world: the Most Holy Wound of our Lord's right hand. I was there all day long, kissing and adoring. How truly lovable is the sacred humanity of our God! Pray that he give me that real love of his and with it completely purify all my other affections. It's not enough to say, "Heart on the cross!" Because if one of Christ's wounds cleans, heals, soothes, strengthens, enkindles, and enraptures, what wouldn't the five do as they lie open on the cross? Heart on the cross! O my Jesus, what more could I ask for? I realize that if I continue contemplating in this way (Saint Joseph, my father and lord, is the one who led me there, after I asked him to enkindle me), I'll end up crazier than ever. Try it yourself! . . .
>   I'm quite jealous of those on the battlefronts, in spite of everything. It has occurred to me that, if my path were not so clearly marked out, it would be wonderful to outdo Father Doyle. But . . . that would suit me quite well, since doing penance has never been very hard for me. That, I'm sure, is the reason I'm being led by another path: Love. And the fact is it suits me even better. If only I weren't such a donkey!
>   Take care, my son. *Dominus sit in corde tuo!* [The Lord be in your heart!]
>   Much love. From the Wound of the right hand, your Father blesses you.
>
>   Mariano[169]

                         *   *   *

[168] *Apuntes,* no. 1576.
[169] AGP, RHF, EF–380606–1.
    The Father Doyle referred to is the Irish Jesuit William Doyle, a volunteer army chaplain who died in August 1917 in the battle of Ypres. He was known for a cheerful but rigorous spirit of penance in little things. The anecdote of "the 'drama' of the butter" in *The Way* (no. 205) refers to him. See Alfred O'Rahilly, *Father William Doyle, S.J.* (London, 1925), p. 168.

Isidoro, in one of the letters he sent to the other members of the Work in the republican zone, wrote: "When we had grandfather with us, we didn't take full advantage of his presence. I have often thought about this. He is the high-powered dynamo that infuses us with energy." [170]

"Do the things that need doing"—this was one of Father Josemaría's stated principles. "One begins as best one can. They don't get left undone, for lack of instruments. . . . They get begun." [171]

The material means were often in short supply. In Utrera, while waiting for the train to Burgos, Father Josemaría noticed that the cassock that Bishop Olaechea had given him was falling apart. "My cassock," he says, "which I have mended so often, is losing its lining." [172] And that was typical, because although he sometimes had money at his disposal, he never had a peseta to spend on himself. Now and then he would send the bishop of Avila Mass stipends for his priests, even though he himself had renounced the receiving of stipends. While straining to raise a million pesetas, he always traveled third-class and spent almost nothing on food. In the monthly newsletter he asked the young men at the battlefronts for donations to cover travel costs and also to give to people in need. [173] But for daily expenses he limited himself strictly to money kept for this purpose in a small box that had once contained a Burgos cheese. Their accounting, as José María Albareda explained to him one day, was done "by the vectorial system." Deposits into and withdrawals from the box were indicated by arrows pointing in or out. The Father laughed, and expressed amazement that two mathematicians (Pedro and Paco) and one scientist (José María) were doing worse accounting than his mother's cook did in Barbastro. The mathematicians thereupon adopted the standard credit-and-debit system. [174]

---

[170] AGP, IZL, D–1213, 340.

[171] AGP, RHF, EF–380406–2.

[172] AGP, RHF, EF–380419–2. In his journal entry for June 4, 1938, he writes: "I've really worn myself out sewing. I think I've put more stitches in this cassock than the tailor did" (*Apuntes*, no. 1574).

[173] For more on the stipends sent to the bishop of Avila, see AGP, RHF, EF–380320–1, EF–380325–1, and EF–380331–2.

From Burgos, Father Josemaría wrote in an undated letter to Antonio de Dalmases Esteva: "May Jesus protect you. I don't want to lose track of you, son. The experiences we shared in our journey from the Red tyranny, in search of freedom, are, I think, a sign from God that we should stay united for our whole lives. Write to me often, and I'll give you news about the others. If you need money, clothes, etc., ask me with the same confidence with which you would ask your father" (AGP, RHF, EF–SD3800–1).

[174] See Casciaro, pp. 146–47.

On rare occasions Father Josemaría did overcome his reluctance to spend. One Sunday afternoon, he asked the house treasurer how they were doing financially and was told that they did not have enough to pay the hotel bill due the next morning. "But," he asked, "is there enough for a treat?" He wanted to lift the spirits of his sons. So they did have a treat—and the next morning, after breakfast, a money order for several thousand pesetas arrived, sent from Santander by Manolo Pérez Sánchez, one of the students who had frequented the Ferraz Street residence.[175]

5. *"A lesson on charity"*

Father Josemaría took retreat resolutions seriously. Resolutions 4 and 5 from his retreat in Pamplona were "The women" and "Do the law dissertation."[176]

Only two of his journal entries contain mention of the apostolate he carried out with women in Burgos in 1938. He gave spiritual direction to a daughter of General Martín Moreno, to Carmen Munárriz, to a sister of Vicente Rodríguez Casado, and to some friends of those women. "I had the study circle for the girls," he writes in one entry. "There were seven."[177] Thinking of the oratory he wanted to set up in Madrid, he encouraged them to make vestments and altar cloths that would complement the sacred vessels he had gotten in Pamplona. "We've taken out of the case all the liturgical objects made for us in Pamplona," he writes to José María. "Really, they are magnificent. So these daughters of mine are lining the inside of the tabernacle with silk."[178]

These very well-intentioned young women either did not join the Work or did not continue in it. But they remained objects of the Father's spiritual affection, as did his daughters in the Red zone: Hermógenes García, Antonia Sierra, and Lola Fisac.

He wrote to Isidoro: "The poor old fellow is very uneasy about his little granddaughters back in Madrid. Send him some news of them,

---

[175] AGP, RHF, T–00159/1, p. 76.

[176] See *Apuntes*, no. 1445 (23 Dec 1937).

[177] *Apuntes*, no. 1575 (5 Jun 1938). In a letter to Isidoro Zorzano, he says: "I give a talk each week to a group of girls, one of whom is Amparito, Vicentín's sister" (AGP, RHF, EF–380801–1).

[178] AGP, RHF, EF–380504–1.

and also of the grandmother and the aunt and uncle. He always thinks of them so much, and with so much affection!"[179]

Isidoro filled him in, but did not tell him everything. He did write, "Grandmother, aunt and uncle, and the rest of the family are still doing fine," and "The little girls are delighted to be able to help the grandfather when he comes. Hermógenes continues to keep grandmother company; we're enjoying fine weather, and they are taking advantage of it to go for walks." But he left out something that would have deeply troubled the Father, something that he did write to those in his own zone: "Since the last bombardment at Castellón, which leveled the Hospital Provincial, which is where Antonia was, we have had no news of her. Pray for her." Fortunately, she was soon located. So Isidoro then wrote to the Father, "Antonia is still in Castellón, and is very happy because she hopes to see grandfather soon."[180]

The matter of his doctoral dissertation illustrates his persistence and determination to squeeze everything he could out of the time and circumstances available to him. On that memorable day when he went to the residence of the archbishop of Burgos to request ministerial faculties, he had, as we mentioned before, run into a priest he had known in Madrid. This was Father Manuel Ayala, now secretary of the seminary, and before that, secretary of the pontifical university. Father Manuel promised to provide him with source material for his dissertation.[181] Obviously he would have to start from scratch, since all his source material and research notes on his original topic, the priestly ordination of men of mixed race in Spanish colonial America, had been left behind in the Ferraz Street residence.

He now chose as his topic a curious case in the history of canon law. The abbey of Las Huelgas Reales, half a mile outside Burgos, had been established by King Alfonso VIII, in the twelfth century. It had a church and chapels, living quarters, courtyards, and a garden. Its rooms housed more than a hundred nuns. At that abbey princes were married, kings were crowned, and several sovereigns were buried. The abbess had a prelate's jurisdiction over a dozen convents in Castile and León, and over about fifty villages and hamlets; this included legal jurisdiction, both civil and criminal. The abbess

---

[179] AGP, RHF, EF–380118–1.

[180] AGP, IZL, D–1213, 327, 354, and 370. The young woman ended up hospitalized in the National Sanatorium of Estivella: see AGP, IZL, D–1213, 372.

[181] See *Apuntes*, no. 1479 (10 Jan 1938).

conferred benefices, approved confessors, gave preaching faculties, decided matrimonial and civil cases, demanded tribute, and imposed excommunications. During ceremonial royal visits, it was de rigueur that the sovereign and the abbess be seated side by side, indicating equality in dignity. In 1873, when these special jurisdictions in Spain were abolished, the abbess became subordinate to the archbishop of Burgos.[182]

Between one trip and the next, whenever he had a few hours free, Father Josemaría would go to the abbey and spend the morning in the bookkeeper's office, where he would be brought folios, books, and files from the library. He would set out early in the day, as soon as Pedro and Paco, having attended his Mass, had left for their respective offices. (During his first several months in Burgos, he said Mass at the house of the Teresian Association or at the Church of Santa Clara, which was next to the boardinghouse. Later he said Mass sometimes at the Carmelite monastery, sometimes at the cathedral, and, for an extended period, at the Church of Saints Cosmos and Damian, at an altar with an ornate altarpiece of our Lady. At this time there were more priests than altars in Burgos.[183])

*   *   *

Monday, June 6, was the day he contemplated the wound in our Lord's right hand. He did not get much research done that week, because on Tuesday he got a telegram from Ricardo Fernández Vallespín saying, "Wounded not seriously." [184] He took the next train to Avila, and from there he took the train to Carabanchel Alto, on the Madrid front, very worried the whole time. Among the hundred young men comprising the extended family of Ferraz students, they already knew of ten deaths. Four had died in Madrid: Eraso, Llanos, Gastaca, Suárez del Villar. Pepe Isasa and Jacinto Valentín Gamazo, both of whom were members of the Work, had been killed at the front. Jaime Munárriz, a medical student, one of the first to go to Porta Coeli, also died in battle. In a high fever, he had been heard calling out for Father Josemaría. The names of the dead appeared monthly in the

---

[182] See Josemaría Escrivá de Balaguer, *La Abadesa de las Huelgas: Estudio teológico jurídico* (Madrid, 1944), p. 33.
[183] See Casciaro, pp. 170–71.
[184] See AGP, RHF, T–00162, p. 41, and T–00159/1, p. 72.

pages of the newsletter. "What a group we have in heaven!" the Father wrote.[185]

On Saturday, at four in the morning, after three nights of not sleeping a wink, the Father returned to Burgos. Later he wrote to Juan Jiménez Vargas:

> As for Ricardo, it's a miracle that the hand grenade that wounded him didn't kill him. He has wounds all over his body; it's like one big tattoo. And yet only three or four are of any importance, and even they are not serious. . . . I expect that he will recover soon and have no worse repercussion from it than the initial shock.
>
> How moving it was to be so close to Madrid! Almost—not almost—it was like being in Madrid. I had some bad moments.[186]

An officer had taken him to the Carabanchel observation post. Using the battery gunsight, he had a good view of war-damaged Madrid, including the partially destroyed building at 16 Ferraz Street.[187] In his letter to Isidoro about Ricardo's "hunting accident," he mentioned this and then said:

> Therefore the grandfather had a doubly hard time—because of his grandson, and because he was only three or four miles from his other grandson Alvaro, whom he is not allowed to visit. However, with some wonderful binoculars, he could see the house and everything around it, and so he could pretend to be where his heart longed to go. In fact, he was closer to Alvaro than he had been in the insane asylum.[188]

"But business is business," he added, "and these separations are necessary. How often, before reaching France, I was on the verge of returning to my own country, but Jeannot stopped me! Things have

---

[185] See AGP, RHF, D–03691, and *Apuntes,* no. 1461 (2 Jan 1938). In the newsletters the names of the following are listed: Carlos Aresti, Zapico, Juan Antonio Mas y Sánchez, Antonio Alfonso Ochoa, Jaime Munárriz, Gil de Santibáñez, A. Costilla Sandoval, F. Mendieta Larrea, Diego Chico de Guzmán, Rafael Moreno, Manolo Isasa.

[186] AGP, RHF, EF–380611–2.

[187] See AGP, RHF, T–00162, p. 41.

[188] AGP, RHF, EF–380612–1.

turned out for the best. You can't even imagine the work that has been done here."[189]

In March, a nationalist offensive to reach the Mediterranean had begun. Fierce fighting broke out on the fronts at Teruel and in northern Aragón, where some of his sons were. In June, Castellón was taken. Then the tide turned, and the last week of July brought a spectacular republican offensive.[190] The Father was now very glad he had let himself be so carried away by his affection as to go to Teruel to visit Juan, because now there were no furloughs.[191]

Some time back, General Orgaz had suggested that he become an honorary military chaplain, so that he could attend to his sons.[192] Why not do this now?

Service as a regular chaplain would not do, as he explained to the bishop of Pamplona, since being assigned to a particular unit would prevent him from traveling to other fronts.[193] The bishop advised that he take up the matter with the military authorities, and suggested that he might be named a military juridical consultant with the National Service of Ecclesiastical Affairs.[194]

Whatever he did, he wanted to do it with the blessing of the bishop of Madrid. Bishop Eijo already knew of the matter through his vicar general, Monsignor Casimiro Morcillo. When Father Josemaría wrote to the bishop, he made some observations that he thought might be helpful, but made it clear that for him the bottom line was that "my vocation is to be one hundred percent a priest."[195]

*   *   *

---

[189] Ibid.

[190] On July 24 began the republican offensive that resulted in the so-called Battle of the Ebro. This was the fiercest battle of the war, and one of the longest ones. It lasted until November 16. In October there was a danger that the conflict would be complicated by a general war in Europe, as a result of the crisis in the Sudetenland caused by Hitler's pressure on Czechoslovakia. On December 23, 1938, a month after the nationalist counterattack on the Ebro, the general offensive of the nationalists against Catalonia began.

[191] See AGP, RHF, EF–380607–2.

[192] See AGP, RHF, EF–380607–3.

[193] Ibid.

[194] See AGP, RHF, D–15219.

[195] AGP, RHF, EF–380807–1. The bishop's reply was taking a long time to arrive. So, at the request of the National Service of Ecclesiastical Affairs, Father Josemaría wrote on October 4 to Monsignor Morcillo: "I would be grateful if you would be so kind as to ask our bishop to give me his opinion, so that I can follow it fearlessly" (AGP, RHF, EF–381004–1).

Shortly before Ricardo's "hunting accident," Father Josemaría learned that Father Carmelo Ballester was staying at the Burgos seminary. Father Ballester was the one who had done the edition of the New Testament that Bishop Olaechea gave him in Pamplona and that he used during his retreat. He was consecrated bishop of León on May 15. Father Josemaría could not attend the ceremony because he was visiting the Aragón front, but he sent a silver tray with the new bishop's coat of arms engraved on it. "The gift is modest, but attractive," he wrote to José María. "Moreover, he deserves it, even though he doesn't understand us—yet!" [196]

Bishop Ballester invited him to spend a few days with him in his residence in León. León being halfway between Burgos and Santiago de Compostela, and Father Josemaría being pressed for time, he made some very detailed calculations so as to get several things done on the one trip, including visiting the shrine of Saint James in Santiago de Compostela "to gain the jubilee indulgence and to pray for everyone." [197] Following the centuries-old tradition of making pilgrimages to the tomb of Saint James the Greater, Spain's patron saint, many devout people sought the holy year indulgence—this holy year having been extended from 1937 into 1938 because of the war.

On the night of July 15, Father Josemaría was in León, "being spoiled by this holy bishop." From the bishop's residence he wrote to those in Burgos, "Pray for me that this Saint James Jubilee will purify me and enkindle my soul." [198]

Having spoken with Bishop Carmelo about the Work, he met with Father Eliodoro Gil, the priest who mimeographed the copies of the monthly newsletter. Father Gil was to join him on the pilgrimage, and so was Ricardo. He arrived in León on July 16, the feast of Our Lady of Mount Carmel (Bishop Ballester's patron saint).

On July 18, after Father Josemaría said Mass for the Teresians, the three of them went to the station, and found that their train had just left. Father Eliodoro called a parishioner of his who was a taxi cab driver, and he took them to Veguellina de Orbigo (some twenty miles from León), where they caught the train to Galicia. The incident would forever remain fresh in Father Eliodoro's memory because of a

[196] AGP, RHF, EF–380429–1. See also *Apuntes*, no. 1423 (19 Dec 1937), and AGP, RHF, EF–380223–1. Father Ballester had given him some of his books.
[197] AGP, RHF, EF–380611–2. At Santiago de Compostela, a holy year occurs whenever July 25, the feast of Saint James, occurs on a Sunday.
[198] AGP, RHF, EF–380716–2.

meditation Father Josemaría gave on the way from León to Veguellina. As they were riding through the verdant valley of Orbigo, enjoying the view of rich fields of alfalfa, beets, and hops, they passed by a waterwheel. A donkey, with eyes covered, was walking in a circle, drawing water to feed the irrigation canal. Father Josemaría spoke of the monotonous, persevering, and ostensibly fruitless work that is indispensable to a fruitful garden. Consider, he said, the importance of that humble obedience of "treading the right path, wearing blinders, but enlightened by the inner light of faith, knowing ourselves instruments in God's hands." [199]

In Santiago de Compostela they stayed at the inn of La Perla. On Tuesday, July 19, with Ricardo serving, Father Josemaría celebrated Mass in the crypt where the remains of Saint James are venerated. "How much I prayed for our family, and for the grandmother, and for Aunt Carmen and Uncle Santi!" he wrote Isidoro.[200]

*   *   *

After the journal entry of June 6 that speaks of the wound in our Lord's right hand, there is an unusual gap of almost two months, ending with an entry that begins: "Tuesday, August 2: I think I should note down the lesson the Lord gave us yesterday about charity." [201]

The incident, which is recorded at length (though not in its entirety), was certainly a tragic one. It troubled Pedro Casciaro to the point of traumatizing him, as he himself says.

When Father Josemaría got back from Santiago de Compostela, on the afternoon of July 20, Pedro told him that a policeman had shown up at the hotel, asking that the Father report to the office of Commander Primitivo Vicente Gallo. He went the next day. The Commander wanted information about Pedro Casciaro and his father. "I told them everything they wanted to know about Pedro," he says, "and all that I knew about the good activities of his father, though in Albacete he was one of the leaders of the republican left." [202]

Very serious allegations against Pedro and his father had reached

[199] See AGP, RHF, T–07987, p. 10, and *Sum.* 7766.
[200] AGP, RHF, EF–380801–1. For more on the jubilee, see the August 1938 issue of *Noticias*, in AGP, RHF, D–03691. There it is said that at the Mass in the crypt, a professor served as acolyte; this is an affectionate reference to Ricardo. Father Josemaría also spoke of Ricardo in a letter to Bishop Santos Moro of Avila: AGP, RHF, EF–380803–1.
[201] *Apuntes*, no. 1577.
[202] Ibid.

the ears of Commander Gallo. Supposedly the father was a Mason and communist who was responsible for, if not an agent of, the deaths of many people in Albacete, and the son, also an active communist, had crossed over to the nationalist zone in order to spy in the headquarters of General Orgaz.[203]

This was the third time these serious allegations had been made. Military justice was swift; the situation had to be cleared up as soon as possible. But it would not be easy, since no one in the Work had been in Albacete at the time of the events in question, and since, truth to tell, there did seem to be an element of truth in the accusations, since Mr. Casciaro was still in political office.

The accusers were a Mr. Jorge Bermúdez and his wife, Teresa. Commander Gallo advised Father Josemaría to go visit them.[204]

The couple belonged to Albacete's middle class, which consisted mainly of landowners, manufacturers, and government officials. Before the Republic was proclaimed, Mr. Bermúdez, a rightist, worked in the city's treasury department. Living across the street from him was Mr. Casciaro, a high-school teacher who was a left-wing activist. But despite their political differences, there was no personal animosity between them. Mr. and Mrs. Bermúdez had a good social position and were well-to-do.

Around 1934, however, a reversal of fortune forced them to liquidate their goods by public auction and move to another city. In 1936 they settled in Burgos, and by the time of these accusations, Mr. Bermúdez had a position of prestige and influence in this city's treasury department: he was administrator of properties and land taxes.

Some days before the policeman showed up at the hotel, Pedro and Mrs. Bermúdez had run into each other on the street. It was not a pleasant surprise for either of them. They had not seen one another since the auction, at which Pedro had bought a chandelier, a suit of armor, and some swords from the Philippines, after haggling with Mrs. Bermúdez.[205]

On Monday, August 1, at ten in the morning, Father Josemaría and José María Albareda went to see Mr. Bermúdez in his office, while Miguel Fisac (who was on leave in Burgos) went with Pedro to speak with Mrs. Bermúdez in her home. On the way to the office, Father

[203] See Casciaro, p. 160.
[204] See *Apuntes*, no. 1578 (2 Aug 1938).
[205] See Casciaro, p. 159.

Josemaría prayed "to the guardian angel of the man we were about to visit, and to José María's, and to the Little Watchmaker [his own guardian angel], so that the meeting would go well."[206]

Bermúdez did admit him and José María to his office, but was right away so irate that the priest had to remind him that they "had come there to discuss that troublesome matter in a gentlemanly and Christian way." Father Josemaría then began the discussion by asking how Mrs. Bermúdez could truthfully claim to have seen Pedro doing propaganda work for the Popular Front in Albacete during the 1936 elections, when Pedro was in Madrid, at the Ferraz Street residence, at that time. "I can't believe," said the Father, "that the Lord would grant him bilocation to work against the Lord's cause."

At that moment there may have flashed in the official's mind the image of two children, his son Rafael and little Pedro, walking home together, in around 1929, after their "Spanish Explorers" expeditions, because he said, "It's true that little Pedro was a good boy." But then he added, "However, he is now a man, and it could be that he has come to be a traitor like his father—who is a red!"

Father Josemaría replied, "I've dealt with little Pedro day after day since he became a man, and I can answer for him. With all due respect to your wife, what she said about him is false."

But Bermúdez did not want to know the truth. He just kept persisting, reiterating his accusations against Pedro's father, exclaiming, "They should be shot, not put in prison, when Albacete is ours!"

To this the Father gently replied that he would put his hands in a fire for Pedro.

"Then you are going to get burned," retorted Bermúdez.

But how could Bermúdez presume to tell him, a priest who knew Pedro through and through, that this young man was not a good Christian and a good Spaniard?

"If he is, let us give thanks to God and I am happy," was the sarcastic answer.

"But you would leave only three Spaniards out of every hundred!" the priest protested.

Bermúdez was not ruffled. "That is what needs to happen," he said. "Otherwise we won't have accomplished anything."

Father Josemaría countered that appalling attitude with a reminder

---

[206] *Apuntes*, no. 1579 (2 Aug 1938).

of the reckoning that every human being will have to give on the day of judgment—an occasion that might not be so far off. What if for Bermúdez it were that very day? What would he say to our Lord?

But even with that he could not soften the man's heart. "Both father and son have to pay," he insisted.

"That isn't Christian. You would have sent Saint Augustine to hell."

"They have to pay," Bermúdez repeated.

In his journal the Father notes, "The meeting took place within the bounds of politeness. We shook hands when we left." [207]

The Father left silent and saddened, deeply disconcerted by the hard and sarcastic tone Bermúdez had kept right to the very end. As Pedro relates it, "He went down the stairs of the building very recollected, almost with his eyes closed, and said, as if thinking out loud, 'Tomorrow or the next day, a funeral.'" [208] Then he went to see Commander Gallo to tell him what had happened.

Meanwhile, the conversation that Pedro and Miguel were having with Mrs. Bermúdez could not have been more acrimonious. She had two sons in the military, one on the front and the other a pilot. Was it right, she asked Pedro, that they were risking their lives while he was living comfortably behind the lines, spying for the reds? Miguel came to Pedro's defense. The conversation grew very heated, insults flying back and forth, and she swore that not one letter of the accusation made by her husband would be dropped. Pedro returned to his office crestfallen. In the Father's journal we read, "The boys' meeting with the wife was terrible. She actually told Pedro that she would do all the harm she could to his father." [209]

In silence, the Father and Miguel had lunch and then returned to the hotel room. The priest stayed deep in thought, with one idea stuck in his mind. "In the afternoon," he wrote in his journal the next day, "the thought kept coming to me that that family was going to suffer a blow. I thought of the son they had at the front." Sitting in one of the wicker chairs on the sun porch and praying, he suddenly said to Miguel, "Tomorrow or the next day, that lady will have a funeral. We will have to express our condolences." [210] The entry continues:

---

[207] See *Apuntes*, nos. 1579 and 1580 (2 Aug 1938). See also Casciaro, pp. 161–62; *Sum.* 6410 (Pedro Casciaro); and AGP, RHF, T–00159/1, p. 78.

[208] Casciaro, p. 162. See also Alvaro del Portillo, *Sum.* 904; and AGP, RHF, T–00159/1.

[209] *Apuntes*, no. 1581 (2 Aug 1938).

[210] *Apuntes*, no. 1582 (2 Aug 1938). See also AGP, RHF, T–00159/1, p. 78.

In the middle of the afternoon, Miguel and I went out for a walk. At a corner, as is customary in Burgos, there was posted a death notice. It was for the man that José María and I had gone to see in the morning. I exclaimed, "I thought it was the son!"

Miguel blanched, and said, "At the time of this man's death, you were talking about it."

We said a Rosary for him and today I offered my Mass for the repose of his soul. I don't want to judge him. I feel sure that the undeniable facts of this case are only a lesson in charity for us.

I have never seen myself so wretched as these past few days.[211]

Late in the evening of August 1, Pedro returned from military headquarters. Trying not to give him too big a shock, the Father told him about the visit he had had with Mr. Bermúdez that morning, and about the man's sudden death early that afternoon. Pedro almost passed out. He had to go lie down in the alcove, on the Father's bed. The Father gently spoke to him, trying to calm him down about the death of Mr. Bermúdez. "He was morally certain," says Pedro, "that God had had mercy on his soul and had granted him final repentance. And he added that from the moment he had left his office, he had not ceased praying for him and his children." [212]

---

[211] *Apuntes*, no. 1582. It was then the custom, at least in the cities of Castile and León, to announce a death by leaving one's front door ajar, with a book for people to sign to express their condolences. Also, before the news appeared in the local paper, notices would be placed on store windows and walls.

On September 24, 1975, at the request of Father Pedro Casciaro and the architect Juan Lahuerta, Don José María Laborda, head of the treasury department of Burgos, held a meeting in his office with some of the people who had worked there at the time of the death of Mr. Bermúdez. The purpose was to clarify certain points. According to the parish records of St. Lawrence the Great in Burgos (in Book of the Dead no. 11), Jorge Bermúdez was given a church burial on August 2, 1938, and had died "of natural causes, on the afternoon of the previous day, at home." Similarly, the death certificate in the registry office (section 3, book 14, folio 263v) says that he "died in his home yesterday (August 1) at 12:30, of angina pectoris."

However, they were able to establish that Mr. Bermúdez had died in his office and then been taken to his home. He had had a visit that day, and when that meeting was over, one employee had remarked to some others, "Don Jorge is not feeling well." They went to his office, and saw him raise a hand to his head and gasp for breath. It lasted a minute. He was fifty-one years old. (See Casciaro, pp. 162–64.)

[212] Casciaro, p. 163. See also *Sum.* 6410 (Casciaro) and *Sum.* 904 (Alvaro del Portillo). Paco Botella says that the Father's comment upon seeing the death notice was, "I thought the one dying was going to be a son of this man—the son who is at the front" (AGP, RHF, T–00159/1, p. 78).

When Pedro seemed somewhat recovered, Father Josemaría suggested that he return to the camp and ask Captain Martos for a leave of three or four days, because of exhaustion; he could spend that time in Bilbao with his uncle. On his way to the camp, Pedro saw on the door of the Church of Our Lady of Ransom the death notice for Don Jorge Bermúdez.

Evidently Captain Martos had already heard what had happened and was a bit superstitious. He was quick to grant the leave. "Of course, Casciaro, you go and rest," he said. "You know I've always had a high regard for you. You don't have anything against me, do you?"

"I left for Bilbao that same night," wrote Pedro Casciaro in 1979. "During those days in Bilbao I did calm down, although that incident had been engraved in my mind for the rest of my life." [213]

*   *   *

The state that the Father went into when leaving Mr. Bermúdez's office—of being so engrossed in thought and prayer that he seemed half asleep—was not something new. On several occasions he had experienced this "waking dream which sometimes lets me know future or faraway events." [214]

Extraordinary supernatural manifestations of intimacy with our Lord—illuminations, interior locutions, the gift of tears, discernment of spirits, perceptible assistance from our Lady and the guardian angels—were regular occurrences with him. So much so that, while everyone else involved was deeply upset by Mr. Bermúdez's death, he saw this incident as simply "a lesson in charity, the lesson that God comes to the defense of his own." [215] While refraining from judging

---

[213] AGP, RHF, T–04197, p. 107.

[214] *Apuntes*, no. 1600 (17 Jul 1939). Of another occasion he gives this description: "In Burgos, before the taking of Madrid, I saw details of what we were going to encounter there. It was like a dream, but a waking one. Thus I *knew* . . ." (*Apuntes*, no. 1598). And of another: "As I left the convent of Santa Isabel, the thought came to me that the church would be burned" (*Apuntes*, no. 1620).

He also had what one might call instructive dreams, such as the one mentioned in his entry for December 12, 1935: "I was saying to the Lord, a few days ago in holy Mass, 'Tell me something, Jesus, tell me something.' And in response I clearly saw a dream I had had the night before, in which Jesus was a seed, buried and apparently rotting, which then became a ripe and fertile spike of wheat. And I understood that this, and no other, was my path. A good response!" (*Apuntes*, no. 1304).

[215] *Apuntes*, nos. 1577 and 1582. In another entry he referred to "that case of charity, or better, lesson on charity, from our Lord in Burgos" (*Apuntes*, no. 1600).

anyone, he said in a letter written the next week: "God knows a lot and *always* acts lovingly." [216]

On August 17, after returning from Bilbao, Pedro Casciaro ran into one of Mr. Bermúdez's sons, a provisional lieutenant in the infantry. They spoke of his father's death. "He told me that it had happened in his office," Pedro wrote the Father, "with no warning, while he was talking to a colleague. It seems to have been a heart attack. I gave him my condolences." [217]

A few weeks after Mr. Bermúdez's death, his other son—Rafael, the pilot—was killed. When Father Josemaría learned of this, he commented sadly, "To a certain extent it was to be expected. Pray for him. I will do the same."

"A few days later," says Pedro, "I saw Don Jorge's widow in the Jesuit church. When I realized that it was she, I tried to leave as unobtrusively as possible. But she saw me, and I think she even looked at me with tenderness." [218]

6. *With pen in hand*

On August 2, the day he wrote that long journal entry about the "lesson in charity," Father Josemaría left for Vitoria to settle certain questions about his doctoral dissertation and about his position as rector of Santa Isabel. He stayed with the bishop, who asked him to give two retreats, one for the diocesan clergy and the other for the community of sisters who staffed his residence. First, however, he was to spend a few days with the bishop of Avila.

From there he wrote to his sons in Burgos on August 8, recounting some events from the trip and expressing admiration for the bishop. "This morning," he says, "I celebrated Mass after the bishop finished his. Every instant I am discovering more points of perfection in the life of this good bishop. May our Lord help me learn from his example, so imbued with simplicity and naturalness." [219] Bishop Moro very gladly

[216] AGP, RHF, EF–380811–1.

[217] AGP, RHF, EF–380819–2.

[218] Casciaro, p. 164.

[219] AGP, RHF, EF–380808–1. See also AGP, RHF, EF–380803–1 and EF–380807–1. In Vitoria he also spoke with Professor Eloy Montero, who taught law in Madrid. "He assures me," he wrote back to Burgos, "that the dissertation is very good (the bootlicker!) and that in a couple of weeks they'll approve it in Madrid" (AGP, RHF, EF–380819–1).

agreed to let him leave there, for safekeeping, the books and other objects that they had been assembling for the future oratory: tabernacle, sacred vessels, candlesticks, vestments. In a tranquillity such as he had seldom enjoyed, Father Josemaría spent the next few days preparing the retreats he was to give in Vitoria. He wrote to those in Burgos:

> How good, how very holy, the bishop is! This place is a school of all the virtues, with a foundation of humility that fills them with fortitude. It is consoling to see how dearly he loves us. I feel quite at home here, except for missing all of you. But if only you knew how much I am with you, each one of you, day and night! This is my mission: to help you be happy hereafter, with God, and now, on earth, giving him glory.[220]

He also wrote to José Ramón Herrero Fontana, who was then ill, and to Ricardo Fernández Vallespín, who had just heard, several weeks late, of the deaths of his sister and his grandmother, and whose father had also died recently. To Ricardo he wrote:

> How can I speak of sharing your sorrow, when all your sorrows are my sorrows?
>
> We heard about the death of your father (may he rest in peace) almost right after you were wounded. Who was going to tell you anything then? I limited myself to saying all the prayers I could for him and to writing (twice) to make sure your family was taken care of financially. Nothing more could be done.
>
> I didn't know about the other deaths. I will also offer suffrages. . . .
>
> How sorry I am that I can't be there to give you an *abrazo!* In desire I put myself by your side, to say with you to the Lord, *Fiat.*
>
> Poor Josemaría would like to say, without tears, that he is now more than ever your Father, if this is possible.
>
> A big hug and my blessing,
>
> Mariano[221]

[220] AGP, RHF, EF–380811–1.
[221] AGP, RHF, EF–380810–1.

In the republican zone, meanwhile, Alvaro and two others were preparing to leave Madrid. They were constantly in his thoughts and prayers. "Where do you suppose they are right now, those sons of mine trying to cross the front? Are they still in Madrid? *Dominus sit in itinere eorum!* [The Lord be with them on their journey!]" [222]

He spent three days, at the Sabadell Hotel, and then left on August 17 for Vitoria. A journal entry dated August 20, during the retreat he was giving at the bishop's residence for the community of Third Order Capuchin nuns, said:

> I see myself as so wretched that often I stick my head in the oratory to say to Jesus, "Don't trust me. I, yes, do trust you, Jesus. I abandon myself in your arms, and leave there what is mine—my wretchedness!" Were I not to do this, I think I would go crazy with so many things churning inside me. I abandon myself to Jesus Christ, with all my wretchedness. And whatever he wants, at each moment, *fiat.*
>
> *Monstra te esse matrem.* [Show that you are a mother.]
> I think the little nuns are making their retreat very well. [223]

There was a lot of work for the nuns to do in the bishop's residence, because of the large number of refugee priests from the republican zone living there. However, they organized things so as not to miss any of Father Josemaría's conferences. "We could hardly wait for his meditations," says Sister Ascensión. "They made us want to fall deeper and deeper in love with Jesus Christ. I have never been on a retreat like that one. I will never forget it as long as I live, and it has always helped me. I don't remember the specific topics of the conferences, but I've always remembered that I have no choice but to be a saint." [224]

[222] AGP, RHF, EF–380808–1.

Isidoro, in letters written to the Father on July 25 and August 5, refers to a planned crossing to the nationalist side by Alvaro del Portillo, Vicente Rodríguez Casado, and Eduardo Alastrué, saying that they are getting ready to make a trip to "be reunited with their grandfather" (see AGP, IZL, D–1213, 386 and 388). These letters probably had not arrived yet. The correspondence with Madrid was done through Manuel Albareda, and it was getting harder to keep up because of the growing volume of letters. From Vitoria the founder wrote to his sons in Burgos, "My God! Don't let there be a cut-off of our communication, via Saint-Jean-de-Luz, with the poor fellows in Madrid" (AGP, RHF, EF–380822–1).

[223] *Apuntes*, no. 1585.

[224] AGP, RHF, T–04388, p. 4.

Father Josemaría's palpable faith in the Real Presence made a deep impression. Sister Juana recalls how moved they all were by the way he "turned toward the tabernacle and spoke with our Lord as if he was seeing him. 'Jesus,' he would say, 'I am crazy with love. Make these also go crazy with love for you.' " [225]

His virtues were quite visible to them. Sister Elvira and Sister Juana were assigned to clean his room. In the morning they would find his bed unmade, but they could tell that he had slept on the floor. Sister Elvira recalls that his breakfast was a little coffee with milk.

The nuns were amazed to see how often his cassock had been mended. "He lived in the most absolute poverty," says Sister María Loyola. "He had only one cassock, which at one point he gave us to repair. It was almost in rags. We tried to mend it as well as we could, and as quickly, because he was in his room, waiting for us to finish. His underwear was so torn that there was no way to put the needle in a part of the cloth that wasn't on the point of tearing. Sister Juana decided to buy him two new sets." [226]

He did have a new hat. Pedro and Paco had forced him to buy one, since the one given him by Bishop Olaechea had been ruined by sun and rain. One day, when Father Josemaría was out, they cut the hat up with scissors and sent a piece with each of the newsletters they were sending to the fronts. Everyone appreciated receiving these reminders of him, and, after reprimanding Pedro and Paco, he did go out and buy a new hat.

Operation Cassock, however, was a total failure. Though not very old, the cassock had had a lot of wear and was made of a cheap material. One time when he retired to the alcove, leaving his cassock in the main room, Pedro and Paco ripped it down the back—an easy thing to do, since the cloth was so worn. And immediately they left for the barracks, hoping that he would have to buy another cassock. But when they got back, they found him carefully sewing it up. He said nothing to them.

It was the hottest part of the summer. People passing him on the street wondered why he was wearing a coat over his cassock.[227]

*   *   *

[225] Ibid., p. 8.

[226] Ibid., p. 6. See also Alvaro del Portillo, *Sum.* 373.

[227] See AGP, RHF, T–00159/1, p. 79, and Casciaro, pp. 156–58. He did not buy a new cassock until the middle of February 1939: see AGP, RHF, EF–390213–3.

Father Josemaría returned from Vitoria to Burgos on August 26. Two days later, accompanied by Pedro, Paco, and José María, he set out for Logroño, mainly to visit José Ramón, who was still recuperating. As he walked through the city, memories of his adolescence came rushing back, some happy, others painful: his family's financial ruin and departure from Barbastro, his years in high school, the prints left in the snow by a barefoot Carmelite. . . . He had, by the way, shortly after his arrival in Burgos, run into that Carmelite, Father José Miguel. He was now living in the Carmelite monastery there.[228]

On September 3 Father Josemaría left for Vitoria, and from there he went to Vergara, to give a retreat for the priests of the diocese. He prepared it very carefully and asked many people to offer prayers and mortifications for its success. Its theme was "Jesus Christ, Eternal High Priest." There is a brief journal entry about it: "Vergara, September 7, 1938: I am happy about the retreat. There are fifty-five priests, and they listen very attentively and seem quite recollected. Our Lady is helping me." [229]

Actually, not all of those attending were priests. A few were preparing for ordination. Guillermo Marañón was one of these. "His love for Christ the Priest shone through all of his words," he recalls. "One saw a man of deep, ardent interior life, who wished to infuse in us what was already his own life and path. His words, clear, ordered, and refined, made his deep faith visible; they were 'burning darts.' " [230]

On September 7 Father Josemaría wrote to his sons in Saragossa:

> It's a fervent group. I clearly sense my mother holy Mary moving me to move them. What a mother our Lady is! Say something to her on my behalf at Our Lady of the Pillar. Kiss her for me. Sometimes love for our Lady is the only noble thing left in the lives of troubled souls. How good she is![231]

*   *   *

[228] "I ran into that Father José Miguel of Logroño, who was my confessor when I was sixteen. We are both delighted": *Apuntes*, no. 1484 (13 Jan 1938). See also AGP, RHF, T–00159/1, p. 72.

[229] *Apuntes*, no. 1586.

[230] AGP, RHF, T–05228.

[231] AGP, RHF, EF–380907–3. He also wrote to Bishop Santos Moro, "I think it has been our Lady who has given the talks" (AGP, RHF, EF–380909–1).

The consistency between Father Josemaría's inner life and his out-ward behavior was readily observable. His contemplative life so clearly came through in his words, gestures, and attitudes that even his handwriting testified to a character that was all of one piece.

His natural gift with words was evident in his writing, which came easy to him. From early on, as we have seen, he found letter writing to be an essential element of his apostolate. With pen in hand, he had a great facility of style that made his thoughts and feelings flow onto the paper. But the pen in hand could not be just any pen.

When the revolution broke out, his old pen got left behind at the Ferraz Street residence. At the consulate, and now for his correspondence of 1938, he had to use different kinds, which for him was a real problem. In more than a dozen letters, he refers to the frustration he feels at having to use a strange pen unsuited to his writing style or his personality. Sometimes he jokes about it. "I'm writing," he tells Paco Botella, "with José María's little pen, which makes me nervous with its delicate strokes." If the ink did not flow abundantly enough to produce nice, thick strokes, he would pronounce the pen "a disaster." But if the ink flowed too abundantly, producing blotches, then the pen was "suffering from incontinence." [232] Typically, however, when he got a good pen, he would give it to one of his sons who lacked one.

His handwriting is strong and distinctive, such that it is surprising to find in some of his letters uneven lines and weak strokes. In a letter written while he was waiting for a safe-conduct pass, he explains: "I am writing with a broken pen, which is worse than the wait." [233] Soon after his pilgrimage to Santiago de Compostela, having lost there a pen that suited him, he writes to his sons in Burgos: "I am starting this letter with a little fine-tipped pen, very fine. . . . Patience! I should have been born in the age of quill pens, so that I could trim them to the style I need." [234] In Vergara, during the retreat for priests, he had to borrow a pen to write a letter, and is embarrassed by the sight of his writing. "What a dainty handwriting, eh? The abbess lent me one of her thin little pens, and that—the pen, not the abbess—is what's to blame." [235] And in a letter written in Burgos to Juan Jiménez Vargas, he

---

[232] See AGP, RHF, EF–380227–1, EF–381218–1, and EF–390117–1.
[233] AGP, RHF, EF–380511–1. See also *Apuntes*, note 1087, and AGP, RHF, EF–381005–1.
[234] AGP, RHF, EF–380808–1.
[235] AGP, RHF, EF–380907–2.

refuses to take responsibility, saying, "The handwriting isn't mine; it's the pen's."[236]

He did occasionally type letters. The first time was in Burgos, on February 7, 1938, shortly after the Corona typewriter was purchased for doing the monthly newsletters. But the anonymity and coldness of typed print struck him as out of keeping with the confidentiality and closeness there should be in spiritual direction.[237] His energetic spirit seemed to pour through his hands when he was writing, but typing never became easy for him.[238] He typed laboriously, with two fingers, making frequent mistakes that he erased with a rubber eraser or scraped off with a razor blade. He "invariably tore the paper," says Pedro Casciaro, and sometimes cut himself with the blade. When writing with a pencil, "he pressed down so hard that he broke the point."[239]

His vigorous handwriting required a sturdy pen that could produce large, thick letters. His sons joked that he wrote with big letters on purpose to fill the page quickly.[240] Actually, though, he could hardly help it. One day, toward the end of March, he was writing to Ricardo on a number of important matters, and in order to save paper, he forced himself to fill a whole sheet of paper with very small writing. Then he turned it over and kept this up—until finally he gave vent to his frustration. "What nice tiny letters!" he says. "I'm exhausted by the effort." Then his distinctive large handwriting erupts across the page, as if he has thrown off a heavy weight. He says:

> Well! No unnatural thing can last. Mariano, back to your big letters! I need a pen that's just right for me, like the one the reds stole from me in Madrid. Something shaped like this [here he drew a picture of a thick pen] and not like the one I

[236] AGP, RHF, EF–381105–6.

[237] But what he liked least was a pen with a very fine point. "My dearest Ricardo," he writes on June 22, "having no other pens at hand than those ones with which you can't write with any vigor, which are incompatible with my temperament, I've decided to do this letter to you on the typewriter—as the lesser of two evils, since neither do I like writing to my sons in American-style machine-produced print" (AGP, RHF, EF–380622–1).

[238] In July a new typewriter was provided by a brother of José María Albareda. But the Father used it only when he couldn't find a pen. See AGP, RHF, EF–380726–1.

[239] Casciaro, p. 170.

[240] See AGP, RHF, EF–380429–1.

am forced to use, which is the fine-tipped kind that a sweet little nun would use. If you happen to come across one that's as big as a warrior's lance and as broad as my ambitions— which are also very deep—please buy it for me.[241]

Those broad and deep ambitions were, of course, apostolic ones. He was confidently looking to the day when the quest for "the glory of God will disperse us to Madrid, Berlin, Oxford, Paris, Rome, Oslo, Tokyo, Zurich, Buenos Aires, Chicago. . . ."[242]

But how did those boundless ambitions, those dreams of grandeur in the making, fit in with a spirit of humility? On the retreat he had made in Pamplona a few months before, he had taken an objective look at himself and found what he considered faults of omission in his governance of the Work, times when he had lacked strength because of false notions about where charity lay, and a need to exercise fortitude. Firmness of spirit, he had come to see, is a first cousin of genuine humility. "Humility, humility, how much you cost!" he had written. "It is false humility that leads one to relinquish the rights connected with one's position. It is not pride but fortitude to make one's authority felt when what one is demanding is the fulfillment of the holy will of God."[243]

Another loose end he wanted to tie up was the problem of how to coordinate his "excessive" affection with the demands of his authority. When, for instance, someone wanted to back out of a vocational commitment to the Work, he usually would refrain from getting into a lengthy discussion about it, for reasons of tact and charity. One day in 1938, however, when one of his sons did back out, Father Josemaría armed himself with fortitude and established a procedure that he would follow thereafter in all such cases: that of speaking in depth with the person in question about the stumbling blocks that had brought the person to this point, and doing so very candidly, without pulling any punches. As he relates it in a letter to Juan, "I got to the bottom of the truth—a system I plan always to follow. Previously I didn't do this, because of some human consideration (good manners, politeness) or a supernatural one (charity), and maybe a little fear of prolonging a bad time. But now I am convinced that true courtesy and

[241] AGP, RHF, EF–380327–2.
[242] AGP, RHF, EF–380407–1.
[243] *Apuntes*, no. 1436 (21 Dec 1937).

true charity demand getting to the heart of the matter, no matter how difficult this is."[244]

However, he never needed to fear that he might sin by excessive severity. The Lord had given him a heart that could not help melting with affection. Witness this letter to his sons in Saragossa:

Vitoria, September 4, 1938
May Jesus watch over you!

Who can fathom the human heart? Can you believe that till the very last minute, I kept looking to see if you would come before the train left? Now I feel a little remorseful for not having been more generous with my Lord Jesus, because I told you not to come to say good-bye to me. That, while being bad, was also good—for making me afterwards keep longing to see you and talk with you a few minutes and give you all a hug. . . .

I'm anxious, and yet at peace, about the ones in Madrid, every one of them. This poor priest never realized how easily the crazy bird caged in his breast could find room—so much room!—for heavenly and earthly loves. Heart! One time back when I was eighteen (don't tell anyone) I composed a few verses—really poor ones, I must say—that I signed, putting into my signature everything in me, thus: "The Priestly Heart." It's no wonder Dr. Vargas can seriously say that I have some unknown "itis" in my chest.

Your Father blesses and embraces you *ex toto corde*.

Mariano[245]

7. *Autumn 1938*

On September 14 Father Josemaría made one of his very few journal entries for that summer:

Feast of the Exaltation of the Holy Cross, September 14, 1938:
I asked our Lord, with all the force of my soul, to grant me the grace to *exalt* the holy cross in all my faculties and senses. A

[244] AGP, RHF, EF–381013–3. See also EF–381013–1, EF–380408–7, and EF–380502–7.
[245] AGP, RHF, EF–380904–2.

new life! A seal confirming the authenticity of my mission. Josemaría, onto the cross! We shall see, we shall see. *Regnare Christum volumus* [We want Christ to reign].[246]

The tenth anniversary of the founding of the Work was approach-- ing, and he wanted to prepare well by making a private retreat. He wrote Isidoro that he planned to "rest in the country for eight or ter days with no other company than Manolito [our Lord]." [247]

On the afternoon of September 25 he took the bus from Burgos to the Benedictine monastery of Silos. He arrived at seven, and at eigh had dinner in the refectory. Later that night, he wrote to his sons ir Burgos.

> At 8:45 I retired to my cell. At 10:15 the gas was shut off. It is now 11:15. The time has been spent praying and writing these pages. It's cold here. I'll do a bit of exercise and say my childhood prayers and the Preces. Then I'll make my exami- nation of conscience, say the three Hail Marys for purity, pray the Miserere [Psalm 51], and go to sleep—*in the bed.*
>
> Juan! How you would laugh if you could see me trying to do calisthenics! [248]

It was a night of fitful sleep, marked by nightmares and interrupted by the hourly chiming of the clock. Mind racing, he prayed for each of his loved ones. "A thousand times today I've thought about each and every one of my children, especially those in the Red zone. Also the Grandmother and my brother and sister, and everyone's parents and brothers and sisters." [249]

Three days later, in a journal entry, he summed up his state of soul:

> Monastery of Saint Dominic of Silos, Vigil of the Feast of Saint Michael the Archangel, September 28, 1938: I have been on retreat for three days now—without doing anything. Horri- bly tempted. I see myself as not only unable to carry the Work

[246] *Apuntes*, no. 1587.
[247] AGP, RHF, EF–380914–2. ("Manolito" is our Lord: Emmanuel.)
[248] AGP, RHF, EF–380925–1.
[249] Ibid.

forward, but even to be saved (my poor soul!) without a miracle of grace. I am cold and, what is worse, almost indifferent, as though I were an outsider looking at "a case" (mine) which had nothing to do with him. I can't pray. Will these days be sterile? And yet my Mother is my Mother, and Jesus is—dare I say it?—*my* Jesus! And there are plenty of holy souls who, right now, are praying for this sinner. I don't understand it! When will the illness come that will purify me?[250]

God continued to purify his faculties and senses with temptations and dryness, letting him experience the dark night of the soul. Unable even to invoke his guardian angel ("the Little Watchmaker"), he found his feelings deadened and his thoughts far from God, "even during Mass!" He saw clearly that his path lay in doing "the most childlike little things," even when it seemed to him that he was just putting on an act, and that it was his duty "to persevere in those heroic tiny details (it not mattering if the feelings are numb toward the good) for months and even years, with my will cold, but determined to do this *for Love.*" [251]

*   *   *

On October 2 he was back in Burgos. The Work was ten years old, and this is what he wrote to Isidoro about that day:

A bad day, for me, the 2nd was, because I found myself drowning in a sea of memories of persons and things dear to me. How sentimental I am! My poor heart! For a year now I've been separated from my loved ones by the demands of the business that is their whole life and future. If I let myself be carried away in a moment of weakness, I would set out and return to my home overseas. But I can imagine what a little scene that would be! [252]

The war dragged on. In his correspondence Father Josemaría often complains that the young men on the fronts are not writing to him, not

[250] *Apuntes*, no. 1588. See also *The Forge*, no. 251.
[251] *Apuntes*, no. 1589 (15 Sep 1938). See also *The Forge*, no. 446.
[252] AGP, RHF, EF–381007–3.

answering his letters. But the fighting was now in its bloodiest stage At the end of July, a powerful republican offensive along the lowei Ebro broke through the nationalist front. This provoked a counter-offensive, followed by a battle of attrition involving air and artillery bombardment. Lasting until November, the bitter confrontation produced more than 125,000 casualties. Amid the attacks and counterattacks, Juan's battalion was cut off, and although eventually they broke out of the encirclement, they lost all of their supplies. When he returned from Silos, Father Josemaría sent Juan some new clothing.

He was still eager to go to the front to visit his sons and many others to whom he had given spiritual direction. Bishop Eijo y Garay had not yet answered his letter of August 7 asking what he thought of the idea of his taking the position of a military juridical consultant to make it easier to do pastoral work at the front lines. So he felt he should tell the vicar general, Monsignor Casimiro Morcillo, that he was being pressured by the National Service of Ecclesiastical Affairs for an answer as to whether or not he was going to accept that appointment.[253] His letter to Monsignor Morcillo and the bishop's letter to him crossed in the mail. The bishop wrote:

> I have thought a lot about your proposal, and after much reflection, I see no way of getting around the prohibition of canon 141, paragraph 1, which bars clerics from voluntary entry into the army. The military judiciary is still part of the army and must act as such in cases of war or civil disturbance. Thus for you to enter the military judiciary would be equivalent to voluntary incorporation into the army. . . .[254]

Father Josemaría thanked him by return mail, assuring him that his letter had given him "a lot of serenity and joy." If possible, he added, "I now feel myself even more a son of my bishop than before." [255]

* * *

But his main concern at this time was elsewhere. During the retreat in Silos, and then on the tenth anniversary of the Work and the days that followed, he kept thinking of Madrid. On October 5 he wrote to

[253] See AGP, RHF, EF–381004–1.
[254] AGP, RHF, D–15226.
[255] Letter to Bishop Leopoldo Eijo y Garay, from Burgos, in EF-381007-2.

Ricardo, "We haven't heard anything from Madrid lately. . . . Madrid! That's another temptation. Can you believe that I would love to go back there, and take up that hard life, amid our loved ones?"[256]

Those who had stayed behind in Madrid in hopes of finding a diplomatic route out of the republican zone—Alvaro del Portillo, José María Barredo, Vicente Rodríguez Casado, and Eduardo Alastrué—saw their hopes fading as the months passed. Don Pedro, the consul, seemed to have lost interest in pressing for their evacuation.[257] One day in June, Manolo Marín, a cousin of Vicente's, left the Honduran consulate, intending to cross the front to the nationalist side. Isidoro then gave up on diplomatic evacuation and prisoner exchange, and (in his capacity as the person temporarily in charge of Opus Dei in Madrid) told the members of the Work that they could do as Manolo had done.[258]

"With the help of Don Manuel," he wrote to Alvaro, "I have thought very carefully about your proposals, . . . and it seems to me that you will be able to carry them out, and that Don Manuel and Doña María will assist you in realizing your desires, which are ours too."[259] He then informed the Father of this decision, writing that they hoped to follow "the example of Mr. Richard." (Ricardo had earlier crossed into the nationalist zone by way of the front.)

They set about obtaining false identity cards. After the Aragon campaign, the Republican army, needing to rebuild, mobilized the classes of 1927, 1928, and 1941—that is, men over and under the ages of those already drafted. Presenting themselves at the recruiting office, Alvaro, Eduardo, and José Maria explained their lateness in reporting by claiming liver problems, defective vision, and even epileptic attacks. The biggest problem was age. Eduardo declared himself a member of the class of 1928—six years older than his real age.

Isidoro had given them copious advice in preparation for questioning. Alvaro's only documentation was the CNT membership card of his brother José. At the recruiting office he said he was 18 (he was actually 24), which would put him in the 1941 "baby-bottle draft," as

---

[256] AGP, RHF, EF–381005–2.

[257] On May 25 Isidoro had written to the Father that the consul had been told "to give up the idea and cease his efforts" (AGP, IZL, D–1213, 360). See also AGP, IZL, D–1213, 373.

[258] See José Miguel Pero-Sanz, *Isidoro Zorzano Ledesma, Ingeniero Industrial: Buenos Aires, 1902—Madrid, 1943* (Madrid, 1996), pp. 245–51.

[259] AGP, IZL, D–1213, 374 and 379.

it was called. The recruiting officer assigned him to a disciplinary battalion; but when they checked his name in the register, they found the name of one of his brothers, Angel, listed for the recruit year he was claiming to belong to. Caught by surprise, the recruiter asked him when his birthday was. "March 11," he said truthfully.

"Well, here it says February 14," the official replied.

"That's my brother. Notice that it says Angel and not José, which is my name."

"But if you're brothers. . . ." The recruiter was having trouble imagining two brothers born the same year, but in February and March.

"We're twins."

The official began filling out a new form. "Date of birth?"

"February 14," said Alvaro.

"That's not what you said before."

"Don't be silly. I don't know what I said before, but I know for sure that if we're twins, I was born the same day as my brother."

"The officer was a bit disconcerted," Alvaro later recorded, "but he didn't give me any more trouble. I also claimed bad vision and a liver problem."[260]

On August 24, the feast of Saint Bartholomew, Vicente and Alvaro left Madrid in army trucks. "Along the way," writes Alvaro, "people tried to guess our destination. Levante? Extremadura? Guadalajara? We hardly take part in the conversation. We really don't care, because we know that wherever they take us, that will be the best point on the front for us to cross over from. After all, our commander-in-chief is Don Manuel."[261]

Alvaro and Vicente spent most of September in training in Fontanar, a small village in Guadalajara. One day, toward the end of the month, another of those providential "coincidences" occurred. Some soldiers arrived to fill up the ranks of the battalion, and among them was Eduardo. The front was hundreds of miles long, and yet the three of them ended up in the same tiny village.

Then came October 2. Alvaro got a pass to spend a few hours in Madrid. He, Isidoro, and Santiago, after a long wait in line at one of the barracks on Atocha Boulevard, sat on the sidewalk to eat their meager rations: a bit of rice, a sardine, and a small piece of bread. When Alvaro told the others that in a few days he, Vicente, and

[260] Chronicle: "De Madrid a Burgos, por Guadalajara," p. 6.
[261] Ibid., p. 14.

Eduardo would be leaving the training camp for the front, he was the one to get a surprise. "Yes," answered Isidoro, "I've already written the Father to say that you will be in Burgos around the feast of Our Lady of the Pillar." [262] Alvaro returned to Fontanar in the middle of the afternoon, carrying in his wallet the consecrated hosts Isidoro had given him. The three of them would keep them by turns. Finally, on October 9, at daybreak, they moved up to the front, and arrived there twenty-four hours later. Between the republican and nationalist lines lay a mountainous no-man's-land that would take about eight hours to cross. After studying the layout, they decided to cross over on the next day, October 11.

The Father, meanwhile, on October 10, offered his Mass in Burgos for them, but with some anxiety, because he had not received a letter from the republican zone since September 5. More worried still were Alvaro's and Vicente's families, and especially their mothers, who for two months had been waiting for them to reach the nationalist zone. The Father calmed them down by reassuring them and giving them work: in their spare time, Doña Clementina and Doña Amparo made linens for the future oratory in Madrid.[263]

[262] Handwritten report of Alvaro del Portillo, written in 1944: original in AGP, IZL, T–94, p. 18. In a letter dated October 5, 1938, Isidoro confirms what he has told the Father earlier. (He mentions having received a letter from him dated September 24—a letter which has not survived.) Referring to Alvaro and his companions, he says: "They will finish their work on the farm about the middle of this month, and will take advantage of this to spend some time with the grandfather."

One day, while praying in front of the crucifix in his office, Isidoro came to understand that on October 12 the three fugitives would cross over into the nationalist zone. (See Alvaro del Portillo, *Sum.* 893).

In the process of beatification of the Servant of God Isidoro Zorzano, the second witness, José Javier López Jacoíste, declares that the refugees "asked him for permission to cross over to the nationalist zone, and twice the Servant of God, after looking at his crucifix, said no, but after the third request he gave them permission and wrote a letter to the founder, who was in Burgos, telling him that these three companions and brothers of ours would be with him on the feast of Our Lady of the Pillar—which is what happened." See *Copia Publica transumpti Processum Servi Dei Isidori Zorzano Ledesma* (Madrid, 1968), vol. 4, fols. 56v–57 and 852.

On July 15, 1943, the day before Isidoro died, José Luis Múzquiz told Francisco Botella that a few days before, when José Javier López Jacoíste was with Isidoro, Isidoro had told him, looking at the crucifix that José was holding, that in 1938, while praying before that crucifix, he had seen that Alvaro, Vicente, and Eduardo would cross over into the nationalist zone. (Isidoro died, by the way, on the feast of Our Lady of Mount Carmel.)

When José Javier asked admission to the Work, the Father had asked Isidoro to give him that crucifix. See AGP, RHF, T–00159, X, p. 23.

[263] In a letter to Isidoro the Father says, referring to Alvaro's mother, "Yesterday Clementina wrote to me from the sands of the Pacific, worried about her son's crossing

Father Josemaría had told Doña Clementina that Alvaro would be crossing over in about the middle of October. With Pedro and Paco and with José María Albareda he was more specific about the date. "Pray," he said, "that they arrive on the 12th, the feast of Our Lady of the Pillar." [264] They took this with equanimity, being accustomed to this supernatural optimism of his.

On October 10 he wrote to Ricardo, "I sense something happening soon. May we correspond to God's mercies. I am overwhelmed when I think of him and then of myself. What little correspondence, up to now!" [265]

On October 11 he wrote to Juan, "I'm expecting events of personal significance to occur any moment now. And I'm getting ready for a real celebration." [266]

On the morning of October 12, when Pedro and Paco left for their offices at military headquarters, they noticed that the Father looked very happy. "I'll let you know when they arrive," he said. When they got back that evening and found him alone, they feared that his spirits might have taken a dive. But no, he was calm, cheerful, and confident. [267]

Probably it was on the next day that he got the good news, from Vicente's father, because all day long he was in a festive and joking mood. "Stay on the alert," he playfully said to Pedro and Paco, "because I'll be calling you at headquarters when they arrive." And a letter to Juan, bearing this date, ends with "P.S. I think our Lady's day was eventful." [268]

Late in the afternoon of October 14, the three finally arrived at the Sabadell Hotel. Immediately the Father called military headquarters, saying, "They've arrived; come back."

---

over. Today I sent her a few lines to comfort her." In another he says, referring to both women, "I speak to them often about their children."

[264] "The fact is," says Pedro Casciaro, "that the Father, in Burgos, and Isidoro Zorzano, in Madrid, knew, in an absolutely supernatural manner, that on October 12, 1938, Don Alvaro del Portillo, Professor Vicente Rodríguez Casado, and Dr. Eduardo Alastrué would cross the front that separated the republican army from the nationalist army" (AGP, RHF, T–04197, p. 163). Francisco Botella testifies to the same thing: see AGP, RHF, T–00159/1, p. 80.

[265] AGP, RHF, EF–381010–3.

[266] AGP, RHF, EF–381011–1.

[267] See Casciaro, p. 179. See also *Sum.* 6411 (Casciaro) and *Sum.* 5652 (Botella).

[268] AGP, RHF, EF–381013–3. "On the day of Our Lady of the Pillar," he wrote to the bishop of Avila, "our Lady gave us the present of three of our own" (AGP, RHF, EF–381027–1). See also AGP, RHF, T–00159/1, p. 80.

Their escape had begun in heavy rain, early in the morning of October 11. After a day of climbing up and down mountains and a night in a cave, they resumed their trek at dawn. Nearing a village from which the sound of church bells was coming, they learned from shepherds that this was Cantalojas and it was in the hands of the nationalists. Only later did they find out that the troops in the village, upon seeing them emerge from a pine forest, had taken them for the vanguard of a republican attack. After explaining themselves, they attended Mass, made a formal declaration, and contacted Vicente's father, an army colonel. He met them the following morning in Jadraque and vouched for them, thus they were able to avoid waiting in a detention camp while an official inquiry was conducted.

En route to Burgos on the 14th, Vicente's mother and sister, who accompanied them, exclaimed, "Look how our Lady has protected you! She must have saved you for something great." [269] Doña Dolores had used the same words in telling her son that he had been offered to our Lady when he was close to dying in 1904. "My son," she had said, "our Lady has left you in this world for something great."

* * *

Father Eliodoro ran into difficulties when he tried to mimeograph the October issue of the newsletter, so Father Josemaría, Pedro, and Paco sent out carbon copies of a typewritten summary. Thus news about Alvaro and the others did not appear in *Noticias* until November. "Alvaro del Portillo, Eduardo Alastrué, and Vicente Rodríguez Casado have succeeded in coming from the Red zone to our lines. With their only recommendations those of their guardian angels, they enlisted in the Communist army and, at the first opportunity, crossed over." [270]

Wanting to spend this time with his sons, Father Josemaría did everything he could to avoid leaving Burgos during those last two weeks in October. Many afternoons he took walks with them along the banks of the Arlanzón River, discussing the next apostolic projects. Only at the end of the month did he go to see the archbishop of Valladolid; and except for two short trips, he stayed in Burgos through November as well.

The Battle of the Ebro, the biggest battle of the war, occupied all

[269] "De Madrid a Burgos, por Guadalajara," p. 45.
[270] AGP, RHF, D–03691. See also AGP, RHF, EF–381010–3 and EF–381011–1.

available forces on both sides. It was almost impossible to get permits for a few days behind the lines, and Father Josemaría had very few visits from the young soldiers. In the mornings, he worked at Las Huelgas on his doctoral dissertation, answered letters, and added new points to his *Spiritual Considerations,* which had first been published at Cuenca in 1934.

8. *The end in sight*

The long-awaited end of the war still did not come. Father Josemaría was vexed at being unable to visit his sons at the front and their being unable to get furloughs to come to Burgos. He wrote to Ricardo:

> There's a lot of talk that the war is about to end any minute now. But if it continues, I'm in favor of setting up a house. Here or in the Congo—let's get a house! As things are, we're spending a huge amount of money, and the apostolate can't be done properly. I really think location is unimportant. If not Burgos, then Belchite. This living in hotels for a year is just too much.

Today I begin a novena of prayer and sacrifice (small sacrifices) to obtain from the Lord immediate light and means, because there needs to be an end to this interim arrangement that makes so many efforts fruitless and is so expensive. Help me.[271]

A sense of having lost the war was said to be spreading in the republican zone, but that was little consolation to Father Josemaría when he thought of how the people in Madrid, including his family, had suffered in those two years of siege. And he did not even know how much worse the situation had gotten since he set out for the Pyrenees. The hunger was terrible. Like beggars, Isidoro and Santiago were going from barracks to barracks, standing in ration lines. Carmen, too, spent hours in line to get a small quantity of food.[272]

In December, Father Josemaría and Paco Botella were left alone in Burgos. José María Albareda now lived in Vitoria, while Alvaro had been sent to Fuentes Blancas (near Burgos), for officer's training.

[271] AGP, RHF, EF–381010–3.
[272] See AGP, RHF, T–07921, p. 28.

Vicente and Eduardo were in similar training programs. Pedro had moved to Calatayud, in the province of Saragossa, when the headquarters were transferred there upon General Orgaz's promotion to commander of the army of Levante [the eastern regional command].

When the manager of the Sabadell Hotel learned that only two people were occupying that room, he immediately assigned two new guests to the now vacant beds. The next morning, December 10, Father Josemaría wrote to José María Albareda:

> When Paco got back, I told him what happened, and he got angry. Really there wasn't any reason to be angry, but I too was angry, since if everything we now don't need had been sent to Avila as I wanted, we would now have more freedom of movement. Where can we go now with such a load of books, clothes, and, as Juan would say, junk?
>
> We went to bed before the new guests arrived, and we got up at seven. So I don't even know what they look like.
>
> This can't go on. We can't work, write letters, have visitors, leave our papers around. . . . And we can't get one minute of that blessed solitude that is so necessary for keeping up one's interior life. Besides all this, every day new people. Impossible![273]

A week before Christmas they moved, with all the odds and ends, to an old boardinghouse on Concepción Street. Their third-floor suite had a tiny living room, a bedroom for the Father, and an alcove with a bed for Paco. They paid five pesetas a day for the flat, plus twenty-five centimos for coal for the small stove that was their only source of heat. The decor was horrendous, but the worst thing about the place was the lack of a place to bathe. To wash in the mornings, they had to use the sink in the boardinghouse's kitchen, according to a schedule worked out with the landlady, who, by the way, had the unusual name of María de la Iglesia [Mary of the Church].

The Father spent Christmas Eve sending Christmas greetings to his children. To Juan he writes:

---

[273] AGP, RHF, EF–381210–1. What Juan was referring to was objects of personal use, not strictly necessary on the battlefront.

May Jesus watch over you, Juanito. . . .

Today I'm writing to the whole family. Just a few letters, since we are still only a few. It grieves me to think that this is my own fault. What good—effective—example I always want to give! Help me ask pardon from the Lord for my bad example up to now.

Don't forget our people in the Red zone. Can you believe that I envy them, living as they do as if in the days of the catacombs? We haven't heard anything from them.

Merry Christmas!

My blessing,
Mariano[274]

In his letter to Ricardo, too, he opens his heart with great simplicity:

I am now optimistic, calm, full of confidence. How good he is! During these days, join me in asking him for perseverance, joy, peace, hunger for souls, unity . . . for everyone.

Oh, Ricardo, if only you and I—especially I!—were to give him all he asks us for, how well everything would go! Prayer, prayer, prayer: this is the best artillery.[275]

Sitting at the table over the coal heater, Father Josemaría continued expanding his *Spiritual Considerations*, wrote letters, and typed up notes, pages for the newsletter, and Alvaro's handwritten account of his escape from the Communist zone. For this account, entitled *From Madrid to Burgos, via Guadalajara,* he wrote the following foreword:

Herein are adventures spanning hardly five months, but brimming with the youthful vigor of three young men who made the effort to escape from the hell of Red Spain, so as better to serve God's plans on this nationalist side.

Every now and then, in the course of the narrative, Marxist military terms appear. These have been left in for the sake of authenticity.

---

[274] AGP, RHF, EF–381224–1.
[275] AGP, RHF, EF–381223–2.

May the supernatural faith that so firmly stayed with the protagonists take hold in the hearts of all who read this.

Then we will all have come out ahead.

Burgos, January 1939.[276]

When he reread that journal of Alvaro's, and saw how constantly his sons had received supernatural help, he was deeply moved. Tears of repentance came to his eyes. "I have asked our Lord," he wrote to Alvaro and Vicente, "not to let me undo by my bad example—a sinner!—what he has so beautifully brought about in you."[277]

On January 9 (his birthday) he wrote another circular letter to his sons: a letter in which he would give "a balance sheet" of the apostolic efforts made during the past year in Burgos.

"I would like to sum up in one word what, after careful consideration in God's presence, my thinking boils down to. The word that should characterize your efforts to pick up again the ordinary activities of our apostolate is *optimism*." He continues:

It is true that the communist revolution destroyed our home and blew away the material means that we had obtained with so much effort.

It is also true, or might seem so, that our apostolic endeavors came to a standstill during the war. And that the war occasioned the loss of some of your brothers.

To all this I answer that, as long as we do not stray from our path, the material means will never be a problem that we can't easily resolve, with our own effort; that this Work of God is alive and kicking and does have fruitful activity going on, like a sown grain of wheat that is germinating under the frozen earth; and that those who lost their spirit perhaps lost it before these turbulent events in our country's history.[278]

Then he turned to the favorable acceptance of the Work by Church authorities and to the advances in the apostolate.

What has our Lord done, what have we done with his help, during the past year? All of you, undeniably, have become more

[276] AGP, RHF, D–15376.
[277] AGP, RHF, EF–390323–8.
[278] AGP, RHF, EF–390109–1.

disciplined. We are in contact with all the Saint Raphael people, who generally respond better than we could have hoped. We have made new friendships that will be helpful in beginning Saint Gabriel centers when the time comes. The bishops are very pleased with our apostolic work. And there are the thousands of little things: the requests for books, the monthly newsletters, the vestments and other objects for the oratory. And more: the greater opportunities for apostolate; getting to know different parts of the country, which will facilitate the Saint Gabriel work; friendships, some of them deep, with a number of university professors whom we didn't know before.

The means? Interior life: *him* and us.

We will find the means, and obstacles will disappear, if each and every one of us makes a perfect, real, operative, and effective self-surrender to God in the Work.

This self-surrender takes place when the norms are lived; when we cultivate a robust piety, including daily mortification and penance; when we try not to lose the habit of professional work and study; when we are eager to understand the spirit of our apostolate better every day; when discretion (not mysteriousness, not secretiveness) accompanies our work. And, above all, when you are continually conscious of being united, in a special communion of saints, with all those who form part of your supernatural family.

Finally, he asks them to keep in their minds and hearts those who were still in the republican zone. "And," he says, "I bid you farewell with words of Saint Paul to the Philippians which seem written for you and me: 'I thank my God in all my remembrance of you, always in every prayer of mine for you all making my prayer with joy, thankful for your partnership in the gospel from the first day until now. And I am sure that he who began a good work in you will bring it to completion. . . .' " [279]

At the same time, the founder felt a real need to have at his side at least a few of his sons to collaborate with him in advancing the Work. When, before the move to the boardinghouse, it seemed that he might be left alone in Burgos, he wrote both to José María Albareda and to

[279] Ibid. The passage is Philippians 1:3–6.

Bishop Santos Moro: "If Juan and Alvaro were to go to Valladolid, I would go there too." [280] He knew each of his sons well and looked to them for support. Now he felt the time had come to choose one of them to be given preparation for the responsibilities of government. In his correspondence in the early months of 1939, one can observe God's hand at work, leading him to the son who would turn out to be such a strong support for him.[281]

When Alvaro was in Fuentes Blancas and, later, in Cigales, a village near Valladolid, he was often able to get away to Burgos to see the Father. Walking along the banks of the Arlanzón River, or sitting at the table in the Father's room, they resumed the long conversations about the Work that they had had from adjoining mats during those nights at the Honduran consulate. The Father wrote to Alvaro:

> Burgos, January 19, 1939
> May Jesus watch over you
> My dear Alvaro:
>   I almost can't pick up the pen, because my hands are so cold. But I wanted to write you. . . .
>   I don't know what to say to you by letter. But when I see you, I'll tell you many things which will please you. There are so many marvelous things to be done! We cannot put up obstacles with childishness that is, in every sense of the word, unbecoming to men. Jesus expects much good service from you and me. And we will do it for him, without hesitating.[282]

In a letter written two months later, he calls Alvaro "Saxum," Latin for "Rock." [283]

> May Jesus watch over you, Saxum.
>   And yes, that is what you are. I see that the Lord is giving you strength and making operative in you this word of mine, "saxum." Thank him for this and remain faithful to him, despite—so many things. . . .

---

[280] AGP, RHF, EF–381210–1 and EF–381224–2.

[281] It was at this time that his affection for his sons began to find expression in epithets and nicknames. See AGP, RHF, EF–390213–3, EF–390200–2, and EF–381013–3.

[282] AGP, RHF, EF–390119–1.

[283] The Father looked for nicknames that had "soul": see, for example, AGP, RHF, EF–390224–4.

If only you could see how great is my longing to be a saint, and to make saints of all of you!

Love and my blessing,
Mariano[284]

*   *   *

Now that the longed-for return to Madrid seemed to be drawing near, his thoughts often turned to what the future there would bring. From time to time he was heard to say under his breath, "How tired I am of Burgos!" [285]

For some time he had been saying, encouragingly, "This is ending," because Madrid had become for him a magnetic attraction, the door of entry into a promising future. He wrote to Pedro, "Madrid! The unknown land. I look to it with optimism because my Father-God is guiding everything. *Fiat.*" But even so, as he wrote to Vicente's mother, he suspected that he would find the capital "a real disaster, humanly speaking." [286]

Doña Dolores, like everyone else, was sick of the war. In the spring of 1938 Isidoro had reported that she was "a bit put out and nervous because of the delay in the grandfather's arrival." [287] What must she be feeling now, a year later? Father Josemaría remembered his loved ones every day in his Mass and prayers. Looking forward to a new residence in Madrid, he wrote to Paco Botella: "I'm keeping everyone in mind—those in the Red zone, most especially. When you write all the others, tell them to ask our Lord to spare for us the Grandmother. I see, clear as day, how much we need her." [288]

In another letter written on the same day, February 13, the eve of the anniversary of the founding of the women's branch, he wrote to Alvaro and Vicente:

> My children! Today, the eve of a day of thanksgiving—one that will, perhaps, go unnoticed by almost everyone—I remember each one with an extra-intense concern and love. I feel a deep urge to beg your forgiveness for the bad example I may have given you, and for the weaknesses

---

[284] AGP, RHF, EF–390323–5.
[285] See AGP, RHF, EF–390111–1.
[286] AGP, RHF, EF–390224–3 and EF–390310–4.
[287] AGP, IZL, D–1213, 348.
[288] AGP, RHF, EF–390213–2.

and wretchedness of this grandfather of yours, which may have scandalized you. I shall spend the entire night near our Lord, in the bishop's chapel. You don't want to know the crazy things we are going to say to each other and what I'm going to whisper to him about all of you.

Vicentín! Pray for your Father.

Saxum! I'm relying on the strength of my rock.

A blessing,
Mariano[289]

"The crazy things we are going to say to each other"—nothing could better get across how enamored he was of the Lord, and how eager to speak with him. On that same day, he also writes to Ricardo: "I'm going to spend the night near the Lord, in the chapel of the bishop's residence. How good he is, letting me get within reach of him. I hope I get him in the Heart!" [290]

On this date the military campaign in Catalonia ended. The president of the Republic (Manuel Azaña) and most of the civil authorities had already left Spain. The soldiers of the republican army of Catalonia had crossed into France and were interned in refugee camps. Negotiations for surrender began.

Father Josemaría had made advance preparations for his return to Madrid, depositing boxes of books and a trunk with vestments and other liturgical objects in the residence of the bishop of Avila.[291] A year ahead of time, he had also gotten permission from the ecclesiastical authorities to enter Madrid immediately after its liberation.[292] Visits to Enrique Giménez-Arnau, a classmate at the Saragossa School of Law, and to José Lorente, Undersecretary of the Interior, had facilitated the obtaining of safe-conduct passes for himself, Paco, Alvaro, and José María Albareda. Passes for Ricardo and Juan had been obtained from General Martín Moreno.[293] And, not forgetting about the hunger in Madrid, he had also bought several wicker baskets and filled them with canned food.[294]

[289] AGP, RHF, EF–390213–4.

[290] AGP, RHF, EF–390213–5.

[291] See AGP, RHF, EF–390213–8 and EF–390321–1.

[292] See AGP, RHF, EF–380303–3 and EF–380406–1.

[293] See AGP, RHF, EF–390303–1 and EF–390303–2.

[294] See AGP, RHF, T–00159/1, p. 86, and AGP, RHF, EF–390224–3.

4

1. *Back to Madrid*

As the days went by, the founder grew steadily more impatient to return to Madrid. He had no illusions about the difficulties that lay ahead—but it would mean the war finally was over and a new era for the Work had begun. "This is ending," he writes in letter after letter. "And soon our family will begin a period of intense activity," he added to Juan Jiménez Vargas.[1] "And we'll have to work with all our soul,"[2] he repeated to Ricardo Fernández Vallespín.

When he wrote to Pedro that Madrid was "unknown territory" that "I look to with optimism," and to Paco that they were now, more than ever, going to need the help of Doña Dolores, he was evidently dreaming of an imminent expansion of the Work in Madrid.[3]

Meanwhile, news came of the death of Pope Pius XI. On March 3, 1939, after the election of Pope Pius XII, he wrote to Juan, "*Papam habemus!* [We have a Pope!] The next time, you and I and others will be living there."[4] As far back as August 1931, he had written, "When the Work of God is well under way, I dream of establishing in Rome a center that will be, as it were, the nerve center of the organization."[5]

He had agreed to give a retreat for the seminarians in the diocese of Vitoria—a commitment he was happy to make, because he found this work with future priests so attractive. But now he postponed it, giving Bishop Lauzurica these reasons:

> (1) The need to be in Burgos for the feast of Saint Joseph, for the reasons you are aware of. Quite a few of the young

---

[1] AGP, RHF, EF-390213-7.
[2] AGP, RHF, EF-390224-5.
[3] See AGP, RHF, EF–390224–3 and EF–390213–2.
[4] AGP, RHF, EF–390303–2.
[5] *Apuntes,* no. 220.

men are coming here on special passes good for only twenty-four hours—not enough time for going to Vergara.

(2) The possibility, highly likely, that Madrid will be liberated when I would be giving the retreat.

(3) If Madrid is liberated and I'm not there from the very first, I would fail in my strict duty to reclaim Saint Elizabeth's as its rector (which some people might try to find fault with). And in my dual duties—the first, very supernatural, and the second, a natural duty—to the Work and to my mother. Both expect me without delay.[6]

In these heartening circumstances, he sent out a circular letter that began:

In the name of the Father and of the Son and of the Holy Spirit, and of holy Mary.

May Jesus bless my sons and watch over them.

I feel God prompting me to write you on this eve of the victorious liberation of Madrid.

As the day draws near for us to return home, we need to think about starting up again our apostolic activities.[7]

This one literally was a circular letter. There were no copies. The original had to be passed from hand to hand and from city to city until everyone had read it. The letter was a trumpet call sounded by the Father to awaken the spiritual energies of his sons. Once the war ended, the new launching of the campaign about which he had spoken so often would begin: the campaign to place Christ at the summit of all human activities; a universal mobilization under the banner *Regnare Christum Volumus*: "We Want Christ to Reign."

I want you to be preparing for the age-old battle, as a militia in the service of the One, Holy, Catholic, and Apostolic Church, by praying the psalm of Christ's kingship with the spirit of a warrior monk, for such is the tenor of our calling.

Every Tuesday, each of us will do this: after invoking our guardian angel with a petition to accompany us in our prayer, we will kiss our rosary, to show our love for our Lady and our

---

[6] AGP, RHF, EF–390310–3.
[7] AGP, RHF, EF–390324–1.

recognition that prayer is our most effective weapon. And then, in Latin, we will recite Psalm 2.[8]

I am speaking of battles and of war, and for a war, soldiers are needed.

Never have our young people been so nobly stirred up as they are now. It would be a great shame not to take advantage, for the growth of our family, of the spirit of sacrifice that unquestionably (amid so many other things, which I won't mention) fills the hearts and the deeds of your fellow students and comrades-in-arms. Begin the sowing. In the name of the Lord of the harvest, I guarantee a rich harvest.

But sow generously. Thus, the world![9]

Before sending that letter, he wrote to José María Albareda:

Paco will write you the details. Just want to let you know that I think I'm going to be setting out for home soon. I'll bring the food we have prepared. You'll need to bring the file and the typewriter.

I've written another circular letter, but I'm not sure when it will go out. When you come, you can read it.[10]

Negotiations were under way for the surrender of the republican forces, with comings and goings between Burgos and Madrid. Father Josemaría followed events closely. On Monday, March 27, he left for Madrid in a military supply truck, sitting beside the driver. He had all his documentation together, including a safe-conduct pass and ecclesiastical permissions. He spent the night in a small village about sixty miles from the capital. The next day, March 28, the republican army surrendered. On that morning, nationalist troops began to enter Madrid, and there among the soldiers was Father Josemaría, wearing a cassock. He was perhaps the first priest to be seen in a cassock on the streets since July of 1936. People rushed to kiss his hand, while he held out his crucifix to them.[11]

---

[8] Thus began a new custom in the Work.

[9] AGP, RHF, EF–390324–1.

[10] AGP, RHF, EF–390323–2.

[11] See AGP, RHF, T–05250, p. 2 (Pilar Angela Hernando Carretero); T–00162, p. 41 (Ricardo Fernández Vallespín); and T–00159/1, p. 87 (Francisco Botella).

Justo Martí Gilabert, who had been a student living at the Ferraz Street residence during the school year of 1935–1936, describes the entrance of Father Josemaría into Madrid with the first troops. "I was standing," he says, "on the corner of Plaza de

The truck he was in went down Ferraz Street, so he was able to see the terribly damaged residence. He then went to his family's apartment on Caracas Street and hugged his mother, sister, and brother, and took possession of the trunk with the documents and other papers comprising the archives of the Work.[12] Then he sought out Isidoro Zorzano and José María Barredo. Ricardo Fernández Vallespín and Alvaro del Portillo came soon after, on furloughs, and in the morning of March 29 they all went together to look at what was left of 16 Ferraz. The damage was greater than the Father had imagined when he had seen the house through the binoculars from Carabanchel. The rooms had been sacked. The walls were pockmarked by explosions. The floor was broken through in many places. Only the façade and the main walls were intact.

Paco Botella arrived from Burgos that afternoon and met them at Santa Isabel, where they had gone to survey the condition of the convent. On July 20, 1936, right after the war broke out, the revolutionaries had set fire to the church. The floor, the pews, the altarpieces, and valuable works of art had all gone up in flames.[13]

España where Bailen Street ends and Ferraz begins, and was facing St. Vincent Avenue. In the emotion-charged atmosphere, what was my surprise and enthusiasm at seeing our Father himself sitting next to the driver of the first truck that came chugging up the hill! I was not yet in the Work at that time, but as a resident in the Ferraz Street house, I had known the Father and received spiritual direction from him, starting in October or November of 1935.

"Since the truck had to slow down when coming up St. Vincent Avenue—which is so hilly that it's also called St. Vincent Hill—and when taking the curve onto Ferraz Street, one almost could not help but see the Father, especially since he was wearing the first cassock seen in the city since July of 1936. The very instant I caught sight of him, I began to shout, 'Father!' The Father answered, 'Justo, my son!' and immediately asked the driver to stop and make room for me. As we embraced, my emotions got the better of me. Just two minutes later, there we were in front of the residence at 16 Ferraz Street.

"The Father took a quick look at the destruction. Only the façade was still standing, and even it was badly damaged by shells fired by the nationalist troops from the hill of Garabitas. That part of Madrid had been practically on the front lines. I recall that the Father spent no more than a couple of minutes looking at that pile of rubble. He then returned to the truck and asked the driver to take us to the apartment building on Caracas Street. On one floor of it lived the parents of José María Barredo." See AGP, RHF, T–06358, pp. 3–4.

[12] See *Apuntes*, no. 1595 (13 Apr 1939).

[13] See the catalog *IV Centenario de la Real Fundación del Convento de Santa Isabel de Madrid*, put out by the Editorial Patrimonio Nacional (Madrid, 1990). The most valuable piece of work lost was Ribera's "Immaculate Conception," the centerpiece of the reredos on the main altar (see pp. 44 and 122). The painting had been donated by King Philip IV; the face, for which Ribera's daughter had been the model, had been repainted by Claudio Coello. See also Antonio Ponz, *Viaje por España* (1788; reprinted by M. Aguilar, Madrid, 1947), p. 426.

* * *

In the second circular letter written in Burgos, the founder had written that there would be no insuperable obstacles for his children, and especially "when you are continually conscious of being united, in a special communion of saints, with all those who form part of your supernatural family." [14] That thought kept him optimistic as he set about the hard work of starting again from ruins. Visiting the Ferraz Street residence again on April 21, he found amid the rubble a parchment he had hung on a wall there. It bore, in Latin, the text of John 13:34–35: "A new commandment I give to you, that you love one another; even as I have loved you, that you also love one another. By this all men will know that you are my disciples, if you have love for one another." [15]

The day after the first troops entered Madrid, a small group of members of the Work had already gathered there. Father Josemaría invited them to sleep in the rectory at Santa Isabel. The afternoon of March 29 was spent cleaning up the place. It had been used as an office for commissars, while the building next door, the girls' school, had become a barracks for army engineers. The whole place was a mess of strewn papers, files ripped open, and broken tables and chairs. But they did salvage some items of furniture in the rector's apartment, intending to paint or repair them in the near future. [16]

Once the place was livable, Father Josemaría persuaded his mother, sister, and brother to move to Santa Isabel. It was here, at the rectory, that Doña Dolores and Carmen began their direct role in the running of the centers of the Work, because for several months the rectory was the only house that Opus Dei had in Madrid. Space was cramped. Living quarters for the two women were fitted up at one end of the place. In a part closer to the front entrance, Father Josemaría occupied a small room with a studio couch. Next to his room was a larger one with four beds—a room that soon became known as El Rancho Grande. [17]

[14] AGP, RHF, EF–390109–1.

[15] See Alvaro del Portillo, *Sum.* 929; *Apuntes*, no. 815 (23 Aug 1932); *Letter 24 Oct 1942*, no. 30; and AGP, RHF, T–00162, p. 42.

[16] Father Josemaría obtained permission from the Director General of Ecclesiastical Affairs to keep part of the furnishings as a small compensation for the losses at 16 Ferraz. See AGP, RHF, T–00159/1, p. 89. The work of reconstruction continued until 1947.

[17] See AGP, RHF, T–00159/1, p. 90.

The mother superior of the Augustinian Sisters soon turned up, accompanied by a novice, intending to occupy the chaplain's quarters, since the rest of the convent had been ruined by the fire. The rector arranged for them to live in community with the rest of the nuns (who were then living outside Madrid) while the church and attached living quarters were being repaired. Since the adjoining building belonging to the Sisters of the Assumption was undamaged, these Sisters turned over some of the rooms in their school to the Augustinian Sisters.[18] The arrangement lasted till August, when Father Josemaría, with the agreement of Madrid's vicar general, Monsignor Casimiro Morcillo, voluntarily turned over his residence to the nuns. It was stipulated that future rectors would still have the right to that residence.[19]

Furniture from his mother's place was brought to the rectory, and although not numerous, the pieces added a touch of homelike elegance to that dreary setting. Doña Dolores and her children lived there from April 9 on. This was the beginning of what Santiago would later call the "transitional stage," referring to the interim service that his mother and sister provided in the Work's centers until the women of Opus Dei could take over domestic tasks.[20] Of both mother and sister, however, it would be closer to the mark to say that the commitment to assist was unconditional and for life. During this "transitional stage" Doña Dolores, whose health had already declined because of physical and moral sufferings, kept selflessly giving of herself till the day she died, while Carmen energetically embraced the life of silent sacrifice that she would keep living, in one form or another, for the rest of her days.

The cleaning and tidying up of the rectory took a considerable amount of time, and not only because of all the clutter and accumu-

[18] As rector, Father Josemaría immediately set about helping both communities not only to reorganize their convent life, but also to rebuild the damaged buildings. He even provided for their material needs: food, etc. See Cecilia Gómez Jiménez, *Sum.* 6512. See also AGP, RHF, T–05039, p. 2 (Consolación Mariana Casas).

[19] The original contract is in the archives of the Archdiocese of Madrid, under "Foundation of Santa Isabel." The contract bears the signatures of the rector, the mother superior, and the vicar general. Its third clause provides for a compensation by the community of 250 pesetas a month for the rector's needs. It is further specified that Father Josemaría renounces this remuneration, but that his successors' right to the sum stands. "The present rector and signatory, for himself and personally and without this serving as a precedent or lessening the rights of his successors in that position, does freely renounce, for the benefit of the community, the receiving of said indemnification, for the entire time that he holds this position."

[20] See AGP, RHF, T–07921, p. 30.

lated dirt. They also had to notify the authorities of their discoveries of a cache of weapons and of a terrible profanation of the tombs in the crypt; the corpses had been thrown around and tossed together. The well in the garden also required a lot of work, since the bodies of a number of people murdered during the war had been thrown into it.[21]

*   *   *

There then began for Father Josemaría days of intense activity. As he had written to his sons on January 9, the supernatural enterprise of the Work had suffered a kind of paralysis in the war years—a stoppage that was, thanks be to God, only an "apparent" one, the reality being something quite different—but now everyone was primed for the "recovery" of apostolic work.[22] (That word "recovery" was used a lot in those days, since shortages made it necessary for people to put back into use objects that had been discarded.)

He now started up again his personal journal. The first postwar entry is dated April 13, 1939, and concerns a divine locution.

> Without realizing it until later, I found myself saying, as I had years ago, *"Dei perfecta sunt opera"* [The works of God are perfect]. At once I was left with the absolute certainty, no kind of doubt, that this was the reply of my God to his sinful but loving creature. I look to him for everything! May he be blessed!![23]

On the previous day he had located his old confessor and immediately gone to see him. "Yesterday," he says, "I visited Father Sánchez, at 28 Velázquez. How happy he was! He embraced me repeatedly, and he still—it's obvious—believes in the Work."[24]

Two weeks later Isidoro writes to Paco: "The grandfather is busy twenty-four hours a day with visits." But there was also plenty of work going on at home. "Since we've finished getting the house set up," Isidoro continues, "we're devoting ourselves to the work we started before, of organizing the files. The fuses are still causing us trouble; the problem is now the mice. Remember how we tried to

---

[21] See AGP, RHF, T–00159/1, p. 91.
[22] See AGP, RHF, EF–390109–1.
[23] *Apuntes*, no. 1595 (13 Apr 1939).
[24] Ibid.

block up their holes? Well, it didn't work; they thwart us every day. We're raising two cats to get rid of the pests." [25]

With the help of the address file, which had been almost totally reconstructed in Burgos, they were able to contact a lot of young men. Father Josemaría spoke with many at length. He gave formation classes to members of the Work who came to Madrid on military leave; he took care of the nuns at Santa Isabel; and he kept up his ceaseless correspondence, encouraging everyone to write to him. To Ricardo he wrote:

> Dear Ricardo,
>
> You don't know how grateful I will be if you don't slack off, and write us often. . . . I think we will have to end up blessing the war. I'm expecting a lot, for God and for Spain!
>
> I have started working, and am very happy. At first, when I got back to Madrid, I thought I might find it hard to get settled. But no, it's just like in 1936, thanks be to God.
>
> A big hug and a blessing,
>
> Mariano[26]

Father Josemaría viewed the war and the many scars it had left on everyone with supernatural optimism. For all its hardships and cruelty, it had served to strengthen souls. Looking ahead, with hope, he wrote to Chiqui: "I assure you that if you fulfill the plan of life I gave you, you will end up blessing the war, because you will have more experience and more strength for doing apostolic work." [27]

Around the middle of May a number of bishops asked him to give retreats to priests and nuns, the first of which would begin in June, in Valencia.[28] As usual, he immediately started asking God to make the retreats spiritually fruitful, and requested others to do the same. He wrote to Bishop Moro, the bishop of Avila:

> My dear Bishop:
>
> May Jesus watch over you!
>
> This sinner is always coming to his bishop with his hand out. I'm due to give several retreats, some (in Valencia and

---

[25] AGP, IZL, D–1213, 422.

[26] AGP, RHF, EF–390427–2.

[27] AGP, RHF, EF–390427–3 (Letter to José María Hernández Garnica).

[28] For a partial list of the founder's preaching activities in these years, see Appendix 6.

Madrid) for priests, and I need your prayers and your paternal and priestly blessing.

Thank you!

Be assured of my love and gratitude.

Josemaría[29]

The first retreat was for university students. His friend Father Antonio Rodilla—now Valencia's vicar general and also the rector of a university students' residence—and Rafael Calvo Serer managed to get a group together quickly enough for a retreat to begin on June 5, in the nearby town of Burjasot. Father Josemaría asked the archangel Raphael to pray that his words would be effective. And, while he was at it, he also wanted to use the retreat to his own spiritual advantage. He wrote to his sons in Madrid, "I'm taking advantage of the scrubbing of these souls to scrub my own. How much I need it."[30]

When Father Josemaría arrived, the students were waiting in the garden, chatting in little groups. Though visibly tired by the long trip, he was very cheerful. As he approached, Monsignor Rodilla commented to those around him, "This man works miracles."[31] Overhearing the remark, Father Josemaría brushed it off with an affectionate gesture indicating that he did not at all relish it.[32]

The college building had been used during the war by the republican army and still had some reminders of their presence. Before the retreat began, Father Josemaría came across a large poster saying: *"Cada caminante, siga su camino"* ("Let each wayfarer follow his

[29] AGP, RHF, EF–390518–6. A little later, on June 2, he communicated in a letter to Madrid's vicar general his plan of work for the summer, to be submitted to the bishop for approval. See AGP, RHF, EF–390602–1.

[30] AGP, RHF, EF–390606–3.

[31] See AGP, RHF, T–02769, p. 1 (Amadeo de Fuenmayor Champin). Monsignor Rodilla had spoken with Father Josemaría for the first time in 1934, in Madrid; see Antonio Rodilla, *Sum.* 5576. The founder referred to him in his correspondence on several occasions: see, for example, AGP, RHF, EF–380327–2 and EF–380412–1. In the second of these letters he describes him as "a holy and learned priest."

[32] In March of 1938, when the founder was still in Burgos, Father Rodilla had written him from Cádiz, announcing an upcoming visit to Burgos. "I want you to infect me with your madness," he wrote. See AGP, RHF, D–15392–2.

The epithet "priest of the miracles" spread quickly among churchmen, friends, and persons receiving spiritual direction from him. "I don't want to be regarded as the priest of the miracles," he said. "I'm just a poor, fat priest working humbly to do whatever good I can": José López Ortiz, in *Beato Josemaría Escrivá de Balaguer: un hombre de Dios. Testimonios sobre el Fundador del Opus Dei* (Madrid, 1994), p. 223. (Hereafter this book will be cited as *Testimonios*.)

own way"). "Leave it," he said. "I like it. Good advice from the enemy." [33]

That phrase served him as a theme for his retreat meditations. He used it in commentaries on the Christian vocation, faithfulness to one's particular calling, and the way leading to a glimpsed ideal.

Realizing that he might be able to visit the Father in Valencia during this retreat, Alvaro del Portillo phoned him, before getting a furlough and setting out. Now stationed in Olot, in the Pyrenees, he had no way of knowing how difficult the trip was going to be. The retreating republican troops had blown up many bridges in Catalonia and across the Ebro River; the highways were badly damaged; and train service had not yet been restored to normal. It took Alvaro three days to reach Burjasot. On the last day of the retreat, to everyone's surprise, a lieutenant of army engineers entered the oratory and sat down in the first row. In a few minutes he was sound asleep. Before God, Father Josemaria commented, this sleep was prayer, the prayer of exhaustion. [34]

In two days the lieutenant had to return to Olot. Waiting for him was a letter the Father had mailed on June 6, before the lieutenant had left Olot for Valencia. It contains the most daring affirmation of spiritual paternity the founder ever wrote: "Saxum! Your Father in heaven (God) and your Father on earth and in heaven (which is what I am) are expecting a lot from you." [35]

Fourteen young men attended the retreat at Burjasot. The day after his arrival, Father Josemaría wrote enthusiastically to those in Madrid: "Very happy. Pester our Lord and this will be a success. Same goes for the matter of the house. Be certain of it! Every moment I get more optimistic." [36]

He asked others for their prayers, too, sensing that he had finally found the rich source of vocations to Opus Dei for which he had so long been hoping. "This is going very well," he wrote at the end of the retreat. "Yesterday the Lord sent another one—four new people, altogether. And all very solid. I pray that they will persevere." [37]

---

[33] *Letter 9 Jan 1959*, no. 35. See also Alvaro del Portillo, PR, p. 1689; AGP, RHF, T–02769 (p. 1), T–00159/1 (p. 93), T–07805, D–12799, and T–12942; and Alfonso Méndiz Noguero, "Cada Caminante siga su camino: Historia y significado de un lema poético en la vida del fundador del Opus Dei," in *Anuario de Historia de la Iglesia* 9 (2000): 741–69.

[34] See AGP, P01 1975, p. 789.

[35] AGP, RHF, EF–390606–1. See also EF–390613–2. This second letter shows Alvaro's departure from Olot as having taken place on the morning of June 13.

[36] AGP, RHF, EF–390606–3.

[37] AGP, RHF, EF–390613–2.

After the retreat, Father Josemaría spoke with a young man who had been unable to attend, but who had heard about the Work and wanted to be admitted. "He too is trying to push open the door," he wrote.[38] A month later he wrote to this young man, José Manuel Casas Torres, "What can I say to you but yes and onward? Marvel and be grateful to him, on seeing that he wants you for such great things."[39]

For now, José Manuel was the last of this cluster of Valencian vocations that began in Burjasot. (The first was Amadeo de Fuenmayor.) But, convinced that he had not exhausted this vein, Father Josemaría decided to return to Valencia as soon as possible, in order to turn into reality the dream interrupted in 1936—when he had been about to expand the Work to other cities.

2. *The Way*

In Burgos Father Josemaría had soon found many obstacles standing in the way of his giving regular spiritual direction to the young soldiers with whom he was in contact. The soldiers were dispersed, on different fronts. The means of transport were precarious. Time for traveling was hard to come by. Safe-conduct passes had to be obtained—but still did not always guarantee being able to reach the front.

Letters were also a problem. On his return to Burgos from a trip, he might find many waiting for him, but usually the opposite was true. Mail was slow even when the military post offices were functioning normally, and service was often interrupted as units moved about.

When writing to his sons, the priest would always remind them of the need to carry out their norms of piety and, especially, to spend some time in mental prayer every day. The monthly newsletter, *Noticias*, helped its readers revive good habits that might have been forgotten and offered points for meditation. But this means of bringing a breath of interior life to those on the front lines was too infrequent.

Father Josemaría therefore thought of his book *Consideraciones espirituales*, which had been published in Cuenca in 1934. His plan

[38] AGP, RHF, EF–390615–1.
[39] AGP, RHF, EF–390716–1.

was to reprint it in a smaller format so that the soldiers could slip it into their pockets. But difficulties in getting it printed forced a postponement.[40]

While still at the Sabadell Hotel, he began writing new points to add to those in the 1934 edition, using the same method that he had used in Madrid with his "Catherines." When an idea, an apostolic possibility, or a flash of inspiration came to him, he immediately jotted it down in abbreviated form, intending to expand it later. More than once when Pedro and Paco returned from work in the evening, the Father greeted them by waving a handful of little pieces of paper. Later he would read his notes to them and comment on them at length. He called them "little bagpipes," because they were charged with meaning that had to be drawn out of them, much as when someone draws a prolonged note out of a bagpipe.[41]

One day, upon returning from headquarters, the two soldiers had a surprise. The "little bagpipes" had been laboriously typed out by the Father and carefully divided into little stacks arranged according to subject. All three beds in the room were covered with them.

But even so, it was still a few months before the book was ready for publication. The printing was delayed first by the Ebro River campaign and then by the campaign in Catalonia—not to mention the wartime paper shortage and the anticipation of an imminent return to Madrid. At the beginning of 1939, when Pedro was in Catalayud, the Father wrote to him from Burgos: "I would like you to take charge of the printing of my book. Are there printers there who could do this? I only need eighty more considerations; it's a matter of days." [42] A letter

---

[40] Although in his letters he referred to *Considerations*, he was also thinking of another book, as we shall see. He wrote to Bishop Moro, "After these have come out, I will be delighted to spend time with my bishop and write the third one": AGP, RHF, EF–380400–1. (The second book was *Holy Rosary*.)

For complete and detailed information on the history and content of *Consideraciones Espirituales* and of *The Way*, see: *Camino, Edición critico-histórica preparada por Pedro Rodríguez* (Madrid: Rialp, 2002).

[41] "When he was just sketching out an idea on some scrap of paper or other," says Pedro Casciaro, "the Father called those papers 'slips,' but when he had reworked them on a bigger piece of paper, he called them 'little bagpipes.' But in either case, the phrases were always very concise. . . . He used the holy Gospel a lot in his preaching, developing his explication around two or three of these 'little bagpipes.' He gave marvelous meditations and talks based on this material. I think he called them 'little bagpipes' because he did not read these concise phrases but, rather, expanded them, making them 'resound'" (AGP, RHF, T–04197, p. 144).

[42] AGP, RHF, EF–390111–1. Pedro answered, "Delighted to take care of the printing of your book" (AGP, RHF, D–15717).

written a week later to José María Albareda contains this laconic postscript: "27 to go." [43]

His goal was 999 points, an expression of his devotion to the Blessed Trinity. The spiritual symbolism of numbers, or, as he sometimes called it, "the theology of mathematics," was familiar to him, and 9 was a number he was especially fond of.[44]

In February 1939, on one of his trips to Vitoria, Father Josemaría brought along the typed manuscript of the book to show to Bishop Lauzurica. The day after the bishop read it, the Father wrote to Pedro: "How is the cover for the book coming along? It's urgent. The bishop likes it; yesterday he told me to do a big printing." [45]

That same week, Pedro sent the design for the book to Burgos. Father Josemaría wrote back: "I like the cover. I'll make a few suggestions when we know the size, so you can draw up the final version." [46] But Pedro was not satisfied, and immediately started doing more sketches. He wrote to Paco, on February 19, "I'm sending you a design for the cover of *Considerations*. I'm not completely satisfied with it, so I'll do one or two others. If Mariano likes the idea, he can send me the title, *Considerations*, written in his own handwriting, to use for the cover, either in black or in red." [47]

Five days later, Pedro wrote again, saying, "I am waiting for the word 'Considerations.' " And again he got no answer. Had the author lost interest?

On the contrary, the author wanted the book out as soon as possible. But he had sent an urgent request to the bishop of Vitoria to write a preface. It came a few days later, dated "Feast of Saint Joseph, 1939"— a saint's day present for Father Josemaría. The bishop wrote, in his second paragraph: "The spirit of God hovers over these pages. Behind each maxim is a saint who sees your intention and waits for your decisions. The sentences are broken off, so that you can round them out with your conduct." [48]

Publication was delayed by the urgent obligations associated with the war's end and the return to Madrid. On May 18, the Father wrote Alvaro. "Saxum! How bright I see the way, a long one, that lies ahead

---

[43] AGP, RHF, EF–390117–1.
[44] See AGP, RHF, EF–380419–2, and *Apuntes*, no. 1550 (22 Feb 1938).
[45] AGP, RHF, EF–390213–3.
[46] AGP, RHF, EF–390218–1.
[47] AGP, RHF, D–15718.
[48] *The Way*, Introduction.

of you! Bright and full, like a field ready for the harvest. Blessed fruitfulness, that of an apostle, more beautiful than anything else on earth!" [49] Very likely, in using the word "way" [*camino*] he was think-ing of the new title he had decided to give his book. Paco Botella, who helped draw up its index, referred to this title, *Camino*, in a letter to Pedro Casciaro in early June.[50]

When Father Josemaría went to Valencia on June 5 to give that retreat for university students, he brought with him the book, to take to the printer. "The book is at the printer," he wrote the next day.[51] The day that he took *The Way* to the printer was, in other words, the same day that he came across that placard saying, "Let each wayfarer fol-low his own way." [52]

The book was finally published on September 29, 1939.[53]

*   *   *

Considerations dated from the years 1928 to 1934, while the historical setting for *The Way* extends to 1939. But the two books have the same sources: the author's life of contemplation and the daily incidents of his apostolic work.[54]

[49] AGP, RHF, EF–390518–5. See also *Apuntes*, no. 1141 (24 Feb 1934), no. 1160 (16 Mar 1934), no. 1304 (12 Dec 1935), and no. 1596 (13 Apr 1939).

[50] See AGP, RHF, D–15393. It is quite possible that Father Josemaría had already written to Pedro that it would be called *The Way*. In the end, by the way, it was Miguel Fisac, not Pedro Casciaro, who designed the cover.

[51] See AGP, RHF, EF–390606–3.

[52] Father Josemaría's use of that saying as a theme for the meditations he gave in Burjasot is mentioned by Paco Botella, who attended some of them. (See AGP, RHF, T–00159/1, p. 93.) Amadeo de Fuenmayor likewise testifies that "he managed to make good use of it in his preaching." During the retreat, he says, he spoke to the Father about the possibility of his having a vocation to the Work, and he remembers the deep peace he felt afterwards, and the Father's words: "God works *suaviter et fortiter* [gently and strongly]. Recall the circumstances of your life, and you will see how he has been preparing the *way*"(AGP, RHF, T–02769, pp. 1–2). See also AGP, RHF, T–07805 (Carlos Verdú Moscardó) and D–12799 (Roberto Moroder).

[53] Printed by a company called Gráficas Turia, it was about 7 x 10 in. and had 336 pages. The first printing was of 2,500 copies. "I think that when you put the price on the book," the author wrote to his sons in Valencia, "you should set it according to what is standard today, neither more nor less" (AGP, RHF, EF–390628–1). In 1939 the price per copy for direct sales was 8 pesetas; in 1940, 10 pesetas. The retail price in bookstores was 14 pesetas. To Manuel Pérez Sánchez, who was in Gijón, Father Josemaría wrote: "I would appreciate it if you could see if any bookstore in Gijón might be interested in selling my book. If so, give them the address so they can write for them, unless you would like to be a middleman, which would be better. *The Way* is sold at 14 pesetas a copy, and the bookstores get a discount of 20 to 25 percent. *Holy Rosary* is sold at 30 pesetas per hundred, so it can be sold at half a peseta per copy" (AGP, RHF, EF–400122–5).

[54] *Considerations* consisted of 438 points, which became part of *The Way*, often with a slight change in the text. There are some twenty new chapters in *The Way*, including

The principal source for *Considerations* was Father Josemaría's personal journal. *The Way*, on the other hand, included many points, added in Burgos, that came from his correspondence with people to whom he was giving spiritual direction. In both cases, personal references are accompanied by many Gospel commentaries and moral reflections.[55] But the autobiographical element is always at the fore, and the author's personal experiences are constantly reflected in the book.

All kinds of persons and scenes connected with his life make their appearance, though not in any chronological order. There is, for example, Father Somoano, the chaplain of King's Hospital, a soul of great refinement and sensibility. "How that saintly young priest, who was found worthy of martyrdom, wept at the foot of the altar as he thought of a soul who had come to receive Christ in the state of mortal sin!" [56] And Luis Gordon, who, on being asked to clean out the bedpan of a sick person, overcame his natural revulsion by saying under his

---

"Heart," "Examination of Conscience," "Lukewarmness," "Holy Mass," "Little Things," "Calling," and "Perseverance." One chapter of *Considerations*, "Spiritual Childhood," was divided into two chapters: "Spiritual Childhood" and "Life of Childhood."

In the sixth printing, in 1950, what is now point no. 381 was introduced to replace a duplication of no. 940.

[55] Some points in *The Way* came from letters in which Father Josemaría gave people advice regarding problems they had written to him about. Compare, for example, nos. 160–164 with the texts of two letters to Miguel Sotomayor Muro: AGP, RHF, EF–380408–7 and EF–380502–7.

In some instances he picks up something written by the other person, such as "My enthusiasm is gone" (Alvaro del Portillo), and adds a commentary: in this case, "Yours has to be a work not of enthusiasm, but of Love, conscious of duty—which means self-denial" (*The Way*, no. 994).

It can also happen that in copying a paragraph or a few lines from a letter, the author is actually picking up ideas that he himself has earlier sown. Such is the case with the plain wooden cross (without a corpus) that was placed in the first centers of the Work, before the civil war. In *The Way*, no. 277, we read: "You ask me, 'Why that wooden cross?' And I quote from a letter: 'As I raise my eyes from the microscope, my sight comes to rest on the cross—black and empty. . . .'" The letter to which this refers was written by Juan Jiménez Vargas, on May 4, 1938, from the Teruel front. In it he mentions that he has found some pieces of wood, painted black . . . a cross. He then continues with his memories of republican Madrid—a paragraph which, with some editing, became part of *The Way*.

Sometimes, too, Father Josemaría extracts an entire anecdote from a letter and reconstructs it into a point for meditation. Ricardo Fernández Vallespín, for example, in a letter dated December 18, 1938, tells this story: On December 8, feast of the Immaculate Conception, patroness of the infantry, the officers of that branch invited him to dinner. "After dinner," he says, "wine flowing, songs of all types and flavors were sung, one of which stuck in my head: 'I do not like divided hearts. I give mine whole and not in parts.' What a struggle to give my heart completely!" (Compare with *The Way*, no. 145.)

[56] *The Way*, no. 532. (See also vol. 1, pp. 331–33, of this biography.)

breath, "Jesus, may I put on a smiling face!"[57] Then there was that woman who had been a "camp follower," but who on her deathbed had reminded him of Mary Magdalene because "she knew how to love." She had died shortly after praying with him, "Blessed be pain. Loved be pain. Sanctified be pain. . . . Glorified be pain!"[58]

When the protagonist is the author himself, however, and there is reference to a supernatural event, the account is suitably blurred or depersonalized. For example, his receiving of a divine locution while giving Communion to the nuns at Santa Isabel is related as, "There is a story of a soul who, on saying to our Lord in prayer, 'Jesus, I love you,' heard this reply from heaven: 'Deeds are love—not sweet words and excuses.' "[59]

There are also instances in which a divine locution or illumination is presented, but not as such. An example: "Let obstacles only make you bigger. The grace of our Lord will not be lacking: 'inter medium montium pertransibunt aquae'—'through the very midst of the mountains the waters shall pass.' You will pass through mountains!"[60]

Many points refer to events in the author's life, but are related in second or third person so as to erase any autobiographical trace. Here, for instance, is the journal entry on an occurrence in the bishop's residence in Pamplona on December 22, 1937:

> The vicar general consecrated some chalices and patens. I stayed behind in the chapel for a few moments by myself, and I left a kiss on each chalice and on each paten, so that my Lord will find it waiting the first time he comes down to those sacred vessels. There were twenty-five in all, a gift from the Diocese of Pamplona for the front.[61]

In *The Way* this becomes:

> Mad! Yes, I saw you (in the bishop's chapel, you thought you were alone) as you left a kiss on each newly consecrated chalice and paten, so that he might find it there when for

---

[57] *The Way*, no. 626. (See also vol. 1, p. 328, of this biography.)

[58] *The Way*, no. 208. (See also vol. 1, p. 339, of this biography.)

[59] *The Way*, no. 933. (See also vol. 1, p. 318, of this biography.)

[60] *The Way*, no. 12. This locution occurred on December 12, 1931. (See *Apuntes*, no. 476 (13 Dec 1931) and vol. 1, pp. 298–99, of this biography.) The second paragraph of this point in *The Way* refers to their situation during the war (their inability to do apostolate) and to the closing of the DYA Academy on Ferraz Street in 1935.

[61] *Apuntes*, no. 1441.

the first time he would "come down" to those eucharistic vessels.[62]

As is mentioned in its preface, *Considerations* was written without any "literary pretensions or concern about publicity." Basically it was just a collection of thoughts arranged by subject. *The Way*, on the other hand, was from the first intended to be a published book, and its composition, though it began with the idea of enlarging *Considerations*, was governed by a strong unity of spirit and intention.[63]

As the book took shape in 1938, the author, building on the 438 points of *Considerations*, saw the need to develop certain topics at greater length. The number of chapters was increased, the material was rearranged, and greater cohesion was given to the various chapters.

The aim is stated at the beginning: "I will only stir your memory, so that some thought will arise and strike you; and so you will better your life and set out along ways of prayer and of Love. And in the end you will be a more worthy soul."[64]

The objective is no less than the conversion of the reader's intellect and will. As the bishop of Vitoria remarks in his introduction, the points in the book invite the reader to fill them out from his own life experience. The desire to stir readers' consciences is reflected in the style, which abounds in exclamations and questions, in appeals to common sense, in irony and exhortations, in imperatives and fragmentary phrases. Here is a challenge to the reader to improve his life, and the mood it evokes in some readers is a kind of reflective tension. The first chapter is entitled "Character," and it begins with a wake-up call:

> Don't let your life be sterile. Be useful. Blaze a trail. Shine forth with the light of your faith and of your love.[65]

The structural unity of *The Way* is evident throughout, but particularly in its last two points. One of the nine new chapters is the concluding one, "Perseverance." Except for one point, everything in it is new. It opens with a direct challenge—"To begin is for everyone, to

---

[62] *The Way*, no. 438.
[63] See *Spiritual Considerations*, Preliminary Note.
[64] *The Way*, Prologue of the Author.
[65] *The Way*, no. 1.

persevere is for saints" [66]—and ends with a parable, the story of that donkey that Father Josemaría had seen treading a waterwheel on the plains of Orbigo in July 1938, when he had missed his train at the León station. From that country scene he drew lessons about docility and about daily work, humble and monotonous, made up of small and repeated efforts, yet producing splendid results of fruitfulness and service:

> O blessed perseverance of the donkey that turns the waterwheel! Always the same pace. Always around the same circle. One day after another, every day the same.
>
> Without that, there would be no ripeness in the fruit, nor blossom in the orchard, nor scent of flowers in the garden.
>
> Carry this thought to your interior life.[67]

How well this consideration of the fruitfulness of perseverance ties in with that opening line: "Don't let your life be sterile." And how potent is the book's closing point: "And what is the secret of perseverance? Love. Fall in Love, and you will not leave him." [68]

The Way is not a systematic treatise, but a work of reflection which the reader can consult without having to read in some predetermined order. Each section, nevertheless, has its own structure and fits into the framework of the book as a whole.

Take the section on "The Will of God." It varies from the version in *Considerations* in both the number and the order of the thoughts. Clearly the author has tried to make meditation easier by providing a guiding thread of thought. The chapter has a clear introductory overture, a main body of text presenting variations on the theme, and,

---

[66] *The Way*, no. 983.

[67] *The Way*, no. 998. See also Eliodoro Gil Rivera, *Sum.* 7766.

Also relevant are these two paragraphs from the *Instruction* of 9 Jan 1935 (nos. 220 and 221), on the importance of teaching young people not to neglect the little things:

"Get them to reflect on what it takes to erect a magnificent building: one day after another of monotonous work. Little things: one brick and another brick, and a foundation stone that, despite its huge size, is nothing compared to the whole building; beginning and ending the day's work at the same times each day; and perseverance. Nothing great is achieved overnight, and especially not sanctity. How much you can tell them about sanctity and little things!

The blessed perseverance, full of fruitfulness, of the poor donkey at the waterwheel! Always the same, monotonously; hidden and despised because of its humble pace; not needing to know that from its efforts come the aroma of the flowers, the beauty of the fruit in season, the refreshing shade of the trees in summer; all the richness of the orchard and all the charm of the garden."

[68] *The Way*, no. 999.

to conclude, practical considerations that end with this advice: "It takes only a second. Before starting anything ask yourself: What does God want of me in this? Then, with divine grace, do it!" [69]

The considerations that open the chapter form the basis for what follows. The first point proclaims the Gospel truth: "This is the key to open the door and enter the kingdom of heaven: '*qui facit voluntatem Patris mei qui in coelis est, ipse intrabit in regnum coelorum*'—'he who does the will of my Father, he shall enter!' " [70]

In the second point he confronts us with our responsibility for determining the exercise of our freedom. He says, "Many great things depend—don't forget it—on whether you and I live our lives as God wants." [71] (These words come from a 1938 letter to one of those to whom he was giving spiritual direction.[72])

The third point matches up with a journal entry from 1932. It reads:

> We are stones—blocks of stone—that can move, can feel, that have completely free wills.
>
> God himself is the stonecutter who chips off the edges, shaping and modifying us as he desires, with blows of the hammer and chisel.
>
> Let us not try to draw aside, let us not try to evade his will, for in any case we won't be able to avoid the blows. We will suffer all the more, and uselessly. Instead of polished stone suitable for building, we will be a shapeless heap of gravel that people will trample on contemptuously.[73]

This consideration takes up where the journal entry leaves off. The journal note is about what God expects of the first members of Opus Dei, the ones who have to build the Work. It says:

> If it were a matter of putting up a booth for a fair, it would be a quick and easy job. Drive four poles into the ground, a few yards of cloth, some boards and nails . . . and there it is. But

---

[69] *The Way*, no. 778. Like almost all of the other counsels in *The Way*, this point has a tie to the author's own interior life. In his journal entry for October 27, 1932, we read: "Don't make a decision without first stopping to consider the matter in God's presence" (*Apuntes*, no. 853).

[70] *The Way*, no. 754.

[71] *The Way*, no. 755.

[72] This was Manuel Sainz de los Terreros. See AGP, RHF, EF–380117–3.

[73] *The Way*, no. 756.

the Work of God is a building for the ages—it will last till the
end of time—and the Holy Spirit is its architect.

We are the blocks of stone that Jesus wants buried in the
foundations. Blocks of stone that can move, can feel. . . .[74]

Throughout, the book emphasizes eternal life in the kingdom of
heaven, noble participation in the tasks of the present, and the sad
consequences of rebelling against God's invitation to humankind.
Appealing to faith, to reason, to the imagination, and to the emotions,
the author encourages the reader to undertake the ascent of the interior life.

*   *   *

From time to time, a point in *The Way* conjures up the context of an
actual event by the use of vivid images. One example: "Do you remember? You and I were praying silently as night was falling. From
close by came the murmur of water. And, through the stillness of the
city, . . ."[75] This refers to the Arlanzón River, along whose banks the
Father would walk with his sons, or with some soldier in Burgos on
leave.

Burgos also evoked the memory of Rodrigo Díaz de Vivar, better
known as El Cid. In a letter sent to Juan Jiménez Vargas from Burgos,
the Father had written: "The epics—those of our El Cid, for example—
always relate great adventures, but mixed in with down-to-earth details about the hero. May you always pay a lot of attention to the little
things."[76] With slight changes, these lines are included in point 826 of
The Way.

At the Sabadell Hotel, the priest, having nowhere else to go for
using his disciplines, would retire to the alcove, closing the curtain
separating it from the room shared by Pedro Casciaro and Paco
Botella. On one of the occasions when his sons were aware of this, he
justified his conduct with words that are reiterated in *The Way*: "If
they have witnessed your weaknesses and faults, does it matter if they
witness your penance?"[77] But he is, as noted above, careful to eliminate any autobiographical reference.

[74] *Apuntes*, nos. 703 and 704.
[75] *The Way*, no. 811.
[76] AGP, RHF, EF–380327–3.
[77] *The Way*, no. 197. See also Pedro Casciaro, *Dream and Your Dreams Will Fall Short*
(London and Princeton, 1994), p. 151.

In *The Way* we also find a reflection of the patriotic spirit that filled Burgos in those days. The flags and the uniforms and the cheering all remind the priest that Christ also has his army. "Patriotic fervor—which is praiseworthy—leads many men to give their lives in service, even in a 'crusade.' Don't forget that Christ, too, has 'crusaders' and people chosen for his service."[78]

* * *

In calling his book—after careful deliberation—*The Way*, the author chose a title rich in meaning. It suggests the path to be followed in response to the universal call to holiness—the faithful following of the footsteps of Christ, who is the Way, Truth, and Life—and a program of spiritual direction for attaining that goal. It also points to the book's purpose.

> Do you want me to tell you everything I think about "your way"?
>
> Well, it's like this. If you really correspond to his call, you'll work for Christ like the best. If you become a man of prayer, you'll be given that correspondence I mentioned, and hungry for sacrifice, you'll seek the hardest tasks . . .
>
> And you'll be happy here, and most happy hereafter—in the Life.[79]

The Way is demanding. It makes room for the little things, but not for mediocrity. It is a call to holiness of life, which it shows to be the

---

[78] *The Way*, no. 905.

[79] *The Way*, no. 255. The founder wanted to lead each soul along its specific path, as he explained in an interview with the journalist Jacques Guillemé-Brûlon which was published in the 16 May 1966 issue of *Le Figaro*. This part of it also appears in *Conversations*, no. 36: "I wrote a good part of that book in 1934, summarizing my priestly experience for the benefit of all the souls with whom I was in contact, whether they were in Opus Dei or not. I never suspected that thirty years later it would be spread so widely—millions of copies, in so many languages. It is not a book solely for members of Opus Dei. It is for everyone, whether Christian or not. Among those who have translated it on their own initiative are Orthodox, Protestants, and non-Christians. *The Way* must be read with at least some supernatural spirit, some interior life and apostolic feeling. It is not a code for the man of action. The aim of the book is to help men become friends of God, to love him and serve all men. In other words, to be an instrument—which gets back to your question—as Saint Paul the Apostle wanted to be an instrument of Christ—a free and responsible instrument. Anyone who tries to see a temporal goal in the pages of *The Way* is mistaken. Do not forget it has been common for spiritual authors of every age to see souls as instruments in the hands of God."

key not only to one's personal destiny, but also to the history of humanity.

> I'll tell you a secret, an open secret: these world crises are crises of saints." [80]

And although it does not contain the whole spirit of Opus Dei, it does contain the essential elements of the message received on October 2, 1928: the universal call to holiness in the midst of the world, the sense of divine filiation in Christ as the foundation of its spirituality, and the sanctifying and apostolic meaning of human work. It places holiness, so to speak, within arm's reach: "'Great' holiness consists in carrying out the 'little' duties of each moment." [81]

The spiritual efficacy of the book stems from the fact that its pages have been seasoned with the author's mortification and prayer. Many readers have testified to its ability to reach the depths of the soul of someone open to its message. "The spirit of God hovers over these pages," the bishop of Vitoria wrote in his introduction. "Behind each maxim is a saint who sees your intention and waits for your decisions." [82]

Since 1931, the founder had harbored a desire to "write books of fire" that would "race across the world like burning flames and set people ablaze with their light and heat, turning poor hearts into burning embers to be offered to Jesus as rubies for his royal crown." [83]

---

[80] *The Way*, no. 301. The entire book resonates with the universal call to holiness, and with the urgent demands that this makes on one's own conscience. One example: "Why don't you give yourself to God once and for all, . . . really, . . . *now!*" (no. 902). This is a question that Father Josemaría frequently asked himself.

[81] *The Way*, no. 817.

[82] Pedro Casciaro, who had heard the founder "play the little bagpipes" and had witnessed his laborious typing of them, wrote forty years later: "All through my years as a priest, innumerable persons have confided to me that the first time they felt our Lord knocking at their heart and their soul to open up to the faith was precisely when a copy of *The Way* came into their hands" (AGP, RHF, T–04197, p. 146).

A few years after the book's appearance, Monsignor Giovanni Battista Montini—the future Pope Paul VI, at that time an official of the Secretariat of State—wrote, in a letter dated February 2, 1945: "I don't want to hide . . . the pleasure I have gotten from reading it. Its pages are a deeply felt and powerful call to the generous hearts of young people, to whom it opens up elevated ideals and teaches the path of reflection and serious judgment, disposing them to live an integral supernatural life. This work, now in its second printing, does not need wishes for its success; we already see the consoling reality of the bountiful fruit it has produced in the university world" (AGP, RHF, D–15086).

[83] *Apuntes*, no. 218 (7 Aug 1931).

This was the spirit in which *The Way* was written, as was *Holy Rosary*, whose second printing appeared at the beginning of October 1939, shortly after *The Way* was published.[84]

3. *Political circumstances*

That cruel and bloody civil war had brought Spain to the brink of collapse. It would take fifteen years for the country to return to normal. And that was just with regard to material goods. The human losses could never be recouped.

In the newsletter, *Noticias,* for March 1939, Father Josemaría refers to the end of the "transitional period" and the beginning of more stabilized conditions. "We are moving," he says, "from the madness that characterized these times to the well-trodden path that will lead us to the definitive conquest."[85] The devastation and lack of material resources, as reconstruction began, was self-evident. Yet his circular letter of January 9, 1939, expressed undaunted supernatural convictions.

> Obstacles? I'm not worried about the obstacles from outside: we will overcome them easily. I see only one formidable obstacle: your lack of filiation and fraternity, were such ever to occur in our family. Everything else—scarcity, debt, poverty, scorn, slander, lies, ingratitude, opposition by good people, misunderstanding, and even persecution by authorities—all of that is of no importance when Father and brothers are fully

---

[84] The first edition of *Holy Rosary* was published in Madrid in 1934: "*Santo Rosario,* by José María, with ecclesiastical approval. Pub.: 3 Juan Bravo, Madrid." The second edition ("José María Escrivá, *Santo Rosario* with ecclesiastical approval, pub. Gráficas Turia, Valencia" appeared in 1939; the date of its imprimatur was October 2, 1939. It consisted of 16 pages of about 6 × 9 inches. The last page carried a notice concerning other publications by the same author:
The Way (Introduction by His Excellency the Bishop of Vitoria)
Liturgical Devotions (Introduction by His Excellency the Bishop of Tortosa)—forthcoming
Apparently it was to *Liturgical Devotions* that Father Josemaría was referring when he wrote the above-mentioned letter (AGP, RHF, EF–380400–1) to the bishop of Avila mentioning that he had two books under way. As is the case with *The Way,* there is no written reference to the negotiations concerning this book. There is only a casual mention by Francisco Botella, who says that Isidoro was working on "ordering the material that the Father was giving him, for a book that the Father wanted to publish on liturgical devotions," and that the Father "had already begun this work when they were staying at Santa Isabel." See AGP, RHF, T–00159/1, p. 102.
[85] AGP, RHF, D–03691.

united through Christ, with Christ, and in Christ. There will be no bitterness that can rob us of the sweetness of our blessed charity.[86]

Every Spaniard knew people who had fallen in battle or been murdered; the total was about three hundred thousand. And then there were all those who had been in prison or exile. Bridges, highways, homes, and factories had to be rebuilt or repaired. Cars, trucks, ships, and all types of machines were in short supply, as were household goods, clothes, and food. Reorganizing and rebuilding would take time, and would require help from abroad. To make things worse, the gold reserves of the Bank of Spain had either been used up in the war or shipped to other countries. Agricultural production had fallen off sharply, too, while drought would keep the country ill fed and prolong food rationing until 1951.[87]

Unfortunately, the end of the war did not mean the end of old hatreds. The spirit of revenge was widespread. In a radio message on April 16, 1939, two weeks after the war ended, Pope Pius XII expressed to the Catholic faithful and hierarchy of Spain his "paternal congratulations on the gift of peace and of victory." Appealing to the generosity and nobility of the Spanish spirit, which, he said, he hoped would soon reestablish the nation's life in accord with "Catholic faith, piety, and civilization," the Pope then said:

> We therefore exhort the rulers and the pastors of Catholic Spain to enlighten the minds of those who have erred, pointing out to them with love the roots of the materialism and secularism from which have sprung their unfortunate errors. ... And we have no doubt that those others, the ones who like prodigal sons seek to return to the Father's house, will be welcomed with benevolence and love. It is your role,

[86] AGP, RHF, EF–390109–1.

[87] The war destroyed 30 percent of maritime freight tonnage, half of the country's locomotives, 8 percent of homes, and a third of the cattle. In 1939, industrial production was 31 percent below that of the last prewar year, agricultural production was down 21 percent, the workforce had been reduced by half a million, and per capita income was about 28 percent lower. In the five years after the war, malnutrition and sickness caused a minimum of 200,000 deaths above the prewar mortality rate. See Ramón Salas Larrazábal, *Pérdidas de la guerra* (Barcelona, 1977); Larrazábal, *Los datos exactos de la guerra civil* (Madrid, 1980); and Stanley G. Payne, *El régimen de Franco, 1936–1975* (Madrid, 1987), pp. 260 and 267.

esteemed brothers in the episcopate, to counsel everyone, in their efforts to establish a lasting peace, to follow the principles taught by the Church and proclaimed with such nobility by the Generalissimo: justice with regard to the crime and benevolent generosity toward those who have erred.[88]

But the principles actually applied to the conquered were very different. In 1939, special courts for political "cleansing" were set up. This repressive apparatus was constructed on three laws: the "Political Responsibility Law," enacted on February 9 and retroactive to the revolution of October 1934; the "Purging of Functionaries Law," enacted on February 10; and a law enacted on March 1 for the repression of Masonry and communism.[89]

Many citizens remained in prison for years or spent extended periods at forced labor. Others were fined, lost their jobs, or were forced into exile. In the midst of all this, Father Josemaría urged forgiving and forgetting as the right line of conduct. As a fugitive in revolutionary Madrid, he had generously offered his sufferings, in reparation for all Spaniards, trying not to categorize people as good or bad. Now he strove to change the attitudes of those who were demanding vengeance. In April 1938, on a trip from Utrera to Salamanca, he met on the train an officer of that mind-set. Afterwards, from Córdoba, he wrote to his sons in Burgos:

> A second lieutenant, who had suffered terrible harm to his family and to his estate at the hands of the reds, said that he

[88] *Acta Apostolicae Sedis*, vol. 31 (1939), pp. 151–54.

[89] Annual statistical compilations give the following numbers for the people imprisoned in the postwar years. At the time of the surrender there were 100,292 prisoners in the nationalist zone; by the end of 1939, 270,719; in 1940, 233,373; in 1941, 159,392; in 1942, 124,423; in 1943, 74,095; in 1944, 54,072; in 1945, 43,812; in 1946, 36,379.

Ramón Salas Larrazábal calculates the number of executions from 1939 to 1945 "for political violence" at about 28,000. After 1945, he says, they became increasingly rare. (See his "Tiempo de silencio, cárcel y muerte," in *Historia del franquismo* 16 [Madrid, 1985], pp. 18–19.) Later studies have revised these figures; some have put the number of executions at more than 35,000. But firm figures for this tragic epilogue to the civil war are lacking. For more on this subject, see Josep Maria Solé i Sabaté, "Las represiones," in *La Guerra Civil: Una nueva visión del conflicto que dividió España*, ed. Stanley G. Payne and Javier Tusell (Madrid, 1996), pp. 598–604; Angel David Martín Rubio, "Las pérdidas humanas (a consecuencia de la Guerra Civil española)," in *La Guerra Civil Española (Sesenta años después)*, ed. Miguel Alonso Baquer (Madrid, 1999), pp. 321–65; and Gonzalo Redondo, *Política, Cultura y Sociedad en la España de Franco: 1939–1975*, vol. 1, *La configuración del Estado español, nacional y católico: 1939–1947* (Pamplona, 1999), pp. 105–108.

would soon have his vengeance. I told him that I too have suffered as he has, in both my family and my estate, but that I want the reds to live and be converted. These Christian words had a strong impact on his noble soul, consumed with a desire for violence, and he became more thoughtful.

I recollected myself as best I could and, as is my custom, invoked all the guardian angels.[90]

On one occasion Father Josemaría went to see someone who had lost several relatives at the hands of communists. This person wanted to put up a large cross at the highway crossroads where those relatives had been murdered. "You shouldn't do it," the priest told him, "because your motive is hatred. It wouldn't be Christ's cross; it would be the devil's."[91] The cross was not put up. The person learned to forgive.

But not everyone did. One day several months after the war had ended, Father Josemaría had to take a taxi to Madrid, and, as was his custom, began to speak to the driver about God, about the importance of sanctifying one's work, and about the need to leave behind the tragedy that Spain had just passed through. The driver said nothing until Father Josemaría had reached his destination. Then he said, "Listen, where were you during the time of the war?"

"In Madrid," the priest answered.

"Too bad they didn't kill you!"

Staying calm, Father Josemaría asked him, "Do you have any children?" And when the driver nodded yes, he added a good tip to the fare and said, "Here, buy some candy for your wife and your children."[92]

Spain came out of the war heavily militarized, with power concentrated in the person of the chief of state, who was also the chief of government, of the army, and of the one and only political party, the National Movement.[93] An exaggerated nationalism reigned in Spain,

---

[90] AGP, RHF, EF–380419–2.

[91] See Josemaría Escrivá, *The Way of the Cross*, Station 8, no. 3.

[92] See Javier Echevarría, *Sum.* 2945.

[93] Franco created the one party, the National Movement (Movimiento Nacional), in an attempt to unify by decree all those who had supported the military uprising. Its creation in April 1937 provoked several violent incidents that were suppressed severely. Up to 1943, one can speak more properly of the Falange (Falange Española Tradicionalista) and of the JONS (Juntas de Ofensiva Nacional Sindicalista) than of the Movement

to the detriment of freedom of thought, freedom of expression, and freedom of association. Existing alongside this authoritarian current, nevertheless, were the ideologies of other parties—monarchist, republican, traditionalist, and democratic. The political regime born of the civil war would in time become known as Francoism. The regime was not easy to define. Its internal cohesive force derived from Franco himself and his personal, authoritarian exercise of power, which was sustained by a constant replacement of cabinet members. The policies of the regime had an essentially pragmatic character, especially in its early years, when Franco had to confront the dangers posed by the Second World War and maintain the country's independence.[94]

The years of struggle, pain, and privation had been experienced by Spain's Catholics as an authentic crusade, and recognized as such by the Spanish hierarchy.[95] All over the country, this fervor now rekindled religious faith and popular enthusiasm. As religious persecution had been a distinctive sign of the republican regime, so protection of the Church was one of the defining characteristics of Franco's Spain. In the long years of his dictatorship, periods of close collaboration alternated with flare-ups between Church and state, but the atmosphere remained cordial and the Church continued to be more or less independent. The civil war was scarcely over when, with the

---

as such, since since it was these political groups that almost exclusively controlled all political activity in those first years of the regime. See Payne, *El régimen*, pp. 180–91.

Franco always desired an integration of all Spaniards in the National Movement. But whether he achieved it is another question. A good part of the Spanish population had political ideas quite different from those of Franco's regime of "national unity." For more on Franco's thinking in this regard, see his speeches of 19 Apr 1937, 3 May 1939, and 4 May 1939, given in Valencia; of 20 May 1939, in Madrid; of 22 May 1939, in León; and of 22 Jun 1939, in La Coruña. These speeches can be found in *Palabras del Caudillo* (Madrid: Editora Nacional, 1943), pp. 16–17, 104–107, 118–22, 127–28, and 153–57.

[94] Franco's regime has been written about abundantly, but is still subject to debate. The more impartial historians speak of an "open debate," which, of course, we are not trying to settle here. Instead, we are simply going along with what seem to us to be the most widely accepted opinions. See Glicerio Sánchez Recio, "Líneas de investigación y debate historiográfico," in *El primer franquismo, 1936–1959* (Madrid, 1999), pp. 17–40; Ricardo Chueca, *El Fascismo en los comienzos del régimen de Franco: Un estudio sobre FET-JONS* (Madrid, 1983); and Redondo, *Política*, vol. 1, pp. 27–115.

[95] The bishops do not use the word "crusade" in their collective letter of 1 Jul 1937; here they speak of a battle fought for religious motives. But most of them did use that word in their individual statements. The first to do so was the bishop of Pamplona, Marcelino Olaechea, on August 23, 1936. See Gonzalo Redondo, *Historia de la Iglesia en España, 1931–1939*, vol. 2, *La Guerra Civil, 1936–1939* (Madrid, 1993), pp. 69–83. See also the pastoral letter "Las dos ciudades," written by the Most Reverend Enrique Pla y Daniel and dated 30 Sep 1936. It can be found in Antonio Montero, *Historia de la Persecución Religiosa en España* (Madrid, 1961), pp. 688–708.

state's help, the rebuilding of churches and convents was begun. Pastoral work flourished. Seminaries were again filled. The number of practicing Catholics increased. But (and here was the first source of tension between Church and state) episcopal sees, vacant because of the assassination or death of bishops during the war, remained vacant while a concordat between the government and the Vatican was sought.

At the end of the war, Spain considered itself officially Catholic, as were its authorities. And therefore these authorities felt that the Concordat of 1851, which had been suspended but never officially abrogated by the Republic, remained in effect. In this Concordat the Spanish kings were accorded the privilege of designating candidates for bishop. General Franco, as chief of state, tried to claim that privilege. The Holy See, however, maintained that because of the profound changes that had taken place over the course of the preceding century, the Concordat was no longer in force. Actually, Pope Pius XII's opposition to recognizing the government's right to "patronage and presentation" of candidates for bishop stemmed from certain clashes between the civil authorities and the Church. The government had, for example, prohibited the publication of several pastoral letters, and even of *Mit Brennender Sorge,* Pope Pius XI's encyclical of 1937 condemning Nazism. Pope Pius XII also feared that ratification of a cultural agreement between Spain and Germany could lead to the establishment of an anti-Christian ideology in Spain. Then there were the problems having to do with internal Spanish politics, such as the government's fear of Basque and Catalonian nationalist elements and, on the part of the Church, the hardships suffered by some Church authorities in these regions who disagreed politically with Franco.[96]

Conversations between Spain and the Holy See produced an accord, dated June 7, 1941. Besides the general provisions (which incorporated the first articles of the Concordat of 1851) and an agreement on the part of the government not to legislate on matters falling under the jurisdiction of both ecclesiastical and civil courts, the accord also

---

[96] The question—not an easy one—has been, and probably will remain, the subject of numerous studies. See Redondo, *Historia,* vol. 2, pp. 69ff.; Redondo, *Política,* pp. 229 ff.; Antonio Marquina Barrio, *La diplomacia vaticana y la España de Franco, 1936–1945* (Madrid, 1983); José Andrés-Gallego, *¿Fascismo o Estado Católico? Ideología, religión y censura en la España de Franco, 1937–1941* (Madrid, 1999); José Andrés-Gallego and Antón Pazos, *La Iglesia en la España contemporánea,* vol. 2 (Madrid, 1999), pp. 34–88; and Payne, *El régimen,* pp. 209–20.

contained a formula for the presentation of bishops for vacant sees. This was the formula: After confidential consultations between the government and the nuncio, a list of six suitable candidates for each position would be presented; from this list the pope would choose three candidates, whose names would be communicated to the government through the nuncio; the chief of state, within thirty days, would then officially choose one of them.[97]

Ecclesiastical appointments made years earlier by the authorities of the Republic now had to be formalized from a canonical perspective. This was the case with Father Josemaría's appointment as rector of the Royal Foundation of Santa Isabel. It had been made by the president of the Spanish Republic in 1934 and was recognized de facto by the Church authorities (the bishop of Madrid-Alcalá and the archbishop of Saragossa, as we have seen). The Holy See now having accepted the exercise of the rights of patronage by the new Spanish chief of state, Bishop Eijo y Garay wanted to formalize the appointment, which Father Josemaría had been exercising with his permission since 1934. The bishop headed his list of candidates for this position with these words: "I propose in first place the exemplary priest who now holds this position, and who in my judgment is most highly suited for the same."[98] On February 3, 1942, Father Josemaría was named rector for a second time, in virtue of the appointments made by the new civil authorities. With this act, his incardination in the diocese of Madrid-Alcalá was firmly fixed.[99]

*   *   *

[97] Concerning the negotiations, see Redondo, *Política*, pp. 407–13; and Marquina Barrio. Concerning the accord, see *Acta Apostolicae Sedis*, vol. 33 (1941), pp. 480–81.

[98] See the archive of the general secretariat of the archdiocese of Madrid-Alcalá, "Patronato de Santa Isabel." See also the Patrimonio Nacional archive, "Patronatos Reales," "Patronato de Santa Isabel," file 182/21.

By a law enacted on March 7, 1940, there was created the National Heritage (Patrimonio Nacional), to which all goods of the former Crown Heritage reverted. This law established the composition of the Administrative Council, whose members, as well as all the personnel of the National Heritage, were appointed by the chief of state. In addition, as already mentioned, all official appointments made during the time of the Republic had to be reviewed, in accord with the law enacted on February 10, 1939.

[99] As soon as he was notified of the appointment, Father Josemaría informed the archbishop of Saragossa, under whose jurisdiction he had been until 1934. See AGP, RHF, EF–420205–1 and D–15514, 2.

His canonical conferment was received from the hands of the bishop of Madrid-Alcalá on February 11. See Benito Badrinas Amat, "Josemaría Escrivá de Balaguer, Sacerdote de la diócesis de Madrid," in *Anuario de Historia de la Iglesia* 8 (1999): 605–34.

As years earlier the founder had written that "the Work of God was not thought up by a man to solve the sad situation of the Church in Spain since 1931," [100] so now it was not his business to become involved in the new tensions between traditional Spanish Catholicism and emerging cultural trends. He concentrated instead on fruitful, quiet priestly work—first of all, on renewing the spiritual vigor of the Spanish diocesan clergy, and then on carrying out with self-denial his own particular ministry, in a difficult political era. He tended to those in need, regardless of their creed or political affiliation or ideology. Bishop Javier Echevarría recalls reading a letter written shortly after the death of a man who had been marginalized and persecuted after the civil war: his widow thanked Father Josemaría for having spent time with her husband "in the years when no one, not even his closest friends, dared show any affection for him, because he was in prison, on charges of being a Mason." [101]

The priest had made the decision, extraordinary at the time, never to engage in any behavior that signified adherence to a political group. This included abstaining from the widespread practice of giving the Roman, fascist salute—arm extended, hand open—which most people saw as just a symbolic declaration of opposition to communism, with its clenched-fist salute. At official ceremonies, or when the national anthem was played, he simply stood in an attitude of respect.[102]

In strenuously steering clear of all partisanship, the founder not only kept intact the universality of the Work, but also safeguarded the Christian freedom of those who participated in its apostolates—their right to their own feelings and convictions in political, social, scientific, or patriotic matters. This respect for the opinions of others is borne out by an anecdote told by Juan Bautista Torelló, a member of the Work. In 1941, a time when nationalistic feelings were running high in the Falange, the walls and façades of Barcelona were covered with patriotic graffiti, such as, "If you are Spanish, speak Spanish!" or "Spaniard, speak the language of the empire!" Juan Bautista had a long conversation with Father Josemaría in which he told him that he belonged to an organization for the defense of Catalonian culture—an organization that the police considered clandestine and anti-Francoist, since use of the Catalonian language was then outlawed. The founder

---

[100] *Instruction* of 19 Mar 1934, no. 6.
[101] Javier Echevarría, *Sum.* 2946.
[102] See Alvaro del Portillo, *Sum.* 647.

reminded him of the freedom that he had in this matter. It was his affair, and no one in the Work would question him about it. "But since you have mentioned it to me," added the priest, "I want to give you some advice. Try not to get yourself arrested, because, being so few, we can't afford the luxury of one of us being in jail." [103] There were at that time no more than half a dozen members in Barcelona.

Toward the Francoist regime the founder maintained an attitude of independence. He appreciated the fact that it had restored peace after years of anarchy and religious persecution. But he stood aloof from government supporters who tried to take credit for so much sacrifice and heroism in defending ecclesial and personal rights, or who tried to give all the credit to one person—regardless of how important a role he might have played in the civil war.[104]

In his relations with civil authorities, the founder took great care not to get involved in political questions or to have the Work's apostolates manipulated for political purposes. However, there were people who would not let him keep his distance. Upon moving to Rome, he therefore decided to make his visits back to Spain few and far between. "This was," he said, "one of the reasons why I have not lived in Spain since 1946, and have not returned there since then except on rare occasions and for just a few days." [105]

*   *   *

The Spanish Civil War had not yet ended when Hitler's Germany began the territorial expansions and annexations that led to a European and eventually a world war. Spaniards watched in amazement as Soviet and Nazi forces, which a few months earlier had been

---

[103] Juan Bautista Torelló, PR, p. 2437.
[104] See Alvaro del Portillo, *Sum.* 654.
[105] See Alvaro del Portillo, *Sum.* 656.

In his approach to membership in an academic organization, the National Council on Education, there is an example of the care he took not to get involved in politics. When this organization was set up in 1941, the Minister of Education was Don José Ibáñez Martín—someone whom Father Josemaría had known in Burgos three years before and who now wanted to have him on the Council. At the added urging of the bishop of Madrid, he accepted, with an eye to the apostolic possibilities of the position. (His appointment as one of five Council members representing private education appears in the diocese's "Official Bulletin" of February 3, 1941.) Soon, however, he realized that his apostolic role would be very restricted, and for this and other reasons he decided to eliminate all personal contact with the Minister. (See Alvaro del Portillo, *Sum.* 384.) The Minister regretted this; and when calumnies began to be spread against members of Opus Dei about their supposed assault on the universities to obtain tenured professorships, he testified to the injustice of the slander.

fighting each other on Spanish soil, cynically made a pact to split Poland between them. The Nazis invaded Poland in September 1939. The following May, German troops occupied Belgium and Holland in order to launch an assault on France. They quickly crossed France, from north to south, reaching the Spanish border at Hendaya in June.

The Spanish government initially adopted a policy of neutrality, but in June 1940 that became modified to one of nonbelligerency, a stance that it would maintain (with some wavering) until 1943, during the years of the spectacular German advances and victories. During this period the country was faced with serious threats, reflected in its foreign policy. It found itself forced to negotiate with its old Axis allies. On October 23, 1940, at Hendaya, Franco met with Hitler, and on February 12, 1941, in Bordighera, he met with Mussolini. In the spring of 1943, however, the government changed course again and adopted a position of strict neutrality. From then on, it tended more and more to favor the Allies. But in the end, Spain did not enter the war.[106]

A large faction of the Falange supported Nazi totalitarianism, and, together with a number of government ministers, sought to haul the country into supporting the German cause. In the first years of the war Franco faced a delicate balancing act. After its occupation of France, Germany's desire to cross Spain, take Gibraltar, and move into Africa was so strong as to seem irresistible.

Father Josemaría, meanwhile, was worried about his sons, almost all of them being of military age. He pictured them again being scattered on different fronts, with the Work's development being paralyzed once more. On October 1, 1940, a few weeks before the meeting between Franco and Hitler, the ones who could do so got together with him in Madrid (this being the eve of the twelfth anniversary of the founding of the Work), and he asked them the same question he had asked them before the civil war: "If I die, will you continue the Work?"[107]

Nazi ideology was rapidly infecting university students. Some did not understand why members of Opus Dei would not, collectively,

---

[106] See Javier Tusell, *Franco, España y la II Guerra Mundial: Entre el Eje y la neutralidad* (Madrid, 1995).

[107] See Alvaro del Portillo, *Sum.* 937. Through those days the founder kept praying for peace, using the words of the psalmist, "The Lord is my light and my salvation; whom shall I fear?" (Ps 27:1). See also AGP, RHF, D–15428.

fall in with the orders and directions of the Falangists, who were then the dominant political group.[108]

Father Josemaría's opinion of Nazism is clear from the following anecdote. In August 1941, he encountered Domingo Diaz-Ambrona and his family on the Madrid-Avila train. They had not met since the Civil War. Passing by the family's compartment, he noticed their four-year-old daughter with them, and stuck his head inside the compartment to say, "I baptized this child."[109] During the conversation that followed, Don Domingo was surprised by how much the priest knew about the situation of the Church and of Catholics under Hitler's regime, and by his love and appreciation for freedom. Díaz-Ambrona had just returned from a trip to Germany, and had noticed the fear that some Catholics had about expressing their religious convictions. This having made him suspicious of Nazism, he was seeking more information. Like most other Spaniards, he had been influenced by the propaganda that sought to depict Germany as the conqueror of communism, and had not heard about the dark side of the Nazi system and philosophy.[110] Father Josemaría, on the other hand, was very well informed on this subject. "It was not easy," says Don Domingo, "in Spain at that time, to find people who would condemn the Nazi system so categorically or who would denounce its anti-Christian roots with such clarity."[111]

---

[108] Nazi Germany and the Soviet Union continued collaborating until June 1941, to the confusion of those who wanted to see the European conflict as a continuation of the "Spanish crusade against communism," as the civil war was often called. When the Germans turned against the Soviets, there was an outburst of popular fervor, encouraged by some sectors of the Falange, but opposed by others in the government and the army. For those favoring a fascist radicalization of the regime, it was the moment to put the "lukewarms" on the ropes—in particular, those most involved in setting domestic policy. Falangist radicals stepped up their campaign, begun weeks earlier, to subordinate the army to directives emanating from official Falangist organizations. The question of the creation, mode of recruitment, and command of a division of Spanish volunteers to fight against the Soviet Union alongside Germany soon became a bone of contention. Behind the attempt to assert control some saw the threat of a purge. See Tusell, *Franco*, pp. 268–73; Redondo, *Política*, pp. 389–406 and 414–17; and Gerald R. Kleinfeld and Lewis A. Tambs, *La División española de Hitler, La División Azul en Rusia* (Madrid, 1983), pp. 17–32.

[109] See chapter 10 above, and *Immersed in God*, pp. 23–25. Father Josemaría had not seen the family since the day he baptized this child, whom they had named Guadalupe.

[110] One reason Spanish Catholics knew so little about Nazism was their difficulty in obtaining a copy of Pope Pius XI's encyclical *Mit Brennender Sorge*. Dated March 14, 1937, it was published in Spain only in the diocesan papers of Calahorra and Vitoria in February and May of 1938, respectively, and in the magazine *Razón y Fe* in the latter month. A similar fate befell the collective pastoral letter that the German bishops issued at Fulda on August 19, 1938. It appeared only in the diocesan papers of Calahorra and Toledo. See Redondo, *Historia*, vol. 2, pp. 208–10.

[111] See Alvaro del Portillo, *Immersed in God*, pp. 23-24.

Spanish policy began to change in 1943 as the course of the war shifted, with the Allies going on the offensive and the Axis armies beginning to retreat. So in the spring of 1945, when Nazi Germany was about to surrender, the world turned its attention to Spain, recalling the presence of Italian and German forces there during the civil war, and its subsequent fluctuating neutrality. No one could tell what might come of the strong pressure brought to bear by communists and other exiles eager to settle accounts with Franco's dictatorial regime.[112]

In the meantime, Opus Dei was rapidly spreading throughout Spain, and the founder was doing groundwork for the first steps in Italy and Portugal. Grasping the gravity of the international situation, he prayed all the harder. And in his prayer he saw clearly that "come what may," their hope had to be centered on Christ. On April 19, 1945, he added to the Prayers of the Work the invocation from the psalm: "The Lord is my light and my salvation; whom shall I fear? Though a host encamp against me, my heart shall not fear; though war arise against me, yet I will be confident" (Ps 27: 1, 3).[113]

4. *The Jenner Street residence*

When, in 1938, in Burgos, the founder kept saying that he needed fifty men who loved Jesus Christ above all things, he was already thinking of Madrid. For him, the end of the civil war and the chance to resume the apostolate in the capital city were virtually synonymous. Isidoro's letters transmitting the Father's concerns reflect his eagerness to open as soon as possible a residence to replace the one on Ferraz Street. But the Work still did not have its fifty men, and except for Isidoro, the few it did have were all outside Madrid. José María González Barredo, although he had a professorship at the San Isidro Institute in Madrid, was in northern Spain, attending to other matters. José María Albareda had to travel a lot for professional reasons. Chiqui was in San Sebastián, and Rafael Calvo Serer was in Valencia. Alvaro, Vicente, and Eduardo were stationed at Olot (in Gerona). The others, also still in military service, were scattered around the country.

A letter written by Isidoro at the end of April 1939 gives an idea of how things stood:

---

[112] It should be noted that the Spanish communists had very bad relations with the rest of the exiles, especially the socialists.

[113] See AGP, RHF, D–15428.

First, I've received a letter from Chiqui. Imagine, he's now in San Sebastián, of all places. Juan is spending a week of furlough with us, but he leaves tomorrow. Barredo is in Vitoria with Albareda for professional reasons. Ricardo is still in Alcoy; even Paco has left us. It's not fair! Grandfather was just reminding us that we need to think about a place for continuing his business, but if everyone in his family is gone, it's clear that it's going to be held up. Grandfather, as always, is extremely busy, and we're spending our time organizing and filing papers.[114]

Money also was short. Father Josemaría had launched a fund-raising appeal in the newsletter for April 1938: "Are you doing everything possible so that our Lord will give us the two million pesetas we need?" [115]

On May 1, Isidoro, who had been the only one fully available to assist him, went to work for a railroad company in Madrid. The eight-hour workday left him little time for other activities. And thus the whole weight of the Work fell on Father Josemaría's shoulders.

His schedule was especially tight that June, as we have seen. In the first half of the month there were the two retreats that he gave in Valencia, and in the last week, the retreat in Vitoria for seminarians. "Pester our Lord," he said, "and things will work out, as will the matter of the house." [116] But the end of the month came, and the house they were searching for had not materialized. Father Josemaría's concern is evident in a letter written from Vergara. "My thoughts seem to be more in Madrid, and in other places, than in Vergara," he says. "I am a bit repentant at having left so many things unfinished." [117]

Then, suddenly, the difficulties seemed to vanish. While giving a retreat in Vitoria for university professors, he received a letter from Isidoro, sent on July 1, containing the news he had been hoping for: "We expect that when you return we will already have moved into

---

[114] AGP, IZL, D–1213, 428.
[115] AGP, RHF, D–03691. In a letter to a friend in Bilbao, he mentions trying to get a loan that one can pay back in installments, and says, "The financial problem is holding me up here." See AGP, RHF, EF–390518–2.
[116] AGP, RHF, EF–390606–3.
[117] AGP, RHF, EF–390626–2. In a letter to his mother, he said much the same thing: "The truth is that I want to finish things here. More than anything, because I keep thinking about all that needs to be done there" (AGP, RHF, EF–390626–1).

our new place."[118] The place was a building at 6 Jenner Street; they had rented two fourth-floor apartments.

Refurbishing and painting began right away. The floors were refinished, there was a top-to-bottom cleaning, and furniture from Santa Isabel was moved in. In mid-July, amid the confusion of the move, Father Josemaría began to show signs of physical exhaustion. His sons talked him into going to Avila for a few days of rest and quiet work. As soon as he arrived there, he wrote to his sons in Valencia: "The ones in Madrid are awfully few, for the work involved in the move. They wouldn't let me help them, and since I do have about seven more retreats to give (including two for priests, in Madrid and in Avila), I could see that I did need some rest. But my conscience still bothers me a lot."[119]

However, the company of the bishop of Avila and the tranquillity of the city were a balm. He jotted a note:

> Avila of the saints, feast of Saint Mary Magdalene, July 22, 1939: I'm spending a few days with this holy bishop, resting. I fled from the mayhem of the change of house. It seems like selfishness. Perhaps it is, but I don't think so. The boys wouldn't let me work like them, in the move. And it's true that I'm very tired and still have six or seven retreats to give.
>
> Very happy, in this bishop's residence.
>
> *Omnes cum Petro ad I. p. M.* [All with Peter to Jesus through Mary.][120]

While the work of refurbishing was still going on in one of the apartments, the new tenants had to live amid its stored-up furniture. Father Josemaría would have liked the carpenters, the painters, and the landlord to understand his urgency a little better. On August 10 he blessed the center, but this did not seem to speed things up very much. "The house is coming along slowly," he wrote to Eduardo, "because the painters and carpenters are taking their time. Everything is still all piled up. This holds up the oratory, the retreats, everything. But God knows best!"[121]

---

[118] AGP, IZL, D–1213, 436.
[119] AGP, RHF, EF–390720–1.
[120] *Apuntes*, no. 1602.
[121] AGP, RHF, EF–390813–1.

His unease stemmed not so much from impatience as from a new crisis of soul. A strong passive purification had begun. He felt unsettled, anxious, irritable, dissatisfied. It was a struggle to remain in control of himself. He wrote in his journal, "August 12, 1939: Very concerned, because I'm not as I should be. Everything gets on my nerves. And the enemy does all he can to provoke my bad temper. I am very humiliated." [122] His internal suffering was intense. "I continue to go through some terrible days of interior crisis," he says. "I wouldn't wish this on anyone." And, as on previous occasions of this kind, he cries out for help: "*Tu scis, Domine, quia amo te!* [You know, Lord, that I love you!] Saint Joseph, my father and lord, my guardian angel, intercede for me." [123]

August brought applications from prospective residents for the coming academic semester. It was decided to rent a third apartment (on the third floor) in which would be the living quarters for Doña Dolores, Carmen, and Santiago, the residence's kitchen and dining room, and Father Josemaría's office. Isidoro and Pedro went to Albacete to pick up some of the Casciaro family's furniture ("very elegant," Isidoro called it) and bring it to Jenner. [124]

While they were finishing the setting up of the residence, Father Josemaría made a trip to Valencia, where in June he had left a half dozen young men who felt they were called to Opus Dei. In August, the Valencian group rented an apartment at 9 Samaniego Street. Because it was so small, consisting of just a couple of rooms and a corridor, it was nicknamed "El Cubil" ("the den"). From September 10 to 16, the founder gave another retreat for Valencian students, which produced several more vocations. [125] The Father encouraged them to think about setting up a student residence for the following year. But having put so much effort into the retreat meditations, as soon as it was over he was overcome by exhaustion. On the following day, September 17, as he was beginning Mass in the Valencia cathedral's Blessed Sacrament Chapel, he felt ill, and was taken to the sacristy. From there he insisted on going to El Cubil, though it was not the best place for a sick person. The only bed in the apartment was an army cot—four planks on iron legs, with no mattress or blanket. He spent

---

[122] *Apuntes*, no. 1603.
[123] *Apuntes*, no. 1604 (12 Aug 1939).
[124] See AGP, RHF, T–00159/1, p. 95, and AGP, IZL, D–1213, 447.
[125] See José Orlandis Rovira, *Años de juventud en el Opus Dei* (Madrid, 1993), pp. 35–48.

several hours wrapped in old curtains and shaking with chills and fever.[126]

Upon returning to Madrid, he busied himself with the residence oratory, since he wanted to have our Lord in the tabernacle as soon as possible. He had chosen the most respectable room for the oratory: a room on the fourth floor, next to the living room. They had covered the walls with pleated burlap to deaden sound. A strip of wood going all the way around the top of the wall had carved into it, in Latin, a line from Acts 2:42, "They devoted themselves to the apostles' teaching," and a line from the hymn *"Ubi Caritas," "Congregavit nos in unum Christi amor"* ["The love of Christ has brought us together"]. The letters had been highlighted in red by the young men who helped set up the oratory. Between the words they had inserted traditional Christian symbols: a cross, a basket with bread, a vine branch, a dove . . .

Near the entrance, against the wall to the right, was a wooden cross, stained dark walnut. And on the wall to the left, near a window looking out on the street, was a corbel with a statue of our Lady. A single bench stood against the back wall. In that sober, simple, and attractive room, attention was directed to the altar.

Construction of the altar and tabernacle was entrusted to a cabinetmaker who lived on the outskirts of Madrid. The tabernacle was of wood, with a canopy. Father Josemaría asked that it be lined inside with cloth of gold. But the glue that the cabinetmaker used for attaching the lining left a persistent odor, so Father Josemaría directed that from time to time some cotton with a little cologne on it be placed inside. The simple altar was covered with a damask frontal, of the liturgical color of the day. The altar cloths almost reached the floor. The candlesticks, three on each side of the crucifix at the center of the altar, were made of the least expensive material available: chromium-plated metal, cut in pieces and welded.[127] (As we shall later see, this detailed description is not superfluous.)

---

[126] See AGP, RHF, T–01234 (Antonio Rodilla); Alvaro del Portillo, *Sum.* 867; and Orlandis, pp. 50–52.

[127] See AGP, RHF, T–00159/1, pp. 95–96, and T–04151, p. 30. As for the vestments, Isidoro wrote that Pedro had designed "some chasubles that have drawn high praises for their color and shape." (See AGP, IZL, D–1213, 451.)

For the setting up of this oratory, new permission from the bishop was not needed, since this was just part of the transfer of the Ferraz Street center to the site. Father Josemaría simply requested written confirmation of the previous permission. See AGP, RHF, D–15107.

At first sight, the oratory seemed to have a motif of crosses: the crucifix on the altar; the wooden cross on the wall; the crosses at the base and intersections of each of the candlesticks; the crosses on the frieze; and the fourteen crosses of the Stations of the Cross. Years later, in one of his circular letters, the founder mentioned this:

> In the oratory (a small room, lacking even benches, despite being the best room in the house) we had put up the Stations of the Cross. And I told my sons: "How valiant we are! We've put up all these crosses. Are you ready to carry all of them?" [128]

*   *   *

Doña Dolores and her children—Carmen, Santiago, and Father Josemaría—settled into the third-floor apartment that also contained the kitchen and dining room for the residents of the center, and an area for ironing, sewing, and so forth. After so many hazards and disruptions, they were together again as a family. No doubt this was what Providence intended, but it also had something to do with Father Josemaría's unfortunate experiences with domestic staff in the first centers of the Work. Although he had tried to create a home in the old student residence at 50 Ferraz Street, deficiencies in this line made it difficult to develop a real family life. Clearly, the feminine touch was essential.

During the time of the Ferraz Street residence he had consulted his mother and sister about domestic problems, but this had not been enough. It was at the Honduran consulate, when he was thinking about the future of the Work, that he had come to realize that the only solution was to get the collaboration of his mother.

Family life in the Santa Isabel rectory had been a pleasant experience. Doña Dolores and Carmen had taken charge of laundry and cooking. That had lasted for only a few short weeks, because in August, as per the agreement that he had made, Father Josemaría gave the rectory over to the Augustinian nuns. But now, as if it were the most natural thing in the world, his family moved into the Jenner Street residence.

Did Doña Dolores know what she was getting into? Father Josemaría gave her a book on the life of Saint John Bosco, hoping that, in

[128] Letter 29 Dec 1947/14 Feb 1966, no. 45. This like some of his other longer letters, remained in his files and was not sent out to the members of the Work. The double date is due to the fact that in 1966 he finished revising and polishing the 1947 text.

imitation of Don Bosco's mother, she would collaborate in the Work. Not long after, she said to him: "You don't want me to do what Don Bosco's mother did, do you? I'm really not up for that." "But Mama," he replied, "you already are!" At that, she gave a good-natured laugh and said, "And I'll continue doing it, quite happily." [129]

Actually, she was ready to help Father Josemaría in every way she could. She deeply loved this enterprise that she recognized as coming from God. She had accepted the title of Grandmother and had grown fond of her little group of grandchildren. With Carmen it seems to have been much the same. [130] Still, these two generous women may not have realized how much work they were taking on.

The family's accommodations were not all that pleasant, since they were confined to the service quarters. Nor did they see Father Josemaría very often, even though his room opened onto the same hallway as theirs. He spent half his time away from Madrid, and when he was there, twenty-four hours were not enough for all he had to do in a day: fulfill his duties as rector, give spiritual direction to a host of people (young men and women, professionals, priests), give several classes of formation daily, and, some evenings, take part in a get-together with the residents before going to bed. So as not to interfere with the operation of the residence, Carmen and the Grandmother would go to Mass in a nearby church. [131]

The 1939–1940 academic year began with about twenty students living there, some of them old-timers from the Ferraz Street residence. A year later, the number almost doubled. The transformation wrought since then by washing machines, refrigerators, and other household conveniences makes it hard to imagine what a burden the two women had suddenly taken on. At first their only helper was Eusebia, a household worker they had brought with them from Santa Isabel. Later, Carmen had to recruit and instruct others. Only good will and tenacity made it possible for them to meet all the demands, especially that of providing three good meals a day for all these

[129] Alvaro del Portillo, *Sum.* 512.

[130] An anecdote related by Francisco Botella gives us some idea of how great Carmen's renunciation was, and of how fully she gave herself to the service of the Work. One day, he says, he and Pedro went down from the residence to the apartment below to keep the Grandmother company, and "while she was showing us some old photographs, she said: 'The reason Carmen never did marry was for us—for Josemaría and for all of you—it was so that she could stay with us and accompany us. She had several very good proposals.'" See AGP, RHF, T–00159/1, p. 99.

[131] See AGP, RHF, T–07921, p. 21.

young people, at a time of great scarcity, with no resources other than ration cards.

Doña Dolores and Carmen did not expect to be paid. Only the hired household workers received a salary. At 6 Jenner Street, debt was a constant reality. One young man, when he applied for admission as a resident, was asked for a cash advance, without being told that it would go to buy a bed for him.[132]

The presence of the feminine touch could be seen in details of cleaning and decorating the house, the preparing of meals, the ironing of clothes, and the care given to the altar linens and other liturgical objects. Residents adapted their behavior to fit this pleasant atmosphere. Courtesy, proper attire, punctuality, and consideration for those who were studying were hallmarks of the residence.

At the start of the 1939–1940 academic year, Father Josemaría, in order to be able to engage personally and directly in apostolic activities, handed over part of his work to Alvaro del Portillo and Isidoro Zorzano, naming Alvaro the secretary general and Isidoro the general administrator of the Work.[133]

Jenner residents invited friends to come by to speak with Father Josemaría. One who came over in October was an engineering student named Fernando Valenciano. The priest spoke to him about the formation offered at the residence. "He showed me great affection," Fernando recalls. "He told me that it was my house, that I could go to whenever I wanted, and that it had an oratory. And then we said good-bye. It was a very short visit. I was very impressed by his cheerfulness and supernatural tone, and by how warm and human he was."[134]

The next week Fernando got a phone call telling him that Father Josemaría would be giving a formational class at eight that evening. It was a class he never forgot, because of the spiritual depth of its content and the clarity, simplicity, exigency, and good humor with which the priest presented it. The eight or nine students attending were encouraged to put into practice what they had heard on certain very specific points: prayer, interior life, study, holy purity, fraternity...[135] On Saturday afternoons, Father Josemaria would give a

---

[132] See Miguel Alvarez Morales, *Vicente Mortes* (Madrid, 1995), pp. 65–66.
[133] See AGP, RHF, T–00159/1, p. 97.
[134] Fernando Valenciano, *Sum.* 7070.
[135] Ibid.

meditation in the oratory, followed by Benediction and the singing of the *Salve Regina*. On December 23, Fernando asked to be admitted to Opus Dei.

Others, such as José Luis Múzquiz, had been mulling over this possibility for some time. José Luis had first met the founder in 1935, while finishing his civil engineering studies. He had then taken part in circles (small group classes of formation) held at the Ferraz Street residence. When the civil war began, he was on a study trip through Europe. In 1938 he ran into Father Josemaría in Burgos, and then traveled there on several occasions from the front at Guadalajara, where his unit was stationed. In 1939 he continued to receive spiritual direction from him, first at Santa Isabel and later at the Jenner Street residence. And finally, he tells us, on a day of recollection, right after hearing a meditation given by Father Josemaría, "without his having expressly invited me, I told him that I wanted to join the Work. And he simply said to me, 'May God bless you, it is something of the Holy Spirit.' This happened on January 21, 1940." [136]

Most of the vocations were coming, as the founder put it, from the ascent of "an inclined plane" on which individuals grew gradually in their interior life while acquiring the spirit of the Work. This was the case, for example, with Francisco Ponz, who had been a student of José María Albareda's at the Institute of Huesca. In 1939 José María spoke to him about the formation classes at the Jenner Street residence, and during the first semester he attended them weekly. When he got back to Madrid after the Christmas break, he was invited to a day of recollection to be held at the residence on Sunday, January 21. At eight that morning, he heard for his first time a meditation given by Father Josemaría. It made an indelible impression. And then came Mass. "The way the Father celebrated Mass," reports Ponz, "the sincere tone of voice, the full attentiveness with which he prayed the different prayers, without a trace of affectation, his genuflections and other liturgical rubrics, all impressed me deeply. God was there, really present." [137]

At the Father's suggestion, Paco Botella explained the Work to him in detail that same day. He bought a copy of *The Way* and spent a lot of time reading it, usually just before going to bed. On February 10, on his way to the residence, "while that streetcar was making its run," he

---

[136] José Luis Múzquiz, *Sum.* 5791.
[137] AGP, RHF, T–04151, p. 10.

says, "I resolved not to think about it anymore, and simply to entrust myself to the Lord and to the Father, permanently dedicating myself to God in Opus Dei."[138] The priest received him in his office, a tiny room, about eleven feet square, that also served as his bedroom. A crucifix stood on the simple table.

> The Father, in a very paternal and supernatural way, wanted to make a few points clear to me. . . . He made me see that our Lord's call was supernatural in character, God's action and not man's. . . . To be in the Work meant committing oneself to a lifelong struggle to grow in Christian virtues, to attain sanctity according to the spirit that God had entrusted to him. . . . From that moment I felt intimately and warmly bonded, for life, to my new family, Opus Dei.[139]

Of course, as new young people came along, it was necessary to make sure they really grasped the spirit of Opus Dei, if they were going to really live it. Because somewhere down the road, as the Father warned Francisco, that initial enthusiasm would most likely wear off, and they would experience temptations against the path they had chosen.[140]

To strengthen the recent vocations, he organized two weeks of intense formation, one during Holy Week and the other to be given in the summer. With the residents gone home for the holidays and vacations, the members of the Work could live together as a family. The Father gave meditations, had get-togethers in the afternoons and evenings, offered tips and explanations, and infused in them his cheerful optimism. Those who had been in the Work for some time were asked to give talks about aspects of its life and customs. There were also opportunities to read the founder's "Instructions" and circular letters, as well as the journal of the crossing of the Pyrenees and other writings.[141]

The second "study week"—later the founder would call these weeks "workshops" or "*Convivencias*"—was in August. The heat was terrible, especially for the Grandmother, whose room faced west and

---

[138] Francisco Ponz, *Mi encuentro con el Fundador del Opus Dei, 1939–1944* (Pamplona, 2000), p. 38.

[139] Ibid., p. 39.

[140] See ibid.

[141] See ibid., pp. 47–50, and AGP, RHF, T–00159/1, p. 114.

became like an oven in the afternoon. Doña Dolores found the heat hard to bear, as did Father Josemaria. Soon, though, they were to leave that apartment. The Work was growing so rapidly that the founder, looking as always beyond the limits of what then seemed feasible, had begun to dream of new centers. In January 1940, with the Jenner Street residence barely up and running, he wrote to his sons in Valencia: "We are also looking for a mansion here, a big house. We need it, so we'll get it." [142]

An apartment was needed, too, for graduate students working on their doctoral dissertations or beginning their professional lives. That, in turn, would free up more room for students at the Jenner Street residence.

On July 22, 1940, Isidoro wrote to Francisco Javier de Ayala: "We have found the apartment we want, and we're hoping it won't be long before we also find the house we need." [143] In August they did. It was a building on Diego de León Street (at the corner of Lagasca) in good condition, although for their purposes some remodeling would need to be done. In November the Father, the Grandmother, Carmen, Santiago, and several members of the Work, including Alvaro del Portillo, went to live there. [144]

5. *Serving the Church*

The civil war had barely ended when Father Josemaría found himself immersed in an apostolate very dear to his heart. The three years of persecution against the Church had stirred up the faith and generosity of the Catholic population. Seminaries were full, and the religious congregations had vocations in abundance. Bishops, starting with those of Valencia and Vitoria, asked Father Josemaría to give retreats for their seminarians and diocesan priests. How could he refuse? Soon there were calls from everywhere in Spain: Navarre, Madrid, León, Huesca, Avila, Lérida. . . . From the summer of 1939 to Christmas of 1942, he preached some twenty seven-day retreats. [145] It was a critical period for the spiritual resurgence of the Spanish people. "The confidence I had in Father Josemaría's priestly spirit, and my conviction of

---

[142] AGP, RHF, EF–400127–1.
[143] AGP, IZL, D–1213, 463.
[144] See AGP, IZL, D–1213, 467.
[145] See AGP, RHF, D–15013, D–15014, D–15015, and D–05212.

the good that his words would do to the priests of Avila," wrote Bishop Moro, "led me to entrust to him, together with another priest, the retreats for clergy that we organized at the end of the civil war. These were very important moments for bringing the diocese together, for uniting the clergy with their bishop and with one another in true fraternity. My priests in Avila needed words of guidance and encouragement for their interior life." [146]

From early youth, Father Josemaría had had a high esteem for priests. He hoped that the new seminaries that had been opened in Spain around 1930 would be seedbeds of exemplary clergy.[147] First in the Seminary of Saint Francis de Paolo in Saragossa and later in Madrid, he had liberally spread among seminarians and priests the extraordinary spirit of his interior life. "When he spoke to priests, or had to direct them," recalls Archbishop Pedro Cantero, "he would say simply and humbly that it was like 'selling honey to a beekeeper.' But he did sell it, and with great benefit to those who heard him." [148]

In the years of the war, most seminarians had to discontinue their studies, and most priests were unable to make a retreat. Both groups were in need of spiritual guidance, of a time-out to reflect on the dignity of their vocation and ministry. Father Josemaría wanted to help the bishops by enkindling the souls of his brother priests. "I'm giving one of those retreats for priests that the hierarchy so often entrusts to me," he writes to Alvaro on July 1, 1940. "What joy it gives me to serve the Church! I would like this to be our aim always: to serve." [149]

He was also giving talks, meditations, and days of recollection to religious and to laypeople, as he mentions in the same letter:

> On the feast of Saint Peter, I gave a day of recollection for the Catholic Action university students in Valladolid. The Sunday before, the Catholic Action students in Madrid had their day of recollection, which I gave them in Chamartin. And before that, in Alacuas, a little town near Valencia, I gave another day of recollection, to the Catholic Action students from Valencia.

[146] Santos Moro, in *Testimonios*, p. 251.
[147] See *Apuntes*, no. 55 (16 Jun 1930). In speaking here, in his journal, of "seedbeds of gentlemen in cassocks," Father Josemaría was expressing his hope that future seminaries would be schools not only of sanctity, but also of outstanding human virtues.
[148] Pedro Cantero, in *Testimonios*, p. 89.
[149] AGP, RHF, EF–400701–1.

After the priests' retreat in Avila in 1940, Father Josemaría returned to Madrid to tend to the people of the Work. July ended with another retreat for university students, at the Ortí Residence in Madrid. After that he went to León, to give yet another retreat—one for which the bishop there, Bishop Carmelo Ballester, had booked him three months in advance.[150]

In the first week of August, from León, he wrote to his sons in Madrid: "There are a hundred and twenty priests on this retreat. A lot of work, but since they are wonderful, I hardly notice the tiredness." [151] But the tiredness was noticeable to others. Father Guillermo Marañón, a priest of the diocesan curia in Vitoria who attended one of his retreats, took the liberty of warning him about it.

> I see that you have practically solved the problem of perpetual motion. I think what you are doing is wonderful, considering how great a need there is for in-depth priestly work like yours. But you should also take care of your health, "which isn't everything, but is useful for everything." Forgive me for taking it upon myself to give you advice, but the affection I have for you moves me to, and I know you won't take it badly.[152]

But there was something more than just tiredness. On August 4, several days into the retreat, he wrote in his journal: "I don't feel well, although I'm not showing it. My throat hurts and I feel a pain in my back. I had to lie down fully dressed, for half an hour." [153] Clearly he felt that he was on the brink of exhaustion, and that he should be giving more time to the formation of his children. "I think," he continues, "that from now on I should turn down all work outside of Opus Dei—unless there is a formal request from the hierarchy. Despite all my wretchedness, I continue receiving light in regard to Opus Dei's immediate apostolic work. How good Jesus is!" [154] And on the same day, he wrote to his sons in Madrid a few lines communicating that tentative decision: "I don't know what to tell you: perhaps that from now on I'll try to avoid commitments outside of our work. Although I

[150] See AGP, RHF, D–15289/1.
[151] AGP, RHF, EF–400800–1. See also *Apuntes*, no. 1617 (4 Aug 1940).
[152] AGP, RHF, D–15716.
[153] *Apuntes*, no. 1617.
[154] *Apuntes*, no. 1618 (4 Aug 1940).

love serving the Church in her priests, I have more pressing duties toward you." [155]

But he kept up his service to diocesan priests, trying to fit it in with service to the Church in the Work, and did not cut down on his preaching, hard work though it was. Compounding his exhaustion were the first symptoms of a serious illness. But he did not complain. After the retreat in León, he wrote to his sons in Madrid: "How am I? Fatter! And more tired. But very happy." [156] Yet, from a letter written just one year later (to Alvaro del Portillo, after a retreat in Avila for university students), one can get some idea of what he must have been suffering at this time. "Tomorrow," he says, "against my inclinations—as almost always!—I leave for Jaca.... They've done some devilish things to my mouth—even scraped a bone. My face is all swollen. But it's necessary to go to Jaca! So I'm going." [157]

Throughout 1941 he continued to regain the weight he had lost during the civil war. He looked healthy and robust. But he was suffering intensely from thirst and fatigue. He had to have his tonsils removed, and from time to time suffered attacks of rheumatism in various joints.

A journal entry for June 21, 1940, written in Madrid, gives an idea of the ardor with which he preached: "Lately I've given a lot of retreats for priests. They tell me, 'You preach with your whole soul ... and with your whole body.' How wonderful it would be if that were true!" [158]

"Love shone through every one of his words," says Archbishop Pedro Cantero. "His eloquent words presented a vivid and powerful image of our Lord. He had an enormous power of persuasion and conviction, a fruit of the authenticity of his faith. He knew how to capture and transmit the profound meaning of the Gospel scenes. In his words they could be seen for what they are: living realities that demand a response. His listeners were moved to make acts of love and reparation and to formulate specific resolutions to improve their lives. His words came from the heart and spoke to the heart." [159]

His way of expressing himself "seemed to me the most ardent and convincing I had ever heard," says Father Joaquín Mestre Palacio. "To

---

[155] AGP, RHF, EF–400804–1.
[156] AGP, RHF, EF–400807–1.
[157] AGP, RHF, EF–410820–1.
[158] *Apuntes*, no. 1612.
[159] Pedro Cantero Cuadrado, in *Testimonios*, p. 75.

hear him speak was to realize immediately that everything he said came from the depths of his heart. His faith was obvious. His love for Christ shone in his eyes. The purity and holiness of his life were clear as day. He spoke as he lived." [160]

Father Josemaría tried to have a personal conversation with everyone on the retreat, to give advice, help them solve problems, or confirm them in their vocation. He encouraged the priests to be united, so that none of them would suffer the chill of loneliness, rejection, or indifference. In some years he spoke with over a thousand priests, and got to know them at some depth. And what did he think of them? "I don't know any bad priests," he said. "So many have opened their hearts to me in private, and I've never found anything but gold, pure gold." [161]

If a priest did not come to him, he went to the priest.

> I remember one time, one of them didn't come. I went looking for him, I went to his room, and I said to him, "Well, my brother, what's the matter? Everyone has come to speak with me except you." And then he told me a really tragic story, about a horrible calumny. And I said to him, "But those brothers of ours who are close to you, they're not standing by you?" And he answered, "I'm the only one standing by me." That coldness hurt me. I was young. I took his hands and kissed them. He started to cry. But I think he ended up not feeling alone anymore.[162]

A great many of those priests kept as a treasure their notes on the talks and the advice he had given them. They reread and meditated on them often, even into old age, in order, as one said, to "recapture those graces and see things again in the same clear light." [163]

The bishops expressed deep gratitude for this work with priests. "I don't want one more day to go by without my telling you thanks, thousands of thanks, for the good you have done for our priests," wrote the bishop of León, Carmelo Ballester. "Yes, you have done them a tremendous amount of good, which makes my soul rejoice. Blessed be God!" [164]

---

[160] AGP, RHF, T–00181, p. 15
[161] See Alvaro del Portillo, PR, p. 406.
[162] Ibid.
[163] AGP, RHF, T–00181, p. 15 (Joaquín Mestre Palacio).
[164] AGP, RHF, D–15289.

Knowing how much the founder disliked being praised, Bishop Olaechea preferred to express his feelings to Alvaro del Portillo, the secretary general of the Work.

> Pamplona, November 22, 1941
> My dear Alvaro:
>
> My beloved friend Father José María, that so-good Father that God has given you, has given a retreat to all the new parish priests of this blessed diocese of Pamplona, whose clergy are so exemplary. I say "to all" even though we have not had the last retreat yet, since we're hoping he'll be giving that one too.
>
> I won't go into detail. Suffice it to say that not one of the retreatants has had one word to say that was not about how greatly they appreciated and were edified by the job he did.
>
> May God preserve him for us for many, many years, for the great glory of his holy Church. Take good care of that treasure.
>
> > Kindest regards,
> > Marcelino[165]

The bishops had, in fact, an extra reason to be grateful: Except for food and lodging, he would not accept any recompense for his services. If they protested, he would tell this story:

> There once was a priest who, on all the big feast days of the villages, went there and gave a sermon and stirred up everyone's fervor. He was very eloquent, and, moreover, charged only one peseta. But the bishop found out, called him in, and said, "What's this. One peseta for the word of God? One peseta for the Holy Spirit? Aren't you ashamed?" "No, Your Excellency," replied the priest, "since there's no putting a price on the word of God!" [166]

---

[165] AGP, RHF, D–15224.

[166] See Alvaro del Portillo, PR, p. 667. Father Eliodoro Gil, who knew him very well, stresses that "he never wanted to receive any financial compensation for his work on behalf of the diocesan clergy." See AGP, RHF, T–07987, p. 5.

6. *Expansion to the provinces*

After appointing Alvaro del Portillo secretary general of Opus Dei, the founder handed over to him part of his work and correspondence. Gradually the secretary general began to receive visitors on behalf of the Father, to talk with those who had joined the Work recently, and to give advice when Father Josemaría was away on his travels.[167] Soon he was taking care of the formation and spiritual direction of many people in the Work.

This freed Father Josemaría to accept more requests from the bishops to preach in their dioceses. Between 1939 and 1944, he labored to elevate the spiritual level of a good part of the Spanish clergy. He gave retreats not only for diocesan priests, but also for communities of nuns and religious-order priests and for members of Catholic Action. To the latter "he gave a great number of retreats, always for free. He acted as confessor and spiritual director to the lay people who gave the biggest impetus to this association in Spain."[168]

His love for the Work was deeply grounded in his love for the Church. In a letter to one of his sons, he asked: "My son, do you love the Work a lot?" and then immediately added, "That love is the assurance that you love Jesus Christ and his Church."[169]

In his work with the souls of his brothers in the priesthood, he felt very close to Christ. He knew he was doing the will of God and felt the tangible guidance by the Holy Spirit. "Your Father 'touches' the Holy Spirit," he wrote to his sons in Madrid. "How much he helps, pushes, urges on! Help me to be holy."[170] As he had recorded in his journal on July 17, 1939, he had had a glimpse of this apostolic work before the war even ended. "In Burgos," he says, "before the taking of Madrid, I saw details of what we were going to encounter there. It was like a dream, but a waking one. Thus I *knew* I was going to give retreats to priests, as in fact has happened."[171]

---

[167] A list of the apostolic trips of the founder of Opus Dei in the Iberian Peninsula from 1939 to 1946 is found in Appendix 7.

[168] José López Ortiz, in *Testimonios*, p. 227; see also Alfredo López Martínez, *Sum.* 5739. Among the communities he gave retreats to were the Hieronymites of Parral (Segovia), the Augustinians of El Escorial, and the Piarists of the Calasanctus School in Madrid.

[169] AGP, RHF, EF–400127–1.

[170] AGP, RHF, EF–400701–2.

[171] *Apuntes*, no. 1598.

More than a simple anticipation of events, this supernatural illumination supplied a divine endorsement. That is the only credible explanation for his willingness to preach in so many dioceses, while leaving his children virtually abandoned. Yet he was greatly concerned for their spiritual needs and prayed for them many times each day, wrote them frequently, and from time to time visited those who did not live in Madrid. He knew the recent vocations were in good hands, as a letter to Alvaro del Portillo from Avila makes clear.

> May Jesus watch over my sons!
> I have your letter in front of me, Alvaro, and am going to answer it point by point. Correct the date for Bishop Santos Moro's birthday: it's June 1. I will write to the bishop of Barcelona for his feast day.
> Those little ones—the children's battalion, Ignacio calls them—are the apple of my eye. When I think of them, I see, in a very special way, God's paternal hand blessing us. Dedicate all your efforts to them! [172]

It was in August of 1940, while giving a retreat to the clergy of León, that he received that "enlightenment about Opus Dei's next efforts." [173] It was a clear announcement from the Lord about the development of the Work. He therefore tried to cut back on his diocesan activities, but found it impossible to cut out all such commitments, with the result that he found himself just as tied down in the summer of 1941 as he had been the year before. If he did on occasion manage to say no to a bishop's request, it was because he could not be in two places at once. On October 1 he wrote to the vicar general of the diocese of Huesca:

> My esteemed friend:
> I received your letter today, and am very grateful for your invitation. But this summer I've given eleven retreats. And I've received a paternal indication (I'm very fat and in poor health) prohibiting me from accepting any more preaching assignments until I have gotten some rest, after the retreat I'm already signed up to give for the priests of your diocese.
> You don't know how sorry I am to miss out on that

[172] AGP, RHF, EF–400701–2.
[173] *Apuntes,* no. 1618.

triduum, which will give so much glory to Christ the King. It's hard for me, but I know that by obeying I am doing what is pleasing to him.[174]

In the end he had no other recourse but to take refuge in the authority of Bishop Eijo y Garay—a resolve he put in writing, to make it stronger: "I need to give up all work unrelated to Opus Dei. For this, I will ask the help of my father the bishop of Madrid. He can shield me with his authority, refusing to let me give retreats, etc."[175]

* * *

Once the Jenner Street residence was in operation, Father Josemaría encouraged his sons to make weekend apostolic trips outside Madrid. They began traveling to university cities near Madrid and to some provincial capitals to meet people whom God might call to the Work. As apostolic work expanded in Valencia following his visits of June and September, 1939, and his retreat for students in Burjasot, the cramped space of El Cubil was not enough. So, even though the members in Valencia had barely finished setting up this very modest apartment on Samaniego Street, he set them a new goal: before the 1940–1941 school year, they should begin a student residence.

The founder communicated his urgency for the promotion of his spiritual "business." In the summer of 1939, he wrote his sons in Valencia, "Three things get in the way, and I can't imagine you being held back by them: doubt, hesitation, inconstancy."[176] He was confident of their spirit of prayer, sacrifice, and willingness to work, but he reminded them, "Don't leave things for later, or for tomorrow. 'Later' and 'tomorrow' are two bad words, symptoms of a pessimistic and defeatist attitude, which, along with that other one, 'impossible,' we have erased for good from our dictionary. Today and now!"[177]

Weekends were very short then, since people everywhere worked all day Saturday. These apostolic trips meant catching rickety old trains on Saturday evening, headed for Salamanca, Valladolid, Saragossa, Bilbao, or Valencia. It was not unusual to travel all night long.

[174] AGP, RHF, EF–411001–1.
[175] *Apuntes*, no. 1854 (9 Nov 1941).
[176] AGP, RHF, EF–390716–4.
[177] AGP, RHF, EF–400127–2.

Sundays were spent seeing friends and meeting friends of those friends. Late on Sunday they would board a train for Madrid, arriving home at daybreak on Monday morning.[178]

Those weekend travelers became very familiar with northern Spain. Sometimes one group would meet another at a transfer station in Venta de Baños, Valladolid, or Medina del Campo. Paco Botella recalls joining up several times in Medina del Campo with some who were returning from Salamanca, and waiting with them in the station café until three in the morning. They would order something to drink, so that they could sit at one of the tables, and, in the weak light of a bare bulb, they would use the time to study, leaving the drinks untouched.[179] (This was so that they could receive Communion the next morning. Back then one had to fast from midnight, from both food and drink.)

After his trips to Valencia, Father Josemaría turned his attention to Valladolid. On Thursday, November 30, 1939, he took the train there, accompanied by Alvaro del Portillo and Ricardo Fernández Vallespín. They arrived late. It was a cold night, and a dense fog covered the city. Carrying their luggage, they walked the streets until finally they found a hotel with vacancies. In a meditation the next morning, the Father told his companions, "We are in Valladolid to work for Christ. Even if we don't meet anyone, we should not consider it a failure." [180]

They had brought a list of students' names and addresses, and that morning they contacted them at home and arranged to see them at the hotel in the afternoon. Father Josemaría spoke with all of them, enthusing them with his apostolic zeal and fomenting the ideal of sanctity in their hearts. So deep an impression did his words make that when the afternoon ended, no one wanted to leave. When they finally did part, Father Josemaría promised to make other trips and expressed the hope that these students would introduce him to friends who might also be able to understand the apostolic spirit of Opus Dei. On Saturday, December 2, he returned to Madrid.

He never complained, but his health continued to be a matter for concern. Because of his rheumatic pains, they bought a used car to spare him long trips on unheated trains. It was an old Citroën that in normal times would have been consigned to the junkyard. On

---

[178] See Francisco Ponz, pp. 57–60.
[179] See AGP, RHF, T–00159/1, p. 101.
[180] See Alvaro del Portillo, *Sum.* 861.

December 26, having gotten it repaired and having invoked Saint Raphael and the guardian angels, Father Josemaría, Alvaro del Portillo, and José María Albareda set out for Saragossa in the car. It went a few miles and then broke down, forcing them to return to Madrid. The Father, who had already been suffering from a high fever before they set out, now went to bed.[181] Two days later, accompanied by Alvaro, he again set out for Saragossa, this time by train. They spent a day there and another in Barcelona, and were in Valencia for the first days of the new year.

On January 31 the Father again went to Valencia, this time with Pedro Casciaro and Ricardo Fernández Vallespín, in the old Citroën. (Ricardo was driving.) Their confidence in the car can be gauged by the fact that before leaving Madrid, they bought a towrope to take along. About forty miles into the trip, the car refused to go any farther. While they were trying to unscrew one part, another one broke. The gasoline caught fire. But, recalls Pedro, "the Father, who had been praying the Divine Office since we set out, encouraged us. He said that we had to get to Valencia any way we could, since it was becoming obvious, from how hard the devil was trying to prevent us from getting there, that our stay in that city would be very fruitful." [182] After two days of breakdowns, they arrived. A good number of young men were waiting for them.

Obstacles did not discourage Father Josemaría. He did, as he wrote to his sons, feel very much in touch with the Holy Spirit and urged on by grace. His words moved people to commit themselves completely to God, some of them setting aside plans they had nurtured for years. One day, at the seashore, he saw his efforts mirrored in a little boy.

> In 1940, on a beach in Valencia, I had an opportunity to observe some fishermen—tough, strong men—dragging their net ashore. A little boy had joined them and was trying to do as they were doing; he, too, was pulling on the net. He was only getting in the way. But I saw that the toughness of those

---

[181] See Alvaro del Portillo, *Sum.* 859.

[182] AGP, RHF, D–15204. Thanks to many unpleasant experiences with the Citroën, Father Josemaría ended up knowing something about cars—at least the names of the parts that often failed during their trips. "You won't believe it," he would write a month later to the group in Valencia, "but the car has been fixed. It's running well, and moreover, thanks to its previous devilries, I now know that it has a distributor cap, hose clamps, and ball bearings" (AGP, RHF, EF–400227–1).

men of the sea had been softened. They didn't shoo the little boy away, but let him think that he was helping them.

I've told you this story many times, because it moves me to think that our Lord God also lets us lend a hand to his works, and looks at us with affection when he sees us trying to collaborate with him.[183]

Did it make sense for those young students and recent graduates to commit themselves to an enterprise whose only visible manifestation was its founder and his companions? It happened frequently that from just a couple of conversations in a hotel room, or after a walk in the city or the countryside, there sprang a radical change of life. It was evident that the Lord was liberally pouring out his grace. Conscious of this and of the exceptional character of the times, Father Josemaría chose, for heading and forming the first vocations, people who were very young and who had been in the Work for only a short time, but who "showed a maturity of judgment and supernatural sense."[184]

The increase of vocations did, however, create some new problems. "Is the family going to grow a lot?" Isidoro writes in the spring of 1940. "The news from all is amazing. So we have to keep insisting on the matter of a house. This is most essential for the development of the apostolate. What can be done with the family if it can't find shelter? It's impossible to create a home atmosphere without a house."[185]

After going three months without making an entry in his journal, the founder wrote:

Wednesday, May 8, 1940: Some months have gone by without any Catherines being written. It's not surprising, since my life is so hectic that I don't have time for anything. But I do regret it. . . . News? A lot. It's impossible to choose things for recording here. Just this one, external thing: we have centers in Valencia, in Valladolid, in Barcelona (the center in Barcelona

---

[183] *Letter 29 Sep 1957*, no. 65.
[184] AGP, RHF, T–04151, p. 27 (Francisco Ponz Piedrafita). See also Alvaro del Portillo, *Sum.* 626. He appointed as director of El Rincón (in Valladolid) Javier de Silió Gómez-Carcedo, who was still very young, and as director of El Palau (in Barcelona) Rafael Termes. Both had been in the Work only a very short time.
[185] AGP, IZL, D–1213, 455.

isn't up and running yet, since the rental contract hasn't been finalized), and—soon—in Saragossa.[186]

The apartment in Valladolid had been set up within the previous month, and had been given the name *El Rincon* (The Corner). In Valencia a place had been found, at 16 Samaniego. It would be renovated during the summer and begin operations as a student residence in October.[187] The apartment in Barcelona was at 62 Balmes Street. The founder got news about it on July 1 and on that same day wrote from Avila to Barcelona a letter that would soon prove prophetic:

> May Jesus watch over my sons.
>
> We already have a house in Barcelona! You can't imagine the joy this news gives me. It is, no doubt, due to the blessing of that bishop—"I bless you with all my heart, and I bless the house!" said our Bishop Miguel Díaz Gómara, the last time I was there. This blessing explains the success of your search for El Palau. The sure path for us to follow, in our spirit, is never to separate ourselves from the bishops' ecclesiastical authority.
>
> I feel that El Palau will, silently, give much glory to God.[188]

7. *"How to fit Opus Dei into canon law"*

In July 1940 an apartment was rented on Martínez Campos Street, not far from the Jenner Street residence, and the older members of the Work moved there. Some had just completed their studies, while others were preparing for university teaching. Father Josemaría had high hopes of beginning what he referred to as "the intellectual apostolate." [189] He saw an urgent need for apostolically motivated university professors. "Dissertations! I need two dozen Ph.D.'s," he frequently told his sons.[190]

---

[186] *Apuntes*, no. 1610.

[187] The founder visited Valencia on several occasions in 1940 to promote the apostolate there and the setting up of the residence. On July 31 the Valencian group left El Cubil and moved to 16 Samaniego Street. The Father blessed the new center on September 20. See Alvaro del Portillo, *Sum.* 626; AGP, RHF, T–00159/1, p. 97 (Francisco Botella); and AGP, RHF, T–02769, p. 3 (Amadeo de Fuenmayor).

[188] AGP, RHF, EF–400701–1. This bishop was the one who ordained Father Josemaría. For more on him, see vol. 1, pp. 91, 105–6, and 112–13, of this biography.

[189] See *The Way*, no. 978.

[190] See AGP, RHF, EF–400704–1.

As early as 1927, at Madrid's Larra Street residence for priests, he had spoken about the important role of intellectuals. Over the years he had become even more convinced of the immense apostolate waiting to be done in that field. Speaking to the other priests at the Larra Street residence, he had compared outstanding intellectuals to snow that melts on the mountaintops in the spring and runs down to irrigate the valleys. This idea had apparently taken hold, for in sending news about the apartment on Martínez Campos, Isidoro wrote: "There are several dissertations under way, and several people are preparing for competitions for professorial positions. These matters are something we should all care about, since they constitute one of the foundations for the growth of our business." [191]

Intellectuals, indeed, are the source of the ideas that guide society, and therefore any serious attempt to re-Christianize social structures must start with them. In an early letter, addressed to those who in time would carry out this apostolate, the founder wrote:

> We want to serve everyone. Our field of apostolate encompasses all men and women, of all races and social backgrounds. But to reach everyone, we must first try everywhere to reach the intellectuals, knowing that any attempt to influence society must go through them. Because they are the ones who see the big picture, the ones who are behind every movement that is at all effective, the ones who organize and give shape to society's cultural, technological, and artistic developments.[192]

[191] AGP, IZL, D–1213, 467. Addressing this subject of the teaching apostolate, the founder wrote to his children a letter which opens with considerations concerning the rights and the mission of the Church in the area of teaching and the duties of Christians in this regard:

"I would now like to point out to you, my beloved daughters and sons, the urgent need for men and women who—with the spirit of our Work—take an active role in the secular sphere of education. This very noble profession is of utmost importance for the good of the Church, whose principal enemy has always been ignorance, and also for the life of civil society, because 'righteousness exalts a nation, but sin is a reproach to any people' (Prov 14:34), and 'by the blessing of the upright a city is exalted, but it is overthrown by the mouth of the wicked' (Prov 11:11).

"There is, as I was saying, an urgent need to form good teachers and professors, with in-depth preparation—with knowledge of their field, with pedagogical skills, with a solid grasp of Catholic doctrine, and with personal virtue—who, by their own merits, by their professional efforts, gain prestige in every teaching sector" (*Letter 2 Oct 1939*, nos. 3–4).

[192] *Letter 9 Jan 1932*, no. 87.

Both in private conversations and in his preaching, Father Josemaría repeatedly taught the importance of making one's God-given talents bear fruit, and of winning professional prestige by sanctifying one's work and sanctifying others through it. One should, that is, make from professional efforts not a ladder for exalting oneself, but a pedestal for exalting the Lord of creation. Each individual should work with full personal freedom and responsibility in his or her own professional area.[193] Some of these ideas communicated by the founder inspired several professionals, including José María Albareda, to offer the suggestion for the law that, in November 1939, brought into being the Council for Advanced Scientific Research.[194]

In this area, as in all others, the Father taught not only by word but by example. In the fall of 1939, at the abbey of Las Huelgas and at other archives in Madrid, he completed the research for his own doctoral dissertation. Given the demands on his time, this was no small accomplishment. Then, on December 18, he attained the doctorate by presenting *A Canonical-Historical Study on the Ecclesiastical Jurisdiction "Nullius Dioecesis" of the Abbess of Las Huelgâs of Burgos*. It was awarded the highest possible grade.[195]

Father Josemaría also taught several government-organized courses which laid the groundwork for the Official School of Journalism that

---

[193] See Casciaro, p. 172.

[194] The first secretary general of this council was Albareda. On the conversations between him and the founder about the promotion of scientific research, see Enrique Gutiérrez Ríos, *José María Albareda—Una época de la cultura española* (Madrid, 1970), pp. 147–74; Casciaro, p. 172; and Alvaro del Portillo, *Sum.* 590. See also *Apuntes*, no. 57 (16 Jun 1930).

[195] See his student file in the archive of the law school of Madrid's Complutense University.

One of the members of the panel judging his dissertation was José López Ortiz, Professor of History of Law at the University of Madrid. He testifies, "His work was so obviously thorough that the date for the defense of his dissertation was moved up to the end of December, which is why I was on the panel. The title was *The Abbess of Las Huelgâs*. This work of juridical investigation was carried out with a skill and a style that were truly extraordinary. Everyone on the panel was impressed, and the dissertation was rated 'Outstanding' " (*Testimonios*, p. 210). Father Josemaría spent the first days of April 1944 in Burgos, doing research to expand and deepen this study before getting it published. "There comes back to my mind," he writes to the abbess, "that blessed charity you all showed me in the bookkeeper's office, in putting up with the bothersome requests of this poor researcher. Especially those two very gracious little nuns, who must have been absolutely worn out after all the running around they did to bring me materials from every corner of the archive" (Letter to Mother Esperanza de Mallagaray, O.Cist.: AGP, RHF, EF–440405–1).

Two weeks later, with the book already at the print shop, he asked the abbess for some final data: see AGP, RHF, EF–440419–1.

opened the following year. Both the bishop of Madrid and the director general for the press had urged him to teach the courses on general and professional ethics.[196]

*   *   *

With the weekend trips to other cities, a network for apostolic activity was being built up throughout central and northern Spain. By the beginning of 1940—nine months after their return to a Madrid reduced to chaos by the war—the Work had stable activities under way in Valencia, Valladolid, Barcelona, and Saragossa. But Father Josemaría wanted it established as soon as possible in many other parts of the country, and, in prayer, he had worked out a very specific plan, at once realistic and ambitious. On January 27, 1940, he wrote: "Very soon we will go to Seville, Granada, and Santiago. With this we will have completed our plan to the letter." [197]

He had gotten the letters of introduction that he would need to present to the ecclesiastical authorities in those cities. But not all these letters were entirely solemn-sounding. The one signed by the bishop of Pamplona and addressed to the archbishop of Santiago said:

> The Rev. José María Escrivá, bearer of this letter, is a rogue who can outfox the devil. He has many very gifted young men following him who are true apostles. I know the spirit that animates them, I am edified, so much so that I consider myself part of his household.[198]

The bishop of Vitoria wrote to the archbishop of Granada: "With these lines I wish to present Father José María Escrivá, a priest of

[196] To the director general, Enrique Giménez-Arnau Gran, he wrote: "Dear Enrique: I have received the appointment of professor at the School of Journalism. I thank you for this, and since the bishop of Madrid is especially interested in my taking on those classes, I will do so gladly, in the hope that I will be working for God and for Spain" (AGP, RHF, EF–401025–1). A few months later he wrote to the bishop of Madrid: "I have started working at the School of Journalism, with the joy that comes of obeying. I have already sent the syllabus to Your Excellency, by way of Monsignor Morcillo," (AGP, RHF, EF–410122–1).

Pedro Gómez Aparicio was the secretary for those "Special Courses for Journalists" established in August 1940. In the July 14, 1975 issue of *La Hoja de Lunes de Madrid* he gives his recollections of Father Josemaría's classes. The Official School of Journalism was founded on November 17, 1941; its director was Juan Aparicio López; and it operated until 1975, when it was replaced by the School of Information Sciences.

[197] AGP, RHF, EF–400127–2.

[198] AGP, RHF, D–15719 (Letter of Bishop Marcelino Olaechea, 14 Jan 1940).

Christ and a true apostle in the fullest sense of the word. I don't ask that you be attentive to him, because soon you will realize what he is like." [199]

Here, clearly, we have the bishops' perspectives on what Father Josemaría had in his journal referred to as his "holy and apostolic shamelessness." [200] And it is also clear, that Father Josemaría also was acquiring a growing reputation for sanctity, as one bishop sang his praises to another. But even so, the bishops often failed to grasp the full ecclesial significance of Opus Dei. [201]

Of them all, Bishop Eijo y Garay may best have understood what a profoundly new thing Opus Dei was in the life of the Church. On September 2, 1939, he and the founder had a five-hour conversation during which he expressed the view that the time had come to give Opus Dei a juridical structure. But Father Josemaría's reaction was restrained. Next day he made this journal entry: "September 3, 1939: Was with the bishop of Madrid yesterday, talking, about five hours. It went very well. It's obvious that God is taking care of everything. What a shame that I'm an obstacle! Bishop Leopoldo showed real affection." [202]

Putting the matter out of mind, Father Josemaría concentrated on his work—until a note came from the vicar general telling him to prepare the papers for official approval. After consulting with his confessor, Father Sánchez, he wrote in his journal: "Praise God! I will do it. Nevertheless, it seems to me that there's no need to hurry." [203]

As he prepared the documents, he came to realize why he had been so reluctant to move quickly. In his journal he wrote:

> I can only account for my reluctance to draw up the statutes for the bishop, as still another exterior proof of the divine origin of the Work. If it was a merely human thing, I would have been in a big rush to get those papers together— now that everything is facilitated—and obtain the official

---

[199] AGP, RHF, D–15720 (Letter of Bishop Javier Lauzurica, 31 Jan 1940).

[200] See *Apuntes*, no. 178 (20 Mar 1931).

[201] On November 25, 1939, he wrote in his journal: "The hierarchy loves the Work, but only halfway understands it; they don't really get it" (*Apuntes*, no. 1606).

[202] *Apuntes*, no. 1605.

[203] *Apuntes*, no. 1607 (25 Nov 1939). This entry begins, "My confessor and the vicar general of Madrid have told me, *as an order*, to prepare the required material for the first official approval of the Work of God."

approval. But since it is entirely God's thing, and he wants it to last until the end, haste is not necessary. The Work began in 1928, on the feast of the holy guardian angels, and will continue forever. As long as people are wayfarers on earth, the Work will exist! [204]

When he had the papers worked up, he asked Alvaro, Juan, Ricardo, and Chiqui to help put them in order.[205] At the end of June 1940, with the project well along, he showed the material to the priest in charge of canonical matters in the diocese, Father José María Bueno Monreal. It covered the regulations, governance, customs, spirit, and ceremonies of the Work. Examining these papers together, they came to the conclusion that there was no appropriate juridical framework for this ecclesial reality.[206] The effort came to a temporary halt. The founder wrote, "We are confronting the serious problem of how to fit Opus Dei into canon law." [207]

This stumbling block came as no surprise to him. He had, in fact, been aware of it from the beginning. Soon after Opus Dei's founding, foreseeing that somewhere down the line it would need ecclesiastical approval, he wrote of having "to determine clearly the fields of action" of its members.[208] The young priest was well aware that the impetuous winds of the Holy Spirit were erasing boundaries that theologians and canonists had for almost two thousand years been using to mark out different fields of apostolate in the Church. Already in 1930 he wrote, "I see that fervor, a zeal for the glory of God, like a cyclone, is making us want to be, through him and for him, everywhere." [209]

From the beginning, he had carefully recorded in his journal all of God's inspirations. In June of 1930, upon rereading what he had written thus far, he was astonished by the broad, boundless fields of action opening before his eyes. He filled up sheet after sheet of paper, trying to list and categorize the immense variety of apostolates. He writes:

---

[204] *Apuntes*, no. 1609 (5 Feb 1940).

[205] See *Apuntes*, no. 1615 (21 Jun 1940).

[206] See José María Bueno Monreal, in *Testimonios*, p. 39.

[207] *Apuntes*, no. 1613 (21 Jun 1940). See also Amadeo de Fuenmayor, Valentín Gómez Iglesias, and José Luis Illanes, *The Canonical Path of Opus Dei*, trans. William H. Stetson (Princeton, 1994), pp. 78–90.

[208] *Apuntes*, no. 42.

[209] Ibid.

When I look over these sheets, I am amazed to see what God is doing. I would never have dreamed of these works the Lord is inspiring, in the form they are taking. At first, all that can be seen is a vague idea. And then, him, turning those shadowy sketches into something clear, specific, and doable. Him! To whom be all glory.[210]

The newness of the Work's message and the secularity of the Work required a special juridical format. Apostolic activities could not grow spontaneously if encumbered with rules and regulations that enclosed a living reality in a rigid framework. From time to time the founder mentions this problem in his journal. One example: "In this year of 1936, we have begun to live the life of poverty with more perfection. We're seeing what I have so often said: that it is useless to draw up rules, because it has to be the very life of our apostolate that, in due time, gives us our guidelines."[211]

On the day that he wrote that note, he was pondering whether or not the time was right to seek approval for the Work. He writes:

Certainly, all indications are that if I were to ask the bishop for the first ecclesiastical approval of the Work, he would grant it. . . . But it is a matter of so much importance that it requires a lot of thinking about. The Work of God has to present a new form, and the path could easily be damaged.[212]

[210] *Apuntes*, no. 65.

[211] *Apuntes*, no. 1307 (25 Jan 1936). When in 1935 the time came to begin the Saint Gabriel work (that is, the apostolate with persons of all conditions and states: single, married, widowed, etc.), the founder noted in his journal, "Thanks be to God, we are growing. Our clothes are getting too small for us," meaning that a juridical format was required that could encompass this expanding apostolate. See *Apuntes*, no. 1290 (14 Oct 1935).

[212] *Apuntes*, no. 1309 (25 Jan 1936). In a letter to all his children the founder returned to this idea. "When Heaven deems that the time is right," he says, "a channel will open, in the structure of apostolates in the Church, for the broad river of the Work, for which the present circumstances do not provide a suitable site. It will be an arduous and laborious challenge. Many obstacles will have to be overcome. But God will assist us, since everything in the Work is his will" (*Letter 11 Mar 1940*, no. 46).

The founder faced a similar problem when it came to trying to express the new concepts that the Work brought with it. "To express myself," he says, "I am using words that necessitate a new terminology. If I were to invent one, people wouldn't understand me. In due course we will have to use that new terminology" (*Letter 29 Dec 1947/14 Feb 1966*, no. 14).

[213] The reports were often absurd. For example, Father Josemaría noted, it was said of the members of the Work that "whenever we knelt down, we put our hands behind us,

And now here was the archbishop of Madrid asking him to draw up the papers required for getting that first approval. But much as he searched for a canonical solution, he could not find one. One did not yet exist.

8. *A change of confessors*

The Jenner Street residence was operating at full capacity soon after it opened. As the only fixed site for Opus Dei's apostolic activities, its study room, visiting rooms, and oratory were heavily used by residents and other students attending classes of formation. Its doors were open to all, and its pleasant atmosphere led many students to bring friends there.

However, a resistance to taking these classes became noticeable among some students. Here and there, critical comments began to be heard in university circles. There were rumors of strange things: of an oratory decorated with Masonic and cabalistic symbols, of Communion given with perfumed hosts, of crosses without a corpus.[213]

It was not the first time Father Josemaría had been the target of such gossip.[214] Feverish imaginations in search of the bizarre found cause for scandal in all kinds of perfectly innocent things: in this case, the Christian symbols engraved on the frieze of the oratory, between words from a Latin hymn; the bare cross; and the slight fragrance given to the tabernacle in an attempt to hide the odor of carpenter's glue. Seeking to curtail the gossip, the founder asked the bishop of Madrid to grant an indulgence for kissing that big wooden cross in the back of the oratory, so that people would understand its Christian meaning. A plaque soon appeared bearing a decree dated March 28, 1940, in which Bishop Eijo y Garay granted a fifty days' indulgence for each time that someone "devoutly kissed the wooden cross in the student residence."[215]

Then, however, there came to the founder's attention new false

---

as some kind of odd ritual. What really happened was that we knelt on the floor, since we didn't have any kneelers, and some people instinctively put their hands behind them" (*Letter 29 Dec 1947/14 Feb 1966*, no. 61). For more on this matter, see AGP, RHF, D–03545/3 (a letter, dated 21 Jun 1941, from Bishop Eijo y Garay to an abbot); Alvaro del Portillo, *Sum.* 414; José Luis Múzquiz, *Sum.* 5800; and Pedro Casciaro, *Sum.* 6327.

[214] See *Apuntes*, no. 751 (15 Jun 1932), no. 1240 (10 Mar 1935), no. 1267 (7 May 1935), no. 1290 (14 Oct 1935), and no. 1292 (28 Oct 1935).

[215] See AGP, RHF, D–15074.

accusations and louder grumblings—and not from students this time, but from mature and responsible people. At first Father Josemaría refused to believe what his friends and sons were telling him. He tore up the notes telling him what was happening. He just could not believe that such lies could be spread among Christians. But before the civil war, in the years of the DYA Academy and the Ferraz Street residence, he had also suffered false accusations: he had been labeled crazy and a heretic, and the Work called a sect or a Masonic conspiracy. So now he hoped that this pestilential new outbreak would likewise wither if greeted with silence. But the rumors grew. Some students propagated the story that Father Josemaría used special lights in the oratory to make it appear that he was levitating, or to hypnotize those present.[216]

Few of those notes from the first months of 1940 have survived. The ones that Father Josemaría did not tear up, he passed on to his bishop. By spring, however, he could no longer ignore the evidence of what was going on. The students spreading this gossip—who had visited the residence and attended classes of formation—all belonged to the Marian Sodality of Madrid.

Feeling enmeshed in an invisible web, the priest suffered greatly from these calumnies. He determined to open his heart to Bishop Leopoldo:

> Madrid, April 23, 1940
> Father: How I would like to have a chance to speak with you at length. . . .
> I'm sending a note that I misplaced several months ago, because although I'm sure I'm not telling Your Excellency anything new, it's still a matter of some concern. The enemy never sleeps! . . .
> Father: Don't forget my people (who are so much your sons!), nor this sinner,
>
> Josemaría[217]

Because of one trip after another to give priests' retreats, he had been unable to see his confessor for several weeks. The next time he did see him, on May 22, he and Father Sánchez agreed that "even if

---

[216] See Alvaro del Portillo, *Sum.* 414, and Pedro Casciaro, *Sum.* 6327.
[217] AGP, RHF, EF–400423–1.

it can only be once a month, because of my trips, I will go to confession only to him."[218] He would certainly have discussed the gossip and calumnies with his confessor. And here, for a few weeks, all record of these events ceases, except for a few references that give no details.[219] Father Josemaría clearly preferred to forgive and forget. Evidently, though, the rumors about him and the Work were continuing and becoming more and more elaborate.

"Father," he wrote to his bishop, "I pray for you often, and I ask our Lord God that you continue to see the Work that he has placed on my shoulders as God's and as your own."[220]

A few weeks later, on August 23, he went to Segovia to make a retreat at the Carmelite monastery where the remains of Saint John of the Cross are preserved. He was assigned cell 36, which had on its door a plaque reading, "Pax. Declinabo super eam quasi fluvium pacis. Isai. 66 v. 12" ["Peace. I will extend prosperity to her like a river"]. Next day he wrote:

> I really needed this retreat. The sinner Josemaría must become a saint. Besides, I've had no lack of tribulations, recently though I haven't said anything about them in these Catherines and my supernatural vision has improved so that I can bear them joyfully.
>
> I won't make any notes on this retreat.[221]

When he returned to Madrid on August 28, new rumors and calumnies were awaiting him. On September 15 he wrote to the bishop of Murcia:

> My revered and very dear Bishop:
> I thought about not saying anything to you on the following matter until I could have the pleasure of seeing you in Barcelona. But I have consulted with Monsignor Casimiro Morcillo, and he has advised me to inform you without delay.

---

[218] *Apuntes*, no. 1611.
[219] See AGP, RHF, EF–400701–2 (a letter to Alvaro which refers to "the Judas affair"), and *Apuntes*, no. 1614 (21 Jun 1940).
[220] AGP, RHF, EF–400806–2.
[221] *Apuntes*, no. 1619 (24 Aug 1940).

I have reliable information that an official of Catholic Action for Young Men of Murcia has literally said that the Work (which I have been engaged in for twelve years in close union with my bishop and the bishops of the other places where I work) is in danger of excommunication by the Pope; that he (the official) is perfectly aware of all that is really going on, but that we only tell the bishops what suits us, etc.

All of this is total slander, and I leave it to you to judge its gravity.[222]

For the most part he kept his sufferings to himself. But to the bishop of Pamplona he wrote, "Don't forget to pray for us, and especially for me, because I always have the cross on my back."[223]

At the beginning of September he had gone to see Monsignor Morcillo, and then two or three of the individuals linked to the calumnies and rumors. He wanted once and for all to put an end to the calumnies and to the disturbances that the devil had stirred up through these people whose intentions may not have been bad but who had acted recklessly.

He also decided to ask the advice of his confessor, Father Sánchez, concerning the Jesuit priest who was in charge of the Marian Sodality, Father Carrillo de Albornoz.[224] There was strong evidence that this priest was spreading the rumor that the Work was a heretical secret society, Masonic in origin. Father Sánchez suggested that he speak face to face with him.

He did so. He told Father Carrillo of the rumors being attributed to him, and explained to the best of his ability the work being done with students at the Jenner Street residence. And then he tactfully gave the priest a way to save face. He proposed an agreement: If either of them heard any pejorative criticism in the future—against the Work or against the Marian Sodalities—he would tell the other as soon as possible.[225]

---

[222] AGP, RHF, EF–400915–1. Bishop Miguel de los Santos y Díaz de Gómara was appointed bishop of Cartagena (Murcia) in 1935, but was later also the apostolic administrator of Barcelona, until 1942. Hence the mention of both Murcia and Barcelona.

[223] AGP, RHF, EF–400910–1 (Letter to Bishop Marcelino Olaechea).

[224] See *Apuntes*, no. 1622; AGP, RHF, D–15200 and D–15204; and Carlos López Pego, *La Congregación de "Los Luises" de Madrid: Apuntes para la Historia de una Congregación Mariana Universitaria de Madrid* (Madrid, 1999).

[225] See *Apuntes*, no. 1626 (15 Nov 1940).

But the murmurings were not coming only from the religious side. Seemingly overnight, the priest's good name had gotten entangled in political intrigues as well. Seeking to clarify his position, Father Josemaría made a visit to the Ministry of the Interior. "I don't get involved—not in the least—in matters not pertaining to priesthood," he wrote in his journal. "I am a priest and only a priest. Some people are trying to drag my name into political and professional matters. God save me!"[226]

Then he went to see the vicar general—to fill him in on this new problem, and, though he does not say so directly, for consolation at a time when he was hurting. "Casimiro encouraged me," he gratefully records after the visit.[227]

From September 17 to 23 he was in Valencia, helping get the student residence there launched. The day after his return to Madrid, he went with Alvaro del Portillo to see Father Sánchez again, at the Jesuit residence on Zorrilla Street, and presented his confessor with a copy of the documents he had submitted for getting the Work approved. He did this at least partly because the ascetical practices and life of piety outlined there had much to do with his own interior life, but perhaps also as a sign of trust in his confessor.[228] Then he spoke of his latest concerns—and got, as a response, an additional one. "There are those," said Father Sánchez, "who doubt that you are in good graces with the bishops." What he was saying did not come as any news, but the tone in which he said it struck Father Josemaría as odd.

They went on to talk about the discretion with which members of Opus Dei had been carrying on their apostolate since 1931, when the Work was still in its infancy and the Church was being violently persecuted. A similar prudence also was observed with regard to the spiritual direction of new members. By a free personal decision, they confided fully only in those who had a full knowledge of the Work and its spirit, and who were therefore in a position to give them sound advice. Father Sánchez knew perfectly well that this was the only sensible thing to do in such circumstances. In fact, it was what he himself had always recommended. Thus one can well imagine Father Josemaría's surprise at hearing him now say, without batting an eye, that whatever had to do with a vocation to the Work should be

[226] *Apuntes*, no. 1623 (14 Sep 1940).
[227] *Apuntes*, no. 1624 (15 Sep 1940).
[228] See Alvaro del Portillo, *Sum.* 329.

discussed unreservedly with any confessor. How could it happen that the Jesuit was now taking this position, when for years he had been recommending that members of the Work receive spiritual direction only from priests who knew and loved it? As a director of souls, the founder immediately saw the grave consequences of such a change. He wondered at the fact that his confessor had "in a few hours changed an opinion he had held for years." [229]

Things were moving fast. Father Josemaría decided to go right away to see the bishop of Madrid, who was in Alhama de Aragón for a few days' rest. They lunched together on September 27 and had a long conversation about the Work. On the next day he wrote:

> Yesterday I was in Alhama de Aragon, with the bishop of Madrid. What a father we have in him! How well he under-stands and identifies with the Work of God! I told him the latest tribulations. He was moved. He sees God behind every-thing, but he also sees the narrow-mindedness of some per-sons. In summary, he told me he wants to grant the decree of establishment and approval of Opus Dei as soon as he gets back to Madrid.[230]

They spoke of his visits and meetings of the past few weeks, and of Father Carrillo: "The thing about the Jesuits, he sees the same way I do—that one must not confuse an individual member with the whole Society. The bishop, the same as me, very much loves and venerates the Society of Jesus." [231]

The founder next met with Father Sánchez two weeks later. (As before, he was accompanied by Alvaro del Portillo.) Coming directly to the point, he told his confessor that to his great sorrow he had noticed a radical change in his attitude toward the Work, and that after much thought, he had concluded that he could not in good conscience continue seeing him for spiritual direction, since he had lost confidence in him.

---

[229] See AGP, RHF, D–15713. The political circumstances in Spain between 1931 and 1939, together with the newness of the Work at that time, dictated a low profile for the apostolic activities of its members. To avoid causing a commotion or incurring a persecution, the founder took care—and his spiritual director supported him in this—to act "with holy discretion." See *Apuntes*, no. 486 (16 Dec 1931, no. 734 (24 May 1932), no. 799 (5 Aug 1932), and no. 1216 (10 Jan 1935).

[230] AGP, RHF, D–15713.

[231] Ibid.

Father Sánchez, obviously somewhat upset, replied brusquely that the Holy See would never approve the Work, and cited a canon in support of his view. This unexpected outburst came as a severe blow to Father Josemaría, but he answered calmly that since the Work belonged to God, he would guide it to a safe harbor.[232]

The meeting was over. Father Sánchez returned the papers the founder had given him. But all the way home, a question kept running through Father Josemaría's mind: Why did this man, who had so often assured him of Opus Dei's divine origin, now doubt it? When he got back to Jenner, the first thing he did was to look up the canon cited by Father Sánchez. Much to his relief, he found that it had no bearing on the approval. Then he opened the envelope that had in it the returned papers, and with them he found a sheet with five or six names: a list of students who had frequented the Jenner Street residence for the purpose of secretly informing Father Carrillo of what went on there. Had Father Sánchez left that sheet there by accident? Or had he "accidentally on purpose," out of friendship, provided him this information?[233]

November passed without major incident. Father Josemaría kept in mind what Bishop Leopoldo had said at the end of their visit in Alhama de Aragón: "Look, Josemaría, up to now our Lord wanted you to take as your model the good thief, and say, 'I deserve to be on the cross.' But from now on, your only model is Jesus on the cross. So may sufferings come—without any justification!"[234]

Also, the Lord was preparing him for bitter sufferings ahead by granting him a divine locution.

For a while now, I have often caught myself saying, "*Aquae multae non potuerunt extinguere caritatem*" ["Many waters cannot quench love": Song 8:7]. I interpret these words in two

---

[232] Alvaro del Portillo, *Sum.* 330.

[233] See ibid. The founder interpreted it as a final demonstration of affection on the part of his confessor. "Alvaro accompanied me," he writes, "and was present at my last two meetings with that venerable Jesuit father. In the last one, I asked him to return to me the 'Codex,' as our statutes were then called. And he did so. I had left it with him because it contained things connected with my soul. And he, Father Sánchez, as a final demonstration of affection, placed among the papers a sheet with the names of the people who, in company with Father C. de A., had been going around spreading stories, rumors, and interpretations that were the false foundation—not the occasion—for that campaign that is still going on" (*Letter 29 Dec 1947/14 Feb 1966,* no. 20).

[234] AGP, RHF, D–15713.

ways: one, that the multitude of my past sins cannot separate me from the Love of my God; and the other, that the waters of the persecution we are now undergoing will not impede the apostolate of the Work.[235]

Father Josemaría's reaction to the persecution was both very human and deeply supernatural. At first he refused to believe people could do such evil things. Later, when forced to acknowledge the facts, he tried to put a good face on their intentions. ("I know his intention isn't bad," he said of one of the rumormongers, "but he doesn't understand anything about our spirit, and he gets everything confused and mixed up."[236]) And as a last resort, in the face of irrefutable evidence, he could only forgive and forget. "Although I don't want to mention this," he writes, "I will just say that it is hard to believe in the good faith of those who systematically spread calumnies. I forgive them with all my heart."[237]

In mid-November he gave a retreat at Madrid's major seminary. One day he left from there to visit the Undersecretary of the Interior, and on his way he ran into Father Carrillo de Albornoz, "the religious who instigated this last tribulation that has gone on now for so long."[238] With no rancor and with perfect naturalness, he shook Father Carrillo's hand and said, "I'm pleased to see you, Father. God bless you!" Aware that Father Carrillo, instead of keeping their pact to communicate criticisms, was going around calling him "either crazy or evil," he added, "Don't you remember our gentlemen's agreement?"

"I already spoke about all that last night, at nine, with the vicar general," Father Carrillo answered hurriedly, breaking away.

On the next day the founder wrote in his journal:

---

[235] *Apuntes*, no. 1625 (4 Nov 1940). He referred to these favors obliquely, using the expression "drops of honey." *Letter 29 Dec 1947/14 Feb 1966*, no. 20.

[236] *Apuntes*, no. 1622.

[237] *Apuntes*, no. 1625.

[238] Angel Carrillo de Albornoz was born in 1905, entered the Society of Jesus on July 15, 1925, and was professed on August 15, 1941. In 1940 he was named director of the Spanish Confederation of Marian Sodalities, and on April 5, 1948, he became director of the General Secretariat of the Marian Sodalities, and was transferred to Rome. In 1951 he left the Jesuits. See R. Mendizábal, "Elenchus Scriptorum qui, in restitutam Societatem Iesu cooptati, eam deseruerunt," in *Catalogus defunctorum in Renata Societate Iesu ab a. 1814 ad a. 1970* (Rome, 1972), p. 605.

November 15, Madrid: . . . In the afternoon, I found myself experiencing a deep interior joy on account of that tribulation. And I feel a greater love for the blessed Society of Jesus, and sympathy and even affection for the religious causing this whole mess. Besides, I understand that he is a very likable man, and certainly a very good person. May God bless and prosper him! This morning I told all this to my spiritual father, José María García Lahiguera.[239]

*   *   *

Father Sánchez and Father Josemaría did not see each other again until November 22, 1948. By then the Holy See had granted the *Decretum laudis* for Opus Dei and pontifical approval of its statutes. The founder traveled to Spain and visited all of the superiors of the Society of Jesus, except for the one in Seville, who refused to receive him. In Madrid, with the permission of the provincial, he went to see Father Sánchez, who received him with great joy. They spoke of old times, and, inevitably, they did touch on that sore spot. Father Josemaría tells us:

He was very happy to hear what I told him about the expansion of the Work. I tried to draw him out a bit, saying to him, "I really suffered, Father. At the sight of that relentless attack made on me by such good people, I even thought at one moment, Could I be mistaken, and it's not from God, and I'm leading souls astray?"

And he immediately protested, with great earnestness: "No, no. It's from God. It's all from God."[240]

Father Valentín Sánchez Ruiz died in Madrid on November 30, 1963. When the news reached Rome, the founder celebrated holy

[239] *Apuntes*, no. 1626. Born in 1903, in Fitero, Navarre, José María García Lahiguera was ordained in 1926, in Madrid. After the civil war he was a professor, superior, and spiritual director at the Madrid seminary. He would serve as Father Josemaría's confessor until 1944. From 1950 to 1964 he was auxiliary bishop of Madrid; from 1964 to 1969, bishop of Huesca; and from then on, archbishop of Valencia. He was also the cofounder of a contemplative order of sisters approved in 1967: the Oblates of Christ the Priest. He died in 1989. See Salvador Muñoz Iglesias, *José María García Lahiguera: un carisma, una vida* (Madrid, 1991); and Vicente Cárcel Ortí, *Pasión por el sacerdocio: Biografía del Siervo de Dios José María García Lahiguera* (Madrid, 1997).

[240] *Apuntes*, no. 1873 (22 Nov 1948).

Mass for him and wrote to the Opus Dei Counsellor in Spain. The letter reflects the deep emotions he felt at hearing the news. "That venerable religious," he says, "didn't have anything to do with the Work, but he had a lot to do with my soul, which cannot be separated from Opus Dei." The letter concludes:

> May he rest in peace, for he was good and apostolic! I turned to him—especially when our Lord or his most holy Mother made themselves manifest to this sinner, and I, after being frightened because I did not want that, had felt clearly and strongly in the depths of my soul a wordless "*Ne timeas!* Don't be afraid; it is I." Every time this happened, the good Jesuit, after hearing me out a few hours later, would say to me with a fatherly smile, "Be at peace: this is from God."
>
> Forgive me. I am a poor man. Pray for me, that I may be good, faithful, and cheerful. I have felt the need to tell you all of this so that you will pray to our Lord for that soul, who was, I think, very pleasing to him.[241]

241 AGP, RHF, EF–631206–2 (Letter to Florencio Sánchez Bella).

5

"The One Who Loves God's Will"

1. The death of the Grandmother

It was the founder's habit to face adversity calmly, trusting God and letting time do its work. Did not Opus Dei have centuries ahead? But this trustful abandonment to Divine Providence coexisted in him with a dynamic temperament that led to decisive action corresponding to his burning love for God and his acute sense of responsibility for his mission.

In those early years, Father Josemaría worked almost exclusively with men—priests and students, tradesmen, artists, and other professionals—but "without losing sight of the need to seek out souls among women." [1] This was something that he realized would take some time. When, in a journal entry made on February 14, 1932, he recorded the "happy event" of the arrivals of the first female vocations, he realized that it was just two years since our Lord had asked him to work also with women. Here was an enterprise that called for a sense of urgency, but not haste.

As we saw earlier, he turned over the spiritual direction of these women to some priests who were close to him, but who never altogether grasped the idea of dedicating oneself to God while remaining in the midst of the world. The women's isolation from the mainstream of Opus Dei during the three years of the civil war had produced substantial alterations in their interior life and spirit, and had bred a spirituality far removed from the secular character proper to the Work. The failure of the priests to properly guide them "was such," says the founder, "that I had to let those women go in 1939." [2] On April 28 of that year, he informed one of them, Ramona Sánchez, of his "intention to make a complete break with all of the girls," saying that they

[1] *Apuntes*, no. 1872 (14 Jun 1948).
[2] *Apuntes*, no. 381 (8 Nov 1931); the sentence quoted is evidently a note that the founder added later, upon rereading this entry.

325

should "follow another path, either entering a convent or getting married," and asking her to communicate this to the others.[3] Later—after they had left the Work—he helped some of them enter religious congregations.

Now he had to start over again from scratch. Or almost. There was still one girl left in the Work: Lola Fisac. She, as we also saw earlier, had requested admission in 1937, while the founder was at the Honduran consulate. When he was able to leave that refuge (as the consulate's "Chief Supply Officer"), he had thought seriously of going to Daimiel, the village in La Mancha where Lola lived, to bring the Blessed Sacrament to her and her brother. Events had moved too quickly for him to make the trip until the war was over, but two years later, on April 18, 1939, he traveled to Daimiel and stayed with the Fisacs, sleeping in the living room and spending the daytime in a small study, doing work or speaking with people. As for Mass, the churches in the area had been either sacked or desecrated, and were still closed. Only one priest had escaped the massacre of clergy and religious. But he had kept a set of vestments and a portable altar in his house, and there Father Josemaría said Mass, the day after his arrival, for the intentions of the Fisac family.

On April 20 he and Lola had a long conversation. After she recounted the details of her daily life, the Father wrote the aspiration "Sancta Maria, Spes nostra, Ancilla Domini, ora pro nobis!" ["Holy Mary, our hope, Handmaid of the Lord, pray for us!"] at the top of a sheet of paper and then wrote out for her a plan of life. He started with mental prayer—a half hour "in the morning, at a fixed time"—and then jotted down "awareness of the presence of God," dedicating each day of the week to a particular devotion. Next came spiritual reading—*The Story of a Soul,* by Saint Thérèse of Lisieux. Then, examinations of conscience: a general examination regarding obligations toward God and neighbor, and a particular examination relating to living in more awareness of the presence of God and to doing one's work conscientiously. Finally, frequent spiritual communions and acts of love and reparation. He concluded: "Live the communion of saints," and write him in Madrid every eight or ten days.[4]

---

[3] *Apuntes,* no. 1596. See also AGP, RHF, T–05827, p. 6 (Felisa Alcolea Millana); AGP, RHF, T–05828 (Sister Ramona Sánchez-Elvira); and José López Ortiz, *Sum.* 5289. On Father Josemaría's advice, Ramona became a Daughter of Charity, in 1940.

[4] AGP, RHF, AVF–0057. See also AGP, RHF, T–04956, pp. 1–2 (María Dolores Fisac).

Lola went to Madrid several times during 1939. On her first trip, in May, she spent a few days with relatives who lived across the street from Santa Isabel. She was able to visit with Father Josemaría and go to confession to him, and to meet Doña Dolores and Carmen.

It was only to be expected that, being so isolated from the rest of the Work, she would suffer some difficulties. Hence the Father wrote to her:

> May Jesus watch over you.
>
> Don't be upset; you're doing fine.
>
> The Lord always builds on what is nothing! He needs every kind of instrument, from the carpenter's saw to the surgeon's scalpel. What difference does it make? All that matters is to let oneself be used.
>
> Coldness or fervor—the important thing is that the will *wants to*. It is—it should be—of no concern to you how fervent or cold you feel.
>
> I bless you.
>
> Mariano [5]

By the time of her next visit, in the second half of September, Father Josemaría had moved from Santa Isabel to the Jenner Street residence. And on her third trip, at Christmastime, she stayed with Doña Dolores in the Jenner Street apartment. Lola could then feel the joy and peace of spirit of seeing something actually in progress. They were days in which there was nothing more than housework, the tasks of domestic service, and the company of the Grandmother, but for her they were unforgettably happy days.

On Christmas Eve, while setting up the crèche on the upper floor, the residents came down from time to time to ask the Grandmother for one thing or another. And she, recalling the long-ago days when her husband would put up the crèche with the help of the children, told them something that her son would include in *The Way*: "You have never seemed more a man to me than now, when you are so like a child." [6]

During that stay, Lola met Amparo Rodríguez Casado, a young woman who had just joined the Work. (She had been in a group of

---

[5] AGP, RHF, EF–390619–1.
[6] *The Way*, no. 557. See also AGP, RHF, T–04956, p. 4.

girls to whom Father Josemaría had given spiritual direction in Burgos.) One day he sketched for the two of them the apostolic panorama of the Work. He presented it in broad strokes, while making it clear that this was not a case of castles in the air, but something firm and objective. He painted the picture with such vividness and enthusiasm, says Lola, that "it seemed to us something amazing and extremely attractive. I was a bit frightened." [7]

(For 1939, there are gaps of one, two, or even three months between entries in his journal. In one of the last entries for that year, we read: "My concern is the women. Well, actually, my first concern is myself." [8])

The year 1940 was a long one for Lola. When she got back from Madrid to her little town, her eagerness to begin realizing the vast apostolic panorama Father Josemaría had proposed made it hard to be patient. The founder had to calm her down.

> May Jesus watch over you!
>   That impatience of yours for apostolic work is pleasing to God, as long as it doesn't take away your peace. Try to use it as a spur toward seeking God's presence in everything. That is sure to help make the time come more quickly.
>   Unite yourself to the intentions of the Father. Never forget the immense value of the communion of saints. Then you'll never be able to say that you are alone, since you will always be accompanied by your sisters and by the whole family.[9]

The Father nurtured her eagerness carefully. Three weeks later, he wrote again (on the anniversary of the founding of the women's branch) in which he said, "Never lose your peace for any reason. One's nerves must always be kept under control." [10] And the following month: "Calm down. Be calm, with joy and peace. This is the watchword." [11] On May 8 he wrote in his journal, "Some months have gone by without writing anything down. It's not surprising, since my

---

[7] AGP, RHF, T–04956, p. 4.
[8] *Apuntes*, no. 1607 (25 Nov 1939).
[9] AGP, RHF, EF–400122–3.
[10] AGP, RHF, EF–400214–1.
[11] AGP, RHF, EF–400306–1. A week later he was finally able to write to her, "I think our Lord will soon arrange things in such a way that you can work as you would like to" (AGP, RHF, EF–400314–1).

life is so hectic that I don't have time for anything. . . . My big concern is the feminine part of the Work." [12]

Then came the breakthrough. On May 10 he wrote to Lola announcing that some new women had come to the Work. "Amparito will tell you about the new additions to our family," he said. "Soon we will have the little house we need!" [13] On June 21 he noted, "The women's branch, praise God, is under way." [14]

But the pace remained slow. The "little house" did not open until autumn. Located on Castelló Street, it was a small, rented apartment, which the women furnished with items from their parents' homes. Father Josemaría immediately started giving classes of formation to them. But this lasted only until December 6. Lola explains: "We soon had to give up the apartment, because with both the Father and ourselves being so young, the situation caused some raised eyebrows in the neighborhood." [15] The priest would tolerate no gossip on this point. Plus, he knew from Doña Dolores that some of the girls who frequented the apartment, "instead of talking about apostolate, were spending their time talking about boyfriends." [16]

Lola did not know, however, about all the other gossip and slander besieging the founder and the Work at this time. A journal entry captures the atmosphere of those days:

September 16, 1940: Yesterday morning I went to see the vicar general to update him on these tribulations. Casimiro encouraged me and said to me, "There will come more, perhaps regarding the Sixth Commandment. But don't worry. Along with a thousand calumnies against the Jesuits, and the opposition of prelates and learned men to them, Saint Ignatius also had to suffer accusations of having taken loose women from their homes for evil purposes. It wouldn't surprise me to see you in jail one day for your priestly work. All of this is a very good sign." [17]

[12] *Apuntes*, no. 1610.
[13] AGP, RHF, EF–400510–1.
[14] *Apuntes*, no. 1612.
[15] AGP, RHF, T–04956, p. 6. See also Alvaro del Portillo, *Sum.* 597.
[16] See AGP, RHF, T–04678/1, p. 106 (José Luis Múzquiz).
[17] *Apuntes*, no. 1624. Father Josemaría first met Monsignor Casimiro Morcillo in Madrid in 1929; he was the priest the founder had stopped on the street to ask for prayers for a personal intention. (See volume 1 of this biography, p. 235.) During the

Meanwhile, both the furnishings of the Castelló apartment and the activities conducted there were transferred to a section of the house on Diego de León. The remodeling was still under way, and although a few people were living there, including Doña Dolores, all three of her children, and Alvaro del Portillo, it was a cold and inhospitable place that winter, because the heating system did not work properly.

The women of the Work occupied a completely separate part of the building. In the evenings they would gather in a room on the first floor to sew vestments for the new oratories, and the Father would spend time with them, giving them pointers on their professional work and on the spirit of Opus Dei. In that room, as he put it, "four young girls and a poor priest" were paving a road for the ones who would come later.[18]

He often preached a meditation for that small group of women, preparing them for incorporation into Opus Dei. But, as had happened with some of the young men before the war, some dropped out of contact over the next few months.

Quite often, Doña Dolores and Carmen took part in the get-togethers with the women.[19] Especially the Grandmother, who liked to listen and seldom intervened.[20]

She lived in a second-floor room overlooking the intersection of Diego de León and Lagasca. The room had a glassed-in porch, with a table that had a small heater beneath it. Here she did her work. She was always sewing, knitting, or reading. The women of the Work who passed through Santa Isabel's in the thirties cannot recall having ever seen her idle there either. "She was a great lady," says Sister Ramona, "always smiling and cordial. She devoted whole days to sewing clothes for the boys who were helping the Father—and she was pretty old."[21]

When prelates and other distinguished individuals were invited to dinner (which, at Diego de León, happened fairly often), the Grand-

---

civil war he was in Burgos. When Bishop Eijo y Garay was reorganizing the diocese of Madrid, he asked Monsignor Francisco Morán and Monsignor Morcillo to be his vicars. (See José Luis Alfaya Camacho, *Como un río de fuego: Madrid, 1936* [Barcelona, 1998], pp. 197–247.) In 1938 Monsignor Morcillo was appointed vicar general. In 1943 he became auxiliary bishop of Madrid; in 1955 he became archbishop of Saragossa; and when he died he was archbishop of Madrid-Alcalá.

[18] AGP, RHF, T–04956, p. 6.
[19] AGP, RHF, T–07921, p. 2 (Santiago Escrivá de Balaguer).
[20] Ibid., p. 31.
[21] AGP, RHF, T–05828, p. 5.

mother presided at the table, as the lady of the house.[22] And sometimes their compliments would put color in her cheeks, her pale complexion and silver hair highlighting the effect. "We are having guests today," she would tell Lola. "What bothers me the most is that I blush as if I were fifteen."[23]

Between the frequent retreats Father Josemaría gave outside Madrid and the heavy workload he had when he was in Madrid, whole weeks went by without Doña Dolores seeing her son, even though they lived under the same roof. She would say to Lola, as a soft refrain, "I haven't seen my son today"; "I still haven't seen him, he has so much to do"; "Nothing; he hasn't come."[24] At times it may have been for the best, since in that winter and in the spring of 1941 he had so much slander to put up with and all that the Grandmother could do when she learned of it was to suffer in silence and pray. "My son, you don't get one good day," she said sadly when they did meet.[25] But at least, at the very end of her life, she had the consolation of seeing the Work officially approved by the bishop of Madrid.

Hardworking and resilient, she seldom had to take to bed because of illness. Her only known health problem was occasional attacks of rheumatism, though the wartime privations undoubtedly had weakened her resistance.[26] Other than for Mass or to go shopping, she seldom left the house.

One day in April, by way of exception, some of her "grandsons" took her on an outing to El Escorial. The next day, she came down with a terrible headache and thought she had a bronchial infection. Later she developed a high fever and seemed to have some ordinary illness that was running its usual course. The two doctors who saw her, Juan Jiménez Vargas and a colleague of his, were not greatly alarmed.[27]

---

[22] AGP, RHF, T–07921, p. 31.

[23] AGP, RHF, T–04956/2, p. 4.

[24] Ibid., p. 5.

[25] AGP, P01 1978, p. 1099.

[26] In a letter written in August 1940, Father Josemaría had asked, "What's this about the Grandmother coughing up blood? She told me this herself, on the phone, but I didn't quite get it" (AGP, RHF, EF–400806–1).

[27] "How is the Grandmother doing?" asks Father Josemaría, in a letter dated April 14 (AGP, RHF, EF–410414–2). See also AGP, RHF, T–00159/1, p. 111 (Francisco Botella). Dr. Juan Jiménez Vargas adds, "It is important to point out that the Father left Madrid to give a retreat to priests in Lérida because the doctors (Alfredo Carrato and myself) assured him there was no reason to think his mother's illness would take a turn for the worse, and that it did not, of course, appear to be life-threatening. Our Father did not

Father Josemaría had been invited by the apostolic administrator of Lérida, Bishop Manuel Moll Salord, to give a retreat for the priests of his diocese.[28] As his date for departure approached, he kept asking the doctors about his mother's condition, and they kept setting his mind at ease, telling him that she seemed to be improving. So, on April 20, after asking her to offer her sufferings for the retreat, he said good-bye to her. As he was leaving the room, Doña Dolores, from her bed, said in a low voice, "This son of mine!"[29] It was as if she foresaw the sacrifice being asked of her.

The Father called from Saragossa and was told by Alvaro that his mother was continuing to improve. But even so, he had a premonition of the sacrifice being asked also of him. Upon arriving at the Lérida seminary, he went to the tabernacle and prayed, "Lord, take care of my mother, since I am looking after your priests."[30] Then he went to his room and wrote to the vicar general of Madrid:

> I just arrived in Lérida, and my conscience is bothering me because I didn't tell you I was coming here to give a priests' retreat. I didn't have enough time to see you. I only spoke with Lahiguera.
>
> I left my mother (in Madrid) pretty sick. Ask the Lord that, if this be his will, he not take her from me yet. I think he and I need her on earth.[31]

Twenty-four hours later, the Grandmother suddenly took a turn for the worse. The symptoms were those of traumatic pneumonia. She was given the last sacraments, and on the morning of April 22 she began a serene passage from this life to the next. She was, in fact, so calm that "on the morning of her death," relates Santiago, "I went to her room and said good-bye and left for the university, the same as every day."[32]

---

seem very convinced, but he left because the doctors were so sure about it" (AGP, RHF, T–04152–VIII, p. 22).

[28] See Laureano Castán Lacoma, in *Beato Josemaría Escrivá de Balaguer: un hombre de Dios. Testimonios sobre el Fundador del Opus Dei* (Madrid, 1994), pp. 105–107. (Hereafter this book will be cited as *Testimonios.*)

[29] See *Letter 8 Aug 1956*, no. 45.

[30] Ibid. Father Josemaría, despite what the doctors were telling him, had the feeling that "his mother's condition was very serious" (Juan Jiménez Vargas, *Sum.* 6713).

[31] AGP, RHF, EF–410420–1 (Letter to Monsignor Casimiro Morcillo).

[32] AGP, RHF, T–07921, p. 32.

As she was dying, Father Josemaría was preparing a talk on the role that a priest's mother has in her son's life. Here is his account:

> Halfway through the retreat, at noon, I gave them a talk. I spoke about the supernatural work, the incomparable role, that falls to the mother at the side of her priest-son. When I finished, I wanted to stay recollected for a little while in the chapel. But almost immediately the apostolic-administrator bishop, who was also making the retreat, came in, looking very pale, and said to me, "Alvaro is on the phone for you." And what I heard from Alvaro was, "Father, the Grandmother has died."
>
> I went back to the chapel, with not one tear. I saw right away that the Lord my God had done the best thing. And then I cried like a baby, praying out loud (I was alone with him) that long aspiration I so often recommend to you: *"Fiat, adimpleatur, laudetur, . . . iustissima atque amabilissima voluntas Dei super omnia. Amen. Amen."* ["May the most just and most lovable will of God be done, be fulfilled, be praised . . . above all things. Amen. Amen."] From then on, I have always thought that the Lord asked of me that sacrifice as an outward sign of my affection for diocesan priests, and that my mother in a special way continues to intercede for this work.[33]

The governor of Lérida, Juan Antonio Cremades, whom he had known since his years in Saragossa, placed a car at his disposal. But, because of a series of mishaps, it did not reach Madrid until four in the morning. Father Josemaría went into the oratory of the Diego de León center, where Doña Dolores's body was lying. After a quiet and restrained shedding of tears before his mother's remains, he asked Alvaro to join him in reciting a *Te Deum*.[34]

When he left the oratory and was filled in on some of the details about the death of the Grandmother, he filially protested, in a low voice, "My God, my God, what have you done? You're taking from me everything, absolutely everything. I thought these daughters of mine very much needed my mother, but you've left me with nothing.

---

[33] *Letter 8 Aug 1956*, no. 45. See also *The Way*, no. 691.
[34] See Alvaro del Portillo, *Sum.* 518. See also AGP, RHF, EF–410430–1 (a letter thanking Juan Antonio Cremades for his help).

Nothing!"[35] Then he got ready to say the Mass *de corpore insepulto* [before burial]. It was followed by others said by priest-friends of his.

The burial took place that afternoon. The funeral procession was led by Father Josemaría, Santiago, and Father José López Ortiz. Doña Dolores was buried in Madrid's La Almudena Cemetery.[36]

For Father Josemaría the whole episode underlined, among other things, the fact that God wanted to use him as an example for his children. He had not been able to be present at the death of either of his parents.[37] The more he thought about this, the more he saw in it a call to teach by way of his own experience lessons on detachment, because the day would come when many of his children, having traveled far and wide as the Work expanded, also would be absent when their parents died.

Two days after the burial, he gave a meditation in the oratory where his mother's body had lain. Looking at the tabernacle (as he often did), he prayed, "Lord, I am happy that you have shown this confidence in me. Because even though my children try to be present when their parents die, this won't always be possible, because of the needs of the apostolate. And you have wanted me, Lord, to lead by example also in this."[38]

2. *Approval of the Work as a Pious Union*

The last few months had been turbulent ones. In her final days, Doña Dolores had had to bear the pain of seeing her son publicly denigrated. Two days before her death, Father Josemaría wrote to Alvaro from Lérida: "Ask the Grandmother to offer up the sufferings of her illness for my intentions, which are none other than to ask the Lord that he cut short these trials—if this is his will—and that as long as they continue, he grant us joy and a supernatural outlook and a lot of charity in dealing with them."[39]

The end of the civil war had, as we have mentioned, brought a rebirth of piety and religious fervor to Spain. Associations and confraternities were reestablished, and the Marian sodalities run by the

---

[35] AGP, RHF, T–04956/2, p. 8 (María Dolores Fisac).

[36] See AGP, RHF, T–07921, p. 32 (Santiago Escrivá de Balaguer). The death certificate is in the Civil Register of Madrid, section 3, vol. 218, p. 301.

[37] See "The death of Don José," in chapter 3 (vol. I), pp. 134-138.

[38] AGP, RHF, T–04678/1, p. 21 (José Luis Múzquiz).

[39] AGP, RHF, EF–410420–2.

Jesuits were once more thriving in the principal cities. The head of the one in Barcelona was Father Manuel María Vergés, a gifted preacher with an imposing physical presence, a powerful voice, and a lot of zeal for the advancement of the sodality.[40] No important religious ceremony took place in the city without official participation by sodality members.

One of the biggest events was the solemn novena of the Immaculate Conception, which concluded on December 8. In 1940 Father Vergés announced that the preacher for that year's novena would be Father Angel Carrillo de Albornoz, S.J.; he would be coming from Madrid for that purpose. It promised to be a memorable event.

The novena was to take place in a church on Caspe Street—a church that was close to the Jesuit provincialate and to the Jesuit high school that was home to the sodality. Among the crowd of students who came to hear the preacher from Madrid were Rafael Escolá, who was studying industrial engineering, and his friend Juan Bautista Torelló, who later became a psychiatrist. On the first night of the novena they were greatly surprised to hear Father Carrillo quote from *The Way*. Rafael had joined the Work two months earlier and was using that book for his daily meditation, and Juan Bautista, though not yet a member, knew it almost by heart.

Not realizing what Father Carrillo was getting at, the two friends, without giving much importance to it, kept count of the references made to *The Way* from the pulpit. "Today there were seven!" "Today, eight!"[41] Actually the preacher was dissecting the book and extracting what he considered to be not in conformity with Catholic teaching, in order to warn sodality members against what he would later characterize as "the new heresy" being spread among the young. But neither Rafael nor Juan Bautista understood this. They could not imagine that a priest would publicly condemn a book bearing the bishop's imprimatur. At this time the only thing that struck them as strange was that the preacher did not name either the source or the author of these quotes.[42]

[40] This Jesuit, Father Manuel María Vergés i Furnells (1886–1956), had been director of Barcelona's "Sodality of Mary Immaculate and of St. Aloysius Gonzaga" since 1923. In 1953 he became superior of the House of the Sodalities of Our Lady. See Frederic Udina i Martorell, *El Pare Vergés, S.I., Apòstol de la Joventut / La Congregación de la Immaculada, 1923–1953* (Barcelona, 1995). See also the commemorative booklet for the centennial of Father Vergés's birth (Barcelona, 1986).

[41] See AGP, RHF, T–04837, p. 8 (Rafael Escolá), and Juan Bautista Torelló, *Sum.* 5195.

[42] Ibid.

The founder, meanwhile, knowing nothing about this attack, was urging his sons in Barcelona—few as they were, and little as they yet knew about the spirit of the Work—to be daring in their apostolate. Certain that our Lord would take them by the hand and give them whatever graces they needed to rise to the occasion, he encouraged them—when El Palau had just opened and was still without furniture—to establish a student residence. He wrote to them, "Will we have a *big house* in Barcelona by the next school year? It's up to you." [43]

Toward the middle of January 1941, Father Vergés gave what Santiago Balcells, a sodality member who was present, was to call "a sermon that made history." Santiago had heard of the Work but had not yet taken any real interest in it, though he was aware that his brother Alfonso was reading *The Way* and frequenting El Palau. (Alfonso, in fact, had let his name be used on the lease for that apartment, since of all the university students in Barcelona who were in contact with the Work, he was the only one who was old enough to sign a lease legally.)[44] Santiago would never forget the main points of that sermon, partly because they were so much discussed afterward among sodality members. He relates:

> As I recall, Father Vergés began by saying that very serious things were going on in the sodality because among us there were traitors. It was possible, he said, that some of us had in good faith been taken in by the propaganda of an association that, without the approval of the pope, or even of the bishop of the diocese, . . . was making itself out to possess a new spirituality, with new virtues. "Coercion, intransigence, shamelessness—since when are these things virtues?" he asked. . . .
>
> "Evidently," he said, "this 'new spirituality' permits its members to lie, because I know for a fact that some people who have denied to me that they are members are in fact members. They're also naïve, because if even among us priests and religious who are tonsured, wear a habit, and are subject to a regimen, things happen and occasionally some-

[43] AGP, RHF, EF–401115–1.
[44] See AGP, RHF, T–00158, p. 6. Alfonso had met the founder in 1938, during a visit that the Father made to Juan Jiménez Vargas at the Teruel front. Later, in September 1939, he took part in a retreat given by the founder at Burjasot. But it was not until 1943 that he asked admission to the Work.

one gives up the cloth, what's going to happen with these young men in suit and tie, who with nothing distinguishing them are free to go wherever they like? Practically speaking, there is no chance that they will persevere."[45]

If we put ourselves in the atmosphere of that time, it is not strange that some people (Father Carrillo and others) mistakenly thought that preaching about sanctification in the middle of the world was both dangerous and erroneous and that they would take strong measures as a result of their feelings. As we shall see, the founder of Opus Dei always felt that those in the Church who opposed the Work so strongly were doing it thinking that they were serving God by doing so (*Putantes obsequium se praestare Deo,* Jn 16:2).

In discussing certain events which are now a matter of past history, we should note that, for the faithful of Opus Dei who knew about them, they were a motive for a greater adherence to God's will, without making a negative judgment about the intentions of anyone. In this too they followed the example of Father Josemaria. We now see as a confirmation of what the Father predicted, that with the passage of time, other people, without seeing the situation in the framework of those years, repeated those false affirmations through an irresponsible and uncritical inertia. And there were also some who did so motivated by a desire to attack the Church.

Santiago, one of the few persons present who had any suspicion of what Father Vergés was getting at, pricked up his ears. The preacher then read article 28 of the Constitution of the Sodalities of Our Lady, which forbade members to join "any other association that was similar or had similar aims," and said that as the director and the person responsible for their souls, he intended to act in accord with it. His listeners were still wondering to whom he was referring when, unexpectedly, the speaker wrapped up his exhortation by saying that "he knew which ones were going around to the apartment at 62 Balmes Street, and that all those who went to that apartment, whether or not they belonged to the association over there, would be expelled from the sodality and erased from the Book of Our Lady."[46]

---

[45] AGP, RHF, T–07025, pp. 8–10. In regard to "holy coercion," "holy intransigence," and "holy shamelessness," see *The Way,* nos. 44, 387-391, 396, 398, 399, and the corresponding notes of the critical-historical edition prepared by Pedro Rodriguez (Madrid: Rialp, 2002).

[46] Ibid. See also Juan Bautista Torelló, *Sum.* 5195.

Those words had quite an impact. When the talk was over, some of those present came up to Santiago and asked about his brother Alfonso. But not even Santiago knew yet what had happened to his brother just an hour earlier.

This is Alfonso's account:

> One Sunday, when I was at the weekly meeting of the sodality, the Father Director, who was Father Vergés, S.J., called me aside and, with no preliminaries, told me that I was "expelled from the sodality." And when I, obviously surprised and having no idea what his reason was, asked him, "Father, why?" he just pointed to the door and said, "You are expelled as a traitor and a Judas to the sodality." [47]

This expulsion was followed by others. Father Vergés, acting on the reports of watchers he had posted in a café on Balmes Street, across the street from El Palau, thought he was acting responsibly.

Behind those thunderous attacks on this association that they felt was on a mistaken path and that was out to "reap what others have sown" (in other words, steal religious vocations) on the "pretext" that it was possible to attain sanctity in the midst of the world, was Father Carrillo. And, as had happened in Madrid, along with the doctrinal condemnations came fanciful reports about strange goings-on, probably the products of thoughtless students who allowed their imagination free rein. It was claimed that people at the Balmes Street apartment nailed themselves to the wooden cross in the oratory, and that they retreated into the solitude of mountaintops to meditate. (The latter story no doubt sprang from the fact that on their excursions to the mountains, they would say the Rosary while hiking or even stop to pray at the top.) [48]

---

[47] AGP, RHF, T–00158, p. 6.

[48] See Juan Bautista Torelló, *Sum.* 5195, and also AGP, RHF, T–04837, p. 9 (Rafael Escolá). As for the story about the cross in the oratory, Father José Luis Múzquiz testifies that one of the calumnies being spread back then was that "we were crucifying ourselves on that wooden cross." Years later, in a conversation with Bartolomé Roig, Father Múzquiz recalled that the first thing he had heard about the operations of the Work in Barcelona came to him from some students, friends of his, who told him that there were some students at Balmes Street who were performing "bloody rites on a wooden cross." When Father Josemaría found out about these rumors, he had that cross put away for later, or for another oratory, and replaced with a much smaller one. "That way," he joked, "they won't be able to say that we are crucifying ourselves, because we won't fit" (AGP, RHF, T–04678/1, p. 110).

*   *   *

In a letter dated January 14, 1941, briefly alluding to the suffering caused him by the slandering of the Work, the founder tells a friend that God "knows how to sweeten bitterness with honey," despite the fact that there are "too many people who do not understand or do not want to understand."[49] Bishop Eijo y Garay of Madrid, wanting the truth to be known, decided to proceed with the approval of the Work.[50]

Father Josemaría and the diocesan canonist, Father José María Bueno Monreal, having reached a dead end in their attempts to find a really suitable place for Opus Dei in canon law, took the stopgap measure of settling for the least inadequate solution. Because the members of Opus Dei were not religious but ordinary faithful, Father Bueno would later explain, "the only juridical path open in the canonical schema in force at that time was that of lay associations. Among these, Opus Dei clearly could not be a third order, nor a confraternity or sodality. So the only possibility left was for it to be classified as a pious union."[51]

After examining the bylaws and other constitutional documents of Opus Dei, the bishop returned them to Father Josemaría in the second week of February 1941, along with a sheet of paper on which he had penciled a few minor observations. A month later the founder gave him the definitive text, along with that sheet of paper. When the bishop saw those notes, he said to Father Josemaría, "If you see before God that it would be better not to go along with what I suggested, then don't, because you're the one to whom he has given the inspiration of the Work."[52]

---

[49] AGP, RHF, EF–410114–1 (Letter to Emiliano Amann).

[50] See AGP, RHF, D–15713.

[51] José María (Cardinal) Bueno Monreal, in *Testimonios*, pp. 39–40. This settling for the juridical status of a pious union did not close the door to future juridical possibilities. What was opted for was not an establishing, but a simple approval. "The provisional character of the decision was thus highlighted in anticipation of future developments. Thus was achieved the practical purpose for this intervention of the ecclesiastical authority on behalf of Opus Dei: public recognition of its existence by the bishop of the diocese, manifestation of the appreciation and support of the hierarchy, and the proclamation that in its nature, ends, and norms of life, there is nothing contrary to Church teachings": Amadeo de Fuenmayor, Valentín Gómez Iglesias, and José Luis Illanes, *The Canonical Path of Opus Dei*, trans. William H. Stetson (Princeton, 1994), p. 92.

[52] AGP, RHF, D–15402. On the same occasion, the bishop gave Father Josemaría a copy of the request being sent to Rome for permission for the founder to use a portable altar when celebrating Mass for young people or university students at retreats and monthly days of recollection. The bishop had signed the copy with these words: "A

On March 20, Father Josemaría sent to the chancery office a petition for approval of Opus Dei as a pious union. On March 24, around noon, the phone rang at Diego de León, and Father Josemaría answered. It was the bishop. He had issued the decree of approval. The founder shared the joyful news with Doña Dolores, Carmen, and the three or four others who happened to be home, and then went to the oratory to say a *Te Deum*.

Elsewhere, the first to receive the news were those at El Palau. The telegram said simply, "Approved. Mariano." [53]

On March 25, Monsignor Morcillo gave the decrees of approval to Father Josemaría. [54] In passing, he mentioned that just after the decrees were signed, Archbishop Gaetano Cicognani, the papal nuncio, had happened to stop by the bishop's residence. Bishop Eijo y Garay, he said, could hardly wait to tell the archbishop what he had just done.

---

request that I wrote, submitted, and personally recommended in Rome in May 1940. Leopoldo, Bishop of Madrid-Alcalá." When handing him the document, he said, "This is for in case I die. Keep it in your files, as irrefutable proof of how you always turned to your bishop in connection with your apostolic work." See AGP, RHF, D–15402 and D–15714–1. For the text of the statutes ("Regulae"), see Fuenmayor, Gómez-Iglesias, and Illanes, pp. 480–82.

[53] When praying the Preces of the Work with his sons that evening, the Father repeated the prayer for the bishop three times. And on that same day he wrote to Father Eliodoro Gil to give him the news. See Alvaro del Portillo, *Sum.* 551; José Luis Múzquiz, *Sum.* 5843; AGP, RHF, EF–410324–1 (Letter to Father Eliodoro Gil Rivera); AGP, RHF, T–07025, p. 18 (Santiago Balcells); and AGP, RHF, T–04696, p. 8 (Laureano López Rodó).

[54] There were two decrees: one of approval of Opus Dei, and another concerning custody of the documents that had been presented for obtaining the approval. The first one reads:

> Having reviewed the preceding petition of Father José María Escrivá de Balaguer, and after having examined in detail the documents on the statutes, regulations, norms, customs, and ceremonies of Opus Dei, founded by the said priest and carried out with our blessing and with that of our vicar general since 1928, we have decided by the present decree to canonically approve Opus Dei as a pious union in conformity with canon 708 of the current Code of Canon Law. And we ask our Lord God, through the intercession of Saint Joseph, on whose feast day we have the pleasure of canonically approving such an important work of zeal, to grant that none of the great fruits we are expecting from it will fail to materialize. For the safeguarding of the copies of the *Statutes*, etc., what is stipulated in the special decree shall be complied with.
> Madrid, March 19, 1941
> Signed and sealed: Leopoldo, Bishop of Madrid-Alcalá

The decree of custody of the documents reads:

> Having on this date canonically approved Opus Dei, a pious union founded with our authorization and blessing in the year 1928, and taking into account the discreet reserve that needs to be kept for the greater glory of God and

"Your Excellency," he said, "we have just approved the Work of Father José María Escrivá."

"Yes, . . . oh, yes, he wrote a book of maxims . . . *The Way*," said Archbishop Cicognani, sounding as if trying to recall something he had been told by someone.

When he left, Bishop Eijo y Garay asked Monsignor Morcillo, "Do you think the nuncio has been warned against José María?"

"Escrivá told me that those people wanted to bring his book to Rome to have it condemned," Monsignor Morcillo replied. "Could they have done that already?"[55]

From March 30 to April 5 Father Josemaría was in Valencia, giving a retreat for the young ladies in Catholic Action, and during that time, when he had a chance to read the decree more closely, he found his joy at the bishop's approval of the Work somewhat diminished. The original text, which had been prepared with such affection by Bishop Eijo y Garay, had been changed substantially. The nuncio, as the bishop had suspected, knew all about the rumors and slanders against Opus Dei, and, fearful of wounding third parties or involving Church authorities in a confrontation, had counseled the bishop to eliminate anything that could in any way be interpreted as excessive. Bishop Eijo y Garay had therefore had to change the text from one of clear, strong, unreserved praise, for an institution promising great spiritual benefits for the diocese and for the universal Church, to one that, though still laudatory, lacked the force needed to proclaim the truth once and for all.[56]

But the Lord, as always, sweetened the bitterness with honey. For that retreat in Valencia produced two vocations of women. On April 6, the day after the retreat, Encarnita Ortega and Enrica Botella went to the residence on Samaniego Street, to be introduced by Father Josemaría to the members there.

---

efficacy of the Work, we stipulate that the copies of the documents on its statutes, regulations, norms, customs, spirit, and ceremonies will be kept in our private archives.
Madrid, March 19, Feast of the glorious Saint Joseph, 1941
Signed and sealed: Leopoldo, Bishop of Madrid-Alcalá

These decrees were (as was customary with such documents) kept in the private archive of the Diocese of Madrid-Alcalá. The texts can be found in Fuenmayor, Gómez-Iglesias, and Illanes, pp. 482–83.

[55] AGP, RHF, D–30002 (a note dated 25 Mar 1941).

[56] See Alvaro del Portillo, *Sum.* 551, and Javier Echevarría, *Sum.* 2151 and 2152.

At Mass that morning, he had been given a divine locution assuring him that the nuncio would not allow himself to be swayed by the attacks on the Work. He describes in a letter what had happened:

> On Palm Sunday in 1941, at Mass, after Communion, I was contemplating the dark outlook and the—at least humanly speaking—powerful forces opposing us, and on our side I saw nothing but my weakness as our only defense. Deeply distressed, I set out before the Lord the current situation. And the interior locution—without words, like almost all those I've received in my life, but very clear and precise—was this: "For things to get better, they have to get worse; you will have easier access to the nunciature than to the bishop's residence." This, at the time, did not seem possible. When I got back to Madrid I gave Alvaro a written account, and he was—like me—amazed but sure of its authenticity. Events soon confirmed the divine message.[57]

He went to see Bishop Eijo y Garay, who expressed his joy saying. "At least this persecution has resulted in the Work's getting its approval, since neither you nor I had been in any hurry about that before."[58]

3. *Events in Barcelona*

Bishop Eijo y Garay had expected his approval to staunch the torrent of—objectively slanderous—criticism. But the attacks soon resumed— even more forcefully. The divine locution that "for things to get better, they have to get worse" was already beginning to come true. This time the center of the storm was Barcelona.

---

[57] *Letter 29 Dec 1947/14 Feb 1966*, no. 12. A sheet of paper 1941 has been preserved on which Father Josemaria briefly described this locution on that April 6,: AGP, Sec. L. 1, Leg. 16. See also Alvaro del Portillo, *Sum.* 551.

[58] AGP, RHF, D–30003. The Work, as mentioned earlier, was approved, but not established, as a pious union. Canon 686 of the 1917 Code stated: "No association that has not been established or at least approved by a legitimate ecclesiastical authority will be recognized by the Church." Unlike other associations (confraternities, for example), a pious union could be either established (i.e., formally constituted as a corporate entity) or simply approved. In the latter case, said another canon (708), the ecclesiastical authority's act of jurisdiction "does not constitute the association as a corporate entity, but gives it the right to exist and the capacity to obtain spiritual graces and especially indulgences." See Fuenmayor, Gómez-Iglesias, and Illanes, p. 92.

Just after Father Josemaría arrived in Lérida to give that priests' retreat during which his mother died, Alvaro del Portillo phoned him to say that a new and severe attack on Opus Dei had broken out in Barcelona. That very day (April 20, 1941), he sent his sons in Madrid a letter of instructions on how to deal with it, and asked Alvaro to pass them on to those at El Palau.

> I won't write them; you do it, and tell them that they should be very happy and grateful to our Lord, and not allow themselves even one word—or even one thought!—that is uncharitable. Tell them they can be sure that Jesus is going to do great and wonderful things, for his glory, in Barcelona, if we bear this as he wants us to. . . .
>
> Do they, in Barcelona, have Ribadeneyra's biography of Saint Ignatius? If not, send them a copy. I want all of you to have a devotion to and a love for Saint Ignatius and his blessed Society.
>
> Ask the Grandmother to offer up the sufferings of her illness for my intentions, which are none other than to ask the Lord that he cut short these trials—if this is his will—and that as long as they continue, he grant us joy and a supernatural outlook and a lot of charity in dealing with them.
>
> May you all have a great love for the Church! I give everyone permission to do some extraordinary penance—*with prudence and after asking permission.* But above all, let everyone approach the tabernacle and the Blessed Virgin with constant prayer and petition.
>
> *Gaudium cum pace!* If we had all the riches in the world, we could never repay God for this joy that you and I—sinner that I am!—have in our souls and on our faces, from seeing that we have been deemed worthy to suffer for Jesus Christ.[59]

[59] AGP, RHF, EF–410420–2. In a letter, dated May 12, to his sons in Valencia (AGP, RHF, EF–410512–1), he explains in more detail what they should do if "presented with the same propitious circumstances" as are his sons in Barcelona:
+ May Jesus bless my sons and watch over them.
My dear children:
The Lord has permitted that holy people, very dear to my heart, are slandering us and doing us harm. Should you also find yourselves affected by the storm of persecution—a divine seal authenticating supernatural undertakings—I give you these instructions, that are so in keeping with the spirit of Opus Dei: (1) always heed the directives of the ecclesiastical authority,

The campaign began with visits by a number of religious to the homes of those who had requested admission to Opus Dei or were frequenting El Palau. They peppered parents and other relatives with arguments against Opus Dei backed up by their moral authority. In the face of this barrage of criticism, who could defend the cause of a new organization represented by a handful of young students and having no public or official endorsement from the Church? Rafael Escolá gives us a good picture of the situation:

> They visited my family to tell them that the Work was "a very dangerous heresy," that we were "being duped, little by little," that the founder was "diabolical," and that we were forbidden to go to confession. Because we did mental prayer, they called us "illuminati." They also claimed that we prac-ticed "invented rituals" . . . My brothers and sisters tried to dissuade me from what they called my "mental confusion." My whole family suffered for years, until the truth, little by little, became clear to them.[60]

This family had already had its share of suffering during the civil war: Rafael had been jailed by the Communists while still a boy.[61] And now to be told that this son who had been saved from death was headed for hell!

José Orlandis, another member of the Work, was in Barcelona to see his father, who was convalescing in a hospital. In a letter to Father Josemaría, dated May 21, he described the conduct of the people of the Work and the sufferings they experienced in connection with their families:

---

i.e., the archbishop and his vicar general; (2) never say anything to anyone outside the house about such events, if they take place; (3) be very charitable, never on any pretext saying one word against the persecutors; (4) much joy and much peace; (5) much prayer, much study, and many small mortifica-tions.

Everything is going very well. I didn't know that the Lord loved us this much. How well my sons in Barcelona have conducted themselves! I don't expect anything less from my sons in Valencia, should they be presented with the same propitious circumstances.

Gaudium cum pace!

You are loved, envied (!), and blessed by your Father,

Mariano

[60] AGP, RHF, T–04837, p. 10.

[61] See Joan Marquès Suriñach, *Testigos de la Fe durante la Guerra Civil (1936–1939): Sacerdotes y laicos cuentan sus vivencias* (Girona, 1994), pp. 31–55.

They are putting into practice what you wrote them from Lérida and not permitting themselves even uncharitable thoughts. And as for the Jesuit fathers who have most directly and actively opposed the Work—expelling its members from the sodality, publicly calling them Masons or something similar, and in some cases making even their mothers and brothers and sisters mourn them as heretics headed for perdition—when they speak of these priests, they do it as you said to. They speak of them with affection, in a tone of voice not at all put-on. They excuse the conduct of these priests by saying they are motivated by zeal and convinced they are doing the right thing.

And what I'm telling you about their families considering them heretics is no exaggeration. Rafa Escolá is suffering tremendously. "You can't imagine what it's like," he told me yesterday. "At home, my mother and all five of my brothers and sisters see me as a heretic on the road to perdition. All day long they keep me under observation, tracking my every least move, and everything I do seems suspicious to them. If they see me sad, they say, 'That's only natural. You're sad because you know what an evil path you've taken.' And when they see me filled with joy and peace, to them this is even worse. 'Now he's a lost cause,' they say. 'There's no hope of his turning back. The evil has taken hold of him; he must already be a hardened heretic.' My mother can't speak to me or even look at me without her eyes filling up with tears. And the worst thing is that there has come between us a kind of coldness." But Rafa's reaction to all this pain and suffering is truly admirable: "I am happy to be able to offer this to God for the Work, and in the midst of these trials I feel a great joy that our Lord is letting me suffer a little for him."

And all the others have this same spirit that Rafa has.[62]

To all this there was soon added a distributing of flyers in ecclesiastical circles—anonymous flyers filled with false accusations against the Work and its founder.[63] More bad news seemed to be coming

---

[62] AGP, RHF, D–15286.

[63] Father Rufino Aldabalde received and kept one of these flyers. In it (see AGP, RHF, EF–410514–1), he wrote, "Given by a Jesuit father to the superior of St. Philip Neri in Barcelona on May 7, 1941." It reads [*cont. page 346*]:

every day. Each morning Father Josemaría would ask Alvaro, "My son, from which direction will they attack us today?" [64]

The founder knew that while God was their ultimate support, he too was responsible for the strength of the Work and the peace of his sons, and so could not allow himself to become pessimistic or lose his serenity. On May 12 he wrote to Rafael Termes, the director of El Palau:

> + May Jesus bless my sons and watch over them.
> My dear sons:
> We should rejoice that our Lord has seen fit to treat us in a divine manner.
> What can I tell you? Be happy, *spe gaudentes* [rejoicing in hope]. Bear suffering with charity, with never a word against anyone; *in tribulatione patientes!* And be filled with a spirit of prayer—*orationi instantes!* [constant in prayer!].
> An embrace from your Father,
>
> Mariano[65]

He rejoiced in soul to suffer for Christ, but his body showed the strain, and he wound up sick in bed. Thanking the bishop of Barcelona for his condolences on his mother's death, he wrote:

> I've dragged myself out of bed to write you this letter—I am suffering a lot! And yet I wouldn't trade places with the happiest man on earth. The last thirteen years have been like

---

Opus Dei
Rules and Directives for Its Members

Be reticent with your spiritual director, always keeping from him the fact that you belong to Opus Dei.

No religious-order priest is Catholic. / Do not go on retreats. / Perfection is found only among us. / Say nothing to your confessor about the Work, because we believe he cannot understand us. / The outlook of the religious congregations is not adequate for the 20th century. / Father Escrivá, author of the book *The Way*, is the spiritual director of the institution. / We have to be few and select. / We do not accept religious-order priests, but we do accept diocesan clergy. This practice has been in effect for a little over a year. / Cardinal Gomá said before he died that Catholic Action should expel such individuals, since they are looking to it for members. / Holy coercion. Holy shamelessness. Holy intransigence. / Where you see a wooden cross without a corpus, that is where you have to be crucified.

[64] *Letter 29 Dec 1947/14 Feb 1966*, no. 8.
[65] AGP, RHF, EF–410502–2.

that. The spirit is willing, with the grace of God; but the body, at times, breaks down.

I want you to know that I feel a deep gratitude toward our Lord, because at the same time that he has permitted persons so holy and so dear to my heart to maltreat us, he also has arranged, knowing our weakness (mine that is), that the bishops who know us should to a man encourage and console and defend us.[66]

His health stayed bad for quite a while, though he tried not to show it. Two weeks later, he was also sick in bed when a call came from Bishop Eijo y Garay. As soon as he could get up, he wrote to Bishop Leopoldo:

My esteemed and very dear Bishop:

They tell me that you called yesterday evening. I was in bed. Yesterday the Lord didn't let me celebrate Mass or receive Communion. All morning I had a slight fever and was throwing up. Today I'm fine. It's the *animalis homo* rebelling, because the "other man" is very happy.[67]

On one of those nights when he was feeling especially upset by the insults made to his honor as a priest, he got up and went to the oratory. (At Diego de León, the oratory was next to his bedroom.) Prostrating himself before the tabernacle, he prayed, "Lord, if you don't need my good name, why should I want it?"[68] Then, leaving things in God's hands, he peacefully went back to bed.

An idea, nevertheless, kept gnawing at him. If the decree of approval was not enough to silence the gossipers, might not the honor of the Work be vindicated if he, its founder, were to appear before an ecclesiastical tribunal that would render judgment on his orthodoxy? On May 4 he wrote to Bishop Leopoldo:

I don't have any tears left for crying: Our Lord has asked of me my good name and my mother. I think I've given them to him with all my heart. The body, at times, gives out, but deep in my soul I constantly experience the truth of those words we read in today's Gospel, "*et gaudium vestrum nemo*

---

[66] AGP, RHF, EF–410430–5.
[67] AGP, RHF, EF–410517–2.
[68] *Letter 29 Dec 1947/14 Feb 1966*, no. 38.

tollet a vobis!" ["and no one will take your joy from you": Jn 16:22].

My bishop: Hasn't the time come for me to be judged by a tribunal, so that this whole affair can be brought into the clear light of day?

Just the thought that I could be straying, even slightly, from the teachings of the Holy Roman Church—my Mother!—is very painful to me.

Your Excellency can do with me as he wishes. The Lord has given me a great sense of security regarding my actions—a sense of security resting on the certitude that I have never done or said anything without the approval of the bishop of whatever place, and especially the bishop of Madrid and his vicar generals.[69]

That same day, a Sunday, just when he had finished giving his sons a meditation during exposition of the Blessed Sacrament, the phone rang, and it was Bishop Eijo y Garay. In the note he wrote the next morning about that call, the founder said: "I want to put it on record that the words of our bishop are a source of great joy. They savor of God. Today all these worries don't seem to be weighing on me—I think I'm even beginning to enjoy them. Laus Deo!"[70]

4. *Opus Dei: "An extremely hot topic"*

With the attacks on the Work continuing unabated in Barcelona, repercussions started to reach other cities. Father Josemaría, besides continuing to seek excuses for the perpetrators, also spoke and wrote to some of them in the hope of getting them to mend their ways. One of these was Father Angel Basterra, a Jesuit priest with whom he had been on friendly terms in the years of the Republic and who was now circulating the accusations in Bilbao. Trying not to provoke more dissension, he communicated to him by letter the news that the Work had been canonically approved. In this letter he says:

Just two comments: that the people spreading these rumors do not know the facts; and that I have never said one word

[69] AGP, RHF, EF–410504–1.
[70] AGP, RHF, D–30004, nos. 31–32.

about the blessed and most beloved Society of Jesus that was not filled with respect and affection for it. And now, when the conduct of certain of its priests is causing me so much suffering, I am carefully reading Ribadeneyra's biography of Saint Ignatius, and I find my love and veneration for the Society and its glorious founder growing, if possible, even stronger. I am learning a lot from the fortitude with which Ignatius and his first followers bore persecutions, calumnies, and misunderstandings coming from exemplary religious.

The truth will come to light. In the meantime, I feel, not forgiveness for those offenses, but affection for the people behind them and a willingness to forget what they have done.

In addition, I am happy to be able to communicate to you that on this past March 19, feast of my father and lord Saint Joseph, the Work received canonical approval.

For the sake of charity, my dear Father; for love of the Church; because of the unfortunate scandal being given to so many souls; for the sake of justice; and in remembrance of those bitter days that the first members of that most beloved Society of Jesus went through, I beg that you, recalling the many good things you said about our apostolic work before the calumnies reached your ears, do all that you can with your prayers and your influence to put an end to this unfortunate campaign (which is being carried out in every place and way possible, including from the pulpit), from which only the enemy of souls benefits. No, that's not true, since we ourselves feel such supernatural interior joy that we will gladly suffer for Jesus and for the service of the Church (our vocation being none other than this), and never from any of us will there be one word of protest against those good priests, who are instruments of God. He is treating his Work in the divine manner in which he usually treats new foundations.

Pray for this sinner, who loves you and who will always continue to love all of you.

Josemaría[71]

---

[71] AGP, RHF, EF–410430–4. For more on the previous relationship between the founder and Father Basterra, see *Apuntes*, no. 1319 (28 Feb 1936), no. 1326 (25 Mar 1936), no. 1330 (18 Apr 1936), no. 1519 (31 Jan 1938), and no. 1520 (1 Feb 1938).

By now, though, many lay Catholics had been confused by the anonymous flyers and by the derogatory statements made in sermons.[72] Upset by the rumors, some sought clarification and advice at Montserrat, a Benedictine monastery which was a focal point of spiritual life in Catalonia and which was not far from Barcelona. Dom Aurelio María Escarré, the coadjutor abbot of Montserrat, acting on the suggestion of Bishop Marcelino Olaechea of Pamplona, whom he had queried about Opus Dei, wrote to the bishop of Madrid a letter requesting information on it. The relevant paragraph reads:

> Now I need to ask you a favor. An extremely hot topic at the moment is that of "Opus Dei," the foundation of Father Escrivá, a priest of your diocese. Many people have consulted us on this matter, especially in the confessional, and so that we might know what advice we should give, we would like some clear guidelines. . . . I humbly ask you to expedite my request, in light of the urgency of the situation here.[73]

In the midst of all that confusion, three members of the Marian sodality asked admission to Opus Dei, in January, March, and April of 1941. The three were Laureano López Rodó, Juan Bautista Torelló, and Jorge Brosa. Laureano submitted his resignation from the sodality in writing, without waiting to be expelled. Later, Father Vergés visited the family.[74]

---

[72] A story told by Laureano López Rodó illustrates how things were at that time in ecclesiastical and religious circles. "I recall," he says, "that on one occasion Father Pascual Galindo, a priest-friend of the founder, came to Barcelona and visited us at El Palau. He insisted that, on the next day, we attend the Mass he would be saying at a high school run by nuns; it was at the corner of Diagonal and Rambla de Cataluña. We went to the Mass, and we received Communion (which back then was not a common practice). The superior and some other nun present there were very 'edified,' and they invited us to have breakfast with Father Galindo. In the middle of breakfast, Father Pascual said to the superior, 'These are the heretics for whose conversion you asked me to offer the Mass.' The poor nun almost fainted. She had been made to believe that we were a vast legion of card-carrying heretics, and she found that we were a handful of ordinary, run-of-the-mill students who attended Mass devoutly and received Communion" (AGP, RHF, T–004696, p. 5).

[73] Letter of Dom Aurelio María Escarré to Bishop Leopoldo Eijo y Garay, dated 9 May 1941. The correspondence between Dom Escarré and Bishop Eijo y Garay is in Montserrat's archive, except for the abbot's letter of 3 Nov 1941 to the bishop, the original of which is in AGP, RHF, D–03545–5.

[74] See AGP, RHF, T–04696, p. 7 (Laureano López Rodó). See also Juan Bautista Torelló, *Sum.* 5196, and AGP, RHF, T–07025, p. 10 (Santiago Balcells).

Juan Bautista suffered more than most. Not only was he expelled from the sodality, but he had two brothers who were Jesuits, a sister who was a nun, and a mother who had been widowed. While studying at the university, he had been teaching math at a Jesuit high school to help support the family. After his expulsion, he lost this teaching position.[75]

As for Alfonso Bacells, in whose name El Palau had been rented, he was on that account considered directly responsible for all the activities that took place there. His brother Santiago recalls that, because the apartment was in his name, Father Vergés refused to believe that he was not in the Work.

Those priests, thinking it their duty to eliminate what they considered a grave danger, brought the civil authorities into the case. Alfonso was summoned before the governor of Barcelona, Antonio Correa Veglison. The governor told him that he wanted to know what kind of activities were going on in that apartment, and that it would be useless to try to hide anything. He already knew everything, he said, because he was good friends with the Jesuits. He knew from them that the Work was "a sect of illuminati, or something of the sort." And, he said, if Alfonso did not spill the beans, he and all the others would end up in jail.[76] Alfonso's explanations helped calm him down, but he remained on the alert lest Father Josemaría show up in Barcelona.[77]

---

[75] Juan Bautista Torelló, *Sum.* 5195.

[76] See AGP, RHF, T–00158, p. 8 (Alfonso Balcells), and T–04696, p. 4 (Laureano López Rodó). Father José Luis Múzquiz testifies that on July 24, 1941, Father Josemaría, "after a telephone conversation in which we were told that the governor of Barcelona, as a result of what Father Vergés had told him, wanted to take forceful measures against us, had us immediately say an Our Father for that priest" (AGP, RHF, D–15406).

[77] See *Letter 29 Dec 1947/14 Feb 1966,* no. 35. See also Alvaro del Portillo, *Sum.* 419; Juan Bautista Torelló, *Sum.* 5195; and AGP, RHF, T–04837, pp. 9–11 (Rafael Escolá).

On September 1, Dom Escarré wrote to Bishop Eijo y Garay about Correa Veglison: "I do have a very clear idea, after getting myself informed by a number of very reliable sources, of what the governor is saying and doing. Certainly he is a devout person, and therefore I think he is well-intentioned, but he is very biased in this matter. He has spoken out too quickly and has acted erroneously in giving more credence to Father Vergés than to the Church hierarchy. He is imbued with what that priest, who is the main source of the persecution in Barcelona, has said to him against Opus Dei, and so it is no wonder that he gives credence to that whole myth about a mysterious, deceitful secret society. If Father Vergés weren't pulling his strings, he would have turned to the abundant sources of sound information and taken the sober and impartial view that it is his duty to take" (AGP, RHF, D–03545–4).

Two months later he wrote: "I believe you have heard about the change of opinion of the governor with regard to Opus Dei. It is due especially to the two letters that Your Excellency was so good as to send me, which I had an employee deliver to him so that he could get a better grasp of the facts. Now it is quite clear that if he did anything

In this postwar period, when civil liberties were dangerously dependent upon religious beliefs, Alfonso Balcells found himself compromised by his ties to the Work in still another context. In May a doctor he had known from medical school told him that efforts were under way to keep him from taking the competitive examination for a position at the hospital clinic, because of his membership in a heretical sect. He went immediately to the bishop of Barcelona, Bishop Miguel de los Santos Gómara, who received him warmly and advised him to write to Bishop Eijo y Garay and tell him in detail what was happening.[78]

The bishop of Madrid sent this brief response, dated June 2: "Our Lord God will reward all of you. Suffer this for him and for his Work, and with much charity and forgiveness. Steps are already being taken to ensure that this outrageous assault does not succeed. I am also writing to your bishop. I think the storm will quickly be calmed."[79]

In January 1943, after a year of postgraduate work abroad, Alfonso asked admission to Opus Dei.[80]

*   *   *

Things did not get better; on the contrary, they kept getting worse. On May 2 Father Josemaría wrote to his bishop:

> The terribly difficult situation of my sons in Catalonia, which has now gone on far too long, is breaking my heart. I'm writing these lines because I can't hide anything from my bishop and I need to open my heart like a son to Your Excellency.[81]

The founder was in danger of being arrested if he went to Barcelona. Then again, that threat existed even in Madrid. There, too, anonymous denunciations had been made to the civil authorities. Those were the months when the vicar general, Monsignor Morcillo, was warning him in all seriousness, "José María, watch out, they may put you in jail any day."[82]

---

against Opus Dei, it was due to the influence of Father Vergés, S.J." (AGP, RHF, D–03545–5).

[78] See AGP, RHF, T–00158, p. 8.

[79] AGP, RHF, D–30007.

[80] See AGP, RHF, T–00158, p. 9.

[81] AGP, RHF, EF–410502–1.

[82] *Letter 29 Dec 1947/14 Feb 1966*, no. 50.

He concluded that he had to go to Barcelona to see his sons and to speak with the bishop, and by the middle of May he was looking for the right moment to do so. On May 19 he wrote to Father Sebastián Cirac, "It's possible that we'll see each other very soon."[83] Father Cirac (the canon in Cuenca who had overseen the printing of *Consideraciones espirituales* in 1934) stood up for the Work throughout this difficult period.

The founder had ordered his sons to refrain for the time being from any external apostolic activity at El Palau and to suspend until further notice their meetings with students who might have vocations to Opus Dei.[84] But these prudent measures had no discernible effect. And so, recognizing that he had to confront the source of the problem, Father Carrillo de Albornoz, Father Josemaría drafted a letter to him. Bishop Eijo y Garay revised it slightly, changing several words that seemed to bespeak excessive humility.

> Madrid, May 20, 1941
> Rev. Father Angel Carrillo de Albornoz
> My dear brother in the Lord:
>
> I write you these lines, that are filled with cordiality and sincere affection, to make it known to you that one hears on all sides that you are the source of a campaign of defamation against the brother who is writing this letter, and against his poor priestly efforts, which the Holy Church has approved. . . .
>
> In that campaign of defamation, tactics are being employed which no ordinary Christian could use. As long as it was aimed only at my poor self, which richly deserves every form of abuse, I kept quiet. . . . But I think I have a duty to tell you, before our Lord God, that people unconnected with me are being hurt.
>
> I have been told, through various channels, that you intend not to stop until you see Opus Dei destroyed. To this I say only these words from Acts: "*Si ex hominibus est consilium hoc*

---

[83] AGP, RHF, EF–410519–1.

[84] He wrote to Rafael Termes, the director of El Palau, "Don't concern yourself right now with doing any proselytizing. Let God act. However, do this for me: increase your life within, having more love every day for the Holy Roman Church" (AGP, RHF, EF–410506–1).

aut opus, dissolvetur; si vero ex Deo est, non poteritis dissolvere illud ne forte et Deo repugnare inveniamini" ["If this plan or this undertaking is of men, it will fail; but if it is of God, you will not be able to overthrow them. You might even be found opposing God": Acts 5: 38–39].

Father Carrillo, the truth will come to light, and I am sure that we will end up being good friends. I have nothing to-ward you except fraternal good will and an earnest desire to forget everything that could obscure that affection.

In the meantime, be assured that we will never utter a word against those who are so cruelly persecuting us. With the grace of God, we will always be prepared to suffer with great joy whatever we may have to for Jesus Christ and for the service of our Mother the Holy Church. That is our vocation. Your brother and devoted servant in Christ,

Father J. M. Escrivá [85]

He sent the letter in care of Father Daniel Ruiz, superior of the house in which Father Carrillo lived, enclosing a note to Father Ruiz saying, "I humbly request that you read the attached letter and, if it seems opportune to you, put it in the hands of Father Carrillo." [86] He had high hopes of everything getting straightened out.

The next day, May 21, he made a phone call to the nunciature to tell Archbishop Cicognani that he was thinking of going to Barcelona. "Use an assumed name," the nuncio advised, thinking of the mea-sures taken by the governor.[87] Father Josemaría planned to be back in Madrid by the twenty-third, and asked for an appointment for Satur-day, the twenty-fourth, at the nunciature.

A few hours later he left for Barcelona by plane, with a ticket in the name of José María Balaguer. Upon arriving, he went to the bishop's residence to report to Bishop Miguel de los Santos and find out how things stood locally, then, having arranged as a precaution to stay with Father Sebastián Cirac, he met his sons at Father Cirac's house. There, at the dining room table, he gave them a spiritual pep talk. "Since we are children of God," he said, "we should always be joyful. Even if they crack our head open? Yes, even if we have to go around

[85] AGP, RHF, EF–410520–1.
[86] AGP, RHF, EF–410520–2.
[87] See *Letter 29 Dec 1947/14 Feb 1966*, no. 35.

with a cracked-open head, since that would be a sign that our Father-God wants us to go around like that."[88] After talking with each of them, one on one, he returned to Madrid.

When on Saturday, at noon, he arrived at the nunciature, he was told by the porter that the nuncio was at that moment speaking with the Jesuit provincial. Archbishop Cicognani came in soon and took him to a different sitting room. "Meeting the provincial wouldn't have bothered me in the least," Father Josemaría thought to himself, "since neither in my head nor in my heart do I have anything against the blessed Society of Jesus."[89]

The nuncio wanted to hear about the Work. Father Josemaría told him all about its nature and mission: service to the Church, sanctity in the midst of the world. He spoke in detail about its spirituality and about its docility to the local bishop, and also volunteered a good deal of information about his own life. Then he asked the archbishop if he had seen the anonymous flyers against Opus Dei that were being circulated in Barcelona, and when he said no, Father Josemaría went on to describe them. Archbishop Cicognani said that he also had not seen the statutes of the Work, but would like to, and Father Josemaría promised to bring him a copy.

"He gave me a very friendly good-bye. I left with a very good feeling," he wrote in a note on that meeting.[90]

As he weighed up the facts, the nuncio saw the situation more clearly. And so when the founder came a second time, on June 10, bringing the promised copy of the statutes, their conversation was even friendlier. Father Josemaría had the opportunity to explain how the members of the Work were reacting to the calumnies and insults and trying to live collective humility in service to the Church.

Right after that visit, he wrote to Bishop Eijo y Garay, describing the nuncio as "very friendly" and adding, "I have an even better feeling than I had the other time. He understands our way perfectly."[91]

Archbishop Cicognani started hearing more and more about the commotion. It was a subject that came up often in his conversations with the bishops. Not being fond of dissensions to begin with, he found this one inexcusable, especially since it involved priests. In

[88] AGP, RHF, T–04696, p. 6 (Laureano López Rodó).
[89] AGP, RHF, D–30006 (a note dated 24 May 1941).
[90] Ibid.
[91] AGP, RHF, EF–410610–1. (This and other private letters were personally returned to the founder by Bishop Eijo y Garay.)

mid-June, the bishop of Pamplona, having just spoken with Archbishop Cicognani, told Alvaro del Portillo, "The nuncio is for Father Josemaría."[92]

Meanwhile, the hopes for a possible retraction by Father Carrillo collapsed like a house of cards. Indeed, the reply from Father Daniel Ruiz suggested further complications ahead.

> Madrid, May 23, 1941
> Father José M. Escrivá
> My dear brother in Jesus Christ:
>
> On my return to Barcelona I received your letter dated May 20, with the one for Father Angel Carrillo de Albornoz. Since you left it to my discretion whether or not to give that letter to the person it was addressed to, it seems to me appropriate that I write you directly, expressing my views on the matter it deals with. As superior of the residence and as director of the San Luis Sodality, I am well acquainted with the thoughts and doings of Father Carrillo de Albornoz, since he and I are of one mind.
>
> I am extremely surprised that you can say so matter-of-factly and with such conviction that a violent campaign has been unleashed against your Work. To me it is obvious that the reality is the exact opposite: that is to say, that you people have done things intended to discredit and defame the Society of Jesus and, in particular, the Marian sodalities. It causes one to suspect that an attempt is being made to defame us *precisely* by making us out to be adversaries of your Work, without this being the case, and without any evidence that it is.
>
> I know for a fact that it is completely untrue that Father Carrillo has undertaken any such campaign. There is no such campaign. There is simply (and not by Father Carrillo's instigation) a natural reaction of legitimate self-defense, *not against a work approved by the Church,* but against the hardly noble tactics used by certain members of that organization to discredit our Marian sodalities and even the Society of Jesus itself.[93]

[92] AGP, RHF, EF–410619–2.
[93] AGP, RHF, D–30005.

The only recourse left was a direct appeal to the Jesuit provincial. Bishop Leopoldo offered to prepare the way before Father Josemaria took that step. On May 29 the bishop met with the head of the Toledo province, Father Carlos Gómez Martinho. They had a long conversation, in which the bishop spoke earnestly and energetically. That afternoon he sent the provincial a long letter reiterating what he had said that morning.

> My dear Father Provincial:
>
> As you requested, and continuing our very positive conversation of this morning, I am writing you these lines about the pious union canonically established with the title of "Opus Dei," [founded] by the worthy priest Father José María Escrivá.[94]
>
> How truly sad that people so good and so devoted to God should be fighting—clearly for motives of zeal and *arbitrantes se obsequium praestare Deo* ["thinking they are offering service to God": see Jn 16: 2]—against this institution that not only I, who have approved it, but all the bishops I know who are familiar with it, hold in the highest esteem. . . .
>
> I can assure Your Reverence that the Opus is truly Dei and has been from its conception through every new stage of its development. That Work was conceived only to serve God, and it is engaged only in sanctification of souls and in works of apostolate. . . .
>
> The people who belong to Opus Dei are not, by that fact, in danger of losing their souls, nor are they in any way heretics or Masons or illuminati. Such accusations are being voiced not only to those thought to be in the Work, but to many who have no connection with it and, worst of all, to the mothers of members, and of students who do have a connection with the Work. Even the confessional is being used for this purpose. All of this is creating truly tragic family situations.
>
> Believe me, Father, none of these charges have any basis in reality. It is not true that it is a secret society. Not only was it born with the approval of the diocesan authorities,

---

[94] Actually, as we noted earlier, the Work had been approved as a pious union, but not "erected" as such.

but, since that birth thirteen years ago, it has taken no step of any importance without seeking and obtaining such approval. . . .

Certainly it does not deserve to be attacked by good people. And, nevertheless, they are attacking it. This would be a cause of astonishment and sadness, had the Lord not gotten us so familiar with this phenomenon. How many other works very much of God have met with the same fortune! . . .

Dear Father Provincial, I ask that you, for love of God and of the Church, help me put an end to a storm from which only the enemy of our souls stands to gain.

If, with regard to all these accusations thrown at the Work, you would like me to clarify some particular point, let me know and I will be glad to do so. I consider it a great service to the Church to do whatever I can in support of Opus Dei.

I send you my blessing and commend myself to your holy prayers.[95]

Two days later, on May 31, Father Josemaría went to see the provincial, at Areneros School. They spoke for two hours on various subjects, including the question of Opus Dei getting vocations from among sodality members. After this meeting, Father Josemaría only had time to send Bishop Eijo y Garay a brief note, since he was about to set out for Pamplona. The note read: "I think this is the end, thanks be to God and to my bishop, our father. May God reward you! I insisted that they rectify this whole thing, and he promised me that they would."[96]

Buoyed up by this hope, he wrote from Pamplona to his sons at El Palau: "It appears that the tribulation is coming to an end. Let us bless God and always be ready to accept whatever he wants. *In laetitia!* [Joyfully!]"[97] And to Alvaro del Portillo: "We need to ask our Lord, in this month of his Sacred Heart, that this may really be (if it is his will) the end of the persecution."[98]

From Pamplona Father Josemaría went to Valladolid and, a few days later, Valencia. His visits to the bishops in these cities tempered his hopes. On June 13 he wrote to Bishop Eijo y Garay, and told him

[95] AGP, RHF, D–15287.
[96] AGP, RHF, EF–410531–2.
[97] AGP, RHF, EF–410601–2.
[98] AGP, RHF, EF–410601–3.

that the bishops were all agreed in thinking that the attack would now come from some other direction.[99]

*   *   *

At long last the coadjutor abbot of Montserrat received the awaited reply of the bishop of Madrid concerning the matter "of great interest" about which he had inquired. Bishop Eijo y Garay wrote, in a letter dated May 24: "Many thanks for your letter of the 9th, which I received yesterday, the 23rd. I don't know why the long delay. . . . Yes, I know all about the commotion being stirred up against Opus Dei in Barcelona. It's obvious that it is a thorn in the side of the Evil One. The sad thing is that people very devoted to God are the instruments of the harm being done."

Then he turned to his main point:

> From the time it was founded in 1928, Opus Dei has been so much in the hands of the Church that the diocesan ordinary, that is to say, either my vicar general or myself, has known of and, when necessary, guided all of its steps. Everything from its first cries to its current groanings has resounded in our ears—and in our hearts. Because, believe me, Most Reverend Abbot, the Opus has been truly Dei from its conception on through every new stage of its development.
>
> Father Escrivá is an exemplary priest, chosen by God for the sanctification of many souls. . . . In a word, I have nothing to say against that Opus. It is, I repeat, truly Dei. And, nevertheless, it is good people who are now attacking it. This would be cause for astonishment were it not that the Lord has accustomed us to seeing that same phenomenon occur with other works very much his own.[100]

Bishop Leopoldo's letter was not brief, but it left a number of unanswered questions in the mind of the abbot. On June 15 he wrote

[99] AGP, RHF, EF–410613–1. In this letter he goes on to say that the bishop of Pamplona "expects that there will still be something," and that the bishop of Valencia said to him, "If any gossip turns up here, you have me entirely at your service. I think that, in one form or another, it will turn up again." And in another letter to Bishop Eijo y Garay, he says that the bishop of Valladolid, " told me that in spite of everything, 'estote parati' ['be prepared']" (AGP, RHF, EF–410610–3).

[100] AGP, RHF, D–03545–2. See Appendix 4 for the complete text of this letter.

again with a long list of specific questions: Where and how did Opus
Dei originate? What are its aims? Why do some say it is shrouded in
mystery and is secretive? What is the truth about the "iconoclastic
leanings" attributed to its members? How do they live? And why are
they accused of hating the religious orders?

Bishop Leopoldo answered in detail. He began, "Reverend Father
Abbot: Yesterday I received your letter of the 15th, and I am happy to
dedicate a bit of time to answering your questions." Pages later, he
went on to say:

> What is really amazing is the spirit with which the members
> of Opus Dei have borne this great trial. I see their letters,
> because Opus Dei shows me everything, and I admire and am
> edified by the holy joy with which they suffer for their voca-
> tion, which the gale only serves to embed more deeply in their
> souls. There is not one complaint or word of ill will toward
> the religious who so harshly persecute them. Their greatest
> consolation is seeing that all the bishops in whose territories
> they have houses are with them; that we are encouraging and
> defending them. God will have to reward those who *arbi-*
> *trantes se obsequium praestare Deo* [thinking they are offering
> service to God] have pressed this war, but all that Opus Dei
> wants out of it is the good that our Lord wants to draw from
> this tribulation. And it will come about.[101]

5. *Bishop Eijo y Garay as pastor*

Bishop Leopoldo Eijo y Garay of Madrid-Alcalá ruled his diocese with
a firm hand. He energetically applied the Holy See's instructions to
restrict the flow of priests to the capital from other dioceses, and
during the time of the Republic he stood up to attempts of the civil
authorities to interfere in Church matters, refusing to recognize the
government's nominations for Church posts.

Father Josemaría, from when he first came to Madrid as a young
priest, had been subject to the diocese's strict rules and had conducted
himself in an exemplary fashion. His consultations with the vicar

[101] AGP, RHF, D–03545–3. See Appendix 5 for the complete text. See also AGP, RHF,
D–03545–4 and D–03545–5.

general (Monsignor Morán), his punctual applications for renewal of his ministerial faculties, and, above all, his ardent apostolic zeal had commended him to Bishop Eijo y Garay from the start.

Then, during the time Father Josemaría spent in Burgos in 1938, their mutual esteem quickly evolved into a warm friendship. As had Cardinal Soldevila earlier, Bishop Eijo y Garay, a perceptive man with a lot of experience in governing, discovered the exceptional qualities of this young Aragonese priest: his daring and prudence, his drive and refinement of soul, his obedience and sincerity. (In 1943, when the bishop had to send to Rome a synopsis of what he knew about the founder of Opus Dei, he wrote of him: "The distinctive notes of his character are his energy and his capacity for organization and government; with an ability to pass unnoticed. He has shown himself most obedient to the Church hierarchy—one very special hallmark of his priestly work is the way he fosters, in speech and in writing, in public and in private, love for Holy Mother Church and for the Roman Pontiff." [102]

Their harmony of will produced a deep mutual trust. The founder made it a habit never to take one step in his apostolic activities without first obtaining permission from the competent authority and afterward making what he called his "rendering of accounts." [103] He did this with great naturalness, making no secret of his esteem and affection for the bishop, and in difficult moments he turned confidently to this shepherd of God's flock. "I've been tempted not to send my Father this letter," he once wrote him, "but I am going to send it. It is of the essence, no doubt about it, that my bishop know all about—I say this again—even the breathing of this poor son of his." [104] And in August 1940, as attacks on the Work were mounting, Father Josemaría expressed to him the hope "that you may continue to regard the Work that he has laid on my shoulders as something of God and as something of yours." [105]

Bishop Leopoldo's first step in defending the Work was always to obtain information—when possible, firsthand. Father Josemaría bent

---

[102] See Fuenmayor, Gómez-Iglesias, and Illanes, pp. 490–92.

[103] See AGP, RHF, EF–400806–2.

[104] AGP, RHF, EF–410530–1. About that close relationship between the founder and his bishop, Father Bueno would later write: "It was a friendship that started at the very beginning of Josemaría's work in Madrid. Josemaría related to him with a very filial trust, and Don Leopoldo had great affection for him" (*Testimonios*, p. 22).

[105] AGP, RHF, EF–400806–2.

over backwards to understand other people's motives, and never to assume bad intentions, and so quickly disposed of reports he received on the subject of attacks. The bishop asked that in the future he keep them, and that he inform him of every detail. Indeed, by the spring of 1941 the attacks had become so virulent that they could no longer be ignored. On May 14 Father Josemaría wrote to the bishop:

> Father, in order to keep Your Excellency up to date on what is going on, I'm sending you this sheet of paper, a copy of a flyer that the Fathers [of the Society] distributed fairly widely in Barcelona among churchmen. I think Lahiguera has brought another copy with him.
>
> I would like to discuss several matters that I don't think should be dealt with in a letter or on the phone. I know very well how little time my bishop has. Nevertheless, I make bold to request that you grant me a quarter of an hour, whenever you have a free moment. May God reward you!
>
> I haven't heard anything from Valencia, nor from the person who went there by plane yesterday. I guess nothing new has happened; otherwise they would have called. I'll let you know as soon as I hear anything.[106]

And on May 15:

> My Reverend Bishop—Bothering you once again. Seems like this is becoming a daily bulletin. But it's good that Your Excellency always be able to say of this poor son of his that he knows all about "even his breathing."
>
> Still no word from Valencia.
>
> As for Barcelona, I'm sending you an account of the most recent talk given by Father Vergés, plus several paragraphs from a letter, which I think are interesting.[107]

The rumors proliferated. The founder half-jokingly dubbed the swarm of stories and innuendos "gossip papers."[108]

---

[106] AGP, RHF, EF–410514–1. Father Jose Maria Garcia Lahiguera was at that time spiritual director of the Major Seminary of Madrid.

[107] AGP, RHF, EF–410515–1.

[108] See AGP, RHF, EF–410409–1 and EF–410420.

Bishop Leopoldo refused to tolerate the least gossip about Opus Dei or disparagement of its founder.[109] "Father Escrivá," he wrote to the Jesuit provincial of Toledo, "is an exemplary priest, chosen by God for apostolic enterprises; humble, prudent, self-sacrificing in work, docile to his bishop; of outstanding intelligence and with a very solid spiritual and doctrinal formation." [110]

* * *

Since the canonical approval had not put a stop to the storm in Catalonia, Father Josemaría appealed to the authority of the ordinary. Bishop Miguel de los Santos Gómara, having only recently arrived in the diocese of Barcelona as apostolic administrator, tried without success to calm things down. He even went personally to the University of Barcelona, as was noted by the woman who was his housekeeper, "to speak to the Rector and the Dean, about the agitation that the "Luises" were carrying on against Opus Dei." [111] On September 14, Bishop Diaz Gomara wrote to Sebastian Cirac, who was in Madrid:

I am very sorry that the campaign against O.D. is continuing, and even more that they have dared to do what you tell me against Escrivá and Albareda. The truth will out and as his

[109] Bishop José María García Lahiguera recounts this anecdote: "The bishop of Madrid-Alcalá, Bishop Leopoldo Eijo y Garay, had a detailed knowledge of Father Josemaría's apostolic work, since the Father had never taken one step, in his work as founder, without the permission and approval of his bishop and his vicar general. Well, then, one day, when the bishop had just finished the ceremony of conferring Holy Orders in the chapel of the seminary of Madrid, while all of us present, seminarians and the newly ordained, were waiting in silence for him to remove the sacred vestments, Bishop Leopoldo said in a loud voice, so that everyone could hear, these or similar words: 'Reverend Rector, Opus Dei is a foundation approved and blessed by the hierarchy, and I will not stand for anyone speaking against Opus Dei.'

"The bishop thus used this solemn occasion, at which so many people were present, to give a public and personal testimony to the supernatural character of Opus Dei and, while he was at it, put a stop to any gossip and criticism that might have been going on in the seminary. The rector at that time, Father Rafael García Tuñón, appreciated and admired the virtues of Father Josemaría, and had invited him to give the retreat at the major seminary. Clearly the situation had to be serious, as I say, for the bishop to so publicly, and on such a solemn occasion, give such a warning" (*Testimonios*, pp. 156–57).

[110] Letter to Father Carlos Gomez Martinho, S.J., Provincial of Toledo, May 29, 1941 (AGP, RHF, D-15287). A similar description, with almost identical wording, is found in the bishop's letter to the Coadjutor Abbot of Montserrat, on May 24, 1941, in Appendix 4 (AGP, RHF, D-03545-2).

[111] Letter of Mercedes Serrano Langarita to the founder, Saragossa, 27 Dec 1973; in AGP, Sec. E.1.2, Leg. 382.

"Luises" was a name that was used in many parts of Spain (though not in Barcelona) to denote the members of the Marian Sodality.

bishop (Don Leopoldo) said to me a few days ago, the Lord expects a lot from the Work if he is putting it through such a trial.[112]

Thus there fell to the bishop of Madrid this heavy task of answering letters, receiving visits, clearing up questions, consoling the afflicted, reprimanding the gossipers, and comforting those they injured—at a time when he was already working so hard, trying to revive a diocese that had been paralyzed for three years and to resolve a thousand intricate problems involving Church personnel and properties. And that is to say nothing of the endless round of meetings, gatherings, and ceremonies. Often the bishop worked late into the night, tackling at the end of the day, when no one else was there, the mountain of papers piled up on his desk.[113]

The founder, too, had a great capacity for work. But ever since he had abandoned into God's hands the whole matter of his good name, he had slept wonderfully. When any concern threatened to interfere with his sleep, he would say, "Lord, let me sleep, because tomorrow I have to work for you." [114] On his shoulders fell the weight of Opus Dei and its apostolates, the endless work of spiritual direction, and the many trips he was making. For, unable to say no to the bishops' requests, he was still giving priests' retreats in many dioceses during these months.

In the spring of 1941 he wrote to his bishop, "It's looking to me like I'm going to have to give up this work that lies outside my particular vocation, because Opus Dei is more than enough to exhaust my poor energies. But I will do whatever Your Excellency would prefer." [115] Bishop Leopoldo did not let him off the hook. He had him keep giving those retreats, not only because of the good they were doing for so many souls, but also because he knew that firsthand contact with the founder—hearing him speak, witnessing his zeal—was the best antidote to the lies about Opus Dei.

---

[112] AGP, Sec. E.1.1, Leg. 166.

[113] Being a conscientious worker who did not like to leave loose ends, the bishop often wrote long letters. His letter of 1 Sep 1941 to Dom Escarré ends with these words: "Pardon me if I have gone on too long. I stayed up tonight much later than I was planning to, so that I could write to you. It's almost three in the morning. But Opus Dei is well worth it, and you are well worth it" (AGP, RHF, D–03545–4).

[114] *Letter 29 Dec 1947/14 Feb 1966*, no. 37.

[115] AGP, RHF, EF–410405–1.

One night, when he was already in bed and trying to put out of his mind the calumnies suffered that day, Father Josemaría got a phone call.

> It was Bishop Leopoldo, with his warm, expressive voice. "Simon, Simon," he said to me, "*ecce Satanas expetivit vos ut cribraret sicut triticum: ego autem rogavi pro te ut non deficiat fides tua, et tu aliquando conversus confirma—filios tuos!*" ("Simon, Simon, behold, Satan demanded to have you all, that he might sift you like wheat, but I have prayed for you that your faith may not fail; and you . . . strengthen—your sons!" [See Lk 22: 31–32.]) And then he hung up.
>
> I went back to bed smiling, more serene (if possible) than ever—joyful, because our Lord was tossing us about like wheat being sifted. And because there were people—so many, not just the bishop—who were praying for me, so that I could confirm my sons in the strength of their vocation.
>
> I never saw myself as unfortunate in that whole period, or ever in my life. I got through it all; I accepted God's will.[116]

Father Josemaría was not the only target. The more the bishop stepped forward to defend Opus Dei, the more criticism he got. Father Josemaría wrote to him:

> I'm sending you copies of several letters that arrived yesterday from Barcelona. You cannot imagine, my Father, how sorry I am that they are trying to smear Your Excellency with the mud they are throwing at Opus Dei. . . .
>
> Will you forgive me, Father, for all these troubles that, despite my best efforts, we are causing you?
>
> I am suffering a lot! But at the same time, I am very happy and filled with peace. I wouldn't trade places with the happiest man on earth. I love God's holy will![117]

It was said—and printed in anonymous flyers—that the bishop of Madrid had let himself be deceived, that Rome would reverse his action, that he was protecting heretics. . . . But the bishop did not

---

[116] *Letter 29 Dec 1947/14 Feb 1966*, no. 37.
[117] AGP, RHF, EF–410429–1.

back down. He was determined to keep fighting until the truth prevailed.[118]

As noted earlier, in June 1941 the Spanish government reached an agreement with the Holy See regarding the presentation of candidates to fill the episcopal sees. Besides those vacant as a result of wartime martyrdoms, others also had recently opened up.[119] Among these was the archdiocese of Toledo, because of the death of Cardinal Gomá in 1940. Since its head was the primate of Spain, filling it was an obvious priority. Late one night, when saying good-bye to Bishop Leopoldo after a long conversation, Father Josemaría remarked that as bishop of Madrid, he surely would be a candidate, but that as things were going, he most likely would be rejected. "Bishop, leave me in the street—ditch me!" he exclaimed. "Or at least make it look for now like you're ditching me, and then pick me up again later. Because otherwise you stand to lose the miter of Toledo."

Bishop Leopoldo became very serious and said, "I am not going to ditch you, Father José María. Because it's not the miter of Toledo that's at risk—it's my soul!"

"Some time later," the founder recalled, "he let me know that he had indeed been excluded from the list."[120]

The priest's gratitude to his bishop operated on both the natural and supernatural levels. "I do not fail to pray for you several times a day," he writes in one letter. "And tomorrow, as at other times, I will

[118] An anonymous flyer delivered by two Jesuit priests to the archbishop of Santiago de Compostela read in part:

Opus Dei: It is said to be backed by Bishop Eijo y Garay, the bishop of Madrid-Alcalá.
—It is said that its director, Father José María Escrivá, has been suspended.
—It is rumored that Rome is going to intervene, to ban it.
—The Society of Jesus is strongly opposed to it.
—They say they do not fear even pontifical prohibitions, because if they are made, it will surely be only because the Pope is badly informed.

(See AGP, RHF, D–15006. To guarantee its authenticity, the archbishop sent this flyer to Father Josemaría with his own seal on the envelope.)

[119] During the civil war the following appointments were made in the nationalist zone: in September 1937, Cardinal Pedro Segura Sáenz as archbishop of Seville and Bishop Javier Lauzurica as apostolic administrator of Vitoria; in January 1938, Bishop Manuel Arce Ochotorena as bishop of Oviedo; in February 1938, Bishop Antonio García as archbishop of Valladolid and Bishop Carmelo Ballester as bishop of León. See Gonzalo Redondo, *Historia de la Iglesia en España, 1931–1939*, vol. 2, *La Guerra Civil, 1936–1939* (Madrid, 1993), pp. 335–39 and 411–13.

[120] *Letter 29 Dec 1947/14 Feb 1966*, no. 50. See also *Letter 14 Sep 1951*, no. 14.

On October 31, 1941, Bishop Enrique Pla y Deniel of Salamanca was named archbishop of Toledo. In 1940 he had founded the Pontifical Ecclesiastical University of Salamanca. In 1946 he was named a cardinal. He died in 1968.

celebrate my Mass for my bishop and his intentions. Never will I be able to thank you enough for all the benefits I have received from your hands." [121] And others knew how much that staunch support of his bishop meant to him. Bishop Santos Moro wrote from Avila, "I've had the pleasure of reading the magnificent letter of the bishop of Madrid to the abbot of Montserrat defending Opus Dei. Having defenders like him must to a great extent sweeten the bitterness of the persecution. Blessed be God." [122]

It must indeed have done so, especially since Bishop Leopoldo was so obviously happy to do all that he did.

The affection that the founder and members of Opus Dei had for Bishop Leopoldo, as well as the support they were giving him with their prayers and mortifications, found expression in a little gift that Father Josemaría gave him for his saint's day. It was a painting of a young donkey, the same sort of gentle, strong, hardworking, docile, and humble animal that carried our Lord on his triumphant entry into Jerusalem. On November 26, he wrote the bishop: "This little donkey wanted to reach you on the feast of Saint Leopold. May my bishop receive it affectionately, seeing how happy it is to come to the bishop's residence. It will be very docile, and comes loaded down with all the respectful affection of these sons of Your Excellency." [123]

Bishop Leopoldo, for his part, was well acquainted with the priest's simplicity and sincerity. On March 10, 1942, a leader of the Falange, then at the height of its power, came to consult him about the "secret and Masonic" society founded by Father Josemaría. The bishop said to him:

To think that Father Josemaría Escrivá is capable of creating anything secret is absurd. He is as frank and open as a child! Father Josemaría—and please don't let this reach his ears—is a good man, a real saint. And what a patriot! But above all, he is a holy man. We are accustomed to venerating the saints only when they are raised to the altars, and tend to forget that they were people who walked on earth, just as we do. Father Josemaría Escrivá—have no doubt about it—is a saint whom we are going to see canonized on the altars.[124]

---

[121] AGP, RHF, EF–410625–1.
[122] AGP, RHF, EF–410806–1.
[123] AGP, RHF, EF–411126–1.
[124] AGP, RHF, T–04695, p. 22. (Eduardo Alastrué was present; it was he who noted down these words.)

The bishop felt it an honor to have been chosen to support the founder of Opus Dei. Once he was even heard to pray, "Lord, although when I appear before you I won't be bearing much of value, at least I'll be able to tell you, 'In these hands was born Opus Dei; with these hands I blessed Josemaría.' " [125]

6. *A panoramic vision*

Barely two weeks after his visit to the Jesuit provincial (Father Carlos Gómez Martinho), Father Josemaría found it necessary to contact him again, this time by letter. During a brief stay in Valencia he had been told by his sons and some friends of his that there had been "threats made in public and in private by Father Segarra to repeat the spectacle of Barcelona." [126] This was something he looked to the provincial to prevent.

> Dear Father Provincial:
> You can't imagine with what joy I recall our meeting at Areneros. Both of us wanting to love God and serve the Church, I just knew that our meeting would be marked by cordiality and mutual understanding. . . .
> Certain Fathers of the Society read to a number of people a letter—from another Father, one from Madrid—that was the start of this sorry campaign. How pleasing to our Lord it would be, and how consistent with justice and charity, were this Father now nobly to retract his accusations! By now, I think, no one can call me a Mason, heretic, reprobate, lunatic, etc., etc., without suffering pangs of conscience. Or say that Opus Dei is all those insulting things it is being called by word of mouth and in writing. [127]
> All the same, what had happened in Barcelona did happen again in Valencia, with the same tactics and maneuvers employed: criticisms of *The Way*, [128] accusations before the civil

---

[125] AGP, RHF, T–04885, p. 2 (Lourdes Bandeira Vázquez).

[126] AGP, RHF, EF–410614–2.

[127] Ibid.

[128] In Valencia Father Segarra was going around saying that *The Way* had been copied from a German source. Francisco Botella went to see him to testify to the book's composition, but Father Segarra refused to make a retraction and told Francisco that the book would be condemned. (See AGP, RHF, T–00159/1, pp. 108–109.)

authorities, visits to families of members of Opus Dei. Parents were told that their children were headed straight toward eternal damnation.[129]

This unexpected outbreak of calumny led Father Josemaría to ask Father Gómez Martinho to intercede with the provincial of Aragón.[130] At this point the misunderstandings had spread so widely through Spain that the founder was not too surprised when he received one day a letter from a convent in Segovia, expressing concern.

It was from the superior of the Marian Reparatrix nuns, Mother María de la Virgen Dolorosa Muratori, the one who had lent him the humble wooden tabernacle for the first oratory, on Ferraz Street. On August 6, 1941, he wrote to her:

> Deeply respected and esteemed Mother, in Christ:
>
> I often remember you with affection, both because of my love for the holy Institute of Mary Reparatrix and because of the favors I personally owe to you. May God reward you!
>
> Your letter brought me joy—and pain, at seeing that even there at your convent you're hearing about this opposition by good people, this persecution that we've been suffering (for

[129] Florencio Sánchez Bella and his brother Ismael were present when such an incident took place at their home. Florencio says, "They told so many lies, perhaps thinking they were acting in good faith, that my parents threatened to throw us out of the house if we went to any Opus Dei center again" (Florencio Sánchez Bella, *Sum.* 7492).

Amadeo de Fuenmayor recalls that one time when his mother went to Barcelona to visit one of her daughters, "she was visited by a Jesuit who did not know her at all. He asked her if she was my mother, and then said he had come to warn her that her son was 'in danger of damnation.' He also told her that she could and should dissuade me from this path I had taken, that of Opus Dei, never mind the fact—which I probably would have mentioned—that I was by then an adult. And he warned her against Monsignor Antonio Rodilla, the vicar general of the diocese, saying that he was one of us. Thus my poor mother had nowhere to turn, since, because of his advanced age, she couldn't go to the archbishop either. (This was Prudencio Melo y Alcalde, the archbishop of Valencia.) I asked her if the priest had given any reason in support of his dire judgment about me. She said to me, 'You members of Opus Dei have been deceived into believing that it is possible to be holy in the midst of the world.' Here was the cause of my going so sadly astray. Here was the great heresy that would drag my soul to the precipice if I did not leave Opus Dei" (AGP, RHF, T–02769, p. 4).

These visits to parents and other relatives of members of the Work spread to other cities in Spain. Javier de Ayala testifies: "Some Fathers of the Society, there in Saragossa, seriously upset my family, accusing the Servant of God of having founded a sect, a kind of Masonry, something similar to the ancient Illuminati, who ended up in hell" (Javier de Ayala Delgado, *Sum.* 7586).

[130] In this letter, dated June 14, 1941, he refers to the situation as one of "constant persecution."

more than a year and a half now) on account of our vocation, on account of our Love for Jesus Christ. . . .

Mother, for love of God, tell that venerable community not to stop praying for us, that we might always see, in persons and events, the hand of our Father in heaven. That way we will keep undergoing *cum gaudio et pace*, as we have been till now, whatever he wills. What joy comes of fulfilling the holy will of God! [131]

Father Josemaría certainly did not expect the matter to end up in the hands of the civil authorities, but he had little doubt that the blaze would go on spreading.[132] Accusations that the Work was a heresy, a secret society, a Masonic group opposed to constituted authority, and much else were familiar by now in the public and academic sectors. Especially dangerous were the allegations made to the Tribunal for the Repression of Masonry, which had been established on September 10, 1940.

Early in July 1941 this tribunal took up the case, in closed proceedings. According to the tribunal reporter, González Oliveros, a group of persons directed by Father Escrivá were accused of forming a branch of Masonry with ties to Jewish sects. The president of the tribunal, General Saliquet, inquired about the lifestyle of the group's members, and among other things was told that they lived in celibacy. When he expressed skepticism, he was assured that the celibacy of Opus Dei members was a confirmed fact.[133] He then decided to dismiss the

---

[131] AGP, RHF, EF–410806–1. For more on Mother María, see *Apuntes*, no. 1258 (26 Mar 1935). In this letter of August 6, the founder also set out his answers to the accusations being made "by good people":
(1) That we have never taken a step anywhere without the express approval of the local ordinary. (2) That the Work is canonically approved. (3) That it is untrue to say that we have mysteries or secrets; such things have never had any place in our apostolic activity, nor will they ever, nor do we have any need of them. (4) That we suffer all the injuries they do us (and they do everything they can to injure us) with a holy joy and in silence; while they slander us, we work. (5) That we wholeheartedly forgive those who spread these stories to denigrate us; and we believe they are acting in good faith."

[132] He did, at any rate, suspect this strongly enough to write to the bishop of Madrid, "I wonder if it wouldn't be a good idea to inform the civil authorities of this matter, before this underhanded campaign manages (indirectly!) to do so, so that those civil authorities don't for one minute believe any of the idiotic things being imputed to us. How happy the enemy of souls would be to see us being harassed from that quarter too!" (AGP, RHF, EF–410525–1).

[133] With regard to this matter and the accusation before the tribunal there is a statement by Dr. Luis López Ortiz, who was then the secretary general of the tribunal: see

matter, since he could not see any reason for Masons to live in celibacy. The other members of the panel fully agreed.

Although the tribunal conducted its proceedings in secret and ordinarily those accused did not even know about them if they were found innocent, an exception was made in this case, as if to make up for the injustice of the accusation itself, and members of the tribunal visited the Jenner Street residence. They asked Father Josemaría to show them the oratory, where, according to the accusers, he pretended to levitate and there was a frieze with cabalistic symbols. As he ushered them into the oratory, he jokingly referred to his ample girth saying, "It would take a first-class miracle to get me even a few inches off the ground." [134]

But the accusations of a political nature kept coming. During these early years of the Second World War, the Falange had a major presence and influence in the government, and it made no secret of its preference for a totalitarian one-party state. Anyone taking any other political stance was deemed unpatriotic and risked being persecuted. At the same time, however, enemies of the Church and opponents of the Francoist regime were accusing the founder of erring in the other direction. Years later he recalled having been branded a Mason and "also a monarchist, an antimonarchist, a Falangist, a Carlist, and an anti-Carlist." At the height of the Second World War, "the same people, or people prompted by them, went to the embassies of the Allies to say I was a Germanophile and to the embassies of Germany and Italy to say I was an Anglophile." [135] To have accusations like these in the possession of the Falangist National Movement was like sitting on a time bomb.

The political allegations were put together by Falangists in a "Confidential Report on the Secret Organization Opus Dei." [136] It said of the members of Opus Dei:

AGP, RHF, T–04214. Other testimonies to the same effect include José López Ortiz, *Sum.* 5271; Alvaro del Portillo, *Sum.* 425; and Silvestre Sancho Morales, O.P., *Sum.* 5399. (At this stage of the Work's existence it was not yet possible for married persons to be incorporated into it.)

[134] The delegation was made up of the following magistrates: Dr. Juan José Pradera Ortega, Dr. González Oliveros, and Dr. Luis López Ortiz. See Alvaro del Portillo, PR, pp. 564–65, and Juan Jiménez Vargas, *Sum.* 6710.

[135] *Letter 29 Dec 1947/14 Feb 1966*, no. 36.

[136] This report has been published in Jose Luis Rodriguez Jimenez, *Historia de la Falange Española de las JONS*, Alianza, Madrid 2000, pp. 420-423. Of this four-page document, dated 16 Jan 1942, there is a typewritten copy in the General Archive of the

In their conception of life they defend internationalism, asserting that for a Catholic there should be no borders, nations, or homelands.[137] ... This organization goes against the goals of the state, by reason of (1) its secretiveness, (2) its international character, (3) its interference in intellectual life and in the system of ideas promoted by the Leader, and (4) its sectarianism, which obliges the state to appear unjust in its grantings of professorships, scholarships, etc. ... Its members act as if they adhered to the Movement, when really they only await its fall, trusting in the permanence of Catholic doctrine, the shield of its shadowy ambitions.[138]

Prelature. The friend who showed the founder the document was Father (later Bishop) José López Ortiz, who gives the following testimony:

> On one occasion I got hold of an internal document of the Falange (the one party, Franco's) in which he was grossly slandered. I considered it my duty to show him this document, which had been lent me by a friend of mine. The attacks were so savage that while Josemaría was sitting there in front of me and calmly reading those sheets, I couldn't keep tears from my eyes. When he got done, and saw how upset I was, he burst out laughing and said to me, with heroic humility, "Don't worry, Pepe, because everything they're saying here is, thank God, false—but if they knew me better, they could have truthfully said a lot worse things, because I'm nothing but a poor sinner, who loves Jesus Christ madly." And instead of tearing up that string of insults, he gave the papers back to me so that my friend could return them to the Falange headquarters, from which he had taken them. "Take them," he said, "and give them to that friend of yours so that he can put them back where they belong, and that way he won't start getting persecuted."

(See *Testimonios*, pp. 241–42.)

[137] See Joaquín Alonso Pacheco, *Sum.* 4659. The ultranationalistic sector of the Falange was scandalized by point 525 of *The Way*:

> To be "Catholic" means to love our country, and to let nobody surpass us in that love. And at the same time, it means to hold as our own the noble aspirations of all the other lands. How many glories of France are glories of mine! And in the same way, many things that make Germans proud—and Italians, British, Americans and Asians and Africans—are also sources of pride to me.
>
> Catholic! A great heart, an open mind.

[138] For many months, when the power of the Falange was at its height, the notion that the Work was a secret society and an enemy of the party put the founder and members of the Work in grave danger. One of many documents testifying to this is a letter sent by Father Josemaría to the bishop of Madrid in February 1943 (AGP, RHF, EF–430217–1):

> Father, I just reread the last page, and I don't think it's clear enough. They have ordered that we be audited by the tax department (everything is in order), and I have been told by a reliable source that they are trying to get Alastrué arrested on the monstrously calumnious charge of his "belonging to a secret society that is an enemy of the Falange and is conniving with the British embassy." And the person who gave me that information also told me

The situation in Spain, as the founder would later write, "was not propitious, from any point of view, to a young and *new* foundation to go forward. The environment was not favorable."[139] There was more at issue than slanders and verbal injuries. An ambassador—a friend of his who was well informed—told him that some extremist members of the Falange had decided to eliminate him.[140] A section of the "Confidential Report"—amusing, but at the same time alarming in light of the close ideological ties between certain sectors of the Falange and German nationalists—concerned the presence in the Jenner Street residence of a map of Germany covered with pigs supposedly representing the German people (actually it depicted livestock production).

In that report it was also claimed that members of the Work, in addition to seeking political power, were trying to gain control by obtaining teaching positions in universities and in centers of scientific research.[141] And thus it happened that when some of them went to take the qualifying exams for professorships, they found themselves targets of discrimination. The story that they were seeking teaching positions by devious means made the rounds so widely that even friends had a hard time not believing it.[142] Father Josemaría wrote to a priest acquaintance:

---

this afternoon that they are trying to find out all they can about Alastrué's friends, so that they can haul them all in.

Forgive me, dear Bishop. I have a lot of consoling things to tell you, to balance out these calumnies.

[139] *Letter 29 Dec 1947/14 Feb 1966*, no. 39.

[140] See Alvaro del Portillo, *Sum.* 417.

[141] Bishop López Ortiz testifies: "Serving as megaphones for these falsehoods were a number of ideologically liberal university professors who—I don't think I'm making a rash judgment in saying this—did not take kindly to having convinced Catholics in the lecture halls. They started a rumor that a group of professors and other persons linked to university life, including the minister of education, Ibáñez Martín, and José María Albareda, the secretary general of the recently established Council for Advanced Scientific Research, wanted to hand over the university to Opus Dei. The whole affair was quite ridiculous, and that it caught on at the time can be understood only if one keeps in mind the nationalistic atmosphere of the country in those days and the jealousy that led certain persons and movements to circulate the counterfeit money" (*Testimonios*, p. 225).

[142] Cardinal Bueno Monreal (*Testimonios*, p. 24) writes: "After these misunderstandings, there also came outright calumnies, alleging occultism and heresy, that flourished for a time. Without going into details (which I have forgotten anyway), I confine myself here to the charge that Opus Dei aimed to control university teaching positions in order to dominate the country ideologically. Such an absurd idea could be taken seriously only by someone who had previously accepted as valid the accusation that Opus Dei is a cult or a kind of Masonry—and who also had an overactive imagination. Yet this particular charge was circulated persistently for several years. And in this case it was not just a matter of opposition by 'good people.' Some who were not so good chimed in,

Look, you know that Opus Dei, which is free from any concern regarding earthly ambitions, seeks only "the Christian perfection of its members through the sanctification of ordinary work." Opus Dei is a supernatural work whose only concern is the interior life of souls. But opposition is inevitable. And the Lord has permitted us to suffer, as the main opposition, persecution by good people. And joining those good people are others who are not so good, who hate the Holy Church and Catholic Spain. . . .

Members of the Work know very well that they cannot please God without carefully observing all of society's procedural niceties and all the demands of Christian morality. So you can reject out of hand all that rubbish about their angling for jobs they aren't interested in.

They say I work with university students? It's true. But is that a crime? I see it as a special service to the nation. The Lord could just as well have moved me to work with illiterates. But it's flatly untrue that I'm trying to "take over" the universities. The Work is not for making professors; it's for forming saints, in all spheres of society, whose only ambition is to love Jesus Christ (and, therefore, the nation) and silently do good.[143]

But the slanders kept coming. And, bothersome enough as they were in themselves, Father Josemaría also had to keep track of them all, because his bishop had directed him to.

---

in an attempt to deny Catholic citizens, as well trained and qualified as anyone else, their right to practice their profession as they wanted and were able to."

See also José Orlandis Rovira, *Años de juventud en el Opus Dei* (Madrid, 1993). On page 182, in a chapter entitled "La leyenda de las cátedras" ("The Fable of the Professorships"), Orlandis says: "[It was claimed that] the minister of education, Ibáñez Martín, and the secretary of the recently created Council for Advanced Scientific Research, Albareda, had 'handed over' the university to Opus Dei. It should be noted that in 1941, when this campaign was at its most intense and Opus Dei was said to be dominating Spanish universities, only one member of Opus Dei—Albareda—had a tenured professorship. And if, with the actual promotion statistics in hand, we look at the whole duration of that virulent campaign revolving around the 'takeover of professorships,' we see that only eleven members of the Work obtained tenured professorships in the five-year period of 1940 to 1945, a space of time in which the total of new tenured professors in the universities was 179."

[143] AGP, RHF, EF–420108–1. This priest, Father Fermín Yzurdiaga Lorca, was a member of the Falange's National Council.

"Again I have to take up my pen, out of obedience, to record gossip and rumors. All for God!" [144] In this note, made during a retreat he gave in December 1941 for university women affiliated with Catholic Action, he records a conversation with one of the retreatants, a chemistry student named María Teresa Llopis, in which she admitted that she had been sent to spy on him. Now sorry for having gone along with this, she told him of a plot being hatched by members of Valencia's city council, with the backing of the police commissioner, to close down the residence on Samaniego Street.

"Does the house have a well?" she asked.

"Yes, my daughter," replied Father Josemaría. "It's a very old house. I'm sure many houses in Valencia have wells like that."

"Well, they claim that the things with the Masonic symbols have been thrown into the well. And they also claim that there are secret passageways."

The note concludes: "I went back to our house, and as I write this, late on Friday night and into Saturday morning, I can't help but smile at the amateurishness of these calumnies. But another detail about the place got missed: in this house there are seven stairways! Great title for a horror story: 'The House of the Seven Stairways.'"

The joking tone suggests that he did not take the young lady's warning too seriously. But if he did take her story as being just one more among so many, he was wrong. The city authorities, using a sanitary inspection as a pretext, really did try to close down the residence. Father Josemaría moved quickly to right this wrong, asking an architect with the city government in Madrid to look into the matter and verify that the action was purely arbitrary. He wrote to this architect, Antonio Rodilla:

> It is important to keep this injustice from happening. So I hope that you—acting for the glory to God—will visit the mayor, and if necessary the governor, and clear this matter up, getting them to leave us in peace, without us having to put out so much as a brushful of paint, since there is absolutely no need for it. What they want to do is to make us close down the house, or at least to interrupt our work with souls, and to get money from us. I don't know if you've heard, but

[144] AGP, RHF, D–30001.

they've already found an excuse for giving us a fine. We paid
it, although it was not at all clear what it was for, just to avoid
more trouble. Clearly that wasn't enough for them.[145]

Spying on centers of the Work, and on the apostolic activities being
conducted from there, continued for years. In 1943 an agent of the
Falange's intelligence service was sent to elicit information at the
Diego de León center in Madrid, under the pretext of seeing how food
supplies were being handled. The founder soon discovered what the
visitor was really after, and he showed him the door—but not without
first making friends with him.[146]

On January 13, 1945, when the war in Europe was drawing to a
close, he wrote to Father Roberto Cayuela, S.J.:

Dear Father:
   I'm sorry to have to write you about some sad events, but a
very close and trusted friend must hear about both the pleasant and the unpleasant.
   Again, in various cities, several Fathers of the Society have
started attacking Opus Dei. . . .
   It's not just a matter of communicating to you this and that
thing being said. It is as if, implicitly or explicitly, the Gospel
were being turned on its head. It's as though they were saying, "The harvest is little and the workers are many." In the
mind of a great general—that great Captain depicted by Saint
Ignatius—there is room for millions of people to be channeled
in an expanding diversity of functions. And in the plans of the
universal King, the eternal Priest, whom we greet these days
as *"dominator Dominus,"* there is room for infinitely more
than any human mind can conceive. Today's challenge is not
just to cultivate what lies uncultivated, but to increase the
productive capacity of what has already been planted; to
make what is fertile even more so; to get the workers to think
of themselves, too, in terms of harvest.
   How shocked we would be if we were to read in the paper
that American planes were bombing British soldiers. This is
one of the saddest things that could be imagined. Can it be

[145] AGP, RHF, EF–420214–1.
[146] See AGP, RHF, D–15415 (José Manuel Casas Torres).

that there is more harmony among earthly allied forces than among people who every day hear in the eucharistic meal, "Love one another"? If these things are going on among us who are united with Rome, how will the Lord ever give us unity with our separated brethren? And that they are going on is shown by dozens and dozens of testimonies. Their sheer numbers are enough to wear one out, but their content is deeply distressing.

You already know what a deep friendship I feel for you and how grateful I am for your prayers.[147]

In a letter written to Father Carrillo de Albornoz from Rome on June 3, 1950, one can see a sincere desire to pardon the person who started the campaign against the Work:

Rev. Father Angel Carrillo de Albornoz, S.J.
London
My dear Father Carrillo:

I received your warm letter dated the 15th of the last month, and I too am sorry things aren't working out so that you can visit this house.

When you return to Rome, I hope we can have a long conversation and get together often. If I should happen to be out, you already know Father Alvaro del Portillo, and I'm sure the two of you will always find it very easy to communicate.

With sincere affection, I send my warmest regards and ask your prayers for Opus Dei and for this sinner.[148]

---

[147] AGP, RHF, EF–450113–1.

[148] AGP, RHF, EF–500603–2. Here is the letter that the founder was answering:
Secretarius Centralis, Congregationum
Marianum, Rome, May 15, 1950
My respected and dear Monsignor:
Despite all my good intentions, I find myself about to take off, and without having found a free moment to go see you. My health hasn't been at all good these days, and I've had to make arrangements for this office to keep functioning in my absence.
I hope that when I get back we can put our idea into effect. In the meantime, feel free to send anything you wish to my address in England: Manresa House, Roehampton / LONDON, S.W. 15.
United in prayer, I remain very much yours in our Lord,
Angel Carrillo de Albornoz, S.J.
President, Central Secretariat of the Sodalities of Our Lady

Encarnación Ortega was present when the founder learned that Father Carrillo had quit the Jesuits. She testifies, "The Father was deeply pained. Salvador Canals reminded him that this was a man who had organized a terrible smear campaign against the Work. The Father cut him short: 'But he is a soul, my son; he is a soul.' And he stayed there a while looking very sad, undoubtedly praying." [149]

7. *A saying of saints*

Saint Teresa of Avila relates an occasion when she encountered a deep lack of understanding. Her confessor was attributing to diabolical intervention some supernatural events she had told him about, and good people around her were accepting that explanation. She suffered terribly until Saint Peter of Alcantara came on the scene. When he heard about all this, Saint Teresa says, "He had the greatest compassion on me. He told me that one of the worst trials on earth was the one I was suffering, which is opposition by good people." [150]

The opposition suffered by the founder lasted a long time. The first troubles dated back to the mid-thirties. In May 1936 he recorded in his journal, "Recently, that I know of, religious from three different orders have attacked us. Opposition by good people? The devil's doing." [151]

The phrase recurs in a journal entry dated September 14, 1940: "Much tribulation. Misunderstandings and slanders. Snare-setting by evil people and opposition by good people. God alone knows the supernatural reason, but to a great extent the human occasion has been M. I realize his intention isn't bad." [152]

Later he summarized this period in his life:

> Along with the "opposition by good people," there were—
> and still are—foolish individuals who used a lot of half-truths,
> not a few errors, and plenty of premeditated slanders, to
> organize an uproar against us. And then all this was spread

---

[149] AGP, RHF, T–05074, p. 19.
[150] *The Life of Saint Teresa of Jesus*, chapter 30.
[151] *Apuntes*, no. 1346 (31 May 1936).
[152] *Apuntes*, no. 1622. There is no record of who "M." is.

far and wide by other people through ignorance or stupidity, not bad will.[153]

Patience and prudence led him to let some years go by before composing a written account of what had happened during this time of persecution. He first drafted this letter in 1947, revised it three times to soften its language, and finally finished it in 1966. That is why it bears two dates.[154] It begins:

> Now that the waters have somewhat subsided, I am going to carry out the instructions given me from on high, by persons who have authority in the Church, telling me to communicate something about events that I tried to keep quiet about, though I couldn't entirely prevent my children from learning about them.[155]

Rather than a complete historical account, the letter sketches a number of incidents and anecdotes at random, setting them down with little concern for chronology or style. Specifics are omitted, as are the names of those responsible. Nor is judgment passed on their intentions and motives. "I'll skip over the gory details and spare you many implausible, harsh incidents that would sound like something out of the Middle Ages," the author remarks.[156]

In any event, the letter does not seem to have been written according to any carefully organized plan. Despite his willingness to comply with those orders from "on high," Father Josemaría makes no attempt to get to the bottom of what happened. Instead, what we have is a collection of isolated impressions, a "family conversation" made from memory and without consulting written records.[157] Obviously the founder had mixed feelings about recounting this whole chapter of

---

[153] *Letter 29 Dec 1947/14 Feb 1966*, no. 47. "They are trying to start a fight, big or small": AGP, RHF, EF–410525–1 (Letter to Bishop Eijo y Garay). Father Josemaría refused to get drawn into the "uproar." He also felt that false information could have repercussions in the future. One of many examples was in Germany in 1983, when a TV network attacked the Work. Court decisions favoring Opus Dei later forced the station to retract its false statements.

[154] See *Letter 29 Dec 1947/14 Feb 1966*, nos. 3 and 18. As we mentioned earlier, he decided to file this letter in the General Archive of the Prelature (AGP) and not send it to the centers of the Work.

[155] Ibid., no. 2.

[156] Ibid., no. 4.

[157] Ibid., no. 13.

the history of the Work, since a family letter is not the best format in which to write any kind of history.

The problem was that Father Josemaría deeply disliked speaking about himself, even in third person, and yet wished to obey the person in the Vatican who had told him to tell his children what had happened. Wanting, as usual, to "hide and disappear," he left out intimate personal details about himself that were an integral part of the history of the Work during the "opposition by good people." He explained, "It's hard for me, my children, to write this letter. But others have suggested that I should tell you something about what has been going on in my soul." [158]

The focus of the letter is on how to draw spiritual profit from trials and opposition and not lose one's peace and joy. There are deeply spiritual lessons to be drawn from almost every paragraph.

*   *   *

Although it is impossible to impose much order on the chaotic assortment of deeds and words, murmurings and falsehoods, that made up the smear campaign, one can discern a few phases. At the start, around 1940, Father Josemaría was the target of isolated criticisms and gossip, which he referred to as "tribulations." A bit later, when there was irrefutable evidence of an organized campaign against himself and the Work, he began to speak of "opposition by the good." Eventually, the campaign became a "cruel and persistent persecution." [159]

For the founder it was no easy thing to use such strong language. The attacks were coming from persons belonging to an order he loved wholeheartedly. That was the case, too, with the abbot of Montserrat; but, as Bishop Leopoldo wrote to the abbot on September 1, 1941, what else but "persecution" could such a harsh and unbridled assault be called? The bishop wrote:

> What seems strange to me is that, seeing how hard things have been made for Opus Dei in your part of the country, you can say "if the opposition it is undergoing can be called persecution." Is it not a most cruel persecution to call this Work, which Your Reverence knows and esteems and is rightly interested in, Masonry, a heretical sect, . . . a den of iniquity where souls are irretrievably lost? To call its members icono-

---

[158] Ibid., no. 11.
[159] See AGP, RHF, EF–410601–3 and EF–410614–2.

clasts, people who have been hypnotized, persecutors of the Church and of religious life, and so many other insults of this kind? To stir up the civil authorities against them and try to get their centers closed and their founder put in jail and condemned in Rome? And, most tragic and painful of all, to sow discord by every possible means, from the confessional to visits to the families of those who love Opus Dei. If this is not persecution of the harshest sort, what is?[160]

In the midst of it all came this inexplicable event that we related earlier: Perhaps because he had been misinformed, perhaps because he could not believe that one of his brothers in religion would stoop to calumny, Father Daniel Ruiz, the immediate superior of Father Carrillo de Albornoz, made common cause with the latter and even accused the founder of having defamed the Society of Jesus.[161]

His sensitivity to the supernatural meanings of events soon moved Father Josemaría to discern a deeper significance in these sad occurrences. From the start, he saw the persecution as a trial sent by God, and sought to draw from it the good that God intended. Although he keenly desired that the uproar cease, he felt that it was in God's hands. To Bishop Leopoldo he wrote, "I ask our Lord insistently that all of *that* may come to an end, if such be his will. With this qualifier attached to it, my petition implicitly contains the request that, indeed, God may will an end to this persecution that we are suffering, this persecution by good people. In any case, FIAT [may his will be done]."[162]

*   *   *

One day, during a walk on the outskirts of Madrid, Monsignor Morcillo asked Father Josemaría, "Do you know that you have

---

[160] AGP, RHF, D–03545–4.

[161] See AGP, RHF, D–30005 (Letter of Father Daniel Ruiz to Father Josemaría, dated 23 May 1941).

The bishop of Madrid wrote to Dom Escarré on May 24, "Yesterday I read a letter from the superior of a Jesuit residence in which he says that it is a defamation of the Society of Jesus to claim that it is persecuting Opus Dei and seeking its destruction. Your Reverence, you know what is going on over there, so you can judge for yourself." (See Appendix 4.)

In his meeting with the founder at Areneros School on May 31, 1941, Father Carlos Gómez Martinho, the provincial of Toledo, said the same thing Father Ruiz had said. Afterwards, Father Josemaría wrote this note: "He says that they're the ones suffering persecution, because the best ones are leaving."

[162] AGP, RHF, EF–410525–1.

been denounced to Rome, to the Holy Office, as possibly being a heretic?"

Father Josemaría was filled with joy. He said, "How happy you make me, Casimiro! Because from Rome, from the Pope, nothing can come to me but light and good." [163]

All the same, the Work's immediate future was now jeopardized, since any ecclesiastical institution with universal aspirations had to have Rome's approval. And, tired as he was, Father Josemaría had ten weeklong retreats to give in that summer of 1941.[164]

At the beginning of autumn, before the new school year began, Father Josemaría was so exhausted that he had to rest for a few days. Accompanied by Ricardo Fernández Vallespín, he went to La Granja, a village near Segovia, and spent his time there writing and taking walks.

One rainy Thursday morning, September 25, he stayed in the hotel and wrote to Alvaro del Portillo:

> Today I offered the Holy Sacrifice and everything in the day for the Roman Pontiff, for his person and intentions. After the Consecration, I felt an impulse to do something that made me cry—even though I am certain the Work will be greatly loved by the Pope. With tears in my eyes, I looked at Jesus in the Eucharist lying on the corporal and told him in my heart, "Lord, if you want it, I accept *the injustice.*" You can guess what that injustice is: the destruction of the entire Work of God.
>
> I know it pleased him. How could I refuse to make this act of union with his will, if he was asking it of me? Once before, in 1933 or 1934, at what cost only he knows, I made a similar one.
>
> My son, what a beautiful harvest the Lord is preparing for us, after our Holy Father gets to knows us *truly* (not through calumny) and sees us for what we are—his very faithful ones—and blesses us![165]

[163] AGP, RHF, D–15011. See also *Testimonios*, pp. 405–406 (Silvestre Sancho Morales), and AGP, RHF, AVF–0027. (The Holy Office is now called the Congregation for the Doctrine of the Faith.)

[164] See AGP, RHF, D–15013 and D–15014.

[165] AGP, RHF, EF–410925–1. That week, September 21–27, he stayed at the Hotel Europeo in La Granja: see AGP, RHF, D–15410.

Just as in 1933, although this time within the Mass, Father Josemaría felt himself interiorly moved to offer in holocaust to God his foundational mission, together with all the apostolates of the Work. In a heroic act of detachment, Father Josemaría offered the sacrifice, in union with the divine will, of something much more precious to him than his own life.

That offering was the culmination of nine years of docility and complete submission to the will of God. In 1932 he had written in his *Apuntes*, "Lord, your donkey wants to deserve to be called 'he who loves God's will.'"[166] So many acts of love and obedience had taken place since then, in union with Jesus' suffering on the cross. With this second expression of loving acceptance of God's will, the founder had shown himself deserving of this title he wanted, and our Lord never again subjected him to that great trial.

Viewed from a spiritual perspective, the cross is a sign of God's special love. Suffering and happiness had consequently become one and the same thing to Father Josemaría. All that mattered to him was God's will. Later on, reflecting on what they had suffered back then from those persecutors, he would say, "They brought us closer to God. They crucified us alongside Christ and made us see—I now see it clear as day—that the sufferings we men undergo are just."[167]

But this correspondence with the divine will did not come easily, as he explained to Alvaro del Portillo:

> Alvaro, pray a lot and ask people to pray for your Father. Jesus is permitting the enemy to make me sensitive to the enormous injustice of that campaign of incredible lies and mad calumnies. And the human impulse is for the *animalis homo* to rise up. By God's grace I always reject those natural reactions (though they seem to be, and perhaps are, products of a sense of rectitude and justice) in favor of a joyful and filial "fiat" (of divine filiation: I am a son of God!) that fills me with peace and joy and makes me forget.[168]

And despite that resolve, he was shocked at the changes he saw in himself. In November 1941, while on retreat, he wrote in his journal:

---

[166] *Apuntes*, no. 711, 28 Apr 1932.
[167] *Letter 29 Dec 1947/14 Feb 1966*, no. 10.
[168] AGP, RHF, EF–410925–1.

This is the big thing I have discovered: I am naturally cheerful and optimistic; however, all these years of struggle and of sufferings of every type have changed my personality, without my realizing it until now. It's hard for me to smile. I have that eighty years' worth of gravity that I asked our Lord for when I was twenty-six—plus a lot of bitterness.

This is objective fact, just as it is also a fact that I've lost my *gaudium cum pace* only very rarely and only for a moment, despite all the trials, both interior and exterior. . . .

But I'm getting off the point: I have frequent bouts of ill humor, I'm somber, I seem sad. And God doesn't want that; it's not the spirit of the Work. I try to make sure that our houses are cheerful places, and they are. I should be the first to give example. What a good mortification—one ready at hand, and unnoticed! If my spiritual director approves, I'll do my particular exam on cheerfulness. It's no small thing!

Resolution: To smile, smile always, for love of Jesus Christ. Madrid—House of the Vincentian Fathers, November, 1941.[169]

*   *   *

Within just twelve months, starting in the autumn of 1940, the campaign against Opus Dei spread so widely and with such force that it seems almost miraculous that the Work survived. In his account of a conversation with the bishop of Madrid in January 1941, the founder wrote about Father Carrillo: "He has—with the best of intentions—gotten the smear campaign perfectly organized throughout Spain, and according to Father Segarra, it will also reach Rome."[170]

The first solid news that an official denunciation of Opus Dei to the Holy See was being prepared came in June 1941. From Barcelona Father Sebastián Cirac wrote to the bishop of Madrid:

Most esteemed Bishop:

I feel it is my duty to communicate to Your Excellency that the Jesuit provincial recently arrived in Rome, where he delivered by hand to the superior general of the Society some negative judgments on Opus Dei. And the superior general

---

[169] *Apuntes*, nos. 1855 and 1856.
[170] AGP, RHF, D–30010.

was so taken in by them that he had them sent to the congregations of the Holy See.

This news comes from a reliable source, and has already been communicated to the bishop of Barcelona by a friend. It might not be good for Father José María to know about it yet. In the meantime, as the bishop here has directed, we are preparing the defense of the truth, of the justness and virtue of the cause, despite the amount of work and the little time I have.[171]

Bishop Leopoldo immediately replied:

Dear Father Sebastián:

When my retreat ended, they gave me your letter. There's no date on it, and no postmark on the envelope, so I don't know when you sent it.

That is sad news. What a shame! But there's no need to worry. Our Lord God is in charge. I agree that there's no need for Father José María to hear about this. His reaction will be a holy one, I know, but it will be a physical blow to him. Right now he is giving a retreat.

I don't think they will do anything over there without consulting the bishops, or at least asking their opinion. When the time comes, God our Lord will assist us.

This does not mean you should not do all that you can. May our Lord, who will repay you, give you light.

Our main concern has to be that nothing in all of this do any harm to souls. And such harm would be done, and on a grand scale, by anything that would cast discredit upon the holy Society of Jesus. The greatest glory of Opus Dei will lie in always blessing the Society.

---

[171] On the top of the sheet there is a handwritten note: "Received 6/13. Answered 6/15."

Father Josemaría's old friend Father Sebastián Cirac held a doctorate in philosophy and literature, from the University of Madrid, and three other secular and ecclesiastical doctorates. At the time of the campaign against the Work, he was teaching Greek literature at the University of Barcelona. During this period, when for members of the Work not even the mail was a safe mode of communication, the founder told Alvaro del Portillo, "Until the cyclone passes, it would be best to write to our people via Cirac" (AGP, RHF, EF–410420–2).

Since the Opus is truly Dei, God will come to the rescue of what is his own and help us defend it well.

I think it would be best that this news not be made public.

Please inform me of any new developments. I will be most grateful.[172]

The news remained unpublicized. In September, during the week he spent in La Granja, Father Josemaría visited the bishop of Segovia, Luciano Pérez Platero. In their conversation the subject of the strong opposition of the Society of Jesus to Opus Dei came up, and the bishop said that he had a brother who was a Jesuit at Loyola, and who had told him that his fellow Jesuits had received only sketchy and unfavorable information about Opus Dei, so that it was difficult for them to make an objective judgment. Then the bishop said to Father Josemaría, "Did you know that they have taken the matter to Rome? My brother told me this."

"I know they've gone to the Holy Office," replied Father Josemaría. "And you can't imagine how happy I felt, even physically, when I found out. Now the Pope knows about us, even if badly, by way of slanders!"[173]

Soon, though, he realized that this was something new: a formal accusation. Even though he had expected this, he was crushed at first and felt the impulse to rebel. But with God's grace and his sense of divine filiation he recovered his peace and joy.

Bishop Leopoldo knew that the Roman Curia, with an eye to letting conflicts cool down, took up such denunciations in the order in which they arrived, which could mean a long wait. And in the meantime a number of Spanish bishops were sending to Rome, via the nuncio, their own perceptions of things. But the accusers had significant advantages. The Jesuits' superior general, Father Wlodimir Ledochowski, not only had sent the Holy See a report with numerous appendices (A–M), but (apparently because of the alarming nature of the information sent him from Spain) had in the accompanying letter

---

[172] AGP, RHF, D–30011. (Bishop Leopoldo provided this copy in 1963, shortly before he died.)

[173] See AGP, RHF, D–30012. His mention of a physical feeling of happiness is clearly a reference to something that had happened several months earlier, on the occasion of that walk that he took with Monsignor Morcillo. In his account of that conversation, he says that when Monsignor Morcillo told him that he had been denounced to Rome, "I jumped for joy right there on the road" (AGP, RHF, D–15011).

declared that he considered Opus Dei "very dangerous for the Church in Spain." He went on to say:

> The fact that His Excellency the Bishop of Madrid supports and promotes the Work by every possible means is not surprising. Nor am I surprised that a few bishops are in favor of the founder, Father Escrivá. Indeed, he does live an upright priestly life and his book *The Way* does contain sound ascetical teaching, expressed in an attractive way. But anyone who has a full picture of the Work will realize that this book is intended for the "uninitiated"—even though there are signs in it of a covert inclination to dominate the world with a form of Christian Masonry. For example, in point 911, "When will we see the world ours?" And if, then, some say that this "Opus Dei" is something of no great importance, that is because the Work, due to its secretive character, has almost no external visibility. Or it may be a skillful maneuver with which to deceive the Church authorities. But it is beyond doubt that it does currently exercise great influence and is also attracting the attention of the civil authorities.[174]

8. A platinum scalpel

From the first, as we have mentioned, Father Josemaría felt certain that the attacks on him were in some way a test allowed by God for the purpose of purifying him. And one of the things that confirmed him in this certainty was the kind of instrument that the Lord was making use of. As he explained, and Don Alvaro relayed to the bishop of Madrid, "How can we not see and bless this as a tribulation coming from God, when he uses an instrument so very much his as the holy and beloved Society of Jesus?"[175] Indeed, both he and Bishop Leopoldo thought that those involved were doing Opus Dei a great service. The founder would later, from Rome, write to Bishop Angelo

---

[174] AGP, RHF, D–30009. The quotation is from a partial copy of the letter: a copy dated July 3, 1942. If it is referring to the report to the Holy See mentioned by Father Sebastián Cirac, the letter must be from some months—even a year—earlier. It is in Italian and was probably given to the founder by some ecclesiastic.

[175] See AGP, RHF, D–03545–4 (Letter of 1 Sep 1941 from Bishop Eijo y Garay to Abbot Escarré).

Dell'Acqua that the Society of Jesus "has been, for Opus Dei, like a platinum scalpel in God's hands." [176] He urged members of Opus Dei to cultivate "a devotion to and a love for Saint Ignatius and his blessed Society." [177] In 1947 he wrote: "I am certain that when, many years from now, this document comes into your hands, you will have in your hearts—the same as we do now in ours—nothing but charity and forgiveness. And that you will love the hammer that has pounded us in such a way as to bring forth the beautiful sculpture that is the Work.[178]

Some Jesuits of course tried to put a stop to the attacks being made by their brothers in religion, but without success. The founder was deeply concerned about all these attacks, in great part because he feared that the calumnies and the techniques used to spread them might be utilized by others, as in fact did happen, with enemies of the Church adopting accusations first circulated by religious.[179] And there were Catholic laypeople and diocesan priests who continued to spread calumnies against Opus Dei.[180] But, as a help toward focusing on the supernatural fruit that would come from all this, he recalled how as a child he had seen old women pierce the early figs with needles so that they would ripen more quickly and be sweeter and more juicy. The persecution similarly was helping his children mature

---

[176] AGP, RHF, EF–650914–1.

[177] See AGP, RHF, EF–410420–2.

[178] *Letter 29 Dec 1947/14 Feb 1966*, no. 58.

[179] On innumerable occasions these calumnies propagated by churchmen were the arsenal used by enemies of the Church. Almost half a century after these events, representatives of certain political groups of a non-Catholic ideological orientation raised questions in the Italian parliament regarding the "secretiveness" of Opus Dei. The government, after looking into the matter and consulting the Holy See, completely rejected this charge against the Prelature. For the unabridged documented response by the Ministry of the Interior, see "Camera dei Deputati, Atti Parlamentari, Resoconto Stenografico n. 561, del 24–XI–1986."

[180] Two years after Father Carrillo came to Barcelona, the visits to parents of members of the Work started up again. This time the parents of Rafael Termes, the director of El Palau, were visited by a Catholic Action spiritual advisor. When he learned of this, the founder wrote to the archbishop of Toledo, Enrique Pla y Deniel, and to the auxiliary bishop, Eduardo Martínez. "I am sorry to bother you," he told the latter, "but I need to inform you that a certain Father Cunill in Barcelona has taken it upon himself to upset the parents of Rafael and Jaime by reiterating some of that slanderous nonsense about Opus Dei. There was a stormy scene in the Termes home, although now calm seems to have been restored. How much good a soothing letter from my Bishop would do this family! Don Eduardo, please don't fail to write them a few lines.

"Along with this letter I am also mailing one to the archbishop, since the Catalan priest in question is a spiritual advisor for Catholic Action and is also slandering us there" (AGP, RHF, EF–421205–1).

spiritually. "Our Lord God," he said, "to make us more effective, has blessed us with the cross." [181]

*   *   *

In the spring of 1941 the agitation in Barcelona was continuing unabated in many Catholic homes and ecclesiastical circles. It was also attracting the attention of civil authorities, and was starting to spread to neighboring dioceses.

At the beginning of May, Bishop Manuel Moll Salord of Lérida went to see the bishop of Gerona, carrying with him a copy of *The Way*, given him by the author, that he had been reading on the trip. The bishop of Gerona may well have been surprised to see him walk in with a book that he himself had just the day before heard denounced as heretical. After this visit, Bishop Moll Salord wrote to Father Josemaría:

> I received your wonderful book *The Way*, with the kind words of presentation that you wrote on the title page. I read it with the greatest interest. Or rather, we read it together, Father Angel and myself, on our way to Gerona one fine spring day. Without my realizing it, the Lord was sending me there to right some wrongs concerning you and your books and activities. Just the day before, that bishop had had some visitors who put him on guard against you and your book. I was able to show it to him, *nihil obstat* and *imprimatur* and all, and vouch for you personally, since I had met you a few weeks earlier. I had to do something similar in several ecclesiastical circles in Barcelona, where you are viewed with deep suspicion. What a shame. But I am convinced that this pervasive hostility will end up looking quite ridiculous. Always be united to your bishop and to the bishops of the dioceses where you want to work. Everything else is just an illusive cloud of dust, having nothing to do with God and everything to do with human designs and ambitions.
>
> I have two retreats for priests coming up in October, from the 13th through the 25th. Would you be so kind as to come give them? The last time, you had to leave us with our

---

[181] *Letter 6 May 1945*, no. 45.

appetites whetted, as the saying goes, having given us hardly a taste. What things the Lord does at times! I have often remembered that interruption, as also, before the altar, the soul of the person who caused it.[182]

*   *   *

On January 9, 1939, a few weeks before the civil war ended, the founder wrote his children a letter in which he enumerated the kinds of obstacles they could expect when they resumed their apostolic work: "scarcity, debt, poverty, scorn, slander, lies, ingratitude, opposition by good people."[183] Supernatural considerations aside, for what reasons were all these attacks being made on Opus Dei?

The root of the misunderstandings, suspicions, criticisms, and attacks was the message preached by Father Josemaría about the universal call to sanctity. Even before the civil war, it was being rumored that he had formed a heretical sect which proposed to seek sanctity in the midst of the hustle and bustle of the world. This was, certainly, a radical concept, but at that time it came as a total shock. Here was this young priest trying to arouse Catholics to make an adequate response to the vocation to sanctity inherent in baptism.

Thus Opus Dei came on the scene as a startling and disturbing novelty. For some, its message seemed to conflict with traditional customs and teachings. Many people equated "vocation" with religious consecration and tried to measure Opus Dei by the yardstick of the form of life proper to the religious state, which meant vows, a habit, community life, and external signs of poverty. Opus Dei surprised and in some cases scandalized them.

However, what got the persecution rolling appears to have been the strong competitive spirit of some opponents of Opus Dei. The slanders were of all sorts, some silly, others very dangerous. Among the latter was the claim that Opus Dei wished to destroy the institutions of consecrated life and steal vocations from religious orders.[184] This was a particularly unjust slander, since Father Josemaría made no secret of his deep love for religious, had so many friends in religious

---

[182] Letter of 25 Jul 1941 from Bishop Manuel Moll Salord, Coadjutor Bishop of Tortosa and Apostolic Administrator of Lérida, to Father Josemaría. (The "interruption" was the death of Father Josemaría's mother.)

[183] AGP, RHF, EF–390109–1.

[184] See Appendix 5.

orders and congregations, and continued to give retreats in convents and monasteries.[185]

Some nevertheless feared that "the universal call to sanctity would only prove to be a detriment to the seminaries, religious-order novitiates, etc., and result in a decrease in the number of vocations to the clerical or religious states."[186] When he wrote to Bishop Leopoldo about his meeting of May 31, 1941, with the Jesuit provincial of Toledo, the founder said: "It's all a matter of their thinking they are going to lose vocations."[187] Two weeks later he wrote to the provincial: "Basically, objectively, it's nothing more than a deplorable fight over whether this person or that is going to work with us."[188] And a week after that, Bishop Leopoldo lamented to Abbot Escarré: "And to think, Reverend Father, that this whole storm has come about because two

[185] The founder's many religious-order friends included Bishop Ballester and Father Moreno, of the Congregation of the Mission (Vincentians); Father Morata and Father (later Bishop) López Ortiz, both Augustinians; Dom Escarré and Dom Justo Pérez de Urbel, Benedictines; and Father Silvestre Sancho Morales, a Dominican (rector of the University of St. Thomas in Manila). And as we know, for years his spiritual director was Father Sanchez Ruiz, S.J.

[186] Laureano Castán Lacoma, in *Testimonios*, p. 103. Experience, he adds, has demonstrated the opposite. In places where members of Opus Dei are working, "the spiritual temperature is raised, and, as a consequence, there are more vocations for everyone."

[187] AGP, RHF, EF–410531–2. As we saw in chapter 6 of this biography (vol. 1, pp. 260–61), the founder tried unsuccessfully to find a word that would express the call to sanctity of Catholics not in religious life (laity and diocesan priests, men and women, celibates and married persons), a word denoting a radical dedication of a Christian to the service of the Lord that did not necessarily involve any change in the person's social, familial, or professional situation.

[188] AGP, RHF, EF–410614–2. What Father Josemaría got out of that meeting with the provincial (Father Carlos Gómez Martinho) was a strong impression that the Jesuit was mainly worried about losing potential vocations for his order. Father Carlos González Vallés, S.J., in his book *Las 7 palabras de Carlos G. Vallés* (Madrid, 1995), relates an experience of his own that bears out this impression. As a student in the Jesuit high school in Tudela, he had told his teachers that he wanted to become a Jesuit. His intention was to enter the order after he graduated. But before the beginning of his senior year, he received an urgent letter telling him to change his plans and go right then to the novitiate at Loyola. "It took me several years to catch on to the reason behind that sudden summons. Opus Dei was at that time beginning to become known in Spain and was attracting some of the best young men. Some of those young men had previously thought of becoming Jesuits, and it hurt the Jesuits to lose valuable vocations. That had already happened right there at the Tudela high school, and had set off an alarm among the priests. In my particular case they feared that if I stayed in the school for another year, I undoubtedly would come into contact with Opus Dei and might be attracted by it. They didn't want to lose me and they acted quickly. They wrote telling me to come to the novitiate without delay so that I would be safely within its walls before I heard of Opus Dei. Of course they didn't tell me anything of this and I had no suspicion of it at the time. I obeyed and went. I have now for the first time told this in writing, and I am fully convinced of it."

or three boys who were thinking of entering religious life preferred Opus Dei once they knew about it!"[189]

Father Josemaría well understood that the general health of the Church came ahead of the particular needs of the Work. In 1931, when he had with him only three young men, he wrote in his journal: "The members and associates will not be egotists, in the sense of seeking vocations for themselves alone (or in any other sense). On the contrary, they will foster vocations for the religious institutes, orders, and congregations, and for the diocesan seminaries."[190] Although Opus Dei had its own pressing need for people, he never sought to reap what someone else had sown. As a director of souls, he fostered vocations for the benefit of all the institutions in the Church, without exception. That way of acting is, in fact, part and parcel of the mission and spirit of the Work,[191] as he himself clearly stated:

> You well know that it is proper to our spirit to rejoice at
> seeing many vocations come to the seminaries and religious

---

[189] See Appendix 5.

[190] *Apuntes*, no. 52 (16 Jun 1930). "His love for God's Church was so great that he quite naturally encouraged and praised all the institutions that have come about in order to bring more souls to God" (José María García Lahiguera, in *Testimonios*, p. 159). "He was very happy to see the apostolic work of everyone, and praised God for it. He always said, 'The more people serving God, the better'" (Silvestre Sancho Morales, PM, fol. 104v). "In his apostolic activities, he not only did not try in any instance to trespass on others' fields or to work in fields more or less already cultivated by other laborers or shepherds in the vineyard of the Lord, but expressly and resolutely steered clear of any such effort and tried to go where he saw a scarcity or complete lack of the pastoral care that he might be able to offer" (Joaquín Mestre Palacios: AGP, RHF, T–00181, p. 30). "I recall very well that in those years of 1940 and 1941, in Saragossa, when vocations for the Work were so much needed, Father Josemaría himself steered toward the seminary two young university students, friends of ours. It made him very happy when we told him ... that as a result of our apostolic work, there had been several priestly and religious vocations" (Javier de Ayala, PM, fol. 1477).

[191] See *Letter 29 Dec 1947/14 Feb 1966*, no. 43.

Vicente Mortes notes that a roommate of his at Jenner, Jose Gramunt de Moragas, entered the Jesuits, and Enrique Saracho went to the seminary from La Moncloa Residence (see Vicente Mortes Alfonso, *Sum.* 7224). On the fostering of vocations see Pedro Casciaro, *Sum.* 6353; Florencio Sanchez Bella, *Sum.* 7507; Blanca Fontan Suanzes, *Sum.* 6954.

Many religious acknowledged that they owed their vocations to the founder. Among those mentioned by Bishop Alvaro del Portillo were Father Jose Maria Aguilar Collados, O.S.H., chaplain of the Monastery of San Bartolome de Inca (Mallorca), who in turn recalls that the founder sent two of his friends to join religious orders; the Camaldolese monk Dom Pio Maria Calvo Botas; Father Hugo Maria (Miguel) de Quesada Lucas, who in 1942 entered the Carthusian monastery of Miraflores; Father Bartolome Rotger Castaño, prior of the Carthusian monastery of Montealegre de Badalona (Barcelona); and others. See Alvaro del Portillo, *Sum.* 298, 299, 443, etc.

families. We give thanks to God, since not a few of those vocations are the fruit of the work of spiritual and doctrinal formation we carry out among young people to enkindle the atmosphere around us with Christian fire, to make it more supernatural and more apostolic. It stands to reason that this results in more souls for all the institutions of the Church.[192]

Thinking that way, Father Josemaria found it hard to understand how the question of vocations could stir up such a commotion.[193]

9. The first center of the women's branch

When, in April 1941, Paco Botella learned that Doña Dolores was sick, he went to the Diego de León residence to ask how she was and, if possible, to visit her. Carefully opening the door to her room, he saw the sick woman lying in bed, consumed with fever. At that moment she turned her face toward the door and, seeing Paco, said, "Listen, Paco! I have good news for you. Your sister Enrica is now my granddaughter." [194]

[192] *Letter 11 Mar 1940*, no. 39. He later wrote: "Others unreasonably got angry because, ordinarily, the vocations the Lord was sending us were coming from environments where they themselves were generally not finding any. *No one with a priestly or religious vocation came to us.* Those vocations are of no use to us; our vocation is very different from that of religious. Some had been in contact with religious orders, but had not felt inclined to join them. The best proof that they did not have that vocation is that, knowing all about it, they took another *way.*

"There should have been no surprise in that. There are, after all, no fenced-off fields, no private reserves. This is how people with a one-party mind-set think. But often 'alius est qui seminat, et alius est qui metit' ('one sows and another reaps': Jn 4:37), and our Lord also said, 'et qui seminat, simul gaudeat, et qui metit' (Let sower and reaper rejoice together: Jn 4:36)" (*Letter 14 Sep 1951*, no. 39).

[193] Archbishop Pedro Cantero, who was a close friend of Father Josemaría from as early as 1931, said of him: "The Father had an outlook that was extraordinarily broad, and not at all exclusivist. He always respected the freedom of each person to choose their own way and follow their own vocation. Or, to put it better, he not only respected but sincerely praised anything that was for the service of Jesus Christ and his Church. And, from where he was, he did everything he could to further every good undertaking. I can never forget that he was the moving force in my own decision and that he always warmly supported it. He knew that souls belong to God alone and that God calls where and as he wants. He was the one who inspired my decision, as I have so often written and said, but never did he feel that he had any rights over me. Rather, he was always concerned with helping me live out my vocation" (*Testimonios*, p. 68). Archbishop Cantero served as bishop of Barbastro (1952–1954), and then as bishop of Huelva, before becoming archbishop of Saragossa in 1964.

[194] AGP, RHF, T–00159/1, p. 111 (Francisco Botella).

It came to him as a welcome surprise. In Valencia a few weeks earlier, at Father Josemaría's suggestion, he had spoken with his sister, explaining to her the Work and its apostolates. But her response had been less than enthusiastic. It sounded, she had said, like an "admirable work," but they should not count on her.[195] Paco had then read her a point from *The Way*, a book that Enrica and the rest of the family were already familiar with, since Paco had given them a copy the year before. The point began, "Woman is stronger than man and more faithful in the hour of trial."[196]

Enrica had then taken part in a retreat given by Father Josemaría for young women in Catholic Action, from March 30 to April 5, 1941. And since her brother was in the Work, she had decided to introduce herself.

"Father," she said, "my brother has spoken to me about the Work."

"And I," he replied, "am praying for your vocation."[197]

When Father Josemaría got back to Madrid, he wanted to tell Paco about Enrica's decision, but he let the Grandmother give him the good news.

*   *   *

Another young woman on that retreat, Encarnación Ortega, had found herself wondering what on earth had possessed her to shut herself up for several days in that place. Could it have been curiosity about the author of *The Way*, a book fresh in her memory? Her brother was often at El Cubil, the residence in Valencia, and he had encouraged her to say hello to the Father, but she was not sure she wanted to.

However, when the founder entered the chapel to begin the retreat, her soul was deeply moved. She says:

> His recollection, totally natural, his genuflection before the tabernacle, the way he put his whole self into the preparatory prayer before the meditation, encouraging us to be aware that our Lord was there and was looking at us and listening to us, made me quickly forget my desire to hear a great speaker. Instead I understood that I needed to listen to God and be

---

[195] See AGP, RHF, T–04894, p. 4 (Enrica Botella).
[196] *The Way*, no. 982.
[197] AGP, RHF, T–04894, p. 5.

generous with him. I overcame my hesitancy and, for the sake
·of good manners, did go to greet the Father.[198]

He gave her a quick overview of what the Work was all about: the
search for sanctification in work, a contemplative and apostolic life
out in the streets, divine filiation. . . . The young woman felt a sudden
fright. She was dazzled by what that priest was explaining, aware that
it was something marvelous, and fearful that God might demand
everything of her. She resolved never to speak with Father Josemaría
again. "But in spite of that decision," she says, "I couldn't sleep and
could hardly eat. I saw that God needed some courageous women to
do his Work on earth, and that, without knowing why, I had been
informed of this by its founder. That thought stayed constantly on my
mind." [199]

For the rest of the retreat, she says, "I tried to get some distance from
God's call." If she was shut up in her room, she felt the need for some
fresh air. So she would go outside for a walk through the convent's
orange grove, but still that thought would never leave her head.
Nothing she did would get rid of it. Nor was she safe in the chapel,
where the preacher's forceful words troubled her heart.

One day Father Josemaría gave a meditation on the Lord's Passion.
He began with the Garden of Olives: Jesus' prayer in the midst of
loneliness and desertion; the oppressive weight of human malice and
the horrible evil of sin; the anguish, to the point of sweating blood, at
what he knew lay ahead.

The retreatants, carried along by the priest's words, followed in the
footsteps of Christ. Encarnita tells us:

> And then he said to us, "All of that, he suffered for you. You,
> since you don't want to do what he is asking of you, should at
> least have the courage to look at the tabernacle and tell him,
> '*That*—what you're asking of me—I don't feel like doing!' "
>
> Then he spoke about the scourging, with such force that
> we seemed to be eyewitnesses. And the crowning with
> thorns. And the cross on his back. And each of the sufferings
> of the Passion. After every one of them, he would repeat, "All
> of that, he suffered for you. Have the courage, at least, to

[198] AGP, RHF, T–05074, p. 74.
[199] Ibid., p. 75.

tell him that what he is asking of you, you don't feel like doing!"

At the end of the meditation, while I was trying to formulate a resolution, someone touched me on the shoulder and said, "Father Josemaría would like to see you." [200]

He didn't have to ask her anything. Encarnita went ahead and told him that she was ready for anything. The Father warned her of the difficulties. The life she was undertaking would be hard; the poverty, great; the renunciation of her own preferences, total. She would have to be ready to travel, perhaps far from her own country. And she would have to pursue sanctity in work, finishing her daily tasks heroically, down to the smallest details.

*　　*　　*

In the first week of August 1940, Father Josemaría was in León, giving a retreat for diocesan priests. His friend Father Eliodoro Gil, the pastor of a parish there, San Juan de Renueva, knew a young woman named Narcisa González Guzmán (Nisa, for short); he was her confessor. Nisa liked sports, studied languages, and dressed well. Perhaps she might understand the Work? Father Eliodoro told her that the author of *The Way*, a book Nisa liked, was in León. At that her eyes lit up, so Father Eliodoro arranged a visit.

On one of those hot August mornings the young lady went to the bishop's residence and waited nervously in a huge room. Soon a friendly-looking priest appeared. He came up to her and immediately, point-blank, asked her a question that caught her by surprise: "My daughter, do you love our Lord a lot?" She answered, "Yes—I don't know." [201]

The priest then got down to business and gave her an incisive overview of the Work. As she listened, Nisa began to worry that perhaps the white summer skirt and dark red jacket she was wearing were not appropriate in that austere setting of the bishop's residence—a concern that she expressed obliquely with a question about how one ought to dress. Seeming to sense what she was thinking, the priest reassured her that in Opus Dei one always dressed naturally, not "like a scarecrow." [202]

---

[200] Ibid., p. 76.
[201] AGP, RHF, T–04989, p. 1 (Narcisa González Guzmán).
[202] Ibid., p. 3.

At the end of the meeting, her reaction was much the same as Enrica's and Encarnita's had been at first. But Father Josemaría was not discouraged by such silences or negative responses. With a supernatural stubbornness he just went on praying and mortifying himself for those women.

Nisa tells us:

> The conversation with the Father made a profound impression on me. It seemed to me like an ambitious commitment, one I was not yet ready for. As I left the bishop's residence, I thought: It is something wonderful, and it might be for me, but I don't feel that I have the strength. . . .
>
> I am certain that the Father was praying for me, and he seemed to know the best way of dealing with me. He did not say anything more to me. I went on reading *The Way*, and got to know it almost by heart. Every time I read one of its points, there was something that moved me, that made me grow in love for God, the love which the founder had spoken to me about that first time, and which led me to accept my vocation.[203]

In April 1941 Nisa went to Madrid and asked Father Josemaría for admission to Opus Dei.

* * *

Ten years after the beginning of the work with women, Father Josemaría remained as optimistic as ever. Given that the Work was something of God, he knew that the logic governing its development was very different from that operating in merely human enterprises. He wrote:

> *The logic of God,* my daughters and sons, does not very often coincide with the poor, pitiful logic of us human beings. For that reason we run into obstacles, internal and external, in trying to love God's holy will and carry it out. That is also the reason why the first vocations came at the price of blood. The same thing will happen again from time to time, for the disciple is not above the Master.[204]

---

[203] Ibid., p. 4.
[204] *Letter 29 Dec 1947/14 Feb 1966*, no. 128.

In the face of a steady stream of calumnies, the founder had other things to cope with besides the need to get the apostolate with women under way, and so he strove to transmit the spirit of Opus Dei to his daughters as rapidly as possible. In August 1941 he gave a retreat for them at the Diego de León center. His dynamic, optimistic, fatherly words sparked in them new hopes and dreams. In October he wrote to his daughters in Madrid:

> May Jesus watch over my daughters.
> Everything worthwhile takes effort. The Lord has, for this last while, been letting you experience some little setbacks. But we are already approaching the goal.[205]

Nisa went back to León, where she was to stay until a center opened in Madrid. She received a weekly letter from those in Madrid, and sometimes Father Josemaría also wrote. In November 1941 he sent her a letter saying:

> It might be good for you to come before the house is ready, to help set it up—though the furnishings will be very modest. Please let me know if you can come in case we need to send for you.
> Pray a lot and get others to pray—with prayer we will go where we need to go. Entrust your concerns and ours to Our Lady of the Way. Be very happy.[206]

Months went by without a house turning up. And there were still very few women in the Work.

Finally they found a house, at 19 Jorge Manrique Street, and they moved in at the beginning of July 1942. It was a private home with three stories, a basement, and a garden, but no furniture or decorations. Father Josemaría was giving a retreat in Segovia, but his daughters were very much on his mind, and when he returned he concentrated on impressing on them the basics: a faithful and very loving fulfillment of the norms of piety and of family and professional obligations; a supernatural outlook on everything; and sincerity at any cost.

---

[205] AGP, RHF, EF–411021–1.
[206] AGP, RHF, EF–411105–1.

They were to have a supernatural outlook toward the director of the house, seeing her as a representative of God. Her personality, abilities, age, temperament—these things did not matter. They must not be like the country bumpkin who refused to pray to one of the saints in the village church because he had seen the saint's statue being carved from a tree trunk, and so "I knew him when he was a cherry tree!" [207]

They had to be transparent, totally sincere. "Savagely sincere—but not sincerely savage," he told them. Sincerity was a virtue always stressed by the founder. When the furniture for the director's office— a sofa with matching armchairs, a desk, and a bookcase—were being arranged, a bottle of ink got spilled, staining the desk indelibly. At first they hesitated to tell him, but sensibly decided they should. "It's nothing," he said. "I don't care if desks get damaged; they can always be fixed. What matters to me is that you always be sincere." [208]

In the summer of 1942, from Pamplona, he wrote to them: "Our Lord has his eyes fixed on that little house from which such great things for his glory have to come." [209] In fact, in a real sense, what would germinate into half of Opus Dei was housed in that little center on Jorge Manrique Street. In *The Way* the founder had written, "Don't judge by the smallness of the beginnings. My attention was once drawn to the fact that there is no difference in size between seeds that produce annual plants and those that will grow into ageless trees." [210] And indeed, by their fidelity to grace and to the spirit of the Work, that handful of women would become a multitude that is like a tree in full bloom for the Church.

Usually Father Josemaría spoke about the greatness and heroism there is in doing the little things, the most miniscule everyday tasks, with much love. But now and then he encouraged his daughters by showing them, as it were, what the Work would develop into in accord with the divine law of growth. One afternoon in November 1942 he visited the Jorge Manrique house and met in the library with the three young women there at the time. Encarnita tells us:

On the desk he spread out a chart showing the different projects that the women's branch of Opus Dei was going to

---

[207] See AGP, RHF, T–05074., p. 5.
[208] Ibid., p. 48.
[209] AGP, RHF, EF–420916–2.
[210] *The Way*, no. 820.

carry out in the world. Just trying to follow the Father almost made me dizzy, he was explaining them all to us so vividly: agricultural schools for peasant women, professional training schools, university residences, activities in the fashion industry, maternity homes in cities all over the world, bookmobiles bringing wholesome and educational reading to the most remote villages, bookstores. . . . Slowly folding up that chart, he said: "There are two possible reactions to all this. One is to think it's very nice, but an impossible dream. The other is to trust in the Lord, to trust that if he asks this of us, he will help us make it a reality. I hope you react the second way." [211]

But the reality then and there was hunger and fatigue, scarcity and poverty. One day, while speaking to his daughters about poverty, he went down to the kitchen with them to inspect the equipment. They had to look after their health, he said, because if they came down sick through their own fault, that would be, among other things, a serious failure in poverty. Yet even when it came to where their next meal was coming from, he insisted, they should never stop trusting in their Father-God.[212]

Although he was not one to complain, he continued at this time to be subject to periodic attacks of rheumatism, especially when the rainy season began or the weather turned cold. On October 14, 1941, from Lérida, he wrote to his sons in Madrid: "I'm still taking the pills, because my rheumatism is still bothering me. What an old wreck I am! Pray a lot for this poor fat fellow." [213]

In November of the following year, he was giving a retreat at the Monastery of Our Lady of Parral in Segovia, and the cell he was assigned was next to the tabernacle on one side and the tomb of two monks on the other. "They have put me between Life and death," he wrote to his sons. And then, as though excusing himself for going off the diet prescribed by his doctor, he wrote: "Here I can't stay on the diet. I'm only having bread and potatoes and milk and a few veg-

---

[211] AGP, RHF, T–05074, p. 2.

[212] See AGP, RHF, T–04989, p. 27.

[213] AGP, RHF, EF–411014–1. In a letter dated October 20 he wrote from Lérida to a friend in Madrid, Vicente Rodríguez: "I wanted to see you before I left. It was impossible because even the day before I left Madrid, I was still laid up in bed with this pesky rheumatism" (AGP, RHF, EF–411020–1).

etables. There's no other choice, given the life of penance of these good souls." [214]

As became clear later, his rheumatism and other physical ailments were more serious than anyone realized at the time. If someone did mention them, he would just say, "You have to have something." [215] He tried to hide the symptoms and declined to attach much importance to them.

In the fall and winter of 1942, he left the Diego de León house early every morning to say Mass at the Jorge Manrique center. His daughters, while praying in the oratory before Mass, watched for him out the window. As the time for Mass drew near, he would come into view, wrapped in his cloak, limping from the rheumatism. (The entire street of Jorge Manrique was on a slope.) When he got near the house, he would start to walk normally, and once inside, and all through Mass, he would move with perfect grace. But once he was outside, going either up or down the slope, he would return to limping, to cut down on the pain.

It was a long walk from the one center to the other, through a hilly district not yet fully developed. Father Josemaría often made the trip on foot, but sometimes he took the streetcar, occasionally asking his daughters for a peseta for the ride home.[216]

---

[214] AGP, RHF, EF–421104–2.
[215] AGP, RHF, T–04989, p. 36.
[216] AGP, RHF, T–05074, p. 60.

1. *Two brothers and a sister*

The three Escrivá children, Carmen, Josemaría, and Santiago, were alike in many ways, including the quick tempers that now and then flared up suddenly and just as quickly subsided, without leaving any residue of resentment. Their mother's death did not change their living arrangements, but it did produce changes in their relationship.

Santiago had grown up in circumstances very different from those of his sister and brother. Born just three weeks before his mother turned forty-two, he did not know the comfortable, cheerful home life of the early days in Barbastro. The Escrivá home, though a happy environment, was marked by suffering by the time he was born. Years later, after Carmen and Josemaría had died, Santiago mentioned something he perhaps had not dared speak of when his sister and brother were living.

"Our home," he said, "was never a normal one, in the strictest sense of the word. To me, a normal home is one where children can have friends over, invite them to come for dinner or a snack, etc. I couldn't always do that. I remember that even when I was studying at the university, if someone invited me to their home, I couldn't reciprocate. For my sister Carmen it was the same." [1]

When Don José died, Josemaría took his place, as he had promised to do in the presence of his father's body. That sad Christmas of 1924 was a trial for the whole family, unforgettably so for little Santiago. The only treat they could afford was a piece of marzipan Carmen bought—but it turned out to be spoiled and had to be thrown out. A few days later, the little one suffered another disappointment.

---

[1] AGP, RHF, T–07921, p. 35. Santiago's recollection about Carmen pertains to his own university years. As a young lady, Carmen had very close female friends and several suitors, among them Luis Otal, Baron of Valdeolivos. She gave up the possibility of having her own home in order to help her brother Josemaría in his apostolate.

Although they were in the period of mourning, he still hoped for a toy from the Three Kings. A half-century later he recalled: "I vividly remember the disappointment I got from the Kings. They had left a box for me. I was excited, thinking it was a toy car. But when I opened the box, it turned out to be a pair of shoes." [2]

In April 1927, Father Josemaría went to Madrid to finish his university studies and get his doctorate. Doña Dolores waited in Fonz for the news that the rest of the family could join him. It seemed an eternity to Santiago. "I was waiting for Josemaría to come see us, but he didn't. In my eagerness I dreamed I saw him arriving on a white horse. But he didn't forget me. Every week he sent me some comics." [3]

In November the family joined Father Josemaría in Madrid—he, of course, having no idea that he would soon also have a new family on his hands. Doña Dolores and Carmen looked after Santiago. "Josemaría also gave a lot of time to me," Santiago recalled. "He would take me for walks when he had some free time, especially on Sundays. Sometimes he would take me for a snack to El Sotanillo, where he met the young fellows he was doing apostolate with. I didn't know much about his work, but I would make up part of the group. Later Josemaría couldn't spend as much time with me because he had to tend to the first members of the Work. For me that was like being orphaned again, since Josemaría and Carmen were like parents to me." [4] With the keen sensibilities of a child, including a touch of jealousy, Santi called the newcomers "Josemaría's boys." And his fears in part came true, as the number of visitors to the apartment on Martínez Campos grew steadily and the state of Doña Dolores' pantry gave all too visible testimony to their healthy appetites.

For Carmen life was very different. She was twenty years older than Santi and had no trouble being a mother to him. Along with solid common sense, she had a romantic streak and dreamed of traveling; she also loved to read.[5] But, rejecting the several marriage proposals she received, Carmen voluntarily took on her shoulders the care of the Work, without neglecting her own family.

---

[2] Ibid., p. 5. The Spanish custom of children receiving gifts on the feast of the Epiphany was a long-standing tradition in the Escrivá family. Recall what Father Josemaría wrote to Enrique Alonso-Martínez Saumell in 1938 about having "that trustful hope that filled my whole soul when as a little boy I would write to the Three Kings" (AGP, RHF, EF–380204–1).

[3] AGP, RHF, T-07921, p. 7.

[4] Ibid., p. 9.

[5] Ibid., p. 4

When Doña Dolores died, Carmen was already over forty. The dark and attractive young girl had become a mature woman, with valuable wartime and peacetime experience, firm in her convictions and determined in her actions, and (like her brothers) endowed with an exceptionally big heart.

For Father Josemaría, Doña Dolores's death brought an immediate, pressing concern: Who could take her place in helping form the women who were coming to the Work? He had relied heavily on her quiet demeanor to convey the homelike atmosphere that was needed. Now he complained: "My God, my God, what have you done? You are taking everything away from me, absolutely everything."[6]

But it did not take long for him to realize that, as always, God was ahead of him, knowing and doing what was in everyone's best interests. Doña Dolores received her reward, and Carmen stepped up to fill the void left by the Grandmother. An incident that took place seven years later shows clearly his awareness of how providential this had been.

In May 1948, the nuncio told him that he had read in *L'Osservatore Romano* that Carmen had been received in audience by the Holy Father. Then he added, "I didn't know you had a sister."

"You can see, Your Excellency, how discreetly my mother, may she rest in peace, and my sister have worked alongside me. Without their help, I don't think we could have given the Work the refined air of a Christian home, a family."

He paused, then added: "On the other hand, knowing what hard times we went through, you can see how God's grace spared us calumny about this, too. Carmen is well over forty now, but she was only in her twenties when she and my mother started helping me."[7]

The dignity and respectability of Carmen and Doña Dolores also made it possible for the founder to carry on a thriving apostolate with women. During the years from the fall of 1940 to the fall of 1942 he gave spiritual direction in the confessional to many women, married and unmarried, while waiting for the first Opus Dei women's center to open.

During those years of "opposition by good people," Carmen gave herself wholeheartedly to serving the Work. Assuming Doña Dolores's functions as lady of the house, she conscientiously oversaw the house-

---

[6] See AGP, RHF, T–04956, p. 12 (María Dolores Fisac).
[7] AGP, RHF, AVF-0036.

keeping at Diego de León. She was calm, tireless, and impervious to trivial mishaps. Her duties ranged from hiring and training the domestic help to teaching Christian doctrine to the women.

Carmen enjoyed cooking and was good at it. But these were times to discourage even good cooks, what with food shortages, rationing, and the poor quality of the charcoal used as fuel. The kitchen was in the basement, and Carmen, who lived on the second floor, had to go up and down the narrow, steep stairs twenty times a day. Housecleaning and laundry were other time-consuming chores in a house that soon had more than forty residents. And then there were meals for guests, shopping, repairs, record keeping, and the training of Nisa Guzmán, one of the first women of the Work.[8]

Carmen discreetly took the Grandmother's place in the sewing and mending get-togethers, where she always had some advice to give or some anecdote to tell. She also took over the tasks that had been reserved to the Grandmother, including washing Father Josemaría's underclothing. At Diego de León, "around 1941 and 1942 Carmen sometimes got angry with her brother at finding blood stains on his shirts from his harsh penances—now partly practiced for the advancement of the women's section, which was just getting a fresh start."[9]

"Aunt Carmen," as they called her, won the affection of both the men and women in the Work. It had become a custom for someone who had been away on a trip to return home with a small gift, candy or some other treat. Doña Dolores used to keep these in a dresser drawer so that she always had something special for her "grandchildren."[10] Carmen continued the family tradition, sometimes even buying the treats herself.

Bighearted though she was, she nevertheless was not given to outward displays of affection. In fact, this held true even in her dealings with her two brothers. Thus outsiders hardly knew how deep their mutual affection was, since she was so reserved and Father Josemaría never favored his family in the least at the expense of the Work. This produced an occasional outburst of annoyance from his sister, but she

[8] See Alvaro del Portillo, *Sum.* 512 and 514; AGP, RHF, T–04989, p. 28 (Narcisa González Guzmán); and Francisco Ponz Piedrafita, *Mi encuentro con el Fundador del Opus Dei 1939* (Pamplona, 2000), pp. 94–96.

[9] AGP, RHF, T–04678/1, p. 125 (José Luis Múzquiz). See also AGP, RHF, T–07921, p. 9 (Santiago Escrivá de Balaguer), and T–05074, p. 56 (Encarnación Ortega).

[10] See AGP, RHF, T-04151, p. 42.

would quickly calm down and go back to her tasks. As had been the case for Doña Dolores, there were many days when, even though they lived in the same house, she never laid eyes on him.[11]

Few were aware of how deeply grateful he was for the help he got from his own family. Every favor, no matter how small, made him feel in their debt. And although aware he could never fully repay them, he did what he could with prayer, mortification, and his Masses.[12] He saw this as fulfilling the fourth commandment, which he liked to call "the sweetest precept of the decalogue."[13]

He never forgot a certain trip to the front that he made in 1938. Starting out from Burgos, he transferred in Mirando de Ebro to a train that made a stop in Logroño. When the train passed the cemetery where his father was buried, his heart skipped a beat.[14] He resolved some day to "rescue" his father's remains, relics in his eyes when he thought of all the members of Opus Dei whose spiritual debt to that Christian gentleman extended back in God's providence to a time even before the Work was founded.

Now and then his mother had expressed a desire to be buried beside her husband. So, soon after the first anniversary of Doña Dolores' death, Father José María Millán, a seminary companion from the Logroño days, completed arrangements requested by the founder to have his father's remains exhumed. On April 27, 1942, Ricardo Fernández Vallespín drove Father Josemaría to Logroño to bring the remains of Don José Escrivá to Madrid. Carrying the required permissions and a zinc-lined chest, the two of them went to the cemetery April 29, and found the tombstone already lifted and the gravediggers removing dirt. Soon the coffin appeared, its top caved in. They gath-

[11] See AGP, RHF, T-04989, p. 42; and also Juan Udaondo Barinagarrementería, *Sum.* 5030.

[12] He also included among his benefactors the people who slandered him, "because they help purify us." For that reason, he said, "we have to love them and pray for them." See Juan Hervás Benet, in *Beato Josemaría Escrivá de Balaguer: un hombre de Dios. Testimonios sobre el Fundador del Opus Dei* (Madrid, 1994), p. 203. (Hereafter this book will be cited as *Testimonios*.)

[13] See Alvaro del Portillo, *Sum.* 505. The founder was well aware of how much he was asking of his family. Though it had, in effect, become the vocation of both Doña Dolores and Carmen to collaborate in the development of Opus Dei, this was something he never took for granted. "Dearest Mother and dearest Carmen and Santiago," he wrote to them from León, "may Jesus watch over you! I remember you frequently, and ask our Lord to make you happy to keep helping us in our work. I hope that in a few months the efforts that God and I are asking of you will be less intense. In the meantime, make them for him" (AGP, RHF, EF–400731–1).

[14] See AGP, RHF, EF-380509-1.

ered up the bones, placed them in the zinc container, took it to one of the cemetery buildings to have it sealed, and immediately headed back to Madrid.[15]

Nisa was the first person Father Josemaría saw when he got to Diego de León. She remembered later that he was wearing his short black cape and carrying the chest under his arm, and that in a quiet voice, with the contented air of someone who had at last satisfied a duty of honor, he said to her, "I have here the remains of my father." [16]

The chest was placed in the oratory, on a small table covered with a black cloth. It stayed there until the next day, except for a few hours when he took it to his room, placing it on his bed to avoid setting it on the floor.[17] On April 30, the remains of Don José Escrivá were buried in La Almudena cemetery at the foot of Doña Dolores's coffin.[18]

Years later, after the Diego de León center had been transformed into the headquarters of the Regional Commission of Opus Dei in Spain, Father Josemaría was able to complete his work of filial piety by having the remains of both his parents placed in the crypt there. This was done on March 31, 1969.[19] In showing this respect to his blood family, the founder was acting at the request of his older sons in the Opus Dei family, who saw this as a gesture of gratitude to all the benefactors of the Work, represented by two who had helped from the very start. "Benefactors" had always been understood to include all the parents and brothers and sisters of the faithful of Opus Dei. In 1973 the founder said: "Today when I go to the crypt where the remains of my parents lie, I won't pray only for them. My prayer of thanksgiving and suffrage for their souls will reach out to the parents and brothers and sisters of all who form part of Opus Dei. Naturally I will also pray for all the souls in purgatory, including those who (acting I am sure with a good intention) failed to understand or placed obstacles to the work of Opus Dei." [20]

---

[15] See AGP, RHF, D–05851, D–15013, and D–15014.

[16] See AGP, RHF, T–04989, pp. 57–58.

[17] See AGP, RHF, T–04956, p. 16.

[18] See RHF, D-05851.

[19] A note filled out in connection with the exhumation from La Almudena reads: "José Escrivá Corzán — Tomb, excellent; level 2, section A, plot 5, block 57, letter A, body no. 2; buried on April 30, 1942. Transferred on 31 Mar 1969 to the crypt of Holy Cross Residence" (AGP, RHF, D–05851).

The original burial documents were deposited in the tombs in the crypt. Photocopies are in AGP, RHF, D–07778.

[20] Javier Echevarría, PR, p. 1578.

*   *   *

It may have been 1944 when a student living in Diego de León one day asked the founder why Carmen and Santiago were not members of Opus Dei. "That is their business. Ask them if you like," he replied.[21] But the question has a simple answer: Carmen and Santiago were not called to be members of the Work but to collaborate in their own ways.

2. *The apostolate of apostolates*

In October 1941, Father Josemaría gave a retreat to priests of the Lérida diocese at the invitation of Bishop Moll Salord. The retreat was at the diocesan seminary, where the previous April he had received news of his mother's death during another retreat. Writing his sons in Madrid on October 16, he spoke of having phoned them the day before, complained about the delay in getting through, and asked when a second telephone line they had ordered would be installed. Then he wrote:

> The archpriest of Fraga, the fig capital, is on this retreat. Find out if it would be worthwhile ordering figs in quantity. The price still hasn't been set. Last year figs were 2 pesetas a kilo, but this year it seems that the price will rise to 5 pesetas. If it's worth the effort, let me know. I have to give them the quantity when I place the order. There's no limit.[22]

A list of urgent things to see to followed: securing the kitchen staff for the Jenner Residence, purchase of furniture, setting up the new house. "This letter," he concluded, "seems to have been written by Lazarus in collaboration with Martha. Poor Mary!"

That lament must be taken with a grain of salt, since even when fretting about dried figs, he was moved by the glory of God and paternal affection for his children.[23] Matter and spirit, action and contemplation, work and prayer were inseparably united in his life.

---

[21] See Juan Udaondo, *Sum.* 5031.

[22] AGP, RHF, EF–411016–1.

[23] While this particular transaction seems not to have taken place, a later wholesale purchase of figs provided the pantries of several centers with a great supply. See AGP, RHF, T–00159.

And in some ways his humorous words in the letter just quoted were the heart of Opus Dei's message: the sanctifying value of work done before God with a right intention. He wrote in 1945:

> The spiritual and ascetical formation given us by the Work aims to create in our souls an habitual disposition, an instinct as it were, leading us always to maintain, and never lose, a supernatural outlook in everything we do. We don't live a double life, but a unity of life, simple and strong, joining and fusing all our actions.
>
> When we are generous in our response to this spirit, we acquire a second nature. Without realizing it, we are immersed in God all day long and feel the need to "put" him into everything we do, since without him our actions seem insipid. The time comes when we can no longer tell where our prayer ends and work begins, because our work is also prayer, contemplation, true mystical life and union with God: divinization. And yet with nothing out of the ordinary about it.[24]

Returning to Madrid, Father Josemaría became involved in finishing the setting up of the apartment on Villanueva Street, which they had rented in September and where Alvaro and Isidoro Zorzano were to live. After much searching, they found another small apartment for members in the Work studying for their doctorates or already working. This center was set up in a house at 116 Núñez de Balboa. [25] To set up a new center naturally included providing for the domestic needs of the people who would be living there. The founder called the profession of domestic service the "apostolate of apostolates"—for its great impact on the apostolic activities of the Work. It would become the professional work of some of his daughters.

At this time there were very few women in the Work. The disproportion between men and women was so obvious that during his retreat in November 1941 he resolved to devote a good part of his priestly activities to the apostolate with women, sensing that it would

---

[24] *Letter 6 May 1945*, no. 25.
[25] See AGP, RHF, T–04151, pp. 74–75 (Francisco Ponz Piedrafita). The first Mass in the oratory at the Núñez de Balboa center was said on January 27, 1942, by the priest who was then the founder's confessor: Father José María García Lahiguera.

"very soon make a big jump, both in numbers and in formation." [26] Yet that disparity would persist for several years. Instead of trying to slow down the growth of the men's centers—Diego de León, Jenner, Villanueva, Núñez de Balboa, El Cubil—Father Josemaría encouraged his daughters at Jorge Manrique to carry on their great task in all of them as a specific apostolate.

Other apostolates for them would come later, but now the founder saw the "apostolate of apostolates" as an important service to the Work as a whole. The fact that there were so few women compared to men could hardly be ignored; but trusting in God, he continued to press for the Work's expansion.

Have faith and daring, he urged his daughters: "With only a half-dozen faithful women, we will fill the world with God's light, with divine fire. Have faith in God, and a bit of faith in this poor sinner." [27] Since the Work was just getting started, those who were first had to be ready for anything. Later, only a small percentage of the women of the Work would make domestic work their profession. "There will be daughters of mine who will be tenured professors, architects, journalists, doctors," he told them. But for the time being, taking care of the centers of the Work in Madrid would have to be their main concern.

Since domestic work on this scale was not something young women from middle-class families in Spain had much experience with in those years, he worked with Carmen, between 1941 and 1942, at the task of training them for it. It was not an easy one, because the needs were urgent, and they had to learn as they went along. Carmen took Lola, Nisa, Encarnita, and several others under her wing, teaching them mostly by her preferred method: example.[28] The founder encouraged and exhorted with a lot of patience. He insisted that every task, no matter how insignificant it might seem, be done as perfectly as possible for love of God. "I want you to be faithful in the little things," he would tell them, "in the ordinary, everyday tasks, for that is how we sanctify our lives."

So, for instance, he taught them, as he also taught his sons, how to close doors with love for God: carefully and quietly. Then he would

---

[26] *Apuntes*, no. 1854 (9 Nov 1941).

[27] AGP, RHF, T–04989, p. 11 (Narcisa González Guzmán).

[28] "I worked at her side," says Nisa, "but she was so habitually tactful that she never made to me the least suggestion. Simply by watching her, I learned and improved in many things" (AGP, RHF, T–04989, p. 28).

turn the knob gently to make sure the door was securely closed. And then he would demonstrate the opening of doors.[29] He did his teaching with pleasant words, a smile, and a prayer in his heart. Many of the things he taught his daughters had first been taught him by his own parents.[30]

Encarnita recalled some of his lessons:

> We learned how to make our houses truly attractive—clean, organized tastefully and with an eye for details; neither stark nor luxurious, and with systematic care given things to make them last. We were told emphatically that nothing was ever too good for the oratory. We learned that pictures should be carefully placed, that furniture should not rub against walls, that doors had to be closed well, that flowers and decorations should be arranged gracefully. On entering a room one was to notice at once if anything was out of place or damaged. All of this was particularly important in the care of the oratory, including the placing of candlesticks and altar cloths. We also learned to turn off any lights that weren't needed at the moment.
>
> Flowers for the altar were to go between the candlesticks, and not come into contact with the altar cloth. And they were not to be put in vases with water. In this way, having nothing that could prolong their life, they would be a holocaust for the Lord.[31]

Other maxims expressed aspects of the spirit of the Work as applied to the care of its centers. Was food scarce? Father Josemaría would tell his daughters and sons to have greater trust in God: "If we don't fail him, he won't fail us." [32] But no one was to think that food would rain down like manna from heaven. "You have to use all the human means as though there were no supernatural ones, then have as much faith as if things depended only on God." [33]

He advised the women who supervised the household employees that if they wanted things to go well, they should be "the first ones to

[29] See ibid.
[30] Alvaro del Portillo, *Sum.* 31.
[31] AGP, RHF, T–05074, p. 82.
[32] AGP, RHF, T–04989, p. 27.
[33] AGP, RHF, T–05074, p. 3.

do any disagreeable tasks." [34] As aspects of the virtue of poverty, he taught them to take care in handling fragile objects, to repair anything broken as soon as possible, and to make things last by looking after them: in a word, to live with dignity, without a show of poverty, but with sacrifice, in the knowledge that they were "mothers of a large and poor family" and that "the treasure of Opus Dei is that we know how to live poor." [35]

The founder liked to see them calm and optimistic, working diligently, efficiently, and in an orderly way. He said to them:

> At times it's a pleasure to see how you work. Your interior life is going well, you work tirelessly, you do apostolate. Then suddenly everything grinds to a halt. This can't happen! Your life must have a uniform rhythm, like the ticking of a watch. The secret of it is to imbue everything with God's love.[36]

Finally, they needed to work with an elegant discretion, because "a good administration is neither seen nor heard." [37]

At first, of course, the standards he set for them did not seem easily attainable, but the women learned quickly—from him, and also from mistakes and mishaps, some of which they called "disasters," but Father Josemaría called "experience." [38] They made "notes of experience" to avoid making the same mistake twice. There were lots of small "disasters," as in any home, and occasionally some bigger ones.

One of these happened during the 1942–1943 school year at the Jenner Street residence, when the son of the owner of the building decided to get married. The owner took the occasion to present a formal eviction notice, claiming that the new family would need the floors occupied by the residence. If the case went to court, the owner was sure to win. Deciding to act quickly, before the situation got worse, Father Josemaría, accompanied by Amadeo de Fuenmayor, went to see the landlord. The conversation was courteous but unpromising. The landlord kept citing the law and showed no inclination to make concessions, even though eviction in the middle of the school year threatened serious hardship for fifty people.

---

[34] AGP, RHF, T–05074, pp. 61–62.
[35] AGP, RHF, T–05074, pp. 61 and 62.
[36] Ibid., p. 12.
[37] *Letter 29 Jul 1965*, no. 20.
[38] See AGP, RHF, T–04989, p. 15.

Suddenly Father Josemaría changed his tactics and tone. "I am a priest of Jesus Christ! And I cannot let you throw out of the residence, in the middle of the school year, fifty students whose souls have been entrusted me!" [39] Fuenmayor recalls:

> The tone of the interview changed completely. At the end, as if summing up a long negotiation that had reached a satisfactory conclusion, the Father said with great authority and simplicity: "Let's have our lawyers meet tomorrow and prepare a document with the following clauses. . . ." And he dictated them one after the other. Next day I passed them on to the two lawyers.[40]

After a deposit was made to guarantee that the terms of the agreement would be met, the Residence continued operating until the end of the school year. In the meantime, forced to seek a new location, Father Josemaría saw here an opportunity for a larger residence, which also would be the first one directed entirely and independently by the women's branch—an "administration," as such an arrangement is called in Opus Dei.[41] Accompanied by Aunt Carmen, he took those who would make up that future administration to La Almudena cemetery to visit the grave of Doña Dolores. There they prayed for the success of the new enterprise—a continuation of the one on Jenner Street, where the Grandmother had served so generously.[42]

Two suitable houses were found on La Moncloa Avenue near the university, across the street from one another. Extensive repairs of wartime damage were needed along with remodeling, so that when October came and close to ninety students moved in, the residence was still not ready.

The administration consisted of Encarnación Ortega, Narcisa González Guzmán, and Amparo Rodríguez Casado. (Amparo did not enjoy the best of health.) They benefited from the help and advice of Carmen, though only sporadically and from a distance, since she had

[39] AGP, RHF, T–02769, p. 6 (Amadeo de Fuenmayor). See also Alvaro del Portillo, *Sum.* 608, and AGP, RHF, T–04678/1, p. 102 (José Luis Múzquiz). (Father Múzquiz also mentions complaints made by the other tenants, especially about the noise the students made while going down the stairs to the dining room.)
[40] AGP, RHF, T–02769, p. 6.
[41] See AGP, RHF, T–05074, p. 91 (Encarnación Ortega).
[42] See AGP, RHF, D–15417, and RHF, T–04989, p. 30.

the Diego de León center to look after. The continual traffic of construction workers, painters, and plumbers was certainly not conducive to keeping services running smoothly or to keeping the house clean. And the houses' being on opposite sides of the street added some rather formidable complications. The pantry, for instance, was on one side of the street, and the kitchen on the other. And some of the students' rooms were in the one house, and some in the other.

Months earlier, Father Josemaría had said that the Moncloa Residence would be a "showcase of the Work" that would be looked at by all kinds of people, including those who did not look kindly on Opus Dei and would be trying to find things to criticize. But he had advised them not to worry about that or to pay too much attention to the inquisitive or the hostile, but just to remain conscious of God's presence and do the best they could.[43]

Masons' and plumbers' mistakes, the result of rushed work and poor quality materials (perennial problems in these early postwar years) kept workers underfoot longer than expected. The kitchen facilities were defective; it became harder and harder to get supplies; and the number of residents was very large. The difficulties gradually undermined the women's optimism, energy, and inner peace. They started cutting down on their sleep in order to get more work done.[44]

The days before Christmas were difficult ones. Work piled up. The students, since they were leaving for the holidays, needed to have their clothes back from the laundry earlier than usual. Some of the household employees went to spend a few days with their families. And there were a lot of last-minute Christmas preparations.

It had been some time since Father Josemaría had visited. He came by on December 23, bringing a gift from Aunt Carmen that he presented to Nisa and Encarnita in the dining room: a lacquered wooden tray, with a design of birds with brilliant plumage. Then, pulling up a chair, he sat down to speak with his daughters. All they could think of to say had to do with the thousand and one "disasters" and "catastrophes" going on. But they did speak their minds with trust and candor.[45]

He listened attentively, interrupting from time to time to offer them encouragement and assure them that things would soon get better.

[43] See AGP, RHF, T–04989, p. 15.
[44] AGP, RHF, T–05074, p. 93.
[45] See AGP, RHF, T–05074, pp. 93–94, and T–04989, p. 53.

"And besides," said one of them, "since we have so much work, we don't have time to do the prayer, and so we have to do it while we're working, hardly realizing that we're talking to God. . . ." At which point the other one timidly said to him, "It's that you think up things in your head and ask of us the impossible." [46]

Suddenly Father Josemaría buried his head in his hands and began to sob. Nisa and Encarnita watched sadly, and silently. Some moments passed, then raising his head, he reached out for the wrapping paper from the gift he had brought, cut off a piece, and began to write on it:

(1) without dishes
(2) with workmen all over the place
(3) with passageways obstructed
(4) without tablecloths
(5) without a pantry
(6) without personnel
(7) without experience
(8) without division of labor

At this point he drew a line, as though isolating the difficulties, and then listed the remedies:

(1) with a lot of love for God
(2) with complete trust in God and in the Father
(3) not thinking about the "disasters" until after tomorrow's day of recollection.

December 23, 1943 [47]

Very peacefully and with a smile on his face, he handed them the piece of paper and told them that he would indeed be preaching a day of recollection for them the next day. Then he told them to be sure to have a good dinner on Christmas Eve and wished them merry Christmas.

On December 24 he gave them the promised day of recollection with a spirit full of faith and optimism, expressing his confidence that his daughters would never forget the lesson they had learned. To Encarnita he explained, "I cried, my daughter, because you were not praying. And for a daughter of God in Opus Dei, the most important work, the one that must take priority over everything else, is prayer." [48]

---

[46] AGP, RHF, T–05074, p. 94, and RHF, D–15147.
[47] AGP, RHF, T–05074, p. 95.
[48] Ibid.

3. *The greatest miracle*

As Father Josemaría had foreseen, the trying physical circumstances were soon remedied. By the end of January the construction and repair jobs were finished, and the place was free of workers. Around the same time, the Núñez de Balboa apartment was closed, allowing them to concentrate on the other centers. Now and then he would tell his daughters to "shorten their sails" and lower unrealistic expectations, since "the best is the enemy of the good." [49] But other times he urged them not to rest on their laurels. He attached much importance to anything connected with the kitchen, since a poorly functioning kitchen would undermine the apostolate as well as the financial situation of the residence.[50]

It would, as it turned out, be several years before everything was running smoothly. In large part this was because of a lack of adequate means and experience. Most of the hired workers were inexperienced and had to be taught the basics of household work. To make that little staff an effective team would require not only their gaining some experience and professionalism, but it would be better still if they had some higher motivation. The most serious problem for the "apostolate of apostolates" was a lack of women who were dedicated professionally, body and soul, to the specific work of administration of its centers.

It was about four years from then that it first happened that some of these women turned their domestic work into a means of sanctification and apostolate as members of Opus Dei.

That happy event had been in the making since the days of the "disasters." The 1943–1944 school year had just begun, with nearly a hundred students living in the residence, when some Basque girls, having found that working there was more difficult than they expected, went home. Father Josemaría went immediately to the mother-house of the Daughters of Mary Immaculate for Domestic Service and explained the situation to Mother Carmen Barrasa, who promised to send help as soon as possible.[51]

[49] See AGP, RHF, T–04989, p. 48. When the Núñez de Balboa apartment was moved out of, another center was already being set up at 24 Españoleto Street. The petition for permission to have a semipublic oratory with a tabernacle is dated January 26, 1943; the blessing of the oratory took place on March 15. (See AGP, RHF, D–15148.)

[50] See AGP, RHF, T–04989, p. 48.

[51] See José Luis Múzquiz, RHF, T-04678/1, p. 109; Encarnación Ortega, RHF, T-05074, p. 96.

Mother Carmen had, as it happened, just heard that a young woman named Dora, who worked for the Duke and Duchess of Nájera, was available. She was an exceptional person, and Mother Carmen wanted to do Father Josemaría a favor, so she approached Dora and talked her into working at the residence for at least a short time.

Wearing a nice dress and carrying a couple of suitcases, Dora showed up at La Moncloa, much to the surprise of Encarnita, who was the one who opened the door. After saying that she had been sent by Mother Carmen, Dora gave a quick rundown on herself. She was twenty-nine; her name was Dora del Hoyo; she came from Riaño, in León; and she had served in several private homes, most recently that of the Duke and Duchess of Nájera. (What she did not mention was that she had come to the residence only in order not to hurt Mother Carmen's feelings and was planning on an early return to the Nájera household.)[52]

When Dora was shown the work area of the domestic staff, she immediately perceived the problem: too much work and too few hands. It pained her to see those young women trying to cope with untrained employees, and work up to their eyeballs. The pay was low, the workers lived in dorms, as was common then, and everything had to be done by the hundreds: the washing of clothes, the cooking and serving of meals. And all this, for what?

Dora had a big heart. She was moved by the sight of so much self-sacrifice. So she thought to herself, "All right, I'll stay today and help as much as I can. But tomorrow I'm leaving."[53] Accustomed to the well-ironed lace-trimmed uniforms worn by maids in aristocratic houses, she felt strange at having to don a plain cleaning dress that did not fit very well.

When Sunday came, Dora went to see Mother Carmen to tell her she was quitting. But the good nun, suspecting what she had in mind, managed to be "not in at the moment." And continued to do so week after week, whenever Dora came.

In time, the sight of so much that she could do to improve things engaged Dora's sense of professional honor and responsibility, and she decided to put off leaving. Encarnita, astonished at her domestic knowledge and abilities, felt that she was a gift from God. She says:

[52] See Dora del Hoyo Alonso, *Sum.* 7038. See also AGP, RHF, T–05074, p. 96.
[53] See AGP, RHF, T–05074, p. 97.

Dora had a heart of gold, and the way she worked was a wonder to behold. She was an expert at ironing, dry cleaning, and sewing. She cleaned with incredible thoroughness, served at table without making the smallest mistake, and knew a great deal about cooking. And her behavior was always respectful and natural. She was able to teach the other girls with authority but also with great delicacy. It is true that she had a strong character, but she also strove to master herself.

The first week we decided to take charge of the clothes, Dora suggested starching the fronts of the white shirts, which was then the latest fashion. We didn't yet have an ironing room, so she organized the work by taking advantage of free periods—one in the morning and one in the evening—and using the kitchen and dining room tables. She taught the other girls how to do it, and the residents were very happy with the results. She grew so fond of the residence that she decided to stay until the end of the school year.[54]

Once the administration of the residence was running smoothly, Father Josemaría, who visited weekly, gave his daughters a green light to begin a deeper apostolate with the domestic employees. Perhaps God would give some of them the vocation to carry out this professional work as members of Opus Dei. "From that moment on," Encarnita said, "the question of Dora's vocation occupied many hours of our prayer and work; the Father was also praying for her a lot."[55]

When the Abando Residence was set up in Bilbao in 1945, Dora del Hoyo and Concha Andrés volunteered to work there. On March 18, 1946, both wrote to the Father asking to be incorporated into Opus Dei. Their letters came the following day, the feast of Saint Joseph; and he said that "those two letters were the best present he had ever received on his saint's day."[56]

In the summer of 1946 the first Numerary Assistants gathered at Los Rosales: Dora, Concha, Antonia Peñuela, Rosalía López, and Julia

[54] Ibid., p. 98.
[55] Ibid.
[56] Ibid., p. 99. Father Josemaría always remembered the favor the Daughters of Mary Immaculate for Domestic Service had done him by sending a number of employees to the residence. When the foundress of the congregation, Vicenta María López y Vicuña, was beatified in Rome, he participated in the liturgical ceremony and went that afternoon to the congregation's central house bearing a box of candy and congratulations (see Alvaro del Portillo, PR, p. 587).

Bustillo.[57] The other component of the Work—that of the women—was at last fully developed, after so much fatigue and suffering. Father Josemaría called it "the greatest miracle God has done for his Work," and added, "And that's saying a lot, considering that he's worked more than a few." [58]

The dream first glimpsed on February 14, 1930, was now a firm and stable reality.[59]

4. *The Priestly Society of the Holy Cross*

In the spring of 1940, while the misunderstandings we have already described were mounting, the founder saw his goals beginning to be realized. The Jenner Residence and the apartment on Martínez Campos were underway in Madrid. In Valencia, El Cubil was in operation, and in Valladolid, El Rincón. And a center was about to be opened in Barcelona. All this had been accomplished within twelve months of the close of the civil war, with only a dozen people, very little money, and no other resources except apostolic zeal—and at a time when Father Josemaría was traveling almost nonstop in central and northern Spain, giving priests' retreats at the requests of the bishops.

Now he began to grow uneasy. Like an offensive fought on too many fronts, the Work might begin to unravel, he thought. In a journal note written in May 1940, after referring to the many new apostolic activities, he added: "My great concern is the feminine part of the Work. Afterward, the 'house of studies' for ourselves, and the future priests. *In te, Domine, speravi!*" [In you, O Lord, we hope!]" [60]

---

[57] See AGP, RHF, T–07918, p. 1 (Rosalía López Martínez), and Dora del Hoyo, PM, fol. 1119v. With regard to categories of members of Opus Dei, especially numerary assistants, see Pedro Rodríguez, Fernando Ocáriz, and José Luis Illanes, *Opus Dei in the Church* (Princeton, 1994), pp. 107–20.

[58] AGP, RHF, EF–461206–1 (a letter to José María Hernández de Garnica, written from Rome). In another letter he said, "The numerary assistants—I really mean this—seem to me the greatest miracle that our Lord has done for his Work" (AGP, RHF, EF–470214–1).

[59] "I remember," says Encarnación Ortega (AGP, RHF, T–05074, p. 122), "that day, July 16, 1949, when the first three numerary assistants—Dora del Hoyo, Concha Andrés, and Antonia Peñuela—made the Fidelity, the act of permanent incorporation into the Work. Our Father spent some time with us in a get-together. It was enormously moving. At one point, as though speaking to himself, he said in a confidential tone of voice, 'I see you, and I don't believe it. For a moment it's taking me back to that February 14 of 1930, when I began the Holy Mass not knowing anything, and ended it knowing everything.' You could have heard a pin drop. We hung on every word our Father said."

[60] *Apuntes*, no. 1610.

This concern surfaces again in a letter in July to his sons in Madrid. At the end, he added this postscript: "Two topics of capital importance: the women and the priests." [61]

Both groups were essential, and in the 1930s Father Josemaría had launched initiatives with both, only to see them fail. Yet in both cases the efforts were renewed. It was as if, after preliminary drafts, God had given the founder fresh pages on which to compose the definitive versions. Certain by now that the priests had to come from within Opus Dei itself, Father Josemaría retraced his steps. He wrote:

> In the early years, I accepted the help of a few priests who wanted to bind themselves to Opus Dei in some way. But God soon made it quite clear to me that, although they were good people (some of them outstandingly good), they were not the ones called to carry out that mission. And so, in an early document, I indicated that for the time being—I would later let them know till when—they should limit themselves to administering the sacraments and to strictly ecclesiastical functions.[62]

At the end of 1930, at a time when only two or three laymen and Father Norberto, assistant chaplain of the Foundation for the Sick, were with him, Father Josemaría had written: "The priest members have to come from among the lay members." [63] In 1935, in the face of the lack of unity among some of the priests then following him, he began to detach himself from them.

He was getting more and more requests from bishops to give retreats to priests and seminarians, and although he wanted to cut back on this activity, working and suffering for his brother priests was at the same time one of the "dominant passions" of his life, as he told

---

[61] AGP, RHF, EF–400704–1.

[62] *Letter 14 Feb 1944*, no. 9. In the same letter, he wrote of those priests: "However, since they were unable to understand what our Lord was asking of us, especially in the specific apostolate of the women's branch—two or three of them even becoming like my crown of thorns, because they were leading souls astray and sowing confusion—I soon had to do without their help. Afterwards I occasionally asked other priests, who had no ties of any kind to the Work, to act as confessors for those in the Work and celebrate liturgical functions, until we found an adequate way of meeting these important needs." The "early document" referred to is *Instruction 9 Jan 1935*, and the relevant section is no. 59.

[63] *Apuntes*, no. 138 (26 Dec 1930). He also indirectly said this a month before, in *Apuntes*, no. 101, and two years later, in *Apuntes*, no. 867.

Bishop Leopoldo.[64] Yet his first duty was the spiritual care of his sons and daughters. Where could he get time for everything? But when the campaign of "opposition by good people" against Opus Dei erupted, Bishop Leopoldo judged it more prudent that he continue to accept bishops' requests.

The result was a decision on his part to start relying more on people who had been in the Work for some time and involve them in the giving of apostolic formation and spiritual direction.[65] At around that same time, in 1940, the founder gathered together his older sons one day and told them that he would no longer teach formation classes to the students—they would be the ones giving them.[66] Also in 1940 two "study weeks" for members of the Work were held, the first in March and the second in August while the Jenner residents were away during Holy Week and over the summer. Father Josemaría gave a meditation each day, offered guidelines for their apostolate, took part in the get-togethers and gave classes on the spirit of Opus Dei. Meanwhile, Alvaro del Portillo, Isidoro Zorzano, Ricardo Fernández Vallespín, Juan Jiménez Vargas, Pedro Casciaro, and Paco Botella gave talks on various aspects of the Work's spirit.[67]

Still, the basic problem remained: How to get priests into the Work?

Pressed for time, he told Bishop Leopoldo he wanted to give up his position as rector of Saint Elizabeth's. The bishop refused. He repeated his request, and the bishop said no again. It would take him several years to win his battle to overcome "the affectionate opposition of His Excellency the Bishop of Madrid-Alcalá."[68]

---

[64] "I don't think I'll be done here until July 5," he says. "A marvelous harvest. It's edifying to see the effort these good Navarran priests are making on the retreat. If the Lord had not so clearly marked out another path for me, I would have liked to spend my life working and suffering and praying for my brothers the diocesan priests. They are my other dominant passion" (AGP, RHF, EF–410625–1).

[65] See AGP, RHF, T–04678/1, p. 120.

[66] Ibid., p. 118.

[67] See Alvaro del Portillo, PR, p. 932; AGP, RHF, T–00159/1, p. 104 (Francisco Botella); and Ponz, pp. 47–50.

[68] In December 1945, for instance, he wrote: "My dear Bishop: On several occasions I have manifested to Your Excellency my desire to give up the position of rector of the Royal Foundation of Santa Isabel. Today, with respectful persistence, I reiterate to my Reverend Bishop my hope of relinquishing this position as of next January, and beg him most earnestly to accept this resignation. The position would be very acceptable to another priest, since, although its financial benefits are modest, it has traditionally been a prestigious one" (AGP, RHF, EF–451204–1).

Two weeks later, Bishop Leopoldo having finally given his permission (though grudgingly), Father Josemaría submitted his resignation in a letter to the president of the Administrative Committee for the Goods of the National Patrimony:

His sons could take over a lot of the weight of apostolate and spiritual direction, especially because of the essentially lay character of Opus Dei. "But it is also obvious," he wrote in a circular letter, in 1944, "that for [Opus Dei] to be realized fully, priests are needed. Without priests, the apostolic efforts initiated by the lay members of Opus Dei would remain uncompleted, since they would necessarily have to stop when they came up against what I often call the 'sacramental wall'—the administration of the sacraments, which is reserved to priests." [69]

As he jokingly put it, the situation at that time was that his children had to make their confessions to "Father Come-across"—that is, whatever priest they came across.[70] Yet in the sacrament of Reconciliation sins are forgiven and spiritual direction is imparted, and so, even though members of the Work were entirely free to seek out any confessor they liked, he strongly recommended that they go to priests who knew its spirit well.[71]

In that circular letter of 1944 the founder, in his summing up of the need for priests, wrote:

> Priests are also necessary for the spiritual care of the members of the Work: to administer the sacraments, to assist the lay

---

I have the honor of letting you know that, after overcoming the affectionate opposition of His Excellency the Bishop of Madrid-Alcalá, and with his approval, for reasons of health and because of my many priestly activities, I am presenting my resignation of the position of Rector of the Royal Foundation of Santa Isabel, effective the first day of January of the coming year, 1946.

May God preserve you for many years.

Madrid, December 19, 1945

The Rector

The deputy director of the Administrative Committee sent him an official letter, dated April 17, 1946, communicating his acceptance of the resignation and saying, "In the name of said foundation, and in my own name, I wish to express our deep regret that we will no longer have the benefit of the invaluable collaboration and unsurpassable services that you have provided up to the present." (See the Patrimonio Nacional archive, "Patronatos Reales," "Patrimonio de Santa Isabel," file 182/21.)

[69] *Letter 14 Feb 1944*, no. 9.

[70] See AGP, RHF, T–04151, p. 47 (Francisco Ponz).

[71] In the early forties, Father Josemaría, to facilitate confession for his children, spoke to a number of diocesan and religious-order priests about the spirit and customs of the Work. Among these priests were Father José López Ortiz, in Madrid; Fathers Ramón Roquer Vilarrasa and Sebastián Cirac, in Barcelona; Fathers Eladio España Navarro and Antonio Rodilla, in Valencia; Father Eliodoro Gil, in León; and Father Daniel Llorente, in Valladolid. See AGP, RHF, T–04956, p. 3 (María Dolores Fisac); AGP, RHF, T–04678/1, p. 25 (José Luis Múzquiz); AGP, RHF, EF–411220–1 (a letter from Father Josemaría to Father José María Bulart Ferrándiz); and Ponz, pp. 58–59.

directors in directing souls, to impart a deep theological instruction to the other members of Opus Dei, and—a basic point in the very constitution of the Work—to perform certain tasks of government.[72]

The ardent desire that as founder he had for holy priests in the Work is reflected in a note dated July 1, 1940, written "from the walls of Avila"—an expression he used when staying with Bishop Santos Moro of Avila, whose residence was literally built against the city wall. "A retreat for priests begins today. May we draw out a lot of fruit: first of all, myself! . . . My God: enkindle Alvaro's heart, that he may become a holy priest!"[73]

Four more years would pass before three of his sons were ordained in 1944. "For many years I prayed, trustingly, eagerly, for your brothers who were going to be ordained and for those who would follow after them," he later wrote. "I prayed so much that I can truly say that *all the priests of Opus Dei are children of my prayer.*"[74]

Yet he often insisted that priesthood did not "crown" a vocation to the Work. On the contrary, by reason of their full availability for apostolic tasks and their formation, all numeraries of the men's branch can be said to have the necessary conditions for the priesthood and to be ready for priestly ordination if our Lord asks this of them and the Prelate of Opus Dei invites them to serve the Church and the Work in this way. The first whom Father Josemaría invited was Alvaro del Portillo: "If this is all right with you," he said, "if you want it and have nothing against it, if you with complete freedom say yes to this. I will have you ordained a priest. I call you to the priesthood not because you are better, but in order to serve the others."[75]

Two others were to prepare for the priesthood along with Alvaro: José María Hernández de Garnica (Chiqui) and José Luis Múzquiz. Chiqui was a mining engineer, the other two were civil engineers.[76]

---

[72] *Letter 14 Feb 1944*, no. 9. The priests in Opus Dei were not to be seen simply as assisting the activities of a group of laypeople. Rather, priests and laity were to be regarded as equally essential, as they are in the Church at large. The Work, in fact, was from the beginning seen as a portion of the People of God, "a little part of the Church."

[73] *Apuntes*, no. 1616.

[74] *Letter 8 Aug 1956*, no. 5.

[75] Alvaro del Portillo, PR, p. 958.

[76] Father Múzquiz recalls, "I remember the affection the Father put into it when, in his room in the student residence at 6 Jenner, he asked me if I wanted to be a priest. 'My son,' the Father said to me, 'would you like to be a priest?' 'Yes, Father, I'd love to,' I

The founder's resolutions from November 1941 include: "Pray, suffer, and work untiringly until the priests Jesus wants in the Work are a reality. Speak about this point with our bishop of Madrid, my father."[77]

When he spoke with the bishop it was about the future priests' ecclesiastical studies. Usually these studies were done at a formal center of instruction, such as a diocesan seminary or a pontifical university. But given these students' circumstances, their age and professional backgrounds, it was agreed that they would receive their classes from private professors at the Diego de León center. The director of studies was Father José María Bueno Monreal, since 1927 professor of canon law and moral theology in the Madrid seminary.[78]

With the bishop's approval, a prestigious group of teachers was assembled: two professors from the Angelicum University in Rome, two professors from the seminary in Madrid, and a tenured professor from Madrid's Universidad Central.[79] Cardinal Bueno Monreal recalled that Father Josemaría wanted this program of studies to have "the same rigor and depth as their secular studies, in which each had obtained two doctorates. Thus they studied all the courses being

---

answered him. And he said, 'All right, see Alvaro about the studies.'" (See AGP, RHF, T–04678/1, p. 32.)

In 1945 the founder wrote to his children: "Also pray that no one in the Work will ever in any way feel pressured to take up the priesthood; and, at the same time, that there will always be those who hear the whistle of the Good Shepherd calling them—a divine compulsion, gentle and affectionate" (*Letter 2 Feb 1945*, no. 22).

[77] *Apuntes*, no. 1854 (9 Nov 1941).

[78] Father Bueno had met Father Josemaría in 1927 or 1928, at the School of Law. And, as mentioned earlier, he had helped prepare the documents for the approval of the Work as a pious union. Now he undertook the directing of the studies of the three first members of Opus Dei preparing for ordination. At the end of 1945 he was made the bishop of Jaca; later he became the bishop of Vitoria; and in 1954 he was named coadjutor archbishop of Seville. Four years later he was named archbishop of that city, and a cardinal. He died in 1987.

[79] "Among them," Bishop del Portillo testifies, "there were two Dominican professors from the Angelicum, in Rome, who weren't able to teach there because of the world war. These were Father Muñiz, who taught us dogmatic theology, and Father Severino Alvarez, a professor of canon law. Father Celada, O.P., who had worked for a long time at the Biblical Institute in Jerusalem, was our Scripture professor. Among the professors, several would be elevated to the episcopate, and some—such as Father José María Bueno, who taught us moral theology—became cardinals. Father José López Ortiz, the future military ordinary, taught us Church history. Father Máximo Yurramendi (the future bishop of Ciudad Rodrigo), Father Joaquín Blázquez (the director of the Institute of Theology in Spain), and Father Permuy, C.M.F., were other very competent teachers he chose for us. We did our studies with great intensity" (Alvaro del Portillo, PR, p. 958). See also José María Bueno Monreal, in *Testimonios*, p. 17; José María García Lahiguera (who was then spiritual director at the Madrid seminary), in *Testimonios*, p. 162; and AGP, RHF, EF–420517–1 and EF–440301–1 (letters from the founder).

taught in the seminaries." [80] Reflecting the founder's love for the Church and the Work, this same careful preparation was in future to be received by all his children, laity as well as priests.[81]

In the spring of 1942 the director reported that the students were "very well prepared to pass their exams." Father Josemaría therefore informed Bishop Leopoldo that they were prepared to be examined in the subjects of the two-year philosophy curriculum, and suggested that the bishop appoint a panel for this purpose.[82] The three candidates received the highest possible grades in all their subjects, as he was quick to tell the bishop.[83] He had wanted these three sons of his to have the best possible formation as an example for the thousands who would come after them. As he later explained:

> When I began preparing the first priests in the Work, I went overboard—if one might say so—with their philosophical and theological formation. I did so for many reasons. The second reason, to please God; the third, because many people were looking to me with affection, and I could not let them down; the fourth, because there were people who didn't like us and were looking for an opportunity to attack us; and then, because I have always urged my sons to get the best possible professional formation and could not be less demanding in their religious formation. And the first reason (since I could die at any moment): because I will have to render an account to God for what I have done, and I ardently desire to save my soul. [84]

[80] José María Bueno Monreal, in *Testimonios*, p. 17.

[81] "Father Josemaría," relates Bishop López Ortiz, "spoke to me with great hope and expectation about those three sons of his who were going to be ordained. . . . He told me that all the members of Opus Dei, in order to carry out an effective apostolate through their work, would need to have a preparation similar to that of the priests, even though the vast majority would never be ordained, since that's not their vocation. With all of them having that formation, he, or whoever succeeded him, would be able to call to the priesthood those they saw fit to, while always respecting the freedom of each one with respect to answering that call. The fact that those three studied theology was not, therefore, something extraordinary, since with time that would become a standard practice in the Work, all the members being expected to acquire a solid formation in religious doctrine. This would make it possible for those three to be followed by others, and then still others, with no break in continuity—which is in fact what has happened. He presented all this to me as something belonging to the apostolic character of the Work, and thus clearly coming from God" (*Testimonios*, pp. 232–33).

[82] AGP, RHF, EF–420517-1.

[83] See AGP, RHF, EF–420607–1.

[84] *Letter 8 Aug 1956*, no. 13. See also AGP, RHF, T–04678/1, p. 24 (José Luis Múzquiz).

Two notes he saved are relevant here: "Priestly formation: Opus Dei certainly has to provide this!"; and: "The priesthood is received when one is ordained, but priestly formation. . . ." [85]

Elsewhere he spells out what is implied here: that priestly formation is the business of a lifetime.[86] He aimed to provide the faithful of Opus Dei with formation corresponding to their secular state and therefore compatible with their professional work.[87] Those first three candidates received their pastoral preparation for Holy Orders and their formation in priestly virtues directly from Father Josemaría, while their academic studies took place not in a seminary but at the Center for Ecclesiastical Studies of the Priestly Society of the Holy Cross, which was formally set up in Diego de León in December 1943.[88]

* * *

As we look back on it from the vantage point of the present, Opus Dei's institutional development may look something like a winding path with numerous byways.[89] Yet this was the path the founder had to move along, as God gave him light to see it. Some stretches were lit up by divine intimations; others he had to travel in total darkness; but always he kept forging ahead with a lot of faith.[90]

In June 1930, as he sketched out the juridical structure of the Work and tried to envision a solution that would allow priests to be incorporated into it, he found himself obliged finally to leave matters up to Divine Providence: "God will give us light when the time comes." [91]

[85] AGP, RHF, AVF–0079.

[86] In one instance he says: "Never consider your formation finished. For all your life, with a marvelous humility, you will need to improve your human, spiritual, doctrinal, apostolic, and professional preparation" (*Letter 6 May 1945*, no. 19).

[87] This is one reason why "a 'boarding school' arrangement does not suit the members of the Work," wrote the founder. "From the very start of their vocation they have to strive to live all the priestly virtues right in the midst of the world" (*Letter 6 May 1945*, no. 20).

[88] A center of studies had been in operation for some time at Diego de León when the bishop of Madrid-Alcalá was formally notified of its establishment as the Center for Ecclesiastical Studies of the Priestly Society of the Holy Cross on December 10, 1943, two days after the Priestly Society was established (see AGP, RHF, D-15140).

[89] For more on the institutional development of Opus Dei, see Amadeo de Fuenmayor, Valentín Gómez Iglesias, and José Luis Illanes, *The Canonical Path of Opus Dei*, trans. William H. Stetson (Princeton, 1994).

[90] He himself said this: "Our *iter iuridicum* [canonical path] seems tortuous to human eyes. But, over time, it will be seen that in relation to God it is a constant movement forward" (*Letter 29 Dec 1947/14 Feb 1966*, no. 163).

[91] *Apuntes*, no. 60.

Then the foundational charism present from the beginning would come into play.

He felt at peace and filled with faith when in 1940 he set about seeking the priestly ordination of three members of Opus Dei. Faith was needed because he seemed to have reached a dead end: What he wanted was nothing less than for the future priests to be dedicated exclusively to the service of the Work—that is, to its specific apostolic activities—something apparently conflicting with ecclesiastical law.

The Code of Canon Law specified that one of the requirements for licit ordination and the exercise of priestly ministry was a title of ordination. This was, as is explained in *The Canonical Path of Opus Dei,* a means of "assuring that each cleric had a decent, lifelong source of support." [92] Although the possible titles of ordination were quite diverse, there were basically only two ways of getting one: (a) by joining a religious order, or (b) by becoming incardinated in a diocese, which meant becoming dependent, to a greater or lesser extent, on its ordinary. Given the secular character God intended for Opus Dei, that first alternative had to be rejected.[93] But the titles linked to incardination in a diocese were not the solution either. Opus Dei's apostolic activities went beyond diocesan borders, and so its priests needed freedom of activity and movement. Depending on the bishop of a particular diocese, they could not also be fully available for the needs of the Work.[94]

Father Josemaría knew what that could mean from his own problems working in Madrid but incardinated in Saragossa: The recurring need to renew faculties and permissions, the intrinsic instability of being a priest from outside the diocese—made him feel "like a chicken in the wrong coop." [95]

[92] Fuenmayor, Gómez Iglesias, and Illanes, p. 109. See also the 1917 Code of Canon Law, canons no. 974 and no. 979.

[93] See *Letter 6 May 1945,* no. 11.

[94] Going down the list of titles of ordination mentioned in the Code of Canon Law, the founder, in *Letter 14 Feb 1944,* no. 16, gives the reasons why he could not use them. "None of the titles provided for secular priests," he says, "was suited to our situation. The title 'beneficii' wouldn't do since it required that before receiving Holy Orders one be assigned an office with a benefice attached to it. And neither would the other ones allowed for by canon law. The titles 'servitii dioecesis' and 'missionis' were not appropriate since they required of the ordinand a promise to dedicate himself to ministry in a particular diocese or mission territory. Neither was the title 'patrimonii' or 'pensionis,' which required that one personally have the capital with which to support oneself for life. Nor were the titles 'paupertatis' and 'mensae communis' acceptable, since they were reserved for religious."

[95] See Alvaro del Portillo, PR, p. 346

As a matter of prudence, Father Josemaría consulted experts in canon law on the question of titles. Every once in a while he would optimistically think he had found the answer, but closer examination showed that it would not work.[96] He met often with the bishop of Madrid, and the two of them racked their brains in long sessions, but always to no avail.[97]

Finally, he stopped looking for a solution. But this did not mean he gave up. "Time went by." he says. "We prayed. The three who were to be ordained as the first priests of the Work were studying very hard, putting their hearts into it. Then, one day . . ."[98]

On the morning of February 14, 1943—already a day of thanksgiving for the Work as the anniversary of the founding of the women's branch on February 14, 1930—Father Josemaría left early to say Mass for his daughters in the oratory of Jorge Manrique. They all participated with great devotion, and he was immersed in God throughout the Holy Sacrifice.

As soon as Mass was over, he took out his notebook and wrote on the page for February 14, feast of Saint Valentine, "In the house of the women, during Holy Mass: 'Societas Sacerdotalis Sanctae Crucis' [The Priestly Society of the Holy Cross]." And then, on that same page, he made a little drawing, of a circle with a cross inside it.[99] After making his thanksgiving, he went downstairs, asked for a sheet of paper, and went into a small reception room, while his daughters waited for him in the vestibule. Encarnita later wrote:

> A few minutes later he reappeared in the vestibule, and it was clear he was deeply moved. "Look," he told us, pointing to a sheet on which he had drawn a circle with a cross of special

[96] In June 1941, for example, he consulted Bishop Marcelino Olaechea in Pamplona, and came away mistakenly believing he had found a solution. "I spoke at length with this bishop about the problem of our priests," he writes from there to his sons in Madrid, "and a practical, immediate, and canonical solution became clear, thanks be to God" (AGP, RHF, EF–410603–2).

[97] "Several solutions were suggested to me, all of them bad. The best suggestion was given me by Bishop Leopoldo: to create chaplaincies, such that the priests would in some way remain assigned to Opus Dei. But this would have taken a huge amount of money, which we could not come up with, so it solved nothing" (AGP, RHF, D–13452, no. 159). See also the 1917 Code of Canon Law, canon no. 128.

Another canonist whom he consulted without success was Father Bueno Monreal (see Alvaro del Portillo, *Sum.* 540).

[98] *Letter 29 Dec 1947/14 Feb 1966*, no. 159.

[99] The page has been preserved, see AGP, RHF, D-15077.

proportions in its center, "this will be the *seal* of the Work. The *seal*, not the *coat of arms.*" Opus Dei will not have a coat of arms. It represents the world, and in the very heart of the world the Cross.[100]

Next day Father Josemaría went to El Escorial, not far from Madrid, where Alvaro del Portillo, José María Hernández de Garnica, and José Luis Múzquiz were preparing for their theology exams. With a great sense of unworthiness, almost with shame, he told Alvaro of the grace he had received during Mass the day before.[101] The necessary documents needed to be prepared quickly. Alvaro would be the one to go to Rome to seek approval for the Priestly Society of the Holy Cross.

5. *Death of Isidoro, and the* nihil obstat *from the Holy See*

What was that ray of light that the founder had received? In the midst of his uncertainty, our Lord had put it in his mind to create a society of priests, of which the laymen preparing for ordination would become a part. In this way, without ceasing to belong to Opus Dei, they would be incardinated in it *"ad titulum Societatis."* Together with this solution there "came" (this is the term he used) the symbol of the cross within the globe,[102] a cross whose arms reached all the way across the globe, symbolizing the plan of redemption and also the common priesthood of all the faithful of Opus Dei, from whose ranks the priests would come.[103]

For Father Josemaría, the name Priestly Society of the Holy Cross was not an exaltation of suffering but a proclamation of victory over pain and death. Just a few months earlier, in October 1942, he had

[100] AGP, RHF, T–05074, p. 45. See also AGP, RHF, T–04989, p. 7 (Narcisa González Guzmán). Years later the founder mentioned what had happened that day. "On February 14, 1943," he said, "I was celebrating Mass at my daughters' house (on Jorge Manrique Street), and after Communion the solution I was looking for came to me: the Priestly Society of the Holy Cross! Jesus wanted to crown the edifice with his most holy Cross. I remember well that I made a sketch of the seal—even this *came!*—and gave it to Alvaro" (*Letter 29 Dec 1947/14 Feb 1966*, no. 159).

[101] See Alvaro del Portillo, *Sum.* 540 and 541.

[102] For an instance of his use of the word "came" in this context, see *Letter 29 Dec 1947/ 14 Feb 1966*, no. 159.

[103] On August 7, 1931, which in that year was the feast of the Transfiguration, our Lord let him see that "he would draw all things to himself" when "the Cross, with the teachings of Christ," was put "at the summit of all human activities" (*Apuntes*, no. 217).

written: "Adversities endured for love of God always yield fruit." [104] And now he was convinced that this grace of seeing the solution to the problem of how to have priests in the Work was one of those fruits.

The attacks on the Work were continuing. It seemed as if there would be no end to the adversities and humiliations. But if, like little splinters from the cross, they did keep coming, Father Josemaría would go on accepting them with joy and without dismay, seeing them in their "supernatural dimension," as needful for a soul on pilgrimage to heaven. "For me a day without a cross is like a day without God," he said.[105]

In the thirties he had gone through the hospitals of Madrid begging the patients to offer their suffering for his intentions. He called them "the treasure of the Work," their suffering a divine "caress." [106] Now, the Lord having crowned the Work with his Cross, the founder reasoned that "since we are of the Holy Cross, we will never lack crosses." [107]

José María Hernández de Garnica fell ill in July 1940. Wartime privations, imprisonment in Madrid, the hard life in the penal camp in Valencia very likely were contributing factors. Father Josemaría kept track of him when he had to be out of Madrid. "Be sure to take care of Chiqui," he wrote from León at the beginning of August.[108] And two days later: "I suppose what Chiqui has is not serious. Is he better?" [109] But it was serious. For a few days he hovered between life and death. "I don't know if you have heard," Isidoro wrote another member of the Work two weeks later, "that Chiqui has come through the operation very well. They took out a kidney. It was more serious than the doctors thought at first, but now he is fine, although still in the hospital." [110]

---

[104] *Letter 24 Oct 1942,* no. 66. "Then the supernatural meaning of our dedication is strengthened," he continued, "because we feel—in our flesh and in our soul—that oblation that we have made of our lives to the Lord, which rises up to him *in odorem suavitatis* [with a sweet fragrance]."

[105] AGP, RHF, T–05074, p. 27 (Encarnación Ortega).

[106] Father Josemaría expressed the Christian "philosophy of pain" in terms of common sense principles. "Physical pain, when it can be gotten rid of, is to be gotten rid of," he said. "Life contains enough suffering already! And when it can't be gotten rid of, it is to be offered up. The sick are to be given everything they need; we might have to go without even some basics, but the sick, no." (See Alvaro del Portillo, PR, p. 968.)

[107] AGP, RHF, EF–440216–1 (a letter to Father Maximiliano Canal, O.P.).

[108] AGP, RHF, EF–400806–1.

[109] AGP, RHF, EF–400808–1.

[110] AGP, IZL, D–1213, 466.

Apparently Alvaro was not well either. On August 23, Father Josemaría wrote, "How is Chiqui? Alvaro, have you been to see a doctor? Please!"[111] And four days later, "How is Chiqui doing? Has Alvaro seen the doctor?"[112]

All this was happening while he was doing the preparatory work for Opus Dei's approval as a pious union. In the autumn of 1940 he wrote to the bishop of Pamplona that the canonical path of Opus Dei seemed to be a kind of Way of the Cross, because of the many sufferings accompanying every step forward.[113]

Chiqui soon recovered. But then Isidoro fell ill.[114] In 1940 he was living at the Jenner Street residence, in a little room next to the oratory. (The room couldn't really be said to be his, since it served other purposes as well.) Besides being busy all day at his job at the railroad office, he handled the accounts for the Jenner Street residence and other centers as general administrator of the Work. By 1941, he had begun to feel ill, but he persevered in his quiet life of hard work, through two years of great fatigue and pain, which the doctors took to be rheumatic.

The diagnosis was wrong. By the second half of 1942 his illness was making alarming progress. Father Josemaría grew deeply concerned. "How is Isidoro?" "How is Isidoro feeling?" he wrote.[115]

Just before Christmas 1942, Isidoro attended a retreat preached by Father Josemaría at the Diego de León center. By now, he was very sick. Having this son of his very much on his mind, Father Josemaría said in the meditation on death:

> To you, my son, there will not happen what unfortunately does sometimes happen, even among Christians—an attempt to keep the sick from knowing how serious their illness is until the very last moment, when they're on the point of

[111] AGP, RHF, EF–400823–1.

[112] AGP, RHF, EF–400827–1.

[113] In this letter he proposed to visit the bishop "to show Your Excellency those papers I mentioned, and to hear the advice that my Father-Bishop, in his charity, wants to give me." At the end, after offering to go "whenever it's convenient for you," he said: "Don't fail to pray for us, and especially for me, who am always with the Cross on my back" (AGP, RHF, EF–400910–1).

[114] On the final illness and the death of Isidoro Zorzano, see José Miguel Pero-Sanz, *Isidoro Zorzano Ledesma, Ingeniero Industrial: Buenos Aires, 1902—Madrid, 1943* (Madrid, 1996), pp. 297ff.

[115] See, for example, AGP, RHF, EF–420712–1 and EF–421104–2.

losing consciousness and can't receive the Last Sacraments with full awareness. To you, my son, a brother of yours will come, and with great sensitivity but very clearly he will say to you, "Look, the doctors say that, humanly speaking, there's nothing that can be done. . . . But we are going to pray a lot, asking God for a miracle. And we're also going to use all the human means medical science has at its disposal.

And then, my son, your reaction will be: *Laetatus sum in his quae dicta sunt mihi* [I rejoiced when they said to me], Let us go to the House of the Lord!" [116]

By early 1943 the least movement was causing Isidoro an agonizing shortness of breath. Also the pain was making it hard for him to sleep, and he was waking up exhausted. For a while he continued to make the heroic effort it took for him to rise punctually at the usual hour, but soon even that was more than he could manage. Only at that point did the doctors finally make the correct diagnosis.

Isidoro was taken to a hospital, where the doctors concluded that he had Hodgkin's disease—an illness for which there was no hope of a cure.[117] He spent the spring in the San Fernando Sanatorium, aware that he was dying. Father Josemaría visited often and arranged for the others to take turns staying with him so that he always had company. The visitors looked after him, changing the sheets, adjusting his position, helping him at mealtime. (Even to swallow liquids caused him severe pain.) They also helped him carry out the norms of piety. The founder told them to treat him "as you would a sacred relic." [118]

His confessor was Father López Ortiz. He received communion every day, usually brought to him by Father Josemaría. Luis Palos, who had been a student with him at the Saragossa School of Law and was the sanatorium director's brother, would see him going down the corridor with the Blessed Sacrament, and was deeply impressed by the recollection with which the priest carried our Lord. "It was almost

[116] AGP, RHF, T–04678/1, p. 39. (The "I rejoiced" quote is from Ps 122:1.)

[117] With malignant lymphogranuloma, or Hodgkin's disease, the patient suffered chronic enlargement of the lymph nodes, bringing with it high fever, profound fatigue, loss of appetite, gradual malnutrition, severe anemia, and growing difficulty in breathing. The enlarged lymph nodes had compressed Isidoro's bronchi, collapsing them and reducing the lung capacity by three quarters: hence the severe shortness of breath and exhaustion (see *Posiciones y artículos para la causa de beatificación y canonización del Siervo de Dios Isidoro Zorzano, del Opus Dei*, Madrid 1948).

[118] Javier de Ayala, *Sum.* 7580. See also Ponz, p. 139, and Eduardo Alastrué, *Sum.* 5568.

something you could reach out and touch," he says. "He never said a word to anyone until he had taken off his vestments." [119]

*   *   *

The first thing the founder had done on February 14, 1943, was communicate the news of the Priestly Society of the Holy Cross to Alvaro del Portillo. Alvaro was not only secretary general of Opus Dei but also the founder's indispensable collaborator and right-hand man.[120] He had discovered the depth of Alvaro's spiritual life in 1938 when the two of them were in Burgos,[121] and afterward he became certain that he was the rock on which he could lean, even calling him "*Saxum*" at times (the Latin word for "rock").[122] To Alvaro he communicated many of the supernatural events that befell him; to Alvaro he left the governing of the Work when he had to leave Madrid; to Alvaro he entrusted delicate questions and matters of conscience. He had no hesitation in telling Bishop Leopoldo: "Since I know that Alvaro del Portillo is keeping Your Excellency informed of everything that is happening to us, I have tried to resist my impulses to write to you." [123]

Thanks to divine inspiration, the founder now had the answer to the question of how to have priests in Opus Dei, but still the question was not completely settled, since the answer had yet to be fitted into the juridical framework of the Church. Again he studied the Code of Canon Law, seeking a suitable juridical niche among the rigid, limited possibilities it offered. And again he sought advice from people he had consulted in the past: Archbishop Cicognani, the nuncio; Bishop Eijo y Garay, the bishop of Madrid; Monsignor Calleri, of the nunciature; Father Bueno Monreal, the professor from the seminary; his confessor, Father García Lahiguera; and Bishop Lauzurica, the bishop of Vitoria.

The most helpful of these was the bishop of Madrid, in great part because he fully understood and had no problem with the fact that, the Work being an eminently secular enterprise, the founder felt "a great repugnance" to its becoming a religious institute. He, too, saw clearly that this would violate its nature.[124]

---

[119] Luis Palos Yranzo, *Sum.* 5568.
[120] See AGP, RHF, T–04678/1, p. 75.
[121] See AGP, RHF, T–00159, IX, p. 25 (Francisco Botella).
[122] See AGP, RHF, EF–390224–4, EF–390323–5, and EF–390518–5.
[123] AGP, RHF, EF–410625–1.
[124] AGP, RHF, EF–430228–1.

The founder was anxious to make sure that this difficult juridical operation did not give rise to the least deviation from the true nature of the Work. Studying all the juridical possibilities, he concluded that the Priestly Society of the Holy Cross would have to be a "society of common life without vows." "This," the Code specified, "is not a religious institution, properly speaking, nor can its members be designated by the term 'religious' in its proper sense."[125] Such societies could vary greatly in their setups and rules and, by concession of the Holy See, could incorporate priests as members on a stable basis. Taking this route would go a long way toward solving two problems: that of how to safeguard the secular nature of the Work, and that of how to obtain for the new priests a title allowing them a ministry unreservedly dedicated to Opus Dei.

Here, then, was a satisfactory resolution of the incardination problem—but one achieved at the price of accepting, for want of anything better, a juridical state of affairs that did not fully reflect Opus Dei's secular character.[126] The founder was keenly aware of the inadequacies of that formula and of the fact that it was a recourse forced on him by the pressure of circumstances and canons. Because where in all this was the pious union of laypersons, men and women, who constituted the vast majority of Opus Dei's members? To emphasize that the priests of the Priestly Society of the Holy Cross would not form a separate group but would have a unity of vocation and life with the rest of the members of Opus Dei, the founder established that they would have to come from the ranks of the lay members and that, once ordained, they would provide service exclusively to their brothers and sisters in the Work, most of whom would remain ordinary Christians under the name of Opus Dei, "a work *proper to, united to, and inseparable from* the Priestly Society of the Holy Cross."[127]

---

[125] 1917 Code of Canon Law, canon no. 673. See Fuenmayor, Gómez Iglesias, and Illanes, p. 112.

[126] The societies "of common life without vows" discussed in canon no. 673 arose in the seventeenth century with specific apostolic aims: care for the poor or the sick, priestly ministry, etc. Although members did not make public vows, their common life was similar to that of religious. Concerned lest this new "society of common life without vows" be mistaken for a religious order or congregation, the founder added declarations to its normative texts (*Lineamenta generalia*, no. 1, and *Constitutions*, no. 1), making its secularity clearer, explaining that, as he put it in *Letter 14 Feb 1944*, no. 12, "'community of life' refers solely to the spirit and to the legal aspect, never to a literal living under the same roof."

[127] Although the Priestly Society of the Holy Cross consists of only "a small core" of priests and of laymen preparing to be priests, this juridical language ("the other lay

*   *   *

Two members of the Work, José Orlandis and Salvador Canals, had been living and studying in Rome for six months. During that time they had made friends with many professors and also, on Father Josemaría's advice, with some eminent ecclesiastical figures, so as to get them acquainted with Opus Dei.[128] Now, with the solution to the problem of priests and incardination in place, the founder wrote to them at the beginning of May 1943, two weeks before Alvaro del Portillo was to leave for Italy.

> May Jesus bless my sons in Rome and watch over them.
>
> My dear sons: your brother Alvaro will soon be going over there, and he will give you the details on a lot of things. You can't imagine how I envy you. I so much long to make my own pilgrimage to see Peter. Whenever I stop to think of it, I feel by God's grace an even greater love for the Pope, if that is possible. Be very Roman. Don't forget that the principal characteristic of our family, our family trait, is affection for and adhesion—service!—to the Church, the Holy Father, and the bishops (the ordinary hierarchy) in communion with the Holy See.
>
> And, for this, interior life: prayer, sacrifice, joy, work. And, above all, a filial love for our Mother, holy Mary.[129]

After the necessary documents were prepared, the date for Alvaro's departure was set in consultation with the bishop of Madrid. Father Josemaría and Pedro Casciaro accompanied him to Barcelona, and from there, on May 25, he continued on to Rome. There was a tense

---

members, who form a work *proper to, united to, and inseparable from* the Priestly Society of the Holy Cross") seems to imply that Opus Dei has been absorbed by the Priestly Society. So does the decree of the bishop of Madrid-Alcalá approving the Constitutions of the Priestly Society of the Holy Cross. The decree, issued on January 25, 1944, includes this statement: "By said Constitutions are properly established the nature, ends, activities, ascetical practices, and government of the Society, as well as those of its specific instrument of apostolate, known as Opus Dei" (see Fuenmayor, Gómez Iglesias, and Illanes, p. 498). Yet the pastoral reality of Opus Dei was not only that its lay members remained ordinary faithful but that it was they who most clearly and fully embodied the real essence of the Work.

[128] See José Orlandis, *Memorias de Roma in guerra (1942-1945)*, Madrid 1992, pp. 41 ff.
[129] AGP, RHF, EF–430510–1.

moment when the flight approached a combat zone involving British planes and Italian warships off the Italian coast, but the pilot skillfully circumvented the trouble spot and landed safely in Rome.

On June 4, bearing a letter of introduction from the bishop of Madrid, Alvaro del Portillo was received in private audience by Pope Pius XII. The Pope showed great affection for the Work.[130]

In June, accompanied by José Orlandis, Alvaro visited Cardinal Vincenzo La Puma, the prefect of the Sacred Congregation for Religious—the congregation upon which societies of common life without vows depended, even though they were not religious institutes. He also saw several other Vatican officials, including its undersecretary of state (Cardinal Maglione) and the assessor of the Holy Office (Bishop Ottaviani).[131]

The proposed solution passed muster with all the canonists and was approved by the Sacred Congregation for Religious. Yet the mere fact that the latter was the competent authority with respect to this question suggests how provisional a solution it was.

In the meantime, the international situation and communication between countries were becoming increasingly difficult. It was expected that once the Allies had conquered North Africa, they would invade Italy, a development that would interrupt or at least complicate relations with the Holy See. Fearing this, and hoping for a prompt response from Rome, the founder prepared to present the petition

---

[130] See Alvaro del Portillo, *Sum.* 552, and also Orlandis, pp. 65–69.

Two weeks earlier, on May 21, Francisco Botella, who was in Italy for a few months' stay, had also been granted a private audience with Pope Pius XII. The Pope had asked him about the founder and the Work, and about the opposition they were suffering. (See AGP, RHF, T–00159, X, p. 16.)

José Orlandis relates quite an amusing story about the morning of June 4, the day of Alvaro's audience with the Pope. When he and Alvaro left the house, they could not get a taxi, so they took a streetcar instead. Alvaro was wearing the very impressive-looking uniform of the Spanish civil engineer (a navy blue outfit with gold buttons and a purple sash), and while they were standing on the platform they heard someone say, "It seems impossible—so young, and already an admiral!" The uniform did actually look like a military one, because of the military origin of what was now the corps of civil engineers. So when Alvaro entered the Vatican through the Bronze Doors, the officer in charge of the Swiss Guards had them line up for review. And Alvaro, not missing a beat, returned the officer's salute, reviewed the guard, and then strode up the stairs to the audience hall. (See Orlandis, pp. 67–68.)

[131] Among these other officials were Monsignor Montini (the undersecretary of state); Bishop Ruffini; Cardinal Pizzardo (the prefect of the Sacred Congregation for Seminaries and Universities); Cardinal Tedeschini; Cardinal Vidal y Barraquer; Fathers Larraona and Montoto (Claretians); Father Albareda (a Benedictine, director of the Vatican Library); and some Dominican priests: Suárez, Canals, etc. (See Orlandis, p. 68.)

without waiting for Alvaro to return. On June 13 he submitted a request for diocesan establishment of the Priestly Society of the Holy Cross, attaching to the request a general description of the Society.[132]

On June 21 Alvaro returned from Rome and informed Father Josemaría of the latest developments. On June 22 the bishop of Madrid sent to Cardinal La Puma, the prefect of the Sacred Congregation for Religious, a request that the Society be given the *nihil obstat*.[133]

They waited impatiently for Rome's response. "All the work of the future priests depends on that solution," the founder told his sons. "I'm praying, and doing all I can to get others to pray and offer things up, for its success. There is so much work to be done—every day more. There is marvelous work waiting for our first priests. How much they are needed!"[134]

Meanwhile, Isidoro was nearing the end, and offering up with great peace and patience and hope all the sufferings of a long death agony. Father Josemaría gave him the Last Sacraments. Isidoro was not to see the granting of the *nihil obstat*. He died on July 15, in the middle of the afternoon—alone, no one with him, despite all the care and affection with which the members of the Work had been keeping him company day and night. The news reached Father Josemaría at Jorge Manrique, where he was giving his daughters a meditation. Isidoro was buried the next day, beside the remains of Father Josemaría's parents—the three of them together, united by a single cause. The stone bore words from the liturgy: "*Vita mutatur, non tollitur*" ("Life is changed, not taken away").[135] After the service, Father Josemaría sent a telegram to all the centers of the Work saying, "Isidoro died a holy death yesterday afternoon. Offer suffrages. Maríano."[136]

The same day, July 16, Father Arcadio Larraona, consultor of the Congregation for Religious and an able canonist, sent Cardinal La Puma a very laudatory report on Opus Dei recommending that it be erected as a society of diocesan right.[137] Matters followed their

---

[132] See AGP, RHF, EF–430613–1, and also Fuenmayor, Gómez Iglesias, and Illanes, pp. 111–27 and 484–89.

[133] Literally, the "nothing standing in the way"; in effect, official approval.

[134] AGP, RHF, EF–430725–1.

[135] See AGP, RHF, T–04956, p. 16 (María Dolores Fisac), and Eduardo Alastrué, *Sum.* 5546.

[136] AGP, RHF, EF–430716–1. Isidoro had a widespread reputation for sanctity. On October 11, 1948, proceedings were opened in Madrid for his beatification. See José Luis Múzquiz, *Sum.* 5797.

[137] AGP, Sección Jurídica III/15015.

usual course, and on October 11 the congregation granted the *nihil obstat*.[138]

The bishop of Madrid got the news by telegram on October 18. Bishop Leopoldo, in Vigo at the time, telegraphed congratulations to Father Josemaría. On October 20 Father Josemaría wrote him: "I received your telegram: bless us once more and especially bless this sinful son of yours who always prays for you. . . ."[139]

The founder relayed to everyone the good news by word of mouth and letter. Though less than ideal, that *nihil obstat* at least signified recognition of his apostolic work, legal consolidation of the Work's structure of governance, and a basis for a future inter-diocesan status (that of "pontifical right"). He wrote Dom Aurelio Escarré, the coadjutor abbot of Monserrat:

> The *nihil obstat* granted by the Sacred Congregation for Religious has just come from Rome for the entire Work, including the priests. With the Holy See's *impositio manuum* [laying on of hands] we now share even more fully in the apostolate and life of our holy Mother the Church. *Roma locuta est!* [Rome has spoken!]
>
> Help me, dear Father Abbot, to give thanks to our Lord and ask your monks to join me in giving thanks.[140]

On December 8, 1943, by the decree *Quindecim abhinc annos*, Bishop Eijo y Garay canonically established the Priestly Society of the Holy Cross. The text abounds with praises and expressions of affection, as

---

[138] It was necessary first to obtain the *nihil obstat* of the Sacred Congregation of the Holy Office. It then was communicated to the Sacred Congregation for Religious, on September 29, 1943. See Fuenmayor, Gómez Iglesias, and Illanes, pp. 493–94.

Bishop del Portillo tells a little story about a conversation he had with the founder on that October 11, when the *nihil obstat* had been granted but the news had not yet reached Madrid. "Father," he had said, "you will be happy tomorrow, because it's the feast of Our Lady of the Pillar." And Father Josemaría had replied, "I'm always happy, and especially when it's a feast of our Lady, but of all her feasts my favorite one is today's, because it's the feast of her maternity" (Alvaro del Portillo, PR, p. 712).

[139] AGP, RHF, EF–431020–1.

[140] AGP, RHF, EF–431029–1. Obviously in very high spirits, he added: "The 'gasoline' you said you were sending hasn't arrived yet. I guarantee you that it will be received with joy—and that that joy will be augmented with that vivifying liquid." The "gasoline" was some bottles of liqueur—"Aromas de Montserrat"—that Dom Escarré had promised to send. Later Father Josemaría wrote him again, to say: "The bottles of Aromas were received, and, much to the joy of the tasters, were rendered due honor" (AGP, RHF, EF–431217–1).

if in compensation for the dry formalities of the decree with which in 1941 the bishop had approved Opus Dei as a pious union.[141] One of its sentences reads:

> From its very beginning, divine favor has smiled constantly on this pious institution, shown in a special way by the number and quality of the young men (of solid virtue and brilliant intellect) who have come to it; by the good results it is producing everywhere; and, finally, by the sign of contradiction that has always been a clear hallmark of divine works.[142]

The last phrase was a reference to the "opposition by good people."

As noted earlier, two days after the date of the decree, December 10, Father Josemaría formally notified the bishop of the establishment of the Society's Center for Ecclesiastical Studies.[143] That same day he proposed candidates for appointment to positions in the Priestly Society.[144] Clearly he was wasting no time; the note is written on stationery with the printed letterhead "The Priestly Society of the Holy Cross," is signed "President," and is stamped with the seal "Societas + Sacerdotalis + Sanctae + Crucis + Praeses." On December 12 the bishop officially informed him that the proposed appointments had been approved.[145]

That same week, Father Josemaría went to see the bishop. As they were sitting in the library, talking late into the night, Bishop Leopoldo suddenly suggested that he renew his incorporation into Opus Dei. And so, the founder tells us, "I knelt down and recited, from memory and stumbling over them because I was so overcome with emotion, the words we have in our ceremonial for the Fidelity, which says nothing about vows or promises or anything similar." And he adds,

---

[141] Bishop Leopoldo had, as we mentioned earlier, adopted that neutral tone on the advice of the nuncio. See Alvaro del Portillo, *Sum.* 553.

[142] See Fuenmayor, Gómez Iglesias, and Illanes, p. 495.

[143] See AGP, RHF, D–15140.

[144] In this note he pointed out that according to the Work's constitution, major posts in the Society were to be filled by the president after consultation with the council, but that since the latter did not exist yet, he needed to do the consulting with his bishop. The list of proposed appointments reads as follows: "Secretary General, Alvaro del Portillo; Vice-secretary for the Saint Michael work, José Luis Múzquiz; Vice-secretary for the Saint Gabriel work, José María Hernández de Garnica; Vice-secretary for the Saint Raphael work, Pedro Casciaro; General Administrator, Ricardo Fernández Vallespín" (AGP, RHF, D–15138).

[145] See AGP, RHF, D–15139.

"It seemed natural to him, as it did to me. However, it was the first time that that venerable prelate, already up in years, had received the incorporation of someone who had set up a group of faithful to foster sanctity and apostolate, without the mediation of any type of vows." [146]

6. *The first priests*

Happy as he was about the *nihil obstat*, Father Josemaría nevertheless did not blow it up out of all proportion. His instincts as a founder, together with fifteen years of experience in dealing with foundational matters, told him that although this was an important step, it was hardly the last one that would have to be taken. Indeed, Alvaro del Portillo had just left for Rome when, on May 31, 1943, Father Josemaría finished writing a letter to his children in the Work that shows him to have been well aware that the configuration they now had in place was only a temporary solution. "The ordinaries of the dioceses in which we work all understand and love us," he says, "and—regardless of what juridical form the Work assumes over time—the Church, our Mother, will respect her children's way of being, because she knows we want only to serve her and please God." [147]

Still more surprising is another parenthetical remark, in a letter dated February 14, 1944. Just two months after the canonical establishment of the Priestly Society of the Holy Cross, the founder refers to that establishment as a solution "necessarily temporary, but valid for the time being," one that "will be replaced as soon as there is a better juridical *iter* [path] available." [148]

What was it about this arrangement that made the founder see it as unacceptable in the long run? And what did he hope to change in the short run, as soon as the opportunity arose?

[146] *Letter 29 Dec 1947/14 Feb 1966*, no. 87.

The Sacred Congregation for Religious specified in the *nihil obstat* for the diocesan approval that the Society's president should profess his perpetual fidelity before the bishop and that the latter had powers of post-factum validation and dispensation in regard to any defects of incorporation (see Amadeo de Fuenmayor et al., op. cit., Documentary Appendix 13, p. 525).

The communiqué of the bishop of Madrid-Alcalá to the Sacred Congregation for Religious concerning erection of the Priestly Society of the Holy Cross (19 Dec 1943) states: *"Moderator nuper erectae Societatis Sacerdotalis Sanctae Crucis coram me perpetuam emisit fidelitatem"* (ibid., Document Appendix, document no. 17, p. 497).

[147] *Letter 31 May 1943*, no. 53.

[148] *Letter 14 Feb 1944*, no. 12.

Clearly it was the core reality of Opus Dei that he was determined to protect.[149] The idea of the Priestly Society of the Holy Cross as a foundational solution had come to Father Josemaría from out of the blue, without any effort on his part, obviously as a gift from God. But it was hard work to fit the whole of Opus Dei into the framework of the Code of Canon Law as a society of common life without vows. Throughout the course of its development Father Josemaría always distinguished what was of supernatural origin, and therefore could not be changed or compromised, from what was transitory. This is clear not only from later events but also from the fact that in 1940, a year before even the pious-union approval came through, he was sure that his efforts to find an appropriate canonical setting for the apostolate of the Work would be "an arduous, laborious, and exacting task." [150]

He approached that task with boundless trust in God and enormous depth of vision that kept on growing. He had dreamed of the Work from the start as a splendid apostolic undertaking, a general mobilization of Christians, each serving the apostolic mission of the Church from his own situation in life, that would put Christ at the summit of all human activity. This was the message, the inspiration, he had received. But as soon as he started looking for a permanent juridical place for it in civil or ecclesiastical society (especially the latter), that priest who was dreaming of vast possibilities opened up to him by our Lord himself had to measure and negotiate every step on the way toward realizing them.

Not everything, of course, depended on him. But he threw all the resources he had into what did. One example was the excellent formation given to the three members of the Work who were going to be ordained. He spared nothing in his efforts to make them models of priestly virtue and theological learning. But he ran into a dead end when it came to the question of their incardination. When he began his Mass on February 14, 1943, he had no idea when or how he would

---

[149] In section no. 11 of this letter of 14 Feb 1944, he writes: "I don't have much sympathy with people who take leaps in the dark, because I think it's possible to make progress maintaining the essentials (which are intangible), step by step. That is how the Church, governed by the Holy Spirit, proceeds, so as to build on firm and solid ground."

[150] From the *Letter of 11 Mar 1940*, no. 46: "When Heaven judges the moment propitious, there will open up, in the structure of the Church's apostolate, the channel for the broad river of the Work, for which present circumstances do not provide a suitable site. It will be an arduous and laborious challenge. Many obstacles will have to be overcome. But God will assist us, since everything in the Work is his will."

find a solution to that problem; the thought of founding the Priestly Society of the Holy Cross came to him as a total surprise. This unexpected grace arrived when he was both doing everything humanly possible and trusting calmly, with faith, that sooner or later the solution would come.

Father Josemaría's motto "To hide and disappear" referred to his preferred mode of serving the Church, but he also sometimes humorously referred to it as "passing off a hare as a cat"—the reverse of "passing off a cat as a hare," or making something appear better than it is.[151] Something of this nature happened with Opus Dei after the canonical establishment of the Priestly Society of the Holy Cross. Opus Dei ceased to be a pious union and became "a simple lay association of a pious character," and yet the truth was that its faithful all lived the same contemplative vocation and observed the same norms of piety and the same customs as their brothers in the Priestly Society. The founder summed up this state of affairs in a letter to the new bishop of Barcelona, Gregorio Modrego:

> Although these are not matters to handle in a letter, and I hope (either here or in Barcelona) to have the pleasure of seeing Your Excellency soon and speaking with you at length, I do want you to know that the latest decree, before being made public, was in its entirety viewed favorably in Rome. Opus Dei has ceased to be a pious union and has become a pious work proper to the Priestly Society, with two branches, the men's and the women's, perfectly separated and defined, and with statutes distinct from those of the Priestly Society of the Holy Cross.
>
> All of this is spelled out in the constitutions of the Priestly Society, which have received the *appositio manuum* [approval] of the Holy See.
>
> I also want to inform you that the Sacred Congregation for Religious was petitioned only [for] what has been granted us: to be able to constitute ourselves as a society of common life without vows and, naturally, for the time being, of diocesan right. As for the doors that were opened to us, about which I will tell you more when I see you, I must say, Bishop, that they

---

[151] See AGP, RHF, T–04855, p. 4 (Sabina Alandes Caldés).

treated us very generously in Rome. *Digitus Dei est hic* [The finger of God is here].

From what I have said, it can clearly be seen that the Priestly Society must be distinguished from Opus Dei. The Priestly Society, as long as it is of diocesan right, will be subject to the jurisdiction of the bishops in whose dioceses it has centers. Opus Dei, on ceasing to be a pious union, has become a simple lay association of a pious character, whose members are subject to the bishop in matters of faith and morals, the same as the rest of the Catholic faithful. . . .

I think that for now, Reverend Bishop, that's enough for me to say about the canonical situation of the Work. When I get the chance to see you in person, I'll be very happy to give you more of the details.[152]

Though that canonical solution was clearly temporary, the Priestly Society of the Holy Cross would continue, through later changes, until Opus Dei as a whole acquired its definitive structure as a personal prelature.[153]

*   *   *

The three young men preparing for the priesthood continued their rigorous philosophical and theological studies. When the time came for their first round of examinations, each petitioned the bishop of Madrid-Alcalá in these words: "Believing he has a vocation to the priesthood and desiring to continue his ecclesiastical studies, [N.] petitions Your Excellency to grant him the appropriate permissions allowing him to be examined in the humanities and philosophy, and then admitted to the study of sacred theology." [154]

The philosophy examinations were given, as mentioned earlier, by a panel from Madrid's diocesan seminary. Some months later, the

---

[152] AGP, RHF, EF–440531–1.

[153] Two sentences in *Letter 14 Feb 1944* sum up very well the problem with the canonical situation of "society of common life without vows": "This solution is not *comfortable* for us, because it makes the main thing—Opus Dei—appear secondary" (no. 12), and "Opus Dei—which constitutes our real Work—becomes a part of the Priestly Society of the Holy Cross, when the reality is that the Priestly Society of the Holy Cross is only a small part of the Work" (no. 17).

[154] See AGP, Sección Expedientes, D–660. The phrase about admission "to the study of sacred theology" was a formality; the bishop knew that they were well along in these studies.

theology examinations took place in the Center for Ecclesiastical Studies that was set up when the Priestly Society of the Holy Cross was canonically established. When the three candidates passed those examinations and drew near the end of their studies, Father Josemaría was deeply moved.

Bishop Leopoldo suggested to Alvaro del Portillo that the three be ordained on June 25 and asked him to pass this date on to Father Josemaría. On April 25 the latter wrote the bishop that he had consulted the ordinands' professors, and they saw no difficulty with holding the final theology examinations in early June, and that he would therefore be happy to have the ordinations set for the suggested date. "I can't hide the fact," he added, "that I am deeply moved by the approaching priesthood of these sons of my soul, with unbounded gratitude to God and to my father Bishop Leopoldo. May He fill you with his grace!" [155]

A dispensation was needed from the Holy See to abbreviate the usual time intervals between conferrals of the various minor and major orders. On Friday, May 12, Bishop Leopoldo called Father Josemaría. "The ordinands should start their week-long retreat tomorrow," he told him, "because on Saturday the 20th I'll give them the tonsure and, every few days after that, the other orders leading to the priesthood." [156] So on May 13, Father Josemaría went to El Escorial to preach the retreat required before Holy Orders.[157]

The founder supplied the instruction in liturgy and pastoral theology himself, giving talks on these topics over a period of several months. He was very demanding on the subject of liturgical decorum, insisting that his sons faithfully observe even the smallest details of the rubrics, especially those for Holy Mass, which so much help bring people nearer to the Lord.[158] In pastoral theology he shared his broad, varied ministerial experience in seminaries and universities, in rural

---

[155] AGP, RHF, EF–440425–1.

[156] This is related in a letter from the founder to Dom Escarré, in AGP, RHF, EF–440515–1.

[157] The retreats prescribed by canon law for the different stages of ordination were finished by June 15. That is the date on which Father Josemaría, as president of the Priestly Society of the Holy Cross, certified that each of the candidates had "made the retreats during the time specified by the Code of Canon Law for the reception of Holy Orders, in the monastery of El Escorial, in the house of the Vincentian Fathers (at 21 Fernández de la Hoz), and in one of our houses." See Alvaro del Portillo, *Sum.* 762, and AGP, Sección Expedientes, D–660.

[158] Whenever Father Josemaría went to El Escorial to give a retreat, he stayed at the monastery, in what had at one time been the room of Saint Anthony Mary Claret. The

and city parishes, in hospitals and charitable institutions, and with religious, priests, and lay people of all ages and professions.[159]

As Bishop Leopoldo had promised, the ceremony of tonsure took place on May 20 and the minor orders were conferred over the next few days; the subdiaconate by the bishop of Pamplona on Sunday, May 28, in the oratory of Diego de León, and the diaconate on June 3 by auxiliary Bishop Casimiro Morcillo of Madrid. [160]

The final examinations were on June 12. Three days later Father Josemaría certified to the bishop that the candidates "had completed all of the studies required for priestly ordination." [161] The results of the theology exams were an almost unbroken string of "Meritissimi" (the highest possible evaluation), but all three received a mere "Benemeritus" (Good) in liturgical chant.[162]

In the days before ordination, Father Josemaría received answers to requests he had sent to almost all the bishops of Spain seeking ministerial faculties for the future priests in their dioceses. All said yes, which made him feel very supported by the hierarchy and very grateful for that support.[163]

On the afternoon of Saturday, June 24, he visited La Almudena cemetery. It was a pilgrimage, to the graves of his parents and Isidoro, to offer thanks and to pray that the new priests would be holy ones. He felt strongly that it was especially to his parents and to Isidoro that he owed these first ordinations, which, as this note found in the opening pages of his journal makes clear, he had foreseen at Opus Dei's founding:

---

practical classes in liturgy were given in the chapel that this saint had used. See Alvaro del Portillo, *Sum.* 762, and also AGP, RHF, T–04678/1, p. 43 (José Luis Múzquiz).

[159] Typically, he distilled that experience into the form of brief, clear principles: for example, that a priest must not set himself up as a proprietor of souls, but must function simply as an instrument of the Holy Spirit, who is the one who actually directs souls. See AGP, RHF, T–04678/1, p. 119.

[160] See Alvaro del Portillo, *Sum.* 762, and AGP, Sección Expedientes, D–660.

[161] See AGP, Sección Expedientes, D–660, Tessera Studiorum. "Despite the considerable amount of work those young men had to do," says Bishop García Lahiguera, "they achieved extraordinary results. The professors were astonished by their ability and progress. But I wasn't all that surprised, given the intellectual capabilities demanded by their secular professions and their dedication to their studies—a dedication supported by the untiring zeal of the Father" (*Testimonios*, p. 162). "All three," says Cardinal Bueno Monreal, "already had a first-class education in the humanities and sciences, and worked very hard at their ecclesiastical studies" (*Testimonios*, p. 17).

[162] Gregorian chant was taught by Father Enrique Massó, at both the Diego de León and the Jorge Manrique centers. See AGP, RHF, T–04151, p. 46 (Francisco Ponz), and T–04956, p. 17 (María Dolores Fisac).

[163] See Alvaro del Portillo, *Sum.* 763, and also AGP, Sección Expedientes, D–660.

> The role of the priest in the Work! How often we have spoken about him! He is the nerve of the Work of God. Holy! He should go overboard in virtue, if it is possible to go overboard in this. For the lay members will see themselves in him as in a mirror; and only if the priest aims very high will the others reach the right level.[164]

Kneeling in prayer now at the three graves, he wept with gratitude for the sacrifices that had been made by his parents and Isidoro.[165]

Sunday, June 25, 1944, was a day of great rejoicing. The three young men said good-bye to the founder at Diego de León and went by car to the bishop's residence, where they were to be ordained in his chapel. The crowd was larger than the chapel could hold and spilled over into adjoining rooms. At ten o'clock, Bishop Leopoldo entered and began the ceremony. After Mass, as the new priests were still removing their vestments, people pressed forward to kiss their newly consecrated hands. Among those present were people from the nunciature and from the bishop's staff, priests from Madrid and surrounding areas, relatives and friends and acquaintances of the new priests, members of the Work, and a large number of representatives of religious orders and congregations: Hieronymites, Dominicans, Piarists, Augustinians, Maríanists, Vincentians. . . .[166] In the meantime, while the ceremony was taking place, the founder was celebrating Mass in the oratory of the Diego de León center, assisted by José María Albareda.

Bishop Leopoldo dined at the Diego de León center with the new priests and a few invited guests. Later that afternoon, Father Josemaría introduced him to the members of the Work who had come from other cities for the ordination. Soon the ground-floor living room was full of young people. The family gathering lasted for quite a while as Father Josemaría laughingly described the merits of each of the new priests. The bishop, too, was in very good humor, although it had been a long day for him. The phone rang repeatedly. Many visitors dropped by to congratulate the newly ordained and the founder.

---

[164] *Apuntes*, no. 123 (9 Dec 1930).

[165] Father Josemaría spoke about this in the meditation he gave on the evening of June 25. See AGP, Sección Expedientes, D–660 (account of Teodoro Ruiz Jusué, 26 Jun 1944), and also AGP, RHF, T–04151, p. 79. The ordination of priests who came from the ranks of Opus Dei was the fruit of fifteen years of trustful and persistent prayer.

[166] See AGP, Sección Expedientes, D–660 (account of Teodoro Ruiz Jusué, May 20 to July 28, 1944, p. 20).

At a point when Father Josemaría was briefly out of the room, the bishop poured out his heart to that large group of young people. First he spoke of the enormous joy it had given him to ordain that first group of priests. Then he called to mind the persecutions suffered by the Work in recent years and congratulated all those young people for having harbored no grudges. "How many tears were shed by so many of your mothers because of those calumnies, when you were branded as heretics or Masons!" he exclaimed.[167]

Then he spoke of the founder and his God-given mission to direct the Work and form them. He has a special grace for it, the bishop pointed out. "Take good care of your Father, who needs it and whom we need very much," he said, noting that the heavy burdens he carried had had an effect on his health. And in a lighter tone he added: "It shows how exhausted he is, that he didn't dare go to the ordination this morning for fear we would see him crying like an old grandfather. And being afraid even to stay at home by himself, he asked José María Albareda to stay with him." And then, in a more serious tone of voice, the bishop said, "Of course, it could also be that he was making a sacrifice of something he very much wanted; that it was a case of, 'Since I would enjoy it so much, I'll stay here instead.' " [168]

He ended with affectionate words and gave them his blessing. But before getting into his car to leave, he asked to have a photo taken of him embracing Father Josemaría.

A little later everyone went to the oratory and Father Josemaría gave a meditation. Commenting on some phrases from Saint Paul that he had jotted down ten years earlier, he insisted on prayer and sacrifice, as the foundation for all interior life, and on humility, both individual and collective. "When the youngest of you who are here," he said, "are going gray—or sporting splendid bald spots, like some that you see—and I, by the law of nature, have long since departed,

---

[167] Ibid., p. 2. Bishop Leopoldo went on to tell them about a certain occasion when he had mentioned to Alvaro his worry that the attack campaign carried on by some Jesuits might embitter the members of Opus Dei. Alvaro, he said, had assured him that they knew very well that the campaign was something permitted by God for their good, the proof being that God was making use of a platinum scalpel—something so near and dear to him as the Society of Jesus. When the bishop finished telling this story, Alvaro, who was sitting right there beside him, said, "But, Reverend Bishop, I was only repeating what I had heard the founder say." And Bishop Leopoldo replied, "Like father, like son." See AGP, RHF, T–08253, p. 26 (Manuel Botas Cuervo).

[168] AGP, Sección Expedientes, D–660 (account of Adolfo Rodríguez Vidal, 25 Jun 1944).

others are going to ask you: 'So what did the Father say on the day of the ordination of the first three?' And you will answer them: 'He said that you are to be men of prayer, men of prayer, and men of prayer.' " [169]

He spoke about perseverance and the cross. He told them some members of the Work would soon be leaving for distant lands. He ended by reporting that he had just received a cable from the Vatican. The Holy Father, it said, had granted the three new priests the right to give a papal blessing, accompanied by a plenary indulgence, to all those attending their first Mass.

A solemn Benediction and the singing of the *Te Deum* followed. Phone calls, visits, and family festivities continued. When Father Josemaría retired, late that night, he was worn out by the day's emotions.

---

[169] Ibid.

7

A New Apostolic Thrust (1944–1946)

1. *After the ordination*

The morning after the ordination of the first priests of the Work, Father Josemaría went to see Father Alvaro del Portillo, in the center on Villanueva Street. He asked if Father Alvaro had heard any confessions yet. The answer was no. "Well," he said, "you're going to hear mine, because I want to make a general confession to you." [1] When the time came for absolution, Father Alvaro was so moved (Father Josemaría said later), that he had to help him recite the formula. Alvaro remained his confessor until his death.[2] Indeed, humility and interior transparency often moved him to open his soul to Father Alvaro even outside confession.[3]

The new priests celebrated their first public Masses the following week. Father Hernández Garnica's was on Tuesday, June 27, at 9:30 A.M. in the church of Santa Isabel. Assisting him were Fathers López Ortiz and Bueno Monreal. The church was packed with a large contingent from the Madrid Electric Company, where the new priest had worked as an engineer. Also present were professors and former classmates from the School of Mining Engineering.[4]

Father del Portillo's first public Mass took place the next day, in the chapel of Our Lady of the Pillar High School, run by the Marianists. He was assisted by a Father Aguilar, O.P., and by the principal of the school. As was also the case with Father Hernández de Garnica's first Mass, at the end the papal blessing was given and a *Te Deum* was sung. Lining up to kiss the new priest's hands were many relatives,

---

[1] Alvaro del Portillo, *Sum.* 330; see also Javier Echevarría, *Sum.* 3211.

[2] When in October 1940 Father Josemaría asked Father José María García Lahiguera to be his confessor, he told him that he intended to make his confessions to a son of his as soon as one was ordained. "Which was something I fully approved of," testifies Bishop García Lahiguera, "and even advised him to do" (José María García Lahiguera, *Sum.* 5474).

[3] See Alvaro del Portillo, *Sum.* 331.

[4] See AGP, Sección Expedientes, D–660.

friends, and acquaintances, including engineers and professors from the School of Civil Engineering.[5]

On Thursday, June 29, Father Múzquiz celebrated his first public Mass, in the church of the Monastery of the Incarnation. Those present included friends and former classmates from the School of Civil Engineering and many employees of the national railroad company where he had worked.

Wishing—at all times, but especially at this one—to avoid anything that might focus attention on himself, Father Josemaría had it in mind to stay away from these first Masses, as he had stayed away from the ordination ceremony. His sons and many of his friends understood his reasons for doing this. But on Thursday, deciding to take this last opportunity to make one of the new priests especially happy, he called Ricardo Vallespín and said, "Let's go to José Luis's first Mass."[6] They were part of the large congregation.[7]

*   *   *

Months earlier, in February 1944, perhaps thinking of the priests to come, he had written: "How clearly I see that, especially in the Work, to be a priest is to be continually on the Cross!" Summing up the priest's role as "to sanctify himself and to sanctify others," he declared: "The lukewarm priest: that's the great enemy of the Work. Hence the absolute need for us priests to be saints." Moreover: "Your work, priest, is not only to save souls, but to sanctify them." It is the task of a priest to fill the world with light by preaching Christ: "You are the sun (*lux mundi*) and your people are the moon, who reflect the light they receive from you."[8]

The founder filled several card files with similar reflections, which he used when preaching to priests. There is a constant refrain: holiness, holiness, holiness. On occasion he had encountered lukewarm

---

[5] See ibid.

[6] See AGP, RHF, T–04678/1, p. 44 (José Luis Múzquiz).

[7] Msgr. Javier de Ayala testifies, "I recall how in 1948, when Ignacio Echevarría and I were ordained, although the ceremony was as private as could be—it was in the oratory of Diego de León and attended just by the few people living at that center—the founder did not attend then either. He greeted Bishop Casimiro Morcillo, the bishop who was going to do the ordaining, and very matter-of-factly said to him that 'as always' he would not be there. And to Ignacio and me he said that during the ceremony he would be celebrating Holy Mass in the little oratory of the administration, praying to the Lord for us" (AGP, RHF, T–15712, p. 55).

[8] See *Apuntes*, no. 1861 (11 Feb 1944), and AGP, RHF, AVF–0079. See also *Apuntes*, no. 1854 (9 Nov 1941).

priests, but they were a mystery to him. How, he wondered, could any priest be satisfied with just getting by?

Father Josemaría had no patience with those "who say they are here to serve, but who serve for nothing." [9] But, fortunately, he had good reason to be proud of his priest-sons. Before the ordination ceremony someone had commented, "Now he's ordaining them, and afterwards he's going to kill them with work." [10] And indeed he soon was sending them on apostolic journeys all over Spain. In August Fathers Múzquiz and Hernández de Garnica were already preaching their first retreats, each of which involved more than twenty meditations. But Father Josemaría gave them a lot of help by telling them to "feel free to use my file of meditations," [11] a generous gesture that deeply impressed Father Alvaro.[12] Apparently they borrowed freely, because Father Josemaría had to start building a new file from scratch.[13]

It was murmured that he was a tyrant who overworked those around him. And, wanting his sons and daughters to be saints, he did at times make great demands on them. He also wanted them to acquire a lot of pastoral experience and urged his first priest sons to put heart and soul into the exercise of their ministry. Father Alvaro (or Don Alvaro, as he came to be called by members of the Work) would later recall that, in his first year as a priest, he was asked by the founder to give thirteen retreats—each requiring the preparation of twenty-two meditations—in addition to giving days of recollection, teaching many classes, and all the rest of his work: talks, confessions, spiritual direction, and work connected with the governing of Opus Dei.[14]

But Father Josemaría made still heavier demands on himself. From the time he started giving retreats after the civil war, rarely did he let a month pass without preaching at least one. November 1943 was one of those exceptions. The reason appears in a letter written to Dom Escarré on December 17:

> I was unable to reply earlier to Your Reverence because I had to spend some days covered with gauze and cotton, as a result

[9] *Letter 15 Oct 1948*, no. 30.
[10] AGP, RHF, T–04837, p. 15 (Rafael Escolá Gil). See also Alvaro del Portillo, *Sum.* 763.
[11] AGP, RHF, T–04678/1, p. 80 (José Luis Múzquiz).
[12] See Alvaro del Portillo, *Sum.* 763.
[13] See ibid.
[14] See ibid.

of a little operation. Plus, my only brother has for some time now been fighting for his life, because of a duodenal ulcer. Thanks be to God, he is doing better—although he lost almost all his blood, despite the two transfusions they gave him.[15]

In January 1944 he had to have another operation, this time a tonsillectomy, and was forced to cut back on his intense activity in the various Spanish dioceses.[16] Although he quickly got back to work, a retreat he gave in October for the Augustinian community at El Escorial tested his endurance. At midpoint, he developed a large boil on his neck, with pus draining from several openings. For protection against chafing from his Roman collar, he used a handkerchief—which, being white, was very noticeable in the dark chapel. But not wanting to alarm the friar in charge of the infirmary or to let the retreatants know how ill he was, he preached the retreat through to the end, despite a high fever. And he wrote to his sons in Madrid:

> Send me a couple of black handkerchiefs, for my neck. And please have the one I am sending washed, as well as the one I sent yesterday. They're greatly needed.
> Tell Ricardo to bring the camera when he comes here.
> It's already after four and my friar from the infirmary still hasn't come. But really I can get by without him.[17]

Two weeks later Father Carlos Vicuña, the Augustinian provincial, wrote to Don Alvaro:

> I want to give you a little feedback on the retreat given by Father José María this month to the Augustinian friars at the Royal Monastery of El Escorial. Everyone agrees that he sur-passed all their expectations, and he fully satisfied the wishes of the superiors. Now we trust in God that the fruit will be

---

[15] AGP, RHF, EF–431217–1. In September he had written to Monsignor Antonio Rodilla, "I'm really worn out and need to rest for a few days, as soon as I finish the retreat I'm giving" (AGP, RHF, EF–430911–1).

[16] The tonsillectomy was performed on January 3 (see AGP, RHF, EF–440102–1). He summarized his activities of those weeks in a letter to a friend, José Royo López: "Things have gotten pretty complicated: the illness of my little brother, which was very serious; my two operations, on nose and throat; several trips outside Madrid, when the doctors gave me the green light . . ." (AGP, RHF, EF–440206–1).

[17] AGP, RHF, EF–441008–1.

very abundant. Everyone without exception—all the fathers, theologians, philosophers, brothers, and aspirants—hung on every word. Those conferences of thirty or thirty-five minutes seemed to them only ten minutes long, they were so captivated by that torrent of fervor, enthusiasm, sincerity, and outpouring of the heart. "It came from his heart—he spoke that way because he has interior life and fire." "He is a saint, an apostle." "If we outlive him, many of us will see him raised to the altars." These are some of the comments I heard from those who made the retreat.

What is really remarkable is the unanimity of the praises, especially since we're talking about an audience largely composed of intellectuals and specialists. I didn't hear one word that was anything but favorable. It is true that he came preceded by a reputation for sanctity; but it is no less certain that, far from diminishing it, he confirmed it.[18]

After the retreat, he saw a doctor. Tests confirmed that the symptoms he had been experiencing for some time—the fatigue, the boils, the thirst, the weight gain—were produced by a severe case of diabetes.

*   *   *

A little over half a year after the ordination of the first three priests, the founder wrote a circular letter in which he said:

> All of you, my children, should serve one another, as a good living out of your fraternal relationship calls for you to do. But the priests must not let their lay brothers and sisters perform unnecessary services for them. We priests in the Work are the slaves of the others, following the example of the Lord, who came not to be served but to serve ("*non veni ministrari, sed ministrare*"). We must know how to lay our hearts on the ground, so as to cushion the walk of the others. That is why allowing yourselves to be unnecessarily served by your lay brothers and sisters is something that goes against the very essence of the spirit of Opus Dei.

[18] AGP, RHF, D–03275.

We need priests with our spirit: priests who are well prepared, cheerful, and effective, with a sportsmanlike attitude
toward life, who joyfully sacrifice themselves for their brothers and sisters without seeing themselves as victims, and who
know that everyone in the Work loves them wholeheartedly.
My children, pray hard that they be very cheerful, very holy;
that they do not think about themselves, but only about the
glory of God and the good of souls.

Our priests must have in their souls a basic disposition to
spend themselves entirely in the service of their brothers and
sisters, convinced that the ministry to which they have been
called, within Opus Dei, is a great honor, but above all a great
burden—easy to bear, however, if they strive to be very united
to our Lord, since his yoke is always easy and his burden
light—"*iugum meum suave est, et onus meum leve.*"

Every year I write on the first page of the ordo I use, "*In
laetitia, nulla dies sine Cruce!*" ["In joy, not a day without the
Cross!"], as a way of encouraging myself to carry the Lord's
burden with generosity, always with good humor (though
often it means going against the grain).[19]

This was his repeated message to the recently ordained priests.

Be priests first of all. And then, priests. And always and in
everything, *only priests*.

Speak only of God.

When a penitent wants you, drop whatever you are doing
and take care of him.[20]

2. *Los Rosales and the Zurbarán Street residence*

Bishop Leopoldo was the first to notice a kind of family resemblance
among the Opus Dei priests. Each was himself, of course, but the three
of them shared characteristics rooted in the spirit of the Work and
nourished by constant contact with the founder. Never complaining,
they embraced a life full of sacrifice and apostolic activity. Following

---

[19] *Letter 2 Feb 1945,* nos. 20 and 21.
[20] AGP, RHF, AVF–0079 (February 1944).

Father Josemaría's example, they pushed themselves to and beyond the limit.

Since the founder's apostolic activity usually was reflected in the amount of his correspondence, it is strange that in the files there are fewer than a dozen letters from the autumn of 1945. It is possible that some have been lost. But in any event, it is clear that he was traveling extensively in Spain during these months. On January 19, 1946, from Granada, he wrote to his daughters in Bilbao: "I received your letters, and I'll see to it that your sisters write you often, since I'm not able to do this myself now." [21] A little later, also from Granada, he wrote to his daughters at the Los Rosales center in Madrid to tell them that he hoped to see them soon, "but you will have to have a little patience, because the Father is moving around these days like a poor gypsy." [22]

A letter from Don Alvaro to José Orlandis, written in Bilbao on February 3, suggests how the founder was moving about. "The day before yesterday," he says, "I arrived here with the Father, who has continued on to Asturias and Galicia." A week later he wrote to Salvador Canals in Rome, announcing his arrival plans. (Canals and Orlandis were faithful of Opus Dei who had lived in Rome for three years and who had assisted Don Alvaro in 1943 in the effort to obtain the *nihil obstat* from the Holy See for the Priestly Society of the Holy Cross.) And a week later he again wrote to Canals, "I'm leaving soon. The letters are almost ready—we're bringing some of them, and the rest will be sent to us. . . . I hope to be there within a couple of weeks. The letters will be from Seville, Granada, Murcia, Valencia, Barcelona, Vitoria, Santiago, Valladolid, Madrid, and perhaps Saragossa and Coimbra, as well as Pamplona, Avila, Palencia, and Salamanca." [23] The nature of these letters is clear from a note he sent the next day to José Orlandis, who by this time was in Saragossa: "We enclose some lines for the archbishop. They are a request for a letter of commendation. Every bishop we've asked so far has written one." [24]

Evidently the founder had been crisscrossing Spain tirelessly, in pursuit of such letters from bishops. But why? A petition to the Holy See, written in consultation with the bishop of Madrid-Alcalá, makes clear the reason. The Latin text translates as:

[21] AGP, RHF, EF–460119–1.
[22] AGP, RHF, EF–460124–2.
[23] Letter of Alvaro del Portillo to Salvador Canals: San Sebastián, 9 Feb 1946.
[24] Letter of Alvaro del Portillo to José Orlandis: Pamplona, 10 Feb 1946.

Most Holy Father:

Humbly prostrate at the feet of Your Holiness, the priest Josemaría Escrivá de Balaguer y Albás, President General of the Priestly Society of the Holy Cross, earnestly entreats that you deign to grant the *Decretum Laudis* (Decree of Praise) and the approval of the Constitutions of said Society.[25]

Mention is then made, in half a dozen lines, of the milestones in Opus Dei's history: its founding in 1928, its approval as a pious union in 1941, the canonical establishment of the Priestly Society in 1943 in the diocese of Madrid. The document continues:

Thanks to divine assistance, the Priestly Society of the Holy Cross has kept growing, to the point where, both because of the number and select quality of its members and because of the nature and development of its activities (which are fruitfully being carried out not only in a good number of [Spanish] dioceses but also in several nations of Europe and the Americas), the said Society requires an approval that will give it greater stability and range than "diocesan right" affords.

In the last paragraph, the founder speaks of the "timeliness and efficacy" of the apostolate of the Priestly Society of the Holy Cross. The document is signed in Madrid and dated January 25, 1946.

The point was that the Holy See's granting of the *Decretum Laudis* would give Opus Dei the pontifical backing it needed to expand to dioceses outside Spain. The bishops' letters accompanying the petition were testimony to the Work's presence in most of Spain's dioceses, as well as in several countries of Europe and of the Americas, and to the bishops' support for the idea of giving it the status of an institution of the universal church, in keeping with the nature of its apostolate.

*   *   *

Having sailed from Barcelona on the steamer *J. J. Sister*, Don Alvaro and José Orlandis arrived in Genoa the afternoon of February 16.[26]

---

[25] AGP, RHF, EF–460125–1.

[26] For more on this trip, see José Orlandis Rovira, *Mis recuerdos: Primeros tiempos del Opus Dei en Roma* (Madrid, 1995), pp. 35ff.

Salvador Canals was waiting for them on the dock. From Genoa they went to Rome, and a few days later Don Alvaro wrote to the founder to bring him up to date on their efforts. Father Josemaría, meanwhile, had been continuing his travels in Spain. On his saint's day (March 19, the feast of Saint Joseph) he received congratulatory telegrams from North and South America, Switzerland, Portugal, and Italy.

On March 24, 1946, late in the evening, he wrote to his sons in Rome. At this time he was giving a retreat for university students, at the Zurbarán Street center in Madrid. "At Zurbarán," he says, "thanks be to God, there is work aplenty. I have two study circles (Saint Raphael), with an average of eighteen people in each; and another one starts up this week; so that will be three. Plus, I am giving the second retreat, and another has already been scheduled." [27] And regarding the new priests, he says: "The young priests are hard at work—there's more than enough work for them all. They'll give you the details. Right now, José Luis is in Seville, but Chiqui can handle everything. It might seem impossible, but he is taking care of both the course at Los Rosales and the apostolic work in Madrid."

That hastily written letter contains important news—about the letters of commendation being sent by the bishops, about the admission to the Work of the first numerary assistants, and especially about a letter from Dom Escarré telling of a meeting with Pope Pius XII in which the Pope had said some very encouraging things about Opus Dei.

Leaving the letter unfinished that night, he took it up the next day with the words, "Continued on March 25, in the evening." But he added only eight or nine lines that night. He wrote some more on the twenty-sixth—and did not get very far that night either. Three days later he began again:

> March 29: I've been in Zamora, to see that bishop, who is also writing a letter of commendation for us. We left yesterday morning and returned at one in the morning today. . . .
>
> Chiqui is in Bilbao, and José Luis, who is now back from Seville, is leaving tomorrow for La Coruña. Once again I'll be alone, although only for a short while. How badly we need more priests!

[27] AGP, RHF, EF–460324–2.

But he was still not finished with that letter. Thirty days later he again took it up, adding entries almost as if it were a diary:

> Continued April 29. I need to make a trip, and between one thing and another I haven't been able to answer Alvaro's letter.
>
> April 30: Just got back from Valladolid—this morning I left our Lord in the tabernacle. How marvelous: one more!

(Father Josemaría counted the centers of the Work by the number of tabernacles.)

That letter also manifests a basic feature of the founder's character: his desire to "hide and disappear." He responded to any insult or unjustified opposition with silence. On June 14, 1972, during a get-together, he said with reference to his forty-something years as founder:

> Many things you will never know, because I have tried to see to it that no trace of them remains. However, you will know enough to be very moved and to give a lot of thanks to God. . . .
>
> Your wanting to know about those events is very good. But you need to understand that as long as I'm still alive they shouldn't be made public, because they have to do with very personal matters of my soul.[28]

Behind the lines of that long, newsy letter begun on March 24, 1946, one can sense the Holy Spirit at work. As had been the case during his time in Burgos, the founder felt that God was preparing him for "a period of intense vibration" when he would be called to "work with all my soul."[29] He also had a premonition that he was about to enter a new period of passive purifications.

*   *   *

Father Josemaría dreamed of having a retreat center run by his daughters. Up to this time, retreats for women were given at the Jorge Manrique center, while most of those for men were given at the Diego de León center or the Moncloa residence.

---

[28] AGP, P01 1982, pp. 1366–67 [Notes taken during a get-together on June 14, 1972].
[29] See AGP, RHF, EF–390213–7 and EF–390224–5.

Sometimes scheduling difficulties made it necessary for Father Josemaría to give two retreats at the same time. One week in December 1942, for example, he had to give two retreats for university students, one at Diego de León and the other at the Jenner Street residence, each with over twenty persons in attendance.[30] As fast as he walked, it still took him a quarter of an hour to get from the one place to the other. Each group got three meditations and a talk every day. And still he found time for a private talk with each participant. He would show up in the oratory on time, still breathing hard from walking so fast, kneel before the tabernacle to say—slowly, clearly, and with great faith—the prayer before the meditation, and then sit down, read a text from the Gospel, and give the meditation, in a good, strong voice. By the third day he was hoarse, and by the fourth he couldn't get out more than a whisper, and yet he spoke with undiminished vigor.[31]

Father Josemaría put himself out as much for a single soul as for a crowd. Take the case of Marichu Arellano. Her brother Jesús was of the Work and living at the Diego de León center. He told Marichu, who was living with their parents in Navarre, to be sure to see Father Josemaría when she came to Madrid. One day in April 1944 she showed up at Diego de León to visit her brother and, while there, to meet Father Josemaría. Here is her account:

> I was struck by his naturalness and cheerfulness. The Father lost no time—right away he started calling me by my name. He asked me about my trip and about what I was doing. I told him that I was thinking of spending a few days in Madrid to get to know the city, to make some purchases, because I was planning to get married soon, and to take advantage of the trip to make a retreat.

He asked her if she would let him ask God to call her to the Work. A little disconcerted, she thought for a few moments. What should she do? What if she did really have that vocation? So she said yes, he could pray. The priest said he would speak with her during the retreat that was about to begin at the Jorge Manrique center.

---

[30] The dates for the retreats were, respectively, December 16–20 and December 17–21. See AGP, RHF, D–15013 and D–15014.

[31] I myself witnessed this.

Marichu was surprised to find only three or four girls at the retreat. She was the only one not yet part of the Work. Nisa González Guzmán, one of the young ladies keeping her company, tells us: "Marichu Arellano was the only one making the retreat. During the five day retreat, the Father gave all the meditations and conferences, and Benediction, with the punctuality he always lived." [32]

*   *   *

One day in November 1944, Father Josemaría told Nisa González Guzmán and Mary Tere Echeverría that he wanted to see them at Los Rosales, a house recently acquired because it seemed suited to be a center for retreats. Located in Villaviciosa de Odón, a small, quiet village a half hour's drive from Madrid, it was large and well laid out, and had its own garden and a small orchard. He chose the best room for the future oratory, and that same afternoon went to see Father Julio, the village priest, and introduced to him Nisa and Mary Tere and the two household employees with them. They took possession of the property that very day. [33]

There was much work to do before the place would be ready for retreats. Father Josemaría himself took charge of furnishing the oratory, using items that had been in storage since the move from the Jenner Street residence to La Moncloa. These included the burlap wall coverings and the frieze with an inscription from the Acts of the Apostles. [34]

On October 29 he wrote to the bishop, asking him to "grant us the required permission to establish a retreat house in Villaviciosa de Odón." [35] A month later, the oratory now ready, he requested permission to have "a semipublic oratory, with a tabernacle . . . while the work on the retreat house is being completed and the definitive chapel is being built." [36]

Some time later it occurred to Father Josemaría that Los Rosales

[32] AGP, RHF, T–04989, p. 38.

[33] See AGP, RHF, T–04945, p. 7 (María Teresa Echeverría).

[34] See AGP, RHF, T–04989, p. 33 (Narcisa González Guzmán).

[35] AGP, RHF, D–15150.

[36] AGP, RHF, D–15152. The application is dated "Madrid, November 30, 1944, Feast of Saint Andrew." By 1944 "La Pililla," near Avila, and by 1945 "Molinoviejo," near Segovia, were also being used for rest and for study weeks. Later both became retreat houses. See Francisco Ponz Piedrafita, *Mi encuentro con el Fundador del Opus Dei* (1939; reprint, Pamplona, 2000), pp. 149–50. See also AGP, RHF, T–05848, p. 67, and T–04151, pp. 78, 83, and 87.

would also make a good women's formation center. By 1945 the Jorge Manrique center was too small for his apostolic vision.[37] On the afternoon that they moved into Los Rosales, he said to his daughters: "Now there are only two of you, but very soon there will be two hundred, two thousand." [38]

All the same, their first winter there was a long one for them. From time to time some of the young ladies living there went to another center to rest or for a change of scenery. Marichu Arellano relates that in April 1945 Father Josemaría suggested that they get a much larger dining room table, assuring them that by the end of that very year the table they had would be too small.[39]

Gradually, more women did come to the Work. A formation course was begun at Los Rosales in July. Father Josemaría gave a morning meditation and celebrated Mass, and then—with the help of his priest-sons, at least one of whom always accompanied him—he gave classes or talks on basic aspects of the spirit of the Work. Carmen Gutiérrez Ríos relates:

> He kept telling us that he especially needed for us to be faithful; that if we were not, we would impede the Work. And one day he said that if we were truly faithful, we would soon spread out, like a fan, all over the world. In the first place, to all the provinces of Spain, but at the same time and later, to the United States, Mexico, England, and so on, through the whole world.
>
> When the Father said this, we had only three centers: Moncloa, Jorge Manrique, and Los Rosales. The Father was dreaming out loud, and inviting us to dream—"Dream, and your dreams will fall short," he told us.[40]

These grand visions of apostolic expansion extended even to the details of ordinary, everyday life, as a story told by María Teresa illustrates:

> One afternoon in 1945, the Father explained to me that he had a great responsibility before God for our formation, for

[37] See AGP, RHF, T–04945, p. 5 (María Teresa Echeverría), and T–04956, p. 16 (María Dolores Fisac).
[38] AGP, RHF, T–04945, p. 7.
[39] AGP, RHF, T–04875, p. 4.
[40] AGP, RHF, T–04999, p. 11.

transmitting integrally to us the spirit of the Work that God had entrusted to him. A few days later, the Father asked for the director. I went up to the foyer of Los Rosales, where the Father was waiting for me. With great patience he asked me, "My daughter, why does this cabinet have a couple of eyebolts instead of a nice latch or a lock?" I answered him, "I don't know, Father." The Father explained to me that a director should know about everything in a house, the reason for every nail. Then he said that he would call the village blacksmith and ask him to put a lock on the cabinet. "Then," he told me, "you should put on the key a cord with a tassel, so that it looks more elegant—doing all this for love of God."[41]

Los Rosales was very soon in operation as a center of studies and formation for women. And that summer the country house of Molinoviejo was used for a formation course for men. Molinoviejo was a modest house situated among pine trees in the foothills of a mountain range, near the little village of Ortigosa del Monte, in the province of Segovia. Eventually, after many alterations, it became a retreat house and conference center.

*   *   *

By 1945 the men's branch had two apartments in Madrid, one on Villanueva Street and the other on Españoleto, plus a university residence (Moncloa) and the center of studies on Diego de León. The women had Los Rosales, the house on Jorge Manrique, and a center for the administration of La Moncloa.

To give more impetus to the apostolate with university women, it was decided to give up the house on Jorge Manrique and move closer to the middle of Madrid. Father Josemaría urged his daughters to pray to the Lord that the new residence they were looking for would be ready by the start of the school year. In October they found a house on Zurbarán Street and immediately started on the remodeling, the moving in of the furniture, and the setting up of the oratory.[42] As soon as the construction workers were finished with a section of the house,

---

[41] AGP, RHF, T–04945.
[42] See AGP, RHF, T–04989, p. 23 (Narcisa González Guzmán), and T–00159, X, p. 4 (Francisco Botella).

the women would furnish and occupy it. Finally they set a date for the first Mass, after which the Blessed Sacrament would be reserved in the tabernacle: December 8, 1945.

The founder's deep and lively faith made him observe and teach the greatest respect for the Blessed Sacrament, as is illustrated by an incident that took place that very evening, during Benediction. Lola Fisac relates:

> The Father asked us to invite our friends and families. We said the Rosary, and then the Father gave us Benediction. The oratory was completely full. People began to give the prayer responses in a haphazard way, not trying to say them in unison. The Father paused, and then started over. But, not catching on, they went on responding every which way. Finally the Father turned around and said to the congregation that that kind of praying was not proper from an earthly or a heavenly point of view, and that it was no way to praise God or converse with him. Then he knelt down and resumed the prayers before the Blessed Sacrament.[43]

He placed the residence under our Lady's protection in a special way: between two windows on the first landing of the stairway, he had them set a plaque bearing an inscription praising the Blessed Virgin. Whenever they climbed up or down the stairs (which they had to do often every day), they could read and pray, "Hail, Mary, Daughter of God the Father; Hail, Mary, Mother of God the Son; Hail, Mary, Spouse of God the Holy Spirit: only God is greater than you."[44]

In the office of the director near the front entrance, where visitors were received, there was a picture of the Annunciation—our Lady kneeling, hands joined in prayer. It had been the altarpiece in the oratory at Jorge Manrique when the founder celebrated Mass there on that notable February 14, 1943.[45] The altarpiece in the Zurbarán oratory was a copy of a work by Claudio Coello depicting Our Lady of the Immaculate Conception.

When classes started up at the university, the women at the center began looking for residents and inviting others to formation classes.

---

[43] AGP, RHF, T–04956, p. 17.
[44] See AGP, RHF, T–04894, p. 14 (Enrica Botella).
[45] See AGP, RHF, T–00159, XII, p. 4, and T–04989, p. 23.

In February 1946 Father Josemaría held his first study circle at Zurbarán.[46] After saying a prayer, he would sit down at the head of a table covered with a rose-colored cloth that matched the living room sofa and curtains. Then the others took their seats around the table. On it stood a gilded wooden lectern in the shape of a shell, on which he placed the Book of the Gospels. After reading a few verses and making a brief commentary, Father Josemaría would speak about some aspect of the interior life or about some particular virtue. Then came an examination of conscience, in which he encouraged them to make at least one concrete resolution. At the end he would invite them to bring a friend next time. And upon beginning the next week's session, he would summarize, or ask someone else to summarize, what had been said at the previous one, so that, as he put it, "your friends know what we're talking about and are brought up to date." [47]

Work and prayer were starting to bring women to Opus Dei, but the work was far from easy. Besides the ongoing spiritual direction of these girls, there were also the ever growing numbers of formation classes in the rose parlor and meditations in the oratory.[48]

*   *   *

Many people found that meeting the Father awakened new aspirations in them and opened unexpected horizons. Carmen Canals was one of these. In May 1946 she attended a retreat he gave at Zurbarán and was impressed by the dynamism of his words, his love for our Lady, and the care with which he prepared the participants for confession. She spoke with him twice. The first chat was a very short one in which he just asked her if she was able to follow the meditations, if she prayed, and if she went to Mass frequently. In the second one, she asked to be admitted to the Work. "I told him I wanted to join Opus Dei," she says, "and the Father said no. I don't recall much more about that retreat." [49]

Carmen kept coming to the residence for a while, and then stopped. Four years later she made a retreat at Molinoviejo. "And I was moved," she says, "at again hearing ideas that I had been keeping in my soul almost without realizing it." [50] She decided again to join the

[46] See AGP, RHF, T–04894, p. 21.
[47] See AGP, RHF, T–04912, p. 2.
[48] See AGP, RHF, T–04894, p. 21f.
[49] AGP, RHF, T–04912, p. 1.
[50] Ibid., p. 2.

Work, and on March 12, 1950, she did so. Not long after, she found herself at Los Rosales, in the big dining room, listening to the founder speak about sincerity and love for the Church and for the pope.

On leaving the class, Carmen went over to greet him, and tell him that she was concerned about his reply when she had said she wanted to join the Work some years earlier. The Father relieved her concern saying that, since that time, the prayers of her two brothers, who were in the work, and his own had twisted the Lord's arm and won her vocation.[51]

What a gift he seemed to have for being able to tell whether someone had a vocation to Opus Dei! Another illustration is the case of the Gutiérrez Ríos sisters. One of them, Lolita, made a retreat at the Jorge Manrique center, and the other, Carmen, picked her up there when it was over. She saw the place, noted the cordial atmosphere that reigned there, and was taken by a certain something that she couldn't put her finger on. A few days later, on April 6, 1945, she met Father Josemaría. Carmen tells us:

> Before I went to that house, my sister had been going there, to help out at Jorge Manrique, and she had met the founder there. As the years have gone by, she has mentioned many a time to the family and to friends something that is very clear to her: the Father's respect for everyone's freedom. The Father, back then, said to her, "Lolita, these ladies want to 'catch' you, but don't let them." And Lolita adds that although she very much does love and has always loved the Work and the Father and all the members of the Work whom she has met, she has never felt the least symptom of a vocation to the Work, despite the great affection and enthusiasm with which she collaborated back then in Opus Dei's apostolic activities.

In contrast, from the first moment that the Father met Carmen he told her without hesitation that she was fully qualified to undertake the path of Opus Dei.[52]

It often happened that he gave someone of whom he had no previous knowledge just exactly the right advice. And his sons and daughters were open books to him. Encarnita Ortega recalls an illustrative

[51] Ibid., p. 3.
[52] AGP, RHF, T–04999, p. 9.

incident in 1943, when, working in the Administration of La Moncloa, the work was becoming difficult for her:

> The Father dropped by with a bishop and came into the kitchen, where I was. I tried to be very polite and keep a smile on my face, so I was astonished when the Father, passing by, said in a low voice, "What's the matter?" And he gave me a look that filled me with strength. Those words were enough for me to be able to begin again, with a great desire to be faithful.[53]

3. *"A truly priestly soul and a fully lay mentality"*

His daughters were young, and some of them lacked experience in many of the arts involved in managing the centers; Father Josemaría patiently shared with them his own considerable experience. And a similar patience marked his responses to the inevitable mistakes that occurred in any family.

His sons and daughters made more than a few mistakes, but following the advice of Father Josemaría, they made notes of their experiences which they reviewed from time to time to avoid tripping over the same stone again. Within a few years the women of the Work were working confidently and efficiently.

Father Josemaría was a constant source of new ideas and solutions to problems. For instance, that of what to do with Los Rosales, which was getting too expensive to maintain. At times it served as a good place to rest, and during the summer, formation classes were given there. Given the situation of food shortages and rationing, Father Josemaría suggested turning it into a small farm that would have a steady clientele: the residents of La Moncloa, Zurbarán, and Diego de León.

He also suggested setting up a workshop for the making of vestments. For this project there was precedent, going back to the days when Carmen, Doña Dolores, and the women who came over to receive spiritual direction from him collaborated in making things for the oratory of the Ferraz Street residence.[54] Later, in Burgos, a group of

---

[53] AGP, RHF, T–05074, p. 22.
[54] Cf. *Meditation 19 Mar 1975*, AGP, P09, p. 223; cf. also, RHF, T-05828 (Ramona Sánchez-Elvira), p. 5.

young women had worked under his direction in the "tailor shop," making amices, purificators, albs, and corporals intended for the first postwar oratory in Madrid.[55] And after that there had been the get-togethers at Diego de León, with Doña Dolores and Carmen, during which altar linens were made.[56]

Now the green dining room on the second floor of Los Rosales was converted into a sewing room. Father Josemaría demonstrated in advance his confidence in his daughters' skills with a request for a complete set of chasubles to go with a portable altar that he would, when necessary, take with him on trips. The chasubles were finished on the eve of the feast of Saint Joseph and sent to Madrid the next morning. Pleased with how they had turned out, Father Josemaría went to Villaviciosa de Odón that afternoon to congratulate his daughters. That day was one of special joy and celebration for him, because he had just received the requests for admission of the two first numerary assistants. Besides congratulating the makers of the vestments, he made a quick tour of the house, since he wanted the numerary assistants to come there as soon as possible to start their formation.[57]

In the weeks that followed, Father Josemaría focused most of his attention on the second group of prospective priests. The first three had barely been ordained when he invited six more laymen to begin preparing for priesthood. The oldest were Pedro Casciaro and Francisco Botella.[58] All of them were university graduates and several were professors. For the most part, they were taught by the same instructors who had taught their predecessors.[59]

On May 7, 1946, they received the tonsure. Bishop Leopoldo administered the minor orders over the next couple of days, at his residence.[60]

---

[55] Cf. Letters to Amparo Rodríguez Casado desde Burgos, in AGP, RHF, EF-390221-1 and EF-390321-1.

[56] AGP, RHF, T-04956, p. 6 (María Dolores Fisac).

[57] See AGP, RHF, T-04894, p. 21 (Enrica Botella), and AGP, RHF, EF-460324-2 (a letter from the founder to his sons in Rome).

[58] For records of the examination, see AGP, Sección de Expedientes, D-660.

[59] The professors included Fathers Silvestre Sancho Morales, O.P.; Fernando Rodríguez-Permuy, C.M.F.; José María Bueno Monreal; Benito Celada Abad, O.P.; Justo Pérez de Urbel, O.S.B.; and Severino Alvarez Menéndez, O.P. See AGP, RHF, T-00159, XII, p. 21 (Francisco Botella). See also AGP, RHF, EF-440828-1 and EF-450908-1 (letters from the founder to Fathers Silvestre Sancho Morales, O.P., and Nicolás García, C.M.F.).

[60] The orders of porter and lector were conferred on May 8, with the founder attending. The orders of exorcist and acolyte were conferred on the next day.

The now Auxiliary Bishop Casimiro Morcillo selected Sunday, June 2, as the day for conferring the subdiaconate. He was at that time making a pastoral visit to the villages along the Guadarrama Sierra, one of which was his birthplace: Chozas de la Sierra (today, Soto del Real). He wanted to celebrate the ordination ceremony there, as a way of catechizing the villagers. The village authorities, for their part, saw here an opportunity to honor the bishop. On the great day, balconies were decorated with colorful quilts and embroidered silk shawls bordered with lace. Following the mayor's unveiling of a marble plaque in the main square, there was a procession to the church. First came the six ordinands, dressed in albs; then the bishop; and then the parishioners and the children waving palms and green branches. When the ceremony was over, there was a return procession, with the new subdeacons now wearing their vestments.[61] Two weeks later, on June 15, they received the diaconate from the hands of the now-Bishop José López Ortiz, in the oratory of the Diego de León center.[62]

Those six members of Opus Dei were ordained as priests three months later, on September 29, 1946.

*   *   *

A few months before his own ordination, Don Alvaro had run into Dr. López Franco, an old professor of his from the School of Civil Engineering. When he told him that he was going to be ordained, the professor replied, "Well, congratu—" and then stopped, having gotten choked up. Then he said, "Pardon me, but I am very moved. Congratulations."[63]

When Chiqui's colleagues at Madrid Electric heard that he was going to be ordained, they said, "Look at that José María, becoming a priest, when he had such a good life ahead of him!"[64]

Even Father Josemaría, much as he wanted to see priests in the

---

[61] See AGP, Sección Expedientes, D–660.

[62] See AGP, RHF, T–00159, XII, p. 28.

[63] AGP, Sección Expedientes, D–660.

[64] Ibid. On the occasion of the 1944 ordination, Father Josemaría wrote: "There are, however, few who understand this new pastoral phenomenon that is taking place within the Work of God: young men with university degrees and already working in their profession, with life and all its human prospects wide open to them, who go off, without any stipend, to serve all souls—especially those of their brothers and sisters— and to work hard, because there will hardly be enough hours in the day for them to get their spiritual work done" (*Letter 2 Feb 1945*, no. 3).

Work, found it hard to accept the idea that some of his sons would no longer be laymen. He wrote:

> I won't try to hide from you the fact that this first ordination of brothers of yours has caused me at the same time much joy and much sadness. I love the lay character of our Work so much that I felt real pain at seeing them become clerics. And yet the need for priests was so clear that it had to be pleasing to our Lord God that those sons of mine were ordained.[65]

In February 1945, after the first three priests had been engaged in pastoral ministry for some months, he wrote of what he had come to see as a kind of fusing of the priestly spirit and lay character in the vocations of all the members of Opus Dei:

> Now that priests have been ordained in our Work, I want all my children, priests and laypersons, to keep something firmly fixed in your minds and in your hearts—something that can never be regarded as merely external, but that is, on the contrary, the very hinge and foundation of our divine vocation.
>
> Always and in everything, each of us, whether priest or layperson, must have *a truly priestly soul and a fully lay mentality.*[66]

The sacrament of Baptism gives every Christian a share in the priesthood of Christ. This baptismal priesthood, this priesthood of the faithful, is a profound reality of Christian life. It is important to distinguish it from the ministerial or ordained priesthood, that conferred by the sacrament of Holy Orders, and yet to be mindful that the laity also have their own ministry.

The lay state also has a distinctive characteristic, one which within the Mystical Body of Christ forms the specific ministry

---

[65] *Letter 2 Feb 1945*, no. 13. "As the ordination of the priests drew near," recalls Francisco Ponz, "one could see that the Father was deeply moved. It was clearly going to be a very important step in the history of the Work" (AGP, RHF, T–04151, p. 81).

Years later the founder could say, "Now I am very happy every time sons of mine are ordained. We have a hunger, a thirst, an absolute need for priests." See AGP, RHF, T–05848, p. 69 (José Ramón Madurga).

[66] *Letter 2 Feb 1945*, no. 1.

proper to the laity: that of assuming their personal responsibilities in the professional and social spheres in such a way as to imbue all earthly realities with a Christian spirit, *so that in all things God may be glorified through Jesus Christ.*[67]

But what is that "truly priestly soul?" And how do the laity actively share in Christ's priesthood, making "operative within their souls the royal priesthood that the faithful receive in the sacraments of Baptism and Confirmation"?[68] His answer was "the Holy Sacrifice of the Altar, in which Christ the Priest renews the sacrifice he made on Calvary." This is "the root and center of our spiritual life": to give through this Sacrifice "adoration, honor, praise, and thanksgiving to the Blessed Trinity."

> Thus, closely united to Jesus in the Eucharist, we will achieve a continual awareness of the presence of God in the midst of the daily tasks of this earthly journey, seeking our Lord at all times and in all things. Having in our hearts the same sentiments Christ had on the Cross, we will make the whole of life into constant reparation, assiduous petition, and ceaseless sacrifice for all humankind. For God will give you a supernatural instinct to purify all your actions, elevating them to the order of grace and turning them into instruments of apostolate. Only thus will we be contemplative souls in the midst of the world, as our vocation requires, and become truly priestly souls, turning all that we are and have into a continual hymn of divine praise.[69]

He insistently taught this for the rest of his life. It was, in fact, something he spoke of on the day before he died. In the Mass he celebrated on June 25, 1975, he included a prayer "for all the priests of the Work" and "for the numeraries who are going to be ordained within a few days," related Don Alvaro, "and he prayed to the Lord that all of his daughters and lay sons—all of them—would always have a priestly soul: a longing to co-redeem."[70] And on that same day—the anniver-

---

[67] Ibid., no. 7.
[68] Ibid., no. 10.
[69] Ibid., no. 11.
[70] Letter of Don Alvaro del Portillo to the members of the Work: Rome, June 29, 1975.

sary of the ordination of the first three priests of Opus Dei—he told his children that at Mass "he had prayed hard for all of them, and specifically that every one of his daughters would be very deeply imbued with a priestly spirit."[71]

4. *Retreats about life and about death*

It was Father Josemaría's custom during his annual retreats to jot down the inspirations he received and his resolutions, to facilitate discussing them later with his confessor. (In some of those years, however, he made only brief notes, or none at all.) The notes, beginning with his retreat in 1932 in Segovia's monastery of Saint John of the Cross, make up an appendix to his *Apuntes íntimos*. The last are from the retreat of February 1944, after which he had no need to take notes, because his confessor was Don Alvaro, who was always with him.

At first glance, the notes from 1943 and 1944 might seem to suggest that the "opposition by good people" had dropped off, there being hardly any mention of this matter. But the reality was far different, as is indicated by a resolution from the February 1944 retreat: "Stay calm! Stay calm, in order to see things, persons, and events from the perspective of eternity. The wall blocking our passage is, humanly speaking, formidable, but the instant we really raise our eyes to heaven, what a little thing it is!"[72] The next entry in his journal explains his agitation:

> While saying Nones this morning, I got distracted and started thinking about the battles that have always been waged against the Church by heretical sects.

[71] Ibid. In the morning of the next day, June 26, the founder went to Villa delle Rose, at Castel Gandolfo, to say good-bye to his daughters, since he was planning to leave Rome a couple of days later. At a short get-together, during which he asked them to pray for the fifty-four men who were to be ordained a few days later, he said to his daughters: "I'll tell you what I always tell you when I come here: you have priestly souls. And your brothers who are laymen also have priestly souls. You can and should help us with those priestly souls of yours. Thus, with the grace of God and the ministerial priesthood of those of us who are the priests of the Work, we will carry out an effective apostolic effort" (AGP, P02 1975, p. 601; these words were tape-recorded).

A little while later he started feeling ill and had to return to Rome. He died there at noon, at Villa Tevere.

[72] *Apuntes*, no. 1857.

I thanked our Lord God for the consolation of a blessing from the Holy Father—a blessing filled with affection for the Work—which the Pope sent us by way of Father Canal, O.P. And bitter sentiments (which do not rob me of my peace) assailed my soul at the thought of a lying tract evidently put together by an apprentice of Judas, some Masons, and perhaps a priest, who seem to have a tremendous hatred for the Work and for this sinner.[73]

One memory led to another. "I also happened to think of the destructive efforts that a certain religious priest is even now making in Barcelona."[74] This priest was an elderly man who, for no apparent reason, says the founder, "goes around saying whatever he feels like against the Work, and especially against me."[75]

The churning of these thoughts disturbed him deeply. But turning back to the breviary, he found peace.

All of the above, and my awareness of the world situation and especially the situation in Spain, with the scheming of Spaniards who hate Christ's Church, caused me deep distress. I returned to praying the Divine Office, and the first verse I came upon was this one from Psalm 58 [59]: "*Et tu, Domine, deridebis eos: ad nihilum deduces omnes gentes*" ["And you, O Lord, will laugh at them; you will hold all the nations in derision"]. And my heart was filled with a more than human joy and peace. I continued with the Divine Office. A bit later, I suddenly received an interior illumination, clear, unmistakable, totally certain. It did not come in words, but it was this: "But, child, don't you know that it is I?" And at that moment there came to me a clear recollection of that verse and the conviction that the Lord, with these words from the psalm, was reaffirming his "*non praevalebunt*"—his statement that there is nothing anyone can do against the Church—and saying there is nothing anyone can do against the Work, an instrument of God for the service of the Church.[76]

---

[73] *Apuntes*, no. 1858. (Nones is one of the hours of the Divine Office.)
[74] *Apuntes*, no. 1859.
[75] Ibid.
[76] *Apuntes*, no. 1860.

In that turbulent atmosphere of renewed attacks, it was not long before criticisms began to be heard about the retreats that Father Josemaría was giving all over Spain. His oratorical gifts were truly exceptional. Carlos Bousoño, a young poet who met him at La Moncloa, would exclaim during the meditations, "He's a genius! A real genius!"[77] Of course, the efficacy of his preaching, as he himself well knew, depended not on his eloquence but on divine grace and on the prayers and mortifications he offered for those who would hear him. But given both his eloquence and his effectiveness, what opening could his detractors find for attacking him here? A highly unexpected one. They started accusing him of preaching "retreats about life" in place of traditional "retreats about death."[78]

It was, indeed, standard practice at that time to focus most retreat preaching on the "last things": death, judgment, hell, and heaven.

Yet Father Josemaría did not avoid the subject of death—not even when preaching to the powerful people of this world. That letter of March 1946 about which we have already spoken—the letter written in bits and pieces—includes this item: "I have been asked to give a retreat to Jesús [Fontan]'s chief during Passion Week. We'll see how it goes."[79] From April 7 to 12, in El Pardo Palace, Father Josemaría gave a retreat to Francisco Franco and his wife.[80] At this time Spain was enjoying a very fragile peace, one threatened by outside pressures; the country had closed ranks behind the constituted authorities; and a good part of the Church hierarchy was showering praise on the chief of state.

When the retreat was over, Father Josemaría refused to say how it had gone.[81] Nevertheless, eighteen years later something from it came to light. One day he had asked Franco, "Have you never

---

[77] AGP, RHF, T–05848, p. 69 (José Ramón Madurga). Before giving a homily or a conference during those years, he would recite as an aspiration these words from the prophet Jeremiah: "A, a, a Domine Deus! Ecce nescio loqui, quia puer ego sum!" ("Ah, Lord God! Behold, I do not know how to speak, for I am only a youth": Jer 1:6). See AGP, RHF, T–05848, p. 59.

[78] See Alvaro del Portillo, *Sum.* 1247, and Javier Echevarría, *Sum.* 2741.

[79] AGP, RHF, EF–460324–2. Jesús Fontán Lobé was a navy officer; "Jesús's chief" is a reference to Franco. And the person who arranged for Father Josemaría to give this retreat was Bishop Leopoldo.

[80] Father José María Bulart Ferrándiz, who was then the chaplain of El Pardo, says that Franco made a retreat every year, and that it was often Bishop Leopoldo who gave the conferences: see Gonzalo Redondo, *Historia de la Iglesia en España, 1931–1939*, vol. 2, *La Guerra Civil, 1936–1939* (Madrid, 1993), p. 130. Father Josemaría had known Father Bulart for a number of years: see AGP, RHF, EF–411220–1.

[81] A quite understandable reticence.

thought, Your Excellency, about the fact that you could die at any moment?"

A few days later, during a visit with Bishop Leopoldo, Father Josemaría had mentioned that conversation with Franco. The bishop had exclaimed, "You'll never get ahead in life!" [82]

In any case, many priests giving retreats were accustomed to speak of the inevitability of death in hopes that fear would provoke a conversion on the retreatant's part. And at this point those who accused Father Josemaría of a novel approach were not so wide of the mark. Notes taken by some of those who attended his retreats make it clear that he covered the last things in a firm, serious, no-nonsense way, but one that fostered a great freedom of spirit and was always very positive, without scare tactics and sensationalism.

The then-Father Angel Suquía (who would become cardinal archbishop of Madrid) took part in a retreat given by Father Josemaría in 1942 at Vitoria's diocesan seminary. The preacher, he testifies, came across as "a thoroughly supernatural man," a real "man of faith." He then lists some of the topics preached on (among which obedience to superiors stands out as "a central point of the retreat") and marvels at the "love for Christ that blazed in everything he said." [83]

Victor García Hoz, who as a young university professor attended another of Father Josemaría's retreats, gives this testimony:

> For me it was like a new discovery. Even though I had been receiving spiritual direction from the Father for some time, I was greatly impressed to see how in a retreat, . . . along with the classic themes of Christian meditation, he brought in the human virtues—cheerfulness, friendship, generosity, and, above all, work—as a part of the Christian vocation. [84]

What really distinguished his "retreats about life" from those that some called "retreats about death" was not whether the realities of the last things were presented, or how bluntly, but to what end. For Father Josemaría, these truths were stimuli for growing in friendship with

---

[82] See AGP, RHF, EF–640614–1.
[83] AGP, RHF, D–05226. See also AGP, RHF, D–15407 (José Fernández).
[84] AGP, RHF, T–01138, p. 14.

God. What he wanted to induce was not fear but the filial love that brings us to our Father-God.[85]

And so, when he was accused of deviating from the traditional methods by giving "retreats about life," he searched his heart and came up with the conclusion, "Well, what can I preach about if not that eternal life to which we are called?"[86]

In 1942, in a retreat for young people of the Work, he reminded them of the recent death of Antonio Moreno, one of the first members of Opus Dei in Valladolid. All of those present were amazed when, turning toward the tabernacle, he said, "Here we are—choose those whom you want to take to yourself."[87] And when it came to preaching on judgment, he liked to pass on to the penitent retreatant the consoling words that Bishop Santos Moro of Avila had written him in 1938, at a time when he was troubled by the thought that the Lord would demand a strict accounting from him: "No, for you he will not be a judge, in the harsh sense of the word, but simply Jesus."[88]

*   *   *

Even more telling on these matters than the testimony of people who attended his retreats is the testimony that he himself left in his personal notes. There is, for example, this excerpt from the resolutions he made during the February 1944 retreat:

> To this day, I have often found consolation in the thought of death. I've said, To die? What a blessing! In the future, I will at least once a day see myself at the moment of death, in order to view the day's events in that light. I have a lot of experience of the peace produced by that consideration.[89]

He recalled the loneliness and fatigue of the early days, the period when he was trying to get Opus Dei started. He thought, too, of how, when at last he had collected a handful of followers, God had put him

---

[85] Father Josemaría always "took an optimistic view of the life and death of a Christian who is conscious of being a child of God." Whenever he was at the bedside of a dying person, says Bishop Javier Echevarría, he would speak very confidently about "the God who is waiting for you, who loves you, who gave himself up so that you would never lose him" (Javier Echevarría, *Sum.* 2741).

[86] Javier Echevarría, *Sum.* 2741.

[87] AGP, RHF, T–04678/1, p. 39 (José Luis Múzquiz).

[88] AGP, RHF, D–10989. See also *The Way*, no. 168.

[89] *Apuntes*, no. 1857.

to the test by taking some of those young people to himself, leaving him to seek solace in the thought that now he had intercessors in heaven.[90] Another resolution he made during this retreat of 1944 was to say every night, "Lord, I accept death when you wish, as you wish, where you wish." [91]

*   *   *

His retreats, then, were marked by a healthy optimism that encouraged acts of faith, hope, and love. For himself, he sought to cultivate perfect contrition born of love. The expression "sorrow of Love" appears frequently in his *Apuntes*, suggesting the path he followed in his own interior life. "Don't forget," he wrote in *The Way*, "that sorrow is the touchstone of Love." [92]

The fruit of genuine love for God is repentance, manifested by a sincere abhorrence of sin. "Sorrow of love. Because he is good. Because he is your friend, who gave his life for you. Because everything good that you have is his. Because you have offended him so much. Because he has forgiven you. He! You! Weep, my child, with sorrow of love." [93]

Feeling the weight of fallen human nature, he felt the barrier that even slight sin places between God and someone who loves Him. In 1930 he had written, "I want, Lord, to want truly, once and for all, to have an immeasurable abhorrence of anything that smacks of sin, even venial sin. I want the kind of compunction that those who have pleased you the most have had." [94]

For a long time he had sought through our Lady's intercession the

---

[90] See AGP, RHF, AVF–0098. On November 21, 1932, he had written in his journal (see *Apuntes*, no. 871), "When José María and Luis died, there came to me—through cowardice—desires to die. Why shouldn't I have to die? And despite the weight of my sins, I saw death as a solution. I reject this—you know, my God, that I accept death when and how you want it." (The references are to Father José María Somoano and Luis Gordon.)

In the early years he kept in his room a skull, which he nicknamed the Bald Lady, to remind him of death. His journal entry for November 24, 1932, includes this sentence: "If you are an apostle, death—the Bald Lady—will be for you a good friend that makes your path easier" (*Apuntes*, no. 875). See also *Apuntes*, no. 1710 (22 Jun 1933).

[91]*Apuntes*, note 659. Bishop Alvaro del Portillo (who wrote these notes of commentary to the *Apuntes*) adds here, "And then he peacefully fell asleep." See also *Apuntes*, no. 871 (21 Nov 1932), and AGP, RHF, T–04151, p. 51 (Francisco Ponz). A meditation given by Father Josemaría on April 17, 1948, contains this statement: "To lead a truly priestly life, it is good often to think about death": AGP, RHF, T–05253, p. 29 (Federico Suárez).

[92] *The Way*, no. 439.

[93] *Apuntes*, no. 1108 (7 Jan 1934); see *The Way*, no. 436.

[94] *Apuntes*, no. 23.

priceless gift of perfect contrition. On October 7, 1932, during the retreat he had made at the Carmelite monastery in Segovia, he had written in his journal:

> It's fair, gentle Lady, for me to ask you for a present, a proof of your affection: contrition, compunction for my sins, sorrow of love. Hear me, O Lady, my life, my hope. Take me by the hand—and if there is anything in me now that is displeasing to my Father-God, make me see it, and between the two of us we'll tear it out.[95]

And almost two years later he had made the same request. On July 16, 1934, he had written in his journal:

> My Mother, our Lady, I kissed the floor and made the sign of the cross (after crying out our "Serviam!"), in the name of the Father and of the Son and of the Holy Spirit, and prayed to you the Memorare. I got distracted, but then put myself once again into the prayer, and I know you have heard me. My dear Mother! Again I invoke you, right now, as I'm writing on this paper. You know well what I need. More than anything else, sorrow of love. And to cry? Or without crying. Just let my sorrow be for real, so that we clean very well the soul of Jesus' little donkey.[96]

5. *Trips through Andalusia and Portugal*

Soon after the first three priests were ordained, Father Josemaría gave them some advice, including practical pointers, for their apostolic trips.[97] Among others things, he recommended greeting the diocesan

---

[95] *Apuntes*, no. 1647.

[96] *Apuntes*, no. 1741.

[97] In a notebook dated 1944, Father José Luis Múzquiz found the following guidelines given by the founder regarding trips (see AGP, RHF, T–04678/1, pp. 6–7):

> *Purpose* of the trips: Helping in the formation of the others. Informing. Directing and fostering the apostolates.
> *Means*
> > *Prayer:* Bringing to your prayer the purpose of the trip, the characteristics of the people, the problems, the instructions you have to give.
> > *Mortification:* Keeping order and using time well. [*cont. page 478*]

bishop as soon as possible and visiting any priests they knew in the area.

Most of these trips were to cities with universities. From the beginning, Father Josemaría in his apostolic zeal reached out to everyone—artisans, manual workers, professionals. . . . But he always made university students a priority. He found the openness and generosity of young people a fertile ground for sowing divine love. "Youth gives all it can—it gives itself without reserve," he wrote in *The Way* (no. 30).

The apostolic work in cities with universities or technical institutes was growing steadily throughout most of Spain. Only the far south lacked a center of the Work.[98] Father Josemaría decided to go to Andalusia to speak with the bishops about Opus Dei. He hoped to open two university residences, one in Seville and the other in Granada, and give a boost to the fledgling apostolic endeavors in the south.[99] Accompanying him were Father José Luis Múzquiz, who had lately been visiting these provinces, and two architects: Jesús Alberto Cagigal and Ricardo Fernández Vallespín. (He wanted the architects' professional opinions concerning the conversion of several houses into university residences.)[100]

Their driver was Miguel Chorniqué—a calm, good-hearted man who was an excellent mechanic. His role in these trips was indispens-

---

Interior life: Having awareness of the presence of God, being cheerful, united. . . . Being mindful of charity, fraternal correction, obedience. (Going by the instructions, and not one's own opinion, is the source of efficacy.) *Norms:* Not put off to the last hour.
Poverty: Common sense. . . .
Before the trip: Thinking about the things one will need to say; reviewing the correspondence from the last trip and the particular things that need to be done. The particular tenor that needs to be given to the trip. . . . Notifying people in good time; thinking if someone else will be accompanying us; asking a blessing for the trip; not forgetting to bring people's addresses.
During the trip: One needs to talk with the director, with the other members of the Work, with all the people involved. And visit the bishop, the priests one knows, friends, etc.
After the trip: Taking stock of the spiritual fruits, the problems and difficulties that came up; making a report; sending notes; not forgetting the pending tasks; turning in an expense report, etc.

[98] Since October 1943 some members of the Work had been living in Seville, but at Casa Seras, a residence hall belonging to the School of Hispanic-American Studies.

[99] See AGP, RHF, T–04678/1, p. 46.

[100] There are two descriptions of this trip: one by Father José Luis Múzquiz (AGP, RHF, D–15204–26), and the other by Jesús Alberto Cagigal (AGP, RHF, D–15204–27).

able, given the prohibitive problems with public transportation, the poor condition of the cars available to them in those days, and the equally poor condition of the roads, badly damaged during the civil war and still not well repaired, due to Spain's economic problems. Father Josemaría and Miguel had had over the past two years many close calls on those roads. They had, in fact, escaped unharmed from so many accidents that Miguel would later testify, "I was convinced that when I was going with the Father in the car, nothing would or could ever happen to us." [101]

On Tuesday of Holy Week, March 27, 1945, a beautifully sunny day, they set out early, taking the road for Extremadura, with Miguel at the wheel. (The car was a Studebaker Champion.) As soon as they got out of Madrid, the founder and Father José Luis started up a sing-along. A little later, as they rounded a bend, they could see in the distance the snow-capped Gredos Mountains. They stopped to eat in Trujillo, a place known for its noble, austere palaces and homes from the days of the conquistadors. They also stopped in Mérida, because Father Josemaría wanted to give the architects a chance to stretch their legs and to see the Roman ruins and the archaeological museum in that city. Then, continuing their drive south, they crossed cultivated fields, vineyards, and olive groves.

It was getting dark when they reached Seville. The streets were packed with people who had come to see the Holy Week processions, and the hotels had no vacancies. Finally they heard that there were some at Hotel Oromana, in the nearby town of Alcalá de Guadaira. Before going there, however, they joined the crowd to watch one of the processions.

A double row of penitents, with heads covered, were carrying on their shoulders a statue of our Lady that was under a canopy supported by silver poles. Lining the path were flowers—and also

---

[101] AGP, RHF, T–06433, p. 5. "The Father," continues Miguel, "was a tireless worker. I don't know how we managed to keep up with his pace. Just with regard to the traveling itself, we made some unbelievable trips. Don Alvaro, who did the calculations of the mileage, found that the shortest distance we went in a day was about five hundred miles, and the longest, about seven hundred. Even by today's standards that's a lot, but back at that time, with all the various difficulties there were, it was quite a feat. One day we read in the paper that during an electoral campaign—this was probably around 1950, since Churchill was then running again after having lost in 1945—that famous British political figure had traveled some nine or ten thousand miles by plane. I don't know if it was myself or Don Alvaro who pointed out that we had covered the same distance over the same period of time, but by car. The Father was very amused at hearing this."

candles, whose flames were reflected in the jewels adorning the statue. Father Josemaría was totally captivated. As he tells it:

> I stood there looking at it, and became absorbed in prayer. Gazing at that beautiful statue of the Virgin, I forgot I was in Seville, or even on the street, until someone tapped me on the shoulder. It was a villager, saying to me, "Father, that statue isn't any good. Ours is the good one!" At first that almost seemed to me like blasphemy. But then I thought, "He's right. When I show people pictures of my mother, although I like all of them, I also say, 'This—this is the good one.' " [102]

They spent most of the next day looking at several houses. Father Josemaría especially liked one called Monteflorido, on Canalejas Street. It was centrally located and was in excellent condition, with light-colored bricks, tiles, and marble that made for a cheerful, attractive appearance. It also had wrought-iron balconies and window casements, and a pleasant patio garden. In the afternoon, the founder and Father José Luis went to see Cardinal Pedro Segura, who received them with great affection.

On Thursday, Ricardo returned to Madrid, and the others went on to Jerez, frequently coming across lively, well-attended processions along the way. Not finding any hotel vacancies in Jerez, they continued on to Puerto de Santa María, where they found what they thought would be a nice, quiet place to stay. Which it was—until two in the morning, when they were awakened by the noise of drums and blaring bugles, which went on most of the rest of the night.

On Good Friday, Father Josemaría visited a number of people in Cádiz, starting with the bishop. Later, on their way to Algeciras, from the top of the Tarifa hills they could make out the coast of Africa across the straits, and Father Josemaría's thoughts turned to the souls waiting on that huge continent. "Can these straits be a barrier to Christianity?" he said with great emotion. "How much there is to do!" [103]

Algeciras, Estepona, Marbella, Málaga. Just as they were entering Málaga, the car broke down. Father Josemaría took advantage of the delay to visit with the bishop, and then to look up an old friend,

[102] AGP, P04 1972, p. 422.
[103] AGP, RHF, D–15204–26.

Father José Suárez Faura, who had shared with him those difficult years in Madrid under the Republic.

The Studebaker was soon running again, and they spent the night of Holy Saturday in Antequera. On Easter Sunday, April 1, Father Josemaría celebrated Mass at the Trinitarians' house there. At midday they reached Córdoba, where, again, the founder made a number of visits. In the afternoon they went to see the famous Hermitage of Córdoba, an ancient monastery situated among the hills outside the city. Father Josemaría gave a donation to the old monk who showed them around. As they left, the monk gave them each a leaflet of verses connected with the site. One of them translates as:

> Very high is the summit!
> The Cross very high!
> From there up to heaven,
> How little to fly! [104]

Father Josemaría found that eremitic life very edifying, while at the same time noting clearly the need to seek sanctity where our Lord calls us. "It can be lived just as well on the Gran Vía of Madrid," he remarked. "One can be just as close to heaven in Cibeles Plaza as in the beautiful mountains of Córdoba." [105]

They climbed to a high point on the mountainside and did their afternoon prayer there. When they got back to the hotel, Father Josemaría was exhausted. By the activities of the day, or by an attack of his diabetes? It is hard to know, since he didn't complain. And if someone did ask him, he would sometimes respond: "The Father is fine until ten minutes before his death. Whoever needs to know how he is, now they know." [106]

Monday morning, his visits all made, they set out for Jaén. Olive groves and more olive groves, as far as the eye could see. At the bishop's residence in Jaén, they learned that the bishop was away on a trip. So they went on to Granada, spending the night in a hotel near the Alhambra.

On Tuesday, April 3, Father Josemaría celebrated Mass in a nearby parish church, and they visited Archbishop Agustín Parrado. They

---

[104] This poem is "Las Ermitas de Córdoba," by Antonio Fernández Grilo.
[105] AGP, RHF, D–15204–27.
[106] AGP, RHF, T–05855, p. 13 (Ignacio Echeverría Recabeitia).

devoted the rest of the day to looking for a house that might serve as a student residence. In their trip journal, Father José Luis noted that although they kept inspecting houses all afternoon, "the Father likes Carmen de las Maravillas [Manor Marvelous] better than any of the other houses. The entrance is bad, but once you're in there it really does justice to its name." [107] He and Jesús Alberto quickly sketched a new layout for the interior of the manor, which actually was a rather modest house, not in very good condition, whose only truly marvelous feature was the view it afforded of the city and of the Genil River.

On April 4 Father Josemaría celebrated Mass in the cathedral of Almería. The bishop of Granada was not available, so they continued on to Murcia—whose bishop turned out to be sick. On April 5 they returned to Madrid, stopping in several churches along the way to make visits to the Blessed Sacrament.

*   *   *

Once they were back in Madrid and had made the necessary arrangements, the work began of remodeling the houses chosen for the future residences: in Granada, Carmen de las Maravillas, later called the Albayzín Residence, and in Seville, the house on Canalejas Street. By the beginning of August 1945, the Albayzín Residence was ready for occupancy.[108] Residents started arriving, but the work of remodeling dragged on.[109] And the problem of how to make ends meet was becoming acute.

With the start of the school year fast approaching, Father Josemaría on October 3 sent a formal request to Archbishop Agustín Parrado of Granada saying that he wished to establish a student residence (Albayzín) from which he hoped to "obtain great results." On October 22 he acknowledged receipt of the requested authorization and invited the archbishop to celebrate the first Mass in the oratory of the residence.

Work on the oratory went more slowly than expected, and it was four more weeks before Father José Luis Múzquiz was able to inform the archbishop that the oratory was now ready.[110] On November 23 they received official notice of the canonical establishment of the

---

[107] AGP, RHF, D–15204–26.

[108] See AGP, RHF, D–00074–19. See also AGP, RHF, EF–450821–1, EF–460124–1, and EF–460124–2.

[109] See AGP, RHF, D–00074–19.

[110] AGP, RHF, D–15434.

oratory and of the granting of permission for reservation of the Blessed Sacrament.[111]

That care in following prescribed regulations in connection with the oratory of the Albayzín Residence was typical of the founder's approach. On November 30 he sent in two further requests. The first one:

> Since it is the custom of Opus Dei to observe a monthly vigil of love and reparation to Jesus in the Blessed Sacrament, I request that you deign to grant the necessary permission so that in all of the oratories of houses of the Work in the Archdiocese of Granada, solemn exposition of the Blessed Sacrament may be held during the night preceding the first Friday of each month.[112]

And the second:

> In the oratories of houses where members of Opus Dei carry out their apostolic activity, it is the custom, out of love for our Lord who died on the Cross, to kiss the wooden cross always placed in these oratories. Its purpose is to increase our love and reverence for the symbol of redemption. I therefore request that you grant an indulgence each time that the wooden cross in the oratories of the centers where the apostolic work of the members of Opus Dei is carried out is kissed and an aspiration is said.[113]

Less than two weeks later, the residence in Seville was also ready. On Monday, December 10, Father Josemaría arrived there, accompanied by Father José Luis Múzquiz, and the next day, after the morning meditation, he celebrated the first Mass in the oratory of Guadaira Residence. Before giving out Communion, he encouraged those present to ask the Lord, as the disciples in Emmaus had done, "to be our light and to remain with us." [114]

*   *   *

[111] See AGP, RHF, D–15434.

[112] RHF, D-15160.

[113] RHF, D-15161. A 200-day indulgence was granted for kissing the wooden cross: see Reg. lib. 1.B, no. 1081.

[114] See Diary of Guadaira Residence: AGP, Sec. N.3 leg. 137-27. See also Luke 24: 13–29.

In 1945 Father Josemaría made three trips to Portugal. The first, in early February, came as an unexpected result of a visit to the town of Tuy, in northwest Spain, where he had gone to see his good friend José López Ortiz, who was now the bishop of Tuy. Sister Lucia dos Santos, one of the three Fatima visionaries, was at that time living in a convent there, and the bishop arranged a meeting, during which she urged the founder to visit Portugal. He had been thinking of doing so for some time, but as yet did not even have a passport. Sister Lucia placed a call to Lisbon and quickly obtained a visa for him and his companions.[115]

Joining Father Josemaría and Don Alvaro were the bishop and his secretary—the founder's old friend Father Eliodoro Gil. They traveled by car, with (as usual) Miguel Chorniqué at the wheel.

On February 5 they reached Oporto, where they stopped to see Bishop Agostinho de Jesús Souza. Next day they were invited to lunch by Bishop José Alves Correia da Silva of Leiría, and afterward they all went to visit the newly opened Shrine of Our Lady of Fatima. In Aljustrel, Father Josemaría met with some families who had taken part in those historic events, and a photo was even taken of himself with the mother of the other two visionaries, Francisco and Jacinta Marto. In Fatima, on February 6, he prayed for the future apostolic efforts in Portugal and signed and dated the prologue to the fourth edition of *Holy Rosary*.

On February 7, in Lisbon, they met with Cardinal Manuel Gonçalves Cerejeira. He was very friendly, but, in the words of Bishop López Ortiz, "did not understand the novelty of the Work very

---

[115] Twenty-five years later the founder related in detail his first meeting with Sister Lucia. "I was trying to keep it short, since I knew that she was a saint," he said, "but far from being annoyed, she came back to tell me that Opus Dei had to go to Portugal. I answered her that we didn't have passports, but she responded, 'I'll take care of that right now.' She made a phone call to Lisbon and got us documentation for crossing the border.

"We didn't speak at all of the apparitions of our Lady; I've never done that. She is a woman of marvelous humility. Whenever I see her, I remind her that she played a big role in the starting of the Work in Portugal" (AGP, P01 1981, p. 1362).

Regarding that first conversation between the founder and Sister Lucia, Bishop López Ortiz relates: "Among other things, he told her more or less this: 'Sister Lucia, with everything that people are saying about you and about me, if on top of all that we end up in hell! . . .' The Father told me that Sister Lucia became pensive and replied with great simplicity, 'Indeed, you are right.' Josemaría was very happy to see her humility." See *Beato Josemaría Escrivá de Balaguer: un hombre de Dios. Testimonios sobre el Fundador del Opus Dei* (Madrid, 1994), p. 236. (Hereafter this book will be cited as *Testimonios*.) See also Alvaro del Portillo, *Sum.* 875, and Alberto Cosme do Amaral, *Sum.* 6791.

well." [116] Father Josemaría agreed to come speak with him again at greater length.

In Coimbra they were received by Bishop Antonio Antunes, even though he was ill. "He was very outgoing and affectionate and eager to help," says Bishop López Ortiz. "The Father decided to start the apostolic work in Portugal in that city." [117]

From Coimbra they began their return trip, which took them through Oporto, Tuy, Santiago de Compostela, Covadonga, Burgos, and Valladolid. [118] They arrived in Madrid on February 14.

In mid-June the founder and Don Alvaro made a second trip to Portugal, staying a week; and in the second half of September the two of them made a third trip. [119]

By 1946 there were already some faithful of Opus Dei living in Coimbra. As soon as a suitable house had been found, Father Josemaría asked Bishop Antunes for permission to set up an oratory with a tabernacle. [120]

*   *   *

Father Josemaría spent most of 1945 traveling from city to city, planting the Work and its apostolate. [121] On a trip through northern Spain he sent a message from San Sebastián to his sons in Bilbao, telling them that he would be with them the next day, October 9. They had spent most of the summer working on the setting up of the Abando Residence and were eagerly looking forward to his visit.

Father Josemaría came with Don Alvaro and Pedro Casciaro. "He had barely stepped over the threshold," a witness recalls, "when he turned to Pedro and said, 'Please take out your notebook and jot down a few things.' The Father had quickly noticed fifteen or twenty things that were not quite right." [122]

Since the remodeling was still under way, he decided to celebrate the first Mass in the oratory, but not leave the Blessed Sacrament

[116] *Testimonios,* p. 237.
[117] Ibid.
[118] See Alvaro del Portillo, *Sum.* 857.
[119] See Alvaro del Portillo, *Sum.* 627. See also AGP, RHF, EF–450908–1, EF–450913–1, and EF–451105–1 (letters from the founder to Claretian Father Nicolas García, Cardinal Cerejeira, and Father Urbano Duarte).
[120] See AGP, RHF, EF–460521–1. The petition to open a student residence in Coimbra was sent by the founder on February 2, 1946, also from Madrid. See AGP, RHF, D–15174.
[121] See Alvaro del Portillo, *Sum.* 627.
[122] AGP, RHF, T–05848, p. 70 (José Ramón Madurga).

reserved there. The date set was October 11.[123] In the middle of the
Mass a team of plumbers began making a racket with their work—the
oratory windows overlooked a patio whose four walls amplified the
noise of the workers. At Communion time he told those present that
the noise should not be a distraction for them, since they had to
sanctify themselves in the midst of their work.

The inauguration of the Abando Residence was followed by the
inaugurations of the Guadaira and Albayzín residences, as well as of
other centers and residences in university towns.[124]

An indication of the scope of Father Josemaría's apostolic projects is
the requests he sent to Church authorities during the first months of
1946. On January 31 he sent to the archbishop of Saragossa a letter
expressing his desire to launch apostolic work there "as I am doing in
other university cities of Spain," and requesting permission to open a
student residence.[125] Similar requests went the same day to the bishops of Oviedo and Murcia.[126] Two days later he wrote to the bishop of
Coimbra.[127] On February 14 he sent a request for permission to set up
a residence in Santiago de Compostela.[128] Finally, on April 4, he requested permission to set up a semipublic oratory at El Rincón in
Valladolid, "while construction work is going on for a student residence." [129]

In May 1943, two years after the troubles in Barcelona had been at
their height, Father Josemaría went there to have the satisfaction of

---

[123] See AGP, RHF, D–15433. It would, in fact, be another two months before the place
was in suitable shape for the Blessed Sacrament to be reserved there. The Father,
meanwhile, was eagerly looking forward to that day. "When will you have our Lord in
that tabernacle?" he wrote to his sons in Bilbao. "I, too, can hardly wait" (AGP, RHF, EF–
451128–1).

[124] See Javier Echevarría, *Sum.* 2208.

[125] By February 8, 1946, the permission had been granted by the archbishop (see AGP,
RHF, D–15167). On October 24, 1946, the founder requested permission to have a
semipublic oratory, with a tabernacle, in the center at 3 Baltasar Gracián Street. This
permission was granted on November 8, 1946 (see AGP, RHF, D–15168); but what is
today Miraflores Residence would take several more years to be completed.

[126] See AGP, RHF, D–15171 and D–15172. The development of apostolic work began
later at the universities of Murcia and Oviedo than at the other Spanish universities.

[127] See AGP, RHF, D–15174.

[128] That permission was granted on February 27, 1946 (see AGP, RHF, D–15173). The
residence was that of La Estila. Already at the end of the summer of 1944, the founder
had called for the taking of the appropriate steps toward building a residence from the
ground up.

[129] See AGP, RHF, D–15170. Before that residence was built, other centers were
opened. On April 30 the founder wrote, "Just got back from Valladolid—this morning I
left our Lord in the tabernacle. How marvelous—one more!" (AGP, RHF, EF–460324–2).

leaving the Blessed Sacrament reserved for the first time in the tabernacle of El Palau.[130] In a meditation given to his sons before Mass, he assured them with supernatural optimism that "this first tabernacle will soon be followed by some more in Barcelona." [131] They would, he said, reap the fruits of their suffering. It was the moment for a daring apostolate. . . .

All the expansion done on the Iberian peninsula between 1944 and 1946 seemed to be enough to have borne out those words. But by now members of the Work—José María Albareda, José María González Barredo, José Orlandis, Juan Jiménez Vargas, and Rafael Calvo Serer, among others—had gone to various countries in Europe and the Americas to pursue their professions. It was time, the founder concluded, to take the expansion to the international level.

---

[130] See AGP, RHF, EF–430508–1. On May 25 the founder went by plane from Madrid to Barcelona. On the 27th he went to Saragossa and from there back to Madrid; see AGP, RHF, D–15200.

[131] Ponz, p. 135.

Appendices

Diary of notes handwritten by the founder of Opus Dei
from July 20 to 25, 1936

—original in AGP, RHF, D–15223

Monday, 20: Worried about everyone, especially Ricardo.[1] — We pray to the Most Blessed Virgin and to the guardian angels. — About one o'clock, I make the Sign of the Cross, and am the first to leave.[2] — Reach my mother's place.[3] — Talk on the phone with Juan;[4] everyone's arrived safely. — Radio news. — A bad night, hot. — All three parts of the Rosary. — Don't have my breviary. — Neighbors on the 3rd and 1st floors. — Militia on the roof. *Tuesday, 21:* No Mass. — We consider going to live at Ferraz. — Juan (on the phone) says no. — Juan comes over in the morning and in the afternoon; wants me to leave the house (tailor).[5] Need to calm down his parents and ask about Carlos.[6] At two I call Juan and he tells me what's going on. — I call the funeral home: Santa Isabel was torched. — I find a Roman Euchology,[7] and can pray the Office for the Dead. — All three parts of the Rosary, novena to Our Lady of the Pillar. — Juan comes over. — Radio news. — Radio Seville. *Wednesday, 22:* Can't say Mass, and am worried about my people. I call Juan, and he's not in (at 8). — We think they've called, and we try again, and he's not in. — The milkman hasn't come. — Not drinking water for everyone, especially our people.[8] — I pray for the dead. —

[Editor's note: The founder wrote this diary in a kind of shorthand, abbreviating many words.]

[1] Ricardo Fernández Vallespín, who was in Valencia at the outbreak of the war. He had gone there to start a student residence similar to the DYA Residence.

[2] The founder was at the DYA Residence, at 16 Ferraz in Madrid, which was just across the street from the Montaña Barracks.

[3] On Rey Francisco Street, three blocks from the DYA Residence.

[4] Juan Jiménez Vargas.

[5] Father Josemaría needed to get some nonclerical clothes.

[6] Probably Carlos Fernández Vallespín, Ricardo's brother.

[7] A devotional book containing the liturgical prayers for Sundays and the principal feasts of the year.

[8] He was offering for everyone, especially members of the Work, the sacrifice of not drinking water.

489

Juan comes over, and I tell him to send a postcard to Ricardo and another one to Rafael,[9] saying to go to Ricardo's house and get Carlos out of the hospital. — Carmen goes shopping; food is getting scarce. — The people downstairs say they heard on the radio that the government has had Valladolid bombed and that it's completely destroyed. — They say that priests are being taken prisoner. — Mama: Hiding things from her (no radio, except for the Seville station); entertaining her (I played cards, offering it to God). — Santi: If things get worse, the people downstairs can eat their name.[10] — Have decided not to use the phone. Rosary, novena to Our Lady of the Pillar. — My mother says this will end on the feast of Saint James.[11] — We don't believe one word they're saying on the radio. — We keep looking out the patio windows: "Now the patio is empty"; "That's the porter." — Carmen (since there are two men) says, "Now there are two porters?"[12] — We light candles in front of the picture of Merciful Love. — We hear, "Don't fire back at the snipers; wait for another chance; one bullet per target!" And "Don't let them attack by way of Mendizábal."[13] — Can't work on my papers, because I don't have the key.[14] *Thursday, 23:* Spiritual communions. Three mysteries at El Pilar.[15] No Mass! — Santiago tells me we should burn *El Siglo*,[16] so that Mama doesn't see it. — It's awfully hot; yesterday I thought I was getting used to it. — Going to try to get hold of a breviary. — Didn't tell Juan to go to 16[17] and bring me mine, because the boy is very reluctant to go there, even though he passes right by it; says it's not *prudent*. — Juan comes over (at 8:30); hasn't been able to receive Communion, because the churches are either burned or confiscated. — He's going to Isidoro's place, and then to the Residence to get my ID card, etc. He's thinking of going to the post office, to see if there are any letters. — Doesn't think it's possible to bring the prayer book. — I *find* a missal; will say a dry Mass. — Carmen goes shopping; the convents, confiscated. — In the

---

[9] Rafael Calvo Serer.

[10] The surname of the downstairs neighbors was Paniagua—"Bread and water."

[11] That is to say, by July 25 everything would be over and peace would return.

[12] Transcription (of "pr") is uncertain.

[13] These were orders given to the troops and militiamen patrolling the streets. Mendizábal was the next street over.

[14] The key to the trunk where the papers of the Work were kept.

[15] Transcription uncertain. "Mis" could stand for "misterios" (mysteries of the Rosary), or for "misas" (Masses) prayed or celebrated spiritually in the Basilica of Our Lady of the Pillar.

[16] The newspaper *El Siglo Futuro*.

[17] 16 Ferraz Street, the DYA Residence.

morning, José María Albareda and Isidoro come over with Juan; they bring me the briefcase and the keys, and a card from Ricardo. — In the afternoon, at 4, after a truckload of men have left, we hear—along with *gunshots*—people shouting "U.H.P."[18] — The brother of Manolo Sainz de los Terreros has been arrested. — Good news about Carlos. — Hermógenes[19] comes over (at 4:30) and gives us details: Don Ramón and Sales are in prison, at de C.[20] — A feeling of pessimism. — I'm mad at my brother because he told Mama news from *El Siglo* (the bombing of Huesca). — On the patio, no one turns the radio on. — We can't get Radio Seville. *Friday, 24:* No Mass! — The milkman came at 7 this morning. — Juan has come over and stayed for a good while. 50 pesetas for the School of Medicine. — We speak of everyone, especially of Ricardo, and write a postcard for Valencia. — The maid comes. — The heat is horrendous. — Prayer: to our Lord, our Lady, Saint Joseph, guardian angels, Saint James. — Three neighbors. — Yesterday and today we didn't listen to the radio. — A truck with 12- or 13-year-old boys. — 5:00 in the afternoon: on the roof of the Conde-Duque barracks, they've put a sheet with a red cross. Are they afraid of airplanes? — Worried, because Juan hasn't come; he said he would, and I called his house 2 or 3 times and they talked with me (coal). — Tonight (10:00) the *nun* from the apartment downstairs[21] came up to bring good news about Paris, Italy, and Prieto. *Saturday, 25:* Saint James, and Spain to the attack![22] Juan comes over, bringing the keys to get an ID card for Barredo. — Carmen goes shopping; the stores' stocks are running out; vouchers. — The people (*illi*), discouraged.[23] — A red cross on Buen Suceso.[24]

---

[18] "Unión de Hermanos Proletarios" (Union of Proletarian Brethren), an organization of the Popular Front.

[19] Hermógenes García, one of the women of the Work. During the war she served as the link between the founder and the other women of Opus Dei in Madrid.

[20] "Don Ramón" is probably a reference to Ramón del Portillo Pardo, Don Alvaro's father. It is not known who "Sales" or what "de C." was.

[21] A member of the Paniagua family.

[22] Ancient Spanish war cry. July 25 is the feast of Saint James.

[23] "Illi": Latin for "the others."

[24] A church two blocks from Doña Dolores's home.

Appendix 2

Diary of Juan Jiménez Vargas, October 6 to 15, 1936
—original in AGP, RHF, D–15347

(Written in rough draft, on two sheets with the letterhead *Clinical Journal*. The sheets were left on the desk in his house in San Bernardo when he was arrested on the 15th.)

October 6, 1936

Went to look for Barredo at 9:30. Last night Don Alejandro telephoned him, saying we can meet today at nine. He spoke in a way that could have gotten him in trouble.

We had just arrived at his house when his sister came out in tears, motioning to us that we needed to leave because they were making a search.

We visited Vicente. He thinks his house is not safe. He's going to speak with the people in the house across the street, which is the house of the Greek consul, and ask about the psychiatric sanatorium they have in their district.

We were running late, and when we reached the home of the secretary of the Cuban embassy, he had already left.

In the afternoon I returned to Vicente's house. The Greek consul thing is not going to work out. At five a girl came over who lives nearby and knows the people at the sanatorium. I went with her and she introduced me to the director. They have no objection, but they would have to give the name to the Security Office, as they do with all the patients.

Late in the evening, Joaquín came over to my house. Everything is arranged. He went this morning, with Infante, to Suils' sanatorium. The Father can stay there without his name being given to the Security Office.

October 7, 1936

At 10:00 the Father and Joaquín came to my place. And then Chiqui, to go to confession to the Father. Joaquín's maid said to him this morning, "Good morning, Father."

Joaquín called the hospital to have them send a car here, and we told the porter that they would be asking for Dr. Herrero Fontana.

We've hidden the ID card in my house. Suils will surely sign the certificate with a false name.

The Father says, about the underwear he's taking with him, that every item seems to have come from a different person.

Vicente called, asking for "Dr. Vargas" and speaking to me *de usted* [as to a stranger], as we had planned. If they didn't hear us laughing, they should be thrown off track by that.

October 8, 1936

Isidoro went to see Alvaro. He's doing very well. No one saw them enter his house except the porter, who is acting very different. I went with Barredo early in the afternoon to the home of the secretary of the Cuban embassy; he either wasn't in or didn't want to see anyone.

I saw Selesio. They were searching for the ones from Villaviciosa, but when they saw that the house was under the protection of an embassy, they left without doing a search.

Soon after I left home, Joaquín came over. Everything went very well and the Father is fine.

October 9, 1936

I brought the diary to Vicente's house, because we're doing it together. I'm writing it and he's putting in the things it needs—periods, accents, commas, spelling corrections, etc. I was there for quite a while. We didn't do anything useful, but we laughed a lot.

October 10, 1936

I brought Isidoro a New Testament, because in the "search" made by his mother, all that could be found that wasn't burned was the "Guidebook for Sinners." (It got spared because it has a red cover.)

Yesterday I was at Alvaro's house. Nothing can be done at the Mexican embassy. The person who was serving as liaison with the embassy was killed.

Barredo is going to go see his cousin again. He doesn't think anything can be done at San Luis de los Franceses. His cousin would have told him by now if she knew anything, because it's been two days since she talked to him about this.

We are a little worried about the sanatorium. They seem a bit too eager about collecting their payments, which doesn't give us much confidence about how safe it's going to be there. But I already knew this, and it seems to me a reason to give it a try, since they apparently are helpful as long as they get their money.

October 11, 1936

I went with Barredo to Isidoro's house to bring him a book about calisthenics. The three of us went out for a walk to San Luis de los Franceses. It looks like it's been vacated. Apparently what was said to Barredo has to do with the hospital, not the school.

We still haven't heard anything about Sellés. We're concerned about not being able to help him, since in this epidemic of cowardly selfishness that Madrid is suffering from, he and the Leyva family are exceptionally generous.

October 12, 1936

I telephoned Chiqui, and they told me that he can't leave the house because he has a bad cold. I didn't dare try to go see him, because of their porter.

I spent the whole morning at Vicente's house.

After lunch I went to Barredo's house. I saw Sellés on the street. They haven't searched his house.

Isidoro and I kept Barredo company for a little while. Then he left for an English class, and we spent some time in Rosales.

October 13, 1936

Before I left the house I called the doctor on duty at the sanatorium. The Father is fine. We can go see him if we want.

Barredo, Isidoro, and I spent the morning in the park, making as if we were studying English.

Herrero's mother (he wasn't home) says that it would be a crazy idea to visit the Father—that it is understandable if he is worried, not knowing anything about us, but that we must restrain ourselves. She's right, although I can imagine what the Father must be going through, being so completely isolated.

We would love to see him, but we don't want to create new complications out of affectionate foolishness. So I went to Suils' house this afternoon and told him that the Father shouldn't worry about anyone, and should act as if we weren't even in Madrid. No phone calls, or anything. Only if he is in any danger should they contact me at my home. Suils tells me that the Father has been feigning a trauma-induced inability to speak, and that he's now beginning to say something, just a very little, so as to avoid arousing suspicion.

October 14, 1936

In the morning we were at Barredo's house. He went to see Sellés. Isidoro and I walked along the street till dinnertime. After eating I went to Isidoro's house. Elordi came to my house while I was out.

October 15, 1936

Early in the afternoon I went to Barredo's house. We think it would be a good idea to speak with Elordi, to see if we could get the Father a safe-conduct pass as a Basque nationalist. He doesn't have to leave the sanatorium, but last night the police went around Madrid asking for documentation in people's homes and arresting many people. The personal ID card is not enough; they demand evidence of being trusted by the Popular Front. . . .

Sellés is looking for a way that the Father might be able to say Mass at his house. Barredo told me this after Valdés had left, because if he heard about it he would get frightened and throw cold water on the plan.

It is a wonderful thing, this "imprudence" of Sellés. In his house, no, we can't do it there, but I think maybe at the sanatorium we could. It would, of course, have to be done without anybody knowing about it. A little argument took place at Joaquín's house. His mother told me yesterday that she was praying a lot for me because I'm taking my life in my hands by walking around on the streets so much! I told her that I must have nine lives, like a cat, and still have plenty left, because with all the doctors I've been to and all the blows I've suffered in my years, I haven't managed to use up more than four or five.

Appendix 3

Diary of Antonio Dalmases Esteva
—extracts: original in AGP, RHF, T–08246

From the prologue (written in Barcelona in 1960)

Among the fugitives was a priest who was accompanied by seven friends. A priest who celebrated Mass during the journey—a Mass that in my memory has forever stood out from all others. A priest whose companions clearly had great respect for him, and who exuded a strange magnetism. A priest with whom I hardly spoke during those days (we didn't talk while on the move), but who for some reason was the center of attraction for all of us. We parted in Andorra, but I ran into him a week later in San Sebastián, when I was praying in the Church of the Good Shepherd. He came up behind me, put his hand on my shoulder, and told me that we would never again be separated. From that day on, including all through the war, he was my spiritual director, by mail. He cared about me—he made me study languages, while the other soldiers were regrettably wasting their time, and was like a father to me during the whole campaign. But when victory came at last, I inexplicably lost track of him and heard nothing more from him directly. Until one day, twenty years later, when I had just lost my brother-in-law, my father, and my mother, and was going through a big spiritual crisis, another fortuitous event—this time thanks to my wife—seemed to lift a veil from the mystery of my own life and reveal a clear purpose for it. I came back into contact, and forever, with not only that priest who had been a real father to me, but also that whole great and marvelous Work whose initial nucleus had been that little group that accompanied him during our escape and whose story I recorded during those days.

That priest was Father Escrivá de Balaguer.

From the diary

Joining the expedition. There is a low whistle, answered by a similar one, and from where there seemed to have been no one, some twenty men emerge. They're all traveling like us, more or less, with big knapsacks, blankets, scarves, weatherproof coats, and what have you. Everyone is moving silently, in the darkness, single file, saying nothing. At the head is a guide, then us, and behind us the rest. I can't resist turning around often to observe this spectacle. No sound can be heard other than that of our walking sticks hitting the earth. Following behind me are men and more men who, by the light of the moon, look like ghosts, they are dressed so unusually and are so stooped over by the weight they carry on their backs. We have to wind our way up the mountain, because the climb is so steep, and below us we see a line of figures moving like a tired centipede. Apparently they have already been walking for many hours (since six in the morning the day before, they later told me), because they look exhausted and we often have to stop to rest. It seems that someone in the line can't keep up the pace set by the guide, and that's why we have to stop so often.

This daybreak I'll never forget as long as I live. We walk until the sun is starting to come up; just then we reach the place where we are to rest today. As we draw near our destination the path becomes very bad; actually there is no path or anything; and the person in front of me bumps a stone loose and gets his foot caught under it. It takes a long time to get him out, because the same stone his foot is caught under is the one that's supporting him. After a lot of work we finally free him and do a little first aid. Luckily no real damage has been done and he is able to keep going. From one to another the alert is passed back about the dangerousness of that spot.

We take shelter under an enormous rock that rises to about a hundred feet above us. From up there, a waterfall descends into a small stream far below us. The ground around us is all large boulders—a very uncultivated and treacherous terrain. We are on a platform about fifteen feet wide and about ninety feet above that stream. Below us, coming up to our level, is an impassable slope, covered with vegetation; above us, almost vertical rock and the sky.

Here the most moving event of the whole trip takes place: Holy Mass. On a rock and kneeling down, almost prostrate on the ground, a priest with us is saying Mass. He doesn't say it like other priests in churches. He says the prayers out loud, almost crying—as are we, some of us kneeling, some lying down, others squatting or standing, holding onto the rocks so as not to fall. There is no sound except the priest's voice. His clear and heartfelt words penetrate our souls. Never have I attended a Mass like today's. I don't know if it's because of the circumstances or because the celebrant is a saint. Holy Communion is very moving. Since we can barely move, it is difficult for him to distribute it, even though we are all gathered around the altar. We are all ragged, unshaven, uncombed, weary. One fellow's trousers are torn at the knees. Everyone's hands are scratched and bleeding. Our eyes glisten with tears we try to hold back. And there among us, in hosts cut out with scissors, is our Lord God, presiding over our coalition and leading us to freedom. We offer our sacrifices to him for Spain, for our parents, for our brothers and sisters, for the family and friends we left behind, for our companions groaning in the prisons. We ask that one day we might return home. . . .

An abrupt change. We are hungry. We eat and then lie down to go to sleep. I can't sleep. Soon people are coming together to get acquainted and chat. Some have been on other expeditions that got close to the border but were forced to turn back when the border guards started firing. There are eight people from Madrid (among them the priest who has so much impressed me—he seems to be their leader); one from Valencia; four or five from Barcelona; several from the province of Lérida; and the three of us. Everyone is very cordial. When a bottle of cognac is opened, it breaks, much to everyone's chagrin. Now all we have left is what I brought with me. I fill the little bottle attached to my belt and serve out the rest to everyone else. The people from Madrid give me bread while we wait for our meal (we left our loaf at home), and so we pass the time, talking, eating, and repairing our equipment, until the guide comes. He is a young and resolute fellow. . . . He tells us to be ready to leave by four in the afternoon.

Before leaving we say a Rosary, praying it as we have never prayed it before, not even during the worst days of the persecution in Barcelona.

*   *   *

My new friends from Madrid are passing the time separating out the most indispensable items in their kits and throwing out the rest, since they can't carry it all. Shirts, socks, satchels, shoes . . . all left behind. Some of us avail ourselves of these clothes, those that we think we have the strength to carry. The priest encourages everyone. In all of us his company inspires confidence, because he seems to have a mandate from God. He has a strange magnetism that has very deeply impressed me.

*   *   *

We kneel alongside the priest and give thanks to God. He gives voice to the joy we share.

Appendix 4

Letter from Bishop Leopoldo Eijo y Garay of Madrid to Dom Aurelio M. Escarré, Coadjutor Abbot of Montserrat, May 24, 1941

—AGP, RHF, D–03545–2

Dear brother in our Lord:

Many thanks for your letter of the 9th, which I received yesterday, the 23rd. I don't know why the long delay.

I have been with you in spirit in that beloved holy house of yours, though the daily grind hasn't allowed me to go there in person.

Yes, I know all about the commotion being stirred up against Opus Dei in Barcelona. It's obvious that it is a thorn in the side of the Evil One. The sad thing is that people very devoted to God are the instruments of the harm being done, although of course *putantes se obsequium praestare Deo* [thinking they are pleasing God]. I know all about it because, from the time it was founded in 1928, Opus Dei has been so much in the hands of the Church that the diocesan ordinary, that is to say, either my vicar general or myself, has known of and, when necessary, guided all of its steps. Everything from its first cries to its current groanings has resounded in our ears—and in our hearts. Because, believe me, Most Reverend Abbot, the Opus has been truly Dei from its conception on through every new stage of its development.

Father Escrivá is an exemplary priest, chosen by God for the sanctification of many souls; humble, prudent, self-sacrificing, extremely docile to his bishop; of outstanding intelligence and with a very solid spiritual and doctrinal formation; ardently zealous; an apostle of Christian formation of young students, with no other aim or goal than that of preparing, for the good of our country and the service and defense of the Church, a large number of intellectuals and professionals who will in the very midst of the world not only lead a life of holiness but also carry out their work with the soul of an apostle.

And in the mold of his spirit has his Opus been formed. I know this not by hearsay, but by personal experience. The *men* of Opus Dei (and I emphasize the word "men" because even the youngest among them are already men, by virtue of their recollectedness and seriousness of life) are traveling a safe path not only for the salvation of their own souls but also for doing a lot of good to innumerable other souls.

This "secret association," as its detractors call it, did not come to birth without the blessing of the diocesan authority, and has never taken a step of any importance without first getting the "amen" of that approval.

The discreet reserve (never *secrecy*) that Father Escrivá fosters in the members is, more than anything else, an antidote to showing off—the defense of a humility that he wants to be a collective one, for the whole Opus, not just an individual one for its members. Thus it will be a more effective instrument in the apostolate of good example and in the services that *occasione data* [as the occasion arises] it can provide to the Church.

The cultivation of mind and heart through study of religion and practices of piety is very intense; several priests of excellent spirit have assisted in this, although at first it was just Father Escrivá.

In a word, I have nothing to say against that Opus. It is, I repeat, truly Dei.

And, nevertheless, it is good people who are now attacking it.

This would be cause for astonishment were it not that the Lord has accustomed us to seeing that same phenomenon occur with other works very much his own.

Opus Dei deserves nothing but praise. But those of us who love it do not want to see it praised or advertised. Its aim is not quantity but quality; not raking in a lot of people, but forming very well those whom God does bring to his Opus; working quietly and humbly, with interior joy, with an apostolic enthusiasm that, precisely because it does not dissipate itself in big public displays, never wanes; endowing every profession with select groups who, without waving banners or doing anything to call attention to themselves, live in a holy way and foster the good of others. That is the ambition of Opus Dei.

I am familiar with all the accusations that have been thrown at it, and I know they are false. I know that some people are being persecuted, even financially, just because they are believed to be in Opus Dei—and they aren't! I know that the fathers and mothers of the students are being harassed, and that threats of action by the civil authorities are being made, and that every possible means, a thousand tactics, are being used. The Lord will turn all this only to Opus Dei's advantage; but it is sad to see good people discrediting themselves by persecuting something good.

Yesterday I read a letter from the superior of a Jesuit residence in which he says that it is a defamation of the Society of Jesus to claim that it is persecuting Opus Dei and seeking its destruction.

Your Reverence, you know what is going on over there, so you can judge for yourself.

I have not gone into details because Your Reverence has not asked for them. If you would like me to clarify any particular point, please let me know; I will be very happy to explain everything. I consider it a favor from our Lord God to be able to be of use to his Opus.

Please keep me in your prayers.

Affectionately yours in our Lord and in our blessed Lady of Montserrat,

+ The Bishop of Madrid-Alcalá
Madrid, May 24, 1941

Appendix 5

Letter from Bishop Leopoldo Eijo y Garay of Madrid
to Dom Aurelio M. Escarré, Coadjutor Abbot of Montserrat,
June 21, 1941

—AGP, RHF, D–03545–3

Reverend Father Abbot:

Yesterday I received your letter of the 15th, and I am happy to dedicate a bit of time to answering your questions.

Origin of Opus Dei. Some years ago Father José María Escrivá came to Universidad Central to finish his studies. I received very good reports about him, and his conduct was exemplary. Around 1928 he came to see my vicar general, Monsignor Francisco Morán, and told him that, in the face of the need he saw for university students to be given spiritual guidance, he felt strongly moved to dedicate himself to this apostolate. If, he said, this desire was approved and blessed by the bishop, he would see in it the will of God. After exchanging impressions about his plans, the means he hoped to use, the promising group of students to whom he was already giving spiritual direction, and the need he so strongly felt there was for that apostolate, we not only approved but applauded and blessed his holy efforts. And so the work began. He did not take one step of any importance without consulting with the vicar general, Monsignor Morán, through whom I knew all about the Work, and I gave thanks to God.

Purpose. The first fruit began to appear. The students called Father José "the Father," and he imparted his fervor to them and formed them, at that perilous age, infusing in them a profound piety, a spirit of faithful fulfillment of duty, and, above all, a love for Holy Mother Church and a devotion to her hierarchy. The lazy and those who don't apply themselves, the lukewarm and the willful, the bad students or bad Christians, these would not be at home in the group. When it had become more numerous, a student residence was set up, under the guidance of the Father and with the help of some of the brighter and more fervent students. The enterprise grew, in intensity even more than in extension. Some of the better formed, convinced of the usefulness of such an apostolate for the glory of God, wished to bind themselves to the Father in order to help him. Those who had finished their studies and begun to work at their professions kept in constant communication with him. They owed to him the best of what they had and valued, sanctity of life and the desire to do good to souls, each from the vantage point of his own situation. The Father counseled them and encouraged them and went on dedicating himself to those sons of his. The idea came up of opening residences and academies in other places, in order to extend that fruitful work to more students; and these were set up in various university cities (Barcelona, Valencia, etc.), under the direction of the Father and the management of those who wanted to dedicate themselves to that beautiful apostolate. The bishop of each place, without whose permission and blessing he never did anything (just as in the beginning, in Madrid), knew everything that was going on, and applauded and blessed it.

As the years passed, the Work in a very natural way produced more and more fruit. Those formed in its spirit fanned out through all of Spain, more notable for their solid formation than for their numbers, aflame with the desire to serve God and supremely eager to be of service to his holy Church. The conserving of that spirit necessitated organization, a family bonding, communication, and mutual support and encouragement. That organization and family is Opus Dei. Its purpose is to help each person attain sanctity in his profession in the midst of the world—working, always working. That is the meaning of the word "Opus." God placed man in paradise *ut operaretur* [in order that he might work]; the ideal of the Father and his children is to serve God by working in a holy way in their own professions, with eyes always fixed on the defense and service of Holy Church, and with a faithful and selfless submission to her hierarchy, that is, to the Pope and to their own bishop.

Now, then, the founder has never had any intention—I know this because he has always made this very clear to me—of founding a religious institute. Rather, he wants the members to live in the holiest possible way as laypeople. He is happy when some people in contact with Opus Dei decide to join religious orders (as some, in fact, have done—an example is the ones who joined the Hieronymites of El Parral). But he has always wanted—and this, in accord with his wishes, I have fully approved—for the organization born by God's grace in his hands always to be made up of laypeople and be for laypeople. Moreover, he does not want that association *as such* to go beyond those purposes that he intended: namely, to form those students in its residences and to direct and sustain them afterwards, and for them to apply themselves to various good works that, while always being apostolic, are not projects of Opus Dei as such, but are separate from it, although his children would be their life and soul.

One of the virtues that the founder is most interested in inculcating in those he directs is holy humility—not just personal, but also *collective*. He wants the Work not to put itself in the limelight or give itself the air of being something important. He always urges them to work quietly, to pass unnoticed, to sacrifice themselves in silence, to flee from the danger of vainglory, to have the soul of an apostle but not the dressings or the halo of one. He teaches them that their apostolate of good example will be more effective if they do not act conspicuously as members of a pious association. He does not want them to talk about him or Opus Dei, but just to serve, as the opportunity arises. He says that for serving Holy Church it is preferable that they not make a show of how much they want to serve her and of the fact that they have been organized for that purpose.

Secretiveness and mysteriousness. That same spirit which is reflected in those other norms having to do with Opus Dei, as such, not owning anything, or having any magazine, or doing any advertising, is also manifested in not speaking about it or praising it or making a show of being a member, or having the student residences look like as if they were run by a pious entity, or saying that in this or that area of the country there is such-and-such a number of members, etc.

And there you have, Reverend Father Abbot, the occasion that the enemy of souls has seized upon to accuse Opus Dei of being a secret, Masonic society; some, indeed, calling it a white Masonry, but others branding it as diabolic and condemned.

That is what its secretiveness and mysteriousness come down to—a secret and a mystery which have never been anything of the kind to the diocesan authorities, and which (I know this to be true of several prelates, and it is certainly so in my case) these authorities have approved and commended, encouraging the founder.

And so that you, Reverend Father, can with good assurance respond to those who slander the Work by saying that members are forbidden to speak about it to their spiritual directors (under threat of the severest sanctions, they go so far as to say), I am going to set down here, copied verbatim from its list of statutes, the only words touching on that subject. After recommending that members not speak about their apostolate to anyone who does not already know something

about it, and that they not do any consulting on it except with someone who has a good knowledge of it, since otherwise they will very
likely get erroneous advice, it says: "*One should not interpret this point
as a limitation on the* FULL SINCERITY *with which one should open one's soul
to one's spiritual director,* but should always be mindful that it is not
easy for a spiritual director to be able to give good advice with regard
to the Work if he is not very familiar with it."

Iconoclastic leanings! This one would be cause for laughter had it not
caused the shedding of so many tears by mothers who have been
made to believe their sons to be irremediably condemned, just when
they were beginning to be so pleased with the edifying life of piety
they had seen taking shape in them.

All the members have their statues, their crucifixes, their medals,
just like the rest of us. They have in their rooms a picture of the
Blessed Virgin and are advised to give it an affectionate glance whenever they enter or leave. There is nothing the least bit iconoclastic
about the Work. But some *spies* sent ad hoc to find out what was
going on there were shocked to see a wooden cross, a large one,
without a corpus. It is meant to remind each member of Opus Dei
that the cross awaits him, and that he should not flinch from it or
refuse to be crucified for love of the One who ascended the cross for
him. And those who saw that cross-invitation had to have also seen,
and should have reported, and those who did the spreading of the
word should have spread this, that at the foot of that cross there is a
little plaque saying that the bishop grants a fifty days' indulgence to
those who lovingly and devoutly kiss that holy cross and address it
with the words of love that Saint Andrew used when embracing his
own.

Their piety is very deep and sound, entirely orthodox, and in nothing—except its intensity—any different from that of all the Christian
faithful.

So many ridiculous stories have been concocted, such as the one
about Communion taking place with perfumed hosts! I repeat that
this would all be something to laugh at, if it weren't making so many
good souls cry.

Hatred for religious orders. This is one of the grossest calumnies
against Opus Dei; I guarantee you, Reverend Father, it is pure calumny. How could they love the Church without also loving the religious state? They love it, they venerate it, they proclaim it a means of

salvation for those called to it by God. But they feel that they themselves are called not to that vocation, but rather to that of attaining sanctity in the midst of the world and carrying out their apostolate there. This they feel and this they say, without implying the slightest disrespect for the religious state. In fact, the founder himself inculcates into them that they must live in the world in as holy a manner as if they were religious. And they believe that, having been called to this kind of apostolate, they will render more glory to God by following that call than they would if they were to turn a deaf ear to it and become religious.

And it is only natural that, seeing the founder's zealous projects and being eager to put them into operation, they contemplate the glory they hope to give to God by means of Opus Dei.

If those who have heard about this think it implies bad will toward the religious institutes, they are completely mistaken.

Connection with the Bañolas affair? I don't know when the Bañolas organization began; a Jesuit father from Barcelona tells me he believes it was around 1932, in which case Opus Dei began earlier, since it started in 1928. But be that as it may, it is beyond question that the one has nothing to do with the other, since they are poles apart. Opus Dei, from its inception, has always operated under obedience to diocesan authority. Father Escrivá did not begin his Work until it was approved and blessed by the bishop. On everything, he has consulted my vicar general or myself, and has followed whatever advice we gave him. What could this have in common with the Bañolas affair, whose characteristic note was rebellion against ecclesiastical authority?

The approval of Opus Dei was verbal and *ad experimentum* from when the Work was founded until this year's feast of Saint Joseph, when, its statutes having been drawn up, I issued a decree of approval *in scriptis*. I thought the time had come to do that since, in my judgment, they now had enough experience to draw up statutes that had been actually lived out and were not just a product of untested idealism. But, I repeat, it had my approval from its birth. Father Escrivá would not have undertaken this apostolate without it. And it has been growing and developing under my guidance and authority.

And to think, Reverend Father, that this whole storm has come about because two or three boys who were thinking of entering religious life preferred Opus Dei once they knew about it!

The disproportion between cause and effects is so great that there is no natural explanation; we have to attribute it to God's providence. Evidently God has allowed this to happen for his own purposes.

What is really amazing is the spirit with which the members of Opus Dei have borne this great trial. I see their letters, because Opus Dei shows me everything, and I admire and am edified by the holy joy with which they suffer for their vocation, which the gale only serves to embed more deeply in their souls. There is not one complaint or word of ill will toward the religious who so harshly persecute them. Their greatest consolation is seeing that all the bishops in whose territories they have houses are with them; that we are encouraging and defending them. God will have to reward those who *arbitrantes se obsequium praestare Deo* [thinking they are offering service to God] have pressed this war, but all that Opus Dei wants out of it is the good that the Lord wants to draw from this tribulation. And it will come about.

I think, Reverend Father, that I have answered all the points in your interesting and appreciated letter. If you need anything more from me, don't hesitate to ask. And forgive me for writing at such length; next time I will try to be briefer.

Asking once more that you keep me in your prayers, I remain Affectionately yours in our Lord,

+ The Bishop of Madrid-Alcalá
Madrid, June 21, 1941

P.S. I'm enclosing an announcement about the residence in Madrid.

APPENDIX 6

A partial listing of the preaching engagements of the founder of Opus Dei from 1938 to 1946

Between 1938 and 1946, in response to requests from bishops all over Spain, the founder of Opus Dei gave many retreats, days of recollection, conferences, and so forth, for priests and seminarians, men and women religious, Catholic Action groups, and university students and professors. This, of course, was in addition to the preaching he was constantly doing for all those connected with the apostolates of Opus Dei.

This partial listing is drawn from official bulletins of the dioceses, and registration books of the houses, where he gave the spiritual exercises; documents in the General Archives of the Prelature, including the "Chronology" and "Itinerary" of the founder of Opus Dei (AGP, RHF, D–15013 and D–15014); handwritten notations in the margins of his liturgical calendars (AGP, RHF, D–05212 and D–15015); letters of the founder, and of members of Opus Dei and others; diaries of the first centers of the Work; notes and testimonies and written reports made by some of those who attended the spiritual exercises; hotel bills and train and bus tickets used by the founder; and photographic archives.

August 1938

18–25	Vitoria. Retreat for priests.
18–25	Vitoria. Retreat for the nuns at the bishop's residence.

September 1938

4–10	Vergara, conciliar seminary. Retreat for priests of the diocese of Vitoria.

June (into July) 1939

5–11	Burjasot (Valencia). Retreat for university men.
11–17	Alacuás (Valencia). Retreat for diocesan priests, at the convent of the Catechetical Workers.
15	Alacuás. Sermon for the Catechetical Workers.
24–1	Vergara (Guipúzcoa). Retreat for seminarians about to be ordained for the diocese of Vitoria.

July 1939

2–8	Vitoria. Retreat for university professors.
5	Vitoria. Sermon for the nuns of Santa Ana.
20	Avila. Meditation at the Monastery of Santa Teresa.
23	Avila. Meditation at the Monastery of Santa Teresa.

September 1939

10–16	Burjasot. Retreat for university men.

14	Burjasot. Day of recollection for Young Women of Catholic Action.
15	Burjasot. Sermon for the nuns.

January 1940

11	Madrid. Day of recollection for diocesan priests, at the parish of Santa Cruz.

February 1940

4–10	Madrid. Retreat for diocesan priests, at the Paulist monastery on García de Paredes Street.

March 1940

7	Madrid. Day of recollection for diocesan priests, at the parish of Santa Cruz.

April 1940

7	Alacuás. Day of recollection for university men, at the convent of the Catechetical Workers.
9–13	Madrid. Retreat for diocesan priests, at the Paulist monastery on García de Paredes Street.

May 1940

5	Madrid. Day of recollection for university men in Catholic Action, at the church of the Sisters of Saint James.
11	Saragossa. Day of recollection for the directors of Young Women of Catholic Action.
26	Alacuás. Day of recollection for university men, at the convent of the Catechetical Workers.

June 1940

2–8	Madrid. Retreat for diocesan priests, at the Paulist monastery on García de Paredes Street.
23	Madrid. Day of recollection for university men in Catholic Action, at Chamartín.
29	Valladolid. Day of recollection for university men in Catholic Action, at Our Lady of Lourdes High School.

July 1941

1–7	Avila. Retreat for diocesan priests, at the seminary.
21–26	Madrid. Retreat for university men in Catholic Action, at the Ortí Residence, on Narváez Street.

August 1940

1–9	León. Retreat for diocesan priests, at the seminary.

September 1940

1–7	Madrid. Retreat for university women, at the convent of the Reparatrix Sisters.

October (into November) 1940

27–1   Saragossa. Retreat for the directors of Young Women of Catholic Action.

November 1940

2–9   Valencia. Retreat at the major seminary.

7   Valencia. Sermon for the nuns working at the seminary.

13–20   Madrid. Retreat at the major seminary.

December 1940

19   Madrid. Talk at the ceremony of a sister's taking of the habit, at Santa Isabel School.

January 1941

12   Madrid. Day of recollection for university men in Catholic Action, at Del Pilar High School.

19   Valencia. Day of recollection, at the major seminary.

20–25   Alacuás. Meditations for priests from all over Spain, during a week for Priest Assistants of Catholic Action, at Immaculate Conception House.

26   Valencia. Day of recollection for university men, at the residence on Samaniego Street.

March (into April) 1941

29   Valencia. Day of recollection for the seminarians at Patriarch Preparatory College.

30–April 5   Alacuás. Retreat for Young Women of Catholic Action, at the convent of the Catechetical Workers.

April 1941

21   Lérida. Retreat for diocesan priests. (On April 22 his mother, Doña Dolores Albás, died.)

June (into July) 1941

1–7   Burlada (Navarre). Retreat for diocesan priests.

15–21   Burlada. Retreat for diocesan priests.

22–28   Burlada. Retreat for diocesan priests.

29–July 5   Burlada. Retreat for diocesan priests.

July 1941

9–15   Madrid. Retreat for university men, at the Diego de León Street residence.

18–24   Madrid. Retreat for university men, at the Diego de León Street residence.

25–31   Madrid. Retreat for university men, at the Diego de León Street residence.

August 1941

5–12   Madrid. Retreat for university men, at the Lagasca Street residence.

13–20   Valencia. Retreat for university men, at the Samaniego Street residence.

23   Jaca (Huesca). Conference for university men in Saragossa, during the university's summer session.

September 1941

2–8   Madrid. Retreat for university men, at the Diego de León Street residence.

October 1941

13–18   Lérida. Retreat for diocesan priests, at the seminary.

16   Lérida. Sermon for the young members of Catholic Action.

20–25   Lérida. Retreat for diocesan priests, at the seminary.

23   Lérida. Sermon at a retreat given by Father Angel Morta, for young men.

        Sermon for the nuns working at the seminary.

December 1941

14–20   Valencia. Retreat for university women in Catholic Action, at the convent of the Sisters of Domestic Service.

February 1942

1   Madrid. Sermon at Santa Isabel School (on the occasion of Mother Nieves' golden jubilee).

March (into April) 1942

25–29   Madrid. Retreat for the teachers at the Ramiro de Maeztu Institute.

28–April 1 Madrid. Retreat for university men, at the Jenner Street residence.

May 1942

8   Avila. Sermon for ordinands, at the seminary. Another sermon for all the seminarians.

June (into July) 1942

30–July 7   Segovia. Retreat for the clergy of the diocese.

July 1942

8–15   Segovia. Retreat for the clergy of the diocese.

9   Segovia. Day of recollection for the clergy of the city.

August 1942

6–13   Madrid. Retreat for university women, at the Jorge Manrique Street residence.

September 1942

4–10   Madrid. Retreat for university men, at the Diego de León Street residence.

October 1942

4–10   Carabanchel (Madrid). Retreat for the clergy of the diocese of Madrid, at the convent of the Sisters of the Pontifical Crusade.

8   Carabanchel. Sermon for the Sisters of the Pontifical Crusade.

November 1942

2–8   Segovia. Retreat for Hieronymite monks, at the Monastery of Our Lady of El Parral.

December 1942

16–20   Madrid. Retreat for university men, at the Diego de León Street residence.

17–21   Madrid. Retreat for university men, at the Jenner Street residence.

February 1943

14   Madrid. Day of recollection for university women, at the Jorge Manrique Street residence.

March (into April) 1943

27–April 2   Madrid. Retreat for university women in Catholic Action, at the retreat house of the Sister Servants of the Sacred Heart, on Martínez Campos Street.

28–April 3   Madrid. Retreat for young women in the parish of Buen Suceso.

April 1943

13–17   Madrid. Retreat for men in the parish of Buen Suceso.

July 1943

25   Madrid. Day of recollection for young members of Catholic Action in the parish of El Salvador.

August 1943

20–26   Madrid. Retreat for the Piarist fathers at Saint Joseph Calasanz High School.

September 1943

4–10   Madrid. Retreat for university women, at the Jorge Manrique Street residence.

December 1943

12   Madrid. Day of recollection for university men, at the Moncloa residence.

27–29   Madrid. Spiritual direction for the Conference on the

University Apostolate for university professors involved in Catholic Action.

March 1944

4–7   Madrid. Retreat for university men, at the Moncloa residence.

12–17   Madrid. Retreat for university women, at the Jorge Manrique Street residence.

April 1944

3–8   Madrid. Retreat for university women, at the Jorge Manrique Street residence.

May 1944

13–20   El Escorial (Madrid). Retreat preceding reception of the tonsure, for Opus Dei's first three candidates for the priesthood.

June 1944

15–20   Retreat for university women, at the Jorge Manrique Street residence.

October 1944

3–11   El Escorial. Retreat for the Augustinians at the Monastery of St. Lawrence.

February 1945

18–24   Madrid. Retreat for young men in Catholic Action, at the retreat house of the Sister Servants of the Sacred Heart.

March 1945

2–6   Salamanca. Retreat for university men in Catholic Action.

3   Salamanca. Conference at the seminary.

5   Salamanca. Sermon at the university residence.

5   Conference for the Propagandistas [a Catholic Action organization].

6   Salamanca. Sermon for the Josephine Diocesan Workers.

12–18   Madrid. Retreat for professors, in the Oratory of the Knight of Grace.

April 1945

22   Madrid. Day of recollection for university men, at the Moncloa residence.

April 1946

7–12   Madrid. Retreat for the Chief of State [Franco], in El Pardo Palace.

September 1946

21–27   Molinoviejo (Segovia). Pre-ordination retreat for six members of Opus Dei.

Appendix 7

Apostolic trips made by the founder of Opus Dei through the Iberian Peninsula, 1939–1946

1939

1. Daimiel: April 19–20.
2. Valladolid — Burgos: May 31.
3. Valencia: June 5–17.
4. Vergara — Vitoria — Saragossa: June 22 to July 12.
5. Avila: July 19–25.
6. Valencia: September 5–20.
7. Valladolid: November 30 to December 2.
8. Salamanca: December 8–10.
9. Saragossa — Barcelona — Valencia: December 28, 1939, to January 5, 1940.

1940

10. Valladolid: January 27–28.
11. Valencia: January 31 to February 2.
12. Avila — Salamanca — Valladolid — Burgos — Vitoria — San Sebastián — Vitoria — Saragossa — Vitoria — Bilbao — Valladolid: February 15 to March 4.
13. Saragossa: March 15–17.
14. Saragossa — Barcelona — Valencia: March 29 to April 7.
15. Valladolid: April 23–27.
16. Valladolid: May 1–2.
17. Saragossa — Barcelona: May 10–15.
18. Valencia: May 25–26.
19. Valladolid: June 8–9.
20. Valladolid — Avila: June 27 to July 8.
21. Barcelona: July 27–29.
22. León: July 31 to August 10.
23. Valencia: September 17–23.
24. Saragossa: September 26–28.
25. Valladolid — Vitoria — Pamplona: October 11–18.
26. Saragossa — Valencia: October 26 to November 10.
27. Valladolid: November 20–24.
28. Valencia: November 26 to December 3.

1941

29. Valencia: January 18–27.
30. Valladolid — Bilbao — Vitoria: March 9–13.
31. Valencia: March 26 to April 7.
32. Vitoria — Pamplona — Valladolid: April 13–16.
33. Saragossa — Lérida: April 19–22.
34. Barcelona: May 21–23.
35. Valladolid — Avila: May 25–27.
36. Pamplona — Vitoria — Valladolid: June 1–9.
37. Valencia: June 11–13.
38. Pamplona — Valladolid: June 15 to July 8.
39. Valencia — Saragossa — Jaca — Pamplona — Vitoria — San Sebastián: August 13–31.
40. Saragossa — Lérida — Saragossa: October 12–27.
41. Valencia: December 13–23.

1942

42. Vitoria: February 17–20.
43. Valencia: March 6–9.
44. Valladolid — León — Valladolid: April 1–7.
45. Avila — Valladolid: May 6–12.
46. Valladolid: May 21–22.
47. Segovia: July 1–7.
48. Segovia: July 9–15.
49. Barcelona: July 22–24.
50. Vitoria — Bilbao — Pamplona — Saragossa: July 27–31.
51. Vitoria — Pamplona — San Sebastián: September 10–24.
52. Segovia: November 2–8.

1943

53. Valladolid — Burgos: March 22–24.
54. Barcelona: April 10–13.
55. Valladolid — Salamanca: May 19–20.
56. Barcelona — Saragossa: May 25–28.
57. Valladolid: June 8.
58. Burgos — Vitoria: July 2–3.
59. Valladolid: September 26.
60. Barcelona: September 28 to October 1.
61. Seville: December 14–18.

1944

62. Valencia: March 22–25.

63. Salamanca: April 25–27.
64. Valladolid: September 9–12.
65. El Escorial: October 3–11.

1945

66. Valladolid: January 29–31.
67. Portugal: February 3–9.
68. Santiago de Compostela — Valladolid: February 10–14.
69. Salamanca: March 1–7.
70. Seville — Jerez — Cádiz — Málaga — Córdoba — Jaén — Granada — Almería — Murcia — Alicante: March 27 to April 5.
71. Valladolid: April 24.
72. Valladolid: April 30 to May 3.
73. Saragossa — Barcelona — Valencia: May 14–19.
74. Portugal: June 12–20.
75. Valladolid: June 23–24.
76. Seville: June 25–28.
77. Portugal: September 16–27.
78. Santiago de Compostela — Oviedo — Bilbao — San Sebastián — Pamplona: September 28 to October 1.
79. San Sebastián — Bilbao: October 7–14.
80. Valladolid: October 29–31.
81. Córdoba — Seville: December 9–12.

1946

82. Valladolid: January 4–5.
83. Seville — Granada — Murcia — Valencia — Barcelona: January 22–28.
84. Valladolid: April 5–6.
85. Valladolid: April 29–30.
86. Saragossa — Barcelona: May 28 to June 1.

Index